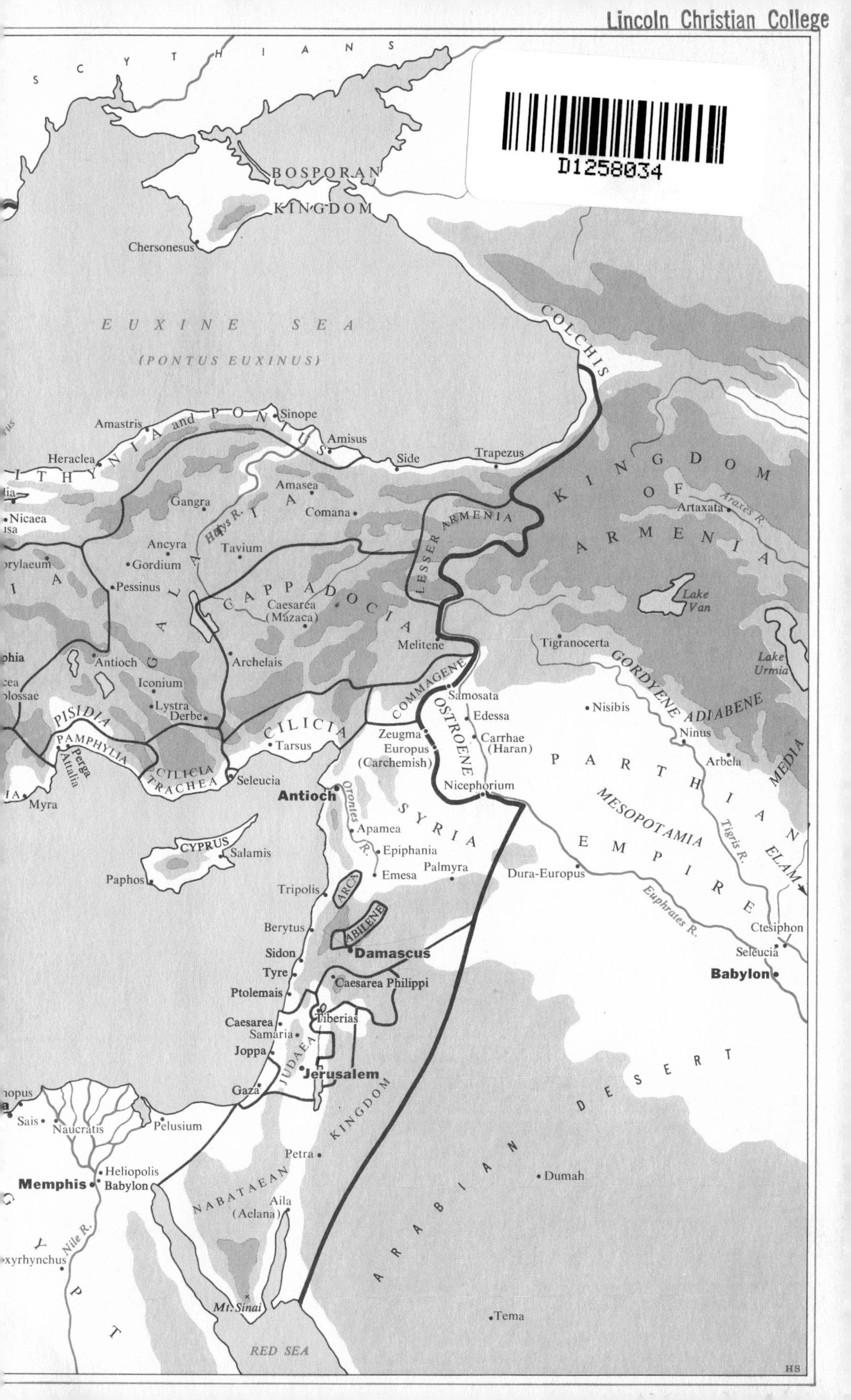
S C Y T H I A N S
BOSPORAN
KINGDOM
Chersonesus
E U X I N E S E A
(PONTUS EUXINUS)
COLCHIS
Sinope
Amastris
BITHYNIA and PONTUS
Amisus
Heraclea
Side
Trapezus
KINGDOM OF ARMENIA
Amasea
Gangra
Comana
Artaxata
Araxes R.
Nicaea
Halys R.
GALATIA
LESSER ARMENIA
Ancyra
Tavium
Gordium
Pessinus
CAPPADOCIA
Caesarea
(Mazaca)
Lake Van
Melitene
Tigranocerta
Antioch
Archelais
GORDYENE
ADIABENE
Lake Urmia
Iconium
Lystra
Derbe
COMMAGENE
Samosata
OSTROENE
Edessa
Nisibis
PISIDIA
CILICIA
Tarsus
Zeugma
Europus
(Carchemish)
Carrhae
(Haran)
Ninus
Arbela
MEDIA
PAMPHYLIA
Perga
Attalia
CILICIA TRACHEA
Seleucia
P A R T H I A N E M P I R E
Antioch
Nicephorium
MESOPOTAMIA
Myra
Orontes R.
Apamea
SYRIA
Tigris R.
ELAM
CYPRUS
Salamis
Epiphania
Paphos
Emesa
Palmyra
Dura-Europus
Euphrates R.
Tripolis
ARCA
ABILENE
Berytus
Ctesiphon
Seleucia
Sidon
Damascus
Babylon
Tyre
Caesarea Philippi
Ptolemais
Tiberias
Caesarea
Samaria
Joppa
JUDAEA
Jerusalem
Gaza
ARABIAN DESERT
Sais
Naucratis
Pelusium
NABATAEAN KINGDOM
Petra
Heliopolis
Memphis
Babylon
Dumah
Aila
(Aelana)
Nile R.
EGYPT
Mt. Sinai
Tema
RED SEA
HS

The Western Heritage of Faith and Reason

THE WESTERN HERITAGE OF FAITH AND REASON

Eugene G. Bewkes · Howard B. Jefferson

Herman A. Brautigam · Eugene T. Adams

and J. CALVIN KEENE

Harper & Row, Publishers

New York, Evanston, and London

This book is in part a revision of EXPERIENCE, REASON AND FAITH: A SURVEY IN PHILOSOPHY AND RELIGION, Copyright 1940 by Harper & Brothers.

D-N

LIBRARY OF CONGRESS CATALOG CARD NUMBER: 63-9052

Contents

II. The Historic Jesus

III. Philosophy and Religion Among the Greeks

IV. Philosophy and Religion in the Greco-Roman World

V. Medieval Philosophy and Theology

VI. Mind and Spirit in Transition from the Medieval to the Modern World

VII. Philosophy, Religion, and Science in the Modern World

List of Illustrations

Photographs

Figures

Maps

Preface to the First Edition

✣✣✣✣✣✣✣✣✣✣✣✣✣✣✣✣✣✣✣✣✣✣✣✣✣✣✣✣✣✣✣✣✣✣✣✣

A survey or general course must present a fairly extensive impression and appreciation of the field which it proposes to cover, and at the same time provide ample content and enrichment. This is a difficult assignment, and many who like the idea have despaired of its realization in practice. Nevertheless, there is increasing conviction among educators that courses of this type which provide general knowledge of a broad field of subject matter can be constructed and made effective. We share this belief out of a long experience with survey courses at Colgate University in most of the major fields of study. These courses can provide breadth as well as a surprising degree of depth, and at the same time meet vital student needs at the college level.

The present volume is designed to provide the subject matter for a survey or general course in philosophy and religion. It can be used specifically for that purpose, and also in connection with courses in the history of Western civilization or the humanities generally, for it provides the philosophic and religious material which is so easily overlooked or slighted in dealing with the development of Western culture.

This volume is not presented either as a condensed introduction to the history of philosophy or philosophy problems or as a short course in Biblical or Christian history. It is rather a very general survey of the part which philosophy and religion have played in Western civilization. The book might well have been described as the adventure of philosophic and religious ideas in Western culture. We have tried to give the college student who has no particular preparation in either philosophy or religion an extensive course which will furnish him with some idea of the way in which the religious and philosophic roots of our cultural heritage took hold and developed in the course of a long history. The volume should certainly do this for the college student; but even so, contact with this survey for the first time is not likely to exhaust its content. We venture to say that more mature students will find here a perspective and a content that will satisfy a long-felt need in this field. Certain historical periods are especially illuminating in showing the interconnection between philosophy and religion, and also in revealing their total effect upon the life of an era. We have endeavored to give the student such ample illustration of this interplay of ideas that he will be in a position to gain genuine insights into the dynamic character of philosophy and religion as cultural forces.

The emphasis and selection of materials are based on more than a decade of experience in teaching a general course in philosophy and religion. The authors have worked together for a long period as a staff handling over 300 students yearly in such a course. The actual arrangement of materials and chapter divisions was the result of cooperative planning. There was a necessary division of labor in writing, however, which was somewhat arbitrary and was distributed as follows: the undersigned wrote Chapters 1, 2, 3, 4, 5, 6, and 18; E. T. Adams 7, 8, 9, and the part on physics in 19; H. B. Jefferson 10, 11, 12, and 17; and H. A. Brautigam 13, 14, 15, 16, and the part on psychology in 19. The volume is in no sense a symposium, but a joint project which grew out of the day-by-day give-and-take of classroom and staff discussion. Consequently we know that students can assimilate this wide range of subject matter. There is an organic unity which unfolds its own story. The material is adaptable to any level of the college curriculum. However, its value as background for later studies and its contribution to student literacy in a relatively closed field make it desirable for inclusion earlier rather than later in the curriculum.

EUGENE G. BEWKES

Colgate University

Preface to the Revised Edition

Many textbooks used in college courses have a limited life, losing their value or appeal after one or two college generations. The original edition of this work was not one of these. It is a remarkable fact that this text, first produced a quarter of a century ago in mimeographed form for use in freshman and sophomore classes, has continued to fill a vital place in American higher education. Since great changes have appeared in the areas of thought covered by many of these chapters, it has inevitably become necessary to bring out a revision in the interests of accuracy and keeping abreast of current interpretations. Over two years ago the undersigned, who had assisted in preparing the first edition in its final stages at Colgate University and has taught it for many years to students at both Colgate University and The St. Lawrence University, was given the assignment of preparing a complete revision. At numerous places this made a fair degree of rewriting necessary, but the general arrangement of the original and much of the materials of the former authors have been retained. The first chapter, on primitive religion, has been eliminated, and a new final chapter replaces the former one.

The original title, *Experience, Reason, and Faith,* has been replaced, in the belief that a title indicating the nature of the contents more precisely is desirable. The new title suggests the historical orientation of the work and at the same time the primary interest in faith, which refers to the Hebrew and Christian religions and theological developments through the past two millennia, and in reason, which concerns both ancient and more recent developments in both philosophy and in science.

For those who will use it as a text, questions have been added at the end of each chapter which may be found useful as study guides. Extended bibliographies conclude each chapter. It is believed that the chronological charts will provide useful outlines by which the student can organize the material for his own thinking. The photographs and drawings should have educational value.

Although the primary intent of the volume is to provide a text for college students which will meet the purposes indicated by Dr. Eugene G. Bewkes in his Preface to the First Edition, it is our belief that in this new edition many educated persons other than students who feel the need of a study that will organize and add to their knowledge of our heritage will discover a valuable guide for use both individually and in study groups. And in this day of uncertainty and "lostness," this work may assist some readers to recover for this period something of the great contribution that our immensely rich past holds for us.

Acknowledgments in a book covering such a panorama of thought and history as this one does are inevitably numerous. They are owed to Thomas Nelson & Sons for permission to quote at length from the Revised Standard Version of the Holy Bible; to all those publishers from whose publications quotations have been taken; and to those who have made the drawings and photographs available. Photographs not specifically credited have been selected from my personal collection.

To Dr. Eugene G. Bewkes, the editor and an author of the original edition, I am particularly grateful for his reading most of the manuscript and offering valuable advice upon it, and for his help in a variety of ways in the preparation of this volume. Special thanks are due also to another of the original authors, Dr. Herman A. Brautigam, and to my colleagues, Drs. Daniel W. O'Connor, Morton S. Enslin, and Douglas Carmichael for extensive assistance with the revision. I am also under obligation to Drs. Dwight M. Beck, Lenore O. K. Congdon and my St. Lawrence colleagues, Drs. Robert B. Carlisle, James D. Coronios, William D. Mallam, Alfred Romer, and Robert G. Wolk for reading sections of the material and making many helpful suggestions. I alone am responsible for errors and insufficiencies, of course. To my wife, Elsa Feichtinger Keene, whose patience, encouragement, and assistance have been constant during the years the book was in preparation, I express deep appreciation.

J. CALVIN KEENE

The St. Lawrence University
February, 1963

I. The Hebrews and Their Religion

CHRONOLOGICAL FRAMEWORK OF PART I

ca.[1] 1750-1650 B.C.	Abraham moves through Palestine into Egypt. The patriarchs: Abraham, Isaac, and Jacob.
ca. 1290 B.C.	Exodus out of Egypt under Moses.
ca. 1200-1020 B.C.	Period of the Judges. No centralized power.
ca. 1020 B.C.	Establishment of the independent United Kingdom.
ca. 1020-1000 B.C.	Saul the first king.
ca. 1000-961 B.C.	David the king. Brings the Ark to Jerusalem.
ca. 961-922 B.C.	Solomon the king. Builds the first Temple.
922 B.C.	Division of the United Kingdom under Rehoboam into Judah (the Southern Kingdom) and Israel (the Northern Kingdom).
900-800 B.C.	Elijah and Elisha prophesy in Israel, the Northern Kingdom. Ba'al worship attacked.
	Rise of Assyria to power.
800-700 B.C.	The eighth-century prophets Amos and Hosea prophesy in Israel, and Isaiah and Micah in Judah.
722 B.C.	The Northern Kingdom, Israel, is destroyed by Assyria.
ca. 626-586 B.C.	Jeremiah prophesies in Judah.
621 B.C.	Great reformation under Josiah. Book of Instruction found.
605 B.C.	Babylonia becomes dominant power.
597 B.C.	Exile. First Jewish captives taken to Babylonia.
586 B.C.	Second group of exiles taken to Babylonia.
	Ezekiel and Deutero-Isaiah prophesy in Babylon.
539 B.C.	Cyrus of Persia conquers Babylon and becomes dominant.
538 B.C.	Hebrews permitted to return to Palestine.
515 B.C.	Second Temple built.
444 B.C.	Walls of Jerusalem rebuilt under Nehemiah.
332 B.C.	Alexander the Great conquers Persia. Greek power dominant.
323 B.C.	Alexander dies. His general Ptolemy takes Palestine and Egypt.
198 B.C.	The Seleucids of Syria take Palestine.
168 B.C.	The Maccabean Revolt begins.
143-63 B.C.	Period of relative independence of Jews. Maccabean family rules.
63 B.C.	Rome annexes Palestine. Pompey rules at first.
63-40 B.C.	Pompey, Cassius, Crassus, and Julius Caesar rule in turn over Palestine.
40 B.C.	Herod the Great, an Idumean, son of Antipater, made king of Palestine by the Romans. Rules 37-4 B.C. Builds the third Temple.
ca. 6 B.C.	Jesus born.
A.D. 66-70	Jewish revolt against the Romans. Jerusalem and Temple destroyed by Titus.
A.D. 132-136	Revolt under Bar-Cochba. Jerusalem destroyed in A.D. 135 and rebuilt by Hadrian as a Roman city named Aelia Capitolina. End of the Hebrew nation.

[1] *ca.* is the abbreviation of the Latin *circa*, and means approximately.

I. History and Religion of the Hebrews to the Eighth Century B. C.

A remarkable feature of twentieth-century thought is that in a cultural period which makes science and its great discoveries pre-eminent, there continues to be a large number of thinkers throughout the world who look to the past for their most important understandings and loyalties. The great scriptures of the world are accepted as sources of "wisdom," and continue to be read, studied, and accepted as foundational to human living. This fact appears to be strange because science finds in the *future* the goal of human thought and discovery; the truth we possess today will be superseded by the discoveries of tomorrow. For scientific thought, the Golden Age of wisdom lies ever before and beyond us. In opposition to this view stands the vast significance attributed to the writings of men who lived centuries before our own enlightened period, in a time when modern science was as yet unimagined. These scriptures, rather than the most recent theories of physics and chemistry, seem to those who accept them vitally important in making truth of a different and ultimately more important kind available. Theirs is a truth by which men can guide their lives, from which they derive their highest values and ideals, and through which they may reach "salvation."

When we inquire why these ancient writings are considered so important, the reply given is that they are the work of men believed to be inspired by God. They are thought to be not just the product of man's own insights but are attributed by those who accept them to a superhuman source. They are, in short, said to contain *revelation.*

The Bible (from the Greek word *biblia,* books), containing the Old and New Testaments, is the most remarkable of these ancient scriptures and, in terms of its influence, the most important Western writing of all time. It has provided many of the basic elements of our culture, particularly in religious and ethical ideals. Were we to trace into the distant past current beliefs regarding the nature of God, the nature of man, the ways in which life is best lived, and the values we hold, we would discover that these understandings find their decisive origins in this Bible.

Other concepts come from a second source, for the taproots of Western civilization are two. One extends back to the country of Palestine and the Hebrews living there, the other to Greece. From the latter have come many of our ideas in philosophy, politics, aesthetics, and physical science. These two roots first arose at different times, the Hebrew starting about the eighteenth century B.C. and the Greek much later. The two peoples lived for many centuries in parallel cultures, physically very close yet with so little contact in the early days that they might just as well have lived on opposite sides of the earth. Eventually they met in Alexander's great empire and merged in the Roman Empire, the Hebrew influence continuing most markedly in its Christian daughter which absorbed into itself and preserved much of ancient Greek thought as well.

It is these movements and their consequences for modern thought which this volume will study. We open our journey into our cultural past by examining first the older of the two heritages, the Hebrew.

The Hebrews and Their Scriptures

Ancient as Hebrew culture is, it arose in the midst of civilizations already existing for well over a thousand years. The Hebrews were located geographically in the ancient Middle East, and during most of their long history were under the sovereignty of powers greater than themselves. Yet, remarkably, they were the only one of those peoples to succeed in maintaining themselves through the centuries as a culture. It was primarily their unique religion which sustained them, making them capable of withstanding those forces of absorption and disintegration which would have removed them as a people from the stage of history.

The Point of View

The Hebrew Bible (the Old Testament) is an extraordinary collection of writings, capable of being understood in a variety of ways according to the interests of the reader. Thus, when taken as a deposit of historical and cultural materials, it is found to be of immense interest and value to modern scholars in many different fields. Historically, it has been shown to be highly accurate in almost all instances where modern discoveries, as in archaeology, have thrown light upon Biblical writings. This accuracy is so striking that an outstanding Jewish scholar, Dr. Nelson Glueck, makes the claim that all archaeological evidence so far uncovered points to the entire historical reliability of the Biblical accounts. Students of anthropology, sociology, and primitive religion find the older sections of Scripture a veritable treasure mine. Nowhere can one find more vivid and accurate reflections of an age now over 3000 years past than in the books of Joshua and Judges. These same books, along with Genesis and Exodus, provide excellent examples of the beliefs and practices of ancient religions.

Again, the Old Testament can be read as remarkable literature, containing a wide variety of literary forms, many highly developed. The cultural value of the Bible as literature is so great that in the various languages of its translation it has colored the literature of all Western cultures, and in many it has formed the foundation of their literary heritage.

Nevertheless, important as these values are, the principal reason these Scriptures have been vitally significant to Jews and Christians in the past is neither of those mentioned. It is rather the *religious* value which is central to the writings, and unless the student today approaches them out of religious interest he will be unable to comprehend fully what their meaning has been —and still is. To the writers and to the Hebrews during their long history, the Scriptures as they developed represented the Hebrew memory of the past in terms of its most important element—the relationship which the Hebrews had over the centuries with their God. They came to see their Scriptures as a group of books containing the word of God to his people, a word given through prophets and understood within the framework of historical experiences. They remembered their history not simply as a series of disconnected events but as a meaningful whole with a vital and ever-present center. As it is written, history has to be given a point of reference if it is to have meaning; the Hebrews found their focus in the God who had delivered them from Egypt and with whom they had established a very special connection. All that happened to them as a nation, within their own boundaries and in their contacts with other peoples, was interpreted in terms of God's relationship with them as the "covenant community."

As understood by the Hebrews, then, the Bible contains the account of how God, their God, has dealt with his chosen people. Others might interpret the same events in different ways, but to the Hebrews the Bible contains sacred history.

The early Hebrews believed that God revealed himself to them in two ways. First, the actual events of their history were understood to be God's acts and therefore revelations of his nature. But further, among the Hebrews appeared certain men called prophets who were thought to be especially receptive to the divine word, capable of receiving directly God's will for his people. Moses was such a prophet who received a call from God to lead his people out of slavery into a promised land. Others of the prophets we will meet in later sections. The significance of these men for us at this point is that the events of history were not left without interpretation and meaning, since these "seers," thought to be especially open to the divine influence through visions and messages, spoke God's direct word to the Hebrews. Their message had to do with the nation's history, and it threw light upon why the nation at that time was as it was and what the future held for it as it responded to the message with obedience or disobedience.

Through God's word, spoken through the prophets, the Hebrews believed they entered into a direct relationship with the divine. Like men, but to a far greater degree, God was believed to be personal, having a will for the nation and concerned with it in a direct way. Although the word that came was not always clear and men had to understand and interpret it, yet it was believed that in basic outlines it was sufficient, and by it they could live. The Biblical record is the drama of God's dealing with the Hebrews as that dealing was understood by its human authors.

Structure of the Scriptures

The writing of the Old Testament Scriptures was done over a period of some 800 years. Not all of it is considered of equal importance. It is well to remember that there was no generally accepted body of Scripture (canon) before the first century of the Christian era when, at a council in Jamnia, Palestine (A.D. 90), a list of scriptural writings acceptable to Palestinian Jews was drawn up. As we now have these in Protestant Bibles they are divided into 39 books, as they are called, which start with Genesis (a Greek word meaning beginning) and end with Malachi. It is interesting to see how these came to be and how they gained acceptance.

Jews today, as over the last 2000 years and more, regard the books of the *Law,* called the *Torah,* as the most sacred books, and their authorship is traditionally attributed to Moses. There are five of these (hence they are sometimes called the *Pentateuch*), namely, Genesis, Exodus, Leviticus, Numbers, and Deuteronomy. It appears that by the year 400 B.C. or somewhat earlier these five were accepted as canonical in roughly their present form. The second division is called the *Prophets* (in Hebrew, *Nebi'im*), itself divided into the two sections of Former Prophets and Latter Prophets. Four books make up the Former Prophets: Joshua, Judges, Samuel, and Kings. Four others make up the Latter Prophets: Isaiah, Jeremiah, Ezekiel, and the Books of the Twelve (Hosea through Malachi, each treated as a separate book in the Christian classification). It appears that by 200 B.C. they also were considered sacred books, yet not on the same level with the books of the Law, or Torah. A third group of writings, some written before 200 B.C. and others later, were designated simply as the *Writings* (in Hebrew, *Kethubim*). At the council of Jamnia, after the destruction of the third Temple, built by Herod, they also were accepted, bringing to 24 the total number of books in the Jewish canon. This least sacred group of scriptural writings includes the books of Psalms, Proverbs, Job, Song of Solomon, Ruth, Lamentations, Ecclesiastes, Esther, Daniel, Ezra-Nehemiah, and Chronicles. Three of these were barely acceptable because of their questionable religious value. These were the Song of Solomon, with its suggestive love poetry; Ecclesiastes, with its skepticism; and Esther, which does not even mention the name of God.

In Protestant versions of the Old Testament, these 24 books are so classified as to make 39. The Roman Catholic version contains 14 additional writings, called the *Apocryphal* books. They can generally be found in Protestant pulpit Bibles also, but are considered by Protestants and Jews to be of less than canonical value. The reason for the difference here is that the Protestant Bible is based on the books included in the Palestinian Jewish Scriptures, while the Roman Catholic follows in content the *Septuagint*. This is a Greek translation of the Scriptures begun about 250 B.C. and continued during succeeding centuries, made especially for Greek-speaking Jews dwelling outside Palestine, chiefly in Egypt. Its name, meaning seventy (often represented by the Roman numerals LXX), is derived from the tradition that 70 (actually 72) scholars cooperated in its translation. The Hellenistic Jews, as these Greek-speaking Jews were called, accepted the same 5 books of the Torah and the 8 books of the Prophets as Palestinian Jews, but added to the 11 Writings 14 additional books, among which are found I and II Maccabees, Ecclesiasticus, Tobit, Judith, and Bel and the Dragon. The name *Apocrypha* (in Greek, hidden) is given to them because some of them make predictions concerning coming events, hidden from most men. Still other books, used in the Eastern churches and only incidentally by the Alexandrian Jews in earlier times, are called *Pseudepigrapha* (in Greek, false writings) because the names of some of them attribute them falsely to ancient figures. Among these are Enoch, Baruch, and the Testaments of the Twelve Patriarchs.

The earliest Christians used the Septuagint version of the Hebrew Scriptures as their Bible. When Pope Damasus I commissioned Jerome in A.D. 382 to make a Latin translation of the Bible, he used various Latin versions and also Hebrew and Greek documents, producing the famous translation called the *Vulgate*. He included the 14 Apocryphal books, with the result that since his time the Roman Catholic church has followed the custom of including these in its versions.

The first English versions were translations from the Latin Vulgate. In the fourteenth century, John Wycliffe rendered portions of Scripture into English. William Tyndale translated directly from both Greek and Hebrew, in 1529 producing the entire New Testament and parts of the Old in English. Various other translations were made but, in order to produce a uniform translation by the best scholars, King James I of England called together approximately 50 scholars who, after seven years of labor, produced the famous *King James Version* (KJV) in the year 1611.

Somewhat earlier the Roman Catholic church had decided to make an English translation since the translations made by Protestants using Greek and Hebrew documents did not agree entirely with the Vulgate, which had been named the official Catholic version in the Council of Trent (1546). The Protestant versions were particularly unacceptable because of their rejection of the apocryphal books (which Catholics term *deuterocanonical*). Because of anti-Catholic attitudes in England, the Catholics doing the work of translating resided in France; consequently, it was in France that their version was published. The New Testament appeared in Rheims in 1582 and the Old Testament in Douay in 1609.

Both Protestants and Catholics have felt the need of more up-to-date translations as time has made the older ones archaic, excellent as they are. Not only have the meanings of words and grammatical structure changed considerably over the centuries, but ancient manuscripts have been discovered in the intervening years which have made more accurate translations possible. In England a *Revised Version* of the King James Version appeared in 1885; the *American Revised Version* (ARV) was published in 1901. A variety of versions have appeared during the twentieth century, culminating for Protestants in the *Revised Standard Version* (RSV), completed in the United States in 1952 as the work of a large committee of scholars. In England the New Testament section of the *New English Bible* appeared in 1961. The high literary quality of the King James Version makes it still a preferred translation, but the Revised Standard Version has achieved such literary excellence combined with its far greater accuracy that it is receiving very favorable attention from Protestants and Jews.

The Catholics produced a new translation of the entire Bible, completed in 1954, as the work of the Englishman Ronald Knox. Although based primarily on the ancient Vulgate, it makes some use of independent Greek and Hebrew sources as well. The *Confraternity Edition* is the most literal of the Catholic translations, of which the New Testament appeared in 1941 as the work of 27 American scholars. In 1943 a papal encyclical recommended that Catholic scholars make greater use of original texts in Hebrew and Greek; as a result, the Old Testament of this edition, appearing after the encyclical was issued, is an entirely new translation which departs far from the Vulgate.[1]

The Writing of the Oldest Biblical Books

The authorship of the Torah, or five books of Law, has traditionally been assigned to Moses. For more than two centuries, students of these books have frequently called attention to the fact that they show many signs of multiple authorship, and that it is questionable whether Moses wrote any large portions or, indeed, any part of them. The reasons for questioning the Mosaic authorship are various. Briefly, it is noteworthy that at no place in the books themselves is it claimed that Moses is their author, although individual sections are referred to as being by his hand. Mention is made of events which occurred in periods later than Moses' lifetime, and his own death is reported (Deuteronomy 34).[2]

More important than these details, however, is the evidence suggesting multiple authorship from within the documents themselves. The most obvious evidence is the fact that certain narratives use the name *Elohim* (translated as God in the ARV) while others use *Yahweh*, or *Yahweh Elohim* (translated as Jehovah or Jehovah God).[3] The significant fact is that as these designations are used, various other terms and certain characteristic styles of writing regularly accompany them. Thus, when Yahweh (translated as Lord in the RSV) is used in the book of Exodus, Sinai is the name used for the sacred mountain where he dwells, and the inhabitants of Palestine at the time of the Exodus are called Canaanites. But when Elohim (God) is used, the sacred mountain is called Horeb and the inhabitants of the land are referred

[1] C. Umhau Wolf, "Recent Roman Catholic Bible Study and Translation," *The Journal of Bible and Religion*, October, 1961, pp. 280-289.

[2] For the Biblical references in this volume, the Revised Standard Version has been used.

[3] The American Standard Version of the Bible has familiarized Americans with the name *Jehovah* as the proper name for God. It now appears certain that this should be Yahweh instead of Jehovah. The name of God was so sacred that Jews did not pronounce it, but substituted in its place the Greek word for Lord, *adonai*. By combining the consonants of Yahweh (in German *y* is interchangeable with *j* and *w* with *v*) with the vowels of *adonai*, an approximation of the name *Jehovah* is obtained.

to as Amorites.[4] The style of writing changes with the name chosen. Further, duplicate stories appear, such as two stories of creation in Genesis 1:1-2:4a and 2:4b-24 and two accounts of the flood, quite clearly woven together to form a continuous story (Genesis 6-9). Three times we encounter the story of a man passing his wife off as his sister—twice of Abraham (Genesis 12:10-20 and Genesis 20) and once of Isaac (Genesis 26:6-11). Two accounts inform us how Moses learned the name of God (Yahweh), in Exodus 3:13-15 and 6:2-6.

Considerations like these, of which the above are only suggestive samples, have led scholars to the conclusion that four different authors or groups of authors cooperated in the production of these first five books. This is a solution deriving from the internal evidence of the works themselves, as we said. No documents have been found to prove this theory, of course, but this is not surprising since there are no Biblical documents extant from pre-Christian times apart from sections of the Dead Sea scrolls. But the majority of Protestant scholars, along with many Jewish and some Catholic scholars, find the evidence so strong that the thesis has come to have wide acceptance.

The reader may wish to examine for himself the two creation accounts in the RSV as an illustration of the point. On inspection he will discover that in the first account (Genesis 1:1-2:4a) the name for the Creator is given as God (Elohim), and that the style of writing is formal, for creation is divided into regular "days," each day concluding with a similar expression ("And there was evening and there was morning . . . ."). The method of creation is by God's word, which alone is sufficient ("And God said . . . ."). The order of creation is a logical one, culminating in the creation of man and woman by the divine fiat. By contrast, in the second account (Genesis 2:4b-24) we find that the Creator is referred to as Lord God (Yahweh Elohim), man is made before plants and trees, and woman is made from man's rib. The style is vivid and personal. God creates not by the word but by *doing*—with his hands he "*formed* man of dust from the ground, and *breathed* into his nostrils the breath of life . . . ." (emphasis supplied). He *planted* a garden and *walked* in it in the cool of day, and he himself *formed* every beast and every bird, *bringing* each to man to be named. Even a cursory inspection of these accounts strikingly illustrates the evidence which led to the so-called *documentary theory*.

According to this theory, it is generally held that the earliest of the four authors or groups of authors came from the southern section of Palestine, called Judah. Because he used Yahweh as the divine name he is called the

[4] Norman K. Gottwald, *A Light to the Nations*, New York, Harper & Brothers, 1959, pp. 104 ff.

Yahwist or *J author* (from the German *J*ahweh). He is thought to have lived between 950 and 850 B.C., during the end of the United Monarchy and the early days of the Divided Kingdom, of which mention will be made below. He drew together oral traditions and probably ancient written documents. His writing is vivid and informal, illustrated by the second creation story, which is his. The next author or group of authors appeared during the following century, probably between 850 and 750 B.C., before the downfall of the Northern Kingdom. Since he came from the northern tribes, poetically called Ephraim, and particularly because he used the name *Elohim* for God, he is referred to as the *Elohist* or *E writer*. Probably during the middle of the seventh century B.C. the code of law found in the present book of Deuteronomy was written, also by an unknown person. Later men edited the history of Israel from the viewpoint exhibited in this material. These writers together are referred to as *D* or *Deuteronomists*. The great Exile in Babylonia during the sixth century B.C., ending in 538, stimulated the fourth school to do their writing. These men, probably writing in the middle of the fifth century B.C., are referred to as the *Priestly* or *P writers*, for they show great interest in the priesthood and ceremonials. They provided much of the framework for the five books of the Law. They use the name *Elohim* for God until Exodus 6:2 ff. when the name *Yahweh* is said to have been revealed to Moses for the first time. These several documents were brought together, probably at various times and by various men, reaching their present state by 400 B.C. or somewhat later, being accepted as authoritative Scripture and assigned to Moses.[5]

These early authors were not attempting to write a complete history of Israel. Each wrote from his own viewpoint, interpreting the events being described according to his understanding of how God had dealt in the past with the Hebrew people.

The Geography of Palestine

Inspection of a relief map of the world of the ancient Middle East reveals that within a relatively small compass of land is found a great variety of geographical features. Bounding this ancient world are large bodies of water: the Mediterranean Sea (the largest), the Black Sea, Red Sea, Caspian Sea, and the Persian Gulf. Three great rivers flow through sections of this land:

[5] Detailed analyses of these four are to be found in Robert H. Pfeiffer, *Introduction to the Old Testament*, New York, Harper & Brothers, 1941, as follows: J document, pp. 142 ff.; E document, pp. 168 ff.; D document, pp. 232 ff.; and P document, pp. 188 ff.

the Nile, the Euphrates, and the Tigris. High mountain ranges isolate large areas—the Taurus Mountains in southern Asia Minor, for instance, and further east the Zagros Mountains of Elam. Breaking into the middle of the region is the Arabian Desert, home since time immemorial of wandering Bedouin tribes and a great natural barrier to armies wishing to cross between Babylonia and Egypt. The crescent of fertile land bounding this desert on its northern end is often referred to as the Fertile Crescent. Along and at the two ends of this crescent lay the centers of ancient civilization in the Middle East: Egypt was the anchor on its western end, Babylonia on the eastern. Assyria, Syria, and Palestine were situated on the crescent itself. This restricted area provided the stage for the enactment of Biblical history, most of which was concentrated in a very small stretch of this land called Canaan (from the Canaanites) or Palestine (from the Philistines), lying at the southeast corner of the Mediterranean Sea.

At the time of the Hebrew nation's greatest expansion, the area it occupied was roughly the size of the state of Vermont. The distance in a straight line from the south end of the Sea of Galilee to the northern end of the Dead Sea is about 65 miles. The Dead Sea itself is a sizable body of water, over 50 miles long and 10 miles wide. For most of their history, the Hebrews were cut off from the Mediterranean Sea itself. The territory which they occupied was chiefly the hilly section between the coastal plain and the valley of the Jordan River. The area "from Dan to Beersheba," taken as the farthest boundaries of Palestine, is about 150 miles long by 75 miles wide.

The physical features of this land are most unusual, unlike those of any other part of the world. The fact that it was *this* piece of land which the Hebrews occupied for so much of their history as a nation had much to do with the determination of that history. The most noteworthy feature is the Great Rift Valley, starting far north of Palestine, in Syria near the Taurus Mountains, and extending south of Palestine into central Africa. The Sea of Galilee, the Jordan River, and the Dead Sea occupy this rift in Palestine. On both its sides are hills and mountains, confusedly thrown up in various forms, cut by stream beds, and giving the impression of general barrenness and vast confusion. These hills fall off to the sea on the west and to the desert on the east.

In moving eastward from the Mediterranean Sea, one finds first a coastal plain, varying considerably in width, providing a very regular coastline with no natural harbors. Farther north, in Lebanon, this plain disappears entirely at places where the mountains spill into the sea. Paralleling this plain to the east is a range of hills and low mountains, called in the Old Testament the

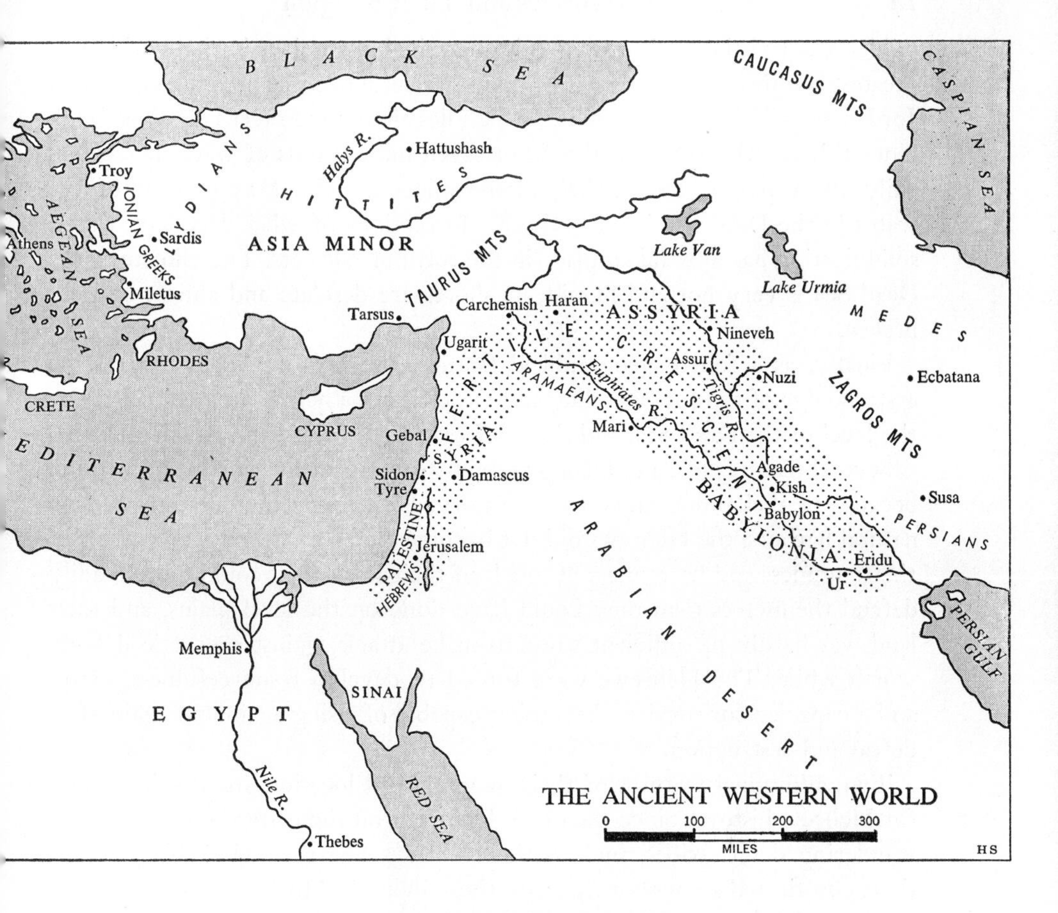

The Ancient Western World

hill country, broken through by plains which extend toward the Jordan River. The most important city of this hill country is Jerusalem, situated at an altitude of about 2500 feet. It was in this area, at one time only 30 miles by 55 miles, that the tribe of Judah received its land. Just west of the Dead Sea the mountains flatten into the plateau of Judea, dropping off in the south to the barren land of the Negeb.

The third main feature is the great depression, or rift, of the Jordan River and Dead Sea, called the Arabah. The Jordan first collects its waters in tiny Lake Hule in the north and flows into the Sea of Galilee, a fresh-water lake 9 by 14 miles in size lying 685 feet below sea level. Gathering additional water from tributary streams flowing out of the mountains on both its sides, the Jordan then flows through the Arabah, at this point an almost tropical wilderness, twisting and turning as it goes, the lowest river in the world. The greatest width of this valley is 14 miles, at its mouth at Jericho where the Jordan empties into the Dead Sea, which lies almost 1300 feet below sea level. Since this sea has no outlet, the six or seven million tons of water it receives daily all evaporate, leaving behind the minerals. About 25 percent of the water in the Dead Sea is mineral salts. In sections of what was once water, solidification has now taken place in the form of salt flats. The climate at the Dead Sea is very hot and humid; its shores are desolate and almost entirely lifeless.

Finally, as a fourth geographical feature, the hills of Moab rise on the eastern edge of the Jordan valley and Dead Sea to a height of 4300 feet above the level of the Dead Sea, and slope off eastward toward the Arabian Desert.

Several features of Palestinian geography are especially worthy of mention because of their importance to its history. First, since the coastline had no natural harbors, the Hebrews did not become seafarers. Second, as a result of the roughness and barrenness of much of their land, they could more readily defend themselves than they could have done on the level plains, and their land was hardly of sufficient value to make attack against energetic defense worth while. The Hebrews were forced to develop resourcefulness, vigor, and a capacity for survival, becoming capable of rising again and again after defeat and destruction.

Two additional features of their geographical location are also important for Hebrew history. Since the open desert lay on the eastern edge of Moab, wandering desert tribes, such as the Hebrews had themselves been at one time, constituted a constant threat to those living in Moab and beyond it into the heart of Palestine. The Biblical book of Judges refers to several such invasions. Another and the most important single geographical feature helpful in understanding Hebrew history is the fact that Israel was located along the coastal route which formed a natural corridor between Egypt to the south and Asia to the north and east. This corridor provided the natural highway for competing armies of the great powers which lay at the ends of the Fertile Crescent, Egypt and Babylonia or Assyria. As these armies marched back and forth to do battle with their rivals, they passed by the plains and hill country where the Hebrews lived, and they usually felt obliged to make their flank safe by subjugating or making allies of the Hebrews. In short, it is clear that the life of the Hebrews in Palestine was an intensely difficult one, as they attempted both to wrest a living from the largely unfriendly land and to preserve their existence in the face of almost constant threat from enemies of the great river valleys and the desert.

The Beginnings of Hebrew Life and Religion

The beginning of Hebrew history in any proper sense of the word is found in the account of the Exodus of the early Hebrews from Egypt, where they had been enslaved under the pharaoh. In the historical memory of the Hebrews, as recorded much later in the book of Deuteronomy (26:5-9), it was demanded that at the time of offering the first fruits of the soil the Hebrews should say:

> A wandering Aramean was my father; and he went down into Egypt and sojourned there, few in number; and there he became a nation, great, mighty, and populous. And the Egyptians treated us harshly, and afflicted us, and laid upon us hard bondage. Then we cried unto the Lord the God of our fathers, and the Lord heard our voice, and saw our affliction, our toil, and our oppression; and the Lord brought us out of Egypt with a mighty hand and an outstretched arm, with great terror, with signs and wonders; and he brought us into this place and gave us this land, a land flowing with milk and honey.

The Exodus and the subsequent formation of the Covenant constitute the great events which remained for Hebrew remembrance the beginning of their history. Later writers carried the story back to the first father or patriarch of the Hebrews, Abraham, and still further to the very beginning of human history and the creation of the world and Adam, the first man. Three outstanding historical events or series of events were taken by the Biblical writers as indications of God's intimate relation to the Hebrews. They looked into the ancient past and saw God calling and making promises to the ancient tribal fathers; they recalled, second, the miraculous escape from Egypt, and, third, the great happenings at Mount Sinai where a "Covenant" was established, binding the people and God together.[6] *Preparation, Exodus, Covenant,* and *fulfillment* are the great words by which the Hebrews understood their national life and their religion.

The origins of the Hebrews are to be sought to the east of Palestine, from which direction they came over the Fertile Crescent onto the stage of history. As regards the details of their migrations, there remain many unsettled problems. They belonged to a drifting westward movement of Semitic stock, one strain of which was the Aramaean, the nucleus out of which the Hebrew nation was eventually to grow. However, for many centuries before they

[6] G. Ernest Wright and Reginald H. Fuller, *The Book of the Acts of God,* Garden City, Doubleday & Company, Inc., 1957, pp. 19 ff.

Ancient Hittite Shrine

Mentioned nearly fifty times in the Old Testament, the Hittites were one of the most powerful people of antiquity in the Near East. This shrine, located at the Hittite capital city of Hattushash in central Asia Minor, portrays the union of two religions or of two peoples.

developed any kind of national consciousness, they occupied no definite area but were simply a nomadic, pastoral people. We designate this the *patriarchal period*. A patriarch was an important chieftain, somewhat like a modern Arabian sheik, who had cattle and portable possessions and led a small group of followers related to him by ties of kinship. In Hebrew tradition, the long patriarchal past is unified under the names of the outstanding chieftains, Abraham, Isaac, and Jacob.

Abraham (or Abram) is believed to have lived between 1750 and 1650 B.C., during the period of Middle Eastern history known as the Middle Bronze Age. This period was in no sense a dark age of simple, primitive people lacking all cultural achievement. Great cities had existed and great cultural achievements had appeared in the Fertile Crescent centuries before Abraham. The wheel had been invented, algebra developed, and great buildings constructed. Writing, chiefly on clay tablets in cuneiform, had been in use for centuries. Though some of the people of Abraham's time lived simply, they had behind them a rich cultural heritage whose influence was present in their traditions and folkways. Abraham's beginnings, as related in the Biblical account (Genesis 11:31), are closely connected with Ur, an important city in ancient times located on or near the Persian Gulf at the mouth of the Euphrates River.

From very early times cultures had flourished along the two great rivers of the ancient Middle Eastern world: the Nile and the Euphrates-Tigris. On the hot plains of the latter, where water was plentiful and crops easily grown, civilizations appeared, grew, and were assimilated by succeeding waves of conquest. During the period 3000-2000 B.C., Sumer, on the Persian Gulf, and Akkad, farther north, were rivals for power. Great wealth was accumulated by Sumer, which in 2360 B.C. was seized by the Akkadians, a Semitic people, under the leadership of Sargon I. Near the close of the millennium Sumer regained her strength and built a great civilization which lasted from about 2060 until 1950 B.C. Elamites, living in the hill country on the eastern edge of the valley, destroyed this culture. In the unsettlement that resulted, another Semitic people, called the Amorites (meaning Westerners, referring to their coming out of the Arabian Desert to the west and south), spread over and took control of the Euphrates valley, establishing the powerful First Babylonian Dynasty, named after its capital city. The greatest king of this dynasty was the famous Hammurabi (*ca.* 1728-1686 B.C.), known primarily for his remarkable code of laws. By 1750 B.C. this Semitic Amorite power had gained control of all Mesopotamia and Syria. It was probably during the time of Amorite dominance that the Semite Abraham migrated from his ancestral home of Ur up to Haran in Syria at the northern part of the Fertile Crescent and then southward into what was later to be called Palestine. Clay tablets written about 1700 contain such names as Benjamin and David, indicating that Semitic influence was both strong and widespread.[7]

A third and later Semitic wave, called the Aramaean, spread over the ancient world between 1500 and 1000 B.C., establishing a number of relatively small states on the western edge of the crescent, among them Moab, Edom, Damascus, Hamath, and Zobah. Their language, Aramaic, became in time the chief language of the Fertile Crescent, eventually replacing Hebrew, sometime after 500 B.C.[8]

From these few remarks it may be seen that the period in which Abraham lived had behind it well over a thousand years of highly significant historical development. And this Middle Bronze Age was itself a period of high cultural

[7] The dates given follow Bernhard W. Anderson, *Understanding the Old Testament*, Englewood Cliffs, N.J., Prentice-Hall, Inc., 1957.

[8] Gottwald, *op. cit.*, p. 90.

development, indicated by its artistic remains, its literature, its elaborate agricultural developments, and its great buildings in the cities, generally centering about a temple tower or *ziggurat*. It was also a time of much commerce, for important trade routes led through Asia Minor and over into Persia as well as down into Egypt. Numerous clay tablets bear witness to the widespread business dealings of the period.

Various other peoples, like the Hurrians (Horites in the Bible) and the Hittites from Asia Minor, enter into the ancient history of the Fertile Crescent, but since they are not central to our account we will pass them by without discussion. It should be mentioned, however, that there was a great mixing of peoples, and our evidence seems to indicate that the Hebrews were themselves the product of such mixture.

A group named the Hyksos, at least partially Semitic, conquered Egypt about 1710 B.C., holding it until about 1570 B.C. It seems very likely that during their rule the Hebrews migrated into Egypt under Joseph, son of Jacob. They were reduced to slavery when the non-Semitic Egyptians once more regained power. Still other peoples, who also included Semites, were called Habiru or 'Apiru. They were wanderers with no settled culture who at times united for purposes of attack upon towns and cities. It is possible and even probable that the early Hebrews of the Bible were a part of these wandering peoples.

Early Religion

A great variety of religious ideas characterizes the ancient world to which the Hebrews belonged. Primitive religion with its animism (worship of spirits inhabiting objects and places) had long been displaced in the more cultured areas by polytheism (worship of many gods).[9] Egypt had a highly developed religion many centuries before the patriarchs. On leaving Mesopotamia, the Aramaean people who became the Hebrews appear to have held to religious beliefs much like those of other dwellers in the Fertile Crescent, and particularly like those of the Canaanites. They appear to have followed polytheistic practices, but a clear understanding of this matter is difficult to obtain with certainty. They possessed a high degree of moral sensibility. They had a strictly regulated sexual morality and a group consciousness which looked upon merit as the basis of leadership. Without straining this point overmuch, it is a fact that the social relationships of the nomadic period had a moral quality which was not superficial but deeply characteristic. It was an impor-

[9] *Ibid.*, p. 97.

tant element in the religious development of the nation. The moral genius of the Hebrews asserted itself again and again under the most untoward circumstances.

The Biblical account contains many references to the ancient animistic background of the peoples inhabiting the land into which the wandering Hebrews first came. Religious ideas and practices may remain many centuries after the cultures which supported them are gone. Also, although people living in the centers of civilization may adopt higher forms of religion, ancient practices and memories of ancient sacred spots continue in the countryside. In the modern Middle East it is still possible to witness ancient ceremonies which persist even though their sources are long forgotten. To take but one example, in Macedonia, in Greece, the ancient custom of *pyrobasie*, or firewalking, continues, now as a part of the Greek Orthodox religion to which the people who practice it belong. Examples like this one could be paralleled throughout the world. So too the Biblical accounts refer to places which hundreds of years before Abraham were considered sacred and still continued to receive veneration in his day from those who came into contact with them. Abraham and his tribe may have been polytheistic, following the general forms of the day, or they may have been monotheistic, which seems very improbable. Yet they appear to have continued ancient animistic practices in their travels through Palestine. We will look at a few examples of such ancient practices.

In the book of Genesis, 12:6, we read that Abraham "passed through the land to the place at Shechem, to the oak [or terebinth] of Moreh." The terebinth or oracular oak was a sacred tree at which Abraham worshiped. In chapter 13:18, we note that Abraham "moved his tent, and came and dwelt by the oaks [terebinths] of Mamre, which are at Hebron; and there he built an altar to the Lord [Yahweh]." These oaks also were sacred. No matter how enlightened Abraham may have been, in these instances we have evidence of practices persisting from a far past. Tradition preserved the remains of an age-old animism which had been universal throughout the Semitic world.

Similarly, there are numerous references to sacred stones or pillars, which are also animistic objects inhabited or "possessed" by spirits. There is no mistaking this in the account of Jacob in Genesis 28:11 ff., even though Jacob himself is said to have ascribed his experience to Yahweh. After his famous dream of the ladder with angels ascending and descending, he awakened, frightened, and said, " 'How awesome is this place! This is none other than the house of God, and this is the gate of heaven.' So Jacob rose early in the morning, and he took the stone which he had put under his head and set it up for a pillar and poured oil on the top of it. He called the name of that

THE HEBREW CONCEPTION OF THE UNIVERSE

The Hebrew conception of the universe assumed a flat earth supported over a watery abyss. A solid firmament held back the waters above the earth and to it were attached the heavenly bodies. At the outermost limits of the earth a circular range of mountains supported the firmament. (The Clarendon Bible, vol. VI, Clarendon Press, Oxford, 1947, p. 20.)

place Bethel [the house of God] . . . ." And then he declared, ". . . this stone, which I have set up for a pillar, shall be God's house . . . ." The form which his act of worship took shows remains of an animism whose origin was extremely remote. Likewise, in I Samuel 4:1 and elsewhere occurs the name Ebenezer. The word *Ebenezer* itself means stone of help, which is very suggestive of the original character of the place. As a matter of fact, sacred pillars persisted until quite late, for even in the porch of Solomon's Temple there were two such pillars (I Kings 7:15, 21), although they were no longer consciously associated with animism.

Another illustration of the survival of primitive forms is found in references to sacred wells. Certain wells were originally presumed to be the possession or dwelling place of some spirit. The habit of reverence for these places persisted long after newer ideas of religion prevailed. An interesting example occurs in connection with place names. In Genesis 14:7 is the following passage: "Then they turned back and came to Enmishpat (that is, Kadesh), and subdued all the country of the Amalekites . . . ." Note that the place which at the time of the writing of this passage was called Kadesh used to be called Enmishpat. Kadesh means sanctuary, and far back in time the same place was called Enmishpat, or the spring of decision. In other words, it was formerly an oracular spring or well, a sacred abode of some spirit. By means of a proper ceremony of incantation, the help of the spirit was elicited. The place name *En-eglaim* appears, meaning the spring of the two calves, giving evidence of an age-old worship of calves, which we know about from other sources. This form of worship persisted also until comparatively late. (See Exodus 32, where a golden calf is worshiped.)

A striking element of the religion of the patriarchs was that they tended to make "covenants" with their God. They not only believed in him but they entered into active, personal relationship with him by forming an agreement. As an example, in Genesis 15 appears the account of Abraham ordered by his God to make a sacrifice. A deep sleep fell upon him and also a "dread and great darkness." Then Yahweh made a covenant with Abraham in these words: "To your descendents I give this land, from the river of Egypt to the great river, the river Euphrates . . . ." This concept of a covenant relationship between God and people was the very heart of the Hebrew religion under Moses.

The Exodus from Egypt

We are informed in the book of Genesis that because of a period of protracted famine in Palestine the patriarchal period was terminated by a migration into Egypt. Extra-Biblical records also refer to various peoples' coming down into Egypt under similar circumstances and being allowed to sojourn in that land. The Hebrews were received in friendship, for one of their own, Joseph, son of Jacob, held a high position under the pharaoh. If the date 1710 B.C. is fairly accurate for the time when the partially Semitic Hyksos overcame Egypt and began their rule, we might have a ready explanation for the cordial relations existing between the Egyptian ruler and the Hebrew immigrants.

Tradition reports that the Hebrews remained in Egypt for a very long time. At the end of this period, it is reported, a pharaoh who "did not know Joseph" came to the throne and reduced the Hebrews to virtual slavery, placing them under taskmasters and using them in building the treasure cities of Pithom and Ramses (Exodus 1:11). Egyptian records indicate that probably during the reigns of the Pharaohs Seti I (*ca.* 1308-1290 B.C.) and Ramses II (*ca.* 1290-1224 B.C.) treasure cities by these names were constructed, and that Asiatic " 'Apiru," possibly including the Hebrews, were used for labor on public building projects.[10] These two cities were probably built in the northeast part of the Nile delta, not far from the present location of the Suez Canal. When we add to these striking parallels the fact that Canaanite cities in Moab and Ammon were destroyed by invaders between 1250 and 1200 B.C., it appears fairly certain that the century of the Exodus of the Hebrews from Egypt was the thirteenth and that either Seti I or Ramses II was the pharaoh who enslaved them. If, as some scholars believe, the Exodus took place in or about the year 1290 B.C., then a stay of 430 years in Palestine and Egypt (Exodus 12:40) would bring the Hebrew migration into Palestine to 1720 B.C., and into Egypt to some years later.

At this point the imposing figure of Moses enters the story to play one of the most important roles of history. Although the portion of the book of Exodus that recounts the amazing story of this great man was probably written some centuries after he lived, it is generally regarded as correct, at least in essence, even though very likely amplified with traditional stories. By a remarkable set of circumstances, Moses was reared in the royal Egyptian household and was given an Egyptian name, related to other Egyptian names like Ahmose and Thutmose. Moses has the basic meaning of *is born* and may simply mean *son* or *child*. If the tradition is trustworthy, he received all the advantages of education and culture which such a milieu made possible. His training included mathematics and military tactics and was the best in the ancient world.

Moses is presented to us as a man who, on the battlegrounds of moral decision, underwent a personal struggle which has repeated itself in the lives of many other men. It was a conflict between personal advantage, success, and pleasure, and his people's disadvantages, hardships, and miseries. Should he identify himself with the untutored rabble which was his people, or should he leave well enough alone and enjoy the position which good fortune had given him? The greatness of men is often revealed by what lies heavily on their minds and by the choices arising therefrom. Moses was haunted by the burdens of his people, and when we read that he murdered an Egyptian taskmaster who had scourged a Hebrew slave with whips, we recognize the final step he took to make himself one with his own kin. His flight from Egypt and his return with his brother Aaron many years later to maneuver and plan for the freedom of his people is a most interesting story. We emphasize only those parts that are momentous from a religious point of view.

Moses' flight took him to the land of Midian, lying to the east of the Gulf of Aqabah (Akaba) on the opposite side of the Sinai Peninsula from Egypt. There he married a daughter of a priest named Jethro, a Kenite, probably

[10] *Ibid.*, p. 117.

of the clan of the Midianites. Like himself, these people were Semites. It may be that their tribal god was named Yahweh; and if, as seems likely, they had tribal connections with the Hebrews in Egypt, Jethro may have pointed out to Moses that their religion centering in Yahweh was actually the original religion of the ancient patriarchs. This theory would help account for Moses' determined effort to fasten Yahweh worship onto the Hebrews in Egypt, who at that time worshiped other gods. Also, it helps explain Moses' conviction that Yahweh "called" him to rescue his kinsmen from Egypt. He believed that Yahweh was the God of his people and had been the God of Abraham, Isaac, and Jacob.

A puzzling feature of this account, however, is the fact that one source of the book of Exodus (6:2-3), states specifically that before the time of Moses God was not known by the name Yahweh: "And God said to Moses, 'I am the Lord [in Hebrew, Yahweh]. I appeared to Abraham, to Isaac, and to Jacob, as God Almighty, but by my name the Lord [Yahweh] I did not make myself known to them.' " The J source, on the other hand, uses the name *Yahweh* for God from the beginning of his writing in Genesis.

However this matter may be understood, it was during Moses' stay with his wife's family that the event took place which decisively affected all subsequent Western history. As he was grazing Jethro's sheep he came to Mount Sinai (or Horeb), where he had a remarkable experience which he understood to be a veritable theophany (appearance of God). It was more than simply an appearance, for, typical of all later Hebrew religion, the vision which came to him was accompanied by the demand that he perform a specific task as the will of God for him. The record gives the happening in this way (Exodus 3:1-6):

> Now Moses was keeping the flock of his father-in-law, Jethro, the priest of Midian; and he led his flock to the west side of the wilderness, and came to Horeb, the mountain of God. And the angel of the Lord [Yahweh] appeared to him in a flame of fire out of the midst of a bush; and he looked, and lo, the bush was burning, yet it was not consumed. And Moses said, "I will turn aside and see this great sight, why the bush is not burnt." When the Lord saw that he turned aside to see, God called to him out of the bush, "Moses, Moses!" And he said, "Here am I." Then he said, "Do not come near; put off your shoes from your feet, for the place on which you are standing is holy ground." And he said, "I am the God of your father, the God of Abraham, the God of Isaac, and the God of Jacob." And Moses hid his face, for he was afraid to look at God.

God then told Moses that he had seen the suffering of the Hebrews and would bring them up out of Egypt into Canaan. He commanded Moses to go to the pharaoh and demand that the Hebrews be granted their freedom.

But Moses wished to know which god it was that was sending him to the pharaoh and to the Hebrews. In reply, God said (Exodus 3:14), "I AM WHO I AM." And he said, "Say to the people of Israel, 'I AM has sent me to you.' " The precise meaning of the name is an enigma and is variously interpreted by scholars, some holding that it means *he will be* or *he causes to be*. Moses accepted his commission, returned to Egypt, and there performed various wonders or miracles, interpreted as acts of God, to persuade the pharaoh to let the Hebrews go out of Egypt, supposedly to make sacrifices to Yahweh. Permission was given finally after Yahweh had slain all the Egyptian firstborn but had "passed over" the homes of the Hebrews, thus instituting the Hebrew feast of the Passover (Exodus 12).

The crowd of Hebrews, however, had not proceeded far on their eastward journey toward the mountain of Yahweh before the Egyptian soldiers started after them to bring them back. At this juncture Yahweh performed another miracle, the mightiest thus far, which again showed his great power.

The Hebrews had reached a point probably near the place where the Suez Canal now runs, in the vicinity of Lake Timsah. In Exodus 13:17 ff. the location is called the Sea of Reeds or Reed Sea (not Red Sea in the Hebrew text). Before them lay this shallow sea or marsh and its papyrus reeds; behind them came the Egyptians in their chariots. Then arose a strong wind which drove back the waters, permitting the Hebrews to pass safely. The Egyptians in their chariots were caught in the returning waters as they attempted to follow the next day; many were drowned, but the Hebrews escaped. So remarkable was this escape that the Hebrews recognized in it the powerful hand of their God, Yahweh, of sufficient might to save them even from the all-conquering Egyptians. So struck were they by it that it still stands today as a central event of their history.

The Hebrews now moved slowly into the mountainous, stony desert they called the wilderness to the sacred mountain of Sinai (or Horeb), traditionally located in the southern part of the Sinai Peninsula. There are, however, good reasons for believing its actual location was farther north, possibly in the vicinity of Kadesh-barnea, where the account informs us they spent much of their time in the wilderness. The description of the mountain as they approached it presents a startling picture of an awesome situation (Exodus 19:18-19). Some scholars have concluded from it that the mountain was at that time an active volcano, but opposed to this theory is the fact that no volcanoes were active in the Sinai Peninsula during historic times. As understood in the tradition, it was the presence of Yahweh that caused the fire and the earthquake.

Moses assembled the people at the base of the sacred mountain and conducted a most significant religious meeting. He saw before him a crowd of people unorganized, undisciplined, and ill-prepared for the semidesert conditions awaiting them. There is reason to think that in this assemblage were some Semitic tribes who had not been in Egypt but who dwelt in the vicinity of Mount Sinai. The only thing in common among these people was a sense of kinship, but there was no genuine feeling of unity. Their religion (or religions) did not as yet create unity, for it was a conglomerate of diverse elements from their own traditions and from the Egyptian environment, with all manner of local variations. They also worshiped idols, relying on material images of gods. Moses was to teach them of Yahweh, the God who was not to be represented in any material way. He wanted them to understand that Yahweh had chosen them, elected them out of his own will and mercy, to be his own people, and that the relation between the people and their God was to be bound for all time by a *Covenant.* This the Hebrews were prepared to accept; and in the fervor of the moment they intended to be faithful to Yahweh alone and put away all other gods, for Yahweh had demonstrated his power over nature and had also overwhelmed the Egyptians. What impressed the Hebrews was that God had done this for *them.* Although they had done nothing to deserve it, Yahweh had chosen them, and in so doing had revealed his care and concern for them.

The Covenant

The great event signalizing the foundation of Yahwism was the deliverance from Egypt; its culmination was the formation of the Covenant, which is the most significant constituent of Hebrew culture and history. From archaeological evidence, it is now known that the making of covenants between individuals was a common practice in the ancient world. Hittite documents and tablets from the Mesopotamian city of Mari report such agreements or treaties. The Hittite documents distinguish between those drawn up between equals, called *parity* covenants, and those made between a king and his vassal, called *suzerainty* covenants. It is this latter type that is reported in the account of Moses at Sinai. In suzerainty covenants there is no parity or equality between one party and the other; the king "gives" the covenant to his subject, and through it the subject receives security and protection. He must of course obey the commands of his king implicitly. Because the covenant is given to him graciously, he should be filled with gratitude toward his sovereign.[11]

The Hebrew Covenant with Yahweh, then, was one in which God,

[11] Anderson, *op. cit.*, pp. 56 f.

sovereign over men, chose to extend his power and benefits to those people whom he had elected to receive them. They were in no sense equal to God; on the contrary, their former position as slaves served to emphasize the fact that they had not been a powerful or successful people found promising enough in themselves to justify God's choice of them. Although they had nothing to recommend them, God had yet graciously extended to them the covenant relationship, offering them his protection and promise for the future on the condition of their accepting his requirements. Gratitude for favors given began the relationship even before the Covenant was formally established.

As the Hebrews reached Mount Sinai (Horeb), Moses received the word of Yahweh, indicating his willingness to covenant with these former slaves (Exodus 19:4-6):

> You have seen what I did to the Egyptians, and how I bore you on eagles' wings and brought you to myself. Now therefore, if you will obey my voice and keep my covenant, you shall be my own possession among all peoples; for all the earth is mine, and you shall be to me a kingdom of priests and a holy nation.

Precisely what it was that constituted the will of Yahweh for his people is not clearly indicated. The commands reportedly received by Moses on top of the mountain (Exodus 20-23) show signs of later accretions, but Yahweh's demands may be thought of as consisting primarily of the Ten Commandments with the addition of a variety of moral laws. Worship of Yahweh alone as God without the use of any physical representations was particularly emphasized. As the Ten Commandments now stand in Exodus 20:2-17, they are probably amplified from their original form; yet in spite of this the original meaning is discoverable. They are apodictic or absolute laws, stating what must absolutely and certainly be done because of God's commands. Following the Protestant way of numbering them, they are: (1) The Hebrews are to give exclusive obedience and worship to Yahweh and Yahweh alone; (2) they are to worship without the use of images of any kind; (3) they are to regard the divine name as sacred; (4) they are to observe the Sabbath as a sacred day; (5) they are to honor their parents. The remaining five commands prohibit murder, adultery, stealing, false witness, and covetousness.

Moses was the agent through whom the Covenant was established. He built a stone altar at the foot of Mount Sinai and placed before it stone pillars representing the tribes making up the Hebrew people. We may visualize the scene. Near the altar stood Moses. Burnt offerings of oxen were made. The blood of the sacrificed animals was caught in basins; half was poured on the altar, representing Yahweh. Moses then read the conditions of the Covenant to the people, who responded, "All that the Lord has spoken we will do, and we will be obedient" (Exodus 24:7). Then Moses threw the other half of the blood on the people, saying, "Behold the blood of the covenant which the Lord has made with you in accordance with all these words" (Exodus 24:8).

In this way was the Covenant sealed in blood and the Hebrews and their God drawn together. As the people lived up to Yahweh's demands under it, he promised to find them a homeland of their own and to protect them, making them a prosperous people and a "kingdom of priests and a holy nation."

The covenant relation with Yahweh carried with it the expectation of a great destiny for the Hebrews. The Covenant was the foundation of their future, the theme song of their national life. It was the basis of their philosophy of history, in the sense that their national failures and successes would be interpreted as Yahweh's punishment or reward for disobedience or obedience toward the Covenant. In later times it formed the keynote of the messages of the prophets. It was a relationship which underwent profound enrichment in future centuries, an enrichment that moved far beyond the simplicities of its original form.

Conceived at first in an elementary form, this Covenant contained implications of universal import which came to fruition under the great prophets and were carried beyond even them into the new religion, at first a cult of Judaism, which came to be known as Christianity. Christianity too saw its relation to God in terms of a covenant, but now the New Covenant, sealed not by the blood of bulls but by the blood of Jesus himself. No one person, not even Moses, could have known in advance all the meanings and ramifications of this agreement with God. It was left for the future to interpret it as the people of the Covenant faced new and more involved situations. The story of that interpretation is largely the story of the Hebrew nation and religion and, we might add, of Christianity as well, with chapters of that story still to be written in our own future.

Understanding of God and Worship Under Moses

Moses' understandings of the nature of Yahweh, the forms of worship used, and their effects upon the people of Israel were all extraordinary at various points. The very name of God, "I AM WHO I AM," has no parallel in early religions. It was possible to interpret this as meaning that God was unique, quite unlike other gods. He was not to be called by a specific name as were other deities; he was not just another *El*, but stood in a class by himself, being just what he was. His being or existence was not dependent upon other powers, not attached or bound to any others. He ruled over nature, making it obey him, as it did in his great deeds directed against the Egyptians and in the crossing of the Reed Sea. He was capable of looking after his people, and therefore controlled history itself. In time, the name of Yahweh would be so interpreted as to imply that all power and wisdom resided in Yahweh and to lead to the belief that Yahweh alone was God, his being involving all life and nature.

In analyzing further the understanding of Yahweh in the early days after the Exodus, we discern elements held in common by the sources making up the early Biblical books. Since Yahweh took the initiative in manifesting himself as protector and deliverer of his people, he was a very powerful being, far above all others. Yet the early Hebrews did not think of him as completely spiritual, for his "glory" could be seen, and within that glory, hidden as it were by the brilliance of the fire or light visible to men, was a form not unlike a human form. This anthropomorphism (in the form of man), as such a view is called, is a marked characteristic of early Hebrew religion.[12] It may be that the early Hebrews needed to think of God in manlike ways since they thought of him as having an actual relationship with human beings. His face may not be seen (but he has a face), for the man who sees it will surely die (Exodus 33:20). But when Moses asked to see God, he was permitted to obtain a glimpse of his back (Exodus 33:23). Not Moses alone but also Aaron and others of the elders saw Yahweh, but presumably in his covering of fire or light (Exodus 24:9).

This same early anthropomorphism is even more noticeable in God's having characteristics of the human personality. Like men, he becomes angry, he forgives, he demands, and he feels compassion. Qualities like these make him a "living" God, able to enter into direct relationship with men. Moses' own experience showed that Yahweh was capable also of revealing himself to and through individuals like Moses or, more frequently, through such events as the Exodus itself. Although very powerful, Yahweh had a personal interest in his people and remained close to them.

There is another and quite opposite side to Yahweh as understood during this period. Above all, he was a "holy" God, and in the Old Testament the word *holy* means not primarily moral goodness but rather the being *other than* or different from man. His nature was quite different from human nature in itself, and the man who met him could feel only fear and trembling

[12] William F. Albright, *From the Stone Age to Christianity*, Baltimore, The Johns Hopkins Press, pp. 201 ff.

awe before him. Holiness refers to the fact that in his difference God both drew and repelled man—he was both fearsome and infinitely attractive, mysterious and yet completely good or just. Possibly awe was the Hebrew's most characteristic response to God, for he recognized that *his* being was in the hands of God while God was who he was, doing what he willed to do.

Still another remarkable aspect of the belief in Yahweh during this period is that he appeared alone; no other divine figures intruded on the scene with him. Various other contemporary religions believed in divine triads or a male god with a female consort, but not the Hebrews, who thought that God was to be worshiped without consort or progeny. There was no suggestion in Yahweh of any of the sexual aspects so commonly attributed to their gods by other Semitic groups, and the myths told about the gods of other religions were not told of him. He was also a "jealous" God, who would not permit worship of other gods. There should be no other gods besides him. Also unique in the world of that time was the prohibition upon making or using any form of representation of Yahweh. No statues of him were allowed, nor have any ever been found in Palestinian archaeological research. Other religions gloried in representing their deities in statues or statuettes, in human form or symbolically, but not the Hebrews. Yahweh's nature was so entirely holy that no physical representation was permissible.

The question of whether this early religion can properly be called monotheistic (having belief in one god) in view of its exalted concept of God is pertinent. So far as the Hebrews themselves were concerned, it is clear that their practices were to be strictly monotheistic, for they were forbidden to worship or serve any other gods. Yet it appears to be unquestionable that they believed in the existence of many other gods who also controlled power—limited yet genuine divinities. Hence the usual and possibly the best term by which to characterize Moses' Jahwism is *henotheism* or the closely related term *monolatry*, meaning the belief in or worship of one god without denying the existence of other gods or the right of other people to worship them. In defining it with these terms, however, the concept fails to express clearly the great gap existing between the Hebrew understanding of God and the understanding other peoples had of their gods. Yahweh was not merely their God, nor merely a bit stronger than other gods. The remarkable characteristics just mentioned placed him in a position by himself, presenting a unique view of the nature of the divine. They mark a new stage in the development of religion.

Yahweh was regarded also as the source of both law and morality, which at that time were the same thing. He represented justice and goodness as the leaders understood justice and goodness. Stating the thought in another way,

Yahweh was the vindicator, the ultimate appeal. He could be relied on to keep his part of the Covenant. Rules and regulations of behavior were to be observed as duties toward him. The breaking of the rules or any moral or religious breach was a personal offense against Yahweh. He was endowed with the human quality of anger, but when Yahweh became angry he had superhuman power at his command. He could punish with a vengeance if he willed.

In the light of our understanding of the meaning of Yahweh in conceptual terms, we next ask about the forms or modes of worship that prevailed at the time of Moses prior to the Hebrews' entrance into the land of Canaan. This is an extremely difficult question to answer. If the Bible were not a highly complex document made up of many sources, we could read the books of Leviticus, Numbers, and Deuteronomy with all their details of worship and practice and regard their accounts as belonging to the time of Moses. However, many of the provisions contained in those books belong to the life of well-established communities and refer to conditions which were not in existence when Moses led his people. Lacking historic perspective, those who finally put accounts of Hebrew religious practices into written form assumed them to be of more ancient lineage than they actually were.

There are certain ritual practices of Yahwism in Moses' day about which we can be quite certain. We know from the account given of the covenant ceremony that at least some simple form of worship or ritual was practiced. The description of the killing of animals and the sprinkling of their blood on the people and on the altar shows a procedure which was very meaningful in that area of the world. The blood represented the essence of life and was universally used as a bond of kinship. There can be little doubt that the Ark of the Covenant[13] covered by a tent was the central object in connection with religious observances. Its exact nature, however, is somewhat obscure.

Simple sacrifices were held; in performing them, Moses and his brother Aaron were probably the leading figures. The simple life and conditions did not require elaborate ritual, nor did they require a separate order of priests. All that would come in time, but at this stage there were probably only a few men, like Aaron and possibly Joshua, who were assigned specific religious tasks concerning the rituals and the preparation of sacrificial animals. One of the religious observances in the wilderness was the Passover, which tradition regarded as associated with the escape from Egypt. In the Passover feast,

[13] The Ark of the Covenant was a boxlike structure which represented for the Hebrews the constant presence of Yahweh. Tradition asserts that it contained stones from the sacred mountain of Sinai on which were written the Ten Commandments.

after sundown an animal was sacrificed. No bone could be broken, and the whole animal was roasted over the fire and eaten by all present as a sacrificial feast.

The elaborate use of sacrifice was no doubt developed *after* the entrance into Canaan and especially during the reigns of the Hebrew kings. Under the kings, royal dignity probably required more impressive ceremonies, and the influence of other religions and their practices no doubt also helped make this development important. It is significant in this connection that the prophets of the eighth and seventh centuries were opposed to sacrifices (Amos 5:25); it is likely that they were opposed not so much to sacrifices in themselves as to the elaboration of sacrifices which had crept in.

Before passing to the next section, which deals with what happened to Yahwism or Mosaism in Palestine, it is worth while to note what effect the religion of Yahweh had upon the people. It sought to eliminate the worship of all other gods at one stroke. Insofar as this was wholeheartedly accepted, its psychological effect must have been extremely important in directing the individual personality and the tribes as a whole in one direction of devotion and loyalty. Recall also that power and goodness were joined in Yahweh. This in itself is a great understanding, and much was to come from it. Its full significance was not at first appreciated, but its practical importance was grasped, and it operated as a controlling element in the moral life of the people. We can hardly overstress this point.

Moses did not originate all the moral standards,[14] but he did give them a more binding status by making their fulfillment a condition of approach to Yahweh. To him we must attribute a new relationship between morality and religion. What is so distinctive about this is not only that proper religious ceremony was desired by Yahweh, but that moral conduct toward others was a condition of the good will of Yahweh. The moral demands were simple and few, but they were strict. No man could be right with Yahweh who was wrong in his moral conduct. Whatever was understood to be good was the will of Yahweh. The effect on behavior of such a situation was necessarily great, even though the entire group did not appreciate fully the nature of these religious ideas.

We now have before us the essential ideas of the Hebrew religion, which we may call Yahwism or Mosaism. The personality of Moses made it what it was. It was characterized by a few fundamental understandings which were like seeds with astonishing germinal possibilities. Equipped with these ideas

[14] For example, many of the covenant requirements are derived from Mesopotamian sources.

and ideals, the Hebrews entered the land of Canaan or Palestine, not at all comprehending the strange fate that was often to confuse them and to produce many changes in religious thinking.

Moses must be understood as one of the world's great political and spiritual leaders. He was a man of vigorous personality who took scattered tribes and united them by infusing them with a common religion and a common aim. Put briefly, his achievement was that he delivered a group of slaves from their chains, welded them into a vigorous, unified people, provided them with their religious and moral standards, led them for a lengthy period under most difficult circumstances, and started them on the long road of historical development which saw two of the great world religions and other elements basic to Western civilization rise out of them. He was outstandingly great as idealist, prophet, and strong administrator, and in the combination of these qualities he stands without a peer.

Hebrew Life in Palestine

The Biblical record states that the period of wandering in the wilderness of the Sinai Peninsula and southern Palestine lasted 40 years. During this time the Hebrews lived the life of desert dwellers, a nomadic type of existence. If the country was as inhospitable as it is today, Moses' following could scarcely have numbered more than 5000 in all, and this is a very high figure for a community living under nomadic conditions. Since it is stated in Exodus 1:15-20 that two midwives served the entire colony, the tribe may have been considerably smaller. These people lived in great poverty and want, facing constantly the danger of death through starvation or at the hands of enemies. It is not surprising that in times of discouragement and despair the people demanded that they return to the "fleshpots" of Egypt where, slavery or no slavery, they were at least assured of food.

The older generation, which was accustomed to the easier life of Egypt, gradually died off and was replaced by tougher new generations adapted to desert life. At last the conditions of their life and the strength of the newer generations made them consider a drive from the south into Palestine which, in contrast to desert conditions, seemed to be a land "flowing with milk and honey," as their spies reported. But this idea was dropped because the way directly north into southern Palestine was too strongly fortified and defended for them to be able to fight their way through; therefore, another approach must be found. Small and less powerful countries lay to the east and south of the Dead Sea, so the Hebrews turned toward them and were victorious against the Amorites and the king of Bashan. These victories enabled them to turn the northern end of the Dead Sea and strike westward across the Jordan River at Jericho and Gilgal.

About the year 1250 B.C., then, some 40 years after escaping Egyptian slavery, the Hebrews stood poised for the great attempt to take and inhabit the land they believed promised them by their God. Their years of wandering had forged them into a vigorous fighting people, entirely different from the whining slaves who had left Egypt. Along with almost all those who had left Egypt, Moses also had died, and the warlike leader, Joshua, had been given the task of conquering Canaan. The book of Joshua, named after the leader, tells the fascinating story of how he proceeded.

The Canaanites inhabiting Palestine at this time were Amorite people closely related to the Hebrews. Those living north of Palestine along the Syrian coast became known as Phoenicians, who were noted seafarers, but the Canaanites of Palestine were agriculturalists, raising figs, olives, grapes, grain, and domesticated animals. Their level of culture was not outstandingly high. Many of them lived in strongly fortified towns which stood primarily in the plains and along the coast. According to the Biblical accounts, Joshua and his forces captured the key town of Jericho, whose walls "came tumbling down," thus opening the road into the highlands where fewer Canaanites lived and the towns were less strongly fortified. The invaders fought their way into the land from the east, and over a period of years they managed to conquer an area of the central hill country, first in the south, then in the north. Many of the fortified towns were not taken, however, and continued to exist in the midst of the Hebrews for a long period (Judges I). Even two centuries later the Jebusite town of Jerusalem had not come into their hands.

The main period of settlement, during which the conquered land was divided up by the Hebrews among the groups that constituted them, called the 12 tribes, was fairly complete by the year 1200 B.C. Much of the conquest was savagely carried out, for the destruction (*cherem*) of conquered towns was at times offered as a sacrificial holocaust to Yahweh, and all human beings in them, including children, were killed. Jericho provides us with the first example of this practice. At the town of Shechem, Joshua established a tribal confederacy where the 12 tribes bound themselves together in a covenant alliance and rededicated themselves to Yahweh and the Covenant established at Sinai. The Ark of the Covenant was placed in the sanctuary of Shiloh. It was at this time that the nation of Israel properly speaking came into being. The name, used variously in later times, referred to the unity of the constituent peoples drawn together by their common covenant obligation.

The Period of the Judges

The strain of incessant warfare forced low cultural and moral standards upon Israel, but as time passed the opposition between Israel and the Canaanites lessened. Living side by side, they intermarried and followed similar modes of life. It appears that they united at times for joint military efforts against invaders. The initial enmity, in any case, gradually passed away.

The epoch of Hebrew history lasting for approximately 180 years (*ca.* 1200-1020 B.C.) from the entrance into Canaan until the appointment of Saul as king is called the period of the Judges. According to our use of the word *judge*, this title is a misnomer, for the men who received the name, as reported in the book of Judges, rarely exercised legal judgment. They were rather deliverers from enemies who oppressed Israel, each possessing the spiritual gifts of enthusiasm and power (*charisma*) believed to be gifts of God. Twelve such judges are named, men who at various times led the Hebrews in battle against Canaanites, Moabites, Ammonites, and Midianites.

The entire period was one of relative barbarism during which it seemed likely that the ideals the Hebrews had brought with them would disappear and their religion would be absorbed by Canaanite forms of worship. The tribes remained a loose confederacy, and all attempts to draw them together into close political union under a common ruler or king were strongly opposed. Many of the Hebrews continued to consider Yahweh their king and thought of themselves as living under a kind of theocracy or rule by God. They deemed it an actual disloyalty if not an insult to Yahweh to choose a human king, suggesting, as such a move would, that Yahweh was incapable of protecting his own people. But the time came when the need for a king was too urgent to be resisted any longer.

The Philistines, whose attacks upon Israel were the occasion of the demand for a monarchy, were probably a remnant of the great Minoan culture on the island of Crete, sea peoples who, after attacking Egypt and being repelled by Ramses III (*ca.* 1175-1144 B.C.), had settled on a narrow strip of the coast of Palestine. From this vantage point they made attacks inland upon the Hebrews and Canaanites, who drew together for mutual support against the common enemy. According to tradition, one of the "judges" who opposed them was a man named Samson, himself married for a time to a Philistine woman. The menace of the Philistines, which expressed itself sporadically, gradually spread from the coast inland until it threatened the entire Hebrew federation. About 1050 B.C. the danger reached a climax with the defeat of the Hebrews at Ebenezer. When on the following day as the battle continued the Hebrews brought forth their Ark as a means of insuring Yahweh's help, the Philistines succeeded in thoroughly routing the Hebrews and in capturing the Ark itself (I Samuel 4). Archaeological evidence indicates that Shiloh, the ancient center of Yahwism after the entrance into Palestine, was destroyed at this time, never again to be the central shrine.

Three centers now appear to have been considered the chief sacred places, namely, Gilgal, Bethel, and Mizpah (I Samuel 7:16), served by the great prophet-priest Samuel. It was under Samuel's direction, in response to the threat of Philistine domination, that a king was finally appointed, who can be described also as the last judge of Israel.

The United Kingdom (ca. *1020-922* B.C.)

Samuel anointed Saul (ruled *ca.* 1020-1000 B.C.) with oil, indicating by this act that Saul was acting as the human incarnation of the spirit of Yahweh, having himself become sacred through the act of anointment. Noted principally for his height and strength, he fulfilled the requirements of a first king creditably under most difficult conditions. With no capital city, no palace, no temple, and only such military might as he could gather to fight along with him, he eventually attacked the Philistines, driving them back toward the coast. His later years were tragic, for Saul suffered from a form of mental illness, possibly schizophrenia, which led him into opposition to the young David and ultimately to defeat and death by the Philistines at Mount Gilboa. His body was nailed ignominiously upon the wall of the Philistine city of Bethshan, whence it was recovered by some of his devoted followers. Scarcely a king by the usual standard of exercise of power, Saul had halted and turned back the advance of the Philistines and had prepared the way for David.

David (ruled *ca.* 1000-961 B.C.) was in a unique position at the close of Saul's reign. He was untouched by the tide of battle which had engulfed Saul. Because of Saul's jealousy and his attempts for years before his death to slay him, David had been able to establish himself in Hebron on friendly relations with the Philistines, who, however, were sufficiently cautious not to want him to participate with them in the war against Saul. David had considerable prestige with his countrymen, and it was easy for them to see in him the man of the hour. Like Saul before him, he was "charismatic," receiving the spirit of Yahweh at times in a state of exaltation. Asked to be king, he willingly accepted, although, to be sure, there was nothing to accept but the name of king accompanied by a backbreaking burden. There was still no court, palace, temple, or treasury.

It is remarkable that David did not set himself up to be king but was *invited* to that position by representatives of the tribes, with whom he made a "covenant" (II Samuel 5:1-5). The idea of kingship is established here on a different basis from that of other Oriental kingdoms. David received his sovereignty from the people, who delegated it to him and retained limitations upon his power. Sovereignty thus had two sources—Yahweh and the people. There were very important consequences of this relation, as we shall see later when we illustrate the action of prophets who could face kings with scathing moral and religious rebuke.

David took up his task, facing difficulties almost as great as those which had confronted Moses over two centuries earlier. His range of operations was extremely limited, but from his capital at Hebron in the western hills he had a fairly impregnable natural position, from which he kept the Philistines quite uncomfortable. The fact that the Philistines were settled in more or less independent communities somewhat like the later Greek city-states meant that David did not have to face their united action.

There is ample justification for the pre-eminent place David came to hold in the history of the Hebrew people, for he executed one bold stroke after another, electrifying the tribes out of dismay into a new pride and national self-consciousness. A flood of confidence and determination was released. The most significant act of audacious bravery on David's part was the capture of the Jebusite stronghold of Jerusalem. The amazing thing is that he managed it at all. This ancient city was located in a position of great defensive advantage. On all but the north side the land dropped away steeply so that defense could be concentrated on that side, where a very strong wall had been erected. In the future course of its long history, Jerusalem withstood many armies. David accomplished its capture probably by drawing the full attention of the enemy to the walls in defense against the attack which was directed there, having meanwhile dispatched a hand-picked group to enter the city through a water tunnel and up a steep shaft into the city. They succeeded in their surprise attack, and David established himself in Jerusalem, secure against any Philistine attempt to dislodge him.

With this city as a base of operations, he could extend his power considerably. Furthermore, Jerusalem now became his capital city. It lay outside the territories of any of the tribes and seemed therefore to belong to all of them. It became a symbol of national unity and the central point of loyalty. Also, as a devoted follower of Yahweh, David had the Ark of the Covenant, which the Hebrews had recovered, brought to Jerusalem, thus associating the national city and the national God. However, Jerusalem did not for a long time become the central point for worship; that was something for the future. In

The Dome of the Rock in Jerusalem

The Moslem mosque shown above is built over a spot sacred alike to Jews, Christians, and Moslems. Near here David erected an altar to Yahweh. Here was the site of the great temple built by Solomon as well as that erected by Herod. Later a Roman temple to Jupiter stood on this place. The Arabs built the present structure, sometimes erroneously called the Mosque of Omar, about the year A.D. *684. The mosque surrounds the sacred rock.*

the following section we shall discuss the religious conditions which parallel this period in national development. It will be well to keep our expectations from rising too high.

From almost every point of view, David was a great leader. He fought successfully against the Philistines and extended his sovereignty over a wide area. The times favored him, for his rule coincided with a period of Egyptian weakness during which her control over Israel ceased. No strong powers threatened from the north. In fact, this favorable external political situation obtained in Palestine throughout the reigns of Saul, David, and Solomon, but the Philistines, also profiting by it, had so threatened Saul that he had been unable to take advantage of what would otherwise have been a possibility in his day also. By his successes against the Philistines, David was able to seize this opportunity. As a statesman, he established a Hebrew government with royal officials and judges, became the founder of a dynasty, and in time established cordial relations with neighboring states, carrying on political and economic relations with them. As an executive, he ran the country efficiently and built up national resources. In bringing the Ark to Jerusalem he did much to strengthen religion. In later Hebrew history it was he above all others, including Solomon, who was regarded as the ideal king, uniting power and goodness. To a large extent he was loyal to ancient Hebrew ideals and ideas, which were never discarded, then or later, but persisted as the national conscience.

It should be noted, however, that under his rule—and probably inevitably so under the circumstances—Israel was increasingly becoming like other nations. No longer was it guided by prophetic, charismatic leadership to the degree that it had been from the time of Moses. The great measure of individual independence which had existed before David consolidated the state around his capital had now largely disappeared in the centralized power he had developed. The strength and prosperity which David brought were obtained at the cost of increasing discontent, arising from the fact that the individual freedom and simplicity of life which had once been the possession of the Hebrews had been sacrificed. It could not have been otherwise before the threat of external enemies, but it meant that in his later years David's popularity fell under a shadow.

What David had begun was carried to its culmination by Solomon (ruled *ca.* 961-922 B.C.), one of David's younger sons. As successor to his father, Solomon inherited the fruits of a great man's labors, and consolidated and expanded David's achievements still further. He built up a small and yet very impressive state, one worthy of high respect from neighboring states. Amazing for the king of so small a country, he was able to obtain as one of his wives a daughter of the Egyptian pharaoh.

Interior of the Dome of the Rock

The holy rock rises in the center. According to tradition it was on this spot that Abraham was on the point of slaying Isaac. The Ark of the Covenant is said to have stood here and here probably was erected the altar of sacrifice of the Solomon temple and its successors. From this rock Muhammad is said to have ascended to heaven on his miraculous steed. It is one of the few unquestionably genuine sacred places in Palestine.

Solomon succeeded in centralizing power fully, and embarked upon large economic enterprises. He kept a stable of blooded horses, and even built a seaport and a copper refinery at Ezion-geber, on the upper end of the Gulf of Aqabah. Unusual among Hebrews, who were never seafarers, he developed a sea trade. His fame reached at least as far as Sheba, in modern Ethiopia, whose queen paid him a visit. His building ventures were spectacular; in his reign the famed Temple was built in Jerusalem by Phoenician craftsmen, along with other great buildings. His harem, also famous, was said to have contained in the course of his lifetime 700 wives and 300 concubines.

All these achievements made for considerable prosperity and almost unbelievable development when it is recalled that not long before his time there had existed only a number of disunited tribes with no wealth worthy of mention. But the cost of this achievement in human terms was very great. The king's personal expenses—his harem, his table, gold and silver inlaid furniture, beautiful buildings—all involved expenses out of all proportion to the resources of the land. The only way of keeping up his state was by imposing heavy, direct taxation on the people and organizing a system of conscripted Hebrew labor (I Kings 5:13). These moves were highly offensive to the independent-minded Hebrews, who kept alive in song and story the memory of the goodness of Yahweh in leading them away from the taskmasters of Egypt and did not relish being put under new taskmasters, even of their own people. As a result, disintegration began in the course of Solomon's reign; outlying subject peoples revolted, and by the time of Solomon's death his kingdom was smaller than it had been at the time of his anointing as king. A seething unrest among the people augured of evil days. The work for which Solomon was most entitled to grateful remembrance was his building of the great Temple, but because he had also built chapels to the gods of his non-Hebrew harem favorites, even this gratitude was qualified.

No other term but stupidity, unless we add moral blindness, is adequate to label the action in Rehoboam (ruled *ca.* 922-915 B.C.), the son of Solomon, who succeeded him. Revolt was in the air already, and only a wise man could have smoothed the troubled waters. The people had had more than enough of tax burdens and conscripted labor. They were annoyed by the centralization of power and longed for the independence they had enjoyed before the time of David. It was not forgotten that the king held no absolute rights over his people, that the political relation rested upon a covenant between king and people no less important than the religious relation, also a covenant, between Yahweh and the people. As Rehoboam came to Shechem to be made king, he was addressed in open assembly by Jeroboam, spokesman of the people, who delivered this petition: "Your father made our yoke heavy. Now therefore lighten the hard service of your father and his heavy yoke upon us, and we will serve you" (I Kings 12:3-4). After three days an answer was given, arrived at by accepting the counsel of young men like himself and ignoring the views of the older and wiser advisers. "My father," Rehoboam said, "made your yoke heavy, but I will add to your yoke; my father chastised you with whips, but I will chastise you with scorpions" (I Kings 12:14).

This reply was of course unacceptable, and revolt followed (I Kings 12:16-20):

> And when all Israel saw that the king did not hearken to them, the people answered the king,
>
> "What portion have we in David?
>
> We have no inheritance in the son of Jesse.

To your tents, O Israel!
Look now to your own house, David."

So Israel departed to their tents. But Rehoboam reigned over the people of Israel who dwelt in the cities of Judah. Then King Rehoboam sent Adoram, who was taskmaster over the forced labor, and all Israel stoned him to death with stones. And King Rehoboam made haste to mount his chariot, to flee to Jerusalem. So Israel has been in rebellion against the house of David to this day. And when all Israel heard that Jeroboam had returned, they sent and called him to the assembly and made him king over all Israel. There was none that followed the house of David [Rehoboam], but the tribe of Judah only.

It is clear from this passage that the United Kingdom, established under Saul a century earlier, developed by David, and continued by Solomon, had broken into two parts—a breach which was never to be healed. The *Northern Kingdom,* at first under Jeroboam I, took to itself the name *Israel,* or sometimes Ephraim, and made Shechem its temporary capital. The tribe of Judah, along with the lesser tribe of Benjamin, remained loyal to Rehoboam as the *Southern Kingdom* and came to be called *Judah* (from which name is derived the term *Jew*). For two generations Israel and Judah were bitter enemies, but they later cooperated at times against common foes.

Even though we have telescoped many centuries into a few pages, we have done so as sympathetic spectators to some of history's most dramatic scenes. We shall see how events like those we have just witnessed affected religious thought, causing men to reflect deeply about the nature of God and human destiny.

Religion in Palestine Until the Ninth-Century Prophets

We have followed the events of the political history of the Hebrews in Palestine through three centuries, and we now return once more to the period of entrance into Canaan at the time of Joshua to understand what happened during this same period to their religion. We recall that as they entered the Promised Land they worshiped Yahweh, with whom they had covenanted at Mount Sinai, having agreed to worship only him and to obey his commands. Their simple, nomadic religion was faced with great dangers as it came into contact with the superior Canaanite culture. Even in defeating the Canaanites militarily, the Hebrews were exposed to the possibility of losing the very religion which provided them with the basis of their faith and the national unity issuing from it. Let us examine briefly the religion of the thirteenth-century Canaanites which posed so great a danger and challenge to the Hebrew religion.

The religion of the Canaanites was polytheistic, bearing marked similarities to the religions of Babylon and Egypt. In great contrast to the concerns of Yahwism, the religion of a pastoral people, the concerns of the Canaanitic religion were agricultural. The generic name for the male fertility god was the Phoenician word *ba'al* (plural, *ba'alim*), meaning lord. Ba'alim with specific names were associated with particular city-states and localities. Ba'al Pe'or, as an illustration, was the god of a widely known glen; Ba'al Berith the god of Shechem; and Ba'al Melkart the god of Queen Jezebel, whose home was Tyre. The ba'alim had female counterparts, *ba'alath*, called familiarly *ashtarts* or the *ashtaroth*. Worship was held in temples and in open-air sanctuaries called "high places." The presence of the ba'al was indicated by a large stone standing on end, called a *massebah*, and the ashtart was represented by a wooden pole, termed the *'asherah*. Sometimes the terms *ba'al* and *ba'alath* were used not of specific gods but of a pair of cosmic high gods.

The ba'al was thought to be the lord or owner of the section of land or the city which worshiped him. He it was, it was believed, who gave it its fruitfulness and who mysteriously brought forth crops from the seed sown. After the barrenness of the hot, dry season of summer, when all vegetation had withered up, came the fall rains, and the crops emerged from the moistened earth. This fertility in crops was thought to result from the sexual union of the ba'al and his ba'alath. It was further believed that by imitative magic man could coerce the ba'alim and in this wise assist in the fertilizing of the crops; for this purpose the temples and high places promoted ritual prostitution. Human enactment of the drama of the ba'al and his consort was thought to lend magical assistance to the powers of fertility and thus to insure good crops and consequent prosperity for the community. Amulets portraying the mother goddess were used as fertility charms by women, and human sacrifice was practiced as a way of offering gifts to the gods.

As soon as the Hebrews began to live peaceably alongside their Canaanite neighbors, they came into contact with these Canaanite forms of worship, so much at variance with their own in which sex played no part and Yahweh had no consort. As the Hebrews began to practice agriculture, the question was undoubtedly raised in the minds of some as to how much power Yahweh, a desert god, had in the land of the Canaanites, and particularly whether he was a God capable of producing crops. To be sure, the best thinkers among the Hebrews must have remembered that Yahweh's power had been sufficient to defeat the Egyptians and that this same power had brought them into Canaan, far beyond Sinai and the wilderness.

The popular drift among the Hebrews, however, was in the direction of a rather complete adoption of Canaanite ways, including religious practices.

Remains of a Ba'al Temple

The remains of an ancient Ba'al temple, dating probably from the early part of the second millennium B.C. *in the city of Byblus in Lebanon. The altar is seen in the center, and behind it large stones set on end, possibly votive stones or phallic symbols.*

After all, these Canaanites had a settled community life, better housing, more secure forms of living, and more sophisticated ways than had the Hebrews. It seemed wise, therefore, the Hebrews might be supposed to have argued, to pay respect at least to the local ba'alim wherever met, for their ability to make the land fruitful seemed proved by the experience of generations of Canaanite farmers.

As time went on and many Hebrews did pay their respects to the ba'alim, some began to treat Yahweh himself as just another ba'al, one among many. At the same time and by the reverse process, Yahweh began to absorb characteristics of the ba'alim. Some of the Hebrews began to believe also, along with the Canaanites, that a given territory had its own particular god or gods which should be worshiped while one was in that territory. An excellent illustration of this widely held belief occurs in the account of Naaman, the

Syrian (II Kings 5:1-19), who after having been cleansed of leprosy by the power of Yahweh carried a quantity of soil from Palestine to Syria in order that he might be able to worship properly the god who had cured him. In effect, such beliefs as those mentioned led toward both polytheism and emphasis upon sexual elements in religion.

The temptation for the Hebrews to worship the ba'alim posed a great threat to the Yahweh religion since it threatened to swallow it up or reduce it to only one of many similar cults. Yet once the conflict was won for Yahweh and the danger of assimilation passed, it proved not to have been entirely bad, for the Canaanite religion contributed to the Yahweh religion in very significant ways. As Norman Gottwald puts it, "A greater depth and expansion of vision, an emotional warmth and color entered Yahwism because of the Canaanites. . . . The Canaanite religion perished but lived on in its victor, both as vanquished opponent and [as] needed corrective. Men often learn much from that which they most bitterly oppose."[15] This could be said some centuries later, but not in the time of the judges, for the danger was then too immediate for anyone to see the deeper values of the relationship.

The center of the attack upon ba'alism came from groups of Hebrews in the east and south of Palestine, away from the cities and the agricultural life of the plains, who retained the pastoral form of life and therefore were not faced with the problem of ba'al worship so directly as were their agricultural brethren who had to deal with the question of crop fertility. These remembered all that Yahweh had done for his people in bringing them out of Egypt and forming a Covenant with them one of whose requirements was, "You shall have no other gods before [or besides] me." Surely God had lived up to his promise by taking care of the Hebrews and bringing them into the land promised to them. Surely, they thought, his power was sufficient even in a new land, and here the Covenant was certainly irrevocable.

The two attitudes, a leaning toward ba'alism versus wholehearted loyalty to Yahweh, indicate a genuine religious conflict. However, Yahwism as such lost ground, for as Yahweh took on more of the character of a Canaanite ba'al, the corresponding behavior took on more of the religious and ethical character of the surrounding people. Instead of simple and rugged rules of ritual and conduct, Canaanite rites prevailed, and the older morality was compromised by acceptance of other standards. Private property in the form of farm land and houses was sought and comforts and luxuries were desired; life became somewhat easier, temptations greater, and morality freer.

The most regrettable aspect of this transformation lies in the fact that among the Canaanites religion and morality were separable, whereas the

[15] Gottwald, *op. cit.*, pp. 151 f.

unique achievement of Yahwism was the close association of the two. That is to say, the ba'al religion permitted certain practices in the name of religion which even the ordinary morality of the time would not have defended. This condition is illustrated, for example, by the acceptance and even justification of ritual murder or human sacrifice, although the common morality was opposed to murder. And likewise, ordinary sexual standards, which have a hard time improving their status anyway, had no real support from a religion which, in its reverence for fertility, upon occasion permitted ritual prostitution. Thus, the trend was away from the few Mosaic fundamentals and simplicities of Yahweh worship, especially on the part of those Hebrews who attached themselves most closely to the agricultural and social life of Palestine. In time there was very little practical difference between the worship of Yahweh and the worship of the ba'alim.

This was certainly the general state of affairs that existed even during the monarchy under Saul, David, and Solomon and well into the period after the break-up of the monarchy into two kingdoms. We must make a qualification of this remark only to the extent of saying that Saul and more especially David were personally loyal to Yahweh. David established Yahweh worship at the newly acquired city of Jerusalem, and by bringing the Ark there he kept alive the name of Yahweh and the memory of his concern for his people. In spite of the fact that Solomon built the Temple, the religious condition in the country at large was what has been described. During the reign of Solomon, Yahweh worship was not at all the exclusive practice; foreign cults were permitted and openly practiced by Solomon's wives and their retainers. Only after the break-up of the United Kingdom did the prophetic movement begin that would restore Yahwism to a supreme place among the Hebrews.

The Ninth-Century Prophets

As we recall from the account of historical events, the division of the United Kingdom was followed by the parallel existence of two kingdoms, the Northern (Israel) and the Southern (Judah).

The Northern Kingdom had a relatively brief existence of about two centuries, for as a political entity it was annihilated by the Assyrians in 722 B.C. We shall not consider in detail its outward political history, which is like following the story of an organization heading into bankruptcy. From Jeroboam I, its first king, to the end, one king followed another in rapid succession.

What is of great interest to us is the rise of an order of men called *prophets* (in Hebrew, *nebi'im*, the plural of *nabi*). A few individuals like Abraham and Moses were prophets in ancient times, but the first known appearance of prophets in regular, professional guilds was in the time of Samuel, in the late eleventh century B.C. These men believed that in states of frenzy and ecstasy, induced sometimes by music and dancing, they became possessed of the spirit of Yahweh and were enabled to speak his word to the people. They displayed an originality and authority which often overrode and superseded the office of the priests. The prophets were a peculiarly important feature of Hebrew religious life, and their contribution was a determinative factor in Hebrew history. The appearance of the prophets in the Northern Kingdom during the ninth century was related to the great problem of saving the Yahweh religion.

There were many Hebrews around the eastern and southern fringes of the country who had not adopted the agricultural and town modes of life to anywhere near the same degree as had those who were permanently rooted in the land. As we have said, these outlying Hebrews had retained more of the ancient ways of life and habits than their brethren in Canaan. Despite such social differences, however, there continued to be a strong bond of kinship and a recognition of the common heritage and common relation to Yahweh on the part of all the Hebrews. If there were to be any revival of Yahwism, it might be expected to gain its stimulus from those who had kept the faith intact rather than from those who had modified it, and indeed, this did happen.

The first outstanding individual in the line of prophets during the ninth century was Elijah. He came from the country east of the Jordan and took up residence in the Northern Kingdom at the time when Ahab was king (*ca.* 869-850 B.C.). Elijah was rudely shocked by what he saw. He learned soon enough about the notorious Queen Jezebel, a Tyrian princess, who brought with her the worship of Melkart, the Tyrian ba'al. Jezebel intended to have her husband reign absolutely as did other Oriental potentates. Politically and religiously this ran against the grain of the two deepest elements in the heritage of Israel: the covenant relation between king and people and the Covenant between Yahweh and his people. Note that here is one of those instances which occasionally occur in history, where a complacent people drifting away from the old landmarks and losing sight of something valuable in their past, rendering only lip service to it, are suddenly confronted with the prospect of cutting loose from it altogether. Then they are in a mood to be aroused by a leader. So it was in Israel, and Elijah was that leader on one side, with Jezebel and her priests on the other. These two are the *dramatis personae* of a very exciting drama. Ahab may be the king, but his part is actually that of a pawn, moved about by the will and cunning of the queen.

The account which follows (from I Kings 21:1-23) is Act I in this tense play.

Now Naboth the Jezreelite had a vineyard in Jezreel, beside the palace of Ahab king of Samaria. And after this Ahab said to Naboth, "Give me your vineyard, that I may have it for a vegetable garden, because it is near my house; and I will give you a better vineyard for it; or, if it seems good to you, I will give you its value in money." But Naboth said to Ahab, "The Lord forbid that I should give you the inheritance of my fathers." And Ahab went into his house vexed and sullen because of what Naboth the Jezreelite had said to him; for he had said, "I will not give you the inheritance of my fathers." And he lay down on his bed, and turned away his face, and would eat no food.

But Jezebel his wife came to him, and said to him, "Why is your spirit so vexed that you eat no food?" And he said to her, "Because I spoke to Naboth the Jezreelite, and said to him, 'Give me your vineyard for money; or else, if it please you, I will give you another vineyard for it'; and he answered, 'I will not give you my vineyard.' " And Jezebel his wife said to him, "Do you now govern Israel? Arise, and eat bread, and let your heart be cheerful; I will give you the vineyard of Naboth the Jezreelite."

So she wrote letters in Ahab's name and sealed them with his seal, and she sent the letters to the elders and the nobles who dwelt with Naboth in his city. And she wrote in the letters, "Proclaim a fast, and set Naboth on high among the people; and set two base fellows opposite him, and let them bring a charge against him, saying, 'You have cursed God and the king.' Then take him out, and stone him to death." And the men of his city, the elders and the nobles who dwelt in his city, did as Jezebel had sent word to them. As it was written in the letters which she had sent to them, they proclaimed a fast, and set Naboth on high among the people. And the two base fellows came in and sat opposite him; and the base fellows brought a charge against Naboth, in the presence of the people, saying, "Naboth cursed God and the king." So they took him outside the city, and stoned him to death with stones. Then they sent to Jezebel, saying, "Naboth has been stoned; he is dead."

As soon as Jezebel heard that Naboth had been stoned and was dead, Jezebel said to Ahab, "Arise, take possession of the vineyard of Naboth the Jezreelite, which he refused to give you for money; for Naboth is not alive, but dead." And as soon as Ahab heard that Naboth was dead, Ahab arose to go down to the vineyard of Naboth the Jezreelite, to take possession of it.

Then the word of the Lord came to Elijah the Tishbite, saying, "Arise, go down to meet Ahab king of Israel, who is in Samaria; behold, he is in the vineyard of Naboth, where he has gone to take possession. And you shall say to him, 'Thus says the Lord, "Have you killed, and also taken possession?" ' And you shall say to him, 'Thus says the Lord: "In the place where dogs licked up the blood of Naboth shall dogs lick your own blood." ' "

Ahab said to Elijah, "Have you found me O my enemy?" He answered, "I have found you, because you have sold yourself to do what is evil in the sight of the Lord. Behold, I will bring evil upon you; I will utterly sweep you away, and will cut off from Ahab every male, bond or free, in Israel; and I will make your house like the house of Jeroboam the son of Nebat, and like the house of Baasha the son of Ahijah, for the anger to which you have provoked me, and because you have made Israel to sin. And of Jezebel the Lord also said, 'The dogs shall eat Jezebel within the bounds of Jezreel.' "

Several things should be noted concerning the above passage. Naboth could not be forced to sell his land to the king. In Israel there still remained the idea that the king was in a sense the servant of the people, that he had covenanted with them to rule, but to rule for the common good. It is to be remembered that the Northern Kingdom, Israel, seceded from the United Kingdom on this very issue. Solomon had played too much the part of absolute monarch, and when Rehoboam succeeded Solomon the overture was made by the elders of the people to get him to alter the policy of his father. But he had been too deeply infected by the principle that the will of the ruler and not the will of the people is sovereign. The result, as we have read, was rebellion and the establishment of the independent Northern Kingdom under Jeroboam. Ahab was in that succession and on that throne, and he had not forgotten the source of his sovereignty; observe that Naboth's refusal had upset the king because he could not carry out his desire, but it had not occurred to Ahab that he could do anything about it. He had simply accepted it. But not so Jezebel: for her the royal will was subject to no review; no writ could run against the king. There was no tribunal to pass judgment on kings. Yet this was where the prophet, the spokesman of Yahweh, came in. After Ahab had accepted the *fait accompli* conceived and executed by Jezebel, Elijah met him face to face and flayed him in the name of Yahweh with all the anger of righteous indignation.

Jezebel had earlier taken up the gauntlet thrown down by Elijah, and the ensuing struggle was very bitter. It became a sharply drawn contest between the religion of Yahweh and the religion of Ba'al Melkart, a contest for which Elijah set the scene. Elijah intended to show that the power of Yahweh was everything and that of Melkart nothing. The account in I Kings 18 may or may not be accurate in every detail, but in any case Yahweh was judged to have shown his superiority to Melkart: there followed a massacre of all the prophets of Ba'al Melkart, an act which seems cruel to us but is to be understood as a sacrifice to Yahweh and, at the same time, a gesture of contempt for Melkart, powerless to protect even his own priests.

Despite these dramatic events, the tide did not turn against ba'al worship until Elisha, the successor of Elijah, influenced Jehu, the army general, to revolt against the royal house. Jezebel was put to death, and Jehu became king. Jehu endeavored to wipe out all trace of ba'al worship, but his efforts were not completely successful. Nevertheless, Yahweh was now recognized as God of the land. For the time being, he and all the moral potentialities and religious possibilities resident in the faith centering in him were preserved for further growth and development. It is not surprising, therefore, that in the history of Hebrew religion the name of Elijah stands out with special prominence. His name is a symbol of prophecy. Even though greater men came after him, the tradition that persisted through all the centuries to the time of Jesus was of Elijah as the pre-eminent representative of the prophetic line.

The steps from the unquestioned acknowledgment of Yahweh as the God of Palestine, more powerful than the previously worshiped ba'alim, to the idea of one God only could not now be many. We can perhaps picture for ourselves that long-ago adventure of the mind. To the thoughtful worshiper, Yahweh was an adequate God. He could do anything necessary for the care and protection of his chosen people. The Exodus from Egypt was proof of that; so was the miraculous care through the sojourn in the wilderness. The Promised Land had now been a reality as a homeland for centuries. In the fight against the Philistines, every battle was as much a contest between Yahweh and the god or gods of the opposing army as it was a conflict between two groups of men in mortal combat. Victories were Yahweh's victories. Observe, then, the implications. Yahweh could withstand the gods of the Egyptians, the Philistines, and the Phoenicians. But what now about the different religions of many of the neighboring kingdoms? We shall presently see Amos answer this question; but even before his time it must have occurred to more than one man contemplating the future of the nation that its continuance would have to depend on the ability and power of Yahweh to control events. The only security against envelopment by some other nation was the power of Yahweh. How could he protect them unless he in some way transcended the gods of their foes? Some such process of thought must have taken place in the centuries following Elijah, for when we turn to the work of the great prophets of the eighth century and after, the universal supremacy of Yahweh is a major assumption of their theology.

Questions for Study

1. What are the two taproots of Western culture, and what has each contributed to our present period?
2. In what differing ways may one read the Old Testament? How did the early Hebrews understand their Scriptures?

3. What three divisions make up the Hebrew Scriptures, and by what dates did these come to general acceptance? Why was the first division considered most sacred?
4. What is the Septuagint, and why was it written? What is the Vulgate? What English translations have been made?
5. For what reasons did the documentary theory of the writing of the first books of the Old Testament come into acceptance? What documents are now identified as present in these first books, and how would you identify these?
6. Draw an outline map of Palestine, indicating the principal geographic features of the land. What significance did Palestinian geography have for Hebrew history?
7. What are the historic origins of the Hebrews? What forms did their early religion apparently take?
8. Why did the Hebrews leave Egypt, and under what circumstances? What was the origin of the Passover? What part did Moses play in these events? Who was Yahweh?
9. What are the most important features of the covenant relationship between Yahweh and the Hebrews at Mount Sinai? What connections have the giving of the Law and the Ten Commandments with the making of the Covenant? What specific demands were laid upon the Hebrews, and what were they promised?
10. In the time of Moses, how was Yahweh understood? What forms did early Hebrew religious practice take? What effects did the worship of Yahweh have upon the Hebrews?
11. How did the Hebrews establish themselves in Canaan? Why were they inclined to worship the Canaanite ba'alim? Why would it have been disastrous to them as a people if they had adopted ba'al worship?
12. Why did the Hebrews become a monarchy? Describe briefly the reigns of the first three kings—Saul, David, and Solomon.
13. Why did the Hebrew nation divide?
14. Describe the nature of the ba'al religion and indicate its differences from the Yahweh religion. Why was it a threat to Yahwism?
15. What is a prophet? How did Elijah and Elisha in the ninth century B.C. illustrate the prophetic role? What great work did they do for Yahweh religion, and how did they do it?

Selected Readings

Albright, William F., *The Archeology of Palestine*, rev. ed., Baltimore, Penguin Books, Inc., 1956.

Anderson, Bernhard W., *Understanding the Old Testament*, Englewood Cliffs, N.J., Prentice-Hall, Inc., 1957.

Baron, S. W., *A Social and Religious History of the Jews,* 2nd ed., New York, Columbia University Press, 1952, 8 vols.

Bright, John, *A History of Israel,* Philadelphia, The Westminster Press, 1959.

Bright, John, *The Kingdom of God,* Nashville, Abingdon-Cokesbury Press, 1953.

Driver, S. R., *Introduction to the Literature of the Old Testament,* New York, Meridian Books, Inc., 1956.

Finegan, Jack, *Light from the Ancient Past,* Princeton, Princeton University Press, 1946.

Gottwald, Norman K., *A Light to the Nations,* New York, Harper & Brothers, 1959.

The Interpreter's Bible, Nashville, Abingdon Press, 1952, vol. I.

Matthews, I. G., *The Religious Pilgrimage of Israel,* New York, Harper & Brothers, 1947.

Mendelsohn, Isaac (ed.), *Religions of the Ancient Near East,* Indianapolis, Liberal Arts Press, 1955.

Mould, Elmer W. K., *Essentials of Bible History,* rev. ed., New York, The Ronald Press Company, 1951.

Oesterley, W. O. E., and T. H. Robinson, *Hebrew Religion, Its Origin and Development,* New York, The Macmillan Company, 1937.

Oesterley, W. O. E., and T. H. Robinson, *A History of Israel,* Oxford, Clarendon Press, 1932, 2 vols.

Orlinsky, H. M. *Ancient Israel,* Ithaca, Cornell University Press, 1954.

Pfeiffer, Robert H., *The Books of the Old Testament,* New York, Harper & Brothers, 1957.

Pfeiffer, Robert H., *Introduction to the Old Testament,* New York, Harper & Brothers, 1941.

Price, Ira M., *The Ancestry of Our English Bible,* 3rd rev. ed., New York, Harper & Brothers, 1956.

Pritchard, James B. (ed.), *Ancient Near Eastern Texts,* 2nd ed., Princeton, Princeton University Press, 1955.

Pritchard, James B. (ed.), *Documents from Old Testament Times,* New York, Thomas Nelson & Sons, 1958.

Rowley, H. H. (ed.), *The Old Testament and Modern Study,* Oxford, Clarendon Press, 1951.

Wright, G. Ernest, *Biblical Archeology,* Philadelphia, The Westminster Press, 1957.

Wright, G. Ernest, and F. V. Filson, *The Westminster Historical Atlas of the Bible,* Philadelphia, The Westminster Press, 1956.

Wright, G. Ernest, and Reginald H. Fuller, *The Book of the Acts of God,* Garden City, Doubleday & Company, Inc., 1957.

2. Popular and Prophetic Religion Before the Exile

Social and Religious Conditions in the Eighth Century B.C.

The greatest period of Hebrew prophetic genius occurred in the eighth, seventh, and sixth centuries B.C. After Elijah and Elisha the supremacy of Yahweh was established, but the character of Yahwism was not far advanced beyond other contemporary religions. The fact of supremacy brought about a considerable development in the ritual of worship and consequently also the promotion of a professional priesthood. It is characteristic of religion that whenever ritual and priesthood develop there is a danger that rites and ceremonies may become ends in themselves rather than means; the proprieties of worship appear to possess inflated values, and the priesthood frequently arrogates a place of primary importance. This tendency, displayed generally by formally established religions, is amply illustrated by the religious life in Israel and Judah for more than a century, from the days of Elisha, in the reign of Jehu, to the rule of Jeroboam II.

Note also the further fact that during this same period the Northern Kingdom enjoyed much prosperity and experienced many changes in the economic and social order. In place of many little farms, great estates were developing. The well-to-do bent the process of justice to their own interest. Moreover, undisguised bribery was common, and accompanying it was a callous disregard of human rights. Consequently, in case after case the hard lot of circumstance was made increasingly bitter by bold and brazen injustice.

Because of it, free men were becoming slaves and serfs to their own countrymen. How do we know this? We certainly would not know it from anything which the priests of this era left behind; their chief concerns in religion were ritual, ceremony, sacrifices, and festivals. We learn of the existing conditions from what the prophets had to say. They had an amazingly clear insight into the relation between religion and ethics. Their thought of Yahweh as the one great God was coupled with the corresponding conviction that the human virtues of justice and mercy should manifest themselves throughout the whole of life, and that this practical morality itself was included under Yahweh's will for men. In the course of their assertions as to what the will of Yahweh was, they brought many indictments against current practices.

In order to get a clear conception of the work of these men, we shall consider them against the background of contemporary events, because from now on national affairs are important chiefly in relation to their religious significance. We shall consider in this chapter the four greatest prophets, whose contribution to religious thought occurred during the eighth and seventh centuries B.C., before the great Exile which took place early in the sixth century. This same period should be remembered also as the latter part of that span of Hebrew history during which the Hebrews were ruled by their own kings. There were no kings after the Exile, except for one very short period. The prophets to be considered here are Amos, Hosea, Isaiah, and Jeremiah. A fifth prophet, Micah, who appeared during the eighth century, will not be examined in this discussion since his message is adequately represented by Amos and Hosea.

The work of Amos and Hosea occurred in the Northern Kingdom of Israel before its fall to Assyria in 722 B.C. They are therefore eighth-century prophets, doing their work about 750 B.C., with Amos probably slightly the earlier. Isaiah and Jeremiah both prophesied to the Southern Kingdom of Judah, which was overthrown by the Babylonians in 586 B.C., but they were far apart in time, for Isaiah prophesied during the latter half of the eighth century, about 742-700 B.C., while Jeremiah appeared more than a century later, possibly 626-586 B.C. or later. Jeremiah was therefore a prophet of the seventh and early sixth centuries.

The Ethical Reinterpretation of the Covenant

Before we examine these men and their message, we must remind ourselves of the attitudes held by pious Hebrews toward their religion. Basic always to their thinking was the idea of the Covenant with their God.

Yahweh had chosen them as his people, telling them what his will was for them. In early centuries, God's will was understood specifically in terms of the Ten Commandments and certain other moral requirements. Great emphasis was placed upon the First Commandment—that the Hebrews were to worship only Yahweh. During the meeting and conflict with the ba'alim, this was the command most frequently broken. In spite of the work of Elijah and Elisha, the problem of the worship of the ba'alim was by no means completely solved; it was still a great issue particularly in the eighth century. Yet it was not as serious a problem as it had been earlier, when the very survival of Yahweh worship had stood in jeopardy. The continuing unfaithfulness of those Hebrews who still did worship the ba'alim quite naturally and properly would receive the condemnation of the prophets, as it did Hosea's.

But with the interest of these prophets in ethical righteousness, a new element, new at least in emphasis, also appeared during this eighth century. For this reason we sometimes call Amos, Hosea, Micah, and Isaiah the prophets who brought about the ethical reinterpretation of the Covenant. Even if the Hebrews had worshiped only Yahweh and had shown their faith by sacrifices and the keeping of holy days, this would not have been sufficient in the eyes of these men. They had come to realize that a righteous God demands righteous people and righteous action, and that formal actions like sacrifices and holy days do not of themselves satisfy God's demands, particularly if the very people who perform them are grasping, merciless, and unjust toward their fellows. Hence the evil actions of formal practitioners toward their brethren showed only too clearly the kind of men they were—men who rightly earned God's condemnation and would therefore in justice be destroyed.

Not during this century did these prophets come to the thought that God would reward and punish individuals—the focus of God's actions was still tribal. The Hebrews *as a people* would be punished for sinful deeds, and in that punishment innocent individuals also would suffer. The basis of condemnation was the evil nature of the people as a whole. By the *kind* of people who made it up, the nation was corrupted and evil and for this reason was regarded by Yahweh as unfaithful.

This understanding was not held by the people of the day. They had heard so much about themselves as God's chosen people that they were quite certain of his care and of the accompanying prosperity. Particularly in the early part of the eighth century, when wealth was so manifest, it seemed that the attention they expected from God was being extended to them lavishly. They even looked for a "Day of Yahweh" when in a supreme outpouring of his gifts God would exhibit their chosenness for all to see.

In short, they thought of the Covenant as a guarantee of privilege, not responsibility, forgetting the ancient dictum that they were to be a kingdom of priests (Exodus 19:6) whose work was to *serve* God.

The great prophets of this century understood the situation, but from quite a different point of view. The priests, presiding over lavish sacrifices, must have felt that these ceremonies exhibited a high degree of religion; and in the observance of religious rites the people sincerely believed they were doing what was well pleasing to God. The prophets, on the other hand, viewed the complacency which ritual religion generated with alarm and concern, and looked upon the current attitude toward religion as a delusion, very far indeed from the will of God. They thought of religion rather as a life of righteousness, mercy, and justice, and asserted that what was pleasing to God was a heart of compassion. The people of Israel were chosen to exemplify an ethical life. Such was the message of the prophets, but it was not the message of the priests, some of whom opposed the prophets. They led the people in the rites and ceremonies and called these good, while greed, injustice, bribery, and inhumanity flourished, untouched by current religious practice.

Against this state of affairs the prophets railed and pronounced doom. Only a change of heart, genuine repentance, and a turning away from these ways could save Israel and be pleasing in the sight of God. Centuries later, Jesus' attack on the Pharisees was made from the same standpoint—that ritual and ceremony can be misleading substitutes for spiritual regeneration. And similarly, fifteen centuries after Jesus, Luther in the Protestant Reformation entered his protest against the Catholic church on the same ground.

The importance, then, of the work of these great prophets can scarcely be exaggerated—not, of course, because they predicted the future accurately, but because they were profoundly religious men who had recognized that the deepest meaning of religion is man's ultimate faithfulness to a righteous and just God. This was the center of their reinterpretation of the Covenant, to be carried still further by Jeremiah when he emphasized the individual rather than the tribal character of the religious relationship.

Amos and Hosea in Israel During the Eighth Century B.C.

Amos

Amos is the prophet who gave us the picture of socio-economic conditions in the Northern Kingdom to which we have referred earlier. He should be read directly, for there is no substitute for his language, which has a tremendous impact upon even the modern reader. We see him, a native of the Southern Kingdom, appearing in Bethel, the capital city of the Northern Kingdom, speaking to a large, festive gathering of leaders who believed that all was well in Israel. Amos surveyed the international scene. One by one, he named the neighboring kingdoms, arraigned them before the judgment of Yahweh, specified the charge, and proclaimed the punishment. As he went down the list, he came to Judah, about which he had something to say, before letting out his climactic broadside against Israel.

> Thus says the Lord [Yahweh]:
> "For three transgressions of Judah, and for four, I will not revoke the punishment; because they have rejected the law of the Lord, and have not kept his statutes, but their lies have led them astray, after which their fathers walked. So I will send a fire upon Judah, and it shall devour the strongholds of Jerusalem" [Amos 2:4-5].

Possibly his listeners were not unhappy to hear of the evil fate about to overtake their neighbors, thinking that this might make Israel even more powerful. But now Amos turned against Israel herself and announced what Yahweh had in store for her:

> Thus says the Lord:
> "For three transgressions of Israel, and for four, I will not revoke the punishment; because they sell the righteous for silver, and the needy for a pair of shoes—they that trample the head of the poor into the dust of the earth, and turn aside the way of the afflicted; a man and his father go in to the same maiden, so that my holy name is profaned; they lay themselves down beside every altar upon garments taken in pledge; and in the house of their God they drink the wine of those who have been fined" [2:6-8].

Then Yahweh reminded them through the prophet of the fact that all they were was the result of his help given in times past, for which they owed him obedience:

> "Yet I destroyed the Amorite before them, whose height was like the height of cedars, and who was as strong as the oaks; I destroyed his fruit above, and his roots beneath. Also I brought you up out of the land of Egypt, and led you forty years in the wilderness, to possess the land of the Amorite. And I raised up your sons for prophets, and some of your young men to be Nazirites. Is it not indeed so, O people of Israel?" says the Lord [2:9-11].

And now he pronounced the punishment for unfaithfulness:

> "Behold, I will press you down in your place, as a cart full of sheaves presses down. Flight shall perish from the swift, and the strong shall not retain his strength,

nor shall the mighty save his life; he who handles the bow shall not stand, and he who is swift of foot shall not save himself, nor shall he who rides the horse save his life; and he who is stout of heart among the mighty shall flee away naked in that day," says the Lord [2:13-16].

"You only have I known of all the families of the earth; therefore I will punish you for all your iniquities" [3:2].

"Therefore because you trample upon the poor and take from him exactions of wheat, you have built houses of hewn stone, but you shall not dwell in them; you have planted pleasant vineyards, but you shall not drink their wine. For I know how many are your transgressions, and how great are your sins–you who afflict the righteous, who take a bribe, and turn aside the needy in the gate" [5:11-12].

The reader of these stirring passages is made profoundly aware that Amos as a prophet of Yahweh was passing ethical judgment and condemnation upon the national scene. As a God of righteousness, Yahweh was demanding justice and mercy in human affairs. Upon injustice and lack of mercy he would bring down disaster, which would be in the form of captivity, a scourge, or a famine. The Day of Yahweh, for which some of the Hebrews were eagerly waiting, would turn out to be a day not of rejoicing but of disaster, not of prosperity and greatness but of doom:

"Woe to you who desire the day of the Lord! Why would you have the day of the Lord? It is darkness, and not light; as if a man fled from a lion, and a bear met him; or went into the house and leaned with his hand against the wall, and a serpent bit him. Is not the day of the Lord darkness, and not light, and gloom with no brightness in it?" [5:18-20].

Those in authority may have thought they were serving Yahweh by sacrifices, rites, and ceremonies, but they were not.

"I hate, I despise your feasts, and I take no delight in your solemn assemblies. Even though you offer me your burnt offerings and cereal offerings, I will not accept them, and the peace offerings of your fatted beasts I will not look upon. Take away from me the noise of your songs; to the melody of your harps I will not listen" [5:21-23].

Such was the charge and such the judgment in store for Israel. Was there no way out, no escape from such a fate, since the sacrifices that were thought to please God were rejected? One way alone remained, and that was by genuine repentance for the behavior against which the charge was brought, namely, for their unethical living. In one lucid verse Amos summed up the solution: "But let justice roll down like waters, and righteousness like an everflowing stream" (5:24).

There was a ray of hope, and yet Amos himself was not hopeful. We have said that he comprehended God in a deeper and greater way than did the people of his own time. We have marked his emphasis upon God as righteous and ethical, but to this we must also add Amos' insight into the great power of God. In order that there be no doubt on the part of his hearers that Yahweh was able to do all that his justice required, Amos explicitly declared of Yahweh that he it was who controlled all of nature, and in so doing, Amos reached the belief that Yahweh was all-powerful.

"... prepare to meet your God, O Israel!"

For lo, he who forms the mountains, and creates the wind, and declares to man what is his thought; who makes the morning darkness, and treads on the heights of the earth—the Lord, the God of hosts, is his name! [4:12b-13]

He who made the Pleiades and Orion, and turns deep darkness into the morning, and darkens the day into night, who calls for the waters of the sea, and pours them out upon the surface of the earth, the Lord is his name ... [5:8].

Several elements of perennial importance to religion appear in these moving passages. Amos attacked the superficialities and externalities of religion and by so doing called upon religion in every age to re-examine itself; he stressed the greatness of God, who might too easily be misunderstood as a mere servant of men; and he had much to say about the ethical heart of religion. The man who acted unethically was acting in ways displeasing to God.

Hosea

Like Amos, Hosea was a prophet of doom, but he showed a degree of qualified optimism concerning the possibilities of restoration and ultimate renewal. Doom was coming upon Israel and God would exhibit his power and justice, but Yahweh's love[1] for his people would outlast his anger and punishment. It is in the writings of Hosea that we find the first great emphasis in the Old Testament upon the love and forgiveness of God.

It may well be asked how the prophets gained new insights into the nature of God and his relation to his people, thus refining the meaning and worth of their religion. The answer to this question is of great importance for any real appreciation of the development of religion. The prophets were all aware of the religious history of the nation. They were also profoundly religious, that is, they had a deep consciousness of the reality of Yahweh and a wholehearted faith that he had a purpose or plan for his people. The

[1] The Hebrew word here translated as love is *ḥesedh*, literally, deep concern.

covenant relationship was real to them. They were intellectually active, and pondered about conduct and national affairs in terms of their experience and understanding of God. They were sensitive in the manner of poets, artists, and musicians. In the course of their religious devotion, they had on occasion such a feeling or awareness of the divine presence that their whole being was stimulated to a high degree of insight into the problems, personal or national, which concerned them so deeply. So, for example, it was with Amos, and so it was with them all.

In the case of Hosea, we have an illustration of the way in which new insights into the nature of God grew out of profound personal experiences. Although not entirely clear in its biographical elements, the account of Hosea suggests that his wife, Gomer, who may have been a prostitute (possibly in one of the ba'al temples) when he married her at the command of Yahweh, was unfaithful to him. The account seems to indicate that she parted from Hosea for a time, having become committed to immoral ways. Later on, the woman became destitute. In the face of this unhappy situation and admitting that justice would have permitted him to dismiss her memory from his mind, Hosea still could not forget her or leave her in her deplorable condition. She had hurt him deeply, and yet he still loved her and wanted to see her restored. In his tribulation he discovered a new clue to God's nature and his attitude toward Israel. The nation Israel also had sinned, and in following after the ba'alim she had in a sense taken them as her lovers because of the gifts of wine and wool she thought these agricultural deities had given her. Israel became unfaithful to her one true husband, Yahweh, who had taken Israel to himself as a bride (to use Hosea's simile) at Mount Sinai in forming the Covenant with her. Here was a parallel that was suggestive in its conclusions. Since Hosea, misused as he was, could forgive and be willing to restore his wife, was it not possible that Yahweh might also forgive and restore Israel once again, after she had suffered the punishment and destitution that were imminent? Hosea believed God would do this.

Using his own personal experience as an analogy to the history of the relations between Yahweh and Israel, Hosea wrote the following passage (Hosea 2:5b-7a, 8-13) in which Yahweh speaks in the first person and the unfaithful wife represents Israel.

For she said, "I will go after my lovers, who give me my bread and my water, my wool and my flax, my oil and my drink."

Therefore I will hedge up her way with thorns; and I will build a wall against her, so that she cannot find her paths. She shall pursue her lovers, but not overtake them; and she shall seek them, but shall not find them. . . . And she did not know that it was I who gave her the grain, the wine, and the oil, and who lavished upon her silver and gold which they used for Baal. Therefore I will take back my grain in its time, and my wine in its season; and I will take away my wool and my flax, which were to cover her nakedness. Now I will uncover her lewdness in the sight of her lovers, and no one shall rescue her out of my hand. And I will put an end to all her mirth, her feasts, her new moons, her sabbaths, and all her appointed feasts. And I will lay waste her vines and her fig trees, of which she said, "These are my hire, which my lovers have given me." I will make them a forest, and the beasts of the field shall devour them. And I will punish her for the feast days of the Baals when she burned incense to them and decked herself with her ring and jewelry, and went after her lovers, and forgot me, says the Lord.

In this way did Hosea represent the sufferings and destruction in store for Israel. But the Israelites themselves refused to acknowledge that Yahweh could or would punish them. Instead of turning to him in repentance under the Covenant while there was still time, they attempted to stave off disaster by forming alliances with Egypt and Assyria. But Hosea assured them that this would help not at all, since it was Yahweh himself who would punish.

When Ephraim [Israel] saw his sickness, and Judah his wound, then Ephraim went to Assyria, and sent to the great king. But he is not able to cure you or heal your wound. For I will be like a lion to Ephraim, and like a young lion to the house of Judah. I, even I, will rend and go away, I will carry off, and none shall rescue [5:13-14].

The punishment that faced them was destruction of cities and lands, and exile: "For behold, they are going to Assyria; Egypt shall gather them, Memphis [an Egyptian city] shall bury them. Nettles shall possess their precious things of silver; thorns shall be in their tents" (9:6).

A striking characteristic of Hosea is that when in one mood he would describe Yahweh as bringing down punishment and judgment, he would immediately afterwards write a passage indicating an ineradicable love for the nation which would prevent Yahweh from abandoning them entirely to destruction. The following passage (11:1-9) illustrates this. The language of tenderness in the quotation is drawn from the relation between father and son rather than that between husband and wife.

When Israel was a child, I loved him, and out of Egypt I called my son. . . . it was I who taught Ephraim [Israel] to walk, I took them up in my arms; but they did not know that I healed them. I led them with cords of compassion, with the bands of love . . . . They shall return to the land of Egypt, and Assyria shall be their king, because they have refused to return to me. The sword shall rage against their cities, consume the bars of their gates, and devour them in their fortresses. . . . How can I give you up, O Ephraim! How can I hand you over, O Israel! . . . My heart recoils within me, my compassion grows warm and tender. I will not execute my fierce anger, I will not again destroy Ephraim; for I am God and not man, the Holy One in your midst, and I will not come to destroy.

The prophet foresaw the day when Israel would realize who her true God was and would return in faithfulness to him. Just as Hosea himself could forgive his wife in her destitution and ransom her, so too the children of Israel would be restored once more and be granted a new beginning in the wilderness of Palestine. They would say, "Come, let us return to the Lord; for he has torn, that he may heal us; he has stricken, and he will bind us up" (6:1).

Again using the analogy of the husband-wife relationship, Yahweh says,

. . . behold, I will allure her, and bring her into the wilderness, and speak tenderly to her. And there I will give her her vineyards, and make the Valley of Achor a door of hope . . . . And in that day, says the Lord, you will call me, "My husband," and no longer will you call me, "My Baal." For I will remove the names of the Baals from her mouth, and they shall be mentioned by name no more [2:14-17].

In that day, the day of repentance and restoration, the Covenant would be renewed, and this time it would be faithfully followed; even war will disappear.

And I will make for you a covenant on that day with the beasts of the field, the birds of the air, and the creeping things of the ground; and I will abolish the bow, the sword, and war from the land; and I will make you lie down in safety. And I will betroth you to me for ever; I will betroth you to me in righteousness and in justice, in steadfast love, and in mercy. I will betroth you to me in faithfulness; and you shall know the Lord [2:18-20].

All of this was for the future. In the present was found worship of the ba'alim, lack of justice, immorality, unfaithfulness on every hand, greediness, struggle for power, and apostasy. The prophet himself was called a fool and a madman by his contemporaries (Hosea 9:7), and although he called himself the "watchman of Ephraim," he was rejected. Like Amos, Hosea also demanded ethical conduct or righteousness as the primary factor in doing God's will: "For I desire steadfast love and not sacrifice, the knowledge of God, rather than burnt offerings" (6:6). But such qualities were not forthcoming. The nation had the spirit of apostasy, called harlotry (5:4), and like Gomer, the wife of the prophet, had to go through the fires of suffering before it would be ready for the greater good God had in store for it.

The disaster which the prophets Amos and Hosea had foreseen did come, for the Assyrians under Sargon II put an end to the history of the Northern

Kingdom, Israel, in 722 B.C. An ancient Assyrian record indicates that 27,290 people were carried away by the conqueror, who settled captured peoples from other nations in the land and rebuilt its capital of Samaria even larger than it was before. Possibly four-fifths of the Hebrew population was left behind under Assyrian control, but as a national unit Israel ceased to exist. The deportees were probably absorbed by the populations of the lands to which they were taken; those remaining behind intermarried with the people settled among them and became the later Samaritans.

Judah, the Southern Kingdom, now stood alone, having saved herself from dissolution by becoming a vassal of Assyria some dozen years before the fall of Israel. It was well that writings like those of Amos and Hosea were preserved, because when catastrophe struck Judah in turn it was not altogether a surprise, and the writings which prophesied calamity also contained elements of hope. With the fall of Israel, the writings of Hosea and Amos became part of the heritage of Judah and were included in its prophetic literature. These, along with the writings of Isaiah, Jeremiah, and others, formed the inspiration that sustained the people from the beginning of the Exile, when the Southern Kingdom fell. These elements of hope kept religious faith in Yahweh alive. Yahweh, the people believed, had not forgotten them, and the future was therefore not dark but full of promise.

In summary, Amos and Hosea took a great step forward in religious understanding. With the Covenant as the background of their thought, that relationship was raised to a new level, both as to the idea of God and as to the nature of the human conduct required by Yahweh. Amos emphasized the justice and power of Yahweh, both conceived universally. He insisted that animal sacrifices were not an original part of Yahweh worship. Furthermore, there was a vital infusion of ethics into religion by the insistence on ethical virtues in human relations as the primary condition of keeping the Covenant properly. In this respect Hosea was exactly of the same mind. Hosea added a new note of love and tenderness to the understanding of the attributes of Yahweh. This new element was important in its implications, for its development by later prophets saved Judaism from complete pessimism.

Isaiah in Judah During the Eighth Century B.C.

We turn our attention now to the Southern Kingdom, where prophetic insights were carried to new depths by Isaiah. His prophetic utterances revealed a greatness of character remarkable for its assurance of and loyalty to the divine commands. Isaiah was a man with a broad national outlook. He seems to have had wide acquaintance with the customs and habits of the peoples in the world around him. Isaiah's role was that of a profound observer and a devastating commentator on the current state of affairs in religion, morals, and politics. He had the unhappy destiny of being in the opposition and spiritually alone for most of his life and of having his patriotism misunderstood. We know that his period of prophesying was a long one, for his call came in the year 742 B.C. and he was still active at the close of the eighth century.

Let us take a brief glance at the setting in which Isaiah appeared. The international scene had changed since the time of Amos. The Assyrian menace to which the earlier prophets had referred had become a reality, and Isaiah himself had lived through those years when the Northern Kingdom, Israel, had finally succumbed to the invaders and had been so ignominiously destroyed, leaving Judah alone to carry on the Hebrew faith and traditions. Isaiah, then, had observed this calamity, had had much to say about it, and was well aware that Judah's continuance was purchased by payment of tribute to Assyria.

The young king, Hezekiah, who had come to the throne in 715 B.C., seven years after the fall of the Northern Kingdom, was in a difficult position. The people were divided into an Egyptian party and an Assyrian party, and some wanted revolt. A period of diplomatic deception followed by armed revolt led to the laying waste of many towns by the Assyrians. In consequence, only by paying heavy additional tribute was Hezekiah allowed to retain his kingdom, which was reduced in size. It was necessary to strip the gold and silver from the Temple in order to pay the levy.

Moral and social conditions during the reign of Hezekiah were bad. Many people, including some priests, led lives of drunkenness, gluttony, and vice, and the prophet Isaiah declared that ruin would fall upon the nation. The political leaders, however, expected to evade divine judgment by subtle diplomacy, and endeavored to make secret alliances with Egypt. These endeavors met with the vehement disapproval of Isaiah, but his objections were of no avail until the threat of disaster induced the authorities to include the prophet in their consultations. Under his urging, religious reforms were put into effect: Hezekiah abolished high places, broke the sacred pillars in pieces, cut down an ancient copper serpent that had stood in the Temple itself, and laid the ax to the sacred pole. The symbols of worship the Hebrews had come to use included representations of deities in animal form, features of totemism, magic, and fertility gods. Each item spoke volumes about the deplorable state of everyday affairs, and each stood in sharp contrast to the spiritual ideals of the prophets.

With this general picture in mind, we may now consider the major features of Isaiah's contributions to religion—the call of the prophet, his exalted conception of God, the union of religion and morals, the principle of punishment for sin, his philosophy of history, the idea of a remnant, and the idea of a Messiah. These have much in common with and developed from the ideas of Amos and Hosea.

The account of Isaiah's *call* to be a prophet (Isaiah 6:1-5) is a classic of religious literature. It can be dated precisely, for we are told that it took place in the year that King Uzziah died, which was in 742 B.C., 20 years before the fall of Israel. Isaiah was standing in the Temple in Jerusalem and looking toward an altar, probably situated in front of the Holy of Holies, on which were burning coals. As he looked, he had an ecstatic vision, and saw

> . . . the Lord [Yahweh] sitting upon a throne, high and lifted up; and his train filled the temple. Above him stood the seraphim; each had six wings; with two he covered his face, and with two he covered his feet, and with two he flew. And one called to another and said: "Holy, holy, holy is the Lord of hosts; the whole earth is full of his glory." And the foundations of the thresholds shook at the voice of him who called, and the house was filled with smoke. And I said: "Woe is me! For I am lost; for I am a man of unclean lips, and I dwell in the midst of a people of unclean lips; for my eyes have seen the King, the Lord of hosts!"

It was the *holiness* of Yahweh that first struck Isaiah; then, by contrast, he was filled with fear at the thought of the uncleanness of both his people and himself. God's holiness suggested both God's ethical and moral perfection, but even more his awesome greatness and "otherness" above his creation. The vision was not merely a vision of God but, in the way typical of all Hebrew prophecy (going back to Abraham and to Moses' vision of the burning bush), it was God's way of calling a man into his active service. In Isaiah's case, that service was to last more than 40 years.

As Isaiah was filled with awe and fear, one of the strange creatures of his vision, a seraphim (a Babylonian symbolic figure, partly human and partly animal), brought a burning coal from off the altar.

> And he touched my mouth, and said: "Behold, this has touched your lips; your guilt is taken away, and your sin forgiven." And I heard the voice of the Lord saying, "Whom shall I send, and who will go for us?" Then I said, "Here am I! Send me." And he said, "Go, and say to this people: 'Hear and hear, but do not understand; see and see, but do not perceive.' Make the heart of this people fat, and their ears heavy, and shut their eyes . . . ." Then I said, "How long, O Lord?" And he said: "Until cities lie waste without inhabitant, and houses without men, and the land is utterly desolate, and the Lord removes men far away, and the forsaken places are many in the midst of the land" [6:7-12].

Isaiah was called to present a message much like that of Amos and Hosea: the message of sinfulness, condemnation, and possible restoration.

As we turn now to the *prophetic message* of Isaiah, we may not overlook the fact that the ideas of a Hebrew prophet are not developed as are the ideas in an essay. They come more like molten lava, flowing out, as it were, from the inner heat and pressure within a burdened and responsive soul. Isaiah dramatizes what he has to say by various literary devices, designed to impress the imagination and memory of his hearers. For example, we learn a great deal about Isaiah's understanding of God and the nature of man's relation to him in an interesting passage which pictures a great trial, the people being arraigned for judgment before Yahweh. Isaiah, writing in the latter half of his life, represents Yahweh as presenting his case against his people (1:2b-6, 10-20):

"Sons have I reared and brought up, but they have rebelled against me. The ox knows its owner, and the ass its master's crib; but Israel does not know, my people does not understand."

Ah, sinful nation, a people laden with iniquity, offspring of evildoers, sons who deal corruptly! They have forsaken the Lord, they have despised the Holy One of Israel, they are utterly estranged. Why will you still be smitten, that you continue to rebel? The whole head is sick, and the whole heart faint. From the sole of the foot even to the head, there is no soundness in it, but bruises and sores and bleeding wounds. . . .

Hear the word of the Lord, you rulers in Sodom! Give ear to the teaching of our God, you people of Gomorrah! "What to me is the multitude of your sacrifices? says the Lord; I have had enough of burnt offerings of rams and the fat of fed beasts; I do not delight in the blood of bulls, or of lambs, or of he-goats.

"When you come to appear before me, who requires of you this trampling of my courts? Bring no more vain offerings; incense is an abomination to me. New moon and sabbath and the calling of assemblies–I cannot endure iniquity and solemn assembly. Your new moons and your appointed feasts my soul hates; they have become a burden to me, I am weary of bearing them. When you spread forth your hands, I will hide my eyes from you; even though you make many prayers, I will not listen; your hands are full of blood. Wash yourselves; make yourselves clean; remove the evil of your doings from before my eyes; cease to do evil, learn to do good; seek justice, correct oppression; defend the fatherless, plead for the widow.

"Come now, let us reason together, says the Lord: though your sins are like scarlet, they shall be as white as snow; though they are red like crimson, they shall become like wool. If you are willing and obedient, you shall eat the good of the land; But if you refuse and rebel, you shall be devoured by the sword; for the mouth of the Lord has spoken."

Despite the fact that Yahweh worship had been firmly established by Hezekiah's reforms and most of the pagan and foreign elements had been officially discarded, Isaiah was convinced that the type of religion that remained was of little value; he had little regard for sacrifices and blood offerings, solemn feasts and incense burnings, which in themselves reveal no moral or spiritual sensibilities at all. He appealed to the minds of the people, and when he said, "Come . . . let us reason together," it is as though he called upon them to think things through with him. Surely it would need only half a moral eye to discern that sacrifices were not in themselves righteousness. The will of Yahweh was that there should be righteousness in all human relations, that greed, avarice, cruelty, selfish luxury, and extravagant tastes should be eliminated. Isaiah strove to make the people see that Yahweh was not an Oriental monarch, taking delight in the smell of incense or the flavor of roasted flesh; Yahweh was the Mighty One, the Holy One, who personified goodness, righteousness, and justice. This idea is the core from which everything else in his teaching flowed, and in terms of which he passed judgment on a wide range of individual and national behavior.

Isaiah's *concept of God* was universal enough to be applied to the whole world of events, both local and international. He looked upon his own people shortly after his prophetic call and found little in their way of life to place them on a higher level than the neighboring nations. He held them responsible for faithless, corrupted, unethical living. Like Amos and Hosea, Isaiah was keenly aware of their injustices, lack of mercy, and exploitation of the poor and the helpless. The source of these evils was their pride in themselves and their achievements, which led them to believe in their own ability to direct the future and to deny in practice the demands of Yahweh. They had thereby broken the covenant relation in which they were responsible partners. Their failure to keep their obligations to Yahweh was sin, and because of it they had to pay the price of punishment. They were to be scourged in the international arena where they had chosen to play the current game of intrigue and armed alliance, for only thus would they learn to rely upon Yahweh, and Assyria would be the instrument of his punishment.

Though men everywhere assumed the existence of many gods, and a nation like Assyria proudly assumed the pre-eminence of its gods, Isaiah and his immediate predecessors had the spiritual audacity to declare the all-powerful moral eminence of Yahweh. Other nations might stride with power and crush little peoples with cruelty, but when Yahweh assigned them to oblivion their brief day would end and they would cease to be.

> Ah, Assyria, the rod of my anger, the staff of my fury! Against a godless nation I send him, and against the people of my wrath I command him, to take spoil and seize plunder, and to tread them down like the mire of the streets. But he does not so intend, and his mind does not so think; but it is in his mind to destroy, and to cut off nations not a few; for he says: "Are not my commanders all kings? . . . shall I not do to Jerusalem and her idols as I have done to Samaria and her images?"
>
> When the Lord has finished all his work on Mount Zion and on Jerusalem he will punish the arrogant boasting of the king of Assyria and his haughty pride. For he says: "By the strength of my hand I have done it, and by my wisdom, for I have understanding; I have removed the boundaries of peoples, and have plundered their treasures. . . ."
>
> Shall the axe vaunt itself over him who hews with it, or the saw magnify itself against him who wields it? . . . Therefore the Lord, the Lord of hosts, will send wasting sickness among his [Assyria's] stout warriors, . . . The light of Israel will become a fire, and his Holy One a flame; and it will burn and devour his thorns and briers in one day. The glory of his forest and of his fruitful land the Lord will destroy, both soul and body, and it will be as when a sick man wastes away [10:5-18].

Here is the insight of Isaiah revealed: his sublime faith that righteousness and justice belonged to God, and that no power of man, however ruthless or wicked, could withstand the purpose of Yahweh to enthrone goodness in the life of the nation. Isaiah stood forth in a day when the whole conduct of his countrymen fluctuated between reliance on some combination of physical power and fear of a combination of the same sort against them. Isaiah wrestled with the problem of finding a dependable force for righteousness. He believed that Yahweh was such a power, and he trusted that power. In one form or another, this is a problem that is always with us. In what shall we put our trust—in the right that is made by might, or in a goodness that is not national, that has no boundaries, but that is universal and eternal? Isaiah accepted the latter faith, affirming that the universal supremacy of moral goodness was one with the universality of God.

His exalted conception of God as the moral ruler of the universe enabled Isaiah to interpret events in terms of the righteous purposes of God, thus providing him with his *philosophy of history*. In other words, here was a chosen people, chosen not by a minor god or gods but by the Mighty and Holy One, and chosen to do his righteous will. This was what the Covenant meant. This conception was so far above the contemporary religious understanding that it ought not to surprise us that its import was only vaguely grasped at the time. It was hard to see that the ways, customs, and habits current in the world were not God's ways. But if the people could not be taught except by punishment and scourging, then only through bitter experience should they learn that it was righteousness alone that exalted the nation; thus, bitter national experiences were interpreted by the prophets as the consequences of unrighteousness.

Whatever Yahweh might have in store for them, however destructive the punishment might be, however devastatingly Assyria might ravish the land, it would not be allowed to destroy God's people utterly. And this brings us to cross-currents in Isaiah's thought out of which he evolved the ideas of the remnant and of the messiah, ideas which came to have a very prominent place in the thought of later generations.

The idea of a *remnant* was first advanced by Isaiah when the Assyrians were laying waste the Northern Kindgom. As much as he believed punishment was due, he nevertheless thought that Yahweh would not leave himself without some remnant from which a new nation could be created. The notion of a remnant was the only form that hope could take, and the day was yet in the far-off future when this idea would be seized upon again as an anchor of hope.

> In that day the remnant of Israel and the survivors of the house of Jacob will no more lean upon him that smote them [Assyria], but will lean upon the Lord, the Holy One of Israel, in truth. A remnant will return, the remnant of Jacob, to the mighty God. For though your people Israel be as the sand of the sea, only a remnant of them will return. Destruction is decreed, overflowing with righteousness [10:20-22].

Before destruction arrived, this teaching was a statement of fearsome things to come, threatening as it did that *only* a remnant should remain; later it became the promise of a future restoration, and so a hope.

Judah's alliance with Assyria prevented the dreaded attack which the prophet had expected from materializing, and the Southern Kingdom, becoming vassal to Assyria, escaped the fate which had befallen Israel. But the danger of destruction continued, for under King Hezekiah revolt against Assyria broke out. The prophecies of Isaiah remained, and at such times of crisis their significance was appreciated. They became particularly significant a century and a half later when Judah followed Israel into captivity.

Finally, in passages of Isaiah's writing which have been widely discussed over the centuries and have been taken as prophecies referring to Jesus, it appears that as the prophet looked beyond the suffering and destruction which were coming he saw a new age which would dawn. A *messianic king* (one anointed by God), he said, would reign in that justice and that righteousness which were so woefully lacking in Isaiah's own period.

But there will be no gloom for her that was in anguish. In the former time he brought into contempt the land of Zebulun and the land of Naphtali, but in the latter time he will make glorious the way of the sea, the land beyond the Jordan, Galilee of the nations. The people who walked in darkness have seen a great light; those who dwelt in a land of deep darkness, on them has light shined. Thou hast multiplied the nation, thou hast increased its joy. . . . For the yoke of his burden, and the staff for his shoulder, the rod of his oppressor, thou hast broken as on the day of Midian. . . . For to us a child is born, to us a son is given; and the government will be upon his shoulder, and his name will be called "Wonderful Counselor, Mighty God, Everlasting Father, Prince of Peace." Of the increase of his government and of peace there will be no end, upon the throne of David, and over his kingdom, to establish it, and to uphold it with justice and with righteousness from this time forth and for evermore. The zeal of the Lord of hosts will do this [9:1-7].

There shall come forth a shoot from the stump of Jesse, and a branch shall grow out of his roots. And the Spirit of the Lord shall rest upon him, the spirit of wisdom and understanding, the spirit of counsel and might, the spirit of knowledge and the fear of the Lord. And his delight shall be in the fear of the Lord.

He shall not judge by what his eyes see, or decide by what his ears hear; but with righteousness he shall judge the poor, and decide with equity for the meek of the earth; and he shall smite the earth with the rod of his mouth, and with the breath of his lips he shall slay the wicked. Righteousness shall be the girdle of his waist, and faithfulness the girdle of his loins.

The wolf shall dwell with the lamb, and the leopard shall lie down with the kid, and the calf and the lion and the fatling together, and a little child shall lead them. The cow and the bear shall feed; their young shall lie down together; and the lion shall eat straw like the ox. The sucking child shall play over the hole of the asp, and the weaned child shall put his hand on the adder's den. They shall not hurt or destroy in all my holy mountain; for the earth shall be full of the knowledge of the Lord as the waters cover the sea [11:1-9].

Here is a prophecy of future peace and righteousness to which the hearts of men have echoed for the 27 centuries that have passed since the time of Isaiah. What was to happen would not be done by men in their own strength but done for them by God. The "zeal of the Lord" would do this, through a child who would become king or, in the latter chapter, through a descendent of David, a second David (Jesse was the father of David), upon whom the Spirit of Yahweh would rest. Through his divine appointment, this messianic king would reign on the basis of true knowledge of God, which meant that his rule would be a reign of faithfulness and righteousness. Such a kingdom would of course be without end, for it would be in complete agreement with the Covenant, whose provisions would be upheld by the power of the eternal God himself.

The vision of the prophet reached beyond the day when justice would rule to a veritable golden age when even the wild beasts and poisonous snakes would lose their destructive natures and be at peace with each other. In this great vision of the peace humanity has so long sought and whose conditions it has so little met, Isaiah repeated the great hope and promise of Hosea (Hosea 2:18).

No such great king came in Isaiah's time, although Hezekiah came nearer to the ideal than did any of the four other kings through whose reigns Isaiah lived. Nor did a messianic king appear in the remaining years of the kingdom up to the time of the Exile. However, the hope that sometime in the future this would happen persisted side by side with the idea of the remnant. Various later forms of these two great ideas will engage our attention, for without them the continuance of the nation after the fall of Jerusalem would have been doubtful.

Jeremiah in the Seventh and Sixth Centuries B.C.

In Jeremiah we reach the last of the great pre-exilic prophets, considered by some writers to be the greatest of all the prophets. Jeremiah was an outstanding religious personality who contributed one of the greatest religious insights found in the Old Testament. Like other prophets before him, Jeremiah also had a call to prophetic service, about the year 626 B.C.

> Now the word of the Lord came to me saying, "Before I formed you in the womb I knew you, and before you were born I consecrated you; I appointed you a prophet to the nations." Then I said, "Ah, Lord God! Behold, I do not know how to speak, for I am only a youth." But the Lord said to me, "Do not say, 'I am only a youth'; for to all to whom I send you you shall go, and whatever I command you you shall speak. Be not afraid of them, for I am with you to deliver you, says the Lord." Then the Lord put forth his hand and touched my mouth; and the Lord said to me, "Behold, I have put my words in your mouth. See, I have set you this day over nations and over kingdoms, to pluck up and to break down, to destroy and to overthrow, to build and to plant" [Jeremiah 1:4-10].

Such calls as these to prophetic service came to sensitive Jews who lived in a state of tension caused by the difference between conditions existing in their society and their conception of what God actually demanded. Jeremiah came from an old, established family long connected with the religious life of the nation; he felt that the spiritual well-being of the nation was his concern. He knew also, of course, the great teachings of the prophets who had preceded him. Before his very eyes he could see the results of the work of the long-lived and evil King Manasseh, Hezekiah's son, who, ruling from about 687 until 642 B.C., had led his nation into a veritable religious dark age. Manasseh had undone all the work of reform accomplished by Hezekiah. He had re-established worship of the ba'alim with its high places and ritual prostitution. Probably in order to please the Assyrians, he had instituted both the worship of the divine spirits connected with the sun, moon, and stars, and also a cult of the dead. Human sacrifice was once again practiced—the king himself sacrificed one of his own sons. Manasseh fostered Assyrian religious practices even within the area of the Temple itself. It is thought that he took strong measures to suppress the prophets of Yahweh.

As a sensitive worshiper of Yahweh, Jeremiah must have felt that something needed to be done about the situation. No great prophet had been heard from for almost three generations. Then one day Jeremiah unmistakably heard the call to himself. Yahweh was telling *him* that he had been chosen from before his birth for just this day and its task. It was useless to protest that he was too young; Yahweh would strengthen him and give him words to speak.

Jeremiah started out as a prophetic voice reminding people of the covenant relationship, seemingly forgotten in the 45 years of Manasseh's reign. Manasseh was now dead, and his place had been taken by Josiah in 640 B.C., 14 years before Jeremiah's call.

The word that came to Jeremiah from the Lord: "Hear the words of this covenant, and speak to the men of Judah and the inhabitants of Jerusalem. You shall say to them, Thus says the Lord, the God of Israel: Cursed be the man who does not heed the words of this covenant which I commanded your fathers when I brought them out of the land of Egypt, from the iron furnace, saying, Listen to my voice, and do all that I command you. So shall you be my people, and I will be your God, that I may perform the oath which I swore to your fathers to give them a land flowing with milk and honey, as at this day." Then I answered, "So be it, Lord."

And the Lord said to me, "Proclaim all these words in the cities of Judah, and in the streets of Jerusalem: Hear the words of this covenant and do them. For I solemnly warned your fathers when I brought them up out of the land of Egypt, warning them persistently, even to this day, saying, Obey my voice. Yet they did not obey or incline their ear, but everyone walked in the stubbornness of his evil heart . . ." [11:1-8].

Yahweh then brought the charge of unfaithfulness against the people, because instead of obeying the Covenant they were serving other gods and living unethically. Because of this sin, he would surely punish them:

"Therefore . . . I am bringing evil upon them which they cannot escape; though they cry to me, I will not listen to them. Then the cities of Judah and the inhabitants of Jerusalem will go and cry to the gods to whom they burn incense, but they cannot save them in the time of their trouble" [11:11-12].

In common with the eighth-century prophets, Jeremiah also was a prophet of ethical righteousness. Although the worship of gods other than Yahweh was the most obvious religious sin of his day, Jeremiah was fully aware of the ethical and moral sins of the people as well. He too attacked the elaborate sacrifices which people offered as substitutes for correct living.

"For from the least to the greatest of them, every one is greedy for unjust gain; and from prophet to priest, every one deals falsely. . . .

"Hear, O earth; behold, I am bringing evil upon this people, the fruit of their devices, because they have not given heed to my words; and as for my law, they have rejected it. To what purpose does frankincense come to me from Sheba, or sweet cane from a distant land? Your burnt offerings are not acceptable, nor your sacrifices pleasing to me" [6:13, 19-20].

Because of the people's terrible and far-reaching disobedience, punishment would be the lot of the kingdom of Judah: destruction, death, and exile. Without repeating what has gone before, we may say that Jeremiah's teaching, like that of Isaiah, included the idea of the lofty moral character of Yahweh and the certainty of punishment for sin. He denounced the popular religion more vehemently than Isaiah had because under Manasseh so much ground had been lost. Therefore, the apostasy of the nation seemed so much worse than formerly. Also, Jeremiah was just as much opposed to the sins of his time as were his predecessors. If this were all that could be said about Jeremiah, we could conclude here, but in the course of an extremely active career his experiences brought about a fundamental change in his outlook in the direction of a more intimate and personal religion. We can appreciate this best if we first take into account a few important events.

About five years after Jeremiah began his ministry, the famous reformation under King Josiah occurred, in 621 B.C. We have mentioned that the earlier reforms under Hezekiah were undone by his son, and we can imagine without difficulty how the prophetic "school" would chafe under conditions during his reign. From rejoicing over the reforms which the prophetic insistence of Isaiah had accomplished through Hezekiah, they were now in dismay over their revocation by Manasseh. It is therefore quite understandable that when the young Prince Josiah ascended the throne as an 8-year-old child, they greeted the new king with hope and possibly with plans to influence him in the direction of a return to Yahweh. When Josiah was 18 years of age, an event occurred which was revolutionary in its impact upon the nation, bringing forth the most thorough reform that Jewish religion had known thus far.

The bare facts are brought out in II Kings 22-23. From this account we observe that extensive repairs on the Temple were being contemplated, possibly in connection with removing some of the signs of Manasseh's apostasy. Josiah's secretary, Shaphan, visited the Temple. While there, the priest Hilkiah informed Shaphan that he had discovered in the Temple a book called the *Book of Instruction.* It was brought to light while repairs were in progress. Shaphan read the book and, greatly disturbed by it, felt that it should be brought immediately to the king's attention. When the king read it, he was alarmed by its contents. It is evident that the book contained many commands disobedience to which would call forth the divine wrath.

The king called officials and leading citizens together, asking and receiving their solemn word that they would stand with him on these instructions. In consequence, there was a widespread reform, the first stage of which was the removal of every mark of idolatry and paganism from the Temple. The purging process extended outward from the Temple through the country as a whole.

A partial list of these reforms shows us the extent of the evil practices of that time. It included the removal from the Temple itself of the vessels intended for ba'al worship and the houses of cult prostitutes. Child sacrifice to Moloch was done away with; horses sacred to the sun were no longer maintained, nor the altars dedicated by Solomon to the gods of his wives. Most important for later Jewish religion was Josiah's destruction of all the ancient sacred places to Yahweh, such as the cult center at Bethel, except the Temple in Jerusalem, thus making for centralization of worship for the first time since the Hebrews entered Palestine. Josiah's reason for taking this action was that the Book of Instruction gave this as Yahweh's will. It was a move, however, that, as might well be imagined, was not popular with the priests of Yahweh who officiated at the ancient sites, for some of these centers had existed from the time of Joshua and antedated by centuries the Jerusalem Temple erected in the reign of Solomon.

Obvious questions are evoked by this recital. What was the Book of Instruction, where did it come from, why was it not known before, and where should we look for it in our present Old Testament? Biblical scholars have tried to find the answers. Briefly, we can say that as we try to locate this "book" in the Bible (for it does not appear in the description of its discovery in II Kings), we have first to remember that it was sufficiently short to be read several times in one day, which the account shows was done on the day it was found. Further, it contained instructions to be obeyed and penalties for disobedience. Also, it would contain a reference to a single center for Yahweh worship. We have every reason to expect that it would be preserved as a sacred writing, since it was thought to be the work of Moses. There is one part of the Old Testament that satisfies all of these conditions, namely, chapters 12 to 26 in the book of Deuteronomy, a book whose name means second law (in Greek, *deuteros nomos*).

As it now stands in the Old Testament, Deuteronomy is one of the five books of the Torah or the Pentateuch whose authorship is ascribed by tradition to Moses. But had Moses left such a book, it is difficult to understand how it could have been so completely forgotten; it would have been preserved along with the other sacred writings. Therefore, since we have no other book similar to Deuteronomy and since it meets all the requirements of the situation recorded in II Kings, it is reasonable to assume that the chapters mentioned are the work in question. Further, examination of this material in Deuteronomy makes clear that its instructions, commands, and penalties pertain in numerous ways to conditions of living and religion which were not and could not have been problems in the days of Moses. Also, in this book and this book alone of the ancient writings is found the explicit statement that Yahweh worship was to be concentrated in one location, as is written (Deuteronomy 12:5-6, 13-14):

> . . . you shall seek the place which the Lord your God will choose out of all your tribes to put his name and make his habitation there; thither you shall go, and thither you shall bring your burnt offerings and your sacrifices. . . . Take heed that you do not offer your burnt offerings at every place that you see; but at the place which the Lord will choose in one of your tribes, there you shall offer your burnt offerings. . . .

Various suggestions have been made to account for the authorship of this material, on the assumption that Moses himself did not write it. One hypothesis that has received wide acceptance among scholars is the view that the book was prepared toward the end of Manasseh's reign and during the first years of the reign of Josiah by deeply devoted men, and that by them, with the cooperation of Hilkiah, it was secreted in the Temple to await discovery. And here it was that Hilkiah "discovered" it. Whether this is in all respects exactly what happened may be doubted, but the men who compiled the Book of Instruction believed they were loyal to the Mosaic tradition; they believed the provisions of the book were in the line of development from Moses through the prophets, and therefore labeled it as from his hand.

We must remember the times. We must remember that these men who lived in the prophetic tradition saw, every day and year after year, that Manasseh's regime drew Hebrew life deeper and deeper into Oriental paganism. Only drastic measures would shake the royal house into reformation activity. The most potent force for such an end would be the fear that Yahweh was about to pour out his wrath because of the violations of his expressed will, and the prophetic group sincerely believed that heavy punishment imminent; they knew that the current customs could be nothing but an abomination in the sight of God. The insights of Amos, Hosea, and Isaiah from which these men took inspiration were in startling contrast to the immoral, unspiritual religions that were prevalent. They plainly read of the opposition of the early great prophets to such practices, and must have felt the moral and spiritual enlightenment of these eminent writers. Their cause, they felt, was a noble one, and under the inspiration of its beckoning they found no difficulty in justifying the particular measures adopted.

Another and more recent suggestion intended also to account for the appearance of the Book of Instruction is one that would accuse no one of deception. This is the view that the book was probably brought down from Israel at the time of her fall a century earlier and kept in Jerusalem among the archives of the Temple, receiving at the time no great attention. The single sacred center of Yahweh worship to which the writing refers may then have been intended to be Shechem, capital of the Northern Kingdom. It is even possible that Hezekiah's reforms had a foundation in this same document, but during the reign of Manasseh any move toward improving Yahweh religion was of course discouraged, so the book simply remained in the Temple. During the changes in the Temple it came to light, and those concerned with improving their religion and destroying foreign religions would naturally be very desirous that it be followed. Accordingly, its origin may go back a century or more before Josiah.[2]

However the origins of this work are explained, the reform under Josiah is itself a fact beyond question. It did bring about changes for the better, and temporarily gave a place of authoritative leadership to the prophetic element. It must not be forgotten, however, that even the reforms under Josiah might not have taken place had it not been for the fact that at this time Judah was briefly free of foreign domination. Assyria would probably not have allowed the reforms, for it was her policy to impose pagan practices upon her vassals. But now Assyria's day was over. Her empire had been weakened by the exhausting efforts to keep out Cimmerian and Scythian

[2] Norman K. Gottwald, *A Light to the Nations*, New York, Harper & Brothers, 1959, p. 338.

invaders, barbarian hordes from the steppes of what is now southern Russia. Before Assyria had time to replenish her manpower, she was overwhelmed by a revived Babylonian Empire, which now once again strode high in the ancient world. It captured and sacked Nineveh, the capital of Assyria, in 612 B.C.

There is some reason to think that Jeremiah may not have wholly approved of the new law book.

> [Thus says the Lord:] "How can you say, 'We are wise, and the law of the Lord is with us'? But, behold, the false pen of the scribes has made it into a lie. The wise men shall be put to shame, they shall be dismayed and taken; lo, they have rejected the word of the Lord, and what wisdom is in them?" (Jeremiah 8:8-9).

If Jeremiah did not wholly support the reformation, it may have been because he had doubts concerning some of its provisions or, more likely, because he felt that the character of the reformation was still too external. He appears to have believed that the reformation would not stave off the punishment that was due. Perhaps a more important consideration still is that Jeremiah had begun to think of religion as an individual and deeply personal thing, whereas basically the Deuteronomic law focused on the unity of the nation and on legal religious requirements for national purification and atonement. As time went on, he could see that religious reliance was increasingly placed on legal and external duties, not on spiritual transformation. How might he have arrived at this insight?

We must think of Jeremiah from the time of his call and earlier ministry as a storm-tossed individual. He was denounced vehemently by his contemporaries—the people, his family, the priests, his king, and even the prophets—and at times stood in danger of his life. The first such threat occurred following the death of Josiah after the battle of Megiddo in 609 B.C. Jeremiah denounced the popular idea that Yahweh would never allow the Temple to be desecrated or destroyed by an enemy (7:1 ff., 26:1 ff.). A prophetic associate was killed for this supposedly treasonous announcement, suggesting as it seemed to the people that Yahweh was not capable of defending himself, and Jeremiah very nearly met the same fate. Other occasions of personal danger and actual arrest were frequent. To be regarded as a traitor when the motives of action could not be more devoted to the common interest is a heavy burden for any man. And what made it so hard was that Jeremiah himself often had misgivings and felt rebellious at the severe demands of his prophetic task. The task compelled him to forego thoughts of marriage and home life, for Yahweh had told him, "You shall not take a wife, nor shall you have sons or daughters in this place" (16:1).

Often his spirit challenged Yahweh and asked why he should have to give up so much and bear so many burdens. At times he became exceedingly bitter toward those who inveighed against him, and he cursed those priests and professional prophets who opposed him. In an astonishing passage (20:7-10, 14-18), out of the bitterness of his soul he cried:

> O Lord, thou hast deceived me, and I was deceived; thou art stronger than I, and thou hast prevailed. I have become a laughingstock all the day; every one mocks me. For whenever I speak, I cry out, I shout, "Violence and destruction!" For the word of the Lord has become for me a reproach and derision all day long. If I say, "I will not mention him, or speak any more in his name," there is in my heart as it were a burning fire shut up in my bones, and I am weary with holding it in, and I cannot. For I hear many whispering. Terror is on every side! "Denounce him! Let us denounce him!" say all my familiar friends, watching for my fall. . . .
>
> Cursed be the day on which I was born! The day when my mother bore me, let it not be blessed! Cursed be the man who brought the news to my father, "A son is born to you," making him very glad. Let that man be like the cities which the Lord overthrew without pity; let him hear a cry in the morning and an alarm at noon, because he did not kill me in the womb; so my mother would have been my grave, and her womb for ever great. Why did I come forth from the womb to see toil and sorrow, and spend my days in shame? [20:7-10, 14-18].

He found it hard to understand why Yahweh had called him and used him in this way, but finally there came to him with great clarity the idea of the New Covenant. The concept occupied an increasing place in his thought, particularly because the nation was on the verge of internal religious bankruptcy and political annihilation from the enemy without.

The Babylonians, after years of planning, had at last overcome the Assyrians and Egyptians and now dominated Palestine. The Hebrew King Jehoiakim stupidly revolted against the Babylonians in 598 B.C., with the result that the following year, under Nebuchadnezzar, they overran Judah. By this time Jehoiachin had replaced his father on the throne. The Babylonians did their work very quickly, capturing Jerusalem and doing great damage. They took the king and most of the leading people, totaling 3023 Jews, and carried them off to Babylonia.

Jeremiah rightly had little faith in the caliber of the populace remaining. In fact, he felt that the future revival of the nation would receive its impetus and leadership from those in exile. This analysis proved correct when, in 588 B.C., the Babylonians returned to put down another rebellion. The Egyptian army made an effort to assist Judah and got as far as the Judaean frontier, whereupon the Babylonians set forth to meet them. A breathing spell was thus obtained by the besieged city, during which time Jeremiah was imprisoned. Shortly after, when the Babylonians returned, his own countrymen cast him into an empty but muddy cistern from which he was rescued by an Ethiopian slave.

The weak puppet king, Zedekiah, in despair at the Babylonians' approach, sought Jeremiah's advice. Jeremiah saw that only surrender would save the city from disaster and so counseled Zedekiah, who, however, did not agree. When the city was finally captured in 587 B.C., it was sacked unmercifully. The Babylonians put all of Zedekiah's sons to death in his presence, and with this for memory they put out his eyes and carried him to Babylon.

Jerusalem was systematically laid waste. The great Temple built by Solomon was burned to the ground, and its precious objects were removed. Everything of value was carried away. Great breaches were broken through the walls. Another group of inhabitants, numbering 832 persons, was lined up and marched off into exile. Some of the poorest and least influential Jews were left behind, "to be vinedressers and plowmen."[3] As Jeremiah tells it (45:13-23), we behold a people stricken with a mortal wound from which there is no recovery.

There is not much more to say about this unhappy ending. Jeremiah was permitted to remain with the survivors who were allowed to stay in the vicinity, and under the leadership of Gedaliah, a member of an old family who was left in charge by the Babylonians, some hope of recovery revived. Gedaliah was a man of wisdom and seems to have been a noble soul. Jeremiah regarded him highly. But even in these perilous conditions, a jealous survivor of the royal family, Ishmael, successfully plotted to murder Gedaliah and all his leading men. This was indeed a stupid measure, for Ishmael had to flee for his life and the survivors were in a panic lest the Babylonians return and put them to the sword. So they fled to Egypt, taking Jeremiah with them against his will. It is known that some of their descendants lived on the island of Elephantine a century later and built a temple there to Yahweh. The last we hear of Jeremiah, he is prophesying disaster for those who have fled to Egypt (Jeremiah 44:1-30).

That there is any further history of the Hebrews at all lies in the fortunes of the exiles in Babylonia. The reader may perhaps wonder momentarily how such a history can have any significance for us. Did the Hebrews never profit from experience? So much of their misery came from the stupidity, avarice, and vanity of their own rulers and leaders. All the more

[3] Still a third group of Jews, numbering 745, were taken into exile five years later. The total number then carried to Babylon was 4,600 (Jeremiah 52:28-30). However, compare II Kings 24:14, which gives the figure of 10,000 taken away in the first deportation in 597 B.C. alone.

reason why we cannot fail to admire the prophetic insights that came out of this environment. The idealism and moral integrity and the spiritual creativity that produced great literature, great religion, and great men were remarkable products of this decadent situation.

The successive events moving toward collapse certainly justified Jeremiah's clear perception of the direction of affairs, and enable us to see how he came to pin his hopes on the New Covenant coming in the future. Compare the following passage (31:31-34) with the quotations from Jeremiah at the outset of his ministry:

> Behold, the days are coming, says the Lord, when I will make a new covenant with the house of Israel and the house of Judah, not like the covenant which I made with their fathers when I took them by the hand to bring them out of the land of Egypt, my covenant which they broke, though I was their husband, says the Lord. But this is the covenant which I will make with the house of Israel after those days, says the Lord: I will put my law within them, and I will write it upon their hearts; and I will be their God, and they shall be my people. And no longer shall each man teach his neighbor and each his brother, saying, "Know the Lord," for they shall all know me, from the least of them to the greatest, says the Lord, for I will forgive their iniquity, and I will remember their sin no more.

The doctrine of the New Compact or New Covenant between Yahweh and the Jews was the rock upon which Jeremiah set his feet. Here he found the firm ground of assurance which his soul had long sought. Perplexity and doubt were now dissolved in his understanding of the divine will and purpose. Just as the personal experience of Hosea give rise to a new understanding of the nature of Yahweh as loving and forgiving, so Jeremiah's struggle between his faith in God and the tragedy of the imminent doom of his people gave rise to this new insight.

Let us remind ourselves once more how the situation must have looked to Jeremiah. Since the time he was a young man he had been prophesying the fall of Judah, and doing so only because of his faith in Yahweh's power, strength, justice, and faithfulness. *Because* Yahweh was God of the Jews, he would destroy them and send them into captivity; *because* he was God, he would go even further—further than almost everyone except Jeremiah even dared imagine: he would destroy the place that the Jews thought of as his own home, the Temple in which he was worshiped, and no place would remain where the sacrifices of Yahweh could be performed! Most of the people and even the prophets were convinced that Yahweh could not go that far, believing as they did that this would be tantamount to the destruction of Yahweh himself as the God of the people. But Jeremiah announced that, rather than a sign of Yahweh's impotence and inability to care for his people, the destruction of the Temple would be an indication of his power and righteous nature. Fortunate it was for the future of the Jews and their religion that he did so, for it was his faith in Yahweh, not in spite of but because of the fall of Jerusalem which he saw about to take place, that made it possible for the Jews themselves to regain their faith in God during the Exile.

So Jeremiah saw destruction as the work of God's own hand. This awareness had a further meaning, and a bitter one: that the old Covenant, established at Sinai under Moses, had been so thoroughly disobeyed and shattered that no real promise remained in it any longer. Under that Covenant the Hebrews had been disobedient for centuries, and there was little reason to think the pattern would be radically different in the future. This was the bitter conclusion of Jeremiah's understanding. But now appeared hope. Because Yahweh was faithful to his people, he would make a *New* Covenant with them. This would not be like the old, written on tablets of stone, mediated to the people through the great external, sacrificial cult which needed the Temple for its performance. On the contrary, this New Covenant would be within the individual, written on his very heart, and God's law would be inward instead of external; it would be part of a man himself.

Jeremiah was thus the great prophet of "inwardness" in the Jewish religion. That which was implied but not expressly stated by the eighth-century prophets as they called for men to live ethically was now made explicit in Jeremiah. It was *this* relation to Yahweh which God would establish that held the meaning of the events of Jeremiah's day. This New Covenant with Israel and Judah would no longer require external ritual, performed for the sake of the group, but would live in every Hebrew, written on his individual heart; and yet at the same time it would make him a loyal member of the covenant people.

When this would happen the prophet did not say. At the moment, the experience of exile was the fate of the nation. But the days were coming when the New Covenant would be given, and when that time came, then finally and in the truest sense of the word, "I will be their God, and they shall be my people." Everyone would know God and would need no instruction. It was in that future time, then, that the fulfillment of the relation between Yahweh and his people would take place.

The expectation of the New Covenant which would be inward and individual became another of the great expectations of Judaism. The early Christians believed that in Jesus and the Christian community it had at last come to pass. At the Last Supper, as Jesus took the cup and said, "This cup is the new covenant in my blood" (I Corinthians 11:25), he must certainly have had Jeremiah in mind. And when later the Christians named their

Scriptures the New Testament and the Hebrew Scriptures the Old Testament, they were actually saying New and Old Covenant, for *testament* and *covenant* are the same word.

The message of Jeremiah, consequently, did not disappear with his death. His prediction of doom was one that was abundantly fulfilled, but the exiles in Babylonia saw in it also the foundation of hope. His was a remarkable life, which continues to this day to inspire devotion to God. His was an example of suffering on behalf of his people which brought into being some of the loftiest insights that have come into the Western religious heritage.

Questions for Study

1. What was the social situation in Israel at the time of Amos and Hosea?
2. Precisely what is meant by "the ethical reinterpretation of the Covenant"? How was this similar to and different from the early interpretation? Be specific and precise. Why did the eighth-century prophets oppose sacrifices and holy days?
3. Explain why it is valid to say that the Covenant was the center around which the Hebrews as a people formed their national existence.
4. What charge did Amos bring against Israel in his prophecies? Exactly how did he say they broke the Covenant, and what did he announce that Yahweh demanded of them?
5. Where did Hosea agree with Amos, and at what points did he bring in different emphases? What hope for the future did he foresee? In what historic events were the prophecies of Amos and Hosea fulfilled?
6. Discuss the call and the work of Isaiah in Judah. Show similarities to the prophets of the Northern Kingdom, and indicate how Isaiah differed from them. What did he have to say about the value of sacrifices? What was his "philosophy of history"? What did he have to say about a remnant? What about the messianic king? Why was this last idea so important in later times?
7. What sort of prophet was Jeremiah, and what were his emphases?
8. What was the nature of the reformation under Josiah, and what was the Book of Instruction?
9. What predictions did Jeremiah make? How were they received by his contemporaries? How were they fulfilled?
10. What was Jeremiah's doctrine of the New Covenant?
11. What meaning was given the Covenant and the duties of the Hebrews under it (a) in the time of Moses, (b) as seen by the eighth-century prophets, (c) as seen by Jeremiah?
12. How was the nature of Yahweh understood (a) in the time of Moses, (b) at the time of entry into Canaan, (c) by the eighth-century prophets, (d) by Jeremiah?
13. What did these great prophets criticize in formal religion, and how did they by contrast understand the nature of religion?

Selected Readings

Anderson, Bernhard W., *Understanding the Old Testament,* Englewood Cliffs, N. J., Prentice-Hall, Inc., 1957.

Bright, John, *A History of Israel,* Philadelphia, The Westminster Press, 1959.

Bright, John, *The Kingdom of God,* Nashville, Abingdon-Cokesbury Press, 1953.

Buber, Martin, *The Prophetic Faith,* New York, The Macmillan Company, 1949.

Gottwald, Norman K., *A Light to the Nations,* New York, Harper & Brothers, 1959.

Graham, W. C., *The Prophets and Israel's Culture,* Chicago, University of Chicago Press, 1934.

Hyatt, J. Philip, *Prophetic Religion,* New York, Abingdon-Cokesbury Press, 1947.

Kent, C. F., *The Kings and Prophets of Israel and Judah,* New York, Charles Scribner's Sons, 1909.

Knight, Harold, *The Hebrew Prophetic Consciousness,* London, Lutterworth Press, 1948.

Lods, Adolphe, *The Prophets and the Rise of Judaism,* New York, E. P. Dutton & Co., 1937.

Matthews, I. G., *The Religious Pilgrimage of Israel,* New York, Harper & Brothers, 1947.

Mould, Elmer W. K., *Essentials of Bible History,* rev. ed., New York, The Ronald Press Company, 1951.

Oesterley, W. O. E., and T. H. Robinson, *A History of Israel,* Oxford, Clarendon Press, 1932, 2 vols.

Orlinsky, H. M., *Ancient Israel,* Ithaca, Cornell University Press, 1954.

Patterson, John, *The Goodly Fellowship of the Prophets,* New York, Charles Scribner's Sons, 1948.

Pedersen, Johannes, *Israel: Its Life and Culture,* New York, Oxford University Press, 1926, vol. II.

Scott, R. B. Y., *The Relevance of the Prophets,* Toronto, The Macmillan Company, 1947.

Smith, G. A., *The Book of Isaiah,* rev. ed., New York, Harper & Brothers, n.d., 2 vols.

Smith, G. A., *Jeremiah,* New York, Harper & Brothers, 1923.

Smith, J. M. P., and W. A. Irwin, *The Prophets and Their Times,* rev. ed., Chicago, University of Chicago Press, 1941.

3. Religion of the Exile

When Jerusalem was sacked and its people made captive by the Babylonians, there was no apparent reason for an observer to think there could be any future for the Hebrews; innumerable countries before them had disappeared. It is one of the most surprising anomalies of history that the Jews did not remain historically dead. The explanation of this fact is found in the survival and further development of Hebrew religion in Babylonia itself. Although Yahweh worship continued among the Jews in Egypt for some time, it showed no creative initiative and absorbed into itself many other religious practices. The Jews remaining in Palestine lacked leadership, and did no more than try feebly to continue the old forms, from time to time offering sacrifices in the ruins of the Temple. It was in what appeared to be the least promising locale of Hebrew life, in Babylonia where the Jews were held as captives, that the future of the Jewish religion was decided.

It is a very important fact that what is today the Jewish religion, with its emphasis on the Sabbath day, its synagogue, its Scriptures, and its devotion to the Law, is a result of the Exile in Babylonia. As Jeremiah had foreseen, the fuller forms of religion were to spring from that Exile. The religion of the Jews today is not that of the period before the Exile, for that practice centered in the Temple in Jerusalem and its services. The Temple was rebuilt and its services re-established when the exiles returned to Jerusalem, but when it finally disappeared in the year A.D. 70 under the

Romans, another form of religion was there, existing side by side with it, which was able to continue. This form we call *Judaism*, as contrasted with the original form which we have called *Yahwism* or *Mosaism*. The latter was established under Moses, but Judaism was the fruit of the Exile.

The survival of the Hebrew religion and the beginning of Judaism can be attributed to two great prophets—Ezekiel, who lived during the first part of the Exile, and an unnamed prophet who is designated Deutero-Isaiah or the Second Isaiah because his messages appear in the present book of Isaiah. Each of these men made a specific contribution, but because Ezekiel was the earlier and the new emphases which led into Judaism began to appear with him, he is sometimes referred to as the father of Judaism. The pious Jew of later times, especially after the final destruction of the Temple, regarded the Exile as a prime example of the way in which Yahweh can bring good out of suffering and evil, seeing in it the guiding hand of God, leading his unfaithful people into a new and more intimate relationship.

Babylon and the Babylonian Exile

In the first years of exile, judging from surface appearances, it seemed very uncertain that the Hebrews would survive as a distinct group with a specific religion. One can imagine how insignificant the average Jew must have felt in the ancient city of Babylon. It was a great city, set in the midst of numerous cities and towns connected by canals, roads, and fortifications. Commercial traffic was enormous. At this period, in the sixth century B.C., Nebuchadnezzar, the king, was at the height of his career. He had the ambition of extending his control of territory and commerce even further. The stream of revenue supported a great army and made extensive building projects possible.

For the immense public works program, including the building of dams, irrigation canals, and great temples, hosts of workers were required. It is likely that one of the reasons for Nebuchadnezzar's removal of the Hebrews to Babylon was their prospective usefulness as laborers in these enterprises. Most of the Hebrews were placed not far from the city of Babylon itself, where much of the work was going on. Many of them lived in villages on one of the great canals, Chebar, which ran east from Babylon to the shrine city of Nippur. Babylon lay on both sides of the Euphrates, connected by a bridge over half a mile long. Miles of streets were paved with brick set in asphalt. High walls surrounded certain central areas of the city. Great buildings, especially the temples and the palaces, would inspire any onlooker with awe because of the magnificence of their dimensions. There are still other features which make the picture even more impressive. The great temple services and the long religious processions in which the King himself sometimes appeared would contribute to the sense of inferiority that was inhibiting the Jewish soul. Among the first captives who came in 597 B.C., some hope of speedy release remained because they still had a national home. But when in 586 B.C. Jerusalem was destroyed and the first exiles were joined by the latest captives, hope dwindled and was replaced by doubt and despair. How fantastic political ambition appeared in the presence of Nebuchadnezzar! And how could the mind fail to ask one pertinent question, "What is Yahweh compared to Marduk, 'Lord of Heaven and earth,' and to Bel, 'Lord of lands'?"

We know enough about the Hebrews to foretell that many of them would cast aside their traditions and become absorbed in Babylonian culture. This would be increasingly the case as their economic status improved. Their captivity allowed them a great deal of freedom. There was no need to guard them, for they could not go away. More and more they became a part of the general population. Many of them gradually found their way into the diversified occupations of the great city, and were merely another of the foreign elements in the polyglot community.

Their commercial interests came to be quite extensive and afforded them one way of adjusting themselves to the circumstances of time and place. An interesting testimony of the business activities of the Hebrews is given by some clay tablets unearthed by archaeologists at Nippur some years ago. The tablets are commercial documents from the files of a great mercantile house, Murashu Sons. Many of them show dealings with Hebrews, as evidenced by the Jewish names, among them Benjamin, Gedaliah, and Hananiah. Since these tablets date from the century following the return from the Exile, they bear witness to the fact that many Hebrews remained in Babylonia and carried on business there.

It is now in order to consider the work of the two men by reason of whom the Exile took its place beside the Exodus under Moses as one of the two greatest episodes in Hebrew history. The Exile, like the Exodus, had to do not only with the survival of a people but, what is of vastly greater significance in the world's history, with the survival of the Hebrew religion in a higher form.

Ezekiel, the Father of Judaism

Ezekiel was in the first group who went into exile in 597 B.C. He must therefore have belonged to the elite, for the flower of Judah was taken at that time. Ezekiel was probably a priest, about 30 years of age. He was well acquainted with the teaching of Jeremiah and was sympathetic with it. The first half of his book, written in exile between the years 593 (when he received his prophetic call) and 586 B.C., was concerned with the situation existing back in Jerusalem. The latter chapters deal with the Exile. His final writing appears to have been in 573 B.C.

Ezekiel's call came in an awesome vision. As he was by the river (canal) Chebar where the exiles were living, he saw a great cloud rise from the north with fire flashing out of it. As it approached, he saw in it "the likeness of four living creatures," each a composite of human and animal forms. Each had four faces, those of a man, a lion, an ox, and an eagle. Over the heads of these creatures was "the likeness of a firmament" and above the firmament "the likeness of a throne." Seated upon the likeness of a throne was a "likeness as it were of the human form," the upper half gleaming like bronze and the lower half as bright as fire. Ezekiel fell on his face before this amazing vision (Ezekiel 1).

Then a voice spoke to him, saying,

> . . . "Son of man, stand upon your feet. . . ." And he said to me, "Son of man, I send you to the people of Israel, to a nation of rebels, who have rebelled against me . . . and you shall say to them, 'Thus says the Lord God.' And whether they hear or refuse to hear . . . they will know that there has been a prophet among them. . . ." [2:1-5].

Ezekiel had received his divine commission and henceforth had to speak when the word of the Lord came to him. At the moment, before the fall of Jerusalem in 586, Ezekiel had only one thing to say to the exiles themselves, which was that they were not to expect to return soon to their homeland. As long as Jerusalem stood, some of them evidently believed it would be a matter of only a few years before they could go back, but Jeremiah had said their exile would last at least two generations, and Ezekiel echoed him. The chief word that came to Ezekiel was intended for the people still in Jerusalem. Over and over, often in acted-out parables, he portrayed the suffering and death in store for the people there. Instead of the exiles' returning to their home, other would be brought into exile and Jerusalem itself would be destroyed. The reason for this disaster was the familiar one of the Hebrews' unfaithfulness to their God, shown in their worship of other gods, even in the very Temple itself. Ezekiel prophesied,

> Then he [God] said to me, "The guilt of the house of Israel and Judah is exceedingly great; the land is full of blood, and the city full of injustice. . . . As for me, my eye will not spare, nor will I have pity, but I will requite their deeds upon their heads" [9:9-10].

We remember that again and again through all the preceding prophets a note of impending doom had resounded, but such prophecies had been for all practical purposes disregarded. Time after time, prophets had said that Yahweh was a God of justice who had kept the Covenant with them, but that they had not kept faith with him. It was therefore possible to maintain that the cup of Yahweh's condemnation had at last filled to overflowing, and that he would allow his wrath to fall upon an unfaithful nation. Ezekiel's own writing is full of this idea. Witness chapter 20, in which he reminds the nation that Yahweh chose Israel as his people and that he had fulfilled his part of the Covenant by bringing them out of Egypt into Palestine. They failed to obey him many times, and each time he forgave them and continued his protection over them. But now he would forgive no longer; the time for punishment and purification had come.

"As I live, says the Lord God, surely with a mighty hand and an outstretched arm, and with wrath poured out, I will be king over you. I will bring you out from the peoples and gather you out of the countries where you are scattered, with a mighty hand and an outstretched arm, and with wrath poured out; and I will bring you into the wilderness of the peoples, and there I will enter into judgment with you face to face. . . . I will make you pass under the rod, and I will let you go in by number. I will purge out the rebels from among you, and those who transgress against me; I will bring them out of the land where they sojourn, but they shall not enter the land of Israel. Then you will know that I am the Lord" [20:33-38].

It was necessary for Ezekiel to fix the idea of deserved punishment in the minds of the Jews so that they would themselves assent to the justice of penalty for sin, and recognize the Exile as a sign not of Yahweh's weakness but of his strength. For after the fall of Jerusalem the situation among the exiles changed. The national homeland no longer existed for them; the Temple was gone, and no Jewish nation in any sense remained. True, some of their countrymen remained in Palestine, but people from neighboring lands moved into the undefended country and mingled with them, much as the Hebrews remaining in the Northern Kingdom had mingled with the non-Hebrews who had come among them.

Now discouragement filled the soul of many of those in exile, and they were tempted to lose their faith in Yahweh. One can readily imagine the attitude they must have held. Yahweh had failed his people; he had allowed them to be taken captive, had permitted his own holy city to be destroyed, and, worst of all, seemingly had been impotent to defend his own home, the Temple. With the passing of the service in the Temple, it seemed they could not even worship Yahweh had they wished to. Such was the direction of their thinking, and in such thoughts as these lay the end of the Hebrew people as a nation. Ezekiel's position was a pivotal one; had he failed at this time to reassure and inspire the Hebrews to hold to their religion, the one rallying point which gave them their sense of unity and therefore their hope of national survival, it is very likely that the account would have closed right there.

But Ezekiel did not fail. Doom had been his message while Jerusalem stood. Punishment from a justly wrathful God had been the former theme, but now with the change of need and the fulfillment of all that had been foretold, it was time for Ezekiel to remind his people of the cause of their disaster and the source of their hope. Just because he had spoken so strongly of the coming of punishment for sin, and because Jeremiah had made the identical predictions, he could now remind the Hebrews that the Exile was punishment *by Yahweh,* not a sign of the greatness of Marduk, chief god of Babylon. And if Yahweh, not Marduk and the other Babylonian gods, had brought evil, he was able also to bring good when the time was ripe. Not immediately, but after the punishment had been completed, he would show the other side of the covenant relation—his care and his power to restore those he had so severely chastised. In one of the most vivid pictures of prophetic imagery in the Bible, Ezekiel brings home his point:

> The hand of the Lord was upon me, and he brought me out by the Spirit of the Lord, and set me down in the midst of the valley; it was full of bones. And he led me round among them; and behold there were very many upon the valley; and lo, they were very dry. And he said to me, "Son of man, can these bones live?" And I answered, "O Lord God, thou knowest." Again he said to me, "Prophesy to these bones, and say to them, O dry bones, hear the word of the Lord. Thus says the Lord God to these bones: Behold, I will cause breath to enter you, and you shall live. And I will lay sinews upon you, and will cause flesh to come upon you, and cover you with skin, and put breath in you, and you shall live; and you shall know that I am the Lord."
>
> So I prophesied as I was commanded; and as I prophesied, there was a noise, and behold, a rattling; and the bones came together, bone to its bone. And as I looked, there were sinews on them, and flesh had come upon them, and skin had covered them; but there was no breath in them. Then he said to me, "Prophesy to the breath, prophesy, son of man, and say to the breath, Thus says the Lord God: Come from the four winds, O breath, and breathe upon these slain, that they may live." So I prophesied as he commanded me, and the breath came into them, and they lived, and stood upon their feet, an exceedingly great host [37:1-10].

The message was a clear one—the valley was the valley of the Euphrates River, in which Babylon stood. The dry bones were the Hebrew nation, now as a nation dead. Their returning to life once more meant restoration. Ezekiel continues:

> Then he said to me, "Son of man, these bones are the whole house of Israel. Behold, they say, 'Our bones are dried up, and our hope is lost; we are clean cut off.' Therefore prophesy, and say to them, Thus says the Lord God: Behold, I will open your graves, and raise you from your graves, O my people; and I will bring you home into the land of Israel. And you shall know that I am the Lord, when I open your graves, and raise you from your graves, O my people. And I will put my Spirit within you, and you shall live, and I will place you in your own land; then you shall know that I, the Lord, have spoken, and I have done it, says the Lord" [37:11-14].

As a result of Ezekiel's message, the Hebrews in Babylonia did come to accept the belief that the Exile had a purpose, that by means of it Yahweh intended to purify the nation. This, then, was the first step toward re-establishing faith in the justice and goodness of God. Thus far Ezekiel reaffirmed the understanding of God which we have already seen in Isaiah and Jeremiah, but he carried the thought further than had they by emphasizing in a marked way the *transcendence* of the God who was able to act in these ways with his people. Since he was transcendent, his restoration of his people was so certain that Ezekiel, speaking for Yahweh, proceeded to describe in detail the restored community, the new Temple they were to build, the purified services, and even the reunion of the Northern and Southern Kingdoms, ruled over by a Davidic king.

> "My servant David shall be king over them; and they shall all have one shepherd. They shall follow my ordinances and be careful to observe my statutes. They shall dwell in the land where your fathers dwelt that I gave to my servant Jacob; they and their children and their children's children shall dwell there for ever; and David my servant shall be their prince for ever. I will make a covenant of peace with them; it shall be an everlasting covenant with them; and I will bless them and multiply them, and will set my sanctuary [the Temple] in the midst of them for evermore. My dwelling place shall be with them; and I will be their God, and they shall be my people. Then the nations will know that I the Lord sanctify Israel, when my sanctuary is in the midst of them for evermore" [37:24-28].

Here as in Jeremiah we hear the promise of a New Covenant, but with a profound difference. In Ezekiel the New Covenant, which was to be an everlasting one and a covenant of peace, would be closely associated with a new Temple and the worship conducted there, while in Jeremiah the New Covenant was to be an inward one, written, as we recall, "upon the hearts of men."

The stress upon the transcendence of Yahweh showed Ezekiel's belief that God had to be approached properly in worship. Even an earthly monarch like Nebuchadnezzar had to be approached with proper ceremony; how much more should Yahweh, before whom Nebuchadnezzar was but a servant, be fittingly addressed! Ezekiel's concern with and frequent reference to cherubims and heavenly creatures was probably likewise a result of his conception of Yahweh as transcendent. Parenthetically, if in Ezekiel's original vision the half-animal, half-human figures who fly about beneath the transcendent Yahweh are understood to be portrayals of the Babylonian gods, represented respectively by the face of a man, a lion, an ox, and an eagle, we then have a particularly vivid indication of how vastly great Yahweh is. To approach so great a God would require, on the one hand, that the worshiper be pure in heart, and yet, on the other hand, Ezekiel taught his relation to Yahweh would be mediated through appropriate acts of formal worship. He emphasized the importance of a religious ceremonial prescribed by law, and spent a large part of his writings (chapters 40-48) in describing in detail the new Temple that was to be built and the services that were to be held therein upon the exiles' return to Jerusalem.

In his emphasis upon a "new spirit" and a "new heart" for the proper worship of Yahweh, Ezekiel shows himself to be in the tradition of the great prophets, but in his stress upon sacrifices and rites he shows himself to be even more thoroughly a priest. God's gifts would be bestowed upon those worshipers who kept God's commandments and participated in the ritual of worship.

As the father of Judaism, Ezekiel marks the starting point of a number of new developments within the Hebrew religion, although most of these came to their full flowering only later, in some instances very much later. Ezekiel was an outstanding figure during the early days of the Exile. We are told that he had his own private home where the elders of Judah met with him to receive advice from him as a prophet of Yahweh (8:1 and 20:1). The exiles were unable to sacrifice to Yahweh, since the Book of Instruction taught that there was only one place where Yahweh was to have formal worship, and that place had been the Jerusalem Temple. Was there any way left for the exiles to worship God? Not in the usual pattern, to be sure, but the eighth-century prophets had taught that Yahweh did not wish sacrifices, so possibly the inability to have sacrifices was not so serious a matter as it first seemed. But *how* could Yahweh be worshiped adequately apart from the Temple form of service? A nonsacrificial type of worship had to be devised, and, although the exiles could not know it, this necessity and their response to it constituted one of the greatest emancipating factors in the spiritualization of Judaism. Of what would such a service consist? To begin with, as a transition from the older forms, the Hebrews could at least celebrate their holy days. Some form of gathering together in remembrance of them was possible, and a memorial meeting could occur.

In a way this is parallel to what happens in countries outside the United States when the American community gathers to celebrate Thanksgiving and the Fourth of July. On such occasions the President's Thanksgiving Day proclamation or Lincoln's Gettysburg Address may be read, and appropriate songs may be sung. In the Hebrew gatherings, the natural thing to do would be to read the stories about the event being celebrated, such as the Exodus and Passover, and possibly to pray and to sing some of the sacred psalms.

Two institutions had their first beginnings in such practices. *The Sabbath day* as a regular time for meeting as a community became important. It will be recalled that there was nothing like this under the sacrificial system, for apart from the Temple services there were no special religious ceremonies on the Sabbath. Such meetings provided a constant stimulus, and the Sabbath as a religious institution arising under these peculiar circumstances became the instrument through which religious life was kept alive. Second, attention was devoted in these meetings to the literature of the past. Many of its passages were undoubtedly read aloud, probably accompanied by public prayer and by exhortation or preaching, possibly by teaching priests. To the participants, these meetings must have been a source of new morale. The Jews were held together by the growing faith that the God who had once delivered them from the Egyptians could and would deliver them from the Babylonians, however imposing they might be. These services of study of the Scriptures and of inspiration continued, and it is from them that the Jewish *synagogue* (from the Greek word meaning to gather together) with its liturgy and worship ultimately developed.[1]

Still another development took place, with which Ezekiel probably had little or nothing to do. The study of the ancient documents in these services brought about the beginning of a great deal of interest in the writings themselves. Scholars worked over them, examined their relationships, compared and joined them together, and eventually placed them into a framework which unified them. We must recall that as yet there was no canon of accepted Scripture; there were rather a number of writings, some of them going back probably as much as 500 years. It was during this period that the so-called Priestly writers (P) arose. The Deuteronomic history was almost certainly brought to a conclusion early in the Exile, probably before

[1] It is not entirely certain that local assemblies were formally organized, but it is likely that they were.

550 B.C. This history consists of an editing of Hebrew history as it appeared in the records from Judges (or Joshua) through the two books of Kings, exhibiting a view in this process that is similar to that shown in the book of Deuteronomy. The P writer or writers did their work by using a number of ancient documents not found in the J, E, or D writings and, in addition, by providing a framework of interpretation reaching back to Adam and the Creation. Their task was probably not completed for a century (for it was about 400 B.C. that the first five books, the Torah, were complete in their present form), but a beginning was made during the Exile itself.

Interest in the Hebrew Scriptures led to the development called *legalism.* The inability to obey Yahweh by sacrifices could be partially replaced by obeying his commands as these are found in the law codes of the ancient writings. Such obedience to the religious Law became eventually the very heart of Jewish religious practices.

Returning to Ezekiel's contributions, we find in his work, particularly in chapters 38 and 39, still another element which played an important part in later Judaism. This is his apocalyptic expectation. As the word is used in Biblical writings, *apocalypse* refers to a revelation presented in cryptic form concerning great events to be brought about by God at the end of an era. In form and spirit, this type of writing is a special development from prophecy. Prophetic teaching proclaimed that since Yahweh was in charge of his world and his people, he would carry out his divine purposes. How he would carry them out is portrayed apocalyptically in ways that only the initiated can understand—numbers, strange animals, cryptic language are usually the forms in which the teaching is presented. In Ezekiel we find one of the earliest examples of such writing. God is shown as fighting for his people to destroy Gog, enemy from the north from the land of Magog. As a consequence,

> . . . my holy name I will make known in the midst of my people Israel; and I will not let my holy name be profaned any more; and the nations shall know that I am the Lord, the Holy One in Israel. Behold, it is coming and it will be brought about, says the Lord God. That is the day of which I have spoken [39:7-8].

A hope such as this was inspiring, but it could also be very dangerous, since waiting for the Day of the Lord, in forgetfulness of Amos' statements that such a day could be one of judgment and disaster, might easily make for undue optimism and eventually lead to loss of faith if disaster struck. Apocalypticism generally flourishes in an atmosphere of captivity and persecution or domination by rulers who frustrate the hopes and longings of a religious group. Ezekiel, sometimes called the father of apocalyptic, set the pattern for this type of literature, which came to be a feature of the Judaism originating from his activities and the Exile.

It has been our intention to emphasize the importance of Ezekiel in the establishment of the Hebrews as a religious community in Exile and in fostering the Judaism which developed after the Exile. He must be credited with the astonishing achievement of lifting the religion of the Hebrews far above anything they had attained prior to the Exile. The Exile itself with the suffering it brought the Hebrews awakened their consciences to an appreciation of what their wise men and seers had been saying for centuries before the disaster. Ezekiel built upon this foundation, and it was largely because of him that Hebrew culture and religion survived.

The Nameless Prophet, Deutero-Isaiah

The great unknown prophet of the Exile is called Deutero-Isaiah (the Second Isaiah) because all the writings from his hand are included in the book of the Bible entitled Isaiah. Historical scholarship has shown that the book of Isaiah contains a great amount of material which, coming from the period of the Exile and later, could not have been written by the eighth-century Isaiah we know about who lived two centuries earlier.

We shall not concern ourselves here with the many interesting discoveries about the composition of the book of Isaiah; for our purpose it must suffice to say that it is divided into three major sections. As we already know, most of the first 39 chapters of the book concern the Isaiah with whom we have dealt. Chapters 40 to 55, for the most part, are the work of a prophet who wrote in the very last years of the Exile when freedom and release were imminent. We shall think of the author of this portion as Deutero-Isaiah. Chapters 56 to 66 may have been written by one man or several men, but in any case they were written when some of the exiles had already returned to Jerusalem and re-established themselves.

Deutero-Isaiah, who must remain for us an anonymous person, is the last of the major prophets to be considered separately, even though some minor prophets did valuable service during the restoration of the Jewish nation. He is not only the last of the great prophets but is possibly the greatest of them all in the profundity of his spiritual insight. Much that he wrote was, as we shall see, immediately appreciated by his contemporaries, but the highest level of his thought occupied a plane which no other person achieved until the time of Jesus. Deutero-Isaiah's best thoughts were like treasures hidden in a field. Jesus came upon them and knew their value. He quoted from them familiarly, and appears to have thought of himself in the terms set forth by this prophet.

The first thing that strikes the reader as he takes up the writings of Deutero-Isaiah is the change in tone over any previous prophetic writing. Instead of accusations against popular and official unrighteousness, there is a new note of joy. In place of impending judgment and calamity, there is pardon and optimism. Instead of an angry Yahweh about to strike, we find a merciful God, gracious and full of compassion. This marked change in tone appears in the very first verses of the material and reappears at various points throughout.

Comfort, comfort my people, says your God. Speak tenderly to Jerusalem, and cry to her that her warfare is ended, that her iniquity is pardoned, that she has received from the Lord's hand double for all her sins [Isaiah 40:1-2].

Ho, every one who thirsts, come to the waters; and he who has no money, come, buy and eat! Come, buy wine and milk without money and without price. Why do you spend your money for that which is not bread, and your labor for that which does not satisfy? Hearken diligently to me, and eat what is good, and delight yourselves in fatness. Incline your ear, and come to me; hear, that your soul may live; and I will make with you an everlasting covenant, my steadfast, sure love for David. Behold, I make him a witness to the peoples, a leader and a commander for the peoples. Behold, you shall call nations that you know not, and nations that knew you not shall run to you, because of the Lord your God, and of the Holy One of Israel, for he has glorified you [55:1-5].

The temper of these passages cannot be missed by the most casual reader. Deutero-Isaiah had the unusual distinction for a prophet of declaring good tidings instead of lamentation and doom. When we remember Amos, Hosea, and Isaiah, however, we recall passages from their writings in which they rather wistfully wished they might talk of the mercy and fatherly tenderness of Yahweh toward his people but could not, for the waywardness of the Hebrews did not permit it. But Deutero-Isaiah was placed in an entirely different historical situation from that of any of his predecessors, which explains a great deal of his optimism. What was this contemporary state of affairs?

When Deutero-Isaiah wrote, about 540 B.C., some 25 or 30 years after Ezekiel, there was an atmosphere of expectancy of release. Through all the years of the Exile the hope of return was present. In the early years it took great faith in Yahweh to keep this hope alive, but Ezekiel kept the light burning. Now it was becoming brighter as Babylonian supremacy declined and the strong probability arose that the Babylonian Empire would be overthrown by the rising power of Persia under Cyrus. Such an overturn presaged the freedom of the Hebrews, and consequently, hope stirred strongly.

Deutero-Isaiah referred to Cyrus as Yahweh's servant and as his anointed (messiah). Why should he use such terms as these of a king who was a Persian, not a Hebrew? This question can be answered from either a secular or a religious point of view. In the secular temper of historical science it can be said that Cyrus was praised even in Greek literature as an ideal king. His successes were tremendous, but he was even greater as a man than as a conqueror. Cyrus represents the transfer of empire from the Semitic stock of the ancient Fertile Crescent to the Aryan stock. With his rise to power he tried to conciliate the vanquished. He did homage to their religions by appropriating them as his own, and thus allied himself with the deepest emotions of his varied peoples. He was a man whose personality, genius, and wisdom in handling his subjects justified his reputation as one of the great figures of history. His name was a household word in those days and, considering his reputation, wisdom, and generosity, it was only natural that the Jews and other conquered peoples should look to him as a probable deliverer.

This appears to be a very plausible explanation, but it needs to be supplemented from a religious point of view, which maintains that the plausible account is merely a surface description, the outward appearance, not the real explanation. The religious view, which was the view of Deutero-Isaiah as well as of all the prophets, was that in the last analysis historical events occurred because God willed them. There was a divine plan and purpose which God would carry through. According to the religious interpretation, Cyrus was the instrument of Yahweh, the one true God, even though Cyrus was not aware of it. And furthermore, the knowledge that Cyrus was the instrument of Yahweh was "revealed" to Deutero-Isaiah prior to the event, just as the prediction of the Exile was revealed to the first Isaiah and to Jeremiah. Thus Deutero-Isaiah exults in the approach of Cyrus, not because of Cyrus' reputation but because Yahweh is using Cyrus for his purposes.

Up to this point we have considered Deutero-Isaiah in the light of the world situation in which he was placed, but we must not forget that he would not have responded as he did to the historical circumstances without a rich background of his own national history and a profound knowledge of what the Exile experience meant to the Jewish soul. At first hand he had heard the exposition of the work of the earlier prophets and the application of their sayings to the Exile. He had been taught their writings. As a Hebrew student in Babylonia, he had been close to Jewish scholars who were absorbed in their efforts of gathering together, writing, and editing the nation's literature. The books of Judges, Samuel, and Kings took form in the Exile. This aspect of literary enterprise was historical in character. Our prophet was also acquainted with another type of literature, writings like Lamentations and many of the Psalms that revealed suffering persons who expressed bitter hatred toward Babylonia and great spiritual unrest. Such writings came from consciences burdened with the nation's sin and remorse. In them was perplexity over the suffering of the innocent. All this was part and parcel of our prophet's inner experience, and he brought to it the touch of his own spiritual genius.

Now we are prepared to follow Deutero-Isaiah's thinking as he traced out on the eve of a new tomorrow an altered design of the covenant relation between Yahweh and his people and the whole outside world.

Deutero-Isaiah's Explicit Monotheism

The Covenant between Yahweh and his people was the theme around which all the prophets played their separate parts. We might very well say that the life and thought of the prophets can be described as an effort to understand Yahweh's will for his people and to declare that will. The nature of the covenant relation depended on the understanding they attained of God. By the time of the first Isaiah, Yahweh was described as the God of justice, and by Jeremiah as a being who dealt with the souls of men. Deutero-Isaiah achieved such a clear-cut consciousness of the reality of monotheism that some scholars hold that only he can be rightly called the first explicit monotheist. It is more nearly accurate to recognize Deutero-Isaiah as the prophet who gave the clearest and most precise meaning and expression regarding a spiritual conception of monotheism. He realized that there could be but one God. Yahweh was that God, and all the other so-called gods were not gods at all but simply objects or statues or graven images. A new insight, not altogether original, yet refreshingly so in a way, was his awareness or revelation that the one God, Creator of the universe, was the one who, in his infinite wisdom, had chosen this people and made a Covenant with them. Let Deutero-Isaiah speak for himself in regard to monotheism, and then we shall follow with his understanding of what this meant in terms of the Covenant.

Thus says the Lord, the King of Israel and his Redeemer, the Lord of hosts: "I am the first and I am the last; besides me there is no god. Who is like me? Let him proclaim it, let him declare and set it forth before me. Who has announced from of old the things to come? Let them tell us what is yet to be. Fear not, nor be afraid; have I not told you from of old and declared it? And you are my witnesses! Is there a God besides me? There is no Rock; I know not any" [44:6-8].

Who can miss the full, explicit nature of monotheism expressed here? There is in Deutero-Isaiah a sweep of vision that includes the whole of things: the created universe, the movement of history fulfilling a purpose, a deep sense of unity pervading the multiplicities of human experience. There is an intuition of oneness, which came into full flower through searching meditation and profound religious feeling. Yahweh is God, beside whom there is none else, nor has been nor shall be. The monotheism of Deutero-Isaiah carries with it a certainty and explicitness not reached by Ezekiel or Amos.

Deutero-Isaiah combined with his monotheism a degree of personal religious intimacy which Greek philosophy did not share but which is found generally among the prophets. It is also a common feature of Hebrew prophecy that it is concerned with the character as well as with the power of God. Deutero-Isaiah followed the tradition of the prophets in this respect, and we can discern in him the influence of the first Isaiah and of Jeremiah especially.

Israel as the Servant of Yahweh

Once the idea of the universality of God was clearly grasped, it was not a long step to the relevant thought that the nation of Israel was in possession of a unique revelation which could scarcely be meant for a single group among the peoples of the world. It must be intended for all nations, and yet through whom could it be proclaimed except those who saw the light? There came to Deutero-Isaiah, therefore, another revelation, the counterpart of his monotheism: that Israel was chosen not to be the recipient of national greatness in material terms but to reveal the oneness, the character, and the demand of Yahweh to the world. All the events of the past he now saw from this new point of view. The history of the Hebrews was the story of God's effort to reveal his will to a chosen people, chosen for a spiritual mission which, as God's mission, must be fulfilled. Babylonia and Persia, for all their greatness, were episodes along Israel's spiritual odyssey. But what now interested the prophet tremendously was how to prepare the people spiritually for their national destiny. The *Servant passages* are the answer to the question.

The Servant passages stand in a class by themselves for spiritual beauty and importance. If the God of the universe is at all describable in terms of Deutero-Isaiah's monotheism, then we must give this prophet credit for revealing with supreme insight the spiritual privileges and obligations of relationship with God. In speaking of the well-known Servant passages, we shall deal with them all as coming from the hand of Deutero-Isaiah, ignoring questions about authorship which might be raised. They are all so manifestly in the same vein and spirit as to constitute one whole.

Four passages stand out as the great Servant Songs. These are found in Isaiah 42:1-4, 49:1-6, 50:4-9, and 52:13-53:12. The reader will find that the figure of the Servant as depicted in these passages appears to be an individual who is quite conscious of his work. Other passages also refer to the Servant, but rather as the nation of Israel which previously failed to understand what Yahweh was doing through her and has only belatedly come to this recognition. These sections are Isaiah 41:8-10, 43:8-13, 44:1-8, 21-22, and 24-28, and 45:1-8. Because of their greatness, these passages are worth closer examination. We will look first at two that speak of Israel as the Servant of Yahweh, chosen for special service.

> But you, Israel, my servant, Jacob, whom I have chosen, the offspring of Abraham, my friend; you whom I took from the ends of the earth, and called from its farthest corners, saying to you, "You are my servant, I have chosen you, and not cast you off"; fear not, for I am with you, be not dismayed, for I am your God; I will strengthen you, I will help you, I will uphold you with my victorious right hand [41:8-10].

> Remember these things, O Jacob, and Israel, for you are my servant; I formed you, you are my servant; O Israel, you will not be forgotten by me [44:21].

In these and similar passages, it is unquestionably the nation that is being called the Servant of Yahweh. But the greatest of the Servant songs are the four referring to the Servant as an individual. Of these we quote the most familiar one (Isaiah 52:13-53:12):

> Behold, my servant shall prosper, he shall be exalted and lifted up, and shall be very high. As many were astonished at him–his appearance was so marred, beyond human semblance, and his form beyond that of the sons of men—so shall he startle many nations; kings shall shut their mouths because of him; for that which has not been told them they shall see, and that which they have not heard they shall understand.
>
> Who has believed what we have heard? And to whom has the arm of the Lord been revealed? For he grew up before him like a young plant, and like a root out of dry ground; he had no form or comeliness that we should look at him, and no beauty that we should desire him. He was despised and rejected by men; a man of sorrows, and acquainted with grief; and as one from whom men hide their faces he was despised, and we esteemed him not.

Surely he has borne our griefs and carried our sorrows; yet we esteemed him stricken, smitten by God, and afflicted. But he was wounded for our transgressions, he was bruised for our iniquities; upon him was the chastisement that made us whole, and with his stripes we are healed. All we like sheep have gone astray; we have turned every one to his own way; and the Lord has laid on him the iniquity of us all. He was oppressed, and he was afflicted, yet he opened not his mouth; like a lamb that is led to slaughter, and like a sheep that before its shearers is dumb, so he opened not his mouth. By oppression and judgment he was taken away; and as for his generation, who considered that he was cut off out of the land of the living, stricken for the transgression of my people? And they made his grave with the wicked and with a rich man in his death, although he had done no violence, and there was no deceit in his mouth. Yet it was the will of the Lord to bruise him; he has put him to grief; when he makes himself an offering for sin, he shall see his offspring, he shall prolong his days; the will of the Lord shall prosper in his hand; he shall see the fruit of the travail of his soul and be satisfied; by his knowledge shall the righteous one, my servant, make many to be accounted righteous; and he shall bear their iniquities. Therefore I will divide him a portion with the great, and he shall divide the spoil with the strong; because he poured out his soul to death, and was numbered with the transgressors; yet he bore the sin of many, and made intercession for the transgressors.

The first of these four passages, from chapter 42, reminds us of the typical emphasis of the great prophets concerning the establishment of justice. The second, from chapter 49, puts us in mind of Jeremiah, who was called from before his birth. Its conclusion is one of the great universal passages in the Old Testament—the Servant shall be a "light to the nations." The third, from chapter 50, again reminds us somewhat of Jeremiah and his daily obedience and suffering. The final one, quoted above, is one of the greatest passages of the Bible, teaching vicarious suffering. The material of this section has been regarded in the Christian tradition as a prophecy of the coming of Jesus Christ as the Messiah, for a number of its ascriptions meet the circumstances of Jesus' life.

Many explanations have been offered by scholars for the meaning of the Servant in these various passages. Some have seen in the references primarily the nation itself; others have seen an individual. Some of the latter group have thought they refer to the prophet himself or to some other historical personage, perhaps Cyrus, Jeremiah, Moses, or Zerubbabel. Still others take these passages as referring to an ideal nation or ideal individual. There are also those who think of them as predictions of events that are still to happen, when in the future the Servant will appear.[2]

[2] For a succinct account of various theories of the Servant, see Norman K. Gottwald, *A Light to the Nations*, New York, Harper & Brothers, 1959, pp. 413-426.

One theory[3] holds that the view gradually changes. Deutero-Isaiah starts with the nation as a whole definitely in mind, and in one sense the nation never leaves his mind; but the deeper his thought goes, the more he appreciates the fact that the great spiritual task of being a Servant will fall upon a comparatively small number, who will be, as it were, a spiritual nucleus energizing the national body. He perceives also as did Jeremiah in times past that in the last analysis the burden sometimes falls upon one leader because he alone is the personification of the task to be accomplished, and without him presumably it would not be carried through. It is reasonable for us to hold, then, that Deutero-Isaiah's Servant represents both the nation and also a looked-for individual, depending on the mode of thought in the particular passage under consideration.

But while our prophet's thought is now on the nation and now on a particular person, there is the same note of service for Yahweh, and the service involves suffering. The character of this service and the reason that suffering or martyrdom is part of it must now briefly engage us, for we have reached the highest level of Old Testament religion.

First, as to the character of the service God lays upon his people, the quotation given from the forty-second chapter is full of a meaning that permeates all these passages. There it will be noted that Deutero-Isaiah has the entire world in mind, and the service to be rendered is to carry true religion to the nations or, as it is sometimes translated, to establish justice in the earth. Many commentators have pointed out that Deutero-Isaiah has here passed far beyond the bounds of narrow national conceptions of religion and has actually discerned service to Yahweh as primarily an effort to spread righteousness on earth. For Deutero-Isaiah, God and righteousness go together. The service of God is the service of man also in terms of mercy, humanity, justice, and law. The prophet is proclaiming an ideal for humanity, an ideal which may be called the love of justice.

Perhaps more definiteness is implied here than appears. In the conduct of human affairs around him, the prophet saw the results of man's inhumanity to man, the misery, cruelty, greed, and avarice which were the attributes of injustice. He declared, therefore, that man's ways were not God's ways, nor man's thoughts God's thoughts. Deutero-Isaiah endeavored to lift men's thoughts above the impoverishment of their lower selves to a new devotion to that omnipotent God whose ways were justice, righteousness, and peace.

Religion in these terms is indeed a service to the world, and Deutero-Isaiah thus brought to full flower the promise of development already discernible

[3] George Adam Smith, *The Book of Isaiah,* London, Hodder and Stoughton, n.d., vol. II, chap. XVI.

in the earlier prophets. But he did more than state what Yahweh's service was. He perceived that such service laid a burden of vicarious suffering, or suffering on others' behalf, upon him who shouldered the task. Why should this be so? Some five centuries later Jesus called attention to the fact that his countrymen had a way of stoning their prophets. It seems to be a perverse habit of mankind to heap sticks and stones and foul epithets upon the prophetic voices, and then later to build monuments to them. The suffering borne by a prophet was suffering by one not himself guilty.

One can follow Deutero-Isaiah's thought here, and understand a certain inevitableness in the suffering of those who walked ahead of the multitude, calling them out of their ignorance and smug moral insensibility, receiving misfortune and persecution as a reply. But it is more difficult for us to follow Deutero-Isaiah in a further step that brought out another aspect of vicarious suffering: that it is redemptive, by which we mean that it heals and makes right the evils because of which it is undergone. In the latter paragraph of the last of the great passages quoted above we note that the prophet states:

> Surely he has borne our griefs and carried our sorrows . . . he was wounded for our transgressions, he was bruised for our iniquities; upon him was the chastisement that made us whole, and with his stripes we are healed. . . . he bore the sin of many, and made intercession for the transgressors [53:4-5, 12].

That the innocent through freely accepted suffering should bring healing and redemption to the guilty—this thought is difficult to understand fully, and yet it became vastly important in Christianity. It *is* possible to understand that the human conscience does sometimes awaken to its own depravity or sterility by the sheer unselfishness of vicarious suffering.

Consider Jeremiah, for example, whose life may have inspired Deutero-Isaiah's thought. Recall how he labored to quicken the minds and consciences of his generation. Consider how he saw the people involved in political arrangements that proved disastrous. And when the day of doom came, he could have escaped it, but he made himself one with his countrymen. He did not deserve punishment, as the Babylonians themselves saw, but he stayed and did suffer, the just for the unjust; he bore their adversities and received their stripes with them. Looking back upon this during the Exile, the people conceived a great respect and reverence for what Jeremiah had done, an appreciation that never came in his own day. He himself was never fully reconciled to his suffering, and so his life was a tragedy and to some extent a mystery. But Deutero-Isaiah could thank God for a life like that of Jeremiah, and thereby this tragedy was transmuted into a blessing and the mystery into a great light. It was men like Jeremiah who bore the burden of the nation's sins, suffering under them and dying for them. With their death, humanity was enriched, for they revealed by their superlative moral and spiritual eminence new possibilities toward which others might then aspire.

Deutero-Isaiah discerned that such lives reveal to all men a quality of goodness that goes beyond the usual interests of the self, a goodness that reaches out to others in a way that counts no sacrifice or pain too great to bear in the service of God and fellow men. Possibly he is saying more than this—that as there are some men who contribute more than their share to the world's suffering, there are also others who, themselves innocent, bear more than their portion of the world's guilt and pain. And by their vicarious suffering they bring healing and overcome evil through their redemptive impact on the lives about them. The prophet appears to have perceived that such redemption was to come in climactic form at some time in the future. He personalized it in his idea of the Servant. Nothing again in Hebrew thought touched this sublime conception of character until men recognized it in the person of the crucified Jesus.

Questions for Study

1. How did Ezekiel understand the reason for the Exile? How did he attempt to restore hope to the Hebrews in Babylonia? What is the meaning of the parable of the valley of dry bones?
2. What was the message of Ezekiel before 597 and what after 586? Why was it different? Why did the destruction of the Temple appear to be a fatal blow to Yahwism?
3. Why is Ezekiel sometimes called the Father of Judaism? What is meant by Judaism, and what developments in Babylonia fostered its appearance? What institutions, basic to Judaism, had their roots in the Exile? How did the Judaism that arose from these elements differ from Yahwism?
4. In what ways was Ezekiel a prophet and in what ways a priest? How were his priestly interests shown?
5. Why is Deutero-Isaiah called the nameless prophet, and when did he live? What is there that is unique about his message, and why was it so different? What political events did he witness appearing that promised deliverance?
6. Discuss Deutero-Isaiah's explicit monotheism, comparing him in this regard with his predecessors.
7. What relation do you see between the Servant passages of Deutero-Isaiah and the Hebrew nation; and Jesus? How does the work of the Second Isaiah affect the understanding of the nature of God?
8. Describe the various meanings and interpretations given the figure of the Suffering Servant by the Second Isaiah. What is meant by vicarious suffering?

9. It has sometimes been stated that the Exile in Babylonia was the most important historical occurrence in the life of the Hebrews. How would you attempt to justify such a statement?

Selected Readings

Anderson, Bernhard W., *Understanding the Old Testament,* Englewood Cliffs, N. J., Prentice-Hall, Inc., 1957.

Bright, John, *The Kingdom of God,* Nashville, Abingdon-Cokesbury Press, 1953.

Buber, Martin, *The Prophetic Faith,* New York, The Macmillan Company, 1949.

Gottwald, Norman K., *A Light to the Nations,* New York, Harper & Brothers, 1959.

Graham, W. C., *The Prophets and Israel's Culture,* Chicago, University of Chicago Press, 1934.

Hyatt, J. Philip, *Prophetic Religion,* New York, Abingdon-Cokesbury Press, 1947.

The Interpreter's Bible, Nashville, Abingdon Press, 1951 and later, appropriate articles in vols. I-VI.

Knight, Harold, *The Hebrew Prophetic Consciousness,* London, Lutterworth Press, 1948.

Lods, Adolphe, *The Prophets and the Rise of Judaism,* New York, E. P. Dutton & Co., 1937.

Matthews, I. G., *The Religious Pilgrimage of Israel,* New York, Harper & Brothers, 1947.

North, C. R., *The Suffering Servant in Deutero-Isaiah,* London, Oxford University Press, 1948.

Oesterley, W. O. E., and T. H. Robinson, *Hebrew Religion, Its Origin and Development,* New York, The Macmillan Company, 1937.

Patterson, John, *The Goodly Fellowship of the Prophets,* New York, Charles Scribner's Sons, 1948.

Robinson, H. W., *The Cross in the Old Testament,* Philadelphia, The Westminster Press, 1956.

Rowley, H. H., *The Re-discovery of the Old Testament,* Philadelphia, The Westminster Press, 1946.

Rowley, H. H., *The Servant of the Lord,* London, Lutterworth Press, 1952.

Rowley, H. H., *Studies in Old Testament Prophecy,* New York, Charles Scribner's Sons, 1950.

Smith, G. A., *The Book of Isaiah,* rev. ed., New York, Harper & Brothers, n.d., 2 vols.

Smith, J. M. P., and W. A. Irwin, *The Prophets and Their Times,* rev. ed., Chicago, University of Chicago Press, 1941.

4. The Foundations of Judaism

The Return from Exile

The prophecies of Deutero-Isaiah concerning the release from the Exile were abundantly fulfilled by Cyrus, king of Persia, after his successful campaign against Babylon in 539 B.C. In 538 B.C. a royal decree gave the Jews freedom to return. A considerable number, although only a fraction of the Babylonian exiles, took advantage of the privilege. Others, economically well circumstanced, stayed where they were, for after a period of 50 years in Babylonia only the older generation would even remember Palestine, and conditions there were so unpromising that it seemed to many far better to remain behind. The wealthier Jews probably provided financial aid to the more zealous Hebrews who were imbued with high hopes of the future awaiting God's people in their ancient homeland. But it took great courage to believe that the new Jerusalem of their dreams could come to earth amid the ruins and broken walls that remained of the once-great city. It is well to notice that beginning at this time we can properly speak of the Jewish *Dispersion.* An increasing number of Jews returned to Palestine, but larger numbers lived outside their tiny country—in Babylonia, Persia, Asia Minor, Egypt, and elsewhere. Many never even visited Palestine. The developing synagogue gave these Jews outside Jerusalem centers for worship, while the Temple, when rebuilt in Jerusalem, became again the main focus of Jewish religion within Palestine.

The leader of the returning exiles was a son of King Jehoiachin, Sheshbazzar, a member of the Davidic line. The exiles returned to the destroyed capital city and reinstituted the sacrificial ritual upon a rebuilt altar in the ruins of the Temple. In this work they received offers of assistance from Jews of Samaria who had intermarried with the peoples brought into what two centuries earlier had been the Northern Kingdom. These people continued to think of themselves as worshipers of Yahweh, but because of their mixed blood they were not accepted by the returned exiles. In consequence, enmity developed between them, an enmity still persisting in the time of Jesus between Jew and Samaritan, as they were called. Under these circumstances, the Samaritans opposed the rebuilding of the Temple, but despite their efforts it was completed in 515 B.C. The second Temple was a poor thing when compared by the older people with the great Temple of Solomon. They "wept with a loud voice" when they saw the foundation being laid (Ezra 3:12). We must pass over the details of the work of reestablishing the Jewish nation except to note that the leaders who carried the main burden of rehabilitation were Ezra and Nehemiah, and that the walls of Jerusalem were once again rebuilt and the city made defensible in 444 B.C. when Nehemiah was governor.

The postexilic period was quite different from earlier times, and with the return from exile a new era in Jewish history began. Politically the Hebrews were destined to relative insignificance. Popular hope never would be reconciled to such a destiny, of course, but the postexilic period may properly be thought of as the history of a religious community rather than of a secular Eastern government. We may state the contrast another way. Before the Exile, with the exception of periods of reformation, politics went its own way independently, more or less indifferent to the fate of religion. After the Exile, the political relations to whatever world power was dominant were determined by the official religious ideas and practices. Religion was now primary. The official religion, despite the fact that it again developed a priestly organization and a corresponding system of worship and sacrifice, was quite different from that which had existed before the Exile. Postexilic Judaism was formulated with the earnest desire that the pre-exilic evils should never exist again. The Hebrews resolved sincerely that the lessons of the Exile should be forever enshrined in an institutionalized practice of religion that would keep Israel faithful to Yahweh.

The most effective way of making certain that religious behavior and practice will follow a prescribed course is to develop a body of law for all adherents of the faith. This was the course followed by the Jewish leaders. Consequently, we can readily understand why the most distinguishing characteristic of Judaism in the five hundred years from the Exile to Christ was the development of the Law. In addition, as we shall point out, some of the world's great literature also came out of this period, indicating reflective thinking on problems about which the human mind will never cease to be concerned, among them the questions of suffering, immortality, and the nature of wisdom.

The Jewish Law

We indicated a distinction between a prophetic and a priestly way of regarding religion when we called attention to certain differences between Ezekiel and Deutero-Isaiah. The legalistic emphasis of Ezekiel flourished and was understood more explicitly than were the loftier spiritual insights of Deutero-Isaiah. As a matter of fact, Deutero-Isaiah did not make much impact upon Hebrew religion and was not appreciated fully before the time of Jesus. The course of Hebrew religion after the Exile followed rather closely the lines laid down by Ezekiel, and prophecy was never again represented by such men as those we have considered until John the Baptist. In fact, prophecy waned until in time it more or less disappeared in the priestly legalism that came into being. The development of priestly legalism was inevitable because of the necessary preoccupation of the returned exiles with such matters as rebuilding the Temple and establishing an appropriate and pure Yahweh worship. Indeed, such minor prophets as Haggai and Zechariah, in the early years after the return, were constantly goading the people to rebuild the Temple, although they were hard pressed by the need to get on their feet economically. These prophets claimed that even the material conditions of life would not be improved until the Temple was rebuilt.

In order to understand the development of the Law, first we should recall that during the Exile serious attention was directed by Ezekiel to the pre-exilic law book, Deuteronomy. We remember that this book had as its aim the establishment of pure Yahwism. It was intended to combine the teaching and traditions of the prophets with the duties of the priests, who were to carry out the necessary services. We also recall that it was a section of this book which brought about Josiah's reform of 621 B.C., a reform, we learned, that was revolutionary in that it centralized worship in Jerusalem. It deprived a great many priests of their functions at the high places dedicated to Yahweh in other parts of the country, so the reform was never wholeheartedly approved by all. In the Exile, however, the Law, as set forth in Deuteronomy, was a revered authority; and it was enlarged upon and in some respects changed by Ezekiel.

The greatest impetus toward the development of legalism was given by the work of a priest named Ezra, also sometimes called the Father of Judaism as is Ezekiel. The dates assigned to him are uncertain; until recently he was believed to have reached Jerusalem from Babylonia in 458 B.C.[1] As a scribe or scholar of the Hebrew religion, he came to investigate the state of religious affairs back in the homeland. He summoned the people together in Jerusalem (Nehemiah 8-10), and, standing by a wooden pulpit, read to them from the "book of the Law of Moses" which he had brought with him. As he read, Levites explained the more difficult passages to the people. After further study of the Law, the people confessed their sins publicly, separated themselves from all foreigners (probably including Jews of mixed blood), and then renewed the Covenant in a great ceremony, saying, ". . . we make a firm covenant and write it, and our princes, our Levites, and our priests set their seal to it" (Nehemiah 9:38). In this act, the attention of the Jews was fastened in a very specific way upon the Law, and their obedience to it was made the very center of covenant obedience. Further, if the book from which Ezra read was actually the first five books of our present Old Testament, as some believe, then we can say that the formation of the first section of the Jewish canon, the section of the Law or the Torah, was complete by about 400 B.C. (assuming the later date for Ezra to be correct).

The development of legalism in Judaism was not confined to the written Law or Torah. A very large body of *oral law* arose because it often became necessary to apply the written Law to an unexpected situation or one not specifically covered by the requirements of that Law. In this way precedents were established which in time also became authoritative and binding upon the Jews. The scribes were the great scholars of the Law, and their task was to study and master it.

Let us note how the process of expansion into every detail of normal life took place. We will illustrate this by selecting the Law regarding the Sabbath day. In Exodus 31:12-17, the people are enjoined to keep the Sabbath holy: ". . . every one who profanes it shall be put to death; whoever does any work on it, that soul shall be cut off from among his people" (Exodus 31:14). Surely, such a demand and such dire consequences make it necessary to know just what will be regarded as work and what will not be so regarded. Is feeding the cattle on the Sabbath work, or is it a necessary duty exempt from the command and the penalty? Is pulling an ox out of a pit work? How about feeding one's family, or bathing the sick? Questions of this nature required answers. As the years passed, new situations would

[1] However, recent theories place him at *ca.* 398 B.C. See Bernhard W. Anderson, *Understanding the Old Testament*, Englewood Cliffs, N.J., Prentice-Hall, Inc., 1957, p. 450.

call for additional answers, so that by the time of Jesus the accumulation of detail on the acceptable way of keeping the Sabbath had become voluminous. The following passage from the historian Schürer indicates what development of the Law meant at the beginning of the Christian era.

On the whole thirty-nine kinds of work were prohibited, but very few are of course anywhere alluded to in the Pentateuch. These thirty-nine prohibited works are: (1) sowing, (2) ploughing, (3) reaping, (4) binding sheaves, (5) threshing, (6) winnowing, (7) cleansing crops, (8) grinding, (9) sifting, (10) kneading, (11) baking, (12) shearing wool, (13) washing, (14) beating, (15) dyeing, (16) spinning, and (17) warping it, (18) making two cords, (19) weaving two threads, (20) separating two threads, (21) making a knot, (22) untying a knot, (23) sewing two stitches, (24) tearing to sew two stitches, (25) catching a deer, (26) killing, (27) skinning, and (28) salting it, (29) preparing its skin, (30) scraping off the hair, (31) cutting it up, (32) writing two letters, (33) blotting out for the purpose of writing two letters, (34) building, (35) pulling down, (36) putting out a fire, (37) lighting a fire, (38) beating smooth with a hammer, (39) carrying from one tenement to another.

Each of these chief enactments again requires further discussions concerning its range and meaning. And here, properly speaking, begins the work of casuistry. We will bring forward just a few of its results. According to Ex. XXXIV, ploughing and reaping were among the forbidden works. But to gather a few ears of corn was already looked upon as reaping. When on one occasion the disciples did this on the Sabbath, they were found fault with by the Pharisees, not on account of plucking the ears, which (according to Deut. 23, 26) was permitted, but because they were thus guilty of doing reaping work on the Sabbath (Matt. XII, 1, 2; Mark II:23, 24; Luke VI:1, 2). The prohibition of making and untying a knot (Nos. 21 and 22) was much too general to rest satisfied with. It was also necessary to state to what kind of knot this applied, and to what it did not. "The following are the knots, the making of which renders a man guilty: The knot of camel-drivers and that of sailors; and as one is guilty by reason of tying, so also of untying them. R. Meir says: Guilt is not incurred by reason of a knot, which can be untied with one hand. There are knots by reason of which one is not guilty, as one is in the case of the camel-driver's and sailor's knots. A woman may tie up a slit in her shift and the strings of her cap, those of her girdle, the straps of the shoes and sandals, of skins of wine and oil, of a pot with meat" (*Shabbath* XV:1-2). And to tie the strings of the girdle being permitted, it was agreed that a pail also might be tied over the well with a girdle, but not with a rope (*Shabbath* XV:2). The prohibition of writing on the Sabbath (No. 32) was further defined as follows: "He who writes two letters with his right or his left hand, whether of one kind or of two kinds, as also if they are written with different ink or are of different languages, is guilty. He even who should from forgetfulness write two letters is guilty, whether he has written them with ink or with paint, red chalk, India-rubber, vitriol, or anything which makes permanent marks. Also he who writes on two walls which form an angle, or on the two tablets of his account-book, so that they can be read together, is guilty. He who writes upon his body is guilty. If any one writes with dark fluid, with fruit juice, or in the dust on the road, in sand, or in anything in which the writing does not remain, he is free . . ." (*Shabbath* XII:3-6).

According to Ex. XXXV:3, it was forbidden to kindle a fire on the Sabbath. This prohibition was supplemented by that of extinguishing a fire. With regard to the latter, the question arose, how it was to be observed, when a non-Israelite approached a fire. "If a non-Israelite comes to extinguish a fire, one must neither say to him: 'put it out,' nor 'do not put it out,' and that because one is not obliged to make him rest" (*Shabbath* XVI:6). It is self-evident that the prohibition to extinguish fire would be extended to lights and lamps. Concerning these it was ordained as follows: "He who extinguishes a light because he is afraid of heathen, robbers, or the evil spirit, or for the sake of one sick, that he may sleep, is free. If it is done, however, to save the oil, the lamp, or the wick, he is guilty. R. Joses declares him in each case free, except with respect to the wick, because he thus prepares, as it were, a coal" (*Shabbath* II:5).[2]

The foregoing cases must suffice to illustrate what is meant by the development of legalism in religion. The instances just given could be multiplied into hundreds of pages of other examples of the Law regarding every area of life—birth, marriage, preparation of food, purification of the body, provision for the needy.

The development of legalism had important implications. When such obedience becomes merely external, done out of a sense of duty alone with attention placed solely upon rectitude at every detail, then it readily becomes a very weak form of religious practice. It then attends primarily to the deeds one performs rather than the spirit in which they are performed, and it can easily lead to pride in one's own goodness when he obeys the commands to the letter or despair when he fails. Under these conditions legalism earns the evil reputation which it has among Christians, largely because of Jesus' criticism of some of the legalists of his day—criticisms echoed, incidentally, by other deeply religious Jews.

But this is only one side of the situation. The other side is that behind obedience to the Law should—and often did—stand genuine love for God and the wish to perform his entire will. One of the most difficult problems of all theistic religions is to *know* what the will of God is. Men who love him, have faith in him, and wish to obey know how easy it is to be in error concerning what his will for them actually is. This had been a problem in early Hebrew religion, for had the prophets not declared those Hebrews in error who thought they were fulfilling Yahweh's will by offering great

[2] Emil Schürer, *A History of the Jewish People in the Time of Christ*, tr. John Macpherson, Edinburgh, T. and T. Clark, 1898, vol. II, sec. 28.

sacrifices? Consequently, to believe that one possessed God's exact demands in written form was to provide certainty for those men seeking to know and obey God's will, and was cause for great satisfaction. Further, it made religion a matter of obedience to God in every detail of one's life, not just a sporadic performance or a once-a-week celebration of a holy day. For the Jews, sin was believed to be not the result of ignorance, since God's will was clearly known, but rather the result of deliberate disobedience to a known command.

In addition, the Jewish Law must be understood as far more than just a set of commands to be obeyed, since central to it was that great statement which through Jesus came to be known to Christians as the First Commandment and which constitutes the heart of the Shema: "Hear, O Israel: The Lord our God is one Lord; and you shall love the Lord your God with all your heart, and with all your soul, and with all your might" (Deuteronomy 6:4). This surely is in no sense dead legalism, but is the very *sine qua non* of living religion.

The Law and obedience to it were something to be joyous about for pious Jews after the Exile. They obeyed the Law because they wished to do so, because with it as a guide to their feet they could walk through life securely. In the Psalms we find frequent reference to the privilege of having such a guide: "Blessed is the man who walks not in the counsel of the wicked . . . but his delight is in the law of the Lord, and on his law he meditates day and night" (Psalm 1:1, 2). "The law of the Lord is perfect, reviving the soul; the testimony of the Lord is sure, making wise the simple . . ." (Psalm 19:7). "I delight to do thy will, O my God; thy law is within my heart" (Psalm 40:8, a reference to Jeremiah and the New Covenant). ". . . I shall walk at liberty, for I have sought thy precepts" (Psalm 119:45). We might then say that the Law represents the liberty of the disciplined life, lived in the certainty that this Law is, specifically and eternally, the will of God.

That this approach to religion has its shortcomings and dangers we have already noted. When the true love for God grows dim, then the Law can become a burden and its endless details a halter round the neck. Historically considered, one of the serious results of legalism was the gradually developing thought that in the Law God had stated his will in all particulars and for all eternity. This of course meant that one could not go beyond the Law, and that no change or new prophet could be accepted.[3]

[3] For further discussion of this theme, see Morton Scott Enslin, *Christian Beginnings*, New York, Harper & Brothers, 1938, chap. 6, and John Bright, *The Kingdom of God*, Nashville, Abingdon-Cokesbury Press, 1953, chap. 6.

The Rabbinic Literature

An extensive literature centering in the Law and its meaning for Jewish life developed during the centuries following the Exile. As both cultural and political conditions changed, it was necessary to discover new interpretations of the Law to cover the new situations; hence, as has been mentioned, a large body of oral teaching appeared which in its turn became binding upon loyal Jews. The sheer quantity of this material required that it be reduced to systematized form. The Midrash and Mishna, followed eventually by the Talmud, were the principal writings that resulted.[4]

The *Midrashim* (the plural of the Hebrew word *Midrash*, explanation) were a reduction of the oral law in the form of commentaries on the Torah. These commentaries took two forms. The *Halakah* (Hebrew for practice or rule) took up the legal points, having to do with the details of the Law, dealing with them in great detail and frequently without quoting the particular written Scripture with which it was dealing. The *Haggadah* (Hebrew, to relate) took up those parts of the Scripture not chiefly legal in form and content and expounded them in terms of the teaching and preaching values to be found in them.

The *Mishna* (Hebrew, instruction) was the second form into which the oral Law was reduced. Instead of a verse-by-verse treatment, as in the Midrashim, the Mishna classified its materials under six principal headings: Seeds, giving agricultural and other laws; Festivals, expounding Sabbath and other festival regulations; Women, stating rules on betrothal, marriage, divorce, and adultery; Injuries, a summary of the laws governing civil and criminal actions; Holy Things, giving the rules for sacrifice and Temple procedures; and Cleannesses, the regulations having to do with ritual uncleanness and purification. Forming a part of the section on Injuries is the famous Pirké Aboth (Sayings of the Fathers), which is now included in Jewish prayer books.

Out of the several Mishna collections appearing in the Christian era the one edited by Judah, called the Patriarch or the Prince, was especially favored and eventually was taken as the true Mishna, receiving veneration nearly equal to that of Scripture itself.

This Mishna, written to explain and interpret the Law as it had developed in unwritten form, was so complex and contained so many contradictory accounts, taken as it was from 150 scholars, that it in turn needed explanation and interpretation! The *Talmuds* arose as an answer to this need

[4] This discussion is based largely upon Enslin, *op. cit.*, pp. 104-110.

as the "Mishnas of the Mishna," so to speak. Two of these were written—the Palestinian, written about A.D. 450, and the Babylonian, far more extensive and completed about A.D. 500. The former was not completed; therefore it is the Babylonian Talmud that is used chiefly by Jewish scholars today. The procedure followed in the Talmuds is that of quoting a section of the Mishna, then of offering interpretations upon it. These interpretations, not part of the Mishna material, are mostly from later scholars and together are styled the *Gemara* (Aramaic, completion). The material of the Talmuds is mostly discussion of points of the Law (Halakah), but other accounts also appear.

Still other forms of rabbinic literature developed, but for our purposes these need not be discussed here. The significance to modern Judaism of the Talmud is that it is second in value only to Scripture itself.

Worship Under the Law

Before closing this brief section, we should consider the forms which worship took in a religion so dominated by religious Law. Two types of worship are to be distinguished, the Temple worship and the synagogue. From the standpoint of postexilic Judaism, the former appeared to be the more important. It seemed to testify to the reality not only of a national religion but of a national existence. The Temple was a place of pilgrimage. It was the fulfillment of past hopes for loyal Yahweh worshipers, and the center of all present hopes for a great future. The forms of worship carried on there revealed the effort to keep Israel faithful to the Covenant so that no guilt should pile up against a day of wrath, and no prophet should ever again have to denounce the impurities of Temple worship. The transcendent holiness of God, so stressed by Ezekiel, was not forgotten. The sinfulness of man, therefore, which stood in dark contrast to the purity of God, must be put away.

The manner in which the worshiper was brought into proper relation with God was through participation in sacrifices, among which were the guilt offering, the sin offering, the incense offering, and the daily morning and evening burnt offering, all of which are set forth in the Law. In later times, the fire used for the morning and evening burnt offering was made perpetual. Certain sacrificial requirements attended all these offerings, each standing for a cleansing from sin. In some mysterious way, the blood of the victim (its life) provided an atonement, and the conscience of the worshiper was freed from a sense of guilt. Lest there be any sins unrequited by the particular sacrifices, the annual Day of Atonement, recorded in Leviticus 16, was instituted, the purpose of which was to provide atonement for the whole people.

Side by side with Temple worship and its priests was the continuous development of the oral Law, the keeping of which was generally regarded as an essential duty of the worshiper, whether he had the advantage of the Temple services or not. This brings us to the synagogue form of worship. Synagogue worship, as we saw, appears to have developed from the religious gatherings during the Exile, which never were discontinued. Indeed, this mode of worship extended wherever Jews were—and they were scattered everywhere. It was regarded at first as a temporary substitute for Temple worship, but even after the rebuilding of the Temple the synagogue was recognized as fulfilling a genuine need. In the long run it proved to be more important than the Temple. The synagogue congregations made no effort to duplicate the services in the Temple, but they did have meetings at which the written Law was read and expounded. This exposition had much to do with the development of the oral Law.

We have tried to show the process by which obedience to the Law increasingly permeated all of life, and to indicate how the sacred and secular were merged into one intricate pattern of duties prescribed by the religious Law. It is a fact that this made at times for undue externalism and a preoccupation with the letter rather than the spirit of the Law. There were also other important aspects of Judaism which will receive attention after a brief consideration of major political changes—changes which powerfully affected the religious life of the Jews.

Political Fortunes of the Hebrews, 538-63 B.C.

With the exception of one brief period, the entire political life of the Hebrews after the Exile until the conquest by Rome was subordinate to one or another of the great world powers. The first was, of course, Persia, which continued dominant until its defeat by Alexander the Great in 332 B.C. The Jews during the Persian period were ruled by a succession of governors, the early ones Jewish but most later ones aliens.

When the Persians went down in defeat before Alexander the Great, it made very little political difference to the Jews, although culturally Hellenistic (Greek) ideas were in time to have a marked effect upon their thinking. The Greeks ruled Syria as well as the rest of the world of their time, but they interfered little with Jewish affairs, which were, after all, quite insignificant from a material standpoint. Alexander died in 323 B.C., and his empire was broken up, divided by the fortunes of intrigue and conflict among various generals of the army. One of these was Ptolemy, whose portion was Egypt and part of Syria. Later, in 198 B.C., Palestine was dominated by the Seleucids, a dynasty begun by Seleucus, an ambitious general, who managed to carve out for himself a territory which began on the west with the Aegean coast of Asia Minor and extended across Persia to the Indus River in India. His capital city was Antioch.

This dynasty of the Seleucids now coexisted in the ancient world with three other powerful dynasties: the house of Ptolemy, possessing Egypt; the house of Lysimachus, holding a part of Asia Minor and Thrace; and the house of Cassander, in control of Macedonia and Greece. The plots, counterplots, intrigues, and wars that marked the relationships of these groups during the third century B.C. do not concern us greatly, but they do help us appreciate the environment in which the Jews tried to live their religious life. The Jews were an intimate part of the turmoil. As a completely subject people, they were required to pay a heavy burden of taxes, and were ever apprehensive about their fate in a war-torn world. More than once they resisted efforts to despoil the Temple of the treasures that had again been accumulated over a long period of time.

The Maccabean Period

The involvement of the Jews in the intricate swirl of world affairs is illustrated by the momentous revolt which inaugurated the Maccabean period, described in the apocryphal books of the Maccabees and in the writings of the Jewish historian, Josephus. The Jewish family of the Maccabees suddenly and unexpected rekindled the hope of freedom and independence. There was always the star of hope, but it was usually a very remote star. The Seleucid dynasty was the ruling power in Syria. The culture it represented was Hellenistic, as we would expect from the fact that it was originally connected with the empire of Alexander. From the time of Alexander Hellenistic culture had permeated the whole ancient world. The Jews were affected by it, so much so that they were divided among themselves with respect to their acceptance or rejection of Greek habits of life and ways of thinking. At least from 198 B.C. to 174 B.C., there were many Jews who desired to Hellenize the city of Jerusalem. About 174 B.C., this movement became sufficiently articulate that appeal was made to the Seleucid ruler, Antiochus IV, or *Antiochus Epiphanes* (ruled 175-164 B.C.), to help forward this "modernizing" program. A pro-Hellenist party now ruled in Jerusalem under the initiative of Joshua (or Jason), who had been appointed high priest. Greek customs, clothing, and language were used by the younger people in Jerusalem. A gymnasium was erected in which Greeks and Jews contended in games. When he visited the city, Antiochus was received with a torchlight parade. We are, of course, oversimplifying a very complex political-religious situation, but let it suffice to remark that there were divisions and lines of cleavage among the Jews themselves.

About 171 B.C. Antiochus, the ruler, appointed a new high priest in Jerusalem, Menelaus, which infuriated the conservative Jews. They felt that all the efforts of the king to Hellenize the Jews were in effect efforts to destroy their religion and to heathenize them. Furthermore, the Syrian government placed repressive taxes upon the Jews. When war broke out between Egypt and Syria over control of Palestine in 170 B.C., the Jews staged a revolt of their own, in sympathy with Egypt. In retaliation, Antiochus carried off the precious objects of the Temple. Two years later the Syrians again attacked Jerusalem, ordered the end of sacrifice to Yahweh and Sabbath observance, made the practice of circumcision and possession of the Scriptures capital offenses, and finally crowned their repressions by erecting an altar to Zeus on top of the altar to Yahweh in the Temple and on December 25, 168 B.C., offered a sacrifice of a hog upon it. These acts united the Jews and turned them against the Hellenism which had once seemed so attractive to some of them. They now felt that only fighting could save them.[5]

The reaction to these Syrian measures proved to be an exploding volcano that let forth its pent-up wrath upon an astonished ruler. Alien interference with the Jewish faith was exactly the spark needed to inflame the zealous. A revolt was led by Mattathias, a priest, who with his sons was prepared to defend Judaism to the death. It is known as the Maccabean Revolt because of the early leadership of one of the sons, Judas Maccabeus (Judas the Hammerer), who was the soul and mind of the rebellion. First, the revolt aimed to purge the land of apostate Jews who had turned toward Hellenism; next, it attempted to gain full religious liberty. Obviously such a rebellion would be countered by strong military measures on the part of the Seleucid authorities. But to our astonishment no less than that of the contemporary Syrians, the Jewish rebels repeatedly overcame military expeditions which sought to rout them. During a lull in the fighting, Judas Maccabeus demolished the altar to Zeus, rebuilt the altar to Yahweh, and, just three years after the sacrifice of the hog to Zeus, reinstituted sacrifices to Yahweh. This great success is observed annually by loyal Jews in the Feast of Lights, or Hanukkah.

Judas had succeeded in obtaining religious freedom, but he now sought

[5] Accounts of these events are found in the apocryphal books of the Maccabees and in Josephus, the Jewish historian. See also Enslin, *op. cit.*, pp. 8 ff.

political freedom as well. In his efforts to maintain his position, he sought to ally himself with the rising power of Rome, which now for the first time is heard of in connection with Jewish affairs. In fact, a treaty was entered into with Rome (I Maccabees 8). However, nothing came of it so far as assistance to Judas was concerned, and Judas was finally killed by the Syrians in 160 B.C.

After Judas was slain in battle, his brothers rose in his place, and the conflict continued. Jonathan followed as leader and obtained marked success, due partially to the preoccupation of Syrian rulers with trouble nearer home, following the death of Antiochus. He actually controlled a wide area, and, in defiance of Syrian power, he left no doubt that he intended to be in charge indefinitely. He also became high priest of the Jews. But Jonathan was murdered by a Syrian general who, under the guise of friendship, pretended to do him honor. And again another brother, Simon by name, took Jonathan's place about 143 B.C. He demanded entire political independence from Syria, including freedom from taxation; and Syria had to agree.

Thus, in the year 143 B.C., 25 years after the revolt began, Judah entered upon a period of 80 years of relative independence from foreign control. The Jews were once again their own masters. Especially was this the case under Simon who, as high priest also, ruled as a religious leader but not as a king. To the orthodox Jew, this was an ideal situation, and in retrospect it stands in great contrast to those far-off days when pagan rites were more served by the Hebrew kings than was the religion of Yahweh. But this state of affairs was only temporary. Peace never seemed to reign long in the ancient world, where treachery cast its shadow on every high place. Simon and two of his three sons were murdered by his own son-in-law, a Jewish army officer. The remaining son, John Hyrcanus, escaped and was able to reach Jerusalem, where he was accepted as lawful high priest, successor to his father. After some preliminary troubles with the Syrian power, which refused to relinquish its claim to suzerainty over Palestine, a fairly long period of peace followed.

With John Hyrcanus firmly established as high priest (134-104 B.C.), religious and political leadership were merged. Political freedom and emancipation from Syria, such as it was, seems to have been aided more by Roman suggestions to Syria to keep hands off than by Hebrew strength at home. In any case, John Hyrcanus was ambitiously intent upon enlarging the borders of his land. There is some ground for supposing that he allowed the idea of kingship to attach itself to his title as high priest. With his personal prestige and Maccabean blood, it would not have been impossible for him to believe that destiny beckoned him to be king. If he did not appropriate that title, his son Aristobulus I did; in any event, a dynasty was started, most likely by Hyrcanus himself. Aristobulus was recognized as king as well as high priest; so also was his brother, Alexander Jannaeus, who shortly thereafter succeeded him. Two other members of this family followed each other in turn down to 63 B.C., but the high religious motivations which activated the first Maccabeans gave way in their successors before political ambition and royal vanity. The worldliness of these Maccabean high priest-kings produced a religious party of protest from which the party of the Pharisees developed. They were ultraconservative Jews who abode strictly by the Law and hated Greek ideas and ways.

This period ends as tragically as did those earlier kingdoms which fell before Assyria and Babylonia. Pompey, the Roman general who was extending Roman power in Syria and Asia, intervened in a conflict between two Jewish royal brothers, Hyrcanus II (grandson of John Hyrcanus) and his brother Aristobulus II. Pompey was inclined to distrust Aristobulus, who was the high priest at Jerusalem, and laid siege to Jerusalem in 63 B.C. When the Romans completed their work three months later, Jerusalem was again a shambles. With the exception of the royal family of Aristobulus, who were taken to Rome, prisoners did not interest the Romans. They slaughtered thousands of the inhabitants. Upon leaving, the Romans put Hyrcanus II in charge as high priest and made him a Roman official, called an ethnarch. The Jews continued as a religious community, subject to Rome, in which condition we shall still find them at the time of Christ. Their history as an independent nation had come to an end, and their nationhood itself was lost in A.D. 135. They remained stateless until the year A.D. 1948, when the modern state of Israel was established.

Religious Problems of Judaism

The Problem of Hebrew Destiny

A great deal of attention in postexilic Judaism was centered on the problem of Hebrew destiny. We stated earlier in this chapter that the Temple was a living promise of a great future. Very high hopes about that future were carried in the Hebrew heart. But the golden age of the future never seemed to come, and all promise of it continually failed of realization and was perpetually postponed. This made for pessimism and despair, especially so whenever national welfare was critically threatened, as in the days of Antiochus Epiphanes and his attempted abolition of the Hebrew religion.

The repeated frustration of national hopes raised a serious problem for Hebrew thought, involving the validity of the prophetic promise and the faithfulness of Yahweh.

The immediate solution to this problem was *apocalyptic thinking*, mentioned earlier in the discussion of Ezekiel. Marked by the use of bizarre and grotesque imagery, of cryptic numbers and figures, apocalyptic is in its essence a form of prophecy taken to extremes or an extension of prophecy. In apocalyptic, the Jewish faith in the coming rulership of God and the consequent greatness of Israel found its expression. The apocalyptic writings purported to disclose a glorious impending future which God was preparing for the Jews and would bring about by the use of his omnipotent might. Elements of apocalyptic are found in Old Testament books like Ezekiel, Isaiah, Joel, Zechariah, and most especially in the book of Daniel, a second-century B.C. work in which this form of writing is seen fully, particularly in chapters 7 to 12. In the New Testament, the book of Revelation is apocalyptic. The writers of the apocalypses claim divine revelation and are themselves usually unknown, frequently adopting the name of a great man of the past like Daniel, Enoch, Baruch, or Moses as the name of their work.

The general idea of the apocalyptic writings was not a new one. Actually, it was a logical expectation on the basis of the Jewish faith in the Covenant. At least as early as the eighth century B.C. there had been the expectation of the Day of Yahweh, a day of great joy when God would bring his promises to fulfillment. That was six centuries before Daniel; in the meantime much history had passed. While there might be greatness and prosperity for a time, these periods were always followed by danger and hardship. Even during the 80 years of relative independence which followed the Maccabean Revolt, the greatness and successes won were accompanied by bitterness, hatred, and strife among the Jews themselves. Was this to be an endless story, going round and round in ever-continuing cycles?

Such a thought was not acceptable. History had had a beginning in the will and deed of God, as he created the world and man; history had continued meaningfully in the covenant relationship with Yahweh, and it would reach a climax, a great and wonderful culmination, as the result again of the act of God. Because the Jew had such great faith in God's concern for his people and his power to carry out his designs, he accepted the apocalyptic ideas. We recall that in the eighth century B.C. Hosea had looked for a golden age when war would cease and justice and mercy reign (Hosea 2:18-20), and that during the same century Isaiah also looked for a time when even the natural enmities of animals would disappear and men would beat their swords into plowshares and their spears into pruning hooks

(Isaiah 2:2-4, 11:6-9). But the need for swords and spears never seemed to pass; only too frequently Joel's advice to beat plowshares into swords and pruning hooks into spears (Joel 3:10) had had to be followed. Faith in Yahweh and his care for his people promised that the tide of history *would* turn. The time of the end was coming, and not far distant, when God would bring his purpose to its fulfillment.

There was no one set pattern for these writings, but generally they followed the scheme of picturing evils, portents, and "woes" which were to appear before the end. Then into the midst of man's history God himself would come to establish his Kingdom by direct intervention. At times God's intervention was portrayed as taking place through a chosen or anointed one, a *Messiah*, to whom had been entrusted the work of acting as God's agent and preparing the scene for God's appearance. In the book of Daniel (chapter 7) this chosen one is called the Son of man, a superhuman being who would come on the "clouds of heaven" and be given "an everlasting dominion." In the apocryphal book of Enoch, the phrase *Son of man* is used also, referring to a superhuman being who would bring the kingdom of God to men. These different expectations of an anointed one who would usher in the end of the ages led to a variety of messianic hopes.

It is readily seen that apocalyptic would make its greatest appeal at times when men seem least able to solve their problems by their own abilities. In these extreme circumstances, only two alternatives would seem to exist for those who have trusted God's plan for his people—either to surrender faith in God and his purposes, or to believe that he is able and ready to take the hopeless situation into his own hands, bringing it to a great and wonderful conclusion. The danger with apocalyptic, particularly in times when man is capable of doing much to guide his own destiny, is that a false "trust in God"—false because it expects God to do what men should be doing themselves—undermines all human effort, based as it is on a misconception of God's relation to man. It is understandable that in the twentieth century, as man's self-confidence is threatened by powers he has developed but may not be able to control, apocalyptic plays a considerable part in thought once again, and books like Ezekiel, Daniel, and Revelation are examined carefully for clues they may contain concerning the time of the end.

The Problem of the Afterlife

It may strike the reader with some surprise to learn that until the post-exilic period there was remarkable unconcern about life after death, or at least no discussion of it. To be sure, from primitive times there had been the belief in a shadowy sort of continued existence. It was assumed that at death one was "gathered to his people," but we find no indication in the early Scriptures of any great speculative interest in the subject. This may be the result partly of the general lack of emphasis upon the individual. It was the *nation* of Israel that had its Covenant with Yahweh, not the individual, who suffered or prospered as his nation was punished or rewarded by God. In the earliest records, a man was spoken of as having died or gone to his people, but only occasionally and remarkably rarely in the older books (the Torah and the Prophets), is there mention of a man's having descended into Sheol (Hell). Exactly how this word is meant is not clear. In some instances it may simply be another way of saying that the man died. On the other hand, because Babylonian ideas influenced Hebrew thought and the Babylonians held to a definite idea of Sheol as an actual place in the depths of the earth to which the souls of men go, the Hebrews may also have taken the term *Sheol* as referring to an abode of the dead, a specific hollow place located in the earth (since the Hebrews buried the dead) in which some form of continuance of what was once a full man took place.

In two of the several instances that the word *Sheol* appears in the Pentateuch, we find Jacob saying, "I shall go down to Sheol . . . , mourning," and ". . . you would bring down my gray hairs with sorrow to Sheol" (Genesis 37:35 and 42:38). Both statements seem simply to mean the end of life. In some of the dozen or so times that Sheol appears in the division of the Prophets, it seems to carry the same denotation. Thus, ". . . Sheol has enlarged its appetite" (Isaiah 5:14); "When it [Egypt] goes down to Sheol I will make the deep mourn for it" (Ezekiel 31:15); and "His greed is as wide as Sheol" (Habakkuk 2:5). The thought that seems basic to these statements —that death is the end of the individual life—appears also in the Writings, the third section of the Old Testament as classified by the Jews. Ecclesiastes, a book probably written under the influence of Hellenistic ideas, has a positive disbelief in any kind of continuance after death. The author writes:

> For the living know that they will die, but the dead know nothing, and they have no more reward; but the memory of them is lost. Their love and their hate and their envy have already perished, and they have no more for ever any share in all that is done under the sun [Ecclesiastes 9:5-6].

The author of the book of Job, of uncertain date, seems to hold a similar view. He writes, "So man lies down and rises not again; till the heavens are no more he will not awake, or be roused out of his sleep. . . . If a man die, shall he live again?" (Job 14:12, 14), to which question he is suggesting that the answer is no.

There are other passages, however, in which the word *Sheol* appears which imply that something continues after death, and that this soul (if it may be termed such) actually occupies a place under the earth along with the souls of all the other dead. Take, for example, Isaiah 14:9-11:

> Sheol beneath is stirred up to meet you [the king of Babylon] when you come, it rouses the shades to greet you. . . . All of them will speak and say to you: "You too have become as weak as we! You have become like us!" Your pomp is brought down to Sheol . . . ; maggots are the bed beneath you, and worms are your covering.

Also, Ezekiel 32:21 reads, "The mighty chiefs shall speak of them [the Egyptians], with their helpers, out of the midst of Sheol: 'They have come down, they lie still, . . . slain by the sword.' " The famous story of Saul's consulting the medium or witch of Endor (I Samuel 28) in order to ask advice of the dead Samuel certainly implies some sort of personal continuance. The shade of Samuel asked, "Why have you disturbed me by bringing me up?" (verse 15).

From these illustrations, it would appear that belief in Sheol did carry the thought of continuance of personal individuality, but in a much reduced and unattractive form. Further, there was no sense of reward or punishment in Sheol; these came within one's lifetime, and the dead were all alike in the same shadowy condition.

In Hebrew thought, Yahweh seems to have had no relation to Sheol, for his justice and faithfulness were intended for living people, not the dead. This view is especially remarkable in view of the all-consuming interest the neighboring Egyptians had in achieving a desirable afterlife with the help of their gods, and the interest in Babylonia also in what happens after death. In Greek thought, Zeus was a god of this life, but then the god Hades was appointed to look after the underworld. Hebrew thought had no god of the underworld. Note what is said about Yahweh's relation to Sheol:

> I am reckoned among those who go down to the Pit; I am a man who has no strength, like one forsaken among the dead, like the slain that lie in the grave, like those whom thou dost remember no more, for they are cut off from thy hand [Psalm 88:4-5].

> For Sheol cannot thank thee, death cannot praise thee; those who go down to the Pit cannot hope for thy faithfulness. The living, the living, he thanks thee, as I do this day . . . [Isaiah 38:18-19].

At best the idea of Sheol left much to be desired. It had nothing to say to the teaching of a Jeremiah or Ezekiel that God's relation to man was individual as well as national, for this teaching raised the question of God's justice if he allowed a righteous man to die miserably. Further, it missed being a truly spiritual conception and was devoid of ethical significance. Because of its unsatisfactory nature, other solutions to the problems of man's death were sought during the postexilic period, particularly in the two last centuries B.C. and the two first centuries A.D. Most of these attempted solutions do not appear in the Old Testament canon; accordingly, they will not be discussed here except in a general way.

There were two possible answers to the problem. One of these taught the resurrection of the body, while the other moved in the direction of belief in a continuing spiritual existence with God. Of the two, the former came to be the more widespread, at least before the time of Jesus, and it was accompanied by a growing belief in rewards and punishments. It was popular because it fitted into the general thought pattern of Hebrew understandings in a way that a spiritual continuance beyond death did not. We recall that the prophets had spoken of the great future of Israel, and the apocalyptic writings had predicted a Day of Yahweh when the consummation of all God's great plans for the nation would take place. The resurrection of the body was a concept that fitted well into these ideas, for it promised that those who had died before the great Day arrived would return, human beings once again, to participate in it.

At three places in the Old Testament the idea of continuance after death in full being appears with some degree of clarity. Isaiah 26:19 concerns the day of salvation: "Thy dead shall live, their bodies shall rise. O dwellers in the dust, awake and sing for joy! For thy dew is a dew of light, and on the land of the shades thou wilt let it fall." This verse has a resurrection of the righteous, of "*thy* dead." In Job 19:25-27, a much-disputed passage of uncertain translation, the suffering Job cries, "For I know that my Redeemer [or Vindicator] lives, and at last he will stand upon the earth; and after my skin has been thus destroyed, then without my flesh I shall see God, whom I shall see on my side. . . ." This passage points to a spiritual relationship with God rather than a bodily resurrection.

Our last and most important selection is a passage in the apocalyptic book of Daniel (12:2-3): "And many of those who sleep in the dust of the earth shall awake, some to everlasting life, and some to shame and everlasting contempt. And those who are wise shall shine like the brightness of the firmament; and those who turn many to righteousness, like the stars for ever and ever." In this passage we find a resurrection of both the good and the evil and a meting out of both reward and punishment. It was a most significant statement in terms of its effect upon future thinking.

On the question of the resurrection of the body, two of the great religious groups among the Hebrews at the time of Jesus, the Pharisees and the Sadducees, differed fundamentally. The principal cause for the differing views was that the Sadducees found nothing about physical resurrection in the ancient Scriptures, and were not in favor of the new development of the oral Law and other new ideas. The Pharisees, on the other hand, were prepared to adopt newer interpretations and concepts. They accepted the belief in the resurrection of the body.

Alongside this more common belief Judaism contained the seeds of another view concerning life after death which was unfolding at the time of Jesus. Out of the lofty concept of God in Deutero-Isaiah, which included the idea of everlastingness, grew the relevant idea that Yahweh had an everlasting interest in those who served him. Since the God of Deutero-Isaiah is the great creator and determiner of destiny, what barrier could death be to him? Certain passages of Deutero-Isaiah indicate that he may have held a spiritual doctrine of the afterlife. Also, in Psalm 73:23-26 we seem to have a suggestion of this same belief:

> . . . I am continually with thee; thou dost hold my right hand. Thou dost guide me with thy counsel, and afterward thou wilt receive me to glory. Whom have I in heaven but thee? And there is nothing upon earth that I desire besides thee. My flesh and my heart may fail, but God is the strength of my heart and my portion for ever.

It remained for the Christians to develop a full doctrine of life beyond death; in them that which was so strangely incidental to ancient Hebrew thought became one of the great central emphases. Man would die, but he would live again in a state of beatitude.

The Problem of Suffering

One of the most difficult problems of religion and philosophy is the problem of suffering or the more general problem of evil. We saw how Deutero-Isaiah found some explanation of the misfortunes endured by Israel by interpreting these sufferings as vicarious, that is, for others. But there are many other kinds of evil and suffering in life which seem to fall at random upon the just and the unjust, as Jesus himself said. Such disasters as plague, pestilence, blindness, insanity, destitution, misery of body and mind, and sudden death are common features of human existence. What is the reason for such calamities, and is a religious man exempt from them?

In an effort to deal with this problem, we may regard the book of Job as representative of the deeper vein of religious and philosophic thought in the postexilic period. This book is widely regarded as one of the great pieces of the world's literature. Beautifully presented in dramatic form, it repudiated a view that had become common in the postexilic period, that under the Covenant Yahweh rewarded the Hebrew nation when it obeyed him and punished when it disobeyed. This idea continued, but it came also to be extended to mean that the individual who lived righteously would prosper, enjoy a long life, and leave behind many children (his immortality), while the one who was sinful would see misery and brevity of life. Reversing this idea, it followed that the wealthy, prosperous man was a righteous person being rewarded for faithfulness, and the suffering person was a sinner receiving his just rewards. It is this view that the book of Job repudiated, as had Deutero-Isaiah in his portrayal of suffering as vicarious.

Let us see the problem with which the author of this great drama struggles. Job is the tragic hero of the piece. As the story opens he is a man of consequence, well-to-do, loyal to God, and respected by all, even by the poor and fatherless because his human sympathy has been extended to them. Had he not been "eyes to the blind, and feet to the lame"? He is a man blessed of God with what the Hebrews and most of us regard as the good things of life—family, prosperity, health, friends. But suddenly, in succession, one form of catastrophe after another falls upon him, both from the hand of man and from nature. The Sabeans take away his herds of oxen and asses and kill his servants; lightning destroys the sheep and shepherds; the Chaldeans take the camels and camel drivers; a tornado strikes the house of his eldest son where all his sons and daughters are banqueting, and they are killed. At last Job himself is smitten with a disease of boils from head to foot, and the drama discloses him as he "sat among the ashes." It is the picture of a man laid low—from prosperity to poverty, from health to sickness. The laughter of his sons and daughters has no echo from the silence of their graves. He is a man suffering with pain and sorrow. All he has left is his soul with its thoughts. He has had faith in God, and that faith was his stronghold; but now there is creeping doubt. His wife has already thrown her faith in God to the winds. Even more, in her bitterness of soul she recommends that he too curse God and let death come. Why has God let things reach this pass? What kind of governance of the world is this? Who can fathom the meaning of this evil?

Job thought in the days of his prosperity that his affluence was a recompense for righteousness, a sign of God's favor. He sincerely loved goodness and mercy and justice and had tried to practice them in his dealings with men. He believed that prosperity was a reward for the good life and that evil was always punishment for sin. Job's friends still adhere to this traditional theology, and so they insist that he must have sinned grievously in secret. But he knows his own character; he has made no change in life or thought commensurate with these tragic devastations and can find no voice of conscience confirming their judgment. He now gives vent to his rebellion and curses the day that gave him birth. How can he believe any more in the moral government of the world? He debates the issue with his friends, constantly maintaining his own innocence and, by implication, the injustice of God. It does not occur to him to doubt the existence of God; nor does he blame his suffering upon a devil. He is a strict monotheist, and for this reason, since all that happens must come from God, the problem is so very difficult. If only there were life beyond the grave; if, like a tree that sends up new shoots after it is felled, one might hope to return, then life's sufferings might be borne. But there is no comfort or recompense in Sheol.

In the agony of his body and soul, Job challenges God to argue the matter with him, confident that in such a debate he could show that he does not deserve this sort of treatment. After a lapse of time, God answers him out of the whirlwind: "Who is this that darkens counsel by words without knowledge? Gird up your loins like a man, I will question you, and you shall declare to me" (38:2-3).

So God proceeds to ask this presumptuous Job, so sure of his knowledge of righteousness and of all things that he dares to accuse God himself of injustice. He asks Job where he was when the earth was created, how the steps of creation were performed, and the nature of the great earth and sea and the wild creatures in them, and he then concludes, "Shall a faultfinder contend with the Almighty? He who argues with God, let him answer it" (40:1). Can Job expect to know the ways of the mind of the Creator; does he know enough to pass final judgment on the universe?

Now at last Job realizes his position before God. He has discovered humility, which in turn leads to repentance. He replies to God, "Behold, I am of small account; what shall I answer thee? I lay my hand on my mouth. I have spoken once, and I will not answer; twice, but I will proceed no further" (40:4-5). But his response to God's challenge goes further than this, for through the agony of his soul and his conflict with God himself he has come to an experience of "seeing" God, of having a direct experience of him. So he concludes the poem by saying, "Therefore I have uttered what I did not understand, things too wonderful for me, which I did not know. . . . I had heard of thee by the hearing of the ear, but now my eye sees thee; therefore I despise myself, and repent in dust and ashes" (42:3-6).

In place of trust in his own moral goodness, Job now has a true faith in God himself, that God whose ways and purposes are beyond all discovery and consequently may not be challenged by puny man. So Job is filled with repentance and with faith. These constitute man's proper attitude before his

God, and these have been reached by Job. He has found a religious, although not a philosophical, solution to his problem; and trust replaces arrogant rebellion.

Job's answer is the best light which the author of the book can throw on the problem of evil. Although not an intellectual solution, it is a far better answer than the doctrine of Job's friends. The earlier theology could make no place for the fact that the righteous did suffer. Job accepted the fact that the righteous could suffer, and at the same time reconciled this fact with faith in God even though intellectually he did not understand.

This is the religious way of dealing with one of life's hardest problems. Is the universe a cosmos or a chaos? Is there moral significance in the world? Is goodness deeper than evil? In the last analysis, is the universe in good hands? In what can men put their trust? The problem of evil is the hardest problem which theologians and philosophers face. The human soul cannot wait until the end of time. It has to live now, and it needs some faith to live by. The dramatist who wrote the book of Job reveals that he himself went through a great struggle with this problem. He turned away from the traditional view, which he found to be false, as did Jesus also. But he felt the need to add something to the belief in the power which created the world: faith and trust in the Creator's moral goodness. These would enable the worshiper to have faith in the existence of an infinite wisdom, operating frequently as an inscrutable providence. Somehow, all things do work together for good; in other words, the practical religious solution is a deep hope turned into an adventurous faith that the power of God is matched by his infinite goodness.

The Nature of Wisdom

Here we deal with another intellectually adventurous phase of Hebrew thought. Philosophy never made its appearance among the Hebrews in the highly advanced, systematic form which was developed by the Greeks. Yet we do know, of course, that the Jew reflected deeply upon life. He did "philosophize," but always in a religious setting; he apparently never departed from the fundamental premise of the reality of God and the Law.

Nothing has yet been said of the wise men or sages. They were Jews, distinct from the prophets and the priests, who exercised an office of practical counsel. Some of our greatest Hebrew literature is the work of sages of the postexilic period.

In Hebrew thought the term *wisdom* has a practical side and a theoretical side. When we examine the wisdom literature of Job, Proverbs, and Ecclesiastes in the Old Testament and the noncanonical books of Ecclesiasticus and the Wisdom of Solomon, we are greatly impressed by the imposing array of practical counsels and observations covering all manner of human relationships and attitudes toward life. We note the great amount of sound common sense; much of the advice is just as useful today in dealing with ourselves and others as it was when written. The same is true of many of the Psalms composed according to the same school of thought. They are, as it were, a distillation drawn from a vast experience. Observing men discerned types of behavior that were admirable and of intrinsic merit and other sorts that were foolish or unwise. They recognize a measure of correlation between clear thinking and sound morals.

The counsels of wisdom comprise a practical ethic, but at the same time they always remain close to the Law of Yahweh. The expressed and implied theme of this literature is that a proper relation to God creates an inner spirit that is expressed in wise conduct. In many of the sayings in Proverbs and Ecclesiastes especially appears the doctrine that the consequence of goodness is prosperity, though Job, the greatest book in the wisdom writings, set this doctrine aside. Generally speaking, practical wisdom meant for the wise man an intelligent choosing of all those things that enrich human relations. He tried, not abstractly but realistically, to indicate the way toward fullness of life.

On the theoretical side, we find some attempt to understand the nature of wisdom itself. The writers of this particular literature, while loyal Hebrews, did speculate beyond the boundaries of orthodox theology. Questions of a religious-philosophic nature which could not be answered by folk tales or myths stirred them. Some of these men shared the lofty monotheism of Deutero-Isaiah, and as well pondered quite consciously about the relation of God to the world of nature and man. They concluded from the wonders of nature that the Supreme Being was infinitely intelligent or wise. The word *wisdom* began to stand out as a divine attribute, and was semipersonified as having almost a separate status of its own. Proverbs 8:22-30 reads,

> The Lord created me [Wisdom] at the beginning of his work, the first of his acts of old. Ages ago I was set up, at the first, before the beginning of the earth. . . . When he established the heavens, I was there, . . . when he made firm the skies above, . . . when he assigned to the sea its limit, . . . when he marked out the foundations of the earth, then I was beside him, like a master workman. . . .

And in the Wisdom of Solomon occur these words: "She [Wisdom] is the breath of the power of God, and a pure effluence flowing from the glory of the Almighty. . . . the brightness of the everlasting light, the unspotted mirror of the power of God, and the image of His goodness" (7:25-26).

The Hebrew authors of these passages have expressed themselves about the being of God in ways which are very closely allied to ideas about wisdom that we find in Greek philosophy, and may in part be derived therefrom. Furthermore, the writer of the second passage also regards wisdom in man as a divine presence or visitation or immanence of the wisdom of God, an idea which we also find in Greek thought.

This designation of wisdom as a manifestation of the power, presence, intelligence, and goodness of God is the clearest evidence of an intellectual effort to find unity, system, and order in the universe. The wise man obviously felt the need to articulate his deeper awareness of the implications of belief in the universality of one supreme God. The Hebrew scholar could have made use of much that had been produced by the Greek thinkers. It so happened that the Hebrew word *wisdom*, so richly laden with a tradition of practical godliness, was the steppingstone between the Jewish religion and Greek philosophy. We have seen only its beginnings here. We shall not now take up the further fruits of this association, which were fully garnered by the great Alexandrian Jew, Philo. However, what has been said here will provide a meaningful point of contact when we later consider the confluence of Hebrew and Greek thought in the Roman world.

Summary

Our study of the development of Judaism has shown us the various sides of Jewish thought. It has illustrated the increasing hold of the Law, characteristic of legalism wherever it appears in religion. At the same time, the postexilic period showed the need for enlarged answers to problems of nature and destiny, a manifestation of growing intellectual maturity. It has given us an awareness also of the cultural and religious conflicts that take place when one form of culture meets another. We saw this not only during the Exile itself, when the Jews tried to maintain their ways in the face of Babylonian customs and beliefs, but again during the Persian and Greek periods, when the Jews endeavored once more to preserve their spiritual identity in the midst of adverse forces cutting away like ocean waters on an island shore.

Questions for Study

1. In what ways did the Hebrew religion and the understanding of the Covenant help to keep the Hebrew nation alive through the centuries?
2. How was it that the Hebrews were permitted to return from Babylonia to Palestine? What happened to them there during the next two centuries?

What two forms of religion existed there side by side, and how did they differ?

3. Why did great emphasis on the Law develop, and precisely what form did this emphasis take? How did the Jews at this period understand the Law, and why was it so vital to obey it? In what way does legalism make religion apply to every aspect of life? What good and what undesirable features do you find in legalism?
4. What is the rabbinic literature, and what principal forms did it take? Identify the Talmud and the Mishna.
5. How, by whom, and when was Persia defeated? What happened to the empire of Alexander the Great after his death? What was the fate of the Jews at this time? What was the relation between the Jews and the Seleucids?
6. Describe briefly the Maccabean period, the way in which relative independence was achieved, and what the Jews did with it.
7. On the basis of understandings of the Covenant, why did apocalyptic messages arise under Syrian and Roman rule? What is the nature of apocalyptic?
8. How was Sheol pictured in ancient times? How did ancient Hebrews think man received his reward for righteousness? What later beliefs concerning man's fate at death modified this ancient view?
9. Discuss the story of Job and its significance. What did Job deny, and what conclusion did he reach?
10. What is the nature of the Hebrew wisdom literature, both practical and theoretical?
11. You have noticed the changed conceptions of God from the time of Abraham through that of Moses to that of Deutero-Isaiah. How would you account for these changes—does God change his nature? Discuss.

Selected Readings

Anderson, Bernhard W., *Understanding the Old Testament*, Englewood Cliffs, N. J., Prentice-Hall, Inc., 1957.

Gottwald, Norman K., *A Light to the Nations*, New York, Harper & Brothers, 1959.

The Interpreter's Bible, Nashville, Abingdon Press, 1951, and later, appropriate articles in vols. I-VI.

Lods, Adolphe, *The Prophets and the Rise of Judaism*, New York, E. P. Dutton & Co., 1937.

Matthews, I. G., *The Religious Pilgrimage of Israel*, New York, Harper & Brothers, 1947.

Oesterley, W. O. E., and T. H. Robinson, *Hebrew Religion, Its Origin and Development*, New York, The Macmillan Company, 1937.

Porter, F. C., *The Messages of the Apocalyptic Writers*, New York, Charles Scribner's Sons, 1911.

Rowley, H. H., *The Re-discovery of the Old Testament*, Philadelphia, The Westminster Press, 1946.

Rowley, H. H., *The Relevance of Apocalyptic*, 2nd ed., London, Lutterworth Press, 1947.

Welch, Adam, *Post-exilic Judaism*, Edinburgh, William Blackwood & Sons, 1935.

II. The Historic Jesus

CHRONOLOGICAL FRAMEWORK OF PART II

40 B.C.	Herod the Great is made king of Palestine by the Romans. Rules 37-4 B.C. Builds the third Temple, known to Jesus.
ca. 6 B.C.	Jesus is born.
4 B.C.	Herod dies. His son, Archelaus, made ethnarch of Judaea, including Samaria, and Idumaea. Herod Antipas made tetrarch of Galilee and Peraea. Rules until A.D.39. Philip rules Iturea, Batanaea, etc.
A.D. 6	Archelaus banished. Judaea ruled by a Roman procurator.
ca. 29-33	Ministry of Jesus.
26-36	Pontius Pilate is procurator of Judaea.
Between 30-33 (?)	Death of Jesus.
66	Revolt against the Romans begins.
70	Jerusalem falls and the Temple is destroyed.
132	Revolt against the Romans under Bar-Cochba.
135	Jerusalem falls, is leveled, and is rebuilt as Aelia Capitolina, a Roman city. Jews forbidden in the city.

WRITING OF THE CHRISTIAN SCRIPTURES

ca. 47-56	The missionary journeys of Paul.
ca. 50-62	Paul's epistles written.
ca. 65-70	The Gospel of Mark written.
ca. 80	The Gospel of Luke and the Acts of the Apostles written.
ca. 85	The Gospel of Matthew written.
ca. 90-100	The Gospel of John, Revelation, and epistles of John written.
ca. 150	II Peter, probably latest of the New Testament writings, is written.

5. The Political-Religious Environment in the Time of Jesus

To understand Jesus it is necessary to consider him in the political-religious setting of the Palestine in which he lived. In this chapter we shall therefore present an abridged account of this aspect of the contemporary scene, beginning with an exposition of the political structure.

The Political Structure

When Jesus was born, the Romans were the power that dominated the Mediterranean world. Pompey established Roman sovereignty over Palestine in 63 B.C. At that time the Jewish high priest, Hyrcanus II, was made a political deputy of Rome with the title of ethnarch. The Romans thus gave recognition to the Maccabean or Hasmonaean house, intending by this arrangement to allay the sting of Roman authority and bring about some measure of political loyalty on the part of the Jews. This state of affairs might have lasted for a considerable time had the Roman republic itself not been entering upon a period of upheaval and civil war as it made the transition into an empire. This section of Roman history is marked by such familiar names as Pompey, Caesar, Crassus, Cassius, and Mark Antony. The whole of Syria figured prominently in these struggles for empire. In consequence, Judaea suffered rather badly in the early stages under Crassus,

Palestine in the Time of Jesus

Gabinius, and Cassius. Julius Caesar, however, dealt kindly with the Jews. In 48 B.C. he restored the civil authority to Hyrcanus II and extended other privileges to the Jews, such as exemption from military service and full religious liberty. But this reprieve was short-lived because of the assassination of Caesar in 44 B.C., which gave rise to troublesome political complications. For a short time after 41 B.C. the Parthians held Jerusalem. In 40 B.C. the Romans appointed a king to rule Palestine, an Idumaean named Herod, later called the Great, but it took him until 37 B.C. to reconquer Jerusalem. Herod, it should be noted, was technically a Jew, for the Maccabean priest-king Hyrcanus I had conquered the territory of Idumaea lying to the south of Palestine, and had forced the Idumaeans to become Jews and to accept circumcision. Thus, the Idumaeans came to be known as "half-Jews." Outstanding among these people was a very clever politician named Antipater who became minister to and actually the power behind Hyrcanus II. Herod was the son of Antipater. He married a Jewess, Mariamne, granddaughter of Hyrcanus II. Herod ruled from 37 to 4 B.C.; Jesus was born at the end of his reign. This same Herod is referred to in Matthew (2:13-18) in connection with the slaughter of infants in Bethlehem.

From the Roman point of view, Herod proved himself a highly capable and successful administrator of the Palestinian territory. He was a great builder—of cities, temples, aqueducts, gymnasiums, and finally of a reconstructed and refurbished Temple in Jerusalem. This, the third Temple, was the one known by Jesus and his disciples. In some respects Herod could be compared to Solomon at his greatest. But because he was not a full Jew, because he had replaced the Jewish ruling house of the Hasmonaeans or Maccabeans and ruled for Rome, and because he tried to Hellenize the Jews by promoting Greek customs and habits of life as vigorously as had the Seleucid, Antiochus Epiphanes, he was both feared and hated by the people he was ruling. His personal life also was a great scandal to the people. Since the family of his Jewish wife, Mariamne, was the Jewish royal family with ambitions of its own to rule again, some of its members, particularly Mariamne's mother, Alexandra, plotted against him. Driven by desperation, Herod murdered six members of the family, including his favorite wife and the aged high priest, Hyrcanus II. In his last days Herod appeared to be insane, murdering indiscriminately and establishing a small harem of wives. His attempts to conciliate the Jews by building them their glorious Temple, made of white marble and overlaid with gold and precious stones, were forgotten in their bitter anger with him.

Herod's death did not improve conditions in Palestine. In his will he left Judaea, which included Samaria and Idumaea, as a kingdom to his son Archelaus, and the remaining territory he divided between his sons Antipas and Philip, as tetrarchs. Antipas was assigned Galilee and Peraea. The Roman Emperor Augustus accepted the provisions of Herod's will, except with regard to Archelaus, whom he designated an ethnarch, not king, of Judaea. After 10 years of tyranny over Judaea, Archelaus was banished in A.D. 6 by Augustus. Judaea was then made a Roman province under a minor official called a procurator, responsible directly to the emperor himself. Of these procurators, the one whose name is familiar is *Pontius Pilate* (26-36), who sentenced Jesus to death.

The two political and geographic divisions of interest to us are Galilee-Peraea to the north and Judaea to the south, including the city of Jerusalem. Let us observe first the general character of Galilee where Jesus was reared. The Roman ruler here at the time of Jesus was the tetrarch Antipas, usually called Herod Antipas, who reigned continuously from 4 B.C. to A.D. 39. Galilee had many large cities and a considerable number of suburban villages, all thickly populated. The city of Sepphoris was second in size to Jerusalem in Judaea. It was therefore the largest city in Galilee and during part of Jesus' life the capital city. Of particular importance is the fact that Jesus lived not more than five miles from Sepphoris, in the village of Nazareth. The importance of this fact is often overlooked. There is every reason to suppose that Jesus had a first-hand acquaintance with this city because it was so near at hand. Nearer still to Nazareth was the large village of Japhia, with a population of about 15,000.

The city of Sepphoris had been very important for many years. Herod the Great had made it his military center. This city passed through one bitter experience which may throw some light on Jesus' attitude toward political authority. After the death of Herod the Great, a Jewish revolutionary, Judas of Gamala by name, gained control of Sepphoris and the surrounding area. He was overcome by the Romans after bitter resistance. The city was sacked when it fell; the populace was severely treated and many were enslaved. However, Herod Antipas rebuilt it on so grand a scale that it was known far and wide as a city of great beauty. Here Herod Antipas himself lived until he built up the new city of Tiberias, named after the reigning emperor, which then became his capital. These events took place during the lifetime of Jesus.

Sepphoris and its surrounding villages had sufficiently tasted the bitter fruits of revolution; they would not therefore have any more to do with revolt, and did not participate in the tragic revolt of A.D. 66 which led to the destruction of Jerusalem in 70. This sheds interesting light on one possible source of Jesus' practice of separating religion from political hatred of Rome. He taught the kingdom of God, which, in the last analysis, was not conditioned by the presence or absence of Roman rulers.

The Jewish Wailing Wall

To this wall have come the Jews since the destruction of Jerusalem by the Romans to bewail the fate of Jerusalem and their nation. These great blocks were part of the substructure of the temple area rebuilt by Herod the Great, shortly before the birth of Jesus. The Dome of the Rock stands on top of the plateau which this wall supports.

What was the political arrangement which obtained between the Roman procurator and the Jewish officials in the province of Judaea and the city of Jerusalem? Jewish officials were, of course, religious officials, for the Temple was the center of Jewish life. Here there was a high priest, usually a member of one of the powerful and wealthy Sadducean priestly families, who was appointed by the procurator. The high priest was chairman of the Sanhedrin or Council of Seventy, which was composed of priests, Pharisees under the name of scribes, and elders. This body had both political and religious authority over the Jews. Its political privileges did not extend outside the province of Judaea, though its religious decisions did.

In Jerusalem, the Sanhedrin was looked upon by the Jews as the object of their first loyalty and their governing body although it appears that the procurator had the privilege of approval or disapproval in matters of capital punishment and, of course, in questions that affected the interests of the Roman government. Otherwise the Sanhedrin exercised complete jurisdiction within Judaea, even to the extent of levying taxes. The Sanhedrin usually tried to present a solid front before the procurator, but within itself there were lines of cleavage because of differences of opinion between the Sadducee and Pharisee members.

Despite the wide authority possessed by the Jews, the Roman legions and the procurator were always on hand, and the Jews writhed under their presence. The Jewish hatred of Roman rule was if possible increased by Pontius Pilate, a brutal official who had no scruples about putting people to death. This hatred was a mixed emotion, composed of political as well as religious elements.

The religious situation was closely related to the political. We should at this point recall the development of Jewish religious life and ideas presented earlier in connection with Judaism after the Exile. All of the elements discussed were actively present in Jesus' generation, but many changes had taken place with the passage of time—variations in thought, changes of emphasis, and a totally different political state of affairs. Consequently, although we do recognize familiar terms and concepts in Jesus' time, his environment was far different from that of earlier periods.

Political-Religious Groups

The Hebrews had always wanted their good things here in this world—family, possessions, long life, and a utopian prospect of each man sheltered in the shade of his own vine and fig tree. Substantial comfort in a Hebrew society under a Hebrew government and worship in the Hebrew Temple, all under the watchful protection of the Hebrews' God—this was the Hebrew ideal. The Hebrews were primarily this-worldly. The hopes for the future that had buoyed up generation after generation were mainly nationalistic hopes. Their kingdom of God, which was to come, was patterned after the ideal just described—a reign on earth of righteousness under a messianic king of God's choosing.

There always seemed to be some foreign power standing in the way of this promised destiny. The yoke of bondage was always near at hand or else actually across their oft-burdened shoulders. Look at the powers holding ascendancy over the Hebrews down through the years—Egypt, Assyria, Babylonia, Persia, Greece, and now Rome! Would there never be surcease from the accursed presence of foreigners? If we could put ourselves in the Hebrew frame of mind, thinking back over this past which even now persisted through the whole of contemporary life, we too might pass through a whole gamut of emotions, from a bitter hatred of the foreign power to a deep resignation to the turn of fortune's wheel. These variations of mood were generated in many minds, and like-minded citizens were attracted to each other. Thus, groups were formed as some of the moods crystallized themselves along party lines. The parties so produced represented different degrees of feeling toward the Roman power and radically different conceptions of what the future of the Jewish religion and state should be. While little is known with complete certainty about these parties, it is generally agreed that the following descriptions may be considered valid.

The Pharisees

In importance, numbers, and strength, the Pharisees were the leading political-religious party. When we think of Pharisees, we also think at once of the Law. The development of the oral Law, accumulated over many generations, and the extensive application of the Law to the whole of life were closely associated with the Pharisees, who rightly regarded themselves as the guardians of the Law. They were strict legalists, the leaders of the synagogues. The Pharisees were puritans but they were not pacifists, and the time was to come when many of them would lose their lives in bloody defiance of Rome. Yet their primary function in Hebrew life was religious. They were dedicated to righteousness, and it was their aim to promote the righteous will of God as set forth in the Law by precept and example. As we shall observe later, they shared a messianic hope, but their task was to spread righteousness. The future advent of the Kingdom was left to the wisdom of God; they believed that in his own time deliverance would come.

In connection with this trust in the wisdom and goodness of God, there is a very important moral-religious problem, that of life beyond death. We know that for generations the Pharisees had tried to please Yahweh by keeping the Covenant through obedience to the Law. Their own consciences testified to their sincerity. Yet God's reign seemed indefinitely deferred. What about all those devout souls who had served the Lord and kept the commandments? What was their reward? The silence of the grave? What blessedness was there in that? That might be a just end for the wicked, but were the good to have nothing more? Should we declare with Ecclesiastes that all things come alike to all, "as is the good man so is the sinner"?

The Pharisee replied *no* with earnest conviction. He believed that justice required a greater reward than annihilation or Sheol for those who served God. Serving God had meant vigorous self-denial and discipline. But if, like the Sadducees, one came to terms with this world and had a broad tolerance toward human frailty, then the feeling of having sacrificed such a great deal in this life would not be so strong. As a matter of fact, the Sadducees and their friends had "the good things of this world." They came nearer the Hebrew ideal of comfort here and now than any other group. The masses, however, had very little. Therefore, the hope which the resurrection doctrine provided corresponded more to their need. The position of the Pharisees was, in consequence, closer to the common man, and accounts in part for their dominant place in the religious life of the nation.

The Pharisees formed the backbone of Jewish religion during the first century of the Christian era, and they alone of the various parties survived the fall of the Temple and the destruction of Jerusalem in A.D. 135. The Judaism which has come down since that time is essentially the religion of the Pharisees.

The Sadducees

This party, quite small by the time of Jesus, was the priestly party. In contrast to the Pharisees with their popular appeal and their association with the synagogue, the Sadducees were the last of the old type of Hebrew religion with its Temple and sacrifices. They disappeared from the scene after the destruction of the Temple in A.D. 70. Because of their associations with the ancient past, they quite readily became the most conservative of the Jewish parties. They were members of the aristocratic, wealthy, priestly families, some of them related to the Jewish royalty of the Hasmonaean line, and therefore politically informed.

Contrasted with the strong nationalism of the Pharisees, as expressed in their hope for God's appearance with his kingdom in his good time, the Sadducees were friendly toward Hellenistic ideas and practices, and so might be called the *social* liberals of their day. They wanted to keep on good terms with the Romans, for as long as this could be done the Sadducees would continue to prosper, receiving as they did the considerable profits of the trade associated with the sacrifice of animals. Religiously, they were conservative in that they refused to accept the oral Law as binding, holding only to the whole of the written Law, which alone they believed came from Moses. Hence, many of the observances that the Pharisees and their followers thought essential to obedience to the will of God the Sadducees rejected as not found within the Scriptures. By the same token they rejected beliefs that had developed during and following the Exile—some of them deriving from Persian and Babylonian sources—concerning angels and demons, spirits, and apocalyptic events, as well as the doctrine of the resurrection of the dead. In all these respects they differed from the Pharisees. Regarding their rejection of the resurrection from the dead and their holding to the ancient Sheol doctrine, an account found in Matthew 22:23-28 illustrates the differences between Pharisees and Sadducees.

The Scribes

The scribes scarcely constituted a party in the formal sense; they were the scholars whose origins go back to the time during or after the Exile. By New Testament times they were probably mostly Pharisees, but not all Pharisees were scribes; that status was achieved by training and work in interpreting the Law.

The Essenes

Although not mentioned by name in the Bible, this group is known from extra-Biblical writings. The Essenes were an ascetic brotherhood of extremely pious Jews, primarily a religious order pledged to holding their property in common and usually to celibacy. They were devoted to the Law, holding to it even more strictly than did the Pharisees. They were especially strict in their observance of the Sabbath. Many of them lived in communities, leading a simple monastic life and spending their time in work, study of the Torah, and prayer. Membership was by conversion only since they did not marry, and one became a full member only after a three-year probationary period. They practiced many lustrations, or formal washings, including baptism, and held to secret teachings. They were similar to the Pharisees except for their greater strictness, but rather strangely subscribed to the doctrine that an immortal soul was held in the body as in a prison house until freed by death, when reward and punishment become the lot of the good and the sinful respectively. At this point they appear to be more closely related to certain ideas found in the Greek mysteries or in Eastern religions than to Judaism with its Sheol or resurrection of the body.

The discovery of the remains of a monastery of an Essene community has provided one of the most exciting archaeological finds of recent times. At a site on the shores of the Dead Sea near its northwestern end were found the living quarters, graves, and a number of ancient documents of this community, named the Qumram community from its site at Khirbet Qumram. The dates of the documents, the first of which were found in nearby caves in 1947, run from the late second century B.C. until about A.D. 70. Because they are in the form of scrolls, they have been named the Dead Sea scrolls. These have the distinction of being the oldest manuscripts in Hebrew as yet discovered, for prior to 1947 no Hebrew documents of any appreciable length were known from a date earlier than A.D. 850.

The community thought of itself as the true remnant of the Jews, living in complete obedience to the will of Yahweh and looking expectantly to the time of the final triumph of God over the forces of evil. Apocalyptic expectations seem to have been especially strong among its members. Their writings refer to a Teacher of Righteousness, one of their leaders who suffered under rulers or priests. Some scholars have supposed that Jesus may have been an Essene and that this very community may have continued his memory as their Teacher of Righteousness, but this view is generally rejected because of numerous dissimilarities. Others have suggested that John the Baptist was a member of an Essene community, but this also is without proof. The community probably disappeared at the time the Temple was destroyed.[1]

The Zealots

The Jewish party strongest in its hatred of Rome and its desire for revolt was the Zealots. The name itself came into use rather late, but they probably stem from Maccabean times or earlier. These people were extreme patriots who abominated the priests for their willingness to cooperate with Rome,

[1] Further information on the Qumram community and the Dead Sea scrolls can be found in the following: Millar Burrows, *The Dead Sea Scrolls*, New York, The Viking Press, Inc., 1955; Millar Burrows, *More Light on the Dead Sea Scrolls*, New York, The Viking Press, Inc., 1958; and T. H. Gaster, *The Dead Sea Scriptures*, Garden City, Doubleday & Company, Inc., 1956.

and were prepared on occasion to use such extreme measures as assassination and revolt. They were regarded by both the Romans and the more moderate Jews as a dangerous element since their unbalanced patriotism constantly faced their country with the possibility of war. In their allegiance to the Law they were at one with the Pharisees. Some of them expected a Messiah, and thought it their task to prepare the way for him by purging the land of alien elements. They probably were not an organized party as such but rather loosely related fanatics, ready to "fight for God" when the call came.

The People of the Land

The groups considered were only a small part of the total Jewish population of Palestine, which at this time may have totaled between one and two million people. Multitudes of rank-and-file Jews, the *am ha-arets,* as they were called, would not have thought of themselves as belonging to any party. They were the ordinary people, the common classes, the uninstructed, who were held in contempt by the learned. They obeyed the Law in the main, but failed to obey many of the small details that the strict legalists felt were so important. On occasion they worshiped in the Temple with a special sacrifice, but ordinarily they worshiped in the synagogue, where they heard the Scriptures read and from these drew their religious inspiration. Some of these were devoutly religious, and among them were found the simple and pure in heart whom Jesus called the "salt of the earth." Jesus, John the Baptist, and the disciples were nourished in just such spiritual soil.

Major Religious Institutions

The Temple

We know that the first Temple, built by Solomon, was destroyed by the Babylonians, and that during the Exile Ezekiel, with faith in a return from Exile, pictured in detail a restored Temple and elaborate ceremonies. When the Jews did return, the prophets of the time seemed never to weary in their insistence that the Temple be rebuilt. It was finally completed in 515 B.C., standing as the tangible evidence of God's presence. Its purified services were the guarantee that the demands of the Law were being carried out, and this meant in turn that the Covenant was being kept. The succeeding centuries only made the foundation of the Temple as the basic institution in Hebrew religion more solid. All parties looked to it with devotion and reverence.

Under Herod the Great, who strove so hard and so vainly to win the affection of his subjects, the Temple was reconstructed in lavish fashion; in fact, it was one of the more imposing edifices even in that day of beautiful buildings. Its position on the eastern elevation of Jerusalem gave it an architectural dominance which perfectly symbolized its religious eminence.

One approached the Temple through a series of courtyards or enclosures. First, there was a large outer court. Here foreigners could congregate, but

The Roman Spoils of the Herod Temple

After his victory over the Jews in A.D. 70, *Titus erected an arch on the edge of the Forum in Rome. This bas-relief appearing on one of its inner surfaces shows the victorious Romans carrying off the great seven-branched candlestick, the table for sacred bread, and the sacred trumpets from the Temple in Jerusalem. (Alinari Photo)*

into the next court Jews alone might enter. In like manner, there were several additional enclosures, each in turn being more selective as to those who might enter. At last came the Temple building itself, where only priests were allowed. Even here there were divisions. The first chamber contained the famous seven-branched candlestick (which was taken to Rome in A.D. 71 by Titus and is shown as part of the loot on the well-known Arch of Titus in Rome). Finally, there was the most sacred chamber of all, the Holy of Holies, into which the high priest alone could come. That is where the Ark of the Covenant would have rested had it still been in existence. Everything else in the way of chambers and courts was but the outer garment of this holy place. Here, the Jews believed, God quite literally dwelt in the midst of his people.

Worship took place every day at the Temple—a morning sacrifice, an evening sacrifice, and, along with these, special sacrifices for festive occasions and for the offering of gifts from individuals. A lamb or some other animal was killed and placed upon the altar in a certain specified manner. The procedure, which never varied, was accompanied by a ritual of song and prayer. The priests were robed in expensive vestments and fulfilled their respective duties with impressive dignity. To Jews at home and throughout the whole Mediterranean world the knowledge that such services were being held was a source of comfort and satisfaction. On special holy days, such as the feasts of Passover, Pentecost, and Tabernacles, the Temple services were very elaborate, and thousands of Jews flocked to them from near and far.

The Synagogue

To the devout Jew, worship in the Temple and worship in the synagogue were complementary. The Temple worship was, of course, the higher form, and it was always a joyful thing to be able to worship there. The synagogue was theoretically a substitute, which, as we remember, was how it originated. But by the first century A.D. the synagogue had become an extremely important religious institution. Though the Temple might retain its unique character, the synagogue had come to have a vital religious significance. It was less formal, and it was a direct means of religious education.

Synagogues existed wherever Jews lived. It was in the synagogues that the Pharisees held their special place of influence. Consequently, the Pharisaic views of Hebrew religion and especially the emphasis on the Law had become the fundamental pattern of Judaism at the time of Jesus. Jesus received the religious heritage of his race principally through the synagogue; here he felt himself to be spiritually at home. The disciples he drew around him had likewise been nurtured in the synagogue. In fact, these assembly places were actually more important than the Temple, though this realization came only after the Temple had been destroyed.

The Law

In a preceding chapter it was shown how the Law developed after the Exile as an increasing regulator of life. The oral Law expanded into ever more minute rules of conduct.

To the credit of this development, we recognize the complete, unqualified monotheism that had become an ingrained aspect of Jewish thought, according to which the one true God was just, which meant that he was a moral sovereign and that the requirements of morality were not subject to human caprice. The Law was believed to be the divine guide which kept mortals on the path of goodness: keeping the Law was keeping the Covenant. All the hopes for the future depended on this. We should bear in mind here the sincerity of intention, the deep desire to do the will of God. The Jews were aware of the weaknesses of human nature—the ready ease with which men slide from good resolutions into carelessness and sin. They knew that the way of moral goodness requires moral effort, so they put the hurdle where one had to rise to it. If one cleared the bar, he was righteous, for he had kept the commandments.

The Law was the Hebrew form of religious and moral control. The increasing extension of the Law to all aspects of human endeavor had the worthy aim of extending the presence of God into every aspect of daily living. The legalist was conscious of a certain satisfaction or peace of mind in fulfilling the Law. This was a part of his reward. Another element of reward was a confidence in a blessed resurrection of the good, which was now a widespread belief. There can be no doubt that many Hebrews found happiness in their religion. There is assurance in the belief that the will of God is known beyond any doubt. It is also true that the religious Hebrew had a message for the sinner; the choice was always open for a human being to turn away from sin and, by repentance, to receive the forgiveness of God.

To its credit also, we may think of the words of the Shema as representing the intention and spirit of the Law. The Shema consists of Deuteronomy 6:4-9 and 11:13-21 and Numbers 15:37-41. We quote the first of these:

> Hear, O Israel: The Lord our God is one Lord; and you shall love the Lord your God with all your heart, and with all your soul, and with all your might. And these words which I command you this day shall be upon your heart; and you shall teach them diligently to your children, and shall talk of them when you sit in your house, and when you walk by the way, and when you lie down, and when you rise. And you shall bind them as a sign upon your hand, and they shall be as frontlets between your eyes. And you shall write them on the doorposts of your house and on your gates.

The words of these verses, or a portion of them, were repeated morning and night by the Jews of Jesus' day, and are still used by many at the present time. The Shema continues to be a regular part of Jewish formal worship services. It comes as near to a creed as Jews have, and is their confession of faith in the one God and in the covenant relation between God and his people.

But there is another side to legalism. The concept of universal monotheism was not so broad in application as to embrace Gentiles within the Covenant. God hated the people whom the Hebrews hated and all those who failed to obey the Covenant. He hated the false worshiper. The Hebrew religion, as a great Jewish scholar has pointed out, had not risen to any sense of obligation toward the unrepentant sinner, even among fellow countrymen.

These people, who had fallen, or were falling, away from the ranks of those who honestly sought to observe the Law, were neglected and shunned by the teachers and by the law-abiding Jews. They were looked down upon and disliked as ignorant, as law-breakers, as unclean. And it was a marked weakness of this legal religion that, while it taught, and its votaries practiced, compassion to the poor and the afflicted, if they sought to observe the Law, it did not teach redemptive compassion and kindness to those who fell away. It did not say, "Seek them out, help them, pity them, and gently bring . . . them back, to the service of God." It feared contamination, and bade the honest observer keep away and keep apart from the negligent and the sinner.[2]

Furthermore, the Law, for all that it was a moral guide and a moral control, overlooked the rich variety and flexibility of life. It attempted to standardize all moral behavior according to one pattern, like a block of houses exactly on the same plan. It left little to individual choice and genius, which suggests a fundamental distrust of human nature. Even though praiseworthy in its intentions, the elaborate extension of the Law went too far, becoming ridiculous in its intrusions, stifling the many spontaneities of human behavior. The Law became for many a burden. The greatest defect of all in legalism is the false notion that goodness is attained by fulfilling commands. Or, to state it differently, legalism centers attention on observances imposed from without to such an extent that the voluntary actions of man as a free moral agent have little room for exercise or development.

The Messianic Hopes at the Time of Jesus

Alongside the dominant place that the Law held in Hebrew religion must be set another feature of that religion, namely, the messianic hopes. The expectation of a Messiah was a common thread which ran through every

[2] Claude G. Montefiore, "Contemporary Jewish Religion," in A. S. Peake, *A Commentary on the Bible*, New York, Thomas Nelson & Sons, 1936, p. 622.

division of Hebrew life and religion in the first century A.D. Because Jesus came to be called the Messiah it is often assumed that the messianic hopes were always those that looked for an individual upon whom the title of Messiah would be placed. This is a misunderstanding, however, since the word *messiah* means simply anointed, and in Old Testament times was used as an adjective rather than a noun. It was applied to the nation of Judah, to Cyrus of Persia, to kings, priests, and others. *Messiah* as a standing title is first used in the Synoptic Gospels. Generally, the emphasis fell upon a messianic age about to appear, a golden age that would arrive when God was prepared to usher it in, not upon the Messiah as an individual. This was the common element within a variety of different conceptions of what God would do. What was this messianic golden age? In general, it meant a miraculous exaltation of the Jews and the universal reign of the one God. But aside from this point we run into all manner of variations, both as to the characteristics of the messianic age and as to the nature of the Messiah and the method of his work.

We may say in general that the masses were hopeful that a human messianic leader, one anointed by God, would rise up in their midst and be a strong deliverer, somewhat in the manner of Judas Maccabeus of glorious memory. A Messiah on these lines would inaugurate an earthly kingdom and would put the fear of God in the hearts of the enemy. This expected Messiah was usually conceived in terms of Isaiah's prophecy (Isaiah 11:1-5, 10). There would be no more foreign conquerors in the land, and Hebrew influence would be great in the world.

This naive confidence in an "arm of flesh" was not held by sophisticated people. Certainly both the Sadducees and the Pharisees understood the nature of the power of Rome too well to expect an uprising that would overthrow the Roman colossus. But whereas the Sadducees accepted the fact of Rome's invulnerability and came to terms with it, the Pharisees at this time rejected the popular view of a Messiah on two other grounds. In the first place, they were not very hopeful of an earth-born prince. They knew their history, so they knew that the Maccabean period, which in former times had promised so much for a theocratic society, had not fulfilled itself. The Maccabean priest-kings had been more worldly than godly. The Pharisees had had their origin in protest against Maccabean godlessness. Consequently, from that time on there was not the same optimism in Pharisaic circles concerning an earthly kingdom set up through revolt and ruled by an *earthly* prince. In the second place, their hopes for a future kingdom rested in the fulfillment of a scriptural promise of a miraculous kingdom, created anew by God and ruled by a *heavenly* prince.

In the book of Daniel, an apocalyptic writing recording visions and dreams, there is a passage of particular importance that records a dream of Daniel's. There are references to various powerful nations that will rise and fall, and then we come to the Hebrew hope:

> And in the days of those kings the God of heaven will set up a kingdom which shall never be destroyed, nor shall its sovereignty be left to another people. It shall break in pieces all these kingdoms and bring them to an end, and it shall stand for ever . . . [Daniel 2:44].

Here was a scriptural promise which fed religious and political hopes at the same time. It is developed further in the extracanonical Psalm of Solomon (17:23), where the messianic idea concerns the nation Israel alone, and the Messiah himself is a perfect ruler. Likewise, there is a variant but supplementary conception of the Messiah in the book of Enoch which is closely related to Daniel 7:13-14:

> I saw in the night visions, and behold, with the clouds of heaven there came one like a son of man, and he came to the Ancient of Days [God] and was presented before him. And to him was given dominion and glory and kingdom, that all peoples, nations and languages should serve him; his dominion is an everlasting dominion, which shall not pass away, and his kingdom one that shall not be destroyed.

In the above passage from Daniel and in similar statements from Enoch, we get the idea of a pre-existent Messiah who will come miraculously "with the clouds" and will rule over all. Here was an expectation that could not fail because God was believed to have promised it. An expected Messiah such as this was what some scribes and Pharisees had in view. Still another important view of the Messiah was one that emphasized his judgment along with his miraculous coming in order to rule. The dead would be raised to face the Messiah as judge; then the new age would dawn and the great era would at last have arrived. Some ideas held that there would be a temporary golden age, of 400 or 1000 years' duration, followed by the Last Judgment and the new world. Some believed the Judgment would precede the 1000 years.

A great variety of such ideas were espoused independently or mingled together, with the result that it is not possible to speak of any one generally held clear concept. All of these flowed into later Christian thought and had their influence upon it.[3] The messianic hope, with or without precision of meaning, pervaded all ranks of religious thinkers apart from the Sadducees.

[3] See R. H. Charles, *Religious Development Between the Old and New Testaments,* New York, Henry Holt & Co., 1914.

All classes were thereby tinged with optimism because the future held out promise of glorious fulfillment through God's expected help.

In the political-religious environment which has now been sketched, Jesus lived his unique life. In the following chapter we shall consider his reaction to that environment and something of the great contribution which he made, despite the limitations of contemporary ideas. Before moving directly into that exposition, it seems desirable to include as a kind of appendix to this chapter a brief explanation of the nature of the New Testament writings and of the gospel sources from which most of our knowledge about Jesus is taken.

The New Testament Writings and the Gospel Source Materials

The Formation of the New Testament Canon

Like the Old Testament, the New Testament is a series of writings, originally individual and unconnected, which eventually were put together in one volume. In contrast to the Old Testament, however, it does not cover a great period of history but centers about one brief span of time, detailing the life, teaching, and death of Jesus of Nazareth and giving the account of the "church" which first came into existence out of faith in the resurrection of the crucified Christ. Because the early followers of Jesus believed that he had established a New Covenant in fulfillment of the prediction of Jeremiah, they thought of these writings as the "writings of the New Covenant," which was later shortened to simply "New Covenant." When translated into Latin this was rendered as the "New Testament," a title which it has retained.

For more than a century, the Old Testament, in the Septuagint translation, was the Bible of the Christians. The remembered statements of Jesus, many of which were probably recorded shortly after his death, were regarded with a special reverence, but they were not at first accorded the same degree of sanctity that the Torah and the Prophets received. Probably the first use of these writings as Scripture arose from reading Paul's letters in the churches and making expositions upon them. At what time the first materials regarding the life and teaching of Jesus were recorded in orderly fashion we do not know.

The first attempt to form a Christian Bible, about A.D. 150, was that of

Marcion, who was later considered a heretic. His Bible included an abridged version of the Gospel of Luke and 10 of the letters of Paul, along with a work of his own writing, the Antitheses. Because Marcion had forced the issue by treating the Christian Scriptures as superior to the Old Testament, which he rejected, and because he was so strongly opposed by other Christians, it was essential that orthodox Christians themselves decide upon an authoritative canon. Three tests for acceptability of material were set up in the latter part of the second century: that the writing have an apostle for its author; that it agree with the "rule of faith" of the church; and that it receive the support of one of the leading churches. But even these tests were not sufficient. During the third century the New Testament, still inexactly determined, came to be held as sacred writing for the Christians, paralleling the Old Testament for the Jews. Most of its books had long been generally accepted; a few, like Revelation and Hebrews, were disputed. In the year 367 Athanasius of Alexandria, in a famous Easter letter, listed the 27 writings which now constitute the New Testament and declared these to be the Scriptures of the Christians.

Inspection of our present New Testament shows that it begins with four Gospels, named Matthew, Mark, Luke, and John. Each of these gives the account of Jesus' life and teaching. Although these four writings stand first in order because they deal with the beginnings of Christianity, the actual writing of them in their present form is generally thought to be later than the letters of Paul. Some Protestant scholars believe that the earliest of the four gospels was Mark, and that it was not written before 65 or 70. The book of the Acts of the Apostles, which gives the early history of the Christian church after the death of Jesus, was originally part of Luke's Gospel, both from about 80.

Following Acts are 21 epistles or letters. The first of these are Paul's, and are the materials of the New Testament written earliest in their present form, probably between 50 and 62. These include Galatians, I and II Thessalonians, I and II Corinthians, Romans, Philippians, Colossians, and Philemon. Ephesians and Hebrews were once considered Paul's writing, but are currently thought to be from a time later than his death. Revelation, an apocalyptic book assigned to an elder named John, and the three short epistles also assigned to him were probably written about 100, possibly about the same time as the Gospel of John. James and I Peter may also have been written about this date. Jude, I and II Timothy, Titus, and II Peter were all probably written in the second century. Three of these, I and II Timothy and Titus, are presented as if written by Paul but reflect a period in the history of the church that was much later than his. Thought to be the last written, II Peter dates from possibly as late as 150. In the discussions during the early centuries concerning these books, the ones most questioned as to their suitability and value were Hebrews, Revelation, James, II and III John, II Peter, and Jude. Many other Christian writings, such as the Epistle of Barnabas, are extant from the second century and later, but for various reasons are not included in the New Testament canon.

The brief sketch that has just been given may serve to suggest a few of the many problems facing the New Testament scholar. Only the specialist can fully appreciate the tremendous difficulties encountered in the effort to reconstruct accurately even the life and teaching of Jesus, seemingly so clearly portrayed in the Gospels. It was only a considerable number of years after his death, when the new religion of Christianity had become well established, that attempts were made to recapture historical circumstances concerning him. Although his letters were written in some instances within less than 25 years of Jesus' death, Paul unfortunately did not feel the necessity for constructing a biographical account; nor did he feel impelled to quote Jesus extensively, as he could have done, for had he not learned the facts directly from the original apostles, who had accompanied Jesus on his mission?

In his missionary service, Paul preached about Jesus and no doubt quoted his sayings. He even refers to an oral tradition (I Corinthians 11:23 ff. and 15:3 ff.) which he received and passed on to his readers. However, apart from these two short sections, none of this oral material known to Paul has been preserved. He was concerned primarily with the significance of Jesus, but he is also a very valuable witness to the nature of early Christianity. At many points in his writings remarks are made which are valuable for their description of events as they very likely occurred. For example, his reference to the Last Supper of Jesus (I Corinthians 11:23-26) is of great worth for an understanding of that momentous occasion.

Increasingly as the years passed the need was felt for written documents containing the life and sayings of Jesus. Christian communities required such materials for apologetics, preaching, and worship, and various efforts were made to acquire them. The very earliest biography of Jesus was that of Mark, written almost 40 years after the Crucifixion. In the course of time, other accounts appeared, each author or editor in turn doing his best to relate the events in the light of the data at his disposal. The preface to the Gospel of Luke is interesting evidence that there were many life stories of Jesus, and it also indicates that Luke was not altogether satisfied with those he did know:

Inasmuch as many have undertaken to compile a narrative of the things which have been accomplished among us, just as they were delivered to us by those who from the beginning were eyewitnesses and ministers of the word, it seemed good to me also, having followed all things closely for some time past, to write an orderly account for you, most excellent Theophilus, that you may know the truth concerning the things of which you have been informed [Luke 1:1-4].

The date of Luke, as already mentioned, is about 80 or 85, and Matthew also was written about the same time. In terms, then, of when they were written, the order of the Gospels is Mark, first, then Luke, Matthew, and John.

The Four Gospels and the Synoptic Problem

There are certain established facts in regard to these Gospels which should be noted. The first three are called the *Synoptic Gospels,* because of their basic similarity in structure and content and because together they present a synoptic or common view. The fourth Gospel, John, stands in a separate category altogether. The Synoptic Gospels have always been recognized as having much in common; they are therefore sometimes printed side by side in parallel columns in order that the likenesses and differences may be readily seen. The accompanying example shows how the tradition in regard to Peter's confession was reported by each of the gospel writers.

Let us examine this triple account to see what conclusions we might reach about the relationships between the three Gospels. It will be noted that Luke's account is different from that of Mark. For some reason, Luke did not choose to mention Caesarea Philippi, though Matthew followed Mark in naming it. Luke has a different setting for Jesus' question: in Mark, Jesus and the disciples are traveling along the road; in Luke, Jesus is alone in prayer. In Matthew, Jesus' question itself is different from Mark's quotation: "Who do men say the Son of man is?" If *Son of man* is synonymous with *Messiah*, as some authorities hold, then by adding *Son of man*, Matthew really nullifies the whole point of Peter's confession. In this case Mark's account is more nearly authentic, less affected by later tradition. Only Matthew's account includes the name of Jeremiah. Matthew also enlarges the answer of Peter with the words, "Son of the living God." The most striking addition of all is the famous saying of Jesus to Peter, containing the words, ". . . you are Peter, and on this rock I will build my church. . . ." Matthew alone has this saying. If Mark or Luke had heard of this, it seems unlikely that they would have omitted it. Consequently, the possibility arises that this saying is secondary, coming from a time in the early church when Peter's name had taken on increasing significance.

MATTHEW

Now when Jesus came into the district of Caesarea Philippi, he asked his disciples, "Who do men say that the Son of man is?" And they said, "Some say John the Baptist, others say Elijah, and others Jeremiah or one of the prophets." He said to them, "But who do you say that I am?" Simon Peter replied, "You are the Christ, the Son of the living God." And Jesus answered him, "Blessed are you, Simon Bar-Jona! For flesh and blood has not revealed this to you, but my Father who is in heaven. And I tell you, you are Peter, and on this rock I will build my church, and the powers of death shall not prevail against it. I will give you the keys of the kingdom of heaven, and whatever you bind on earth shall be bound in heaven, and whatever you loose on earth shall be loosed in heaven." Then he strictly charged the disciples to tell no one that he was the Christ [16:13-20].

MARK

And Jesus went on with his disciples, to the villages of Caesarea Philippi; and on the way he asked his disciples, "Who do men say that I am?" And they told him, "John the Baptist; and others say, Elijah; and others one of the prophets." And he asked them, "But who do you say that I am?" Peter answered him, "You are the Christ." And he charged them to tell no one about him [8:27-30].

LUKE

Now it happened that as he was praying alone the disciples were with him; and he asked them, "Who do the people say that I am?" And they answered, "John the Baptist; but others say, Elijah; and others, that one of the old prophets has risen." And he said to them, "But who do you say that I am?" And Peter answered, "The Christ of God." But he charged and commanded them to tell this to no one . . . [9:18-21].

For comparison, we may notice the way in which the Gospel of John deals with the confession of Peter.

After this many of his disciples drew back and no longer went about with him. Jesus said to the twelve, "Will you also go away?" Simon Peter answered him,

"Lord, to whom shall we go? You have the words of eternal life; and we have believed, and have come to know, that you are the Holy One of God" [John 6:66-69].

The author of John is seemingly following an independent tradition which, although quite different, has reference to the same event in Jesus' life.

The existence of different traditions does not indicate that everything in Mark is necessarily more nearly authentic than some similar but slightly different account in another Gospel. Various standards of historical evaluation are used. The foregoing illustration is just one example of the comparative method, and we have not begun to exhaust this one example. If we turned from the English translation to the Greek original, many other considerations would arise; but these lie outside the province of the present study.

For a number of generations scholars have been aware of the very many problems raised by the fact that the Synoptic Gospels, similar as they are, contain marked differences also. How to account reasonably for these similarities *and* differences is the Synoptic Problem. If one should go through these three writings, placing parallel passages side by side, he would discover first that Luke is by far the longest, with 1149 verses in the Revised Standard Version, and that Mark is much the shortest, with only 661 verses; Matthew contains 1068 verses. He would find that in many sections they all give essentially the same account. When one is shorter than the others it is almost always Mark. Then there are passages in which Matthew and Luke are very similar but for which no parallel exists in Mark. Such sections, like the Sermon on the Mount, for instance, generally consist of the teaching material of Jesus. In addition, there are fairly lengthy sections which appear in Luke alone, and less extensive ones that appear in Matthew alone. Thus, the account of the angel appearing to Joseph in a dream appears only in Matthew (1:18-25), and the story of Mary and Joseph's going to Bethlehem for the census and of Jesus' being born there appears only in Luke (2:4-17). Almost nothing appears in Mark alone. This, then, is our problem—how do we account for the similarities and differences just outlined?

In an earlier day, when the entire Bible was held to be too sacred to be studied like other books, it was assumed that, since the Holy Spirit had inspired its various authors, Matthew, Mark, and Luke had been inspired at some points in similar ways and elsewhere differently. This view was challenged in the period of the Enlightenment, partly because it was too simple an answer and partly also because various Greek and Latin documents of the Gospels were found which did not agree in every detail with each other, thus raising critical problems.

Without going into the details of the question,[4] we can examine the outlines of the solution rather generally accepted by outstanding scholars, though not by Roman Catholics or fundamentalist Protestants, who do not accept standard procedures of historical analysis and criticism for examination of the Bible. Scholars who apply the usual analytic procedures do not claim any final answers, but offer what appear to be the most probable interpretations of the data currently available. According to this historical approach, there were probably many writings about Jesus' teaching and life and about the beginning of the church before any of our present Gospels was written. They may have been in the form either of brief accounts or of more extended and organized writings. We have seen above that the author of the Gospel of Luke refers to the many who had written narratives; hence, it would appear that documents of some length were not rare. Quite naturally, the needs of the growing Christian church concerned with its teaching, preaching, worship, and meeting of controversy and persecution would tend to make for an emphasis upon materials that were helpful in these respects. It is theorized that at least four masses of materials, derived from the earlier writings, were drawn together. The book of Mark is thought to be one of these earlier collections, possibly written by the man John Mark who is referred to in the book of Acts, and through him possibly containing some materials from Peter. We can then say that at those points in which Matthew, Mark, and Luke are in essential agreement, Mark has been used by Matthew and Luke as their common source, since neither Matthew nor Luke knew the work of the other. Sometimes they add to his writing, which accounts for the fact that when the accounts of a particular event differ in length, generally Mark writes more briefly—the other two have expanded his material.

Concerning those extensive sections where Mark has nothing and Matthew and Luke parallel each other fairly closely, as in the Beatitudes, it is supposed that the authors of Matthew and Luke drew on a collection of material that existed but has since disappeared consisting chiefly of teachings ascribed to Jesus. This hypothesized material is called *Q* because the view was developed by German scholars who referred to the material as the *Source*, for which the German word is *Quelle*. It is not known whether Q was one document or several, but there are strong grounds for supposing that it was a single collection of teaching, concerned primarily with Jesus' Galilean

[4] The interested reader will find extended treatment of this matter in Dwight M. Beck, *Through the Gospels to Jesus*, New York, Harper & Brothers, 1954, chaps. 6 and 7, and in Frederick C. Grant, *The Gospels: Their Origin and Their Growth*, New York, Harper & Brothers, 1957.

ministry. Chapters 5-7 of Matthew are the longest single block of this material.

This now leaves us with those considerable masses of material appearing in Matthew alone and in Luke alone. To account for these passages, scholars suppose that the author of the Gospel of Matthew had in his possession other writings not known to the other Gospel writers, possibly, although improbably, a complete document in itself, which is called *M* (since it appears in Matthew alone). And by the same reasoning it is supposed that the author of the Gospel of Luke had still other materials, possibly a complete document, known to him alone, to which is given the name *L* for Luke. Matthew and Luke each organized his Gospel in his own way, presenting the readers with a fairly complex document. It will be seen that this theory of four and more sources for the Synoptic Gospels holds that none of them was written by an apostle.

The diagram below illustrates in a very simple way the basic elements of this theory.[5]

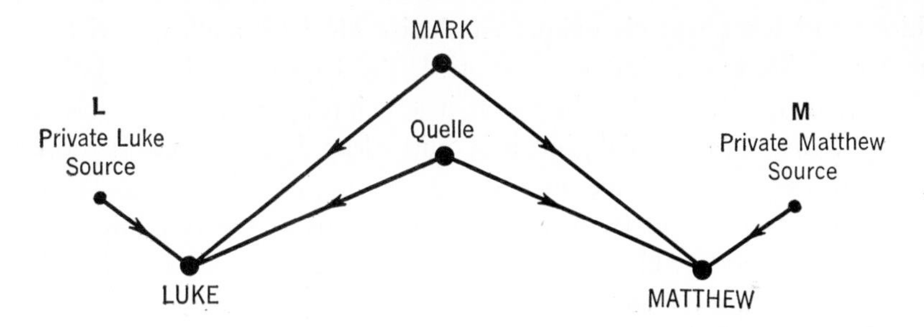

Sketch Illustrating the Generally Accepted Synoptic Theory

When the four Gospels are placed side by side and a synoptic view is made of all the materials, certain general characteristics of each Gospel stand out, a few of which should be noted.

Mark

The Gospel of Mark is an evangelistic work which contains a very early Palestinian and Roman view of Jesus, emphasizing belief in Jesus as the Son

[5] One of the scholars refusing to accept the theory of the Q source is Morton S. Enslin, who holds that the basic issues are met by supposing that Matthew and Luke drew upon Mark and that Luke used Matthew in those sections where they alone have material. He finds that the existence of Q is "an unnecessary and unwarranted assumption." See Morton Scott Enslin, *Christian Beginnings,* New York, Harper & Brothers, 1938, pp. 426-436.

of God, the Messiah. The author has written a Gospel for Gentiles, possibly for Christians at Rome. One of the evidences of its early date is the way in which the author sometimes allows disciples to be shown in an unfavorable light (see Mark 4:13, 6:52, 8:17, 9:10, 32, and 34). The other Gospels either omit this approach or minimize it, which we would expect to be the case after the passage of time. Another characteristic of Mark, which he shares with Matthew and Luke, is the realistic description of the human emotions of Jesus that is fortunately included. This is brought out in Mark 10:13-16, where Mark describes Jesus and the little children, and again in 10:17-31, in the story of the rich young man. Mark also lays special emphasis on the opposition between Jesus and the scribes and Pharisees in regard to the Sabbath. This emphasis suggests that Mark had Gentile readers in mind.

Matthew

Since almost all of Mark is included in Matthew, whom did Matthew address and what was his unique emphasis? He had much material to add to that of Mark: the infancy narrative, the baptism and temptation, the Sermon on the Mount. Matthew was just as interested as Mark was in presenting Jesus as the Messiah, but it is quite clear that Matthew is addressing Jewish readers. As evidence, he offers a genealogy which traces Jesus back to David (1:1-17), and frequently presents Jesus as the fulfillment of Old Testament prophecy. He emphasizes the teaching of Jesus, and finds in it a new law replacing the ancient Jewish Law. At the same time he satisfies the demand for a more complete account than the one presented by Mark of what Jesus did. One of the characteristics of his Gospel is his attempt to relate the teaching of Jesus to the needs of the early church.

Luke

The preface to Luke's Gospel states that he wrote it in order to inform Theophilus, probably a Greek Christian, of the truth of Jesus and the beginning of the Christian church. Luke's interest is therefore historical, and he is sometimes referred to as the first Christian historian. He wrote for both Jews and Gentiles, showing that in Jesus the purposes of God had come to fulfillment.

In the Gospel of Luke we get a deep insight into the rich humanity and spirit of Jesus. It is only in Luke that we find the parables of the prodigal son, the good Samaritan, and the lost coin. We can hardly believe that Mark or Matthew knew about these, for if they had, how could they have left them out? Luke gives us our best knowledge about Jesus' neighborly attitude toward non-Jews. Jesus is represented by Luke as a very human person who had temptations, who prayed, and who felt the burden of a great task. It is Luke who emphasizes the joy of the good news of the Gospel, and he it is that teaches about prayer.

John

It is difficult to characterize John briefly. This Gospel reveals at the very beginning the influence of Greek philosophy, for it opens with a typically Greek rather than Hebrew statement: "In the beginning was the Word [*Logos*], and the Word was with God, and the Word was God" (John 1:1). This opening verse, making use of the Greek term *logos*, is a perfect illustration of the way in which the Christian faith in the messianic significance of Jesus would be made meaningful to people of Greek culture. The philosophic idea of the *Logos*, or divine Wisdom, was the best Greek concept to serve as an equivalent of the Jewish idea of the Messiah. The Gospel of John is not intended to be a history of Jesus' life. Rather, the author has selected various materials in the Christian tradition to support a theology about Jesus which was designed for use in an environment of Greek ideas. He explains what that theology was, for he writes, ". . . these are written that you may believe that Jesus is the Christ, the Son of God, and that believing you may have life in his name" (20:31).

The Gospel of John assumes that the messiahship was known from the beginning by Jesus; there is nothing in this Gospel that suggests any development or struggle in his mind. It is an idealization of his life. This does not mean that the Gospel is not important, but from the earliest times it was recognized that the differences between John and the first three Gospels made it difficult to harmonize them. Some of the differences reveal that the author of John had access to traditions about Jesus which were not the same as the sources for the other Gospels, and these are of great historical value. For example, the Gospel of John does not agree with the Synoptic Gospels on the date on which the Last Supper occurred, and some scholars believe John's account to be the accurate one.

Jesus is pictured in this Gospel as the divine *Logos* through whom the world was made (1:10), and yet at the same time he is described also as the Word that "became flesh" (1:14). John does not swallow up Jesus' humanity in his divinity; on the contrary, he emphasizes the fact of Jesus' being "flesh." He portrays him as weeping on the death of his friend Lazarus, as being weary, as thirsting. Yet he omits the accounts of the baptism, the temptation, the transfiguration, and the agony in the garden of Gethsemane, possibly because they do not show clearly Jesus' own certainty about his being the Word of God. Much of the book is taken up with long discourses by Jesus, very different in vocabulary and idea from the Synoptics—words like *know*, *life*, *light*, and *truth* appear frequently. It stresses the need for spiritual rebirth and is marked by mystical and devotional characteristics which have made it a favorite of Christian mystics through the centuries. It is sometimes called the "spiritual Gospel." In spite of its differences from the Synoptics, its appeal and value can scarcely be exaggerated.

Summary

The foregoing material on the nature of the source materials of Jesus' life and teachings must be understood to be illustrative only. It offers us but a glimpse at problems which have confronted historical scholars. It gives an impression of the way in which the Gospels came into being, and reveals something of the influences that affected the choice of materials. Most of the effort that has gone into this field of research has been motivated by a desire to come as close as possible to the historical Jesus. We believe that conspicuous success has been achieved. On the basis of that work, there is a great deal of assurance that very much indeed can be said with confidence about Jesus' life and message.

Questions for Study

1. Describe briefly the political structure in the time when Jesus was born. What was the relation of Rome to the Jewish nation? Who was Herod the Great, and what kind of rule did he bring? What was the Sanhedrin, and what were its powers?
2. Describe the viewpoints of the Pharisees, the Sadducees, the scribes, the Essenes, the Zealots, and the people of the land. Show the relation of the Pharisees to the synagogue and why they were considered the liberals of the day, and the relation of the Sadducees to the Temple and why they were the conservatives.
3. What was the nature of Temple worship and of synagogue worship? How were they related to each other? Why was it thought important by the Pharisees to work out every detail of the Law and obey it? What was good about this, and what not good?
4. What various forms did the Messianic hopes take at this time? What was

meant by *Messiah*, and how was he variously pictured and his mission understood?

5. What are the various kinds of books that make up the New Testament? In what respects is the New Testament different in structure and content from the Old? How did its writings come to general acceptance? What were the probable dates of writing of the four Gospels, and when were Paul's letters written?
6. What is meant by the Synoptic Problem, and why is there a problem? What solution is offered to it?
7. Distinguish the four Gospels from each other in content. Why were these Gospels written?
8. What expectations not fulfilled within the Old Testament did the Christian writers claim to be fulfilled by Jesus and the new religion? (Think of Isaiah, the Second Isaiah, Jeremiah, and apocalyptic expectation.)

Selected Readings

Beck, Dwight M., *Through the Gospels to Jesus,* New York, Harper & Brothers, 1954.

Crownfield, Frederic R., *A Historical Approach to the New Testament,* New York, Harper & Brothers, 1960.

Enslin, Morton Scott, *Christian Beginnings,* New York, Harper & Brothers, 1938.

Grant, Frederick C., *The Gospels: Their Origin and Their Growth,* New York, Harper & Brothers, 1957.

Guignebert, C., *The Jewish World in the Time of Jesus,* New York, E. P. Dutton & Co., 1939.

Heard, Richard, *An Introduction to the New Testament,* New York, Harper & Brothers, 1950.

Kee, Howard C., and Franklin W. Young, *Understanding the New Testament,* Englewood Cliffs, N. J., Prentice-Hall, Inc., 1957.

McNeile, A. H., *An Introduction to the Study of the New Testament,* rev. ed., New York, Oxford University Press, 1953.

Matthews, Shailer, *New Testament Times in Palestine,* New York, The Macmillan Company, 1934.

Pfeiffer, R. H., *History of New Testament Times,* New York, Harper & Brothers, 1949.

Purinton, Carl E., *Christianity and its Judaic Heritage,* New York, The Ronald Press Company, 1961.

Schürer, Emil, *A History of the Jewish People in the Time of Christ,* tr. John Macpherson, Edinburgh, T. and T. Clark, 1898, 5 vols.

Scott, Ernest F., *The Literature of the New Testament,* New York, Columbia University Press, 1932.

Titus, Eric L., *Essentials of New Testament Study,* New York, The Ronald Press Company, 1958.

6. The Life and Teaching of Jesus

The New Testament as Interpretation

Preliminary to the discussion of the life and teaching of Jesus, it is important to consider the nature of the Gospel writings. We must not think of them as news reports, written shortly after the events happened for the purpose of presenting objective, detailed narratives. Like the Old Testament books, they are *interpretations.* They are concerned with the events involving Jesus which were believed to have happened and were written for a purpose and from one or more particular viewpoints. All of them came out of the community of Christians (the church). Their authors wrote from the standpoint of those who believed that Jesus was the Son of God, the fulfillment—and more than the fulfillment—of Old Testament expectations, and himself in some sense divine. The author of Mark possesses this faith just as strongly as does John or Paul. The ways in which the writers express their understandings vary, but in the main outline of their faith they agree. This brings up a very difficult historical problem: how to separate the actual occurrences from the interpretations given them by the writers. There is no easy or certain answer to this problem; for this reason, scholars generally agree on the impossibility of writing an accurate biography of Jesus.

We recall that while the accounts start at the beginning of Jesus' life and ministry, they were written a generation or more later. Part at least of the beliefs all Christians held by the time the Scriptures came to be put into their present form is contained in Paul's first Epistle to the Corinthians, 15:1-8. In this passage the matter "of first importance" is Christ's death for the sins of man and his well-attested resurrection. Around these central facts everything else is organized. We keep in mind that this letter of Paul was written very early, about 25 years after Jesus' death. Paul's letters, the Gospels, and the other materials of the New Testament were established upon these beliefs. When the story of Jesus is told, therefore, it is related from the standpoint of these understandings of what he did. They provide the viewpoint from which he is seen and his life is comprehended. The critical reader who stands outside the basic faith of the early Christians may find himself unwilling to accept various elements in the accounts. This is to be expected. It raises the question of correct interpretation.

It should also be pointed out that those who knew Jesus while he lived felt in him a mystery which eluded them. Their first approach to understanding him was naturally in terms of the thought forms of their day. Some believed him to be the Messiah of popular expectation, for instance, and yet he seemed to be unwilling to accept the designation. How then should one understand him? He was the "Son of God," but just exactly what does that mean? In I John 3:2, all Christians are called sons of God. The books of the New Testament do not provide conclusive answers to such questions as these. The questions continued on into post-Biblical times and became the great issues of later theological discussion.

If we try to solve the historical questions of the New Testament by appealing to materials from outside the Bible, we discover that there is little we can find that is of help to us. Therefore, as we examine the story of Jesus, we do so primarily on the basis of the Biblical writings, keeping always in mind that they contain historical materials as interpreted by early Christians. We will make no great effort at providing interpretation, following rather the faith of the early community as that is related in the community's accounts of "the Gospel of Jesus Christ, the Son of God."

A further point to keep in mind is that the New Testament writers did not think of Christianity as something entirely new. On the contrary, they thought of it as being based upon the Old Testament. The God of the Old Testament, the idea of a Covenant, the teachings of the prophets, and the wisdom literature and Psalms were all claimed by the Christians as their heritage. Consequently, their literature is filled with quotations and references from the Old Testament, as every copy of the English Bible supplied with footnotes abundantly testifies. Further, the thought forms of the early

Christians were also derived from the Jewish religion—the idea of sacrifice as a way of approaching God and the emphasis upon God's demand for righteousness are examples. To this old, something new is added, namely, the fact of Jesus, the anointed one, but the meaning of the new is sought, at least at first, quite within the framework of the old. With these understandings in mind, we will now look at the Biblical accounts of Jesus.

Jesus' Background and Preparation

We know that Jesus was brought up in the village of Nazareth in the province of Galilee. The facts of Jesus' life up to the beginning of his public ministry, at about the age of 30, are so meager that we are curious for more details. We are dealing with a man who has influenced our culture more profoundly than any other single person, and yet even the date of his birth is not certain. According to the Gospel of Matthew, it took place while Herod the Great was still living (2:1), which would place it before 4 B.C. Luke, on the other hand, while referring also to Herod the Great (1:5), has the birth occur in the year of the census when Quirinius was governor of Syria. The known period of his governorship was the years A.D. 6 to 9. This places the Lukan date not less than 10 years after the one in Matthew. However, it is argued by some that from 10-6 B.C. Quirinius was imperial legate of Syria and it was during this period that the birth of Jesus took place, possibly 7 or 6 B.C. Luke (3:23) states that Jesus was "about thirty years of age" when he began his ministry. Since he states also that John the Baptist began his movement in the fifteenth year of Tiberius, which is A.D. 28 or 29, this also would suggest that Jesus was born a few years B.C.

Both Matthew and Luke report that Jesus' mother, Mary, was a virgin at the time of his birth, and both report remarkable occurrences in association with the birth. In both books the conception of Jesus is presented as a miraculous happening, through the power of the Holy Spirit. Matthew tells the story of the wise men and the star and the flight to Egypt; Luke gives the account of the shepherds who visit the manger and the child. None of the other books in the New Testament makes reference to these matters.

It is tempting to speculate about Jesus' early life, for like all other boys he went through a process of development. The language he spoke was the common Aramaic. He probably knew some Hebrew and even possibly some Greek. He was a member of a large family, according to Mark 6:3: "Is not this the carpenter, the son of Mary and brother of James and Joses and Judas and Simon, and are not his sisters here with us?" Hence, with Jesus, there

The Mount of Olives and Gethsemane

A view of the Mount of Olives from the city wall of Jerusalem across the Kidron valley.

were no fewer than seven children. Tradition holds that Joseph was considerably older than Mary and died before Jesus reached manhood. We notice in this connection that the Marcan quotation just given mentions Mary but not Joseph, at the time when Jesus began his ministry.

In the apocryphal books of the New Testament, stories appear which refer to Jesus as a child wonder-worker.[1] The ordinary childhood pastime of making mud pies is transformed in these stories into the legend that Jesus made pigeons of clay and then successfully bade them fly. Again, in his father's shop Jesus miraculously caused a piece of lumber or a beam that was too short for Joseph's purpose to be extended to the desired length. Serious attention is not given to such bald fiction.

It requires no stretch of imagination to visualize Jesus' home, built of

[1] See the Infancy Gospels in M. R. James, *The Apocryphal New Testament,* Oxford, Clarendon Press, 1924.

stone or brick, square in shape, with a single entrance door, possibly with a window also. Joseph's carpenter shop was either part of or attached to the small house. The home environment was religious; in fact, it was steeped in the history and religion of the Hebrews. The Old Testament names which are familiar to us were the subject matter of daily speech. Sacred story lived for the family, and the wisdom of the Psalms, Proverbs, and other literature was drawn upon readily. The foundation of all Jewish education was the Shema, referred to in the preceding chapter. Jesus, like other children, learned this before he knew its meaning. It was recited morning and night. In school, Jesus learned to read it along with other Scriptures in Hebrew, although the everyday spoken language was Aramaic. We know that he chose an artisan's career rather than that of a scribe. He learned carpentry, and followed this trade for a number of years (Mark 6:3).

There can be no doubt that Jesus knew his own surroundings well. When we consider his thorough mastery of the Hebrew past, the years of contact with other men as a workman, and the manifest keenness of observation of life and nature which characterizes all his sayings, we are compelled to recognize that he was thoroughly aware of all the political-religious cross-currents and of all the hopes and fears of his native land.

Jesus' Response to the Political-Religious Situation

Jesus comes into historic perspective in connection with the dramatic ministry of John the Baptist. John was a colorful personality who had already made a reputation as an effective religious teacher by the time Jesus first came under his influence. He preached that God's kingdom was at hand, and that men had to repent if they were to escape the coming wrath. He proclaimed the imminent arrival of the Messiah and the necessity for moral living. Baptism was practiced by John as a rite of purification symbolizing repentance and cleansing of the soul and, possibly, membership in a religious fellowship. John did not think of himself as the Messiah. He proclaimed the coming Messiah and had a message that emphasized the need of getting ready, because when the Messiah arrived he would act as a judge of the people. He would first separate the righteous from the unrighteous. In other words, John was more concerned with righteousness than he was with the bare fact of membership in the Hebrew community. His message was revolutionary in his day; it marks him as a genuine prophet and enables us to understand why he made such an impact on Jesus.

Yet Jesus was aware of a great difference between himself and John, and the consciousness of his own mission caused him to separate from John. The latter, however, even up to the end of his life, was not quite certain what estimate to put upon Jesus. While John was in prison, where Herod Antipas had placed him, later to behead him, he sent one of his own disciples (for he was the leader of a movement) to Jesus with the question, "Are you he who is to come, or shall we look for another?" (Matthew 11:3). John's arrest and death gave Jesus a very accurate gauge of political boundary lines that could not be crossed without disaster.

The Baptism

Jesus' coming to John at the Jordan River for baptism marked a moment of decision and possibly of crisis in the life of Jesus. Exactly how Jesus himself saw the significance of this act is not indicated in the accounts in the Synoptic Gospels, all of which describe it with only slight variations. It might have meant that he saw in John the leader of a strong nationalistic movement, preparing the way for the glorification of the Jewish nation. This must surely have been the way in which many of those who came to John understood him—the great day when God's rule would begin was finally about to arrive. In view of Jesus' later teaching, this appears not to have been his own understanding of the meaning of his association with John's movement. In any case, the baptism became a point of central importance for him, marking the beginning of his own mission as he stepped out of obscurity. The accounts in the Synoptic Gospels all emphasize this central significance.

MATTHEW

And when Jesus was baptized, he went up immediately from the water, and behold, the heavens were opened and he saw the Spirit of God descending like a dove, and alighting on him; and lo, a voice from heaven, saying, "This is my beloved Son, with whom I am well pleased" [3:16-17].

MARK

In those days Jesus came from Nazareth of Galilee and was baptized by John in the Jordan. And when he came up out of the water, immediately he saw the heavens opened and the Spirit descending upon him like a dove; and a voice came from heaven, "Thou art my beloved Son; with thee I am well pleased" [1:9-11].

LUKE

Now when all the people were baptized, and when Jesus also had been baptized and was praying, the heaven was opened, and the Holy Spirit descended upon him in bodily form, as a dove, and a voice came from heaven, "Thou art my beloved Son; with thee I am well pleased" [3:21-22].

This account reminds us at first glance of the call of men in the Old Testament—of Moses, Isaiah, and Ezekiel, for instance. Yet on closer inspection we find a very important difference. The Old Testament figures responded to their visions with a sense of unworthiness and sinfulness, but this is entirely absent from the Gospel account; the content of the experience was for Jesus an indication of approval from God. According to each of the three accounts, as God's Spirit came upon him Jesus heard himself called "beloved Son" and heard the word of commendation, "with whom I am well pleased." The experience, in short, was of the prophetic type, but with real differences from the experiences of the Hebrew prophets.

The Temptation in the Wilderness

Immediately following the baptism, Jesus went into the wilderness (actually, the barren stone desert of Judaea lying on the heights near the west side of the Jordan River). There he remained, fasting, for a period said to be 40 days, at the end of which time he was tempted. It may be that, having recognized a mission from God, he found it necessary to clarify the nature of that mission. The actual forms the temptations took, we feel justified in believing, were part of his own profound personal struggle to determine the character of his message in relation to the issues of current Judaism. More particularly, this struggle was probably concerned with his effort to gain a clear understanding of the meaning of his call. In the light of such discoveries or revelations as came to him, he was enabled to define his own task and the nature of his sonship and his messiahship.

Temporary retirement from an active life is far from unique in the life of great religious figures. Fasting was quite common among Jews, and it is almost a hallmark of deeply spiritual leaders that they take periods of withdrawal during which they seek quietly to discover God's will for themselves. The fact that for Jesus the temptation experience took the form of three specific trials may lead us to suppose that, however they are to be interpreted, they represented three courses of action, each of which appealed to him as a course his own life might follow. So understood, the devil or Satan or the tempter may well be the tempter everyone knows from his own experience. We take the account from Matthew 4:1-11, which is similar to the one in Luke (for both come from the Q material); Mark contains only a brief statement (1:12-13) without detailing the forms of the temptation.

Then Jesus was led by the Spirit into the wilderness to be tempted by the devil. And he fasted forty days and forty nights, and afterward he was hungry.

The Wilderness of Judaea

It was in a section of this stony desert, or wilderness, that Jesus spent the forty days of fasting and temptation. A Greek monastery clings to the cliffs near the center of the picture.

And the tempter came and said to him, "If you are the Son of God, command these stones to become loaves of bread." But he answered, "It is written, 'Man shall not live by bread alone, but by every word that proceeds from the mouth of God.'" Then the devil took him to the holy city, and set him on the pinnacle of the temple, and said to him, "If you are the Son of God, throw yourself down; for it is written, 'He will give his angels charge of you,' and 'On their hands they will bear you up, lest you strike your foot against a stone.'" Jesus said to him, "Again it is written, 'You shall not tempt the Lord your God.'" Again, the devil took him to a very high mountain, and showed him all the kingdoms of the world and the glory of them; and he said to him, "All these I will give you, if you will fall down and worship me." Then Jesus said to him, "Begone, Satan! for it is written, 'You shall worship the Lord your God and him only shall you serve.'" Then the devil left him, and behold, angels came and ministered to him.

Before discussing the possible meanings of this account, we may profitably notice certain things about it. First, the Spirit which descended upon Jesus at the baptism now leads him into the wilderness. This suggests that the receiving of the call had to be followed by this experience of inward struggle and clarification. Then too, at the baptism Jesus had heard himself called by God his "beloved Son." What does this mean? The Messiah, possibly, but what *kind* of Messiah? This was the central problem. We notice too that the dialogue was conducted to a large degree in terms of statements from the Old Testament. Such varied sources as Deuteronomy, Nehemiah, Daniel, and Psalms appear. This illustrates how the writing of the New Testament is rooted in the Old. Also, we should be aware that the account cannot without great difficulty be taken literally. Questions of how Jesus might have seen all the nations of the world or whether the devil actually did place him on the pinnacle of the Temple miss the level upon which the experience is taking place.

It is not possible to know with certainty what the temptations meant for Jesus himself, but we can attempt to see some of the possible meanings. In the first temptation, if he was the Son of God he was tempted, being hungry, to turn the stones into bread (that is, food). The temptation may have been to think of himself, in being God's Son, as uniquely privileged, able to perform miraculous deeds for his own purposes. His reply to the tempter was, "Man shall not live by bread alone, but by every word that proceeds from the mouth of God"—a quotation from Deuteronomy (8:3). As God's Son, he had a task which reached beyond his own and others' material needs to the spiritual necessities of men. The response made to the temptation was that of indicating where matters of primary importance lay and, consequently, where his own responsibility was to be found—to live by the words that proceed from God's mouth is to live in obedience to God.

The second temptation is related to the first. Does not God watch over his chosen ones to see that no danger comes upon them? The words of the ninety-first Psalm from which "the devil" drew his quotation came as a temptation to Jesus. But he rejected the view that because one serves God the normal flow of life's ups and downs should be suspended, exempting him from accidents and tragedies. One taking this view might test God's providence, even to the extent of casting himself down literally from the Temple pinnacle. Such thoughts were to be rejected: "You shall not tempt [or put to the test] the Lord your God." Jesus accepted sonship, as he accepted life itself, for what it would bring, without special favor. This profound understanding of religion was all-important for those days in the near future when he would face death as the completion to his task. Whatever privileges sonship had, they were not to be found in exclusion from the common lot of man. This understanding marks a great change in religious thought, bringing to full development ideas found earlier only in Deutero-Isaiah.

The third temptation may be understood as one that moves from the personal to the national level. For centuries the Jewish nation had hoped and expected that some day it would become paramount among the nations. In this temptation Jesus may have been rejecting the entire notion of national pre-eminence. Nationalistic hopes were not of God at all! As Jesus had rejected as evil all suggestions in the earlier temptations to think of sonship as uniquely privileged, so he likewise rejected the view that the chosen nation was specially privileged and marked for primary favor at the hands of God. It would be a false messiah who would lead his people toward this goal. It was a temptation of evil to include in the worship of God the belief that such worship promised some exclusive privilege for the nation.

Jesus' answer to this third temptation is clear-cut and decisive: "You shall worship the Lord your God and him only shall you serve." Ascendancy over other nations was not the purpose of the life of Israel; her task was to serve the true God with whom she alone had a special relationship. He was to be *served* by her—this was the one purpose of the nation.

It is possible to see in this temptation an appeal to motives of a more personal sort: as a temptation to Jesus himself to compromise his message, to court favor and gain a great following by relaxing its rigor. So interpreted, the reply is just the same: "You shall worship the Lord your God and him only shall you serve."

Before leaving the temptation accounts, we should notice also that while they tell us what Jesus rejected they do not specifically state what he understood to be his fundamental service. It may well be that in his last statement

—that one shall serve God alone—he found his answer, but it is not clear at this point what this service included for him. The decision he came to was not one that could henceforth be dismissed as settled; for the rest of his life he had constantly to discover what service to God required in his daily relationship with the Father. Toward the end of his life, as he explained to his disciples that he was to go to Jerusalem to die and Peter protested, saying, "God forbid, Lord! This shall never happen to you," Jesus' reply to Peter may well echo something of these temptations. He said to Peter, "Get behind me, Satan! You are a hindrance to me; for you are not on the side of God, but of men" (Matthew 16:21-23).

The implications of the three temptations involve the whole future course of Jesus' ministry and throw light on it at many points. They bear upon Jesus' response to the contemporary political-religious conditions. As a result of his clarifying and emancipating experience, Jesus did not find in the accepted modes of Judaism what could satisfy him fully. His message was to be different from that of all others. Nevertheless, he was a Jew, and he drew upon the Old Testament book of Deuteronomy for each of the answers to temptation. Yet in using the spiritual literature which nurtured him, he not only rearranged its ideas but he expressed new insights. Their newness was so marked that in due course they would inevitably break the bonds of orthodoxy. In our summary of the temptations, we have seen by implication a new religion coming to birth. As Jesus himself said, the new wine could not be held in old wineskins. This fact becomes evident in his attitude toward political-religious parties, and in his changed conception of the meaning of messiahship and of the kingdom of God.

The Beginning of Jesus' Ministry

With his baptism and through the temptations, Jesus had gained a clear understanding of the general nature of his mission as one called of God. John the Baptist had now been arrested, and, aware of the danger in which he too stood, Jesus went into his home district of Galilee to speak, primarily in the synagogues. His first message was identical with that of John, "Repent, for the kingdom of heaven is at hand" (Matthew 4:17). He came to Capernaum, on the Sea of Galilee, and there spoke, with great effect.

> And they [Jesus and his first disciples] went into Capernaum; and immediately on the sabbath he entered the synagogue and taught. And they were astonished at his teaching, for he taught them as one who had authority, and not as the scribes. . . . And they were all amazed, so that they questioned among themselves,

saying, "What is this? A new teaching! With authority he commands even the unclean spirits, and they obey him." And at once his fame spread everywhere throughout all the surrounding region of Galilee [Mark 1:21-22, 27-28].

This passage testifies to the fact that the multitudes were eager to hear Jesus, and indicates that he had a new and different approach to religion.

In the Gospel of Luke we have a specific reference to an appearance of Jesus in the synagogue of his native town of Nazareth. In this passage Jesus announces what his mission is, in fulfillment of Isaiah 61:1-2.

And he came to Nazareth, where he had been brought up; and he went to the synagogue, as his custom was, on the sabbath day. And he stood up to read; and there was given to him the book of the prophet Isaiah. He opened the book and found the place where it was written, "The Spirit of the Lord is upon me, because he has anointed me to preach good news to the poor. He has sent me to proclaim release to the captives and recovering of sight to the blind, to set at liberty those who are oppressed, to proclaim the acceptable year of the Lord." And he closed the book, and gave it back to the attendant, and sat down; and the eyes of all in the synagogue were fixed on him. And he began to say to them, "Today this scripture has been fulfilled in your hearing." And all spoke well of him, . . . and they said, "Is not this Joseph's son?" [Luke 4:16-22].

Along with his preaching, Jesus performed "great works" of healing. Persons possessed with demons (persons whom we would likely call insane) and those with physical ailments came to him, and he cured them. The crowds came, therefore, not only for his message but also (and chiefly) because many sought cures for their ills.

Up to this point it would appear that Jesus was a disciple of John, in that their messages seemed similar; yet one obvious important difference is found in the way in which Jesus spoke *with authority*. Instead of following the usual procedure of the scribes in the synagogues, of quoting ancient authorities on the matters under discussion, he spoke on his own authority. In the above passage from Luke, we note that Jesus read from the book of Isaiah. By applying this to himself and his receiving of the "Spirit of the Lord," he declared the good news of God's fulfillment of his promises—of the arrival of the New Age. Here too inspection shows that his message differed from that of John, for John's message was one predominantly of doom. Although Jesus did call also for repentance, his teaching stressed the positive message of God's care for his people. In this same passage, Jesus claimed to have been anointed by God, which is another way of saying that he had been chosen by God for a messianic mission.

Many were attracted to Jesus and his message. The records indicate that at times crowds numbering thousands followed him. A small number of these were chosen for special intimacy and responsibility, and twelve of them were called the apostles. Although their names are given in the Synoptics, the lists do not harmonize completely. Exactly what function they held is not clear; at one point reference is made to their being sent out by Jesus to declare his message of the imminent coming of the kingdom.

As Jesus began to gain notice, persons of various religious and political interests naturally endeavored to find out where the new teacher stood on current issues. The Pharisees were the first to sound him out. They were suspicious but not immediately hostile, as we may judge from Luke's statement that Jesus accepted hospitality in the homes of Pharisees (Luke 7:36 ff, 11:37, 14:1). However, once they realized that Jesus did not accept their view of the Law, their attitude toward him grew cold and from then on was marked by suspicion and bitterness, as the numerous efforts to embarrass Jesus show. They came to regard him as an enemy, and some of them now associated themselves with the so-called Herodians. Although we do not know enough about the Herodians to deal with them as a separate party, we suppose the term designates those who were loyal to Herod and who favored the extension of his rule in Palestine. Fortunately for Jesus, there were some Pharisees who remained sufficiently friendly to warn him that Herod sought his arrest.

Despite the fact that Jesus had not announced himself as a political Messiah and that the disciples had not recognized him as such, he encountered a serious political obstacle in the threatened arrest by Herod. As in the case of John the Baptist, Herod mistrusted anyone who had great influence and a great following among the people. How could Herod know whether Jesus, like the Zealots, might not have a revolt in mind? It is possible that the famous question put to Jesus, whether it is lawful to pay tribute to Caesar, belongs to this moment in his life, for it does fit the circumstances perfectly:

> And they sent to him some of the Pharisees and some of the Herodians, to entrap him in his talk. And they came and said to him, "Teacher, . . . Is it lawful to pay taxes to Caesar, or not? . . ." But knowing their hypocrisy, he said to them, "Why put me to the test? Bring me a coin, and let me look at it." And they brought one. And he said to them, "Whose likeness and inscription is this?" They said to him, "Caesar's." Jesus said to them, "Render to Caesar the things that are Caesar's, and to God the things that are God's." And they were amazed at him [Mark 12:13-17].

The passage illustrates superbly the political-religious conditions through which Jesus had to thread his way. The question asked was cleverly framed to destroy Jesus either politically or religiously. The questioners, with simulated sincerity, acknowledged his divine commission and sought guidance on the question of paying tribute to Caesar. If he said yes, the political authorities would be satisfied, but the strong nationalists would then accuse him. If he said no, the political authorities would arrest him. Jesus answered the question in an ingenious manner: since the Jews were using the money of Caesar with all that that implied, then they owed something to Caesar. But they owed even more to God.

Jesus continued to be a political menace in the judgment of Herod Antipas, however, because of the attitude toward him of the sizable crowds that followed him. Popular fancy looked upon every new leader as a potential Messiah. There is an illuminating fragment in John (6:15) which states that the people tried to force Jesus to become king. Herod Antipas was not a man to let budding danger reach full flower. Consequently, he reached the decision to arrest Jesus. Being warned, Jesus had to move quickly and take himself out of the territory. Though the Gospels are not clear on the actual order of events, they do contain a number of passages which make up the story of his leaving Galilee. They indicate haste, and a series of appearances in remote spots outside Palestine, like Tyre and Sidon, considerably to the north. From here, after some time, Jesus wended his way back toward Galilee (Mark 7:31). But soon thereafter we find that he went north again into the territory of the tetrarch Philip where, at Caesarea Philippi, the conversation took place between Jesus and his disciples which appears in the preceding chapter. In this incident it appears that for the first time one of the disciples accepted him as God's anointed. Yet the meaning Peter gave this term was quite different from that of Jesus, for when Jesus began to explain that he had to suffer and be killed, Peter protested (Mark 8:31-33). It would appear from this account that Peter expected Jesus to become a political messiah. In the face of this, one can better understand the fears and suspicions of Herod and the Pharisees.

As we examine the teaching of Jesus we must keep in mind, first, that we know only as much of that teaching as the early community of Christians preserved for us and that this included their own interpretations, and second, that the precise meaning of the teaching ascribed to Jesus is not always clear.

The Centrality of Jesus

The first verse of the Gospel of Mark sums up Jesus' teaching in most brief form: "The beginning of the gospel of Jesus Christ, the Son of God." It is the "gospel" (or "good news"), and that gospel which is associated with Jesus Christ, designated by Mark as "the Son of God," is presented in the four Gospels. In other terms, it is a message—a good and promising and hopeful message—brought by Jesus of Nazareth who was accepted at the time the Gospels were written as the Son of God. A person and that person's message are central; the two are united in the minds of those early Christians.

As the followers of Jesus understood their master, they thought of him always as standing within the ancient Jewish view of life, of God, and of man. They did not regard him as one who brought something entirely new, even though by the time the Gospels were written it was obvious that the Jewish religion could not contain the Christian faith. They understood him as the one awaited in many Old Testament expectations. True, he did not exactly fulfill these expectations, but that meant that the Scriptures were not precise in what the "expected one" would be like. The incompleteness of the Old Testament, with its prophecies—in the first and second Isaiah, Jeremiah, Daniel, the apocryphal literature, and the minor prophets—of a future new age, New Covenant, and a messianic leader or anointed one, seemed to the writers to have finally been fulfilled. That which many had longed for but not seen had at last happened, they believed.

The first disciples, as Jews, had looked for this day to come also. Their gospel was good news just because it announced the arrival of the expected one, of the Messiah, God's anointed, and of the new age, God's reign or rule upon earth and in the hearts of men. Jesus said, "Blessed are the eyes which see what you see! For I tell you that many prophets and kings desired to see what you see, and did not see it, and to hear what you hear, and did not hear it" (Luke 10:23-24). Jesus himself (assuming that he is meant by the phrase *Son of man*), the very center of this happening, was greater than the great men of the past: "The queen of the South will arise at the judgment with the men of this generation and condemn them; for she came from the ends of the earth to hear the wisdom of Solomon, and behold, something greater than Solomon is here" (Luke 11:31). "I tell you, something greater than the temple is here" (Matthew 12:6).

The man Jesus, then, was the very center of the proclamation of the good news; he was understood to be the culmination of the hopes of the Jewish past. This implies that the Jewish understanding of Yahweh, their position as God's chosen people, and the covenant relation are all present in the thinking of the Gospel writers as part of the account of Jesus and his mission. In other words, they were not merely telling the story of a man who happened to have some good ideas that he thought others should hear, or of simply a teacher of ethical righteousness. He was far more: the fulfillment of centuries of expectation based on the covenant relation which the Hebrews had had with God since Sinai. As will be seen later, one of the problems of Christianity when it began to approach the Gentiles was that of explaining Jesus apart from this Jewish background.

How, then, did Jesus understand himself and his mission? In terms of fulfillment, we have said, but what can be added to give that word additional meaning? There seems little question that the disciples thought of him as the Messiah, the anointed one of God, and it is possible that Jesus was willing to accept this designation, yet not with its popular political or nationalistic connotation. When two of his disciples, James and John, obviously influenced by these same expectations, came to him and asked him to be given the highest positions in his "glory," his reply was that they did not know what they were asking (Mark 10:38). And even when Jesus appeared to his disciples after the Resurrection, they asked him, "Lord, will you at this time restore the kingdom to Israel?" (Acts 1:6), thereby indicating how thoroughly their thoughts still moved within the circle of Jewish ideas. Jesus' denial that he was such a messiah is contained in an account of his teaching in the Temple in Jerusalem. Many Jews, we will recall, held the expectation that the Messiah would be a "second David," a great political leader descended from the Davidic line. In contradiction of this view Jesus asked,

> How can the scribes say that the Christ [Messiah] is the son of David? David himself, inspired by the Holy Spirit, declared, "The Lord said to my Lord, sit at my right hand, till I put thy enemies under thy feet." David himself calls him [the Messiah] Lord; so how is he his son? [Mark 12:35-37].

Jesus' own understanding of his mission went beyond such ideas as these. At the very least, he held a relationship to God such as we find in no prophet's teaching. His use of "father" and "my father" with connotations of intimacy and certainty about God find no parallel in either the Old Testament or the New. Because of this nearness, he was able to speak with authority rather than as an interpreter of the ancient Law which came down from Moses. In fact, he actually set aside the ancient Law for no other stated reason than his own authority. Note, for example, the fifth chapter of Matthew. In the first two passages quoted below, Jesus broadens and deepens the commands; in the latter two he contradicts them:

> You have heard that it was said to the men of old, "You shall not kill; and whoever kills shall be liable to judgment." But I say to you that every one who is angry with his brother shall be liable to judgment . . . [5:21-22].

> You have heard that it was said, "You shall not commit adultery." But I say to you that every one who looks at a woman lustfully has already committed adultery with her in his heart [5:27-28].

> It was also said, "Whoever divorces his wife, let him give her a certificate of

divorce." But I say to you that every one who divorces his wife . . . makes her an adulteress . . . [5:31-32].

Again you have heard that it was said to the men of old, "You shall not swear falsely. . . ." But I say to you, Do not swear at all . . . [5:33-34].

The significance of Jesus' statements may be lost by familiarity with the teachings. Each of the sayings of "the men of old" given above is taken from the Pentateuch, the heart of the Jewish Law. Yet Jesus felt free, on his own authority, to broaden them and at times actually to contradict them! Here is an authority which was possible only because of his intimate relationship with God. When questioned about the source of his authority, he refused to answer (Matthew 21:23-27).

If Jesus designated himself by the term *Son of man*, as seems unquestionable in some verses, this title is used in a way that implies something more than ordinary man. It reminds us of the use given the title in the apocryphal book of Enoch, where it is written:

And there I saw One who had a head of days, and His head was white like wool, and with Him was another being whose countenance had the appearance of a man, and his face was full of graciousness, like one of the holy angels. And I asked the angel who went with me and showed me all the hidden things, concerning that Son of Man, who he was, and whence he was, [and] why he went with the Head of Days? And he answered and said unto me: This is the Son of Man who hath righteousness, with whom dwelleth righteousness, and who revealeth all the treasures of that which is hidden, because the Lord of Spirits hath chosen him, and whose lot hath the pre-eminence before the Lord of Spirits in uprightness for ever . . . [Enoch 46:1-3].[2]

The "Son of man" of Enoch was a supernatural figure whose task it would be to usher in the kingdom of God at the end of the age. This same book refers to this figure in three other ways also mentioned in the New Testament—as the anointed one (or Messiah), the righteous one, and the elect one. It is clear, therefore, that the Gospel authors had the book of Enoch in mind as they wrote, and applied these concepts to Jesus himself.

When we add to Jesus' speaking with authority and his presumed identification with the supernatural Son of man the many wonders reported of him, we are again aware of the element of the "more than man" in him. He cured people of a variety of physical ailments, including blindness and leprosy, and drove out demons of insanity. He was reported even to have

[2] R. H. Charles (ed.), *The Apocrypha and Pseudepigrapha of the Old Testament*, Oxford, Clarendon Press, 1913, vol. II, pp. 214 f.

raised the dead. His control over nature was shown by his stilling the storm and by the multiplication of food. The belief in his own resurrection from the dead was present very centrally in the minds of all the Gospel writers and its meaning needed to be taken into account. Also, the events at the Baptism and the Transfiguration were highly important items in the biography of Jesus for these writers.

No less startling (and for the Jewish leaders far more reprehensible) was Jesus' claim that he could forgive sin. In Jewish thought, the power to forgive sin belonged to God alone. In Mark 2:5-12, a paralyzed man is brought to Jesus, and the account continues:

> And when Jesus saw their faith, he said to the paralytic, "My son, your sins are forgiven." Now some of the scribes were sitting there, questioning in their hearts, "Why does this man speak thus? It is blasphemy! Who can forgive sins but God alone?" And immediately Jesus, perceiving in his spirit that they thus questioned within themselves, said to them, "Why do you question thus in your hearts? Which is easier, to say to the paralytic, 'Your sins are forgiven,' or to say, 'Rise, take up your pallet and walk'? But that you may know that the Son of man has authority on earth to forgive sins"—he said to the paralytic—"I say to you, rise, take up your pallet and go home." And he rose, and immediately took up the pallet and went out before them all. . . .

All of these occurrences and teachings must be considered together in trying to form conclusions on the basis of the Gospels about Jesus' understanding of himself. All of them reflect the conviction of early Christians that there were in Jesus qualities that could only be called divine, and that he himself was not merely a man.

At the same time that the Gospel writers recognized Jesus' special relationship to God, they recognized also what might appear at first to be almost a contradiction of that relationship. Ordinarily it was supposed that one specially appointed or chosen of God would be under God's special protection. Precisely on this point much of the uniqueness of Jesus appears. He was anointed by God for service, but what is more, for a service which included and pivoted upon suffering! Instead of one who would be borne up by angels or turn stones into bread or receive all the kingdoms of the world, he was to lead the life of a *Suffering Servant.* Jesus turned to the writings of the unknown prophet whom we have called Deutero-Isaiah for Old Testament witness to the task to which he was called. The Gentiles found it natural for their great men to "lord it over them," but it would not be so of Jesus' disciples. "Whoever would be first among you must be slave of all. For the Son of man also came not to be served but to serve, and to give his life as a ransom for many" (Mark 10:44-45). The call to his disciples to live the life of a servant was made on the basis of the example of his own life. He incorporated in himself two roles which had never before been joined in Jewish thought: The Son of man and the Servant in Second Isaiah. His life was one of denial of himself and his own natural inclinations. He was to take up his cross in literal fashion—the ultimate indication of self-denial—and his disciples in turn were to bear their crosses by their own self-denial: "He who does not take his cross and follow me is not worthy of me. He who finds his life will lose it, and he who loses his life for my sake will find it" (Matthew 10:38-39).

In conclusion, then, we can say that contrary to the rather simple messianic hopes of many of the people of his time, including his own disciples at first, Jesus' understanding of his mission as the Messiah combined a special intimacy with God, superhuman elements similar to some of those found in the book of Enoch, and, most basic of all, the belief that his life of obedience to God was to be one of service and suffering.

The Kingdom of God

The heart of Jesus' message as it appears in the Synoptic Gospels is the kingdom of God.[3] This phrase was used very commonly in the Old Testament and at the time of Jesus. It was shot through and through with political and apocalyptic connotations, but the most casual reader of the Gospels is aware of something quite different from these popular usages in Jesus' references to it. Its basic meaning is quite simple and clear: it is the rule of God. As popularly interpreted, this divine rule would guarantee to the Jewish nation the fulfillment of their hopes for freedom, prosperity, and greatness. But as used by Jesus, its purport was as different from the popular meaning as was his understanding of the word *Messiah*. It was the kingdom of the Suffering Servant that he announced, and its introduction into the world was his task, as he acted in obedience to God, his father.

As one reads the accounts of Jesus' teaching on the kingdom, he finds that Jesus did not define it but rather pointed to it in many parables and allegories which were intended to be understood by those who were spiritually sensitive, who had "eyes to see." The focus of the kingdom, of course, is not on man and what God will do for him but on God and man's proper

[3] In the Gospel of Matthew the form *kingdom of heaven* is used, probably as a way of avoiding mention of the holy name of God. One of the marks of the difference between the Synoptics and the Fourth Gospel is that the phrase *kingdom of God,* used so frequently and centrally in the former, is found very rarely in John.

relation to God. Since God is spirit, the kingdom is a spiritual relationship to him who is actually king over all men. The conception of God as king was not new in Hebrew thought, for the Old Testament frequently pictured him thus, emphasizing God's majesty, holiness, rulership, and power. By contrast, man's position as a created being, his subordination, and his need of God were implied.

The rule of God as king is the meaning of the phrase *kingdom of God;* yet when Jesus pictures man's actual relation to God he frequently turns away from the idea of kingship to the more intimate one of fatherhood, and proclaims that God is like a father or is a heavenly father. In the prayer he taught his disciples, he did not say, "Our king who art in heaven," but "Our father." Jesus took an old phrase and gave it a new content which emphasized the nearness of God and his concern for men. The Jewish father's relation to his children was not that of the modern Western father, for in place of the sentimentality frequently found in modern families, Jewish families were governed by the father in love and strict justice. The thought of God as father was central to the good news proclaimed by Jesus.

Concerning the human side of this relationship, men are called upon, as children of God, to place their full trust and confidence in him and to obey him as human children trust and obey their fathers. "Therefore I tell you, do not be anxious about your life, what you shall eat or what you shall drink, nor about your body, what you shall put on. . . . For the Gentiles seek all these things; and your heavenly Father knows that you need them all" (Matthew 6:25, 32). Yet this trust was not a naive one to Jesus; he knew very well that life is full of pain, and predicted suffering for his followers as for himself. No guarantee is given that because one loves and trusts God he will escape difficulties and trouble. But this at least he knows, and this will support him in life or in death—that he is in the care of a loving God who is a father to him.

God's Nature

When it comes to expressing the fatherly nature of God, Jesus uses a number of striking analogies (Luke 15:3-24). God is like the shepherd who has a hundred sheep, and yet when one is lost he leaves the others, seeks for it until he finds it, and then calls together friends and neighbors to rejoice with him over his recovery of the lost sheep. In the same way there is "joy in heaven" over a repentant sinner who is restored to God. Or a woman who has 10 silver coins and loses one seeks until she finds it and rejoices with her neighbors over it. One of the most beautiful parables of the New Testament is that of the prodigal son, a story whose primary aim is to portray the relationship between God and the sinner:

> And he said, "There was a man who had two sons; and the younger of them said to his father, 'Father, give me the share of property that falls to me.' And he divided his living between them. Not many days later, the younger son gathered all he had and took his journey into a far country, and there he squandered his property in loose living. And when he had spent everything, a great famine arose in that country, and he began to be in want. So he went and joined himself to one of the citizens of that country, who sent him into his fields to feed swine. And he would gladly have fed on the pods that the swine ate; and no one gave him anything. But when he came to himself he said, 'How many of my father's hired servants have bread enough and to spare, but I perish here with hunger! I will arise and go to my father, and I will say to him, "Father, I have sinned against heaven and before you; I am no longer worthy to be called your son; treat me as one of your hired servants."' And he arose and came to his father. But while he was yet at a distance, his father saw him and had compassion, and ran and embraced him and kissed him. And the son said to him, 'Father, I have sinned against heaven and before you; I am no longer worthy to be called your son.' But the father said to his servants, 'Bring quickly the best robe, and put it on him; and put a ring on his hand, and shoes on his feet; and bring the fatted calf and kill it, and let us eat and make merry; for this my son was dead, and is alive again; he was lost, and is found'" [Luke 15:11-24].

This masterpiece of parable and short story has so many implications that we may think of it as a summary of much of Jesus' message. With reference to the idea of God, Jesus declares that God is like a father. This father does not prevent people from doing foolish things. They may take their entire inheritance, whether money, their capacities, or whatever else has come to them, and, failing to appreciate its value, waste it. They may indulge themselves in all manner of ways. They may even end up with pigs. God does not step in to prevent it. He just waits. But if, having turned from folly, men in deep and sincere repentance seek newness of life, God graciously grants forgiveness and reinstatement. The analogy of fatherly love at its best serves to portray Jesus' idea of God. To be sure, this is not original, for in the Old Testament there are numerous references to the people of Israel as children and sons of Yahweh. Nevertheless, the course which Judaism had taken had tended to emphasize God as austere judge rather than as loving father. Jesus protests against this austerity and impersonal remoteness when he so greatly emphasizes the divine fatherhood.

We can appreciate the effect of regarding God thus. The multitudes needed something like this. A great many of the common people felt that no one had any real spiritual concern for them. There simply was no emphasis on the thought that God loved all men. In practice, the idea of God's love extended to those who kept the Law, though there is much in Old Testament prophecy that might have produced a more generous application of the concept of love. Jesus had a sincere love and concern for people. Through the entire development of Hebrew religion we have seen the close correlation between personal experience and new religious ideas; so it was in Jesus. He was one of the people, knowing toil, humble circumstances, and frugal fare. He was acquainted at first hand with the many ills of the common man—sickness of body, sickness of mind. He saw pain and sin, but he saw also the downright goodness which flows through human life. He loved people for what they were and for what they might become, and the love he felt for them was like the love he believed God had for them. If human beings in all their evil knew how to give good gifts to their children, how much more their heavenly father! And if the God of the universe was in reality a loving father, it followed also that the father would be more than ready to forgive sinners where there was sincere repentance, as in the parable. Consequently, the Gospel message to all manner of men was and is one of love and forgiveness, graciously bestowed by a heavenly father who eagerly awaits their return that they may receive their proper status as children of God.

Jesus further thought of God as near at hand and everywhere present. He is not located on some mountain top, nor is he confined to a Temple at Jerusalem. God is spirit, and they who worship him must worship him in spirit. He is everywhere accessible to the souls of men.

Jesus believed also that this personal God is the God of nature, with power and knowledge, even to awareness of a sparrow's fall. On the other hand, however, he appears to have thought of God's jurisdiction as orderly and not modified in relation to man's goodness or badness. The rain falls on the just and unjust, he said. The fall of the tower of Siloam destroyed a random group of people, but Jesus held that this fact was entirely irrelevant to their moral or religious condition. Again, he said, when a man is born blind it is not at all a proper question to ask whether he sinned or his parents. Physical infirmity is part of life, and the idea of sin is not at all the touchstone by which we make clear the meaning of these circumstances. What their meaning is Jesus did not say, but he suggested for man's part an attitude of complete trust in God and a consequent acceptance of whatever life brings. If this is thought through carefully, it will be understood why Jesus could say that those who shared his trust in God should have no fear or anxiety about life.

Jesus' view of God carried the profound ethical monotheism of Judaism to a new level. His concept is at once more personal and more universal than that of Judaism. The attribute of love is ascribed to God as it never had been before, and it is applied universally, including all of mankind. God is fatherly, forgiving, and eager to have his children enjoy all the riches of his spiritual kingdom. Entrance into this kingdom of God's will is like the homecoming of a lost son, filling the household with joy and radiance.

The kingdom of God, then, is a kingdom of God's rule, but the rule of a God who is like a father calling his children to turn away from those forms of life which destroy them to a different sort of life. It is a call to accept a new kind of life, one of genuine sonship, with all that that includes of obedience, service, and love. In still another way we can express what this kingdom is: it is a community of those whose lives are governed by love in all its wonder and demand. We will now look in some detail at some of the statements reported in the Synoptics concerning Jesus' teaching on the kingdom.

The Teaching on the Kingdom

The kingdom so long expected is now present, with Jesus the one who announces it and ushers it in. To a question addressed to him by the Pharisees concerning when the kingdom was to come, Jesus replied, ". . . behold, the kingdom of God is in the midst of [or within] you" (Luke 17:21). When accused of casting out demons by the aid of the prince of demons, he replied that if that were the case then the demons were fighting each other and would fall. Then he added, "But if it is by the finger of God that I cast out demons, then the kingdom of God has come upon you" (Luke 11:20). He sent out his disciples to preach the kingdom: "Whenever you enter a town . . . say to them, 'The kingdom of God has come near to you' " (Luke 10:8-9).

The kingdom's full appearance will take place in the near future, but the beginning is already present:

> He said therefore, "What is the kingdom of God like? And to what shall I compare it? It is like a grain of mustard seed which a man took and sowed in his garden; and it grew and became a tree, and the birds of the air made nests in its branches."
>
> And again he said, "To what shall I compare the kingdom of God? It is like leaven [yeast] which a woman took and hid in three measures of meal, till it was all leavened" [Luke 13:18-19].

The first parable suggests that the grain of mustard seed represents the kingdom of God, which is already planted but will grow increasingly, combining the present and the future. Likewise, the leaven or yeast is now at work, and will fulfill its function of leavening the whole in days to come.

The kingdom is no longer merely a hope for the future; it is *now here*, as the future will demonstrate ever more clearly.

Entering this kingdom is the most important thing anyone can do. Outside it, he is alienated, separated from God, in rebellion against that God who, whether one knows it or not, is like a shepherd searching for him, the lost sheep. The supreme good of life lies in man's turning to God. True, man can be like the Prodigal wandering in a "far country" who is eventually reduced to the lowest stage of distress. But man's true good comes when he enters the kingdom. It is of supreme value, and needs to be sought after:

> And do not seek what you are to eat and what you are to drink, nor be of anxious mind. For all the nations of the world seek these things; and your Father knows that you need them. Instead, seek his kingdom, and these things shall be yours as well [Luke 12:29-31].

The value of the kingdom is expressed by Jesus in various ways, all pointing to its primary significance in human life.

> The kingdom of heaven is like treasure hidden in a field, which a man found and covered up; then in his joy he goes and sells all that he has and buys that field.
>
> Again, the kingdom of heaven is like a merchant in search of fine pearls, who, on finding one pearl of great value, went and sold all that he had and bought it [Matthew 13:44-45].

The kingdom is given men by God, but men must do their part or they will not enter it. They must give up the lesser pearls—the lesser values of life—to obtain the supreme one. Recognizing the value of the kingdom, one must resolutely seek for it; if he seeks properly, he will be given it: "Ask, and it will be given you; seek, and you will find; knock, and it will be opened to you. For every one who asks receives, and he who seeks finds, and to him who knocks it will be opened" (Matthew 7:7-8).

But not everyone asks or seeks in this way. When someone asked him whether few would be saved, Jesus answered, "Strive to enter by the narrow door; for many, I tell you, will seek to enter and will not be able" (Luke 13:24). And again, "Enter by the narrow gate; for the gate is wide and the way is easy, that leads to destruction, and those who enter by it are many. For the gate is narrow and the way is hard, that leads to life, and those who find it are few" (Matthew 7:13-14).

The one wishing to enter the kingdom must be ruthless in destroying all that stands in his way:

> And if your hand or your foot causes you to sin, cut it off and throw it from you; it is better for you to enter life maimed or lame than with two hands or two feet to be thrown into the eternal fire. And if your eye causes you to sin,

pluck it out and throw it from you; it is better for you to enter life with one eye than with two eyes to be thrown into the hell [Gehenna] of fire [Matthew 18:8-9].

If any one comes to me and does not hate his own father and mother and wife and children and brothers and sisters, yes, and even his own life, he cannot be my disciple. Whoever does not bear his own cross and come after me, cannot be my disciple. . . . whoever of you does not renounce all that he has cannot be my disciple [Luke 14:26-27, 33].

To deny oneself means that one ceases his self-seeking and his attempts at self-realization, seemingly so entirely natural to human life. Jesus' disciples were not to seek the places of authority, as did the Gentiles; they were taught instead that "whoever would be great among you must be your servant, and whoever would be first among you must be slave of all" (Mark 10:43-44). Jesus told them to avoid being called with special titles and seeking after honors.

The good deeds one performs are not to be done with an eye toward obtaining praise for oneself. On the contrary,

Beware of practicing your piety before men in order to be seen by them; for then you will have no reward from your Father who is in heaven.

Thus, when you give alms, sound no trumpet before you, as the hypocrites do in the synagogues and in the streets, that they may be praised by men. Truly, I say to you, they have their reward. But when you give alms, do not let your left hand know what you right hand is doing, so that your alms may be in secret; and your Father who sees in secret will reward you [Matthew 6:1-4].

Let your light so shine before men, that they may see your good works and give glory to your Father who is in heaven [Matthew 5:16].

The humility of a little child is taken as suggestive of the proper attitude of a disciple of Jesus: "Truly, I say to you, unless you turn and become like children, you will never enter the kingdom of heaven. Whoever humbles himself like this child, he is greatest in the kingdom of heaven" (Matthew 18:3-4). Pride and self-assertion are fatal attitudes for the one seeking the kingdom. This is one reason that those who find the way "that leads to life" are few.

Loyalty to God and his claim upon man is so all-demanding that one must deny himself and his natural desires at every point where they conflict with the demands of God, as Jesus did, even when he had to surrender life itself. The man living for self loses God, and the man living for God offers himself and, paradoxically, finds himself. Jesus said to the crowds following him, "If any man would come after me, let him deny himself and take up his cross and follow me. For whoever would save his life will lose it; and whoever loses his life for my sake and the gospel's will save it" (Mark 8:34-35).

The kingdom of God is found in man's relation to God as king and father. It must be sought. But the first step in entering it must be a complete change of life. One's sense of values must undergo a complete transformation. The word *repentance* is used by Jesus for this radical inner change. Jesus' first teaching was ". . . repent, and believe in the gospel" (Mark 1:15); "Repent, for the kingdom of heaven is at hand" (Matthew 4:17); ". . . there is joy before the angels of God over one sinner who repents" (Luke 15:10). The same emphasis upon repentance is found in the story of the Prodigal Son. The man satisfied with his life as he lives it apart from God cannot find the kingdom, for he does not seriously desire and seek it. But the one who reverses his way of life in genuine repentance is becoming ready for the kingdom of God.

Repentance includes giving up the wrongly lived life and seeking God's forgiveness for one's past. But one cannot be forgiven unless he is of a forgiving spirit himself. This thought is brought out in the parable of a king (representing God) to whom his servant (representing any man) owed vast sums of money which he was unable to pay. When the servant begged not to be punished for his inability to repay, the king freely forgave him. But then the servant went to his debtor, who owed him only a small amount, and threw this poor man into prison because he was unable to pay (Matthew 18:23-35). The account ends: "And in anger his lord delivered him to the jailers, till he should pay all his debt. So also my heavenly Father will do to every one of you, if you do not forgive your brother from your heart." The request is made in the Lord's Prayer, ". . . forgive us our debts, as we also have forgiven our debtors . . ." (Matthew 6:12), and even more specifically:

> For if you forgive men their trespasses, your heavenly Father also will forgive you; but if you do not forgive men their trespasses, neither will your Father forgive your trespasses [Matthew 6:14-15].

> And whenever you stand praying, forgive, if you have anything against any one; so that your Father also who is in heaven may forgive you your trespasses [Mark 11:25].

To be *humble*, to *repent*, and to *forgive from the heart*—these are essentials in finding the new life of sonship with God in his kingdom. The goal toward which one is aiming is nothing short of perfection itself: "You, therefore, must be perfect, as your heavenly Father is perfect" (Matthew

5:48). The single word that best sums up the kind of life which characterizes the member of God's kingdom is the word *love* (in Greek, agápe).[4] God as heavenly father is primarily a God of love. The man, then, who is in God's kingdom loves as God loves. Such love exceeds the normal bounds of love for each other; it extends even to enemies.

> If you love those who love you, what credit is that to you? For even sinners love those who love them. And if you do good to those who do good to you, what credit is that to you? For even sinners do the same. . . . But love your enemies, and do good, and lend, expecting nothing in return; and your reward will be great, and you will be sons of the Most High; for he is kind to the ungrateful and the selfish. Be merciful, even as your Father is merciful" [Luke 6:32-36].

Properly understood, it seems that all Jesus' teaching on the life of the kingdom can be summed up in the two commandments:

> And behold, a lawyer stood up to put him to the test, saying, "Teacher, what shall I do to inherit eternal life?" He said to him, "What is written in the law? How do you read?" And he answered, "You shall love the Lord your God with all your heart, and with all your soul, and with all your strength, and with all your mind; and your neighbor as yourself." And he said to him, "You have answered right; do this, and you will live" [Luke 10:25-28; compare Matthew 22:34-39 and Mark 12:28-31].

The one who would enter the kingdom must have only one ultimate purpose or value to his life: his love for God must be a love of his whole heart, soul, strength, and mind. The person of divided loyalty who attempts to love both God *and* the goods of his life (called mammon) will fail, since "No one can serve two masters; for either he will hate the one and love the other, or he will be devoted to the one and despise the other. You cannot serve God and mammon" (Matthew 6:24).

As used by Jesus in regard to God, the word *love* includes faith, single-minded devotion, repentance, and obedience; and in regard to one's fellow men it includes forgiveness, reconciliation, nonresistance, and service, which are summed up elsewhere in Jesus' teaching, as in the Sermon on the Mount in Matthew 5-7, particularly in the "Golden Rule": ". . . whatever you wish that men should do to you, do so to them . . . (Matthew 7:12). This, said Jesus, is the life of sonship with God, the life of the kingdom of God, the way that man is intended by God to live—yet a way few men find. God is seeking men for his kingdom, however, and wants to give it to them.

[4] We will discover later that the Greeks make reason rather than love the ideal by which life is best lived.

The Kingdom in Its Fullness

Jesus announced that the kingdom of God was present, that the long-awaited coming was being realized in the midst of the people. But this was only the beginning; the kingdom in its fullness was to appear, and that, it seems, quite soon. Many problems cluster about Jesus' teaching at this point, caused partly by lack of agreement between the various Gospels (John, for instance, treats the matter quite differently from the Synoptics). Some of the material may have been derived from apocalyptic writings of the time that were not originally Christian. In the description which follows, the expectation given in the Synoptics will be followed.

That the early Christians expected the kingdom in its fullness in the very near future cannot be doubted, for Paul's letters also reflect this anticipation. We shall examine the teaching from the viewpoint of the judgment, the time of its coming, and the place of Jesus in the full kingdom.

That judgment is coming is emphasized in Jesus' teaching: ". . . it shall be more tolerable on the day of judgment for the land of Sodom than for you [Chorazin and Beth-saida]" (Matthew 11:24). "I tell you, on the day of judgment men will render account for every careless word they utter . . ." (Matthew 12:36). The conclusion to the parable of the sower looks for judgment:

> . . . the harvest is the close of the age, and the reapers are the angels. Just as the weeds are gathered and burned with fire, so will it be at the close of the age. The Son of man will send his angels, and they will gather out of his kingdom all causes of sin and all evildoers, and throw them into the furnace of fire; there men will weep and gnash their teeth. Then the righteous will shine like the sun in the kingdom of their Father [Matthew 13:39-43].

When would the full appearance of the kingdom take place? To this query Jesus replied, "But of that day or that hour no one knows, not even the angels in heaven, nor the Son, but only the Father" (Mark 13:32). Yet it will be in the near future, for "Truly, I say to you, this generation will not pass away before all these things take place" (Mark 13:30). Also (in Mark 9:1) Jesus states, "Truly, I say to you, there are some standing here who will not taste death before they see the kingdom of God come with power." These statements seem to indicate clearly that the great consummation was expected to take place within a very few years. This same belief is expressed also in the book of Acts (1:6), and Paul in his first letter to the Corinthians (7:29) advises against marriage because the time had grown short before the end of the era and the passing away of "the form of this world."

The point is brought out continually that the end of the era will come when least expected; therefore, disciples must be ever looking for it and ready for it (Luke 12:35-40; Mark 13:35-37). The well-known parable of the wise and foolish virgins (Matthew 25:1-13) illustrates this belief. The foolish virgins were those not prepared, and when the bridegroom came they were not able to join in the wedding feast. This passage also ends with the admonition to watch: "Watch therefore, for you know neither the day nor the hour."

The arrival of the kingdom in its fullness is closely associated with the figure of the Son of man. One of the critical problems of New Testament study is whether in these references Jesus meant himself or another being still to come. Opinions among scholars vary, but Christians throughout the centuries have understood him to be speaking of himself. The quotation above (Matthew 13:39-43) refers to the Son of man's sending his angels to destroy the evil. A parallel passage (Mark 13:24-27) states that after days of great suffering the sun will be darkened and the stars fall from heaven, "And then they will see the Son of man coming in clouds with great power and glory. And then he will send out the angels, and gather his elect from the four winds, from the ends of the earth to the ends of heaven." If these and similar passages refer to Jesus himself, then the expectation was that the humble and suffering Jesus would return as victor and judge over all peoples and nations. His humiliation would be replaced by his glory, and all would then know who he was.

Other Teachings of Jesus

The Scriptures and the Law

On the surface, there is a seeming paradox in Jesus' teaching about the Jewish Law. On the one hand, he said:

> Think not that I have come to abolish the law and the prophets; I have not come to abolish them but to fulfil them. For truly, I say to you, till heaven and earth pass away, not an iota, not a dot, will pass from the law until all is accomplished. Whoever then relaxes one of the least of these commandments and teaches men so, shall be called least in the kingdom of heaven . . . [Matthew 5:17-19].

On the other hand, he was very free in replacing commands from the ancient books of the Law with his own teaching:

You have heard that it was said, "You shall not commit adultery." *But I say to you* . . . [Matthew 5:27-28].

It was also said, "Whoever divorces his wife. . . ." *But I say to you* . . . [Matthew 5:31-32].

Again you have heard that it was said to the men of old, "You shall not swear falsely. . . ." *But I say to you* . . . [Matthew 5:33-34; emphasis supplied by author].

The contrast between "*You have heard* . . ." and "*But I say to you* . . ." is noteworthy. Does this mean that the former statement concerning Jesus' respect for the Scriptures is canceled by his own expression of authority? This is surely not the point. Throughout the teaching of Jesus, he referred to the ancient Scriptures with devotion, quoting them as authority for many of his statements. Yet he exercised discretion in the use of these writings, and their authority was not itself absolute. He felt particularly free to differ with the Pharisaic interpretations of the Law. The Pharisees believed God to have a will for every human situation, and the legalistic developments were their attempts to make clear what that will was in every possible circumstance. Yet in the very earnestness of their attempts they stood in peril of losing the goal of religion, the active love for God.

The difference, then, between Jesus and the Pharisees was not one of acceptance or rejection of Scripture—both he and they believed it to be revelation from God—but their respective interpretations were very different. The relation between a God who loves men and men who love and obey God is one which cannot be put entirely into the form of laws codified once and for all for every situation. The parties to a legalistic relationship are an absolute king and his subjects, not a father and his sons. God's will for man is for man's good. We note in this connection the difference in attitude between the Pharisees and Jesus regarding one of the most important laws, that of the Sabbath:

One sabbath he was going through the grainfields; and as they made their way his disciples began to pluck ears of grain. And the Pharisees said to him, "Look, why are they doing what is not lawful on the sabbath?" And he said to them, "Have you never read what David did, when he was in need and was hungry, he and those who were with him: how he entered the house of God . . . and ate the bread of the Presence, which it is not lawful for any but the priests to eat, and also gave it to those who were with him?" And he said to them, "The sabbath was made for man, not man for the sabbath; so the Son of man is lord even of the sabbath" [Mark 2:23-28].

Jesus does not deny Sabbath observance, nor does he reply in terms of his own authority. He quotes an instance from Scripture (I Samuel 21:1-6) in which human need rose above the religious regulations. The Sabbath day itself, in all its sacredness, was made for man. Much of the conflict between Jesus and the Pharisees arose over his freedom in the use of the Sabbath. At one time when Jesus was teaching in a synagogue on the Sabbath he saw a woman who had been ill for 18 years. He called her to him and said, "Woman, you are freed from your infirmity." As he put his hands on her, she could stand straight again and was cured. The ruler of the synagogue was indignant, for as he pointed out, quite properly from his standpoint, cures could be done on the other six days of the week. Surely this woman, ill for so long, could have been cured just as well the next day! But Jesus replied,

> You hypocrites! Does not each of you on the sabbath untie his ox or his ass from the manger, and lead it away to water it? And ought not this woman, a daughter of Abraham whom Satan bound for eighteen years, be loosed from this bond on the sabbath day? [Luke 13:15-17].

From the standpoint of obedience to the details of the Law as the explicit will of God, the Pharisee was perfectly correct; but from the standpoint of one who from his own experience knew that man's relation to God was different from this, it was quite wrong. Everyone takes care of the needs of animals on the Sabbath, even though it requires work; how much more, then, does God want human need ministered to, *particularly* on his sacred day? In their eagerness to be right before God, the Pharisees lost the very qualities which the ancient prophets had emphasized above all—mercy, righteousness, and love itself.

> Woe to you, scribes and Pharisees, hypocrites! for you tithe mint and dill and cummin, and have neglected the weightier matters of the law, justice and mercy and faith; these you ought to have done, without neglecting the others. You blind guides, straining out a gnat and swallowing a camel! [Matthew 23:23-24].

Not the details of conduct but the inner attitudes were for Jesus, as for the prophets before him, the vital matter in true religion. As Amos and Isaiah had condemned the lavish sacrifices and the observances on holy days because men were not just and merciful, so did Jesus condemn the Pharisees because they, with all their legal obedience, failed in inner attitude. When Jesus summed up the meaning of the Law and the Prophets, he did it in terms of two statements—that one must love God with everything he is, and love his neighbor as himself. These are attitudes, containing the essence of God's will on men. One who lives in these attitudes will live in ways that make the details of the Law unnecessary. The real need of man, Jesus says in effect, is not so much a set of rules covering all manner of duties (although, again, he does not reject the Law) but an inner spirit of openness and love, the opposite of pride and egotism, which fulfills life's obligations joyously.

Jesus had more to say to the Pharisees than to remind them of the true meaning of the Law, with which some of them agreed entirely. He attacked them, the most righteous men of their day, in the most damning way possible: they were hypocrites, he said, because their outer claim to righteousness and obedience toward God was denied by their inner attitudes of pride and self-seeking. Note the following statements, the strongest charges Jesus brought against anyone, charges which can be directed against the self-centered, loveless legalists of every day in every religion:

> Woe to you, scribes and Pharisees, hypocrites! for you cleanse the outside of the cup and of the plate, but inside they are full of extortion and rapacity. You blind Pharisee! first cleanse the inside of the cup and of the plate, that the outside also may be clean.
>
> Woe to you, scribes and Pharisees, hypocrites! for you are like whitewashed tombs, which outwardly appear beautiful, but within they are full of dead men's bones and all uncleanness. So you also outwardly appear righteous to men, but within you are full of hypocrisy and iniquity.
>
> Woe to you, scribes and Pharisees, hypocrites! . . . You serpents, you brood of vipers . . . [Matthew 23:25-33].

Jesus did not make the life of religion easier by his interpretation of the Law than the demands of the Pharisees. To love God with the whole mind and soul and one's neighbor as oneself is far more difficult than to obey the external legalistic requirements. Jesus summed up his attitude toward the Law in a single sentence: "For I tell you, unless your righteousness exceeds that of the scribes and Pharisees, you will never enter the kingdom of heaven" (Matthew 5:20).

Divorce and Marriage

A point of the Jewish Law concerning which the rabbis had had considerable discussion was that of the conditions under which a man might be permitted to divorce his wife. This question was put to Jesus by some Pharisees. Instead of discussing the question on the basis of rabbinic interpretation or what might seem practically possible, Jesus shifted it onto an entirely different ground, raising the matter to the intent of God for marriage:

> And Pharisees came up and in order to test him asked, "Is it lawful for a man to divorce his wife?" He answered them, "What did Moses command you?" They said, "Moses allowed a man to write a certificate of divorce, and to put her away." But Jesus said to them, "For your hardness of heart he wrote you this commandment. But from the beginning of creation, 'God made them male and

female.' 'For this reason a man shall leave his father and mother and be joined to his wife, and the two shall become one.' So they are no longer two but one. What therefore God has joined together, let not man put asunder" [Mark 10:2-9].

Several points in this passage are worthy of special attention. The verse from the Torah upon which the Pharisees based their interpretation was Deuteronomy 24:1-4, which Jesus accepted as being from Moses. But here is a prime example of Jesus' attitude toward the Law: even though Moses himself permitted divorce, Jesus is saying, this is not God's intent. Jesus then interprets God's intent himself. He recognizes that there are many instances when divorce seems called for, but these are the result of man's hardness of heart, which is another way of saying rebellion against God. When men truly live as God would have them live, then divorce is to be entirely forbidden.[5] The reason for this is found in the relation between man and woman as God originally created them. He purposely made them sexually different (thus implying the goodness of sex) with the expectation that one man and one woman would join together in marriage in a man-woman unity. Such was God's intention, an intention circumvented by those who turn against God and his will. When the disciples asked him later about his reply to the Pharisees, he elaborated on his statement by adding, "Whoever divorces his wife and marries another, commits adultery against her; and if she divorces her husband and marries another, she commits adultery" (Mark 10:11-12).

Love for Fellow Man

The second commandment, to love one's neighbor as oneself, was quoted by Jesus from the ancient book of Leviticus (19:18). In its original setting, it referred to a fellow Hebrew, not to people of other tribes and religions. In the same way, the last five of the Ten Commandments concern treatment of fellow Hebrews. Jesus, however, recognized no such limitation to the word *neighbor*. Since all men alike are God's children, all men are neighbors and should be treated accordingly. To *be* a neighbor, that is, to express love for one's neighbor, is to act in a neighborly way toward any man. In a superlative story Jesus showed what this means.

But he, desiring to justify himself, said to Jesus, "And who is my neighbor?" Jesus replied, "A man was going down from Jerusalem to Jericho, and he fell

[5] In the parallel Matthew account (19:3-11) the phrase "except for unchastity" is added. This is obviously a later addition, placed there to meet the very conditions that Deuteronomy was meeting.

among robbers, who stripped him and beat him, and departed, leaving him half-dead. Now by chance a priest was going down that road; and when he saw him he passed by on the other side. So likewise a Levite, when he came to the place and saw him, passed by on the other side. But a Samaritan, as he journeyed, came to where he was; and when he saw him, he had compassion, and went to him and bound up his wounds, pouring on oil and wine; then he set him on his own beast and brought him to an inn, and took care of him. And the next day he took out two denarii and gave them to the innkeeper, saying, 'Take care of him; and whatever more you spend, I will repay you when I come back.' Which of these three, do you think, proved neighbor to the man who fell among the robbers?" He said, "The one who showed mercy on him." And Jesus said to him, "Go and do likewise" [Luke 10:29-37].

In this account, several incisive points should be noticed. The man robbed is given no name or place. He is simply a man, presumably a Jew, who has been maltreated and needs help. A priest comes along, sees the man, and passes by on the other side of the road. So does the Levite, another representative of formal religion. The man who stops to take care of the victim is a Samaritan, belonging to the group of half-Jews despised by the Jews from the time of their return from the Exile. Jesus was saying, then, that one may be a representative of formal religion and still not be a neighbor or an example of the true religious spirit. One may, on the other hand, belong to a despised people and yet have the religious qualities of heart which make a neighbor. True neighborliness extends beyond the circle of one's own race and religion to any man in need. The parable of the Good Samaritan is two thousand years old, but its truth is ageless.

Another form of the teaching on love for neighbor is the Golden Rule. In this statement, again, we have the strongest possible emphasis upon consideration and concern for one's fellow man. We note that this is a positive statement; it does not merely say that whatever one does not wish the other to do to him he should not do that himself. Far more inclusive, it says that men should *do* the good thing for the other that they themselves would like. And this action is not made dependent upon the neighbor's doing the same! Whatever kind of conduct one would like for himself, that he should do in regard to the other. As concerns one man's relation to another surely this sums up the demands of ethics and religion.

The Dangers of Wealth

One of the more striking aspects of Jesus' teaching, not because it is different from the rest but simply because it serves to illustrate the wide gap between his outlook and the usual values of human life, is his comment on wealth. Many Jews, we recall, felt that the reward of a good life was God-given prosperity, and that an evil life earned hardship and poverty. Although this connection between one's way of living and wealth was denied in the book of Job, many still held to it. Thus, the disciples were amazed when Jesus said, "How hard it will be for those who have riches to enter the kingdom of God!" (Mark 10:23), for they thought that if those whose wealth showed God's favor could enter the kingdom only with difficulty, then it was practically impossible for the poor, who had not received the divine favor. Jesus added to their astonishment when he continued by saying, "Children, how hard it is to enter the kingdom of God! It is easier for a camel to go through the eye of a needle than for a rich man to enter the kingdom of God" (Mark 10:24-25). This conversation followed immediately after a wealthy young man had inquired of Jesus how he might inherit eternal life. Jesus' reply was, "You lack one thing; go, sell what you have, and give to the poor, and you will have treasure in heaven; and come, follow me" (Mark 10:21). The astonishment of the disciples was so great that they asked, "Then who can be saved?"

One need not search far to understand Jesus' meaning. He has said that one should seek the kingdom of God first and above all; he has added that one cannot serve both God and mammon. It must then follow that the wealthy man has made his choice. His possession of wealth makes it impossible for him to serve God in the single-minded way that one must if he is to enter the kingdom. Wealth by its very nature is a peril. Great concern with money destroys those very qualities and attitudes that we have been studying as requisites to entrance into the kingdom—humility, repentance, forgiveness, the love of God above everything else, and the love of neighbor as oneself. Both the motive and the procedures which lead to the amassing and holding of wealth destroy or overlay man's spiritual nature. Riches disqualify one from wholehearted search for and service to the kingdom. Again we are reminded of the emphasis Jesus (although not later Christianity) placed upon the difficulty of entrance into the kingdom: ". . . whoever of you does not renounce all that he has cannot be my disciple" (Luke 14:33); "For the gate is narrow and the way is hard, that leads to life, and those who find it are few" (Matthew 7:14).

The Rewards of the Kingdom

The Jews of Jesus' day assumed that the coming of the kingdom and membership in it were highly desirable goods in which all would wish to share. But, one might ask, what rewards does one obtain by entering this kingdom? If the questioner is looking for a political kingdom, the rewards he hopes for are political; and if he looks for a time of plenty for everyone, the rewards he expects are economic. But the kingdom announced by Jesus was neither of these; furthermore, it was a kingdom which required sacrifice, the renunciation of all personal ambition, the offering of oneself for service to God. What kind of rewards does such a kingdom hold? In other words, what does one get out of it?

At one point Peter asked this very question, and Jesus replied to him:

> Truly, I say to you, there is no one who has left house or brothers or sisters or mother or father or children or lands, for my sake and for the gospel, who will not receive a hundredfold now in this time, houses and brothers and sisters and mothers and children and lands, with persecutions, and in the age to come eternal life [Mark 10:29-30].

Such a statement needs interpretation, since it is obviously intended figuratively. We are reminded of two other statements of Jesus in this regard. Once when he was speaking, he was told that his mother and brothers were waiting outside for him. He replied, "Who are my mother and my brothers?" And looking around on those who sat about him, he said, "Here are my mother and my brothers! Whoever does the will of God is my brother, and sister, and mother" (Mark 3:33-35). At another time when a scribe said he would follow him wherever he went, he replied, "Foxes have holes, and birds of the air have nests; but the Son of man has nowhere to lay his head" (Matthew 8:20).

In the light of these two sayings, the promise of houses, brothers, mothers, and lands can only be taken to suggest that one who is a disciple of Jesus, a member of the kingdom, finds himself everywhere in the family of God; he recognizes in those about him brothers, sisters, and mothers, and finds his home and his land anywhere and everywhere in God's world.

We can be certain that Jesus did not hold out any prospect of material reward as an incentive for following him. Had that been the motive, his own life would have shown that these are not what the kingdom offers. He understood, as many others before and since him have understood, that the inner quality of one's life is what makes life good or bad. Possessions in themselves do not give human life its meaning or its value. Great possessions, we have noticed, may be a hindrance to true life, and might better be given away. We recall the statement Jesus made about the difficulty wealthy men would have entering the kingdom, and his advice to the rich young man. Throughout Jesus' teaching we sense a distinction between ordinary life, in which possessions and powers figure prominently, and a higher or better form of life which awaits his followers. This distinction is most strongly made in the Gospel of John, but it appears also throughout the Synoptic Gospels. It is noticed in the contrast drawn between the one who "would save his life" and loses it in the process, and the one who "loses his life for my sake and the gospel's" and yet saves it (Mark 8:35). The life lost and the life saved are to be distinguished from each other. The latter is a full, meaningful, real life—life in the fullest sense of the word—because it is lived in harmony with God and with one's fellow men. In this same connection, Jesus asks, "For what does it profit a man, to gain the whole world and forfeit his life?" (Mark 8:36). The life of the kingdom is a life of trust, and hence without anxiety, and a life of obedience, and hence an active and a sacrificial life. It is a life emancipated from greed, avarice, lust, anger, and jealousy, raised above those forces of inner division which, regardless of outer circumstances, ruin life for men.

He who has entered the kingdom of God receives two rewards: a state of deep inner joy and vital goodness, which Jesus characterized by the word *blessedness,* and the continuation of that state after death. As we shall see, among the Greek philosophers the question of the goal of life is also raised; Aristotle defines it as happiness. The word *blessedness* as used by Jesus has even greater connotations of inner joy, peace, meaningfulness, and satisfaction than does Aristotle's happiness. Particularly in the group of sayings called the Beatitudes do we find Jesus's discussion of blessedness:

> Blessed are the poor in spirit, for theirs is the kingdom of heaven.
> Blessed are those who mourn, for they shall be comforted.
> Blessed are the meek, for they shall inherit the earth.
> Blessed are those who hunger and thirst for righteousness, for they shall be satisfied.
> Blessed are the merciful, for they shall obtain mercy.
> Blessed are the pure in heart, for they shall see God.
> Blessed are the peacemakers, for they shall be called sons of God.
> Blessed are those who are persecuted for righteousness' sake, for theirs is the kingdom of heaven.
> Blessed are you when men revile you and persecute you and utter all kinds of evil against you falsely on my account. Rejoice and be glad, for your reward is great in heaven, for so men persecuted the prophets who were before you [Matthew 5:3-12].

Even a cursory examination of this list of "blesseds" indicates the vast gap between the life of the kingdom and its rewards and the ordinary life of men. To obtain mercy, to be comforted, to be called sons of God, to "see God," to be in the kingdom—these are the highest goals of life. Carrying his point further, Jesus gives a parable that makes an even more radical distinction. The group of sayings called the Sermon on the Mount ends with this parable:

> Every one then who hears these words of mine and does them will be like a wise man who built his house upon the rock; and the rain fell, and the floods came, and the winds blew and beat upon that house, but it did not fall, because it had been founded on the rock. And every one who hears these words of mine and does not do them will be like a foolish man who built his house upon the sand; and the rain fell, and the floods came, and the winds blew and beat against that house, and it fell; and great was the fall of it [Matthew 7:24-27].

The second reward that comes to those in the kingdom is the continuation, in blessedness, of life beyond the death of the body. The relation between men in God's kingdom and God is intimately personal, like that of father and children, a relation which will not be dissolved by death. The blessed life is blessed within a lifetime, and continues in blessedness into the "life of the resurrection," in which the blessed dead are "like angels [of God] in heaven" (Matthew 22:30). Jesus says remarkably little about the nature of this state of being. Its actuality underlies his entire teaching, but the emphasis of that teaching falls upon what man should do and become within this lifetime. The achievement of blessedness in this life assures its continuance into the future.

Summary

It has been our interest in discussing the teaching of Jesus to present the material as it appears in the gospels of Matthew, Mark, and Luke. The Gospel of John will be examined in a separate section later. Within the scope of this volume, it is not intended to interpret the teaching of Jesus in terms of modern application. This task is the one which the Christian church has attempted to do through its theologians over the centuries. Some of this interpretation in early days, as it appeared particularly in Augustine and Thomas Aquinas, awaits us in our considerations of medieval thought.

Jesus' Death at Jerusalem

An account of Jesus' death at Jerusalem would be ironical indeed, following a consideration of rewards, if the rewards he had expected were material and were to be gathered fully in this life. This unique person, Jesus, was brought to the end of his life as a criminal for what he was and for what he taught. His continued presence was an implied threat to the authorities in both politics and religion.

Earlier in this chapter reference was made to the time soon after the beginning of Jesus' ministry when he was forced to leave Galilee. The accounts show him to have gone to many different parts of Palestine. For one period, possibly of several months, he seems to have been in and around Jerusalem. Hostility became so intense that he withdrew into Peraea. But he returned later, probably between A.D. 30 and 34. Whether he expected to be killed is not entirely certain. In the Gospel of Mark he is described as stating specifically that in going up to Jerusalem he expects arrest and death (Mark 10:32-34). Certain it is that in going there he was courting disaster, for many regarded him with deep suspicion and hatred. When he entered the city he was greeted by some who saw in him the fulfillment of the messianic hope of a Davidic king, for they said, "Blessed be the kingdom of our father David that is coming! Hosanna in the highest!" (Mark 11:10). He entered the great Temple which Herod had built and there drove out those who sold the sacrificial animals and those who exchanged Roman money for the temple money needed to make purchases of animals. He said, "Is it not written, 'My house shall be called a house of prayer for all the nations'? But you have made it a den of robbers" (Mark 10:17). This act infuriated the chief priests. Both of the major parties of the Jews were now opposed to him. His denunciations of the Pharisees had earned him their hatred, for they recognized that his approach to religion stood in contradiction to theirs. The Sadducees may now have recognized that he was a threat to the accepted forms of Temple worship as well, with possible loss of income if the people should follow his lead.

At Passover time the disciples prepared the Passover meal for Jesus and themselves. This meal has become known as the Lord's or Last Supper, and is memorialized in the rites of almost all Christian churches in one form or another. As they were eating, Jesus took the bread and handed pieces of it to the disciples, and said,

> "Take; this is my body." And he took a cup, and when he had given thanks he gave it to them, and they all drank of it. And he said to them, "This is my blood of the [new] covenant, which is poured out for many. Truly, I say to you, I shall not drink again of the fruit of the vine until that day when I drink it new in the kingdom of God" [Mark 14:22-25].

He then went with the disciples to the Mount of Olives, across the ravine from Jerusalem. There, knowing the danger in which he stood, he went

The Garden of Gethsemane

It was to this olive orchard, according to Roman Catholic tradition, that Jesus and his disciples withdrew the night of the betrayal by Judas Iscariot. The garden contains olive trees of very great age, some of which are reputed to date from the time of Christ. In the background can be seen the Kidron valley, part of the wall of Jerusalem, and the dome of the Dome of the Rock.

into a garden to pray. He "began to be greatly distressed and troubled" and "fell on the ground and prayed that, if it were possible, the hour might pass from him. And he said, 'Abba, Father, all things are possible to thee; remove this cup from me; yet not what I will, but what thou wilt' " (Mark 14:33-36). The cup was not removed from him; he was arrested and brought first before the Jewish authorities and then before the Roman procurator, Pontius Pilate. The charge before the Jewish high priest and elders was blasphemy; before Pilate he was accused of sedition. He was condemned and crucified.

Jesus' career was closed. But within a short time his followers, who had at first scattered, were imbued with a new hope and faith. The report was circulated that Jesus had risen from the dead; various of his disciples and friends had seen him. The result of this assurance of his Resurrection was a new and tremendously powerful movement which spread first through Palestine and then through the Roman world with astonishing vitality. Following chapters will take up the beginnings of the organized Christian movement from this point.

Questions for Study

1. Why is it said that the Gospels are interpretations and not objective biographies? What was the standpoint from which their authors wrote? Why is it difficult to write an accurate biography of Jesus?
2. Who was John the Baptist, and what was his message? What appears to have been the relation between him and Jesus?
3. Why was Jesus' baptism so significant an event? How did this lead to the temptations, and what meanings may be given to them? To what decision did they lead Jesus?
4. What was Jesus' first message? How did he differ from John the Baptist in this? How did his hearers respond?
5. Why did Herod Antipas consider Jesus a threat? How did his disciples apparently regard him at this point?
6. What is the relation between Jesus and his message in the minds of the authors of the Gospels? What relation did Jesus' followers think he held to the Old Testament? Why was his message regarded as "good news"?
7. How is Jesus pictured in the Synoptics as understanding himself and his mission? How did his disciples understand him? How is he portrayed as being "more than man"; how as the fulfillment of Deutero-Isaiah?
8. What does Jesus appear to have meant by the kingdom of God, as concerns its fundamental meaning and the nature of God?
9. What did he say about the presence of the kingdom, its value, why one needs to "deny himself" to enter it, the meaning of repentance and why it is basic, and why one must forgive? What does love for God mean, and how does its meaning differ from that of love for neighbor? Why was love central for Jesus?
10. What was meant by saying that the kingdom would come in its fullness? When was this expected to happen, and what would be the nature of the accompanying judgment?
11. How did Jesus agree with and differ from the Pharisees in regard to Jewish religious Law? Why did Jesus condemn the Pharisees so strongly? Did he object to their high moral standards? What meaning may his condemnation have for some forms of modern Christianity?
12. What had Jesus to say about divorce, and why? What did he hold was the

nature of neighbor love? Why was wealth considered a great danger? What rewards did he promise his followers? In what two ways did he use the word *life*?

13. Why was Jesus executed, from the standpoint of the Jewish authorities and that of the Romans? Why did his movement not collapse with his death?
14. Why did Jesus' followers consider their religion the New Covenant?

Selected Readings

Beck, Dwight M., *Through the Gospels to Jesus*, New York, Harper & Brothers, 1954.

Bright, John, *The Kingdom of God*, Nashville, Abingdon-Cokesbury Press, 1953.

Buttrick, George A., *The Parables of Jesus*, New York, Harper & Brothers, 1928.

Crownfield, Frederic R., *A Historical Approach to the New Testament*, New York, Harper & Brothers, 1960.

Dibelius, Martin, *Jesus*, Philadelphia, The Westminster Press, 1949.

Duncan, G. S., *Jesus, Son of Man*, New York, The Macmillan Company, 1949.

Enslin, Morton Scott, *Christian Beginnings*, New York, Harper & Brothers, 1938.

Goguel, Maurice, *The Life of Jesus*, New York, The Macmillan Company, 1933.

The Interpreter's Bible, Nashville, Abingdon Press, 1951, VII, 3-227.

Jeremias, Joachim, *The Parables of Jesus*, New York, Charles Scribner's Sons, 1955.

Klausner, Joseph, *Jesus of Nazareth*, New York, The Macmillan Company, 1925.

McCasland, S. Vernon, *By the Finger of God*, New York, The Macmillan Company, 1951.

Major, H. D. A., T. W. Manson, and C. J. Wright, *The Mission and Message of Jesus*, New York, E. P. Dutton & Co., 1938.

Manson, T. W., *The Servant-Messiah*, Cambridge, Cambridge University Press, 1953.

Manson, T. W., *The Teaching of Jesus*, Cambridge, Cambridge University Press, 1955.

Manson, William, *Jesus the Messiah*, Philadelphia, The Westminster Press, 1946.

Marshall, L. H., *The Challenge of New Testament Ethics*, New York, The Macmillan Company, 1950.

Schweitzer, Albert, *A Quest of the Historical Jesus*, New York, The Macmillan Company, 1910.

Taylor, Vincent, *The Life and Ministry of Jesus*, Nashville, Abingdon Press, 1955.

Titus, Eric L., *Essentials of New Testament Study*, New York, The Ronald Press Company, 1958.

Wilder, Amos N., *Eschatology and Ethics in the Teaching of Jesus*, rev. ed., New York, Harper & Brothers, 1950.

Wilder, Amos N., *New Testament Faith for Today*, New York, Harper & Brothers, 1955.

Windisch, H., *The Meaning of the Sermon on the Mount*, Philadelphia, The Westminster Press, 1951.

III. Philosophy and Religion Among the Greeks

CHRONOLOGICAL FRAMEWORK OF PART III

GENERAL CHRONOLOGY

ca. 2800-1400 B.C.	Minoan culture flourishes.
ca. 1600-1100 B.C.	Mycenaean culture flourishes.
1184 B.C.	Fall of Troy.
776 B.C.	Beginning of the Hellenic period.
461-430 B.C.	Pericles beautifies Athens.
431-404 B.C.	Athenian-Spartan war. Athens falls in 404 B.C.
336 B.C.	Alexander the Great dominant. Hellenistic period begins.
197-146 B.C.	Rome gradually conquers all of Greece.

THE GREAT PHILOSOPHERS

Thales, *fl. ca.* 600 B.C.

Pythagoras, *fl.* 550-510 B.C. His religious order established in 532 B.C.

Heraclitus, *ca.* 535-475 B.C.

Parmenides, *fl.* 500-450 B.C.

Democritus, *ca.* 460-370 B.C.

Socrates, *ca.* 469-399 B.C.

Plato, 427-347 B.C.

Aristotle, 384-322 B.C.

Antisthenes, *ca.* 446-366 B.C. (founder of the Cynic school).

Aristippus, *ca.* 435-350 B.C. (founder of the Cyrenaic school).

Zeno, 350-258 B.C. (founder of Stoicism).

Epicurus, *ca.* 341-270 B.C. (founder of Epicureanism).

LITERARY FIGURES

Homer, *fl. ca.* 850 B.C. *The Iliad* and *The Odyssey.*

Hesiod, *fl. ca.* 750 B.C. *The Theogony.*

Pindar, 522-448 B.C. Poems.

Aeschylus, 525-456 B.C. The *Oresteia* trilogy: *Agamemnon, The Choephoroe*, and *The Eumenides.*

Sophocles, 495-406 B.C. *Antigone.*

Euripedes, *ca.* 480-406 B.C. *The Suppliants, Electra, Medea.*

7. Greek Religion

As we turn the page from the conclusion of our account of the Hebrews and early Christians to the Greeks, we move back in time from the beginning of the Christian era to an ancient people whose roots, like those of the Hebrews, are embedded in early cultures. Their primitive history is at points less clear than that of the Hebrew people. They appear to be the descendants of two very different ancestral lines: the Mediterranean peoples living on Crete, in Asia Minor, and in Greece proper, and an invading people who spoke the Greek language and are called Hellenes, coming from Europe.

In almost every respect, these two cultures were very unlike. The Hebrews, whose homeland was Mesopotamia or Arabia, were people who lived almost exclusively in a small, restricted area, hemmed in on one side by desert and on the other by their enemies, the Phoenicians and Philistines, who inhabited the coastal plain and shut them off from the Mediterranean Sea. Much of their history tells of their defending themselves both against the great powers of Egypt, Babylonia, and Assyria, and against the desert dwellers who wished to settle on their arable land. For most of their long life as a nation they were held under the control of one or another of the great powers. They of course had no colonies. Generally speaking, they were poor, although in some periods, as in the almost legendary time of Solomon, the king and his nobles at least were very wealthy. Furthermore, they were not a highly creative people. Archaeology has found remains of fine pottery and

Greater Greece in Ancient Times

homes, and the temple and palaces of Solomon were famed for their beauty, but there was no great outflowing of creativity in painting, architecture, sculpture, and other art forms, and the ancient Hebrews developed no great philosophical thought.

The Greeks, by contrast, were at home on the sea, living in valleys of arable land on the coasts of contemporary Greece, Italy, and Turkey. They moved about freely, and knew the world of their day. Much of the time they were the chief power at the eastern end of the Mediterranean. They were tremendously creative culturally, fathering most of the art and intellectual forms that have come down to us as part of our Western heritage —in music, architecture, sculpture, logic, mathematics, metaphysics, and drama. Our physicians still take the oath of Hippocrates, a Greek. We go to a *theater* to see a *comedy* or *tragedy*. The very words and the institutions they represent are Greek, and certain ancient Greek plays like *Oedipus Rex*, *Antigone*, and *Lysistrata* are still to be seen on the modern stage. Many forms of literature, among them the *epic*, *didactic*, and *lyric*, have Greek names because of their origin. Our bank and school buildings are often supported by Doric, Ionic, or Corinthian columns. Students still study geometry in much the form that students of Euclid learned it 2400 years ago. We continue to enjoy Olympic games, often not remembering that they were originally religious festivals of Greece, of sufficient importance to become the basis of the Greek calendar; and the statues inspired by those early athletes evoke admiration and despair among many modern imitators.

Greek and Hebrew Views of the Nature of Life

Looking at these two people in less superficial ways, we find marked differences also in the way in which they understood the nature and meaning of human life, that is, in what the Germans call *Weltanschauung*, or world view. Like most peoples of that period, the Greeks worshiped many gods who they believed held power over human life. Until the seventh century B.C. at least, the Greeks had a basically mythological approach to life, using stories or myths about the gods to explain the world and its happenings. Yet their religion permitted much freedom of thought and action. It was well to obey the gods, but the gods' chief interest was in themselves, in their own realm. As far as man was concerned, it was believed that the gods required only that he pay them proper recognition and offer gifts in the form of sacrifices. Further, these gods were beings of power rather than goodness, for they were themselves not too moral or ethical, nor, in the earlier days, did they establish stringent moral requirements for men.

As we have seen, when the Hebrews thought of the ultimate nature of things, it was in terms of Yahweh; in his will they found the meaning and end of human life. They had no need of philosophy, for they stood in a covenant relationship with God. At least as early as the eighth century B.C., at a time when classical Greece was just beginning to rise, the prophets taught that God was himself an ethical being who demanded ethical living of his faithful people. Their God was not aloof, uninterested in men, but a Covenant-making God who revealed himself through their prophets. For them, all of human life was centered in man's relation to God, and no man was independent of him in any way. Whatever other factors may have been influential (and there were many), the success, independence, outward reach, and achievement of the Greeks in the directions we have indicated were at least partially the result of their not believing in the ultimacy and all-embracing control of their gods over their lives. Because the Hebrew understood that Yahweh and his will were the goal of all human endeavor, he did not sense the same driving need to search into all other aspects of human creativity. Yet in the late Greek period, in the fourth century B.C., in spite of all their efforts men found themselves frustrated. They had "lost their nerve," as Gilbert Murray so aptly describes it, and began to seek for religious solutions to life resembling those held all along by the Hebrews.

It is clear, then, that while the Greeks were far more productive than the Hebrews culturally, from the standpoint of a deep-rooted relationship with the ultimate powers and the being of God the Hebrews held the advantage. The very words used most commonly by these two peoples indicate something of this basic difference. For the Hebrews, the words that stand out as primarily important are God, obedience, Covenant, righteousness, and the holiness of God. The basic words for the Greeks were human excellence, education, destiny, Fate, and *hubris*.[1] A close, personal relationship with God had little or no place in their thinking and practice, but it was fundamental for the Hebrews.

Throughout their history, life for the Greeks was essentially tragic. Ultimately, life lacked the meaning for them which it had for the Hebrew with his kind of God; yet it was not a gloomy "vale of tears." Much that is very good is to be found in life, they thought, for it can be filled with physical, mental, and emotional activities that are valuable. But their fierce love of life and joy in it and their exaltation in human achievement were combined with the belief that all that man does is finally held in the hands of the gods and of Fate. The gods are not always kind—they may destroy everything man has done. Fate may blindly do the same. It was even felt dangerous to be too successful or too happy, for then the gods might become jealous and destroy the happy mortal. Further, there was thought to be no hope of any better kind of existence after physical death or in future history. Since neither gods nor men change their given natures, life will continue much as it now is. The theory, popular in recent times, that the world and man are growing better and better was not part of the Greek view of life. Hades, the underworld where the life-souls of the dead go, is far worse than this life and not a genuine immortality of the conscious, knowing personality. The Greeks' recognition of an unalterable cosmic framework and lack of purpose on the one hand and, on the other, their deep love of all that human life can be in terms of truth, beauty, and goodness created a conflict that produced the Greek sense of tragedy, which underlies their thought from the time of Homer on with the exception of the teaching of the mystery religions and their promise of immortality.[2]

[1] The meaning and significance of this word will be discussed later.

[2] See H. D. F. Kitto, *The Greeks,* Baltimore, Penguin Books, Inc., 1959, pp. 58-62.

The Greek People

It is almost impossible to assign geographical boundaries to the ancient Greek people, for they did not assign such boundaries to themselves. "Wherever were Hellenes [Greeks] there was Hellas [Greece]," and the Hellenes were those who spoke the Greek language. The earliest home of a truly Greek people was probably the southern end of the Balkan peninsula, that part which lies south of Macedonia and points its nose toward the island of Crete in the Mediterranean Sea. To the east lies the Aegean Sea, studded with islands which provide access, by easy stages, to Turkey, and to the west lies Italy, which was settled by Greek colonies as far north as Naples. Still farther west is the island of Sicily, where two of the largest Greek cities were situated—Syracuse and Acragas (now Agrigento). By the sixth century B.C. Greek colonies had spread Greek culture to all these points as well as to coastal areas throughout the Mediterranean world and northeast along the coast of the Black Sea. Later Alexander the Great was to make the influence of Greek culture felt as far east as India. But let us turn back for a moment to a pre-Greek civilization in the Aegean, and then catch a hasty glimpse of the rise and fall of the Greek people.

The Minoans

In the Western world, the most ancient civilizations were those on great rivers: the Sumerian on the Euphrates-Tigris, the Egyptian on the Nile, and in the East, in India, the Indus culture with its great cities like Mohenjo-Daro. All of these civilizations extend back in time to about 4000 B.C. About that same time a culture started on the island of Crete in the Aegean Sea which reached the Bronze Age about 2800 B.C. and then began its climb to greatness. This civilization is now called the Minoan after the title *Minos* given their kings, who were reputed to have had bulls' heads. These people were so mighty a sea power that they did not need to fortify their capital of Knossos, where the remains of their great palace, the famous Labyrinth, penetrated by the legendary Theseus, may still be seen. They reached a remarkable stage of development, marked by marvelously free painting, vases, statuettes, and indications of highly refined taste in dress and amusement. They traded with Egypt and ruled the islands of the Mediterranean. Sometime about 1400 B.C., before the time of the Hebrew Moses, their capital was destroyed, and although the city was later rebuilt, their great power was never recovered.

The Mycenaeans

Centuries before the Minoan civilization lost its power, it had established other centers of culture, on the mainland as well as on the islands. One of these centers was a strongly fortified city named Mycenae, situated on the Peloponnesus, the heart of ancient Greece. About 1600 B.C. a great culture developed, centering in this city, which held supremacy as the Minoan power went into eclipse. The Mycenaean age, as this period of supremacy is called, lasted until about 1100 B.C. The paintings and pottery from this civilization show great similarity to those of Crete, indicating the dependence of Mycenae upon the ancient Minoan culture. Judging by the remains of buildings like the famous Lion Gate and the remarkable tombs, some of which contained great numbers of gold objects of the finest workmanship, this was a very powerful and wealthy culture which reached its zenith about the time the Minoans were being conquered, in 1400 B.C.

Exactly who these Mycenaeans were is a puzzle. One modern interpretation[3] holds that several groups of Greek-speaking people migrated southward at various times into the Balkan peninsula and by way of the Dardanelles into Asia Minor, starting about 2000 B.C., and that one group formed an amalgam with the native peoples on the Peloponnesus, creating the Mycenaean culture. The language used by the Mycenaeans was chiefly Greek, but Minoan was used for some purposes. The leaders of this culture, who became the great heroes in Homer's stories, were the descendents of the Greek conquerors, to whom the name of Achaeans was given. According to Homer, it was these who attacked and destroyed Troy in the year 1184 B.C. Agamemnon of Mycenae was their great leader; others were Achilles, Odysseus, Patroclus, and Nestor.

The Early Greeks

About 1100 B.C. another major wave of conquerors swept over the Peloponnesus and into parts of the mainland of Greece. These Dorians, as they were called, were also Hellenes, using the Greek language, but were less developed culturally than the Achaeans. They destroyed all the cities in

[3] Moses Hadas, *A History of Greek Literature*, New York, Columbia University Press, 1950, p. 9.

The Lion Gate of Mycenae

The great 14th century B.C. *lion gate of the city of Mycenae. The heads of the lions were probably of metal and disappeared long ago.*

their path and founded their own cities, of which Sparta was one of the most important. Greeks from earlier migrations fled before these newcomers, some to Asia Minor where they settled along the coast, calling their territory Ionia and themselves Ionians. Athens escaped destruction, and considered herself the leader of the Ionians. The earliest and some of the greatest cultural contributions of the Greeks came from Athens and from other Ionian cities in Asia Minor where we find Ephesus and Miletus. The last-named city will be heard from again as the birthplace of Western philosophy.

From the mingling of these various native peoples and the Hellenes in their several invasions emerged the people of classical Greece. What they did from 1100 until the eighth century B.C. can only be guessed at, for there are no authentic historical records before 776 B.C., when the first games between the city-states were held in the city of Olympia. This date ushers in the historic *Hellenic* period of Greek history. The first indication we have of the new day about to dawn during this dark age is the remarkable work of the great poet Homer, who wrote about 850 B.C., picturing in his *Iliad* and *Odyssey* the life of the heroic age of the twelfth century B.C.

Unclear as the details of this history are, it is fairly certain that the Greek culture which began with Homer and his epics combined Greek-speaking Hellenes with a native population called Pelasgians by the ancient Greek historian Herodotus. The two cultures did not become completely and indistinguishably mixed for centuries, for even as late as Herodotus, in the fifth century B.C., there were pockets of people in Greece who still spoke Pelasgian. Athens proudly traced her history back to 1700 B.C., long before the Dorians had arrived. Miletus in Ionia believed itself to have been founded by Minoans. Classical Greece was therefore a joining together of two different people, the one "Mediterranean" in type, dark-haired and slightly built, and the other the brown-haired, blue-eyed, strongly built Hellenes. These two strands, unlike in so many respects and particularly in regard to religion, nevertheless succeeded in creating together a unique cultural unity and balance.

The Hellenic and Hellenistic Periods

The Hellenic or historic period of Greek history extends over 450 years between the first Olympiad in 776 B.C. and the conquest of Alexander the Great, who died in 323 B.C. It embraces the golden age of Pericles which produced so many of those artists, sculptors, philosophers, and dramatists to whom the immortality of Greece is due.

Following the conquest of Alexander came that era which is characterized by the spreading of Greek influence to a large part of the civilized world and the loss of political independence to the old city-states. It is named the *Hellenistic* (as opposed to the Hellenic) period of Greek history. This period came to an end as the Romans conquered Macedonia and Asia Minor between 197 and 146 B.C. It may be some consolation to reflect that while Rome may have conquered Greece by force of arms, the victor was largely vanquished in the battle of ideas which resulted from the impact of one culture upon another.

So runs the course of Greek history in very brief outline from almost neolithic times to the growth of the Roman Empire. Many factors of importance to the development of Greek religious and philosophical thought should be pointed out in detail, but we have time to consider only a few.

The City-State and Political Disunity

Perhaps the most important single factor in shaping Greek culture was the relatively early formation of small city-states, generally with fewer than

20,000 citizens. Each city had its own independent government, which was sometimes monarchic, sometimes oligarchic, and sometimes—as in the case of the most famous of the city-states, Athens—democratic. While these states achieved a cultural solidarity with each other, having a common language (albeit with many dialects), common customs, and some community of religious ideas, they never achieved political unity. Confederations were sometimes tried but always failed. At times a "barbarian" enemy, such as Persia, forced the various states into temporary unity, but the common danger had no sooner passed than old state rivalries appeared to keep the Greeks a divided people. Athens, Sparta, and Thebes each dominated the political scene at times, but never for long.

This political disunity had natural causes and cultural effects which ought to be observed. Regarding the former, it should be enough to point out that Greece is a mountainous country with many small valleys, some big enough to support an economically independent people; and where people are economically independent they are likely to insist on political autonomy. But mountains were not the only natural invitation to governmental self-sufficiency; so were the seas, for, as we have noted, Greek colonies were scattered throughout the Mediterranean area in such a way as to be aloof enough from all the rest to make defense against aggression relatively easy and yet accessible enough to make the interchange of goods and ideas possible. The pattern of Greek culture was largely formed by the fact that Greece was a maritime civilization.

But let us consider briefly the consequences of this political disunity which geographical factors had induced. In the first place, it meant that Greece was not likely to withstand the aggression of more united people forever. The Greeks threw back the Persian invasion but lost eventually to Macedonia. Yet their disunity was not without some merit. The many city-states, with their various forms of government, provided an efficient laboratory for the growth of political science. We find that Aristotle was able to study 158 state constitutions (and innumerable revolutions) when he came to write about political philosophy. Of chief importance, of course, was the many-sided genius of the Greeks, which must be attributed in part to their very lack of unification. Finally, even in decay, the city-states were to influence philosophic thought.

A further point remains to be made before we turn to an examination of Greek religion. This is the question of what *kind* of people the Greeks were in the Hellenic period. While harmony was their ideal and while they spoke much about balance, reason, and similar qualities, they were actually people who were inwardly in tension, prone to go to extremes, and forced to fight for self-control. Possibly the Greek inherited his strong sense of form and balance from his Hellenic forebears, and his tremendous drive, his creativeness, his desire for personal expression from his Mediterranean ancestors. The harmony achieved by the Greeks was, then, not one that came naturally to them but one they had to achieve. It was a harmony of tension, between control and vast excitement and passion. A modern scholar has said,

> The doctrine of the Mean [as between the extremes] is characteristically Greek, but it should not tempt us to think that the Greek was one who was hardly aware of the passions, a safe, anaesthetic, middle-of-the-road man. On the contrary, he valued the Mean so highly because he was prone to the extremes. It is we more sluggish Northerners who have a certain furtive admiration of extremes. . . . The Greek had little need to simulate passion. He sought control and balance because he needed them; he knew the extremes only too well. When he spoke of the Mean, the thought of the tuned string was never far from his mind. The Mean did not imply the absence of tension and lack of passion, but the correct tension which gives out the true and clear tone.[4]

Other factors which influenced Greek thought will be referred to incidentally as we develop the conceptions of religion and philosophy of these remarkable people.

Early Greek Religion

There is every evidence that early Greek religion in its various forms included many primitive elements like magic, fetishes, and taboos which probably sprang from animistic roots and which, moreover, persisted throughout the culture long after more enlightened religious ideas had been introduced. As often happens, the majority of people, while not altogether unwilling to accept something new, were quite loath to give up something old and familiar.

In addition to these most primitive constituents, evidence for which can be found at almost any stage of Greek culture, there are two main movements in Greek religion, one leading to the Olympian or state religion and the other to various mystery religions, which provided a more personal kind of religious experience than did the Olympian. In addition to these, there was finally, of course, that body of religious conceptions which emerged as the result of philosophic criticism of earlier forms. We will consider each of these in turn.

The *Iliad* and *Odyssey* of Homer, written, as we said, about 850 B.C. but relating stories of what had happened over 300 years earlier, give the impression that the Olympian religion of classical Greece was the religion of

[4] Kitto, *op. cit.*, p. 252.

the Achaeans and of twelfth-century Greece generally. This supposition was a mistake on the part of Homer who assumed that the religion had not changed. On the contrary, just as we have found that classical Greece herself was the product of the mingling of two very different cultures, so we find that its religion was a combination of two principal forms of religion; the native religion of Crete and the coastlands was united, forcibly it seems, with the religion of the conquerors, the Hellenes. In addition there were smaller cults and local practices. Our question is, what were these two main forms of religion?

On Crete, the basic religion exhibited by archaeology was the worship of a female deity or deities. The same is true of the early religion of Asia Minor and the country of Greece as well in the period before the Hellenes arrived. The names of Athena, Hera, Demeter, Aphrodite, all goddesses in Homer's pantheon, are not Greek at all but belong to divinities worshiped before the coming of the Hellenes. These goddesses are conceived of chiefly as earth goddesses, personifications of the life-giving powers of nature in crops, growth, procreation, fertility, and so forth. The leaders of religion in these cultures were generally women, who were the priestesses. It was, in short, chiefly a woman's religion, for women are thought to be in touch with these powers in ways men are not. In many of their aspects these religions dealt with the subterranean forces of life which give existence, food, and increase, and eventually receive back the body of the dead. Centuries later they provided the subsoil out of which came the mystery religions that we will examine later.

In early Athens prior to the coming of the Dorians, three forms of religious worship are known, all quite different from any in the Olympian religion. The first was the festival of Diasia in which the underground powers were worshiped; fittingly, the snake was its symbol. Among the statues remaining on the Acropolis in Athens after it was burnt by the Persians was one that had been a principal feature of the early temple. It was in the form of a huge snake with three bearded human heads. Burnt sacrifices were made to the god of this cult, called Meilichios (he who can be placated). A second festival, that of fertility, took the sow as its symbol. Although in later times it was given the name of the Demeter-Persephone cult, in primitive times it held festivals called Thesmophoria, of her who carried the *thesmoi*, the seeds. The Anthesteria, which later grew into the Dionysiac mystery, was the third of these ancient festivals. It was originally a three-day festival held to appease and cleanse the dead, who were of course the ancestors.[5] In every instance —in the propitiation of the mysterious underground powers, the solicitation

[5] See Jane E. Harrison's discussion in *Prolegomena to the Study of Greek Religion*, 3rd ed., Cambridge University Press, 1922, chaps. 1, 2, and 4.

The Minoan Snake Goddess

A small statuette of ivory, arms entwined with two golden snakes, representing probably a goddess of the native Cretan religion associated with the powers of the underworld. 16th century, B.C. *(Courtesy, Museum of Fine Arts, Boston)* of the forces of productivity, and the propitiation and cleansing of the dead —the gods of whom Homer sings are not present; we are in a period preceding their arrival.

The Homeric gods, then, combine in themselves not one but two traditions with their respective sets of gods. The dominant one, that of the great male gods with Zeus at their head who live in the upper air of Mount Olympus, was the native religion of the migrating Hellenes. It is said in one place that Zeus forced Hera to become his bride, a tradition which seems to reflect the actual occurrence of the conquering religion's forcing the native religion into its structure. But this did not eliminate the old cults and beliefs, which remained and later reappeared in both primitive and purified forms.

The Olympian Religion of Homer and Hesiod

According to the historian Herodotus, Homer (flourished *ca.* 850 B.C.) and Hesiod (flourished *ca.* 750 B.C.) gave the gods their names, disclosed their functions, and made known their forms. This is a striking statement, for it suggests that before these two men did their great work the gods were not given specific names nor identified with definite functions. It would then appear that Homer, who was the earlier, took crudely conceived deities, purified and idealized them, and fixed the titles and range of activities of each. Thus these gods were manifestations in objective, manlike forms of the great superhuman powers which rule over the universe and man. The old religions, with their crudities and sex worship, were driven aside. The work begun by Homer was completed by Hesiod, who in his *Theogony*, written about a century after Homer's great epics, brought the gods and goddesses of Homer into a unified system, showing who were husband and wife, who their children, and the entire relationship of the Olympian deities to each other.

Homer's *Iliad* and *Odyssey* and Hesiod's *Theogony* actually held for the Greeks the place which the Hebrew Bible occupied for the Jews. These two poets became the religious teachers of all Greece. Their works were read in the schools and out, and the tales they told of the gods were known to all. In short, they provided religious conceptions which, although modified by later poets and philosophers, never ceased to influence the Greek consciousness. Ethical and moral ideals also had their bases in these works; often a quotation from Homer was sufficient to settle a disagreement on questions of this nature.

We can describe Homer's religion as an *anthropomorphic polytheism*, that is to say, the gods had human form and there were many of them. They were of varying degrees of importance. They were like human beings both in physical form and in personality traits. They ate and drank as we do, although it is true that their food and drink were not ours, for they lived on ambrosia and nectar instead of common food. In their veins ran the divine ichor rather than blood. But they could be wounded, even by men, and sometimes had to be carried from the battlefield. They had feelings much like those of men, and petty jealousies were no less evident on Olympus than in Athens. The goddesses were very like ordinary women, quite capable of tears and deceit. But if they were almost human in these many respects, yet there were enough important differences to make them a race apart.

Most important was the fact that they were believed to live for a very long period of time; they were almost immortal—but not quite! They had ancestors, gods who had preceded them many ages ago and had passed out of existence, so there was a time when the Olympian gods were not, and there would be a time when they would cease to exist. In the meantime, however, they had vast ages of time at their disposal. They could not die before their time was up; hence the nagging fear of death which darkened the life of man was not an imminent fear of the gods. Further, the gods were far more powerful than men. They were actually almost omnipotent—but not quite! Poseidon could cross the Aegean Sea in four strides and could shout as loud as 10,000 men. The gods were capable of vast feats, and no man could stand against them; yet they did not have all power, for their power was believed limited by the greater power of Fate, of which we shall say more presently. Finally, just as they were more powerful than men physically, so they outstripped them mentally. They were almost omniscient—but again, not quite! It was possible, for instance, for Zeus to be deceived by Hera, his wife.

So much for the nature of the gods as pictured in the Homeric poems. They were a rather human lot whom we would be more apt to call supermen than deities, vastly more powerful and knowing than man, yet not particularly moral—judged by later standards, they were distinctly less moral than men. To the early Greeks—but not to the later ones—morals and religion were not so closely associated as they generally were in the Hebrew religion. However, even more important to men than knowing the nature of the gods in themselves was knowing the nature of their relationship to the world and the people who lived in it. How should they be approached, and what could one hope to obtain from them?

For one thing, they exercised control over nature. This is scarcely surprising, since in their origins they were manifestations of the powers ruling over nature and man. Their power was also expressed in civic affairs, as evidenced by the fact that Troy's destruction was planned by Zeus, and in the destiny of individuals, as shown many times in the *Iliad*. Thus, every city had its shrines dedicated to some protecting deity, and no home was without its ritual of the hearth whereby the gods could be made friendly.

To classify all the gods of Homer would be a tedious task which he himself was too wise to try, leaving this for Hesiod to attempt, but we might do well to become acquainted with the major figures in his poems. Three who stand out in importance are Zeus, Athena, and Apollo. To be most efficacious, prayers named all three. Zeus, "father of gods and men," was lord and master of all the gods and king of Mount Olympus. Many shrines and temples throughout Greece were dedicated to him. Athena, who according to later legend sprang full grown from the brow of Zeus, was the very personification of wisdom. She was also a goddess of war, and had in fact been born in a full panoply of armor. In Homer she was the favorite of Zeus and was also the patron of the arts. Apollo, sun god and god of the archers, was a many-sided deity. He was a patron of war and yet gentle enough also to inspire musicians, seers, and poets. He was a god of prophecy and had many important oracles dedicated to him, the one at Delphi being the most famous.

Next in importance to these three stand Hera and Poseidon. Hera's importance came chiefly from the fact that she was the proper wife of Zeus. Something of a scold, she needed at times to be disciplined, as when Zeus strung her up and hung heavy anvils from her feet. Yet, being queen of the gods, she demanded respect and presided over the Olympian court. Poseidon, brother of Zeus, had the sea for his special domain, but he appeared on Olympus in council with the other gods. Hades, the third brother, was god of the underworld and ruler of the dead. Hephaestus, god of fire, builder of homes, and skillful artist; Aphrodite, the beautiful goddess who controlled the passions of love and desire; and Ares, embodiment of the war spirit but himself not so good a fighter as Athena, were three additional important figures in Homeric times. There were innumerable other gods of lesser rank as well as a host of divinities not even named who, along with Fate, were responsible for all natural phenomena. But we have seen enough to give us some idea of the beginning of the Olympian deities.

The Oracles

To view the world as governed by personal agencies was one step toward the reconciliation of man with his environment. Nature no longer needed to be considered alien to man and his desires, for she was seen to be presided

The Sacred Way and Foundations of the Apollo Temple in Delphi

Ancient sacred processions followed the way on the right of the photograph to enter the great temple of Apollo whose foundation wall can be seen on the left.

over by beings who could be approached and appeased. How important these deities were to become for Greek history must be judged from the fact that no major civic enterprise was ever initiated nor any important individual act undertaken without asking guidance and protection from the appropriate gods. There were many ways of finding out the will of the gods, including such primitive modes of divination as observing the flights of birds for portentous signs or peering into the entrails of animals for propitious omens. Sometimes, indeed, decisions were thrown literally into the laps of the gods by taking recourse to the casting of lots. But the mode par excellence for determining whether human plans would have the backing of the gods was divination by means of oracles, mediums through whom or places where the gods spoke more directly. These oracles became such important institutions throughout Greece that special consideration must be given to them. Since one can stand as an illustration for the many, we shall confine our discussion to the most famous Apollonian oracle, the one at Delphi.

It was here that Socrates was told he was the wisest man in Athens. He looked upon the oracle as giving him a divine mission to expose ignorance wherever he found it. It was here the mighty king of Lydia, Croesus, came to ask about the advisability of going to war with Cyrus of Persia (who, we recall, was the king who defeated the Babylonians and permitted the Hebrews to return to Palestine). He received the famously ambiguous reply that if he attacked Cyrus "a great empire would be destroyed." History records that he did attack and that a great empire was destroyed, but that it was not Persia. To Delphi came civic leaders to ask Apollo's instruction in founding new colonies; still others sought religious advice on how best to worship certain gods. The oracle's sanction was invariably required to elevate the dead to the rank of hero or to bestow on them such divine honors as came to Asclepius and Heracles, who, although mortal beings, were admitted to Olympus. In short, the oracle was called upon to provide answers to the most vexing problems, whether economic, political, religious, or moral, and frequently the answers received were very wise.

The oracle of Apollo in Delphi was the central authority and constituted the greatest factor in preserving unity in ancient Greece, which we must recall had no Bible and no church. It has been asserted that without the unity and authority which it provided the Greek city-states, Greek society would not have endured the tensions to which it was subjected during the ancient period. The morals of the institution changed with time, of course, and whereas in its most primitive stages it might have recommended human sacrifice as a way of placating the gods, in later days it offered more enlightened—or at least less drastic—ways of achieving the same end.

As we have suggested, much of the advice given by the oracle was wise, which doubtless had much to do with its continued popularity. It is remarkable to realize that this oracle, starting before historical times, continued down into the Christian era. This is partially explained by the fact that the attending priests were learned men who were constantly being consulted by inquirers from both the Greek and barbarian worlds. Thus they acquired a great deal of information. The Greeks as a people, however, trusted the oracle because it was the voice of the god Apollo speaking through his medium. If occasionally, as did happen, the oracle was in error, this could be considered not the failure of the god but of the medium who, being human, was fallible.

The medium through whom Apollo spoke was a woman—in the early

The Oracle Temple of Didymus

Although Delphi was the best known of the Greek oracles, there were many others. Second in fame only to Delphi was this great temple on the southwest coast of Asia Minor, sacred to Apollo. Worshipers entered by small doorways, then faced the stairway. The priests and priestesses had rooms at the top of the stairs, and from there announced the oracle of the god.

days of the oracle a young maiden, in later times a matron aged 45 or 50. It appears that she went through various rituals, including drinking at the sacred spring and chewing laurel leaves; then, seating herself on the sacred tripod, the seat of Apollo, she passed into a trance state and spoke out the divine message, frequently in verse form. The message was recorded by the attending priests and applied to the question asked, with interpretation provided if necessary. At times, but by no means always, the answer might be ambiguous, as in the instance of Croesus' famous question.

One thing more should be said about the character of the oracles' advice.

We have already suggested that such shrines as the one at Delphi became real Panhellenic centers and thus provided a unity to Greek religious ideals that could never have been achieved without them. But at the same time, the pluralistic character of Greek life was expressed here as elsewhere. Cities asking advice on constitutional changes might be advised to "take counsel with the majority," that is, form a democracy; or they might be told to retain their monarchic system. The oracle apparently did not seek so much to unify Greece politically as to satisfy each individual client to the best of its ability. And in religion, too, the oracle continued the pluralistic tradition, for Apollo often advised the worship of other gods, not infrequently even obscure and local ones.

Fate or Moira

There is a concept associated with Homer's picture of the gods which we have mentioned in passing but which deserves fuller consideration because of the important role it played in subsequent theological and philosophical speculation. This is the notion of Fate as a power superior even to the gods themselves. In the Hebrew tradition God created the heavens and the earth. Since he was the ultimate power and goodness, the Hebrews sensed no need for further explanation behind God himself. But to the Greeks the gods were "later than this world's production." This meant that they were not ultimate realities; while wiser, longer lived, and more powerful than men, they still depended on something beyond themselves. In Homer's time this ultimate power behind all, human and divine, was *Moira*, which might be translated Destiny or Fate. Some of its meaning can be discovered in the account of a conflict of the gods described in the fifteenth book of the *Iliad*.

In this story Zeus finds fault with Poseidon and orders him to cease from battle and return to his proper abode, the sea. But Poseidon feels that Zeus has no right to be so domineering, and explains that the three gods, Zeus, Poseidon, and Hades, are all of equal rank, having all been born to Cronus and Rhea. Finding that the universe at their disposal was comprised of three separate spheres, they drew lots: to Zeus fell the heavens, to Poseidon the sea, and to Hades the misty darkness of the underworld. Earth and high Olympus were common to all three; therefore, reflects Poseidon, let Zeus confine his commands to his own undisputed third part and not impose his will beyond his proper realm.

This notion of a "proper realm" for each suggests the setting of boundary lines beyond which even the gods either cannot or may not go. The sense of complete impossibility (the *cannot*) is less evident in Homer than is the second meaning, but it is not absent entirely, and in time it becomes the basis for philosophies which emerge during the early classic period. Once philosophy demands an explanation of the cause of things in naturalistic language, it is quite likely to grasp hold of this early meaning of *Moira* and interpret it simply as necessity. Then the world will be viewed as the result merely of blind mechanical motion, for necessity need not be either moral or purposive. The second meaning of *Moira* mentioned above, as the force that sets limits beyond which even the gods are not allowed to go, is the familiar one which runs through the whole of Greek literature. It is like saying that you may not break the law. Obviously you can break it, but not without setting in motion a certain train of events which according to the modern view might and which according to the Greeks must inevitably overtake you and exact full toll for your trespass. The spirits of vengeance, the Erinyes, are quick to visit any man or god who goes beyond his proper sphere.

When *Moira* is given this second meaning, it becomes a moral force imposing penalties for wrong acts, and as such it plays an important role in the development of Greek ethical understandings. In accord with this understanding of *Moira*, the greatest of human sins is *hubris*. This is the sin of extreme self-assertion, arrogance in thought, word, or deed. Its wages are suffering and death, for the man guilty of *hubris* has overstepped his human boundaries and has made claims for himself not proper to him and so beyond what *Moira* permits. Punishment is certain to be visited upon such a person. It is wrong to want to be like the gods, for this implies an attempt to avoid one's own destiny as a man. The idea that the good man does "naught in excess" is implied in Homer, stated clearly as early as Hesiod, and made explicit in Aristotle's doctrine of the Golden Mean, which we will examine later. This doctrine is one of the rich developments of the early concept of *Moira*, which is essentially a principle of order with implications for both metaphysics and ethics.

Hesiod

So far our picture has been that of the Olympian deities as described by Homer. Some added touches from the pen of Hesiod, who lived a century or more later, must serve to complete our description of this phase of Greek religion. Two works of his which give us much material on the subject are the *Theogony* and *Works and Days*. The former is the first systematic attempt at explaining the origin of the world and the generations of the gods.

According to Hesiod, there have been several dynasties of the gods, and Zeus simply happens to be head of the current one. Before him was the rule of Uranus, who gave way to Cronus, who in turn gave way to Zeus and his cohorts. And men, too, have gone through a series of generations, for there have been five different ages of man, ranging from the perfectly good original age of gold, in which gods and men dwelt together under the reign of Cronus, to the age of iron in which Hesiod lived. The silver, the bronze, and the heroic ages came in between, but in the whole series each age was more degenerate than the last. Hesiod, like the Hebrew prophets, looked back to a golden age such as the Hebrews found in the Garden of Eden before man's disobedience "brought death into the world and all our woe" and forward to a future Utopia. He felt certain (how ancient and how modern he sounds!) that his own age represented the very depths of man's depravity.

In general, there are no fundamental differences between Hesiod's outlook and that of the earlier Homer, except that Hesiod reflects a more settled type of society. Insofar as religion is concerned, one of the chief differences lies in his attributing to Zeus a passion for absolute justice which far exceeds anything like it belonging to the Homeric Zeus. In fact, justice is personified as the daughter of Zeus who is very dear to him; and she has innumerable assistants ("thrice ten thousand") who, clad in mist, go to and fro upon the earth searching out the righteous and unrighteous that the former may be rewarded and the latter punished. All this suggests that Zeus and *Moira* are more closely related than they seemed to be in Homer. Zeus is now looked upon as the determiner of destiny, whereas in Homer Zeus was not wholly master. It is true that there are passages in Homer which are not unlike Hesiod's idea. Chief of these is one found in the twenty-fourth *Iliad* where we are told that Zeus has two urns, one containing evils, the other blessings, and that he determines the destiny of men by giving them portions from both urns, apparently in whatever measure pleases him. But against this passage we must place one from the *Odyssey* in which Zeus repudiates all responsibility for evil and attributes its presence to the perverseness of men who insist on doing things "beyond that which is ordained," and thus incite the avenging spirits who see that men do not exceed their destiny with impunity.

The Problem of Evil

The problem of how best to account for the evil and apparent imperfections in the world is one that was to trouble Greek thinkers as much as it did the Hebrews. Adam and Eve's disobedience in the Garden of Eden and their consequent punishment parallels the Greek story of Pandora, the first woman. Prometheus, son of a Titan and a goddess, had stolen fire from Olympus because of sympathy for man and interest in his welfare and brought it to earth in a hollow reed, thus deceiving Zeus. In retaliation, Zeus made the first woman and for her dowry gave her a box, with injunctions not to open it. Prometheus' brother married Pandora, who soon afterwards, out of womanly curiosity, opened the box and so released all those evils, troubles, vices, and diseases that ruin man's life. Both grief and responsibility in man are thus explained mythologically. Hesiod did not get beyond the adversities of Job in explaining why evils befall some individuals and not others. Wealth, he says, comes to men because they are righteous and poverty is punishment for wrongdoing. The author of the first Psalm in the Bible is no more explicit about such matters than was Hesiod; nor were the prophets of Israel more certain about the corporate character of guilt. Ofttimes, says Hesiod, a whole city will reap the punishment of an evil man who sins and contrives works of foolishness. Sin was foolishness to the Greeks because it meant that a man was stupid enough to fly into the face of Destiny. Later on, Socrates was to remind the citizens of Athens that knowledge is virtue.

Summary

The Olympian deities were brought to Greek consciousness largely through the works of Homer and Hesiod. The gods described by these men were essentially human in characterization except that they lived much longer and were far wiser and more powerful than men. Like men, they were subject to Fate, but they also had considerable control over the fortunes of mankind. They had not created the world but had much to do with what happened in it. They were proper objects of worship for citizens, either as members of the state or as members of the family, and both private and public shrines were erected in their honor. The gods were oracular and willing to dispense their knowledge to men for a consideration. The consideration was ritualistic, sometimes attaining extravagant proportions and demanding enormous sacrifices. There was no real immortality for men, but only a shadowy semiconscious afterlife in which men were more to be pitied than envied.

What happened to the Olympian deities as the result of subsequent criticism by poets and philosophers will engage us in a later section, but let us consider next the movement in Greek philosophy which led to the establishment of the mystery religions, which made up for the recognized deficiencies of Olympianism.

The Mystery Religions

We have seen that the religion the Hellenes brought with them when they conquered the country we call Greece was one that worshiped primarily male gods thought to dwell in the sky. It incorporated into itself figures drawn from the ancient native religions of Crete, Asia Minor, and Greece, which, being concerned with the earth and its functions rather than with the sky, were very different forms of belief. They maintained themselves alongside the Olympian religion, especially in the Greek countryside. The Olympian religion, we saw further, failed to meet human needs at their most ultimate, especially concerning death. What goes into Hades is merely the "breath" of man, his breath-soul, as it might be called, and there is thus no genuine human survival of the personality or self. Even the heroes, who at death go into the Elysian fields, have a miserable kind of continuance. The best that could be hoped for from the gods was health, prosperity, and long life.[6]

As compensation for these deficiencies, some of the ancient pre-Hellenic religious beliefs arose again, now developed and purified. During the sixth century B.C. these religions, emphasizing genuine immortality of the personality or full self of man, came into prominence and gained many adherents in the cities of Greece. The Olympian religion as the state religion still continued in its central position, but two of these non-Hellenic religions became noteworthy alongside it: the Eleusinian mysteries and the Orphic mysteries.

Mystery religions can be thought of as those which encompass certain beliefs and rituals which must not be disclosed to anyone who has not yet undergone the rites of purification (initiation). These rituals were believed to provide the initiate with a better way of living in this life and a blessed existence in a life to come. They were very different in type from the Olympian religion, for while the latter was practiced publicly in open temples served by priests who performed the sacrifices and received the gifts, the mysteries were secret, with practices so hidden that even today we are not certain of them. Only initiates were permitted to attend their

[6] Werner Jaeger, *The Theology of the Early Greek Philosophers*, Oxford, Clarendon Press, 1948, p. 74.

meetings. They were often served by priestesses, and women often held the central positions. Associated with the earth rather than the sky, they dealt with man's deepest feelings rather than his rational faculties. They became far more influential in subsequent philosophical and religious thought than the gods of Olympus, for while the latter found their greatest sphere of influence in the life and culture of the people who worshiped them, the mysteries contained ideas possible of great expansion. The Eleusinian mysteries took their name from the city of Eleusis, situated not far from Athens, where they were said to have originated. Orphism was named after its supposed founder, Orpheus. Each was associated with a myth which provided the basis for its doctrines. One needs to be acquainted with these myths to understand the wide appeal of the religions.

The Eleusinian Mysteries

The myth behind the Eleusinian mysteries is the familiar story of Demeter and her daughter Persephone. According to the story, while Persephone is picking flowers one day she is snatched away through an opening in the earth by Hades, lord of the underworld. For nine days Demeter goes to and fro over the earth without tasting either food or drink, vainly looking for her daughter. Finally she learns from Helios (the sun), whose position in the heavens permits him to see all, that Zeus has given Persephone to his brother Hades to become his bride. In her distress Demeter refuses to go to Mount Olympus but disguises herself as an old woman and wanders aimlessly about the earth until she comes to the house of Celeus, a prince in Eleusis. Here she breaks her fast with a mixture of meal and water and pennyroyal tea, and takes a job as nurse to Celeus' son, Triptolemus. She feeds the child ambrosia and is about to make him immortal by plunging him into the fire when Celeus' wife, who has spied on the proceedings, cries out in fear and so fills Demeter with great wrath. Removing her disguise, Demeter tells the king's family who she is—the earth goddess, giver of all their grains—and demands that the people of Eleusis build her a great temple with an altar where, by worshiping her, they may regain her favor. She later teaches Triptolemus the art of agriculture, and through him men learned how to cultivate the soil and grow crops.

But Demeter is so distressed by the continued absence of Persephone that despite the building of a temple according to her order, she sends a great famine which threatens mankind with utter destruction. This is a matter of concern not only to men but to Zeus also, for starving men cannot

Relief from Eleusis

Executed in honor of the great goddesses of Eleusis, Demeter and Persephone, this relief shows Demeter, on the left, presenting to Triptolemus the grain of barley in order that he may teach men the art of agriculture. Persephone, holding an Eleusinian torch, places a wreath on his head. Athens Museum, 5th century B.C.

be counted on to offer generous sacrifices to the gods—and the gods do like generous sacrifices. So great is his concern, in fact, that he gets all the gods of Olympus to try their hand at persuading Demeter to return to them. Failing in this attempt, he persuades Hades to release Persephone; but not until Persephone has eaten a pomegranate seed in the nether realm is she returned to Demeter. Upon her return she learns that since she has eaten food in the world below she must return there for a third of each year, although she may spend the remaining months in the bright atmosphere of Olympus. Demeter, heartened at having her daughter back again, restores grain to the earth. In Greece it springs up generously in the early spring, grows vigorously in the summer, and yields a bountiful harvest in the fall. But in the winter the earth is and always will be dormant because Persephone must ever spend that time of year with Hades in the underworld.

Such is the myth behind the rites which annually took place at Eleusis. Let us see what it must have meant to the Greeks and what it implied to those who took part in the mysteries.

In the first place, this is plainly an allegory of the seasons. Earth does seem to be alive about eight months in the year and dormant for four. Since nature had become completely personified in terms of deities, there had to be a personal explanation of all this. As the basis of a mystery religion, the story of Persephone and Demeter was much more than just a good pictorial explanation, for it was not only history but prophecy as well. If one of earth's (Demeter's) children could die and live again, perhaps that possibility was open to others as well, and man's mortality might be overcome. To the Greek mind this was an appealing thought. But how did one put on the cloak of immortality? Fortunately, a goddess herself had shown the way in the rituals which she disclosed to those fortunate people at Eleusis. To them had come the key to eternal life in the form of sacred rites, which had to be kept secret lest they be corrupted through too general use of them by men not qualified to understand them. However, any true Hellene was eligible to membership in the mystery society, and in fact a considerable amount of missionary zeal was displayed. The rituals whereby one gained immortality have never been fully disclosed, so safely guarded was the secret, but certain aspects of it have become tolerably clear.

One way to enjoy the privilege of godly immortality was to become godlike. This could be achieved by ceremonial repetition of the activities of the god described in the myth. Thus, the candidate for membership in the Eleusinian cult was first introduced in the spring to the Lesser Mysteries, which were essentially rites of purification and preparation. Then he was treated to the dramatic repetition of important phases in the life of Demeter early in the fall at a festival of the Greater Mysteries. Many aspects of Demeter's life were re-enacted. The candidate fasted as Demeter had fasted when searching for her daughter, and the fast was broken with a mixture of meal and water such as that employed in the myth. The candidate went over some of the same country through which Demeter had traveled and sat on the same stone where she had mourned for her lost child. Finally, as a climax to the long celebration, initiates were probably allowed to handle items which the goddess herself had touched, and were given final instruction in all the mysterious meaning attaching to these rites.

It is not hard to see that religion as it was represented by such mysteries was of an infinitely more personal and emotional type than anything known to the Greeks in the Olympian religion. Here each individual participated in such a way as to be made over into the likeness of the god he worshiped. The fasting and the drama combined to induce an ecstasy of religious fervor to be prized above the more routine experience of ordinary sacrificial worship. The promise that membership in the cult meant immortality was no less pleasing to the Greeks than it is to modern men. Little wonder that the mysteries celebrated at Eleusis came to have Panhellenic significance, that they were made a part of the state religion at Athens, and that they lasted well into the period of Roman domination. It was at Eleusis that the Roman Julian the Apostate, was initiated in his youth; and the sanctuary remained until Alaric the Goth, who overran Rome in A.D. 410, destroyed it.

The Orphic Mysteries

The mysteries celebrated at Eleusis were the most widespread of the Greek mysteries, but they were probably less influential for subsequent thought than was the Orphic mystery, which developed about the sixth century B.C. in connection with the ancient religion of Dionysus. The figure of the god Dionysus is a remarkable one. Not originally an Olympian god, he represented various aspects of human life in the earlier days of his worship. Parades in which phallic symbols were displayed were held in his honor, thus pointing to his power as a nature god who made for procreation. Generally he is portrayed with a bunch of grapes and a pine cone, referring to the wine of Greece which was, and still is, made with pine resin added as a preservative. But the association of wine with Dionysus signifies much more than mere drunkenness, to which the Greeks were not prone. Dionysus is the god who enters into the human body in wine and temporarily releases the soul from the body, bringing ecstasy. In an extreme form, this might mean madness, but Dionysus could also cure madness.

In ancient times, the Maenads (inspired or mad ones, also called the Bacchae) were women followers of Dionysus who, inspired by wine, music, and dancing to the point where they quite lost consciousness of what they were doing, tore to pieces and ate raw any living thing that crossed their paths. Tradition holds that Orpheus, the legendary reformer and purifier of the Dionysiac rites, was himself killed as he tried to interfere with a group of Maenads in their ecstatic madness.

This same god Dionysus was also the father of the drama, for in the festival honoring Dionysus called the Greater Dionysia, ritual dances were held about the altar of Dionysus. As time passed, monologue and then dialogue were added until a primitive form of drama had evolved. The earliest official recognition of drama as a culture form was given in the year 534 B.C. when the first dramatic contest was held.

Dionysus is thus seen to be a complex figure representing the vital, ecstatic, non-rational aspects of life. It appears that during the sixth century B.C. this crude religion, gaining in popularity, was purified and reconstructed by a historic personage named Orpheus, a lover of music.[7] The Orphic religion which now appeared was far more rational and mystical and far less ecstatic and crude than the Dionysus cult. Orpheus gave it spiritual significance. He replaced the temporary ecstasy, brought about through the use of wine and music, by a spiritual ecstasy, brought about through discipline and rites of purification.[8] Unlike the Olympian religion in which even to wish to be like the gods was thought to incur the guilt of *hubris*, this religion specifically aimed at transforming humanity into divinity while in this life, thus assuring immortality, an attribute of the gods.

We turn now to the basic myth of this Orphic religion. This story, which appears in a variety of forms, relates that Zagreus (another name for Dionysus), son of Zeus and Persephone, was torn to pieces by the evil Titans, earth powers who were warring against Zeus himself. They ate the body, but Athena rescued the heart and took it to Zeus. From it Zagreus returned to life as Dionysus, son of Zeus and Semele. A second part of the myth adds that Zeus destroyed the Titans in punishment, and eventually out of their ashes man came to be.

Here, as in the Demeter-Persephone story, we have a myth centered about a nature deity. The god is twice-born, and consequently, as with Persephone, the possibility of immortality is suggested to his worshipers. The second part

[7] Harrison, *op. cit.*, pp. 455, 469, 566 ff.
[8] *Ibid.*, p. 476.

of the myth contains material for explaining man's dual physical and spiritual nature and the necessity of putting off the physical man in order to enjoy true being as an immortal. According to the account, men sprang from the ashes of the Titans destroyed by Zeus' thunderbolt. Now, since the Titans had eaten Dionysus (Zagreus) before their destruction, men made from their ashes contain both a mortal element, derived from the deposed Titans, and also a spark of the divine, from Dionysus whom they had devoured. The goal of a man's life, therefore, was to free the divine and immortal soul from the mortal prison house of the body which was also a part of his natural heritage. One of the sayings of the Orphics, found on a gold tablet lying by the remains of one of their members, was, "I am a child of earth, but also of starry heaven."

The purpose of the Orphic mystery was to provide a means of freeing the prisoner, the immortal soul; the task was no easy one, and had in fact to be done by degrees. The rituals employed consisted essentially, it is thought, in dramatic repetition of the various myths of Dionysus, especially that of his death and rebirth, much as the Eleusinian rituals probably re-enacted phases of the life of Demeter.

We have said that the soul's salvation came only by degrees. This introduces the notion of successive incarnations of the soul, called the doctrine of *metempsychosis.* This belief may well have originated in India, where it was widespread at that time as it is today. It may have come by way of Babylonia and Egypt to Greece. The vegetarianism and the formulas summarizing the idea of the wheel of rebirths are the same in Orphic and Hindu teaching.[9] According to later Orphic belief, the soul that went on at death was not just an unthinking, unfeeling life-soul but a consciousness-soul, the real self, separable from the body. At death it went first to Hades, where the righteous lived for a period more or less pleasantly and the wicked suffered; but the stay there was only temporary, for the soul was fated to pass into another body and begin life over again, either as another person or as an animal, depending upon the extent of its purification. This weary round of existences in various forms continued as long as the soul did not discover the means of escaping from it. To help the soul escape was the primary object of the Orphic ritual and its way of life. Vegetarianism was demanded of members of the cult, for since human souls might inhabit animal bodies, the slaying of animals could conceivably have disastrous results. Certain other foods were forbidden for various reasons, and a moderately ascetic life seems to have been the general rule. Whether the purified soul that escaped the cycle of rebirths was finally united with the god worshiped or

[9] Theodor Gomperz, *Greek Thinkers,* London, John Murray, 1920, p. 127.

lived on in blissful individuality is not entirely clear, but we know that souls were rewarded and punished throughout the course of their transmigrations, especially during their temporary visits to Hades. The Orphic description of souls immersed in mud and filth suggests punishments for the wicked that even Dante could hardly exceed in his picture of the Inferno.

Let us now look briefly at the general religious outlook of the mysteries as contrasted to the Olympian religion. In the first place, the mysteries were other-worldly religions as opposed to Olympianism whose values were all for this world. To the Orphic, man is a son of both earth and heaven, and his heavenly nature can be fully realized through the right rituals. Also, the Olympian gods were worshiped that they might be pleased and so send immediate benefits to the worshiper, whereas the dramatic rituals of the mystery religions were attempts to become godlike and so share in immortality. Orphism was destined to loom large in the philosophic teachings of Pythagoras and Empedocles. It colored the work of Heraclitus, the Eleatics, Socrates, and Plato, and in Christian times it influenced Neo-Platonism, coming directly through it into the Christian tradition.

One tendency in the Orphic mysteries which was new to Greek thought but which was destined to be important historically was the drift toward pantheism, which is also a step toward monotheism. Certain Orphic verses express the thought that there is "one Zeus, one Hades, one Sun, one Dionysus, one god in all." This suggestion of a unity in all things is a far cry from the pluralism of the Olympians and is a foretaste of the more carefully elucidated pantheism of later philosophy.

The lack of rigorous moral requirements in many instances and the idea that simple initiation into the mysteries was both a sufficient and a necessary basis for salvation were to prove repulsive to many Greek minds who were not slow to advance criticism of this notion. When told that association with the mysteries could guarantee salvation of the soul and that no salvation was possible apart from such association, Diogenes is said to have asked, "What do you mean? Is Pataikion the thief going to have a better lot after death than Epaminondas, just because he was initiated?" This type of moral criticism of Greek religious ideas came largely from the poets and philosophers of Greece, and we now turn to view their contribution to the subject.

Religion Among the Later Poets

Among the Hebrews the priests became the conservators of traditional religious ideals, and the prophets were the innovators. The history of Judaism could be largely written in terms of these two classes. But in Greece it was Homer, a poet, who provided the people with a bible and it was the later dramatists and philosophers who refined the religious teachings handed down to them. The philosophers especially remind us of the major prophets of Israel, for they were bold enough to insist that religious ideas are not necessarily good simply because they happen to be old. The fifth century B.C. in Greece saw the development of those great dramatic and philosophical figures whose names are even more permanent than the statues of them which immortal artists produced in the same age. During this period Greece repulsed the Persians, and the Greek spirit expanded with the new feeling of power which victory brings. The dramatists of the times, especially Aeschylus, Sophocles, and Euripides, became, along with poets like Pindar, important religious teachers. Their conceptions were based largely on Homeric ideas, but they refined the earlier notions and so discarded many of the crasser elements which belonged to the sixth century. The real radicals among the new religious teachers were the philosophers like Xenophanes, the Sophists, Socrates, and others, but before turning to them let us take a brief glance at how religion fared among the literati.

A century before the Periclean age, considered the Golden Age of Greece, there appeared a poet whose sentiments about religion are strikingly like those expressed in the Old Testament by the author of Ecclesiastes and by Job. This was *Theognis* (flourished *ca.* 520 B.C.), and while he wrote ostensibly to show the importance of humility and proper worship of the gods and believed that good and evil both came from Zeus, yet like Job he was much troubled by the problem of human suffering. When he tells us that it is best not to be born at all and second best to die young, we see that his despair was equal to that of his spiritual cousins in Palestine. But Theognis' message is not one wholly of despair. Poverty and evil may be the test of a man, sent to try his character if it be good, for the good man will think always of justice regardless of the price it costs him. This marks some moral progress over anything found in Homer, but in most other respects Theognis contributed little to traditional conceptions.

The greater poets and dramatists whom we have just mentioned carried religion to new heights of moral significance. Their work was predominantly of a religious nature. Much of Pindar's poetry was in the form of odes dedicated to the victors at the great religious-athletic festivals like those held in honor of Zeus, Apollo, or Poseidon; and the great tragedians, Aeschylus and Sophocles, produced their plays for performance at the religious festival connected with the worship of Dionysus. While the primary purpose of each of these men was artistic, their subject matter was such as to disclose the current religious tendencies.

Pindar

Pindar (522-448 B.C.) is conservative in his religious outlook and does not depart greatly from the Homeric pattern, but his work shows some new emphases. His gods are thought of as holding all power and as knowing all, whereas Homer presented them as being merely very wise and unusually powerful. Furthermore, Pindar insists on truthfulness as a prime characteristic of deity, whereas for Homer veracity was not an outstanding virtue. Another aspect of Pindar's writing which indicates an increased moral sensitivity is his unwillingness to relate many of the grosser tales which had been told about the gods, and his insistence on absolute justice as a divine trait. For him, as for many of the Hebrew prophets, righteousness and reverence were virtues which heaven rewarded, and no wicked man could know bliss for long. On the question of human freedom Pindar is ambiguous, as are most of his colleagues, and seems torn between the notions that everything is assigned by Fate and that man's own actions bring his fate to pass. Quite in keeping with the Greek tradition, Pindar looks upon excess as the chief sin of man; but unlike Homer he envisions the results of sin as reaching indefinitely into the future, for he has not been untouched by the mysteries, and so shares their doctrine of future rewards and punishments. Morality and religion, as reflected in his *Odes*, were lifted to a higher plane, but he provided no radical innovations, nor could he have been as important from a religious point of view as were Aeschylus and Sophocles.

Aeschylus

Aeschylus (525-456 B.C.), the father of the drama, and Sophocles, his younger rival, derive the subject matter for their plays from the old tales which had been handed down, but in their treatment of them a new morality is fostered. In Aeschylus' famous trilogy, the *Oresteia* (458 B.C.), composed of *Agamemnon*, *The Choephoroe*, and *The Eumenides*, we find the cause, the course, and the cure of sin laid bare in terms as certain as those of the greatest of the Hebrew prophets and with all the force that tragic drama can provide. The highlights of the story which these three plays unfold can be told briefly and the implications for morality and religion pointed to, but the influence which the dramatic presentations must have had on Athenian audiences can only be guessed at.

The Greek Theatre of Epidaurus

This is the best preserved of the ancient Greek theaters, famed for their remarkable acoustics and their striking locations. Although the highest row of seats is nearly 200 feet from the orchestra, every word spoken there in a normal tone of voice can be heard.

According to the conventions of antiquity, it became the task in every case of murder for the next of kin to seek blood vengeance. Greek tradition was in this respect just like the Mosaic code as outlined in the thirty-fifth chapter of Numbers: blood vengeance, places of refuge, and the doctrine of "an eye for an eye" were provided for by both the Hebrew and the Greek traditions. It is altogether possible that Aeschylus wrote this particular trilogy to win the Greeks away from what must have struck him as a very primitive custom.

In *Agamemnon* we learn that a curse has fallen on the family of Atreus and is now made manifest in the life of Agamemnon, son of Atreus, king of Mycenae. Pride has made King Agamemnon a fit subject for punishment, and to placate the gods who deprive him of favoring winds while he and his fleet are sailing for Troy, he sacrifices his daughter, Iphigenia. On his return his wife, Clytemnestra, slays him, ostensibly to avenge her daughter's death but partly for selfish reasons. She thus sets the stage for the next step in the endless cycle of blood revenge. The second phase constitutes that part of the trilogy called *The Choephoroe* which introduces Orestes, son of Agamemnon and Clytemnestra, as the central figure.

The Choephoroe (libation bearers) opens with the exiled Orestes returning home for no other purpose than to avenge his father's blood by slaying his slayer. The horrible dilemma in which Orestes has become involved provides a most intense dramatic situation. His religious duty demands that he avenge his father, but this makes it necessary that he slay his mother, thus breaking the moral code. He does so, however, and is revolted by the deed he has done.

The Eumenides (kindly ones), the concluding part of the trilogy, opens with Orestes seeking solace at the temple of Apollo. The god appears and directs Orestes to go to Athens where he will be tried for matricide by a just jury. The jury is deadlocked, but an acquittal is brought about when Athena, goddess of wisdom, herself casts the deciding vote in Orestes' favor.

We see from the plays that Aeschylus is convinced that men live in a moral universe where things happen according to the will of almighty and eminently just Zeus. Even suffering can be explained, for "Justice doth wait to teach wisdom by suffering," and Fate is made bearable because it is made moral.

The tendency to believe both in Fate and in individual responsibility (with its implication of human freedom) is marked in Aeschylus as in most of the Greek writers; and if the two ideas were never thoroughly reconciled, let those complain who can do greater justice to the facts of experience. Aeschylus says bluntly, "Fate will have its way"; but he then proceeds to show that Orestes escapes what would normally be the fated consequences of his act by acts of piety, obedience to the will of Apollo, and by willingness to be judged by wisdom (as we have seen, the final verdict rests with Athena). Moreover, Orestes is innocent of any other evil than that for which he is tried. "Impious deeds conspire to beget an offspring of impious deeds," but apparently an honorable man, willing to walk according to the law of Zeus, can break the evil spell of Fate which may have dogged his family for generations. To some extent the destiny of individuals is not beyond their control.

That Aeschylus is conscious of introducing something new into Greek religious ideas is evidenced by the fact that the Furies, spirits of vengeance, become in the closing part of the drama the Eumenides, beneficent spirits who protect Athens. Moreover, when the law of wisdom deprives the avenging spirits (before their transformation) from taking full toll for Orestes' crime, they sing:

> Curse on your cause,
> Ye gods that are younger!
> O'er the time-hallowed laws
> Rough ye ride as the stronger.
> Of the prey that was ours,
> Ye with rude hands bereave us.[10]

To this Athena answers shortly, "Be ruled by me!" In sum, Aeschylus seems to be conscious of introducing a new and more moral element into religion, though in his treatment of religion he is less radical than Euripides, of whom we must make brief mention.

Sophocles and Euripides

As somewhat younger contemporaries of Aeschylus, both Sophocles (495-406 B.C.) and Euripides (480-406 B.C.) did much to shape Greek religious ideas. Of the two, Sophocles was far more conservative in temper regarding religious matters, and looked upon piety and discretion as fundamental virtues. He might be compared with the Hebrew prophet Hosea in contrast to the Amos-like Aeschylus who spoke much about divine justice but little about divine mercy. One sentence from Sophocles should indicate this contrast: "Zeus on his mighty throne keeps mercy in all he does to counsel him." Vastly concerned with the tragedy of human life, inexplicable as much of it is, he turned the discords of human suffering and conflict into poetry. Like Aeschylus, Sophocles taught that suffering may be an avenue to wisdom. But for all this, Sophocles was still conservative and retained most of the traditional notions about the gods. The difference between this essential conservatism, common to both Aeschylus and Sophocles, and the more radical temperament of Euripides can be brought out by comparison of one fundamental concept.

According to a fragment from Sophocles, "Nothing to which the gods lead men is base." While this shows some moral progress over Homer, it is still a far cry from the humanistic radicalism of Euripides, who says, "If the gods do aught that is base, then they are not gods."[11] This statement shows a

[10] *The Eumenides*, lines 778-782.
[11] Fragment 19.

willingness to judge theology by standards of justice rather than to judge justice by the traditional standards of theology; and indeed, Euripides, unlike his forerunners, was ready to hold traditional notions up to scorn. The immorality of the traditional gods, the reliance on divinations, and many other religious practices and beliefs of the period are mocked in his dramas. One of his characters says of Hera, who through jealousy has wronged him, "To such a Goddess who shall pray now?" Another, in answer to the question, "What is a seer?" replies, "A man who speaks few truths and many lies." Here is a radicalism not evident earlier, and yet it does not mean that Euripides was bent on ridiculing all religion; it means merely that he had caught a glimpse of something better than was being practiced. He seems to point the way to a monotheistic conception such as that held by some of the later philosophers. Witness the following passage:

> O Earth's upbearer, thou whose throne is Earth,
> Whoe'er thou be, O past our finding out,
> Zeus, be thou Nature's law, or Mind of Man,
> To thee I pray.[12]

This is the articulation of a new spirit that was dawning among the intellectual leaders of Greece, a spirit which found its fullest fruition among the philosophers of the Periclean age.

Those who contributed most to the development of Greek religious ideas from the time of Euripides on were the philosophers. We shall postpone discussion of their notions until we consider their philosophical systems in the next chapters. One of the earliest, who was as much religious teacher as philosopher, may be mentioned here by way of introduction to philosophy proper. He is Xenophanes of Colophon in Ionia, who lived during the latter part of the sixth and the first half of the fifth centuries B.C.

Xenophanes

An intellectual revolutionary, Xenophanes struck out boldly at the anthropomorphism of the period, ridiculing the Greeks for making the gods in their own image by pointing out that the Ethiopians looked upon their gods as black and having flat noses, while the Thracians were sure the gods, like themselves, were blue-eyed and red-haired. If cattle could draw, he said, they would doubtless present the gods as being in their image too. In view of this, it was high time that the Greeks got away from the primitive notions bequeathed them by Homer and Hesiod and developed more rational understandings of deity. All the things that happen in the world about are due to

[12] *The Trojan Women*, lines 884-887.

natural causes, not to the gods. They did not give men civilization, but men in time created their culture and steadily improved it. A more rational conception of a god, he thought, is to be found in pantheism—the doctrine that God is the same as the universe. This doctrine will be found in subsequent writers, and we shall pay fuller attention to it later on. This one god, said Xenophanes, sees, thinks, and hears as a whole. He is unlike man in shape and in mind. There is, therefore, a single god for all men.

The free spirit of criticism manifest in Xenophanes indicates the initiation of a new movement in Greek culture, one destined to offer in the course of several centuries a more radical reconstruction of religious and philosophical ideas than had come about in the whole history of Greek thought up to this time. This new movement is the birth of philosophy proper.

Questions for Study

1. What differences do you find between Hebrews and Greeks in geographical and cultural factors and in their views on the nature of life?
2. Who were the Minoans and Mycenaeans, and what were their achievements? Where did the early Greeks come from? What two cultures mingled to form the later Greeks?
3. Distinguish between the Hellenic and Hellenistic periods of Greek history. What was the relation between the city-state and political disunity?
4. What was the nature of early Greek religion? Distinguish the native religion from that of the Aryan invaders.
5. What was the significance of Homer and Hesiod for the Greek Olympian religion? How did Homer portray the gods?
6. What function did the oracles perform? Compare and contrast these to the Hebrew prophets in function and procedure.
7. What was the importance of *Moira* in Homer's religion? How would such a concept affect one's attitudes toward the gods? How was evil accounted for? How was the afterlife pictured?
8. What lacks in the Olympian religion led people to the mysteries, and how did these make up for the deficiencies? What are the myths, the aims, and the methods of reaching these aims in the Eleusinian and Orphic mysteries? Where does the figure of Dionysus enter the Orphic mystery, and how does it happen that Greek drama arose from ceremonies in his honor? What qualities in human experience are represented by Dionysus?
9. What is the doctrine of metempsychosis? For those holding this belief, what was considered to be salvation?
10. What significant contributions in religious thought were made by Theognis, Pindar, Aeschylus, Sophocles, and Euripides?
11. Think of Hebrew understandings of God and man–God a Covenant-making

God, the meaning of suffering, the nature of man. By contrast, consider Homer's emphases on Fate, the nature of the gods and their relation to man, the nature of man, determinism, and the meaninglessness of life and history. How would you account for these differences?

Selected Readings

Bowra, Maurice, *Ancient Greek Literature,* London, Oxford University Press, 1959.

Cornford, F. M., *Greek Religious Thought*, Boston, Beacon Press, 1950.

Hadas, Moses, *A History of Greek Literature,* New York, Columbia University Press, 1950.

Harrison, Jane E., *Prolegomena to the Study of Greek Religion,* 3rd ed., Cambridge, Cambridge University Press, 1922.

Jaeger, Werner, *Paideia: the Ideals of Greek Culture,* New York, Oxford University Press, 1945, vol. I.

Kitto, H. D. F., *The Greeks,* Baltimore, Penguin Books, Inc., 1959.

Moore, C. H., *The Religious Thought of the Greeks,* Cambridge, Harvard University Press, 1925.

Murray, Gilbert, *Five Stages of Greek Religion,* New York, Columbia University Press, 1925.

Nilsson, Martin P., *A History of Greek Religion,* Oxford University Press, 1949.

8. The Beginnings of Western Thought

When we distinguish philosophy from religion, we are separating two interests of man which have many things in common. We have already discovered that Greek religion involved some speculation about the nature of things, and to the extent that it did so it was philosophical. That is to say, it included a primitive sort of metaphysics or theory of reality. Then, too, Greek religion was concerned somewhat with human conduct, and was in that regard like another branch of philosophy called ethics. When men concern themselves with problems of reality and conduct for their own sake quite apart from their implications for worship, we detect the emergence of a specifically philosophic attitude as distinguished from a religious one. In the tradition of ancient Greece, this more objective attitude appeared first in connection with a man named Thales (flourished *ca.* 600 B.C.), and in the course of several hundred years developed into a number of fairly complete philosophic systems. Not all of these systems were favorable to religious ideas since the speculative intellect may discard earlier notions and may even find itself entertaining ideas opposing the traditionally accepted ones.

Each of us has some elementary sort of philosophy of life. We believe that the world is thus and so, and that we can live best in such and such a fashion. In short, we entertain at least rudimentary notions about metaphysics and ethics. Few of us, however, take the pains necessary to examine our various attitudes and ideas and to make certain that they are consistent with each other. It is at this point that the philosopher differs from the layman. The philosopher makes a business of analyzing his various beliefs, endeavoring to arrange them into a systematic and consistent whole. If he is concerned chiefly with problems of the nature of reality, we describe his interest as metaphysical; if his emphasis is placed on problems of conduct or on determining the meaning of the good life, we describe his interest as ethical. The Greek philosophers were interested in both these problems. We shall discover that they developed a number of different theories about each, and we will acquaint ourselves with the more important of these. Let us begin by looking at some of the first of these thinkers and their theories of reality.

Thales, Father of Western Philosophy

All the things with which we become acquainted in ordinary experience come into being, persist for a while, and then disappear. Even the "everlasting hills" are not *ever*lasting; they simply last somewhat longer than the chipmunk which makes his home there. Eventually the hills too will fall prey to the "gnawing tooth of time." But whence did they come, and whither do they go? What is the stuff of which they are made and to which they return? To ask questions like these is to express interest in metaphysics, and Thales is credited with having been the first Greek to approach such questions philosophically.

What Thales actually did was to pose a question and seek its answer in a particular way. Naturally, others then took up the problem in hope of finding better solutions than the one he arrived at, and so the philosophical venture was begun. What was this important question which has kept the world busy theorizing for some 2500 years? Actually, it was a very simple matter, for Thales merely dared to wonder whether there might be some one fundamental world-stuff which could take the form of chipmunks and mountains and somehow continue to exist when these particular things had disappeared in time. In other words, he approached in a new way the question: what is the true nature of reality?

Most people are content to believe that the world is made up of a number of things; but when you stop to think about it, it does seem reasonable to suppose that possibly these many things all have something in common, some underlying substance which is the basis of all existence. A moment's reflection on a glass of milk may show the reasonableness of thinking along these lines. What is the *stuff* which changes from clover into milk, and then as we drink it is turned by our own body chemistry into bone and flesh and blood? What is the substance that remains throughout all changing forms? This was Thales' question. Somebody had to ask this question before philosophy and science could begin. Before we examine Thales' answer, we must look briefly at the background of his period.

It would be an error to think that an absolute break in thought appeared between Thales and his predecessors. Hesiod, living a century and a half earlier, had also asked about the nature of reality, but his question and the answer he gave it were contained within a framework that is properly called mythological. His solution was given in terms of the gods: Demeter, Aphrodite, Zeus, and others make things happen as they do. A vast difference comes at the point where Thales leaves the mythological framework behind and approaches the problem of nature, called in Greek *physis* (from which we get the word *physics*), in a fresh and amazingly independent way.

The independence of mind that Thales and his immediate successors displayed sprang at least partly from their environment. Thales lived in Ionia, in the city of Miletus. Although overshadowed by the importance of Athens in later Greek history, Miletus was one of the greatest of the Hellenic cities in the sixth century B.C. Founded more than a thousand years earlier, it was a great trading center, drawing its wealth from the hinterland of Asia Minor and maintaining relations with Egypt, Lydia, and the East. In the course of its history it founded more than 40 colonies, some as distant as the Black Sea. Its location on the eastern end of the Mediterranean, where the Meander River meandered into the sea, gave it a commanding position. Because of the complete personal independence the city allowed its citizens, it was possible for them to be quite independent in their thinking of the older ways of looking at things.

Little is known of Thales himself, although a number of stories about him have come down to us. We are told that he was the first Western astronomer, having learned about the stars from the Mesopotamians. He correctly predicted an eclipse. He taught geometry, whose elements he learned from the Egyptians, but is said to have taught them later how to measure the height of their pyramids. To prove that he was not just an impractical thinker, he once leased many olive presses in advance of the harvest, from his knowledge of agriculture foreseeing a bumper crop, and so made a huge profit for himself.

Nothing is left us of what he wrote. The three sayings attributed to him reach us through Aristotle, who quotes him as having said that water is the origin (the *physis*) of all; that all things are full of gods (or alive); and that the loadstone (magnet) has a soul (life) because it moves iron. Exactly what he meant by these statements cannot be known with certainty, but it appears clear that he did not regard matter, as we do, as inert and lifeless in itself and moved by purely mechanical forces. He seems closer in this respect to the thought of Hesiod than to our own, for he saw the world as alive, a world in which objects are inhabited by a life of their own. Thus, the magnet through its life draws iron to itself, and all things must be full of life since they are in motion, acting upon other things. Such a view is called *hylozoism* or *animatism.*

The Greeks generally thought of the world as being made up of four different and distinct substances: earth, water, air, and fire. Since the philosophizing mind looks for a single, unifying explanation of things, it is not content to say that four different substances are the basic reality. Thales, then, looking for the answer to the question of reality, said that there is one basic substance out of which everything comes and to which it again returns. This substance is water. We must recognize that in saying this he meant something other than the inert substance H_2O which we think of as water. He appears to have meant that the living substance called water mysteriously transforms itself into all the other forms of our physical universe; it is the single visible *something* which is the invisible reality and force behind the scenes of all that is and that happens.[1]

Just why Thales chose water in preference to one of the other basic substances is not clear. Possibly it was because his home was by the ocean, and he is said to have taught that the earth floats on the ocean. Possibly too he observed that deltas are built up at the mouth of rivers and supposed that this resulted from water turning into earth. He may have thought of the moisture which collects on the surface of a jug as air turning into water. Further, he may have recalled that Hesiod had stated that Ocean is the genesis of all. Aristotle comments later that Thales may have gotten his idea from the fact that the "nourishment of all things is moist" and "from observing that the germs of all things are moist, and moist things have water as the first principle of their nature."[2]

Be this as it may, what distinguishes Thales fundamentally from Homer, Hesiod, and his other predecessors is that in turning away from their mythological explanations, he put his question and answered it in terms of what his own reason, having examined the facts of human experience, was able to bring forth as a seemingly good solution. With Thales, therefore, philosophical speculation arose. After him it was confidently believed that man's *mind* or *reason* is capable of finding its own solutions as a result of contact with the world of experience.

[1] Richard Kroner, *Speculation in Pre-Christian Philosophy,* Philadelphia, The Westminster Press, 1956, pp. 76-81.

[2] Charles F. Bakewell, *Source Book in Ancient Philosophy,* New York, Charles Scribner's Sons, 1907, p. 2.

In modern times this confidence in the power of man's reason is so fundamental to our scientific research that we can easily fail to recognize the revolutionary importance of what Thales did. From his time onward, Greek and later Western thinkers will stand before the world and say, "If I use my reason clearly and well, I can discover through it the answers to the most basic questions of reality." Not only the world in its changes but the world in its deepest, most mysterious characteristics is thus thought to be open to the reflective mind of man. This is the first and most fundamental contribution of Thales' philosophizing.

There is a second significant intellectual implication in Thales' approach to nature. Its secrets are to be sought *within* the phenomena of nature itself rather than in myths which point beyond nature. We can see in this emphasis and in the emphasis upon reason the beginnings of what we would today call a scientific interpretation of things. Further, Thales assumed that in spite of all appearances to the contrary, nature is one whole. Life, mind, and matter are all to be explained fundamentally in terms of a single, fundamental substance.

It is his discovery of these three principles, each basic to the development of later Western philosophy, that justifies Thales' being designated the father of Western philosophy.

Were this a study of the history of philosophy, it would be interesting and instructive to investigate how far Thales' great successors in the Milesian school, Anaximander and Anaximenes, of whom we know much more than we do of Thales himself, carried forward his search into the problem of the nature of *physis*. Regretfully, we turn aside from these two men, contenting ourselves with remarking that they accept the three principles mentioned above, even while disagreeing with Thales' suggestion that water is the fundamental *physis*.

Following the Milesians a great many thinkers appeared who contributed to the growing stream of speculation. We shall name only four of these who stand out in such ways that we will want to look at each briefly as we carry this account up to Socrates and Plato. These four are Pythagoras, Heraclitus, Parmenides, and Democritus.

Pythagoras—a Mathematical Theory of Reality

Since Pythagoras flourished between 550 and 510 B.C. and founded his great religious order in 532 B.C., he was one of the earliest of the Greek thinkers and one of the most influential in his contribution to later thought. His home was on the island of Samos, just off the coast of Asia Minor, so it is practically certain that he was in touch with his close neighbors, the Ionian philosophers. Some of his thought had a close resemblance to theirs. In this account we will look first at some of the ideas usually attributed to him, and then point out his significance for Western philosophy.

The Pythagorean Order, founded at the old Achaean colony of Croton in southern Italy to which Pythagoras had gone from Samos, was an order closely allied to the mystery religions, especially to Orphism. Like the Orphics, Pythagoras taught metempsychosis. Most people, he said, forget their previous lives when they are reborn, but he claimed to be able to remember all his previous lives. This assertion reminds us of the teachings of Gautama the Buddha in India during this same century, for he also claimed to be able to recall his previous lives. Some human souls, said Pythagoras, might return as animals in a later existence, but he himself had always been a human being. He further taught that the great purpose of human life is to prepare for the real life beyond death. Body and soul are two different and separable entities. The body needs strict attention and control so that it will serve the soul well as its instrument. Special care must be given to the cultivation of the intellect through the study of mathematics, to the disciplining of the emotions, and to the proper care of the body so as to prepare for the next existence. Within the Order, strict rules were enforced concerning personal habits, diet, and study. Pythagoras himself eventually came to be considered a god, a mouthpiece of the god Apollo.

Our chief interest lies in his philosophic ideas, of which we have some general knowledge but lack certain understanding of his meaning at many points. Unlike the Milesians, Pythagoras was not seeking for a simple *physis* of which the whole world is made. His thought took a new direction which had added a fundamental element to the thought of the Western world and provided part of the basis for science. He discovered the significance of mathematics.

Mathematics is an abstract rather than a concrete study. One does not see or touch numbers and numerical relations. Through the senses one can know things that illustrate these relations, but the relations themselves are not sensed. Here, then, is the realm of the abstract that is to be entered directly only through reason. Students today as in that day can experience for themselves the joy—or difficulty—of discovering the realm of the abstract as they begin the study of arithmetic and geometry. Two fields of study may help us realize how the Pythagoreans approached this understanding.

First, they investigated the study of music carefully, for they were deeply interested in harmony, which is more essential in music than in any other art form. They found that if a taut string, as on a musical instrument, is divided in the exact middle, the tone produced by either half is just one octave above the tone produced by the entire string. That is, if the tone of the entire string is low mi, the half-string is high mi. If, next, the same string is divided at the three-quarters point, the tone produced is la above low mi. Should the next division be at the two-thirds point the tone produced is si. The mathematical ratios expressing these relations are 2:1, 3:2, and 4:3 respectively. That is to say, the concordant intervals of the scale can be expressed as 6 8 9 12 when 12 represents the length of the entire string. Many additional relationships can be discovered quite readily by further investigation. These may be as far as Pythagoras carried his experiments, but they are sufficient to demonstrate that mathematical relations are the foundation of harmony in music.

Second, the Pythagoreans studied numbers themselves directly, and came to conclusions about them difficult for us to understand. They said, for instance, that things are numbers, and seemed actually to mean that numbers are just as much things as water is a thing. This is what Aristotle understood them to say when he wrote: "These philosophers evidently regarded number as the first principle, both as being the material cause of things that exist and as describing their qualities and states as well."[3]

It appears certain that in their mathematics they used pebbles laid into geometrical forms, and in so doing are said to have developed the famous Pythagorean theorem in a mathematical way (rather than geometrically, which probably had a far earlier origin). They spoke of "triangular numbers," formed by placing series of successive natural integers in rows like this:

•
• •
• • •

There were also "square" and "oblong" numbers, the former the products of equal factors and the latter products of unequal factors, formed like this, of pebbles or marbles:

square number
• • •
• • •
• • •

oblong number
• • • •
• • • •
• • • •

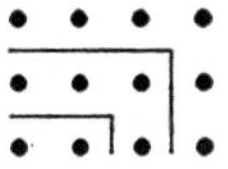

Adding successive odd numbers to a square number produces successive square numbers: 1 + 3 + 5, etc. gives the squares of 1, 2, 3, etc. Adding successive even numbers produces oblong numbers: 2 + 4 + 6, etc.[4]

Although we cannot follow the ideas of the thinkers of the Pythagorean school when they assert that numbers are things, we can follow them in

[3] *Ibid.*, p. 37.
[4] John Burnet, *Greek Philosophy*, London, Macmillan & Company, Ltd., 1953, pp. 45-54.

understanding that in mathematics are found harmonious relationships which are unchanging. Anyone who has dealt with figures must be struck by the fact of the unvaryingness of numerical relationships: 2×5, for instance, is *always* 10. If no step in a geometric demonstration contains an error and each step is based upon already proven presuppositions, the conclusions reached *must* be valid. Furthermore, numbers and geometric relations apply to the real world in which we live—to *this* world, as everyone knows well. Through principles of triangulation the heights of buildings can be determined; in keeping accounts no variation in the behavior of figures is ever discovered. This suggests a principle, implict if not explicit in the Pythagoreans, of the most far-reaching importance for all future thought: that number is the key for understanding the world. We will later see how this influenced Plato in very fundamental ways and became the actual ground upon which modern science was constructed, starting with the ideas of Copernicus.[5] Reality (that which is unchanging) is numbers and numerical relations. Not the objects of the senses, which we see and touch and taste, but these invisibles, known by the mind of the thinker, unchanging, eternal—*these* are the real. This suggests further that beneath the variety of the world there is actual simplicity, that law and not chance rules, and that the universe itself is based on reason.[6] At every point, these ideas are basic to modern thought.

Heraclitus

Possibly the most fascinating figure in pre-Socratic philosophy was that of Heraclitus (*ca.* 535-475 B.C.) who lived in the Ionian city of Ephesus, lying to the north of Miletus. Five or more centuries later, St. Paul visited this same city on one of his missionary journeys and lived and taught there for a period.

Of the teaching of Heraclitus a number of brief, rather cryptic sayings have come down to us. From these and from reports by his successors we can build a fairly clear picture of his thought. His starting point is sense experience rather than abstract or mathematical reasoning. Three elements seem to make up this teaching, each of which we will take up in turn. These are, first, that nothing remains the same, for everything is in a process of constant and eternal change. Second, beneath this process of change there is a basic unity. Third, there is a divine law, which he calls the *logos*, because of which knowledge is possible.

[5] See the discussion of Copernicus, pp. 500-505.

[6] H. D. F. Kitto, *The Greeks*, Baltimore, Penguin Books, Inc., 1959, p. 90.

Looking at the obvious facts of experience, Heraclitus made the statement that in the world of things there is nothing permanent and unchanging. On the contrary, all things are in a process of constant flux. We cannot step into the same river twice, he wrote, for by the second step the river has moved, so neither the river nor we are the same. The tempo of change varies with different things, as we see if we compare the duration of a rainbow, let us say, with that of a mountain or a chunk of lead. Yet all things do change, and we look in vain for anything that remains always the same. The symbol Heraclitus used for change is fire, since the process of burning is one of change in its most obvious form.

From this starting point he proceeded to his main emphases. To have gone no further would have been to maintain that there is no basic unity or oneness in reality, but only a kind of picture-play of changing forms and qualities. He believed, however, that beneath this process of change is a basic unity. There is constant upward and downward motion, each thing moving toward its opposite and back again. "Fire lives the death of air, and air the death of fire; water lives the death of earth, and earth the death of water," he wrote. And again, "This universe . . . always was, and is, and ever shall be an ever-lasting fire, fixed measures kindling and fixed measures dying out." Constant tension between opposites is the basic cause of the universe's constant change and this is desirable, for if there were no tension the entire universe would enter into a static condition that would be death. Heraclitus says in this connection, "Out of discord comes the fairest harmony, and all things have their birth in strife"; and further, "Men do not understand how that which is torn in different directions comes into accord with itself—harmony in contrariety, as in the case of the bow and the lyre."[7]

We note this expression, "as in the case of the bow and the lyre." In the bow the ends provide the power for shooting the arrow by pulling against each other in powerful tension; relax this tension and the bow is useless. It is the tension on the strings of the lyre that makes the harmony of tone possible. This is surely a striking thought—that the nature of reality is not to be found in this or that thing but rather in the state of tension between all things. All things do form a unity, but the unity is not to be found in any one thing, like Thales' water, but in the harmony resulting from the intertransformation of opposites. Heraclitus does find a oneness in nature, then, not a oneness of substance or stuff but a oneness of the changing, moving, dynamic *process* keeping all in perfect harmony and balance.

One might say that this is all very well as far as it goes, but how is this balance between opposites maintained? Why does one set of occurrences or substances not take over and destroy the balance? This question brings

[7] Bakewell, *op. cit.*, pp. 28-35. Fragments quoted are numbers 76, 30, 8, and 51.

us to the third emphasis and the heart of Heraclitus' thought, a notion which makes him still very difficult to understand and which led thinkers in his own time to call him "the Dark." At this point a number of ideas not previously encountered enter into Western thought for the first time, all centering about the Greek word *logos*. Once used, the word *logos* proved to be so potent a concept that it came to be adopted for use in many different ways. Thus, for instance, in Christian thought it reached a development all its own, appearing in the Gospel of John in the New Testament where the first verse states, "In the beginning was the *Logos*"; the *logos* came to be identified with Jesus as the incarnate "Word of God." In itself, *logos* means simply word or concept, but as used by Heraclitus it was given a very different meaning.

He tells us that he found life a riddle, an enigma, as any penetrating thinker must. Nature loves to hide herself. He says that in his search for truth he traveled for himself the road to insight, and solved the enigma. It appears, however, that his solution was one incapable of being put into words, for while the *logos* is the discovery he made, it is not possible to know exactly how he understood it. He seems to be saying that reality cannot be penetrated solely by human thought, but a comprehension of it comes, if at all, by some reach of intuitive insight. As known within his own experience he says of it, "This *logos* is everlasting, but men are unable to comprehend it before they have heard it or even after they have heard it for the first time."[8] Because they lack this knowledge, most people are to be considered asleep, but those who awake into knowledge of the *logos* form the community of the knowers.

Whatever its innermost nature may be, the *logos* is the law of the universe, for the universe too has a law, as has the city-state. But the *logos* is at the same time the law of thought and so a form of knowledge. The thinking mind of man has therefore to respect this *logos*,[9] and it is the thinking mind of the philosopher which may perceive the meaning of the universe. It is man's mind, the individual *logos*, which makes him at home in the universe, for his *logos* relates him directly to the universal *logos*. When Thales said that the real is water, it is hard to see how human nature could be reduced to such a reality, and Pythagoras' numbers seem also to leave man's complex nature unexplained; but in the individual *logos* of Heraclitus which can comprehend the cosmos, man himself is made to stand at the very heart of

[8] *Ibid.*, fragment 1, p. 28. A remarkable parallelism exists between this statement concerning the *logos* and descriptions given by the Chinese sage Lao-tzu of the nature of the *Tao* in the *Tao Tê Ching*.

[9] Kroner, *op. cit.*, p. 92.

reality.[10] Since the cosmic *logos* rules over nature, the strife of opposites continues as the *form* of its activity, bringing about the unity in tension noted above.

As we read Heraclitus carefully, we are certain to be somewhat perplexed, particularly concerning the nature of the *logos* in itself and in its relation to what Heraclitus calls God. Possibly Heraclitus would reply that only as the thinker's intuitive insight awakens can this question be answered. However this may be, we can conclude our discussion by stating that Heraclitus originates the idea that any metaphysical explanation must find an adequate place for man, and that in some way man's conscious mind is closely related to the structure of reality.

Parmenides

In Parmenides (flourished 500-450 B.C.) we find the first great thinker to turn in another of the directions later taken by Socrates and Plato. Before him, the nature of the cosmos held the center of philosophical investigation; he began the study of ideas and concepts and tried to remove inner inconsistencies by logical investigation rather than through physical explanation. His home was Elea, originally a Doric colony in southern Italy, from which comes the name *Eleatics* given to the school of philosophy he founded. Like Heraclitus, he puzzles us, not so much because his meaning is unclear as because what he has to say disagrees so thoroughly with ordinary human experience. His ideas have been so vastly influential, particularly upon Plato and through him upon later Western thought, that he has even been designated one of the greatest philosophers who ever lived. Plato tells us in the *Theaetetus* (184a[11]) that when Socrates was a youth he had met Parmenides and found him "venerable," possessing an "absolutely noble depth of mind," and adds that he himself feared he might not be able to understand Parmenides' words.

We have just noticed that Heraclitus held to a unity of opposites in tension in the world of ordinary experience, but then added that behind this surface fact, unseen and knowable only to intuitive insight, stands the *logos*, the truly unchanging reality which governs us and maintains the world of

[10] Werner Jaeger, *Paideia: the Ideals of Greek Culture*, New York, Oxford University Press, 1945, vol. I, pp. 180-182.

[11] The number following the title of a classic work is the conventional way of locating a specific passage in that work. Many modern translations continue to use these numbers, which refer to the page numbers on which the passages are found in the famous sixteenth-century editions of the classics.

change in harmony. That is to say, Heraclitus found that our normal experiences do not give us truth about reality itself, which truth is "hidden" and can be understood only in a special way. In some ways Parmenides finds himself in a degree sympathetic with Heraclitus, being suspicious also of ordinary experience and believing that one must seek beneath or behind it for truth. Yet his way of approaching the question is different, and is often treated as though it is the opposite of Heraclitus' views, which it is not. Parmenides agrees with Heraclitus in stating that in ordinary experience everything changes, but he insists that many problems are raised by Heraclitus' views which need further study and lead to quite different conclusions when investigated. In this approach, Parmenides can be seen as continuing the work and thought of Heraclitus rather than as representing an opposite viewpoint. His great central emphasis results from his investigation of thinking per se and the relation of thinking to what truly *is*. To state this in another way, for him the logical unfolding of pure thought is the basic factor in understanding.

In order to express his ideas, Parmenides wrote a long poem, important sections of which are still extant, entitled *On Physis* or *On Nature*. An introduction explains that the contents of the poem came directly from Dike, the goddess of right and justice, who taught him herself and is the speaker in the poem. The main sections are two: "The Way of Truth," which expounds his ideas of reality, and "The Way of Opinion," which pictures the way in which other men at their best try to explain the nature of things.

The principal topic of "The Way of Truth" is the nature of *Being* or the Existent. Since the Greek word for being is *on*, this topic is called *ontology*, and Parmenides as the first to discuss it is called the father of ontology. Other thinkers before him started with human experience and attempted to develop their knowledge on the basis of that experience: Thales' water and Pythagoras' numbers are illustrations. But Parmenides starts at a very different point with the question, what is the nature of Being? It is obvious that its nature must be what *is*. Contrariwise, Nonbeing or Notbeing must be characterized by the fact that it *is not*. Logically these two are opposites, and everything that can be conceived of must fall within one or the other class. What it, is; and what has Nonbeing, is not, and therefore does not exist. Further, since nothing can become its opposite, it is impossible for Being ever to become Nonbeing, ever to cease to be; and it is equally impossible for Nonbeing ever to become Being, that is, ever to come into existence. This seems obvious enough, but what happens when we apply this idea to the world of our everyday experience?

In the world of our usual sensory experiences, all objects that we know arise as one thing and pass away as another. Let us now suppose, as we ordinarily do, that a particular object, such as a pencil or a tree, is Being. Parmenides would say that *if* this were the fact then it must be true that before this object became itself it must have been Nonbeing, since it was other than what it now is; and when it passes away it must again pass into Nonbeing, for the same reason. That is, if we think of any of the changing objects of experience as Being, then this is the conclusion to which he believed we are driven. But according to Parmenides' analysis, as examined above, this is impossible, for that which is Being will always remain, since Being cannot become Nonbeing, hence can neither arise from it nor pass into it. His logic drove him to a conclusion which seems inescapable when one understands what he means by Being. This conclusion can only be that the world of sense experience, the world we so readily call real, is itself not a world in which Being is found, just because in it we *do* find change, that is, objects arising and passing away again. It follows that the world of sense experience is not the Real; it is a world not of truth but of *opinion.*

What Parmenides is presenting to our minds is a demonstration by rational analysis of thinking and experiencing that what we have always assumed to be the Real, that is, the Existent or Being, is not truly so at all, but is merely a realm of opinion which we have in some way (and he does not explain how) come to *believe* real. We must not suppose that Parmenides stepped out of the world in which all the rest of men live. He knew as we know that this world appears real and in constant flux, incessantly arising and disappearing. But his trust in the validity of reason and thought would not permit him to stop at this point, just as Heraclitus was not content to stop there. Parmenides goes on to ask what the *true* nature of Being must be if the world of change is not itself Being. His reply is most remarkable.

Being, he says, must be the same everywhere, *undivided* and *identical.* The reason is that if it were to be divided or different at one place from another it could be so only because something other than Being (which would have to be Nonbeing) was the cause of the division or difference. But Nonbeing is *not,* it has no existence; hence it cannot divide or make any differences within Being. Further, Being is *uncreated,* for if it were created it would have to come from either Being or Nonbeing. In the former instance, it would come from itself and therefore would not in fact be created but only continuous. In the latter instance it would arise from what has no existence, and this is impossible, for something does not come from nothing. For a similar reason, Being is also *indestructible.* Also, Being is *immovable,* for if it were to move it would have to move from where it is to where it is not; but since Being alone is, there is no "where it is not," and motion is therefore impossible.

Without proceeding further with his reasoning, we can now state his startling conclusion. Because Being is and Nonbeing is not, Being or the Real must be without birth or death, one, complete, immovable, eternal, ubiquitous, continuous, indivisible, immovable, homogeneous, boundless, and impenetrable.[12] This view may be called extreme *monism*, for all is one pure identity.

Obviously, this is not the way that we, or Parmenides for that matter, experience our world. Where, then, in this understanding is found any place for ordinary experience, which is the experience of many changing, moving, finite, non-eternal things? To this very central question we unfortunately do not know Parmenides' answer.[13] Yet it is obvious that he is seeking for an understanding that reason may find logically coherent. He follows where reason takes him, and "lets the chips fall where they may."

A highly important consequence of this way of looking at the nature of things is that what is and what can be correctly thought are the same. This of course does not mean that reality is only ideas, but it does mean that what is true for the mind must also be true in reality, and vice versa. There is agreement, a confluence, between reality and true thought. This remarkable idea went through Plato into the Middle Ages, and upon it is based the ontological argument for God, to be noticed later in this work. In modern science we agree with the idea in at least one point: if the starting point of our theorizing is correctly established by past experience, then the conclusion reached by correct thinking must be true of the world about us. It is on this basis that new scientific discoveries are made. When man's reason is properly applied to the investigation of his universe, it does reach conclusions which are true not only in logic or thought but in fact as well.

Democritus

The fourth philosopher claiming our attention is Democritus. Since he was born about 460 B.C. and died about 370 B.C., he was a contemporary of Socrates, possibly 10 years his junior. He must have known Plato and Aristotle as well. Yet because he treats of the same problems as the other early philosophers—the problems of nature—he is generally classified as a pre-Socratic.

[12] Jaeger, *op. cit.*, pp. 175 ff.

[13] Philosophic Hinduism as later formulated in the system of the Vedanta holds a rather similar view to that of Parmenides. It states that Brahman alone is, and is beyond all description. However, it goes on to say that the world is in a process of *samsara*, or change and becoming, and while not truly real as Brahman is real it yet holds a position in reality. This system is called not monism but non-dualism.

Among modern thinkers Democritus is sometimes regarded as the greatest of the early philosophers and their culmination. Modern physics and chemistry are heavily indebted to him for his theory of atoms, for this portion of his system was brought into modern thought in the seventeenth century by Gassendi and Galileo. Without it our modern scientific achievements would have been impossible. If philosophy is to be considered important primarily for its contribution to practical knowledge, then truly Democritus must be classified as one of the world's greatest thinkers. If, on the other hand, philosophy is significant for its contributions to metaphysics and problems of Being, then Democritus is not a major figure.[14] It is interesting to note in this connection that the influence of Democritus and his theory upon his fellow Greeks was less than that of any other leading thinker. Socrates, Plato, and Aristotle seem to pay this view little or no serious attention.

Ancient writers state that Leucippus, Democritus' predecessor, was greatly influenced by Parmenides and his view that Being is a single, unmoving, unchanging substance. Parmenides denied that there is a void, or empty space, for that seemed to him to be Nonbeing, and Nonbeing does not exist. The question Leucippus faced and passed on to Democritus was whether there was any way within the framework of nature of solving the paradoxes reached by Parmenides. These men sought for a substance that does not itself change and yet accounts for the changes of nature.

The solution developed by Democritus was one that opposed Parmenides at two very basic points. First, he stated that a void or emptiness actually exists within space—it is a kind of vacuum, and it *is*. Second, in place of the one, single Being of Parmenides he suggested that our world is made up of an infinite number of exceedingly tiny particles, invisible to the human eye. Each of these resembles the One of Parmenides in that it is unchangeable and indivisible in itself, but it also differs from his One because there are vast numbers of them, they move, and they are not all spherical in shape. They differ from each other in size and shape, some being relatively large and rough and others smooth and tiny, with all varieties between. Because there is no void in the particle itself it is indivisible, and since the Greek word for indivisible or uncuttable is *atomos*, the name of *atoms* was given to these theoretical particles. Each atom was thought to be solid through and through.

As these vast numbers of invisible atoms move in the void they group together to form large masses of atoms which are both visible and changeable. These are the objects our senses report to us. In other words, reality

[14] Kroner, *op. cit.*, p. 127.

is made up of an infinite number of unchanging atoms which are in constant motion making the changing objects of our world. The differences between objects are the result entirely of the size, shape, and arrangement of the atoms making them up, not of any difference within the atoms themselves. A well-known quotation from Democritus sums up the point we have been making:

> By convention [customary agreement] sweet is sweet, by convention bitter is bitter, by convention hot is hot, by convention cold is cold, by convention color is color. But in reality there are atoms and the void. That is, the objects of sense are supposed to be real and it is customary to regard them as such, but in truth they are not. Only the atoms and the void are real.[15]

Democritus says that the atoms have always been in motion, and thus there is no need to explain how motion began. As they move about, infinite numbers of vortex motions are set up by the impact of these upon each other. This action is the result of the structure of the system arising from the qualities of the atoms and their mechanical grouping. The density of objects is explained by the quantity of void separating the atoms from each other. Light objects of great size simply have more space between the atoms than small objects of greater weight. Vision is made possible by the fact that physical films stream off objects, as the outer skin is shed by a snake, and these strike the eye. The mind and "soul" are also physical, the atoms which constitute them being only finer in texture and smoother than those which combine to make up the more tangible items of experience. Moreover, since the mind and "soul" are also constructed of multitudes of atoms in combination, they are no more permanent than other things. Their atoms are eternal, but they themselves are changing combinations. Everything, in short, is reduced to the eternal movement of atoms. As old combinations break up, new ones are formed, and so the world goes on, without meaning or purpose of any kind.

This solution to the problem set by Thales can well be considered the best scientific answer possible to the early Greeks. It is not, however, an answer that follows the lines along which Thales understood his world, for the material atoms of Democritus are inert and lifeless, while for Thales matter was living substance, carrying its life in itself. In other words, in his theories Democritus approached the view of matter held by modern man. This is a thoroughgoing materialism, since everything that is, including life, mind, and thought, is explained as resulting simply from the one ultimate reality of material atoms in motion.

Since simplicity is one of the goals of explanation, one cannot help but

[15] Bakewell, *op. cit.*, p. 60, fragment o.

admire the model of the universe which Democritus provided. What could be simpler than explaining everything in terms of one fundamental kind of reality in motion? The old Greek doctrine of Fate is now reinterpreted to mean mechanical necessity, which alone governs the motion of the atoms. Let us examine briefly some of the other implications of this beautifully contrived but oversimplified explanation of the mysteries of existence.

First, let us notice that the universe is interpreted in terms of a mechanical model. Things do not happen because of any purpose or because Zeus or another intelligence wills them so; they happen as they do because the atoms move together out of blind necessity. Teleological (purposive) explanations have no place in such a system, and neither has chance. This concept of mechanical determinism, or necessity, has contributed much to scientific progress, for as long as men believe that things happen because of the will of some capricious agent, their control over nature is impossible. Men may supplicate the gods, employ magical incantations, or resign themselves to whatever circumstances befall them, but until they grasp the principle of mechanical regularity they are greatly limited in their ability to redirect the forces of nature to their own ends.

Yet, important as this principle is, atomic materialism has carried it too far in applying it indiscriminately to both things and persons. It seems that such rigid determinism robs rationality and value of any meaning. How can my ideas be said to be more rational or valuable than yours (or vice versa) if both your ideas and mine are merely the result of completely nonrational atoms indulging in determined movements?

There are still other implications of this view. It is evident that in a universe such as we are here describing there is little or no place for the usual concepts of religion. There is, for instance, no creator god, and the gods that Democritus believed do exist are themselves impermanent atomic combinations which blind necessity has brought together. Further, there can be no personal immortality, since no combination of atoms is eternal. For the same reason there is nothing comparable to concepts of heaven and hell. Again, there is no genuine freedom in anything we do; we do what mechanical necessity forces us to do. There are no purposes or meanings to human life that go beyond the moment, for whatever human ideals there may be, the last word to be spoken is that there really is nothing except atoms moving in the void. It is because of the antireligious and, finally, antihuman conclusion to which this theory leads that many persons dismiss it as far too simple to do justice to the vastness of reality. It may be that Democritus himself did not believe it to be a final solution to the mystery of being, for he wrote, "Verily we know nothing. Truth is buried deep."[16]

[16] *Ibid.*, p. 59, fragment 117.

Later on, this way of looking at things was made popular in Rome through the work of the poet Lucretius, and in its major outlines it has lasted on through the centuries. Democritus' view is not, however, the modern theory of the atom, for a variety of reasons. To mention just a few differences, modern physicists are by no means certain there is a void in nature, and, more importantly, the atom is no longer thought to be solid and indivisible. Since atoms can now be "split," the word *atom* (indivisible) is in fact a misnomer. The modern concept of energy has replaced the idea of solidity. The views of modern physics are rooted in the ancient theory but are now basically very different.

The Period of Socrates

About 450 B.C. a great change appeared in Greek history and thought, and during the century that followed, the chief thinkers considered quite different problems from those already examined. A transition in interest from the study of nature and substance to the question of man himself and the conduct of his life appeared, chiefly in Athens which up to that time had produced no real philosophers. The early philosophers of nature, we recall, came from Ionia, southern Italy, and Sicily. Historical changes brought Athens into prominence as the greatest of the Greek cities while Miletus, which had held that position for a long period, sank into insignificance.

In studying the Old Testament we learned that the Persians were the dominant power in the ancient world for two centuries. The Exile of the Jews in Babylonia came to an end in 538 B.C. when Cyrus, the Persian, who had conquered the Babylonians, allowed captive peoples to return to their homelands. These same Persians conquered not only the Babylonians but also all the great empires of their day, and until the Macedonian Alexander the Great broke their power they ruled all of western Asia.

Early in the seventh century B.C., Lydia, a power in western Asia Minor, had extended her control over the Ionian cities on the coast. Her rule was apparently not overly oppressive, and the Lydians participated in Greek culture, even consulting the Delphic oracle. Their last king was Croesus, famed for his great wealth. He was the king who was encouraged to attack Cyrus by the Delphic oracle's pronouncement that if he did so a great empire would be destroyed. Cyrus' victory over him spread Persian power to the Mediterranean Sea. This was in 546 B.C., just seven years before Cyrus conquered the Babylonians. His son, Cambyses II, conquered Egypt in 525 B.C., and by the time Darius, son of Cambyses II, came to the throne, Persia was the sole power in all of western Asia. All the ancient monarchies were now under her control.

The freedom-loving cities on the coast of Asia Minor were not content to accept this domination, and under the leadership of Miletus and with the aid of Athens and other cities in Greece proper, they rebelled about 499 B.C. At that time Miletus was a far more important city than Athens, but because of her subsequent overthrow, records were destroyed and her early greatness was forgotten. The revolt was so powerful and so determined that it required six years for the Persians to crush it, and when they did they destroyed Miletus almost totally.

The Greek cities on the European mainland, especially Athens, which had aided the cities of Asia Minor, still remained to be dealt with, so the Persians sent a large force against them. The Athenian victory at Marathon and the Spartan delaying action at Thermopylae held them back for a time, but in 480 B.C. the vast hosts of the Persians (said by Herodotus to number 1,700,000 men and a great fleet of fighting ships) captured and burned the city of Athens to the ground. Fortunately, almost all the citizens had escaped from the city before the Persians took it. Following this victory, the Persians lost most of their fleet at the hands of the Athenians in the great naval battle of Salamis. Within the next two years they were forced by circumstances to withdraw entirely from Europe and so no longer posed a threat to the Greeks.

In these momentous events, Athens played the leading role, assisted at times by Sparta, noted for its military prowess. Because of the leadership and power she supplied against the Persians, Athens could claim the preeminence which from that time became hers. In 480 B.C., with Athens as the leading city, the Greek city-states developed a confederacy. Until that time the Greek cities had still preserved essentially the form of government and culture they had possessed since the earliest days, but now great political changes began to appear. Athens claimed and gained increasing power, both economic and political. She forcibly transferred the treasury of the confederacy from the island of Delos to herself, and within a space of 50 years became in effect the head of an Athenian empire totaling some 2,000,000 people, and consisting of 200 cities paying her what amounted to tribute.

This period of 50 years was the Golden Age of Athens, and of Greece with her. Between 461 and 430 B.C. Pericles made Athens into a beautiful city, replacing the buildings burned by the Persians with great marble structures, one of them the Parthenon. Scholars were attracted from all over the world. Great trading ventures were initiated, and wealth poured into the metropolis, whose population touched a quarter-million.

During these years the greatest rival to Athens was Sparta, an inland city on the Peloponnesus. The relations between the two cities during the course of their respective histories had often been marked by bad feeling. The reasons for this may be connected partially with the difference in temperament of the two populaces, which in turn may have resulted from the fact that the Spartans were Dorians and the Athenians Ionians. The Spartans were slow-moving, simple-living, authoritarian, stay-at-home people, governing themselves through an oligarchy and denying citizenship to most of their people. The Athenians, on the other hand, were a freedom-loving, democratic people, very resourceful, versatile, and enterprising, who liked to travel widely. They were intellectually alert and intensively creative. Athens left behind her a great cultural treasure while Sparta left almost nothing.

At the end of this golden age came the event which has been called the greatest tragedy in the ancient world. In 431 B.C. Sparta and Athens made war against each other, a war which the other Greek cities hastened to enter on one side or the other, with the result that it became a Greek world war. There were frequent changes of fortune, but after 27 years of intermittent fighting Athens fell, in 404 B.C. The Spartans destroyed her walls and left to her only 12 ships of the navy upon which Athens had depended so greatly for her strength. Moral and spiritual exhaustion accompanied the physical destruction.

The Sophists

Inner disintegration set in among the Greeks during the middle and end of the fifth century B.C. The old culture patterns, centering in the city-states and the ancient religion, were breaking down. Increasing wealth and power brought with them a new sophistication which made the Greeks question their cultural and spiritual foundations. The purposes of human life had been supplied by the ancient faiths and customs, but as they were discarded or questioned nothing was available to replace them. Chief among those who questioned and rejected the older ideas and faiths were men called Sophists (the knowers, or the wise). They were practical in their interests and either uninterested in or skeptical about the possibility of obtaining knowledge concerning the ultimate nature of things.

The Sophists narrowed their intellectual interests to the practical issues of dealing with men. They taught the arts of logic, persuasion, eloquence, and convincing speech. Believing it impossible to obtain knowledge of things beyond the practical, they were destructive of ideals. Two sayings of *Protagoras*, a leading Sophist, illustrate the point: "Man is a measure of all things," and "With regard to the gods I know not whether they exist or not, or what they are like. Many things prevent our knowing; the subject is obscure and brief is the span of mortal life."[17]

Another Sophist, named *Gorgias*, made a statement that shows he had become a complete skeptic. He was not content to say that there is a reality to be known but that man is unable to know it; he questioned whether anything *is*. In his most famous writing, entitled *On Nature*, he divided his discussion under three heads: "First, nothing exists; second, if anything did exist we could never know it; third, if perchance a man should come to know it, it would remain a secret [with him, for] he would be unable to describe it to his fellow-men."[18]

The conservative mass of people looked upon the Sophists with suspicion and distrust. They were too clever and not serious enough. They taught "wisdom" for money, and although there appears little reluctance in our day to accept money for teaching, in Greek society many men felt that wage earning was beneath the dignity of gentlemen. Their teaching of persuasion seemed an unfair way to win an argument by clever twisting of the meaning of words. One amusing story tells of a Sophist who had taught a young man to win arguments, with the understanding that the teacher's fee should be paid only if the student won his first case before the law. That case turned out to be the master's suing him for his fee!

More serious, however, was the Sophistic criticism of established ways of thinking. Most Greeks of the fifth century B.C., like most people of any other place or time, accepted their beliefs on authority of one sort or another. Among the forms of authority is custom; people are inclined to assume that ideas are somehow authoritatively binding if they are old and have the prestige of a long tradition behind them. Among the ideas inherited by the fifth-century Greeks was one which had been even more pronounced among the early Hebrews—that virtue and justice were absolute requirements of the gods, and that the virtuous and just man would be rewarded with a prosperous life. Job was the chief figure to protest this idea among the Hebrews, and the Sophists did a similar service for the Greeks. It was relatively easy for them, just as it would be easy today, to point out instances where the righteous man suffered and the scoundrel prospered, but this sort of criticism carried them still further. What is the nature of virtue and justice in the first place? When we actually try to put content into these terms, do they not turn out merely to represent the things which are expected of us, by reason of some custom which probably originated in the

[17] *Ibid.*, p. 67.
[18] *Ibid.*

interests of some privileged and dominant class of people? If I am a wealthy man, I will probably believe in property rights as a moral requirement. Also, being rich, I will probably be influential in making the laws for the country, and my moral requirement is likely to have some teeth put into it by being enacted into law.

Some of the Sophists were quick to point out that laws, in the legal sense, were human contrivances, frequently enacted in the interest of influential groups. They were not absolute things which represented absolute values, good for all men at all times. If this was true in the legal sense of the term, it might also apply to moral law. In short, some of the Sophists became complete individualists in their interpretation of laws, legal and moral. What men call justice may be merely a fiction to serve the interests of those in power. Even if there were such things as absolute justice and virtue and goodness, how should we ever be able to determine what they are? A thorough skepticism about man's ability to answer such questions as these led many of the Sophists to reject any notion of an absolute morality. Each man alone was to be the measure of what was and what was not good. Likewise, in metaphysics, each man was to be the measure of what was and what was not real, for why should any one man's interpretation of such matters be any better than another's? All this suggests some kind of intellectual and moral anarchy.

Socrates

The threat to Greek life posed by the Sophists was far-reaching. Had they been content to challenge the metaphysical views of certain of their predecessors, it would not have been serious, for then new views might have been suggested in their place; but the Sophists challenged the very foundation of knowledge, even denying the possibility of knowing truth. When this is done the universe must remain a mystery to man, and, more important still, sincerity, integrity, honor, and all the other virtues that hold human society together are in danger of being undermined. How were these critics of the *status quo* to be answered? There was one man among the Greeks during the fifth century B.C. who, while not concerned with defending authority itself, was able and willing to attack the Sophists in the intellectual arena. The man was Socrates. He was the first Athenian philosopher of note, and his chief interest was in opposing relativism in ethics.

CHARACTERISTICS OF SOCRATES. Like Jesus, Socrates (*ca.* 469-399 B.C.) wrote nothing, so far as we know. His personal impact was such that, again as with Jesus, many turned against him in bitter anger and eventually brought him to his death, while many others experienced a kind of "conversion" which made them look to him in memory as the greatest man they had known. He was a strange man, first of all in his personal appearance. He had a snub nose and strangely protruding eyes. His gait was peculiar, being likened to that of a waterfowl. He was compared in appearance to a silenus or a satyr. He always went barefoot. But far more striking than his physical appearance was his personality. In no sense was he an ordinary man, although he did marry and have children. He gave up his family profession of statue making and spent his time in discussion, regarding it as his divine mission to seek for truth. From his boyhood he had an inner "daemon" or oracle which, he said, warned him of approaching evil. At the close of his life he said that he did not regard death as an evil, because if it had been, his inner voice would have warned him against it. He was also subject to ecstatic trances, during which he would remain for hours in one position. In Plato's *Symposium* we are given this description of one such occurrence, which took place during a military expedition:

> He got some notion into his head, and there he stood on one spot from dawn, thinking, and when it did not come out, he would not give in but still stood pondering. It was already midday, and people noticed it, and wondered, and said to one another that Socrates had been standing thinking about something ever since dawn. At last when evening came, some of the Ionians after dinner—it was summertime then—brought out their pallets and slept near in the cool, and watched him from time to time to see if he would stand all night. He did stand until it was dawn, and the sun rose; then he offered a prayer to the sun and walked away.[19]

He was admired by other men for his disregard of hardship, his self-control, and his ability to refrain from the use of wine, or, when joining in the drinking, to remain sober.

But these personal characteristics are still not the basis of Socrates' great reputation, even while they helped build it and manage to give some sense of the kind of man he was. More importantly, he has been designated a prophet and a rationalist. He called men of his day to inner change, a kind of conversion to righteousness, and so reminds us of the great Hebrew prophets. In addition, he advised all men to follow reason, for it is reason that leads to truth and one must live by truth if he is to live well.

The two main sources of information about Socrates are Plato and Xenophon. The latter in his *Memorabilia* defends Socrates against the charges lodged against him at his trial. Plato, whose picture of Socrates is different

[19] Plato, *Symposium*, 220, in *Great Dialogues of Plato*, tr. W. H. D. Rouse, New York, New American Library, 1956, p. 114.

at a number of points from that of Xenophon, gives an extended account of Socrates' trial in the *Apology* and of his death in the *Phaedo*. In others of his earliest dialogues also Plato uses Socrates as his central figure. Aristophanes, the writer of comedies, refers to him humorously in *The Clouds*; and there are other incidental references to him. In spite of some differences of view regarding Socrates, the following summary of his teachings seems fairly well established.

TEACHING OF SOCRATES. It is clear that considered superficially Socrates seemed to be one of the Sophists, for he raised the same kind of questions about customary morality as they. Instead of accepting uncritically what had come down in tradition, he went about questioning those who claimed the greatest authority in such matters, and by questioning them showed both the one questioned and the bystanders that the supposed knowledge was in reality ignorance. Thus a general, who claimed to be expert in matters of courage, found himself unable to define courage, and a jurist was equally unable to define justice. The effect of Socrates upon many people, especially the younger men, was disruptive, making for skepticism about the old moral and ethical ideals. He prided himself, however, in never teaching for money, and unlike the Sophists he believed that there is genuine truth in matters of morality, ethics, and values, and that this truth can be discovered through the use of reason. He seems not to have claimed to have found this truth, but asked his hearers to join him in the search for it. Virtue, which is excellence, he believed can be taught. In his method and in his attack upon ancient mores, he therefore certainly seemed to be a Sophist and was so considered by many, but in his intention and his conclusions he was entirely different.

Socrates believed that words like *courage*, *justice*, and *beauty* were in no sense to be taken as relative to this person or that but carry unchanging meaning in themselves. To assert, for instance, that this picture or building is beautiful is not, Socrates believed, merely to express a personal opinion but to make the affirmation that the object in itself does contain the quality of beauty, which other men who understand what beauty is should be able to recognize. He believed, that is, that values have a genuine being of their own; in this view he was absolutely opposed to the Sophists.

Further, Socrates' chief interest was in ethics rather than metaphysics. He knew the thought of his great predecessors, but he lived at a time and in an atmosphere which thrust before him as more important than metaphysics the question of how men should live. He seems not to have developed any unified system of thought; rather, he raised issues and insisted that there must be solutions, leaving the finding of these solutions to his followers. He was one who stimulated other men, gathering followers and letting them work out implications and make their own discoveries. It is remarkable that, following his death, schools of thought as divergent as those of Plato, the Cynics, and the Cyrenaics should all claim him as their master.

Socrates felt it his mission to reveal to men their ignorance in order that they begin the search for truth. He made no claims to having knowledge himself, insisting rather that he too knew nothing. When told that the Delphic oracle had named him the wisest man in all Greece, he is said to have commented that if this were true it was because he alone of all the Greeks knew his own ignorance, while others were ignorant even of that. His function in Athens was to sting people awake to a recognition of their ignorance in the hope that they would then seek for wisdom. Plato has him say in the *Apology:*

> For if you kill me you will not easily find a successor to me, who, if I may use such a ludicrous figure of speech, am a sort of gadfly, given to the state by God; and the state is a great and noble steed who is tardy in his motions owing to his very size, and requires to be stirred into life. I am that gadfly which God has attached to the state, and all day long and in all places am always fastening upon you, arousing and persuading and reproaching you. You will not easily find another like me, and therefore I would advise you to spare me.[20]

The method followed by Socrates in the discharge of his mission was the one called since his time *dialectic.* It consists in asking questions and in following out the implications of the answers through further questions until weaknesses and errors are exposed. Other answers are then in turn examined in the same way until answers are found capable of standing up under such an examination. The thought behind this method is that truth contains no contradictions, either logically or experimentally. Untruth does contain contradictions; hence if these can be uncovered the falsity of a position is exposed. Socrates was a master of this form of discussion.

In this connection it is worth mentioning that Socrates was famous also for his irony. In his discussion he frequently encouraged his opponents by praising their ability or minimizing his own until the time arrived when, unable to answer his question, they discovered that they had walked into a trap. An example of this irony is the following:

> But when he began to go mad at our talk, I fixed my eyes on him first so that I was able to answer, and I said, trembling a little, "My dear Thrasymachos, don't be cross with us. If we two have made mistakes in our discussion, we could not help it, I assure you. . . . Pity is more natural for us to expect than anger from clever men like you."

[20] Plato, *Apology*, 30, in *The Dialogues of Plato*, tr. Benjamin Jowett, New York, Random House, Inc., 1937, vol. I, pp. 413 f.

He gave a great guffaw, and laughing bitterly, he said, "By Heracles, here's the famous irony of Socrates! I knew it, and told these gentlemen all along—you will never answer, only play simplicity and do anything rather than answer, if someone asks a question."

"That's because you are a wise man, Thrasymachos," I said.[21]

Behind the teaching of Socrates there were at least three basic convictions, all of which Plato developed further. Socrates believed that virtue can be taught, that is, through serious thought and consideration one's insights and values can be developed to the point where excellence as a human being is reached. Second, knowledge is virtue, and no one sins against his will. At first thought this idea seems difficult to accept, but what Socrates was saying was that every act is done for the sake of some supposed gain to oneself or others. In the doing of a deed, no one aims at harmful or evil consequences, but rather at what he thinks to be desirable. When then a man does evil it is because he mistakes the nature of what is good for himself. Genuine knowledge would teach him what is his own good, and if he had such knowledge he would act virtuously. One needs understanding of the meaning of his life before he knows how best to act: knowledge brings such understanding and, with it, virtue. Sin, on the other hand, is "missing the mark" of what one should be and should live for.

Third, true goodness and true well-being (happiness) are one, Socrates insisted. The evil, unjust man cannot really be happy in the sense in which Socrates uses the word, for in practicing injustice he acts against his own nature and so injures himself. From this understanding arises Socrates' great insistence upon tending the soul, which he teaches is the goal of life. With this teaching he suggests a totally new understanding of what the soul is. He replaces the older view that the soul is merely a breath-soul which gives life to the body with the thought that the soul is in truth the seat of consciousness and the intellectual life. Whether Socrates believed that the soul is separable from the body and naturally immortal seems likely but not certain. In the *Apology* (40 ff.) he leaves that matter unsettled, but it is certain that he believed that the man who serves his soul by living temperately, courageously, and justly lives well, and that on the contrary the man who lives unjustly and intemperately is neglecting his own true welfare. So man's first concern is the care of his soul, and Socrates' task was to call men to this "tendance": "All I do is to go about and try to persuade you, both young and old, not to care for your bodies or your monies first, and to care more exceedingly for the soul, to make it as good as possible."[22]

[21] Plato, *The Republic*, book I, 336, in Rouse tr., *op. cit.*, pp. 135 f.
[24] *Apology*, 36, in Rouse tr., *op. cit.*, p. 442.

DEATH OF SOCRATES. Few accounts of human experience have the power to move the reader as does that of the death of Socrates, the first martyr to philosophy, as Plato records it in his *Apology* and *Phaedo*. It is quite possible to understand why the city of Athens did condemn Socrates, just as it is possible to understand why the ruling Jews of his day condemned Jesus. In view of the situation in which each appeared and the stand he took, death was the fate to be anticipated. Both men could have escaped execution had they run away, and, as we look back upon them, both are seen to represent a level of justice beyond the awareness of their judges.

Socrates died in 399 B.C. by being made to drink the poison hemlock. Just five years earlier the city of Athens had been attacked, starved, and dismantled by the victorious Spartans. One of the Athenians who had aided them was Alcibiades, a one-time disciple of Socrates, who appears as a character in the *Symposium*. Another of his disciples was Critias, hated leader of the Thirty Tyrants who exercised control over Athens for a short period after the Spartan victory. Many of the Athenians held Socrates at least partially responsible for these two men, and they were used as examples to support the charge brought against him of corrupting the youth. But this was not the only reason for the Athenians to wish to destroy Socrates. His method of asking questions was irritating and sometimes maddening. In times of calm self-confidence in a state, it is possible to accept a certain amount of criticism of customary ideas and beliefs, but Socrates had pursued his ways during the Greek war and in its aftermath of Athens' humiliation. He freely examined and criticized traditional standards and, what was worse, offered nothing positive in their place.[23] When he saw the imminent danger of arrest, he could readily have withdrawn from Athens until the danger had blown over, and after his condemnation he could have escaped from his prison, as the *Crito* shows. His conduct during the trial was not one to win him sympathy, for when asked what alternative penalty to the sentence of death he was prepared to suggest, he replied, as Plato depicts the situation,

> Then what do I deserve . . . ? Something good, gentlemen, something good which would be suitable for me . . . . Nothing, gentlemen, is so suitable, as that such a man should be boarded free in the town hall, which he deserves much more than any one of you who has gained the prize at Olympia with a pair of horses. . . .[24]

From the standpoint of many of his fellow citizens, he was a nuisance of the most dangerous kind who deserved to die.

[23] Kitto, *op. cit.*, pp. 152 ff.

[24] *Apology*, 36, in Rouse tr., *op. cit.*, p. 442.

Yet, looking back from our vantage point, totally removed from the situation of fifth-century Athens, we must say that Socrates was quite right and his detractors quite wrong. His message was one that moved on a level where most persons could not comprehend either the man himself or what he was truly attempting to do. He refused to compromise with pettiness and evil. At his trial he refused to beg for his life with tears, and he truly did deserve to be taken care of by the state for his great contribution to human life. Having taught that a citizen must obey the law of his state, even when evil, he could scarcely have fled from Athens after his condemnation. So Socrates was right and his judges mistaken, and the picture drawn by Plato of the last day of Socrates' life will never cease to move men to feel that this was "a man, as we would say, of all then living we had ever met, the noblest and the wisest and the most just."[25]

Although Socrates was dead, his inspiration lived on and, through the influence exerted by the schools of Plato, Aristotle, the Stoics, and the Epicureans, still makes itself felt in our own day.

Questions for Study

1. Distinguish from each other religion, philosophy, metaphysics, and ethics.
2. What distinguishes Thales from the Greeks before his time? What was the significance of the problem with which he dealt; how did his approach differ from the religious approach; and what great contributions to thought did he make?
3. How would you yourself answer Thales' problem?
4. What was the great discovery of Pythagoras? How does he seem to have come to it?
5. Why did Heraclitus say one cannot step into the same river twice? Yet what did he find that does *not* itself change? Explain what he seems to have meant by this. In what respects does his insight seem a more comprehensive one than that of his predecessors?
6. How does Parmenides approach the problem of Being, and why is his solution one that we find difficult to accept? Exactly why did he seem to think there can be no change in Being? What were some of the qualities of his Being? Where do you see the fundamental differences between him and Pythagoras on the one hand and Heraclitus on the other, and which theory seems to you most acceptable? Why?
7. What is Democritus' solution to the problem of change and permanence? What for him truly exists, and how does he account for the vast variety of our

[25] Plato, *Phaedo,* 118, in Rouse tr., *op. cit.,* p. 521.

world? In what sense might one say that he partially unites the insights of both Parmenides and Heraclitus in his theory?

8. What are some of the principal implications of Democritus' theory? What do you find acceptable in it? Where might you criticize it? How does it differ from the modern atomic theory?
9. What were the chief political occurrences during the lifetime of Socrates? What effect did later events have upon the thinking of the Greeks, especially of the Athenians?
10. How would you account for the rise of the Sophists, and what ideas did they hold? Why did their ideas provoke a strong reaction?
11. In what respects did Socrates appear to be a Sophist, and in what ways was he different? What were his chief interests, and how did he carry them out among the Greeks of his time? Why did people object to him and his procedures?
12. What is meant by saying that the method used by Socrates was dialectic? What are the virtues and shortcomings of such a method? What basic convictions did he hold? How and why was he executed?
13. Draw a comparison and contrast between Socrates and one of the great Hebrew prophets, like Jeremiah or Isaiah, and then between Socrates and Jesus, considering the personality of the men, what they stood for, how they approached life, and their influence.

Selected Readings

Bakewell, Charles F., *Source Book in Ancient Philosophy*, New York, Charles Scribner's Sons, 1939.

Burnet, John, *Greek Philosophy*, London, Macmillan & Co., Ltd., 1953.

Fuller, B. A. G., *A History of Ancient and Medieval Philosophy*, 3rd ed., New York, Henry Holt & Co., 1955.

Gomperz, Theodor, *Greek Thinkers*, London, John Murray, 1920, vol. I.

Jaeger, Werner, *Paideia: the Ideals of Greek Culture*, New York, Oxford University Press, 1945, vol. I.

Jaeger, Werner, *The Theology of the Early Greek Philosophers*, Oxford, Clarendon Press, 1948.

Kitto, H. D. F., *The Greeks*, Baltimore, Penguin Books, Inc., 1959.

Kroner, Richard, *Speculation in Pre-Christian Philosophy*, Philadelphia, The Westminster Press, 1956.

Russell, Bertrand, *A History of Western Philosophy*, New York, Simon and Schuster, Inc., 1945.

9. The Great Schools of Greek Philosophy

Plato

The greatest of Socrates' followers was Plato (427-347 B.C.), who had known him for some years prior to his martyrdom. The influence of Plato upon later thought, especially in Europe, has been enormous. In spite of disagreements, Aristotle was deeply indebted to him for many of his basic concepts. As Christianity entered the Roman world and was there adapted to Greek and Roman thought forms, it took a number of Plato's ideas and carried them into later Christian thought. Augustine, the greatest of early Christian thinkers, was strongly influenced by the Neo-Platonic form of Platonism, and our own day is indebted to Platonism in both its science and its religious understandings.

Plato's writing, in the form of dialogues, covers a multitude of interests, including logic, epistemology, metaphysics, politics, and ethics. This writing exhibits no completed system of thought, for Plato seems to have reconsidered many of the views of his earlier dialogues in his later ones, sometimes raising damaging criticism of the earlier ideas. The student who wishes to examine a neat system will find Plato somewhat disappointing; yet it is a mark of Plato's greatness that he was not fully satisfied with his own answers. He appeared to believe that reality is too great for man to comprehend fully;

frequently in his dialogues he had recourse to "myths" as a way of dealing with issues beyond the power of thought alone.

Our discussion will examine Plato's thought in two principal areas: his metaphysics and his ethics.

Plato's Understanding of Reality

The greatest contributors to the thought of Plato, in addition to Socrates, were three men we have already examined, namely, Heraclitus, Pythagoras, and Parmenides. Of these, Parmenides was probably the most influential; many echoes of his teaching are found in the dialogues. One of them, named after Parmenides, portrays him at the age of 65 conversing with the young Socrates.

From Pythagoras, Plato derived his great interest in mathematics. We are told that over the doors of his Academy (which continued in existence for more than nine centuries) he had placed a sign which read, "Let no one ignorant of geometry enter here," and at one time he said that God is always doing geometry. In his personal religion Plato may have been an Orphic. While the Orphics were not Pythagoreans, there was a large measure of agreement between the two movements, including belief in the immortality of the soul and metempsychosis and the thought that the real world is the world of spirit while this human life is basically unreal. Heraclitus taught Plato that nothing in the world of the senses remains constant, and from Parmenides came the thought that the highest reality must be permanent and changeless and is to be known by reason alone.

From Socrates, Plato derived his great moral seriousness, his belief in the value and essential goodness of human life, his interest in ethics, and his conviction that there are genuine standards of right and wrong. It was the example of Socrates which convinced him that virtue and well-being go together and are finally inseparable. Like Socrates, Plato was entirely opposed to relativism in ethics, a view which would make any man's opinion as good as any other's.

THE IDEAS. Plato is classified as an *idealist* in metaphysics because he believed that ideas, not matter, are the real. One like Democritus, who believed that matter alone is real, is called a materialist. Many forms of idealism can be identified; Plato held that in reality there are certain Ideas which have objective existence of their own. These Ideas are unchanging and permanent, and may become objects of thought for thinking men. The name *objective idealism* is generally given to this view. Because most beginning students find it difficult to understand just exactly how Plato meant this, we will attempt to clarify his meaning.

Like Parmenides, Heraclitus, and Pythagoras, Plato sought for the nature of the Real, but unlike these predecessors he was unwilling to seek it in separation from man and his life. When we in our day are asked what we think is real, we more than likely reply that the real is anything that can be touched, seen, tasted—that which can be known through the senses. Plato and his great predecessors would all challenge this view, for reasons already noted. Plato knew about the human senses and what they are capable of discovering, but he denied that they give us knowledge of reality. His reasoning may be understood to go something like this.

When we say we know this chair, table, tree, or dog through the senses, we are talking about something that at one time did not exist and at some future time will not exist. Every object of the senses comes into existence as that object and eventually passes out of existence again. Sensed objects, then, are constantly in a process of change. Hence, before an object arrived on the scene in its present form and after it disappears again, the object is not (it is a nonbeing), and while it is here it is changing its form of being. Because this is true, whatever we know about the object will include contradictories, for a statement made about it now will not be true later. Furthermore, the senses do not always agree with each other. For example, if one hand is placed on a cake of ice and the other on a hot radiator, and both hands are then plunged simultaneously into "warm" water, the first hand will feel the water as hot and the other will feel it as cool. Here we become aware of a puzzling situation—we are trying to make statements about reality, statements that are actually true, and yet the statements made are sometimes contradictory and sometimes only temporarily true. This means that what we know of the world of the senses is rightly called not truth or knowledge but *opinion*. We have to say that we have opinions, not truth, about this cat, or pencil, or man.

Thus far Plato's thought is skeptical, but he escaped skepticism by claiming that there *is* knowledge other than that of the senses. He believed that it is difficult, yet possible, to obtain genuine knowledge, and that such knowledge is of that which does not change, namely, that which does not come into or pass out of existence. Real Being, he insisted, does not come out of Nonbeing, nor does it return to it again. It must then be *permanent*. Here again Plato agreed with Parmenides, though not with his conclusions.

Is there anything in human experience which may be considered unchanging and permanent? It is clear that no "thing" escapes change, but, Plato taught, there are Ideas that are permanent. Let us see how he meant this.

If we consider in the first place some simple object like a tree, we know that there are many trees of a wide variety of sizes, shapes, and types. There are little oaks and great maples, birches with smooth bark and hickories with very rough bark, and so on. Every tree is different from every other, and yet we give them all a common name, *tree*. That is, we give an abstract name to a group of concrete objects because there is something held in common by all those objects which the name indicates. This familiar experience gives us a first clue to Plato's meaning of the word *Idea*. What is usually taken to be an abstraction, the name or *Idea* of tree, man, cat, circle, justice, courage, and so on, is taken by Plato to be the Real, while concrete objects such as this oak tree, that cat, the man John Smith are the changing, about which we have opinions—they are not reality. So he reverses our usual understanding, doing so just because the concrete objects and particular acts we meet in everyday experience change and become something else and are therefore not the Real. But the general idea, the abstraction, continues on without change, he taught. Hence the Idea is the Real. Abstract ideas have a kind of reality that is far above the particulars that manifest them, and they are apprehended not by the senses but by *reason*.

We will now illustrate what Plato is saying by reference to three different areas of human experience, beginning with the field in which we might anticipate the greatest measure of agreement, mathematics. Here, thought Plato, is the most certain and demonstrable knowledge which man's mind is capable of discovering. It was both because it disclosed the nature of permanent truths and because it taught men to think abstractly that mathematics was a required course in Plato's school as a prerequisite to everything else. In this field of study, as every freshman has discovered, there is little room for private opinion. In mathematics we talk about straight lines and perfect circles, but surely no man ever *saw* such things. The world of experience may suggest ideas like these, but it does not seem to contain them. The lines we actually employ in our blackboard demonstration of theorems can be far from straight (and, of course, never are absolutely so) without invalidating our conclusions, which are reached by reason rather than sensation in any case. Here is the surest knowledge we have, and it is attained, independently of sensation, by virtue of reason's ability to grasp realities in their complete abstractness. If we were talking about experienced triangles instead of ideal ones, it would only be more or less true that the sum of their angles would add up to 180 degrees. We should never have demonstrable knowledge that such is the case, but only opinion, for each experienced triangle might vary in its angular structure, however minutely, and our best calculations would thus go astray. Mathematics, then, provides a clue to the fact that knowledge must concern itself with that which does not change, and that the only avenue to true knowledge, and hence to reality, is through reason rather than sensation.

This is not to suggest that the senses do not have their importance in obtaining knowledge, for without the senses there would be no material for reason to work upon. Reason starts with sensory material and seeks for the eternal relations and truths that stand behind the particulars. Recalling the theorems of geometry, we know that they tell of unchanging truth, being just as valid today as they were when first discovered. The actual triangles, circles, and other forms drawn by teachers to illustrate and demonstrate the theorems have long since gone. They were the changing, known through the senses, but the truths which reason has discovered through them remain constant.

A second area of experience with which we can illustrate the Ideas of Plato is that of physical objects, a chair for instance. This particular chair *is* a chair because it manifests in itself the qualities which make an object a chair. Were it to manifest the qualities of a table or a bed, it would be a table or a bed. There have been vast numbers of chairs before this one and will probably be many more in the future, but the Idea of chair is eternal. It is, and someone at some time *discovered* the Idea and fashioned the first rude chair on which he could sit.

The third area is one in which there is likely to be less agreement than in the two already mentioned. Human beings are not only mathematicians and users of objects but they also live by values and ideals. Beauty, justice, courage, love, for instance, are valued by men. Taking beauty for our illustration, we call a picture or a sunset beautiful. What are we really saying? Plato would maintain that we have in mind, however vaguely, an ideal or standard of beauty, and in comparing this particular picture or sunset with that standard we feel justified in calling it beautiful, believing it to exemplify beauty in the way appropriate to it. Plato recognized that there are widely varying *opinions* about what is truly beautiful; yet he insisted that there must be some ideal of beauty, else the statement, "This is beautiful," would be meaningless. The same sort of statement can also be made about justice, courage, and the other ethical ideals to which men aspire. In each case men differ on their actual meaning, but if there is no Idea of each, then the words are meaningless, and this few people would believe. It is the thinker, the lover of wisdom, who is best qualified to discover what the Idea of each is, and even he may make errors; yet there must be such an ideal. The particular example or manifestation of beauty which we see today may no longer be beautiful tomorrow, but beauty itself, the Idea of beauty, remains forever, just as truly as do the truths of geometry.

In short, we are saying that human beings know through their senses an unending and ever-changing series of experiences generated by the physical world about them. Since these arise and pass away and always change, they give us a low form of knowledge, to which the name *opinion* is given. But there is a higher form of knowledge which is real knowledge, available to those men who use their reason properly. This is the knowledge of the unchanging Ideas.

PHILOSOPHERS DISCOVER THE IDEAS. Plato did not intend to claim, of course, that every man's ideas in general or his ideas of the ideals in particular are equally valid. Had he meant this he would have been lost in the same sort of relativism that he condemned in the Sophists. Rather, he asserted that the one and only way in which the eternal truths are to be found is through man's reason, and certainly not through the senses. It is not easy to discover them, but it is possible to do so. Those embarking upon the venture are the *philosophers,* a word meaning lovers of wisdom. Some men (and there are not many of these) are not merely slightly curious about truth but passionately love to obtain wisdom and crave the vision of truth for its own sake. These men point out the directions that human life should follow if it is to be lived well, in accordance with the nature of reality. Plato's concern for society emphasized the ideals of human life and the ways in which these could be discovered and known.

It is obvious that the Ideas are not physical objects and that no sensory description can be given of them. Since they do not occupy space, it is meaningless to ask *where* they are. Only through the proper use of reason can their true nature be known. This concept is not so strange to modern ways of understanding as we might think, for the so-called laws of science may be comprehended in rather similar ways. In any event, for Plato as for Heraclitus and Parmenides, although in different respects, the universe in which we live is conceived of as double-storied: the lower floor is the common one of sensation, which at its best yields opinion, and above is the world of Ideas, in the knowing of which we obtain true knowledge. Each of these Plato further divides (see *The Republic,* 510), but this does not affect the main distinction. Reality, then, is not as it seems, and usual understandings of it are in truth quite mistaken. The wise man must come to see that matters are quite the opposite of the way in which the great masses of people understand them, for these unthinking men live by the senses and therefore by opinion alone. They can be likened to captives seated in a cave, so fastened that they see only shadows on the far wall and not realities, and who, because they are accustomed to these shadows (the ordinary objects of our senses), believe them to be the real (*The Republic*, 514 ff.). The philosopher tears himself loose from his shackles with great effort (the use of reason), and by going out of the cave sees the sun and the objects as they truly are in themselves (the Ideas).

It is evident from this analysis that the world of our senses does have some degree of reality for Plato. It is not just illusion, as Parmenides appeared to believe. The degree of reality it does have it owes to the degree to which it *exemplifies* the eternal Ideas. Thus, a chair has a degree of reality because it exemplifies the Idea of chair, and a cat likewise because it exemplifies the Idea of cat. So is it with a beautiful picture and all else in our experience. Yet since this chair and cat and picture will pass away while the Ideas of chair, cat, and beauty do not, the specific objects are not fully real.

THE GOOD. Chief of all the Ideas is that of the Good. This stands in a special class by itself and is possibly not properly called an Idea at all. It might be more properly called the Idea of all the Ideas, the apex of all being. Everything that is, is only insofar as it exemplifies the universal Good, and all that is must be good just because it exemplifies the Ideas, all of which in turn participate in the Good. At times Plato seems almost to identify the Good and the Beautiful, which reminds us of the close unity felt by the Greeks between goodness and beauty.

Since the experienced world is made in accordance with the Good, it must follow that the whole of existence is shot through with purpose and rationality. In short, Plato conceived the world as thoroughly teleological (purposive) rather than, in the manner of Democritus, as blindly mechanical and determined.

GOD AND CREATION. In his writing Plato refers frequently to God and the gods. The relation of God to the Ideas is one of the unsolved problems in Plato. Scholars generally believe that Plato did not identify God with the Ideas in general or with the Idea of the Good, for God seems to be the principle of motion and action while the Ideas and the Good are intellectual principles. In the various dialogues, written as they were over a lifetime, he has a variety of things to say about the gods. In the *Pheadrus*, for example, he treats the Ideas as superior to the gods, and in the *Laws* he states that the divine being is the soul of the universe, accounting for its life and motion. Plato thinks of God at this point as being related to the entire universe much as human souls are related to our bodies. In addition, because of evil in the world, he concludes that there must also be an evil world soul. In the

Timaeus, the demiurge, the divine artist, is said actually to have created both the universe and the world soul which is at the center of the world sphere.[1] This same demiurge also created man's soul, making it similar to the world soul. Looking at the Ideas as he created, he used them as patterns, copying the world itself after them. However, the actual world cannot be as perfect as these patterns, the Ideas, because the "stuff" with which the demiurge worked placed certain limitations upon his activity, much as even the best of carpenters is limited in the perfection of his work by the materials he uses. Hence, evil is explained at this point as the result of these limitations upon the creator. Finally, it appears that the demiurge himself created neither the Ideas nor the "stuff," but found them ready for his use. Their origin is a mystery.

RECOLLECTION AND METEMPSYCHOSIS. One further aspect of Plato's philosophy which deserves some elaboration is his famous doctrine of recollection. Plato seems to have been so impressed with the Orphic doctrine of metempsychosis that he used it as one of his explanations of how it is possible for man to understand the world of Ideas. According to this view, learning consists in recollecting. In one of its earlier periods the soul became acquainted with reality; hence learning about reality in this life consists actually in the art of contriving to remember what was once immediately evident but has been forgotten. Plato illustrates this theory in a dialogue in which the spokesman, Socrates, is able to have an uneducated slave boy prove a theorem in geometry. Obviously, the slave has not learned the principles of geometry in this life, but through skillful questioning (and without *telling* him anything) Socrates is able to lead him to a correct demonstration. The point is that the boy is simply reminded of something he originally knew but has since forgotten because of the confusion which the partly unreal world of experience has caused in him. Socrates speaks of himself as a midwife to ideas because of his ability to elicit truths from those unable to bring them to light without help. Plato suggests the possibility of generalizing such an experience as this. How, he asks, should we ever be able to identify truth if we did not have *some* knowledge of what it is before we began our quest? The obvious connection between this doctrine of recollection and arguments for immortality need hardly be pointed out. Plato makes the most of it.

SUMMARY. Much more could be said about Plato's metaphysics, but we have tried to concentrate attention on some of the more important aspects.

[1] The teaching of Plato in the *Timaeus* that the cosmos is round like a sphere was carried through the Middle Ages and lay behind the thought of the early astronomers, including Copernicus, that the planets revolve in circles. Kepler discovered the error of this assumption.

We have found that Plato offers a world view very different from that of the atomists, for he presents the world as meaningful and purposive rather than as blindly mechanical. He provides for the possibility of an immortal soul, which was denied by the atomists, and his scheme of things includes in at least one dialogue belief in a creator god, which is wholly foreign to materialism. Little wonder that this philosophy was to prove highly influential in subsequent religious thought. Christianity owes much of its philosophical content to a pagan philosopher who lived four centuries before Jesus.

Plato's Understanding of Ethics

Ethics is a branch of philosophy which attempts to systematize our understandings of what constitutes the good life for man, just as metaphysics attempts to systematize our understandings of the nature of reality. The mistake must not be made of thinking that the phrase *good life* necessarily means being good according to the current moral standards of the day; this is what goodness usually does mean, so that the good man is conceived of as being the man who can be blamed for nothing because he does not act in opposition to generally recognized standards of social living. In ethical theory, however, the good life means the life which is best for a man to live. Generally, ethics does include the teaching that an individual ought to obey the customary mores of his society; yet the teaching given may be quite different, as we noticed in Jesus' statements to the Pharisees, who were highly moral men.

The way in which life is thought to be best lived will depend, of course, upon the kind of world in which we live. For thinking people, the ethics by which they live is therefore determined by their understanding of what reality is *really* like. Therefore, ethics is very closely related to if not actually rooted in metaphysics. Greek ethics illustrates this relationship, for it involves the Greek understanding of reality.

The earliest Greek philosophers provided no genuine development of ethics. Their interest lay primarily in metaphysics. In fact, it was not until the time of Socrates that men even began to analyze the nature of the good life with the same zeal they had shown in analyzing the nature of reality. The Sophists called attention to the problem, and Socrates paved the way for the great thought of Plato's ethics, to which we now turn.

THE NATURE OF JUSTICE. One of the problems bequeathed to Plato by Socrates was that of discovering the actual meaning of those great terms like *courage* and *justice* which Socrates had insisted must have definite meaning, even though he himself failed to discover what that meaning was. In *The*

Republic, one of his longest and most famous dialogues, Plato developed his answer to the question, what is the meaning of justice? In the process of answering this one question he outlined the meaning of the good life generally and so provided material for understanding his ethical system in its entirety. We shall look at several of the major concepts which appear in *The Republic*.

Plato informs us that his motive for taking up the study of philosophy was his desire to deal with man and society; his interest was not just a theoretical one of spinning out fine theories on the nature of things, but was rather to discover the ways by which men can live best.[2] The metaphysical views which he reached, as we have examined them above, are the substructure upon which his ethics is erected. Let us see how this is so.

Since in Plato's metaphysics reality is not the world known to our senses, it is clear that his ethics will not find the good life to be the life of simple physical enjoyment. Reality is to be discovered by men in only one way—through the use of reason. Logically, it will follow that in his ethics Plato will place reason at the peak of man's functions and claim that the proper exercise of reason is the best way for man to live.

As we read in *The Republic* what Plato has to say about the nature of justice, the most inclusive of the ethical qualities, we are surprised to discover that much of the book has to do with education and politics. Instead of going directly to the specified question, Plato digresses; his reasons for doing so are good ones, for he believes that politics and ethics are opposite sides of the same coin. The political structure makes the man, so one cannot be ethical apart from living in a state. In a very real sense the state and the individual are the same. When the good life for the individual is under discussion, there is value in starting with what constitutes justice not in the individual but in the state, for the state is "the individual writ large" (368). This in turn will provide insight into the ethical requirements for individuals within the state.

Plato opens the discussion of justice by having Socrates, whom he uses in the dialogue to represent his own views, look at various suggested definitions and find none of them very acceptable. An ancient story concerning a Lydian shepherd named Gyges is told to illustrate the point that injustice may at times seem very desirable (359 f.). According to this account, Gyges, while tending sheep for the king of Lydia, found a ring which made him invisible when he turned it on his finger. Because of his power to disappear from sight he was able to act unjustly without discovery, so he seduced the queen of Lydia, with her help murdered the king, and became king in his stead. It

[2] Robert E. Cushman, *Therapeia*, Chapel Hill, University of North Carolina Press, 1958, p. 30.

seems obvious that injustice has paid off. So Socrates is asked by his friends in the dialogue to defend his claim that an unjust man who practices injustice without being punished for it and, even more, actually being thought just by other men is less happy than a man who lives an entirely just life and yet is thought by his fellows to be unjust, thus not even obtaining the joy of a good reputation. Thus stated, the problem of justice is placed in its starkest form, and Plato answers it in that form.

THE IDEAL STATE. Plato begins his reply to this question by setting up what he would consider to be an ideal state, within which he will look for justice. Practically considered, such a state would require three distinct classes of people. The largest group by far would be that of the *producers* or *artisans*. These are the people who produce the basic goods and wealth of the state—farmers, manufacturers, merchants, traders, carpenters, and so on. In our day this group would probably also include doctors, property managers, and business directors. Many poor people would be included within this class, but there would also be wealthy men and women, for the production of goods is what these live for, and those who do this well might be expected to have large incomes. The second class would be the *auxiliaries* or *soldiers*, for every state must be able to defend itself against loss of its goods or independence at the hands of a jealous or greedy neighbor. However, this group would be much smaller than the former, and would require very careful training to perform its work of guarding well. The third class, that of the *guardians* or *rulers*, would be a very small one. These philosopher-kings would have the most important function of all to perform, namely, that of directing the state properly and well. If this third class governed solely for the sake of the common welfare and if the other two classes accepted its government over them, then and then only would the state be inwardly harmonious.

In order for his state to be ideal in these respects, Plato suggests an extensive scheme of education. All children alike would begin with the same education, in gymnastic, music, and the other arts. At stated intervals those who showed by their performance that they had gone as far as their natural capacities allowed would be dropped out of the education process and put to the work for which they were by nature best fitted. Those who demonstrated capacity for still further development would remain for additional years. Eventually the best of these would become the soldiers and the guardians. They would have achieved a rounded kind of life, being developed physically, in their "drive" or spirited element, and in the use of their minds.

The purpose of the educational system would be a double one. First, it would develop the latent abilities of the young to their fullest. Second, it would guarantee that each person would find the work for which he was best fitted. Plato believed that human beings are not equal in ability and that their differences should be recognized quite realistically. Since happiness usually accompanies doing one's work well, these people ought then to be very happy in their work.

Another feature of the ideal state would be the communal kind of life that Plato would impose on his two upper classes. He would allow his producers to marry and live in families, but the soldiers and the rulers he would have living together very simply, sharing all in common. The idea behind banishing private property and families was to safeguard the integrity of these most valuable citizens. The public official who holds property and has family interests is unlikely to devote his sole attention to the welfare of the state. There are only too many known instances, for example, of judges' reaching their decisions because of financial rather than judicial considerations. Plato sought to minimize the possibility of men's ruling more for personal gain than for the common welfare. His ideal of self-sacrificing, intelligent, well-educated ruling and defending classes, devoted only to the state, is a very appealing one when compared with the stupid and greedy political ineptitude which is often the lot of other forms of government. Since, however, it is not our purpose to discuss Plato's ideal state for its own sake, we will examine the ethical considerations which Plato attempted to demonstrate by reference to his ideal republic.

We have seen that his state would consist of three classes of people, and that it would be ideal only when each class subordinated itself to the welfare of the state. Obviously, such a state would not be a democracy in any sense, and the fact is that Plato, remembering the experiences in Athens of an uncontrolled form of democracy which led to anarchy, opposed democracy as a very low form of government. For him the ideal form would be better called an *aristocracy*, since it would be governed by a few men who had demonstrated their superior ability as lovers of wisdom. Each of the classes would have its particular function or work to perform. Producers, when they worked properly, would produce bountifully and develop the physical well-being of the state. The soldiers would protect bravely and well, and the rulers would rule and direct wisely. In actual states these tasks are often performed badly and then everyone suffers, for each depends upon the whole for his well-being. Hence, each class has its own proper *virtue*, appropriate to its function within the state. The word *virtue* as used here refers to excellence in doing or being; hence the virtue of each class would lie in the excellent performance of its particular task within the state.

Most important for a state's welfare is that it should have rulers who have achieved the virtue of *wisdom*. The wise are those who are "good in counsel" —who know what is best for their state. They are the men in whom reason has reached its finest flowering. The soldiers in the ideal state would accept what the law of the state tells them is to be feared, and would act unhesitatingly to destroy that which threatens the state under the direction of the guardians or rulers. This is the true meaning of *courage*, their peculiar virtue. The producers, since they are least characterized by reason and hence least able to direct their activities, would need especially to accept the control of the rulers. They value pleasure above all—the fulfillment of their appetites and desires. Their specific virtue is *temperance*, which results when they and the rulers agree on the right of the latter to guide the producers in the use of their appetites and desires.

We are now approaching what we have been searching for, the true meaning of *justice*, which is none of the three virtues already examined. It may be defined in two seemingly different ways: first, as the condition in which everyone in the ideal state is doing his own business and not being a busybody, not meddling in the proper affairs of others; and second, as the condition of harmony in the state which results when each class does its proper work under the control of the ruling class, whose members have achieved wisdom. The state's several parts are all subordinated to the jurisdiction of reason, exercised by the governing philosopher-kings. Justice stands, then, in the closest possible association with the three virtues of wisdom, courage, and temperance.

By contrast, an unjust state is one in which reason is not in control and the several parts are not subordinated to it. In such a state members of one class meddle with the proper work of members of another class or themselves take up the duties of that class as their own, duties for which they are by their natures unfitted. One of the worst things that could happen to a state, to illustrate the point, would be for a person whose nature fitted him to be an excellent haberdasher or plumber and nothing more to force himself by sheer ambition into the guardian or soldier class, or for a man who by nature is just an excellent soldier to take over rulership. Contrariwise, it would be a great misfortune for a state if a man qualified by nature to be ruler should remain a farmer.

Such is Plato's picture of his ideal republic; but is it possible for such a state actually to exist, men being what they are? Plato held no illusions about human strength and purity of motive, for he knew well the irrationalities of human nature and human unwillingness to be ruled by others. When, therefore, the question was put to him: "Is such an order of things possible, and how, if at all?" he gave this reply:

Until philosophers are kings, or the kings and princes of this world have the spirit and power of philosophy, and political greatness and wisdom meet in one, . . . cities will never have rest from their evils,—no, nor the human race, as I believe,—and then only will this our State have a possibility of life and behold the light of day.[3]

But let us return to the virtues, recalling that the picture of the ideal state was drawn simply as a way of identifying justice on a large scale before identifying it in the individual.

THE INDIVIDUAL. Plato believed that a correct analysis of the individual self or soul discloses three aspects or principles, corresponding exactly to the three classes of society. The first of these is the *rational.* Since it alone knows how to govern the soul, it should rule the soul in *wisdom* (which is its virtue), making the spirited aspect its subject and ally, and governing the appetites for the good of the whole. The second principle is the *spirited.* When it follows the direction of reason regarding what to fear and not to fear and acts according to the dictates of reason in the defense of the proper interests of the whole, it exemplifies the virtue of *courage.* The third principle, that of *appetite,* is by far the largest part of the soul, and is quite insatiable if permitted to act without restraint. When it is brought under the control of reason and accepts its lead, it displays the virtue of *temperance.* As these three virtues are present in the individual through the control of reason over his life, then appears the fourth virtue of *justice,* which is again defined as the result of each aspect doing its own business properly. Again, a second definition of justice may be given: that it is the condition of inner harmony in the individual soul which arises when all is controlled by reason so that the individual is wise, courageous, and temperate. It is the harmonious life. Plato describes it thus:

The just man does not permit the several elements within him to interfere with one another, or any of them to do the work of the others,—he sets in order his own inner life, and is his own master and his own law, and at peace with himself; and when he . . . has become one entirely temperate and perfectly adjusted nature, then he proceeds to act, if he has to act, whether in a matter of property, or in the treatment of the body, or in some affair of politics or private business; always thinking and calling that which preserves and co-operates with this harmonious condition, just and good action. . . .[4]

Plato presents a vivid visual image to suggest the inner nature of man and the way in which the three aspects of himself are related:

[3] *The Republic,* 473, in *The Dialogues of Plato,* tr. Benjamin Jowett, New York, Random House, Inc., 1937, vol. I, p. 737.

[4] *Ibid.,* 443, pp. 707 f.

Let us make an image of the soul . . . model the form of a multitudinous, many-headed monster, having a ring of heads of all manner of beasts, tame and wild, which he is able to generate and metamorphose at will [the appetites]. . . . Suppose now that you make a second form as of a lion [the spirited element], and a third of a man [reason], the second smaller than the first, and the third smaller than the second. . . . And now join them, and let the three grow into one. . . . Next fashion the outside of them into a single image, as of a man, so that he who is not able to look within, and sees only the outer hull, may believe the beast to be a single creature. . . .

And now, to him who maintains that it is profitable for the human creature to be unjust, and unprofitable to be just, let us reply that, if he be right, it is profitable for this creature to feast the multitudinous monster and strengthen the lion and the lion-like qualities, but to starve and weaken the man, who is consequently liable to be dragged about at the mercy of either of the other two; and he is not to attempt to familiarize or harmonize them with one another—he ought rather to suffer them to fight and bite and devour one another. . . .

To him the supporter of justice makes answer that he should ever so speak and act as to give the man within him in some way or other the most complete mastery over the entire human creature. He should watch over the many-headed monster like a good husbandmen, fostering and cultivating the gentle qualities, and preventing the wild ones from growing; he should be making the lionheart his ally, and in common care of them all should be uniting the several parts with one another and with himself.[5]

In effect, Plato is arguing that if reason is not to control man's life, what aspect or principle in man knows how to control? Reason alone can judge how life ought to be lived, and can make proper choices and decisions. It develops the specifically human in man, and when it controls it brings harmony into the very soul of man which will otherwise be inharmonious.

It is evident that Plato has moved the discussion of justice from the usual level of just actions to its inner nature within state and individual. In this he is much like the great Hebrew prophets and Jesus, for they too looked first not at what one does but at what one is within. Since actions proceed from what one is, Plato suggests that the man "of temperate and perfectly adjusted nature" will always act in just and good ways, doing what his harmonious nature directs him to do. By contrast, the unjust man is one whose acts reflect his own lack of inner harmony and the uncontrolled nature of his appetites and his spirited principle. Arising from inner strife, this man's actions result in injury to his own soul and to society.

This, then, is our picture of what justice really is and of how the good and wise man will conduct his life. A just life is one lived in accordance

[5] *Ibid.*, 588 f., pp. 848 f.

with the principles of reason, wherein the appetites and passions are subordinated to the interests of the whole man. For Plato, the good man is a well-integrated individual. Today, when many people are consulting psychoanalysts in an attempt to become integrated instead of divided personalities, Plato's picture of the just and well-adjusted man seems like a modern psychological ideal as well as a philosophic one and, indeed, he has been called the father of modern psychoanalysis.

Let us look now at Plato's reply to the original question of whether the unjust man is ever happier than the just, recalling the illustration of Gyges and his remarkable ring. To this question Plato replies that the answer must now be obvious, and that the just man alone can claim true happiness. He points to two main reasons for this. The former is simply a sound psychological observation. A nature in which the various parts are at war with each other is constantly tormented by conflict and frustration. The very fact that people *go* to analysts and clergymen to have their conflicts reduced indicates that they are hardly happy with the state of their souls. Even if the unjust man could grow tough-minded enough not to worry about the state of his soul and if his unjust acts should go undetected, Plato would still insist that the disintegrated soul was absolute evil for him. He would be like a man who had some undetected disease of the body, that was slowly sapping his vitality. Until he found the disease he could not even begin to effect a cure. Hidden injustice can destroy the soul just as surely as hidden disease can destroy the body.

But there is still another reason that the life of the just is better than the life of the unjust, a reason which springs from Plato's metaphysics. We recall that for Plato the very essence of reality was to be found in the eternal Idea of the Good, which was said to be the source of all true being. This means that the just man, because he is by definition more rational, shares more fully in the nature of reality than does the evil one. Since it is man's nature to share in the reality of the Good, he who falls short of this by not being rational never attains to real being. His life is spent in a vague world of semireality. Even if because of lack of knowledge the unjust man should never come to understand himself, wiser natures can see how vain, shallow, and unsatisfactory a life of injustice is. The only one qualified to judge the reality of things is he whose knowledge is great enough to encompass the widest variety. Intelligent men, Plato would say, testify to the fact that the life of reason is superior to a life of the senses. If some sensualist begs to disagree with this judgment, let him hold his tongue; for whereas the sensualist knows only the sensual type of life, being incapable of governing himself by reason, the reasonable man knows both sorts (for everybody has sensation), and consequently he alone is in a position to decide the merits of each type of life. It follows that for Plato as for Socrates before him, man's greatest task lies in tending his own soul. He too might well say with Jesus, "What does it profit a man if he gains the whole world and loses his soul?"

Plato has pointed out a way of life that has been an inspiration to multitudes of men across the ages. The psychological validity of what he has to say can be attested both by those who have tried to follow his precepts and by those who live under the tyranny of some all-consuming appetite or passion. The latter might readily admit that had they been wise enough, they would have curbed their appetites or ambitions before the nobler part of them became enslaved to their baser elements. But Plato has written more than psychology. He stands as one of the most important guardians of the theory that values have a real existence quite apart from our evaluation of them. Good and bad are not relative to the casual judgment of fickle times and periods; the Good is a reality in the nature of things, to be sought for as truth is sought for. It must be sought after and grasped by the mind, and does not have its roots in sentient experience, as some other philosophers seem to suppose. Plato attempts, once and for all, to lay the ghost of relativity in ethics. Goodness does not depend upon the way you or I choose to think about it, but if we would be happy men we would do well to choose to think about it as it *really* is. That this is not an easy task, Plato would agree. That it is the most important task in life, he would insist.

Anyone who understands the spirit of what Plato was writing about in *The Republic* will understand the prayer which he attributes to Socrates in another dialogue, the *Phaedrus:*

> Beloved Pan, and all ye other gods who haunt this place, give me beauty in the inward soul; and may the outward and inward man be at one. May I reckon the wise to be wealthy, and may I have such a quantity of gold as a temperate man and he only can bear and carry–Anything more? The prayer, I think, is enough for me.[6]

Aristotle

"Master of those who know"—such is Dante's description of Plato's famous intellectual successor, Aristotle (384-322 B.C.), who performed the unparalleled feat of encompassing all the knowledge of his day and unifying it within a single focus. One of the most versatile men of history, he ex-

[6] *Phaedrus,* 279, in Jowett tr., p. 282.

plored anatomy, astronomy, botany, biology, psychology, physics, politics, poetics, mathematics, metaphysics, ethics, rhetoric, art, and theology, and made a distinctive contribution to each which continues to have great importance even into our own day. Although it would be most interesting to get well acquainted with this many-sided genius, our remarks here must be limited to his natural philosophy, metaphysics, and ethics.

Much as Aristotle owed to Plato, having spent 20 years of his life after age 17 in Plato's Academy, he was not satisfied with the solutions offered by Plato to the metaphysical problems we have been considering; consequently, in his later life he formulated a world view of his own. His ideas also, like Plato's, have been very important in Christianity and preeminently so in the medieval formulation, particularly in the thought of Thomas Aquinas; and through Aquinas they have made a strong mark on modern thought.

Aristotle's father was a court physician who for a period served Amyntas of Macedonia, grandfather of Alexander the Great. Years later Aristotle was called back to Macedonia to become tutor for four years to the youthful Alexander. It is likely that Aristotle's contact with medicine through his father lay behind his interest in biology, which was his primary concern throughout his life. By contrast, Plato's primary interest in mathematics accounts for a large part of the difference between these two great thinkers, for biology deals with life and the processes of development or growth while mathematics is concerned with unchanging being and relationships. The temperament of the two men also differed greatly, for Aristotle was the cool, detached, scientific observer seeking for Truth rather than for the Good, while Plato was warm, enthusiastic, willing to use myths to account for many of his beliefs, and loyal above all to the Good. Plato showed awe and humility, while Aristotle surrendered these qualities for clarity of thought.

Aristotle's Metaphysics

Plato's understanding of reality seemed weak at one fundamental point to Aristotle. By setting the world of reality—namely, the Ideas and the Good—completely outside and above the world of experience with an independent being of their own, Plato seemed to Aristotle to make these same Ideas incapable of explaining either the existence or the changing character of particular objects, such as trees and animals and men. Plato had tried to deal with this problem by stating that objects exemplify Ideas and participate in them, thus receiving their own being. Yet Plato himself (in the

Parmenides) seems to have questioned the validity of this explanation. Aristotle, on his part, was unwilling to believe that the Ideas had any being at all apart from the individual things; for instance, he would deny that there is any Idea of tree apart from individual trees. He thought there was no use talking about the forms of knowledge as being outside the world of experience, for this world is the one in which we actually live and about which we need to have knowledge. Consequently, while it is true that universal terms like *tree* and *man* must represent some sort of reality and are true objects for thought, yet the universal terms must be thought of as being found in, not apart from, the particular objects of experience. Plato's Ideas must accordingly be brought closer to the particulars which manifest them if they are to serve any real function. The two-story universe of Plato must become a single-story universe. This means, for one thing, that Aristotle seems to us to be more down to earth and practical in his thought than the other-worldly Plato.

Aristotle developed a theory by which he attempted to deal with human experience more fully and with a greater degree of accuracy than did his predecessors, Plato included. He did this neither by embracing the theory of matter as the only real, which Democritus and the early materialists had believed true, nor by accepting Plato's Ideas as the real, but by saying that the real is always a combination of *matter* and *form*. Exactly how he meant this requires explanation, for he did not mean by the term *matter* what is commonly meant today, nor did he mean by *form* what Plato meant by *Ideas*. To understand him at this point is to enter into the heart of his philosophy.

Let us begin by considering again any particular thing in our world, like a tree. We call it a tree because it has those characteristics which belong to the class of objects that go by this name. It cannot be properly classified as bush, flower, or stone. Yet what is important about it is not the fact that it exemplifies the transcendent Idea of tree, as Plato had said, but that *within* this particular tree there is what might be called a tree nature, which constitutes its own individual form. The form of the tree is not merely a pattern or model but is, rather, an inner, active force which gives it the characteristics of a tree and causes those processes of growth and action to take place by which the tree goes through the various stages of tree life. The form, for Aristotle, dwells *within* the particular, being the form of what is reality within the world of experience. Form is always "forming" things, making them become their full selves.[7] It works upon and within "matter."

[7] See Richard Kroner, *Speculation in Pre-Christian Philosophy*, Philadelphia, The Westminster Press, 1956, pp. 194 ff.

Because of its form, then, this tree is, generally speaking, a tree. But we are examining this *particular* tree because of the matter which constitutes it. It is the matter of an object which makes it particular, concrete, and individual. The dog Pixy, for example, is a dog because of the *form* of dog within her; she is Pixy, a living, actual, individual beagle with her own ways of behaving, because of her *matter*. Likewise, every object is a combination of both form and matter, which together always combine to make up reality for Aristotle.

Examining the situation still further, we remark that there is no form without matter and no matter without form, at least within experience. In every instance, there is a single object about which we are speaking, but it is spoken of under two aspects: there is only one Pixy, but we can think of her under the aspect of form—that of dog—or that of matter, which makes her individual—this dog right here.[8] These dual aspects may be considered two different directions in which this particular object points. Let us look at a brick as a way of illustrating the point. A relatively unformed mass of clay (only relatively unformed because it already has at least the form of a mass) is the material out of which a brick can be made. Relative to the clay, the finished brick is form; it is what clay has achieved. Relative to the brick, the clay is matter—something to be formed. The actual brick, which represents accomplished form relative to the matter, becomes, itself, mere matter in relation to the *wall* of which it may become a part. That is to say, anything is matter relative to some higher form, and the wall represents a higher organization of matter than the mere brick. So it is with the whole universe of sensible things: matter and form are correlative aspects of the dynamic process of being itself.

CHANGE OR MOTION. As a biologist and a person interested in the becoming of living being, Aristotle raised the question of how change takes place. His answer is that every change is the result not of a single cause or type of cause but rather, of *four causes*. He finds this to be true whether it is a natural change, resulting from actions of the forces of nature like earthquakes or the movement of water or bodies or the life processes of plants, insects, and animals, or, on the other hand, a change brought about as the result of purpose, whether animal or human.

Try to understand how any particular thing came into being and you will find that in each instance you will need the following four causes to explain it. Suppose you are considering the existence of a manufactured object, made by man, such as a watch. First, you will attempt to discover that out

[8] See B. A. G. Fuller, *A History of Ancient and Medieval Philosophy*, New York, Henry Holt & Co., 1938, pp. 124 ff.

of which it is made, which Aristotle called its *material* cause. Second, there is the watchmaking process, which includes tools, machinery, and workmen, by which materials are made into something, and this is called the *efficient* cause. Third, the materials used did actually go into the making of a watch rather than a fountain pen or some other object, so surely one of the reasons that this thing is a watch is the form into which the materials were cast. This is the *formal* cause. Finally, there would be no watch at all if someone did not wish to keep time, so our explanation is not complete until we list the fourth cause, that for which the thing comes into being. This Aristotle called the *final* cause.

Look next at an illustration of purely mechanical motion, not the result of human action. Here too are found the same four causes. First, there must be a body to be moved—the material cause; then something must set it in motion—the efficient cause; there must be a path to follow in the body's motion—the formal cause; and an inclination within the body resulting from its nature to follow this path (a pile of sand would have no inclination to follow a straight-line path)—the final cause.[9]

In living creatures like man, the material cause is the newborn child or the fertilized germ cell, depending upon the point at which we wish to start our analysis. The efficient cause is food, air, and other factors that aid growth and development. The formal cause is the pattern of man which is being realized in the development that takes place. The inner drive or purpose which causes the process itself to take place is the final cause.

No change can be fully accounted for without mention of these four causes which bring matter and form into a real conjunction, yet of the four one stands out as most illuminating of all, namely, the *final* cause. It represents the inherent tendency because of which the change took place. In short, the end toward which each thing moves, the goal it achieves in its changes, is really the decisive factor in understanding it. This final goal is not external to the change but is inherent in it, just as the oak is in some way inherent in the acorn or the statue in the block of marble. This purpose or goal inherent in a thing Aristotle called its *entelechy*, a Greek word meaning having its goal, or purpose, within itself. How important this concept was for his system of ethics we shall see very soon. In the meantime, the perceptive student will have recognized that Aristotle's approach is quite different from that of modern science, which emphasizes the efficient causes as explanation for actions and tends to deny the other three causes, particularly the final cause with its purpose.

It is possible to use a different vocabulary to express the process of

[9] *Ibid.*, p. 129.

change, and Aristotle does so. Instead of the word *change* he speaks at times of *motion; potential* replaces *matter;* and *actual* is used to represent *form.* Using these words, we can then say that the matter of an object is that which makes the object possible, its capacity or potentiality. Thus, boards are what make possible—the potential—of a table. The form, meaning the realization of this potentiality, is the actuality of the desk. When the desk is built, the boards have actualized their potentiality. Motion is always a process that moves from potential to actual. Everything in nature illustrates this fact. Again we remark that the word *matter* for Aristotle, interchangeable with *potency*, means something very different from what we mean when we use this same word today. The words of this book, for example, are *matter* for the thought of those who read it.

These understandings lead us to further points of central importance in Aristotle's metaphysics. First, the actual (the form) must be *prior* to the potential (the matter) if the latter is to change, since there must be something already formed to change the potential into its own form of actuality. Were the actual not already present, the potential would not leave its state of potentiality. To illustrate, were there no actual fire to ignite logs, which potentially are capable of burning, they would not burn. The actual fire changes the potency into actuality. Since everywhere in nature we discover movement (change) going on, we come to understand that the world is shot through and through with actuality, form, and purpose, which are constantly changing everything from potential to actual states.

Further, it follows from the thought that every potential requires an actual to bring it into actuality that there must be a hierarchy or pyramiding of forms, the upper ones of which bring the lower into actuality. And, by implication, there must be a *supreme* actuality or form at the very apex of the world structure which contains in itself no potency or potentiality needing a still higher form to bring it into actuality; there is nothing in it that cannot be actualized by itself alone. Logically, in terms of the system Aristotle sets up, this pure actuality or form must exist as the ultimate explanation of the movement and change throughout the entire universe. It is called by Aristotle the First Cause or *Unmoved Mover* or God. This concept is centrally important for Aristotle's system since it accounts for both the fact that things exist actually, as products of change, and the fact of motion, or change itself. Since God represents most complete actuality, he moves things not by reason of some mechanical push which he gives them but by virtue of the fact that all potentials tend toward actualization.

Whatever has matter or potentiality as part of its nature (and every *thing* does) is moved to realize its highest form, moving toward God who is the highest actualization. Hence he is the great Mover, but he is himself unmoved since no change occurs in him. It is plain, then, that he moves the entire universe by attraction, as the vision of beauty moves the artist toward realization of his own ability to create or as the beloved moves the lover to herself.

Aristotle's God is obviously not the god of religion, for he does not respond to man's worship—in fact, he is quite unaware of man. He is primarily active reason, who thinks and contemplates. But he does not think about or know man and his world, for to think about these potential and imperfect beings would be unworthy of him. He thinks only of himself and his own perfection, spending eternity in self-contemplation. He is not personal in the sense that there are emotions or moral qualities in him. In short, the God of Aristotle is not a god to be worshiped, adored, and obeyed. He is rather a philosophic being whose chief characteristic is thought and who is brought into the philosophic system to fill a gap that reason cannot otherwise account for. Aristotle had to find an explanation for motion or change, and the Unmoved Mover provides the solution.

We understand, then, that Aristotle sees reality as a great pyramid, with God who is pure actuality or pure form above the apex of beings that are in the process of becoming. The power which draws all these lower beings into higher forms is the result of his attraction. Inorganic substances change rather slightly. Animals and men use the inorganic forms, but transform them into new patterns of organic life and so carry them unto a higher level of fulfillment. Man is able to carry this process of realizing forms even higher as he becomes a rational mind which may find its highest actuality in glimpsing in moments of deepest contemplation the very being of God himself.

The world is in a constant and eternal process of change (there is no creation) in which lower forms of being are raised to higher levels and fall back again toward their starting points. Man is the peak of this ceaseless process. But the forms of living creatures do not evolve—nature includes a series, a heirarchy, of fixed ends, and it is only within the limits of these ends that individual members of species evolve. No animal ever changes into a different or a new species. In short, Aristotle believed in a doctrine of the fixity of the species. The highest development possible for any living creature is to become a fully functioning and fully developed member of its own particular species. Of course, many beings do not become actually what they are potentially capable of becoming simply because of the accidents of life. But if nothing hinders and circumstances make it possible, creatures do achieve what is potential to them, and they do so because of the attractive power of the Unmoved Mover.

A further point needs to be noticed. Every individual of any species, including man, is the result of the conjunction of his matter and form. Each of us combines the form of man and the matter which makes him up. We come into being when this particular conjunction takes place, and we pass out of being again when the body dies and the conjunction is destroyed. There is no personal immortality in the thought of Aristotle.

Our exposition has been somewhat abstract, but certain aspects of Aristotle's way of looking at things should have become clear. In the first place, it is evident that Aristotle sought to be more "realistic" than Plato, for he found the pattern of things to be immanent in the things themselves. Knowledge, for Aristotle, begins with particular experiences and not with any form of recollection such as Plato talked about. In the second place, Aristotle's doctrine of internal design made his philosophy more meaningful in its teleology than was Plato's. Later on it was Aristotle's writings which were drawn upon by Christian theologians as they tried to demonstrate God's existence by means of teleological arguments. Despite his failure to believe in personal immortality and the creation of the world, Aristotle later exerted a great influence upon Christian thought, even though he too, like Plato, lived four centuries before Christ.

Before leaving a discussion of Aristotle's influence on subsequent thought, it should be pointed out that his strength was coupled with a weakness which was not his fault. In the medieval period of European history he came to be accepted as almost as great an authority as the Scriptures, with the consequence that certain mistaken notions which he held in physics and astronomy came to be perpetuated long after they should have been given up; as a result, Aristotle became one of the chief causes for church action against men like Galileo. More recently, his doctrine of the fixity of the species made for difficulties with Darwin.

Aristotle's Understanding of Ethics

With Aristotle as with Plato, any discussion of the good life must necessarily start with the assumption that man is a social as well as a rational being. For Plato, the good of any individual lay largely in his finding his proper place within the superstructure of the state. Personal deprivation, such as Plato spoke of imposing upon the ruling class, was to be accepted because it was necessary for the welfare of the state as a whole, and on this depended the welfare of the individual. Aristotle also imputed great importance to the state. For him the state was the end for which the family originated. Even though the family may have appeared first in time, it is merely the material means for realizing the higher social form of the state.

It must be added, however, that while for Aristotle politics, the science that aims at the welfare of the state, is a higher science than ethics, yet ethics is intimately related to it and is, in truth, a branch of politics. The element of realism and common sense present in Aristotle's philosophy (and sometimes absent from Plato) is demonstrated in his ethics by his denying that in looking for the highest good in life he is seeking for anything as abstract and beyond human experience as Plato's self-existing Idea of the Good. On the contrary, he is concerned with the good for man, and he teaches that to discover what this good is requires that one start with the actual facts of human experience. Any theory of the good life, he believes, must be based on an examination of human nature and what is good for it, not on some preconception of what the good ought to be.

HAPPINESS IS THE GOAL. At the beginning of his theory, Aristotle agreed with what he took to be the general opinion of man, that happiness is the goal of human life. But just what *is* happiness, and how is it to be achieved? To these questions he finds varying answers from earlier philosophers, so his problem turns out to be that of putting specific content into a vague generalization. As Plato tried to give meaning to the word *justice*, so Aristotle turns to finding the meaning of and the means to happiness. In the first place, it is clear that the word does not mean what it is often thought to mean. Happiness is not pleasure, for pleasure is the result simply of satisfying the senses, and the life of pleasure is a vulgar kind of life, suitable not so much to man as to beasts. Neither is money-making the goal, for money, he says, "is merely useful and for the sake of something else." Even the obtaining of honor is not the end.[10] Now, the word which is translated in English as happiness is the Greek word *eudaemonia*, which means literally *well-being*. Hence happiness, the goal of life for man, is human well-being; and our question now becomes, what constitutes well-being for man?

Aristotle thought it obvious that the well-being of any creature depends upon the nature of that creature. The well-being of a cat, for instance, consists in living the kind of life proper to the cat nature—the life of catching rodents, climbing trees, acting in general as cats like to act in the fulfillment of their own peculiar final cause or entelechy. Likewise, a mosquito finds its well-being when it realizes the entelechy proper to mosquitoes. As it lives, grows, and acts as mosquitoes properly do, it reaches its highest form of happiness or well-being. It is clear, then, that when the question is asked of how man should achieve happiness, the answer must be given in terms of the nature peculiar to man. Because his entelechy is a human one, he cannot find

[10] Aristotle, *Nicomachean Ethics*, 1095b, 1096a in Richard McKeon (ed.), *The Basic Works of Aristotle*, New York, Random House, Inc., 1941, pp. 938 f.

happiness by living the life proper to cat, mouse, or dog simply because such is not his nature. This consideration brings us then to the question of what is the nature of man, or, phrased differently, how is man properly defined?

WHAT IS MAN? Aristotle finds that man belongs to the genus *animal.* Biologically—in structure, nutrition, reproduction, need for rest and sleep, etc.—men are to be classified among the animals. Any definition of man must include this fact. Yet man is more than animal. At one supreme point he is different from all other animals, and that is in his possession of reason. He is able to think rationally. Hence, man can be correctly defined as a *rational animal.* Since it is true that happiness or well-being for every living creature is the result of its fulfillment of its entelechy, it must be true that man reaches his greatest well-being when he fulfills himself in his nature as a rational animal. And his greatest happiness as a man must lie in the fulfillment of that in him which distinguishes him from all other animals, namely, his rationality. Of course, man has a vegetative side to his nature, for he takes nourishment and reproduces his kind even as cabbages do. He has an animal side to his nature, for he has sensations even as rabbits do. But his distinguishing feature is his rational element; in this he is unique among the forms of life, and in the fulfillment of this capacity must lie his highest good.

It is remarkable to discover that Aristotle, having started from an entirely different idea than Plato's, has now reached a position very similar to his. We recall that Plato developed his understanding of the Ideas, showing that these are the real and that they can be known in only one way, through the use of reason. Hence, for Plato, using reason as his one way of discovering reality is man's primary function, and reason should direct his conduct as well. Aristotle's approach began with the biological nature of man, and from this he reached the conclusion that to live most fully man must live rationally. From this point the resemblances between the two systems of thought are striking.

According to the doctrine just described, the highest good of man must be sought in the development and exercise of the reasoning faculty. But what is the function of reason? Aristotle shows that reason may be understood as having two functions. On the one hand, it is an instrument for regulating the feelings and desires, which are a part of man's general nature. On the other hand, it is an end in itself, to be cultivated for its own sake. When used in the former way (in its instrumental capacity), it leads to the development of *moral virtue,* and when used as worthy of cultivation for its own sake, it engenders *intellectual virtue.* We will consider these two types of virtue in turn.

MORAL VIRTUE. Some philosophers taught that the life of the senses was entirely evil and that all emotion ought to be suppressed. Even Plato depreciated the importance of the nonrational side of man. Aristotle's common-sense attitude prevented him from sharing such opinions. For him, desire and feeling are a part of the life of man, even if not his highest part, and they are to be used properly rather than suppressed. Natural impulses are in themselves neither good nor bad, but become good or bad insofar as they are controlled or uncontrolled by reason in its attempt to help man realize his highest possibilities. Proper rational control of these natural impulses results in moral virtue, which Aristotle describes as representing a midpoint or mean between excessive and deficient expressions of the impulse. This is the famous doctrine of the Golden Mean, which is simply Aristotle's version of the old Greek notion that extremes are dangerous. We met it first in Homer. Let us see what Aristotle intends by it.

The first thing we notice is that the passions and impulses are not in themselves vices, but are rather the raw material out of which either vice or virtue may develop. Whether they be vicious or virtuous depends upon whether they function in excess and disproportion or in measure and harmony. Aristotle writes:

> Let us consider this, that it is in the nature of such things to be destroyed by defect and excess, as we see in the case of strength and of health . . . both excessive and defective exercise destroys the strength, and similarly drink or food which is above or below a certain amount destroys the health, while that which is proportionate both produces and increases and preserves it. So too is it, then, in the case of temperance and courage and the other virtues. For the man who flies from and fears everything and does not stand his ground against anything becomes a coward, and the man who fears nothing at all but goes to meet every danger becomes rash . . . .[11]

In like manner, Aristotle applies his doctrine of the Golden Mean to many other moral qualities. Following is a partial list of virtues which can be represented as the mean between extremes.

DEFECT	MEAN	EXCESS
Cowardice	Courage	Rashness
Insensibility	Temperance	Self-indulgence
Meanness	Liberality	Prodigality
Boorishness	Ready wit	Buffoonery
Humble-mindedness	High-mindedness	Vaingloriousness
Shamelessness	Modesty	Bashfulness

In the instances listed above, as with all the moral virtues, the Golden Mean is a midpoint discovered by reason and not a mere arithmetical mean.

[11] *Ibid.*, 1104a, pp. 953 f.

Thus, a wrestler might find that a one-pound steak is neither too much nor too little to sustain his strength, whereas the same amount of steak might be far too much for another person. The Golden Mean, in other words, is always relative to the particular individual and the circumstances in which he finds himself. Making the right choice between extremes is an art, achieved, like all arts, only after earnest study and careful practice. It involves not only the exercise of reason but also the building up of right habits, and this is the work of a lifetime.

Moral virtue may then be defined as "A state of character concerned with choice, lying in a mean, i.e., the mean relative to us, this being determined by a rational principle, and by that principle by which the man of practical wisdom would determine it."[12] It must be added that choices are not always those of the mean. For, Aristotle reminds us,

> Not every action nor every passion admits of a mean; for some have names that already imply badness, e.g., spite, shamelessness, envy, and in the case of actions adultery, theft, murder; for all of these and suchlike things imply by their names that they are themselves bad, and not the excesses or deficiencies of them. It is not possible, then, ever to be right with regard to them; one must always be wrong. Nor does goodness or badness with regard to such things depend on committing adultery with the right woman, at the right time, and in the right way, but simply to do any of them is to go wrong.[13]

Development of the moral virtues is obligatory for all who would lead a good life, for it is a way or technique of realizing life's higher possibilities. The college track man who aspires to be an Olympic champion must augment his native ability with the best of training if he is to succeed. In this he is no different from all other people, for they too must train themselves through the careful development of right habits to realize their fullest potentialities. The real failure in life is the person with abilities who fails to develop them and thus becomes a might-have-been. The only way to avoid this fate is by training to become what one would like to be. In order to avoid going on a wild goose chase, of course, it is essential to find out as nearly as possible what one's *real* potentialities are. Socrates' advice to "know thyself" is indispenable to a successful employment of Aristotle's teaching.

INTELLECTUAL VIRTUE. The faculty of reason can be used in two ways, as we said above. As it is used instrumentally in controlling impulses and emotions in man, it leads to the development of moral virtue. But if that which distinguishes man from the other animals is reason, it follows that the full development of this faculty *for its own sake* is man's highest possible accom-

[12] *Ibid.*, 1107a, p. 959.
[13] *Ibid.*

plishment, for virtue consists in realizing one's highest nature. Hence, the best life of all is that of the contemplative wise man or philosopher; indeed, the sage leads a life that is most nearly like that of God, for the Unmoved Mover is best characterized as being engaged in eternal self-contemplation. This final principle of Aristotle's ethics is implied by his metaphysics: it is man's highest nature—his entelechy—to be rational. In fact, Aristotle describes the rational soul as the "form" of the body. Moreover, using reason to the fullest assures the highest bliss, as we can see if we stop to consider the matter for a moment.

He who practices the moral virtues can be assured of a happy life, one filled with a pleasurable sense of well-being, for pleasure is a by-product of doing things well. But if the self-realization that the moral virtues make possible brings so much pleasure and happiness in its wake, how much more, then, will the development of man's highest function, that of the intellect, bring? The sage is not only the best of men but also the happiest, for he shares the bliss of God himself, who leads the life of pure reason.

He who leads a virtuous life will find a pleasant one, but the converse of this is not necessarily true. Some things that are pleasant in themselves may not contribute to a lifetime of happiness, and they must be shunned. Pleasure is among other things the by-product of a well-organized life and must not be considered as itself the primary value. On the other hand, Aristotle was convinced that a life of difficulty and suffering cannot be considered a good life. At this point he appears less ascetic than Plato in some respects, for he gratefully accepts some of the things Plato might consider unworthy as material means to a good life. Perhaps he had Plato in mind (although it is more likely he was thinking of the Cynics) when he wrote, "Those who say that the victim on the rack or the man who falls into great misfortunes is happy if he is good, are, whether they mean to or not, talking nonsense." Aristotle likewise contradicts those extremists who say that money, goods, or any other material means to a pleasurable life are bad. On the contrary, he maintains that happiness "needs the external goods as well; for it is impossible, or not easy, to do noble acts without the proper equipment . . . happiness seems to need this sort of prosperity in addition."[14] To the good man, then, possessions and a degree of prosperity are instruments that aid him in realizing his fullest possibilities. The happy man is the one who "is active in accordance with complete virtue and is sufficently equipped with external goods, not for some chance period but throughout a complete life."[15]

Since we have said much about the good man who for Aristotle becomes

[14] *Ibid.*, 1099b, p. 945.
[15] *Ibid.*, 1101a, p. 948.

the very measure of the good life, let us close our section on Aristotle's ethics with a portrait of such a gentleman drawn for us by the philosopher himself.

> He does not run into trifling dangers, nor is he fond of danger, because he honours few things; but he will face great dangers, and when he is in danger he is unsparing of his life, knowing that there are conditions on which life is not worth having. And he is the sort of man to confer benefits, but he is ashamed of receiving them; for the one is the mark of a superior, the other of an inferior. And he is apt to confer greater benefits in return. . . . It is a mark of the proud man also to ask for nothing or scarcely anything, but to give help readily. . . . He must also be open in his hate and in his love (for to conceal one's feelings, i.e. to care less for truth than for what people will think, is a coward's part), and must speak and act openly. . . . He must be unable to make his life revolve around another, unless it be a friend. . . . Nor is he given to admiration; for nothing to him is great. Nor is he mindful of wrongs; for it is not the part of a proud man to have a long memory, especially for wrongs, but rather to overlook them. Nor is he a gossip . . . since he cares not to be praised nor for others to be blamed, . . . With regard to necessary or small matters he is least of all men given to lamentation or asking of favours . . . .
>
> Further, a slow step is thought proper to the proud man, a deep voice, and a level utterance; for the man who takes few things seriously is not likely to be hurried, nor the man who thinks nothing great to be excited, while a shrill voice and a rapid gait are the results of hurry and excitement.[16]

The Greek Stoics and Epicureans

We have seen how the philosophic spirit of Socrates leavened the work of his most distinguished pupil, Plato; and how Plato in turn transmitted some of that Socratic concern about the good life to his own best pupil, Aristotle. We turn now to two other great schools of thought which, starting in the late Greek period, continued for centuries, on into the Roman Empire—the Stoics and the Epicureans. Although they arose only in the late fourth century B.C., after the time of Alexander the Great, they both sprang from earlier schools of thought which in turn also trace back to Socrates as their ultimate ancestor. Whether he would have accepted them as legitimate progeny is doubtful, but then he had no opportunity to express an opinion on the matter since they appeared after his death. It is a remarkable fact that all four of the most important schools of philosophic thought in Greece were stimulated and inspired by that great but strange man.

[16] *Ibid.*, 1124b, 1125a, pp. 993 f.

Stoicism had its roots in the Cynicism of Antisthenes (*ca.* 446-366 B.C.) who claimed to be practicing the Socratic doctrine of virtue. Epicureanism sprang from the Cyrenaicism of Aristippus (*ca.* 435-350 B.C.). Like Antisthenes, Aristippus had been a disciple of Socrates, and he claimed that the pleasure philosophy which he expounded was inspired by his master. That two such divergent systems of thought as these claim a common ancestry indicates the many-sidedness of Socrates. His simplicity of living, his independence, his lack of regard for public opinion, and his courage may be the factors that influenced Antisthenes, while his human, genial, pleasure-enjoying spirit which we see portrayed in the *Symposium* could well be the starting point for Cyrenaicism. In a succeeding section we shall discuss the pleasure philosophy of this school, and its successor, Epicureanism. For the present we turn our attention to Stoicism and its forerunner, Cynicism.

The Stoic View of Life

CYNICISM. *Antisthenes*, founder of the Cynic school of thought,[17] carried certain aspects of Socrates' teaching to extremes. Socrates had certainly taught that pleasure is not the end of life; he had emphasized discipline and said that a life of virtue is to be sought above a merely pleasant one. Antisthenes exaggerated these ideas to the point where he made virtue and pleasure contradictory notions. "I should rather go mad than feel pleasure," he is said to have exclaimed. He felt that pleasure not only fails when regarded as the *summum bonum* (the highest good) of life, but that it is man's most seductive foe. Many men, lured on by its prospect, walk straight to their doom. The wise man, seeing this, avoids pleasure as he would the plague. We can see that this is certainly an extreme view that is hardly representative of Socrates' teaching. Still, there is some justification for the Cynics' claim to stand within the Socratic tradition. The master himself had been careless of his attire, independent of luxury, and seemingly indifferent to pleasure and pain. Was this, then, not the pattern of the good life which he taught? Antisthenes thought so, as did his followers, especially the famous *Diogenes* (*ca.* 404-323 B.C.). They practiced independence from external goods to the limit.

Tradition holds that Diogenes lived in a tub and begged whatever minimum of food he needed. He seemed unreasonably proud of his humility, and was as likely to abuse as to thank a patron. Although a slave for a time,

[17] *Cynic* may come from the Greek word for dog; it may have been assigned to these people because of the "dog's life" imposed upon them by Antisthenes, or it may have been merely a term of abuse.

he felt himself superior to his master because his master was tied down by things and responsibilities whereas Diogenes was free from this kind of servitude. To sum up this point of view as briefly as possible, the Cynics taught that complete independence from external goods, from public opinion, and from social responsibility constituted the wise man's way of life. Virtue meant mastery of desire, and the good man sought only virtue. If others found some of their acts shocking, the Cynics suggested that it was merely because they were fettered by the artificialities of custom and fear of public opinion, neither of which concerns the good man. Before turning to see how Stoicism toned down the more extreme aspects of Cynicism and built a highly influential philosophy upon it, let us see how strikingly different the individualism expressed in this point of view makes it from the previous philosophies we have examined.

For Plato and Aristotle, the good life involved definite social considerations. The good man was a citizen of the city-state first and an individual afterwards. A conception of the ideal state, based more or less on the actual ones with which they were acquainted, was the constant background for the ethical philosophy of both philosophers. Moreover, both had an aristocratic outlook on life, as is evidenced by Plato's class divisions and Aristotle's defense of slavery. Both seemed to assume that some form of the city-state would survive and that the life of the good man and the life of the state would continue to be interwoven indefinitely. However, through the conquests of Alexander and the subsequent change in the status of the city-states, history decreed otherwise. By the time Stoicism and Epicureanism had developed, men's ideals had had to find a new home; as the political horizon changed, the philosophical outlook changed with it. If one could no longer find his highest realization in being a citizen, if his first allegiance was no longer to the city-state, to what should his loyalty be given? Only two answers to this question were possible. First, the soul could look within and find there an object for its allegiance. This type of individualism, turning in upon itself to find the security which it could no longer find in the external world, was developed into a system of philosophy by Epicurus and his followers. In the second place, if the local city-state had become a rather insignificant part of a world empire, perhaps some larger unit could take its place in man's allegiance. But what was this larger loyalty to be? The Stoics found their answer in a doctrine of universal brotherhood which implied that men were really citizens of the whole world rather than of Athens, Sparta, or other cities. The seed of this remarkable teaching is to be found in the Cynic philosophy, for Diogenes used to boast that he was a "citizen of the world." With him this was possibly a way of avoiding the responsibility of being a citizen anywhere else, but the Stoics developed the idea into a fairly consistent philosophy destined to become influential not only in Greece but especially in later Rome. Let us now turn to the philosophical system which bears their name.

STOICISM. From its very beginning, Stoicism was a cosmopolitan philosophy. It was not specifically Greek, although its founder and early leaders lived in Athens. It appears to have appealed chiefly to Syrians and Romans. The latter adopted it eagerly and popularized and modified it. Within the Roman Empire it gained many famous adherents, including Seneca, the poet, Epictetus, the slave, and the emperor Marcus Aurelius. The very fact that its three great Roman spokesmen held such different social stations indicates its universal appeal, and suggests how admirably the doctrine of world citizenship fitted the needs of an expanding Roman Empire. But let us return to its beginnings in Athens.

Zeno (*ca.* 350-258 B.C.), the founder of this school, was born on the island of Cyprus, and was a Phoenician by ancestry. On coming to Athens, he fell under the influence of the Cynics and was much impressed by their rigorous devotion to virtue. Soon, however, he became weary of their excesses and established his own school in the *Stoa Poikile* (painted porch)—a circumstance which led people to call him and his followers Stoics. Some of his followers became highly influential in their own right, but we shall not attempt to distinguish the contributions of the various members of his school. Instead, we will be content to consider a few outstanding doctrines of the completely developed system of thought, if indeed it can be called a system, for it combined within itself many diverse opinions and went through many alterations during the period of its greatest influence. Indeed, it is quite true to say that Stoicism lacked the intellectual virility and speculative capacity that characterized the thought of Plato and Aristotle. It appeared at a time when there again arose in Greek philosophy much skepticism concerning the capacity of the human mind to grasp reality. It was interested far more in finding supports for man's practical life than in solving intellectual mysteries for their own sake. We will look first at the Stoic view of reality (metaphysics), considered by Zeno quite secondary to practical, ethical interests.

According to the views developed by the earliest Stoics, nature was thought to be a material reality, though not in the sense that Democritus had talked about it. Whereas he had thought of nature as blind and irrational, the Stoics believed it to be both rational and purposive. This rational element within nature they identified as God, the *Logos* who guarantees nature's rational and teleological character. Since God is the soul of the world, this philosophy may be designated properly as pantheism. To state this point in another way, the universe is a material thing which can be understood in two ways: in its passive aspect it is sheer inert matter, but in its active aspect it is universal reason, the *Logos*, or God. While these two aspects can be thought of separately, they are actually an indivisible unit, with God and nature in some sense one.

The God of Aristotle was a remote, rational being, whose one activity was that of contemplating his own perfection. This God, we recall, was "unmoved," by which was meant that nothing outside himself affected him at all. He took no personal interest in the universe or in men and their fate. At the times when the religious impulse feels a deep need for a living, responsive god, such a god as Aristotle's is rejected as religiously valueless. Accordingly, the Stoics turned against Aristotle and his purely rational God, saying that God is certainly not isolated from the world, but that through the *Logos*, which may be considered the innermost essence of the cosmic God, he governs, regulates, and orders the entire universe. As the soul of the universe, he works to perfect the world in beauty and harmony. His highest characteristic as far as man is concerned is his attitude of universal love which points to his concern that men should live life reasonably, according to the universal principles of nature, and by so doing should live well. This God also has foreknowledge and acts providentially. Zeno refers to God not in terms of mind (*nous*) as did Aristotle but rather in terms of spirit (*pneuma*), intending in so doing to emphasize the vitality, will, and love of God. Spirit seemed to Zeno to express the nature of ultimate reality more fully than does mind.

Man is a creature not only in the world but also of it. He is a microcosm, a small edition of nature, which is the macrocosm. Hence, each human individual is, like nature, both body and soul, having within his nature a spark of the divine fire, rationality, or mind. He is literally an offshoot of the *Logos* and so is equipped to understand the world in which he lives. This gift of rationality is the highest characteristic of man, and in its development lies his highest good. The observant student will notice that at this point we have returned once more to the typical emphasis of the Greek philosophers. Plato, Aristotle, and the Stoics follow very different paths, but all agree that reason is man's highest characteristic and that in living the rational life man finds his greatest good.

The ethical theory of the Stoics is closely related to the metaphysical views just discussed. Since the universe is harmonious, rational, and purposive, all that happens within it must be good and reasonable. Virtue for man lies in his identifying himself with the universal law and living in agreement with nature. His reason enables him to understand the reasonable aspects of things, and even where he cannot understand he is assured that all that happens is reasonable. Therefore, he willingly lives in accordance with nature. The good man subordinates his personal will to the will of the universal mind, and indeed only so far as he does so is he truly a free man. Everything that happens in the universe is determined to happen, for the *Logos* decides all things reasonably and well. A later Stoic, Chrysippus, said that even the omnipresent bedbugs are a part of the universal purpose, existing for the purpose of assuring that men do not lie too long abed in the morning! The events of nature cannot be changed, and will therefore be accepted by the wise man. Those who try to make the world serve themselves and demand the impossible are children crying for the moon. They are stupid for two reasons: first, because they are trying to avoid the law of universal necessity; and second, because they do not see that what is impossible would not be good in any case. For if it were good, a purposive universe would have arranged to make it possible.

The doctrine that virtue resides in living according to nature (which is the life of reason) has several very important consequences. In the first place, since the rational soul in each man makes him a son of God, it implies a brotherhood of all men, and this leads to the doctrine of world citizenship which we mentioned earlier. In the second place, since the life of reason is the good life, the place in the scheme of things for the life of sensation and emotion is brought into question. In regard to this the Stoics are even more drastic than any of the philosophers we have met. Whereas Plato and Aristotle sought to control the passions, the Stoics called upon their followers to suppress and destroy them. Even impulses which in themselves may be good, like the impulse of sympathy, must be drastically curbed lest they give rise to false judgments about things. By their very nature, emotions (of anger, love, hatred, for example) are not rational, and under their influence even good men act quite irrationally. "Love is blind" is a true statement. So are all emotions blind, because they tend to lead man away from the reasonable life. It is not enough to be moderate or temperate in regard to them. The truly wise man will live without passions entirely, his ideal being *apatheia*—apathy or emotionlessness. His will will be used to suppress all emotional and hence irrational activity—to pity some poor wretch bowed down with trouble might be the first step toward sharing his emotional attitude in regard to it. Consequently, pity had better be left to weaklings, while the Stoic wise man hardens himself to it and all other emotions.

Another Stoic teaching reflecting a Cynic origin has to do with man's relationship to the world of things and the favors of fortune. All things and events can be divided into three groups: those which are good, those which are evil, and those which are indifferent. We must recall that in one sense everything that happens is, of course, good, since it is the action of the universal mind or God. But seen from the standpoint of the individual human being, the happenings of his life may be thought of in these three different ways. The Stoics taught that the good and evil things are entirely within the control of man, while the indifferent things are external and not within his control, becoming good or evil only insofar as they affect his life in some specific way. Let us illustrate this idea with an example.

Suppose you fall and break a leg. The external fact is a broken bone, which *in itself* is neither good nor bad but strictly indifferent. You can find a dozen broken bones in any butcher shop and discover for yourself that in themselves they are matters of indifference. What is not a matter of indifference about your leg is the way you allow it to affect you. Good and evil reside solely in your attitude toward what is in itself an indifferent matter. Allow yourself to be crushed or downhearted about the whole business and evil has appeared. How? As a defect in your character, for emotion has been allowed to replace reason. In short, the only real evil is not the external occurrences of life but the inner failure of not being reasonable. Triumph over the experience by treating it as a matter of indifference and good has appeared. How? As a triumph of reason over your emotions. In short, the only real good is the virtue of being reasonable. Hence all that is good or evil, being simply virtue or vice, is within the control of man. All else is neither good nor evil but is indifferent. No happening or loss or injury is really disastrous to the good man, because he will let nothing hurt him. Even pain is no evil unless we think it such. This does not mean that disease and pain are unreal but rather that they are not evil.

Critical evaluation of Stoicism suggests that it was more religious than philosophical in nature, more concerned with finding a way for man to live in relation to God than with intellectual understanding. We have indicated that the rational element in man is akin to the nature of God, and that the Stoics' conception of a universal brotherhood of all men is based upon the idea of the fatherhood of God. All this sounds much like later Christianity. The hymn to Zeus of Cleanthes, successor to Zeno, will indicate something of this religious spirit, more theist in actuality than pantheist.

> O God most glorious, called by many a name,
> Nature's great King, through endless years the same;
> Omnipotence, who by thy just decree
> Controllest all, hail, Zeus, for unto thee

Behooves thy creatures in all lands to call.
We are thy children, we alone, of all
On earth's broad ways that wander to and fro,
Bearing thine image wheresoe'er we go. . . .
For thou by knowledge art made strong to reign
O'er all, and all things rulest righteously.
So by thee honoured, we will honour thee,
Praising thy works continually with songs,
As mortals should; nor higher meed belongs
E'en to the gods, than justly to adore
The universal law for evermore.[18]

Here is a perfect blending of the ethical and the religious impulses such as characterized the Old Testament prophets. Compare the closing lines of this hymn with Micah's famous words (6:8): ". . . what does the Lord require of you but to do justice, and to love kindness, and to walk humbly with your God?"

With their strong interest in religion, how did the Stoics think of death? No single answer can be given to this query, for various Stoics held different opinions. Both Zeno and Cleanthes appeared to believe that the individual soul—of the virtuous man at least—continues to exist after the death of his body. Early Stoics held with Heraclitus that there are world eras each of which ends in fire. Those who believed in personal immortality held that souls continue in one form or another until the end of the current era when they too are destroyed in the universal conflagration. The new cycle of nature that then appears will have a new set of souls in it. In Roman times it was held that this present era is eternal and that consequently individual souls will continue eternally.

In keeping with the doctrine of universal brotherhood, the Stoics taught that man has a responsibility to his society. No man lives for himself alone; he is one of a large group of similar souls, all of whom are sparks from the divine fire. Hence, while the Stoic would not seek public office and responsibilities, were his services requested he would be willing to act responsibly and reasonably in society out of a sense of duty. His motive would never be that of seeking praise or honors, and he knew that serving society was a heavy responsibility, and one that reason said should be done by those best fitted for it. The Stoic made an excellent citizen, therefore, for he was responsible without being a seeker after personal advantage.

Still another aspect of Stoic religion which ought to be mentioned is its

[18] Tr. James Adam, as quoted in R. D. Hicks, *Stoic and Epicurean*, New York, Charles Scribner's Sons, 1910, pp. 14-16.

treatment of the problem of evil, a problem which we met earlier among the Hebrews. We have already seen that the Stoics denied any reality to objective evil, for they declared the world to be purposive and good at every point. Yet many experiences which men have seem evil to them. Why is there even the appearance of evil? The problem was complicated by the Stoic teaching that everything which happens is determined by the universal mind, and thus events could not be otherwise; yet man himself is said to have freedom of will. Many Stoics treated this problem of evil and freedom at great length, and practically every possible solution was presented by one or another of them. The chief tendency of these arguments was to assert that things seem evil only to the man who has not developed a sufficiently Stoic character. To the truly virtuous man evil does not even seem to exist. If those poor creatures who feel plagued with the fact of evil would only see things in a proper rational perspective, they would find that it would disappear for them also, for what seems evil to the limited vision of a single individual is really a part of a greater good in the total harmony of things. The child may fancy every bit of denial and punishment to be an evil, but could he reckon in terms of the good intended he might revise his opinion.

Finally, we should notice that like Epicureanism Stoicism was a way of attempting to live successfully during a very difficult period of history. A philosophy such as this would have attracted few if any followers in an earlier period, like the sixth century B.C., when men were optimistic about their capacities and felt in control of their own destinies. But in the fourth century B.C. when Stoicism developed and in the centuries which followed men felt pessimistic about their outer lives and realized that in the great empires after Alexander the individual was often the victim of events beyond his control. Consequently, Stoicism, along with Epicureanism, may be regarded in one aspect as a type of individualism through which men prepared themselves inwardly for any fate fortune might bring them. If one cannot mold the outer world and its events to suit himself, then by suppressing his emotions and feelings the wise man makes himself inwardly unassailable, prepared for whatever happens, pleasant or unpleasant. He builds within himself a citadel which can withstand the bombardments of fortune or misfortune.

The Pursuit of Pleasure

The 600 years between 300 B.C. and A.D. 300 encompass the waning glory of Greece and the rise and decline of Rome. During this period Stoicism had as one of its chief philosophic rivals a school of thought which took its name from *Epicurus*. Just as Zeno the Stoic found his immediate inspiration in the radical thought of the Cynics and developed their views into a consistent and unified philosophy, so Epicurus found a starting point for his philosophy in the pleasure doctrines of the earlier group known as the Cyrenaics, so called because they came from the city of Cyrene, a Greek city on the North African coast. Before considering Epicureanism itself, therefore, let us glance at the earlier and more extreme formulation of a pleasure theory.

CYRENAICS. The founder of the Cyrenaic school, *Aristippus*, had doubtless heard much talk about virtue from his master Socrates, but the thing that seems to have impressed him most about his teacher was Socrates' ability to find pleasure in almost any circumstance. Instead of following the Cynics' lead in taking simplicity and disregard for public opinion as the best Socratic pattern to follow, Aristippus sought to uncover the clue to Socrates' enjoyment of life. Moreover, it probably occurred to him to ask what the virtues so strongly extolled by the Cynics were really good for. To say that virtue makes for the good life and that the good life is the virtuous one seemed to be arguing in a circle. There had to be something of which men did not need to ask, "What is it good for?"—something that any man would recognize immediately as a good in itself. What should this be but pleasure? There is nothing mysterious or esoteric about this idea! What men really want is to lead a pleasant life, that is, a life crammed full of various pleasures.

Socrates was mistaken, Aristippus would say, in trying to distinguish between higher and lower kinds of pleasure. There had been rumors to the effect that pleasures of the mind were somehow superior to those of the belly, but Aristippus found the evidence unconvincing. On the contrary, pleasures seemed to him to be alike in quality, differing only in a quantitative way, that is, only in intensity. The more intense the pleasure, the more we prize it. Viewed in this way, the pleasures of the mind are, if anything, less to be sought after than those of the body. Compare the pallid pleasure of a philosophical discussion with the intense and robust satisfaction to be derived from a well-cooked meal! Why waste one's time in idle prattle about virtue and logic and aesthetics when there are foods to eat, women to love, happy aspects of nature upon which to feast our eyes? The truly wise man, according to this Cyrenaic position, is the one who exploits his capabilities for sensuality rather than his reason, for the most intense pleasures are to be obtained in that way.

To the Cyrenaic, the ultimate good in life was to be found in enjoying a series of particular pleasures. This emphasis upon a continuous series of pleasures for their own sake is quite likely to lead to a philosophy centered on enjoyment of each moment in itself with the pleasure it may bring one. Though Aristippus and some of his followers counted reason a good thing, its value lay not in itself but in the good things it might lead to. The natural consequence of emphasizing momentary pleasures, however, is to neglect consequences and indulge each moment to the utmost; this is especially true when philosophy has a tinge of skepticism about it, for what guarantee do we have that we shall even be alive tomorrow? Trying to calculate pleasures in such a way as to promise a lifetime of happiness seemed to the Cyrenaic a rather irksome if not impossible piece of business. Find the pleasures first—enough of them is all that is meant by happiness!

To give up reasonable calculation of the future and the effects upon it of a present pursuit of pleasures would seem to be a philosophy which many people practice but which few have been willing to defend. To fill this hour with many pleasures may mean that the next hour is filled with pain and grief, so that the wise man may well come to the conclusion that the game is not worth the candle. Since Aristippus himself lived to the ripe age of 85, it may well be questioned whether he himself lived out the full teaching of his school. As a matter of fact, it is known that on the main the school early moved away from this extreme stand, so that by the time of the Epicurean school the Socratic principle of exercising reason in one's conduct was to some degree incorporated into the pleasure philosophy. Before turning to Epicurus himself, let us summarize and evaluate briefly the major principles of the Cyrenaics.

The good life is a life filled with pleasures, preferably those of the bodily sort. Its wise administration consists in making each individual moment of life a pleasant one, never sacrificing a present pleasure for a later one. In this regard, a "bird in the hand is worth two in the bush"! Diogenes Laertius, in his life of Aristippus, tells us that he "derived pleasure from what was present, and did not toil to procure the enjoyment of something that was not present."[19] The shortcomings of this kind of conduct are obvious. In seizing upon momentary pleasures we may and do make bad bargains with life. The notion that we should make the most of each moment has much to be said for it, but if we are going to live only an hour it may be wise to dedicate some of the earlier moments to the service of later ones—thereby gaining a fuller hour than we could by treating each moment separately. Probably the best that can be found in Cyrenaicism is its solemn warning

[19] Book II: 66 in *Lives of Eminent Philosophers*, tr. R. D. Hicks, London, William Heinemann Ltd., Loeb Classical Library, 1949, vol. I, p. 195.

not to take the passing moments too lightly, and its assurance that pleasure is a good. The worst that can be pointed to in early Cyrenaicism is its failure to see that one can live well today only if yesterday he had at least one eye on the future, and that some things may be more important than pleasant physical sensations. Epicureanism modified this philosophy considerably, as we shall see.

EPICUREANISM. Born on the island of Samos, *Epicurus* (*ca.* 341-270 B.C.) was of Athenian descent. In 306 B.C. (a quarter-century after Alexander the Great conquered the Near East), he opened his famous school in the garden of his home in Athens. He was a much-venerated teacher, immortalized in the lines of a later Roman disciple, Lucretius, as a god who first found out the plan of life which is termed wisdom.

The life of Epicurus may itself provide us with something of a clue to his philosophy. We recall that he lived in a period of great social unrest when old standards were disappearing along with the city-states which had supported them. Individual men felt themselves helpless before the great power structures of the day. Finding no home in the vast, impersonal empire, many men turned inward, producing, as we have seen, Stoics on the one hand and Epicureans on the other. The unrest and uncertainty of the surrounding world led to the search for inner security and happiness. Epicurus was one of those who sought the way to inner peace and happiness under these conditions. His was a life of great hardship. Banished at the age of 19 or 20 from his native home, he became a self-made man only after undergoing great difficulties. He was in ill health throughout his life. When he writes that the worst pains are those of the stomach he may be thinking of the fact that he suffered from daily nausea as the result of a stomach ailment. He died at the age of 71 after many days of extreme pain. In the face of the difficulties of his existence, Epicurus attempted to build a life for himself and congenial associates that would offer a refuge from the harshness of their environment and give some degree of satisfaction. His school and the quiet friendship of the Epicurean community gave him and others the kind of life they sought. He must not, therefore, be thought of as primarily an abstract thinker, dealing with purely theoretical problems, but, like the Stoics again, rather as one for whom philosophy became religion, pointing the way to a peaceful and mildly happy life.

In view of Epicurus' desire for peace and quiet joys, it may seem incongruous to number him among the hedonists, that is, those who teach that pleasure is the goal of life. The Cyrenaics quite obviously should be so classified, but Epicurus' philosophy represents a greatly modified form of their teaching, to which he has added something of the atomic materialism of Democritus. Let us notice in the following quotations just how he modified Aristippus. He writes:

> When, therefore, we maintain that pleasure is the end [of life], we do not mean the pleasures of profligates and those that consist in sensuality, as is supposed by some who are either ignorant or disagree with us or do not understand, but freedom from pain in the body and from trouble in the mind. For it is not continuous drinkings and revellings, nor the satisfaction of lusts, nor the enjoyment of fish and other luxuries of the wealthy table, which produce a pleasant life, but sober reasoning, searching out the motives for all choice and avoidance, and banishing mere opinions, to which are due the greatest disturbance of the spirit.[20]

> And since pleasure is the first good and natural to us, for this very reason we do not choose every pleasure, but sometimes we pass over many pleasures, when greater discomfort accrues to us as the result of them: and similarly we think many pains better than pleasures, since a greater pleasure comes to us when we have endured pains for a long time. Every pleasure then because of its natural kinship to us is good, yet not every pleasure is to be chosen: even as every pain also is an evil, yet not all are always of a nature to be avoided.[21]

In these quotations we find that hedonism has undergone very important changes. The first section points to the fact that although Epicureanism is still a pleasure philosophy it has given a new and somewhat strange and negative definition of pleasure. Whereas for Aristippus pleasure was the positive and definite thing with which we are all acquainted through our own experiences, Epicurus thought of it in two ways. There are what he calls active or dynamic pleasures on the one hand, which are what the Cyrenaics had in mind. They accompany the satisfaction of a need like hunger, thirst, or sexual desire. Epicurus was not averse to these and has much to say about their desirability, but he found passive or static pleasures to be the more important sort. To have *no* needs that call for satisfaction, to be in a state of contentment—this is unalloyed pleasure unconnected with pain. Hence the pleasures of eating very simple food, being content with one's lot, enjoying one another's company—these were the pleasures he valued above all. Freedom from pain is thus the highest of all pleasures. The ideal for him and his associates was *ataraxia,* which may be defined as serenity, calm contentment, or peace of mind and body. Paradoxical as it

[20] *Epicurus, the Extant Remains,* tr. Cyril Bailey, Oxford, The Clarendon Press, 1926, pp. 89, 91.

[21] *Ibid.*, pp. 87, 89.

may seem, Epicurus, champion of the life of pleasure, could, by pressing his qualifying suggestions far enough, actually live on the ascetic plane of a medieval saint.

The second quotation suggests that Epicurus brought back into hedonistic philosophy the Socratic principle of reason and calculation which had been lost in the excesses of Cyrenaicism. Only through the exercise of reason can excess be avoided and *ataraxia* be reached.

As it actually existed under its founder, Epicureanism was a very different philosophy from what it is popularly understood to be; the common misapprehension may arise from the forms this philosophy took in the Roman Empire. There was in it no debauchery, for excess brings suffering in its train, and as regards sexual matters the Epicureans are quoted as saying that continuous drinking and revelings are to be avoided and that "sexual intercourse has never done a man good, and he is lucky if it has not harmed him."[22]

LIFE'S GREAT FEARS. The greatest enemy of *ataraxia* is not outer circumstance, painful as that may be, but inner unrest; and the principal cause of inner unrest, said Epicurus, is fear—particularly of the gods and of death. To bring peace to his followers he had to find a solution for these two great fears.

He believed that gods exist and are eternal. Belief in the gods is not in itself frightening, but fear appears as a consequence of wrong ideas men hold concerning the nature of the gods and their relation to men. It is believed, for instance, but quite wrongly, that they spy upon mankind, interfering with and destroying men's pleasures and punishing them for misdeeds. The truth is, Epicurus taught, that the gods do nothing of the sort, for since they are gods they are wise and therefore live for pleasure, as all wise beings do, and to be burdened with the task of supervising mankind is in no sense a pleasure. Only in man's imagination are the gods fearful; in truth, they are remote from human affairs and quite uninterested in them. They need not be feared either during life or after it. Hence, this cause of man's malaise may be safely dismissed.

The fear of death cannot be so easily removed since it is clear that everyone must die. In order to allay this fear, Epicurus had recourse to the atomic theory of Democritus. Up to this point, nothing has been said concerning the metaphysics of Epicurus. Comprehension of the thought of Plato, Aristotle, and the Stoics requires that one start with metaphysics and then examine the ethical teaching based upon it. With the Epicureans, however, this is not a necessary approach, for metaphysics appears to have been im-

[22] *Ibid.*, p. 123.

portant for Epicurus chiefly as it provided a solution to a particular problem, that of death. No one can fully enjoy the pleasures of life, active or static, who is ridden by the fear of his inevitable death. Epicurus teaches, as did Democritus, that an individual is a combination of atoms which have temporarily united to form this being I call myself. The atoms themselves are eternal, but their combinations are not. When death comes, this combination which is I is destroyed, and the self ceases to exist: it is annihilated. This is the fate of all men. Yet Epicurus teaches that it is not to be feared, for as long as we *are*, death is not for us, and when death comes we are no longer about to meet it or have anything to do with it. Therefore, foolish is the man who fears, for why should one fear that which he himself never meets? Such fear is like that of a man who fears a lion which is never present when he is. Epicurus writes:

> Become accustomed to the belief that death is nothing to us. For all good and evil consists in sensation, but death is deprivation of sensation. And therefore a right understanding that death is nothing to us makes the mortality of life enjoyable, not because it adds to it an infinite span of time, but because it takes away the craving for immortality. For there is nothing terrible in life for the man who has truly comprehended that there is nothing terrible in not living. . . . So death, the most terrifying of ills, is nothing to us, since so long as we exist, death is not with us; but when death comes, then we do not exist. It does not then concern either the living or the dead, since for the former it is not, and the latter are no more.[23]

He adds the following: ". . . the man speaks but idly who says that he fears death not because it will be painful when it comes, but because it is painful in anticipation. For that which gives no trouble when it comes, is but an empty pain in anticipation."[24]

To one who is thoroughly enjoying life, Epicurus' logic may not be entirely convincing. Non-existence may not be an annoyance to the non-existent, but such considerations hardly increase its charm for the living. We may well agree with the philosopher that one should not worry about death since worrying does no good without admitting his contention that loss of our being is no evil.

It is evident from the foregoing that Epicurus placed no stress upon responsibility to the society of which one is a part as did Plato, Aristotle, and the Stoics. This fact is possibly understandable in view of the nature of the period in which he lived and the incapacity he and many others must have felt to bring about any changes in the political and social structure. What-

[23] *Ibid.*, p. 85.
[24] *Ibid.*

ever the reasons for it may be, it is nevertheless true that Epicureanism, like the Cyrenaic philosophy which preceded it, promotes an egocentric and individualistic attitude toward life. The individual's pleasure is the important thing. There is no social urge to seek the greatest happiness of the greatest number, a principle of a more modern version of the hedonist view. Marriage and family responsibility will also be avoided, although it is quite possible for an Epicurean to marry and rear a family. Social responsibilities of all kinds will generally not be undertaken. The wise man avoids political life except under extraordinary circumstances. In other words, the Epicurean may enjoy the advantages of society and yet be unwilling to sacrifice his own peace of mind to help make such a society possible, except insofar as mankind finds deliverance in the Epicurean philosophy itself.

In Roman times, the Epicurean life became entirely parasitic in nature, requiring a government and slaves for its own existence while offering nothing to society in exchange. The simple life of Epicurus and his followers demanded less from society, and yet it also contained elements of the same parasitic nature. One chief difference at this point between Epicurus and both the later Epicureans and Aristippus, the Cyrenaic, was that Epicurus alone emphasized a simple life while the others required wealth to live in the way they thought desirable. Epicurus expresses himself on wealth in the following fashion:

> We regard independence of outward things as a great good, not so as in all cases to use little, but so as to be contented with little if we have not much, being honestly persuaded that they have the sweetest enjoyment of luxury who stand least in need of it, and that whatever is natural is easily procured and only the vain and worthless hard to win. Plain fare gives as much pleasure as a costly diet, when once the pain of want has been removed, while bread and water confer the highest possible pleasure when they are brought to hungry lips. To habituate one's self, therefore, to simple and inexpensive diet supplies all that is needful for health, and enables a man to meet the necessary requirements of life without shrinking, and it places us in a better condition when we approach at intervals a costly fare and renders us fearless of fortune.[25]

> He who understands the limits of life knows how easy it is to procure enough to remove the pain of want and make the whole of life complete and perfect. Hence he has no longer any need of things which are not to be won save by labour and conflict.[26]

[25] Diogenes Laertius, *Epicurus,* book X, 130-131, in *Lives of Eminent Philosophers,* tr. R. D. Hicks, Cambridge, Harvard University Press, Loeb Classical Library, 1950, vol. II, pp. 655, 657.

[26] *Ibid.,* 146, p. 671.

In this respect Epicurus is perhaps more comprehensible in his egoism than is Aristippus. Whereas the latter wanted the fruits of hard labor without the effort it required to attain it, Epicurus was quite willing to diminish desire for more than the bare necessities of life in order to render hard work as unnecessary as it was undesirable.

The recurring negativism of Epicurus emphasizes the fact that psychologically he and Zeno of the Stoics had a great deal in common, different as their metaphysical presuppositions were. Both Epicureanism and Stoicism seem to be philosophies of those afraid of life. The Stoic development of virtue was largely for the sake of training oneself to withstand the buffets of any misfortune; the Epicurean withdrawal from life also suggests that philosophy is a sort of insurance against disaster. If we do not trust the world too far it cannot hurt us through frustration. Stoicism was optimistic enough about the ultimate nature of things, which represented a divine harmony, but treated the facts of experience with a haughty disdain which smacked a little too much of simple distrust. In expanding the world of man beyond the confines of particular experience, Stoicism reached an infinite world which psychologically was hardly distinguishable from the infinitesimal world of the self into which Epicurus withdrew because he too distrusted experience. Aristotle would not have thought that man's fullest self-realization could be attained by either of these techniques.

Summary

Among the things which Socrates taught the Greeks was this: that it was the primary business of philosophy to make men wise, in the sense of acquainting them with themselves, that they might lead more intelligent (which for him meant better) lives. Man should devote time to ethics—the study of morality and conduct—if he would be a true philosopher. Speculation about the nature of the world seemed to him of little account unless it led to increased wisdom in the matter of conducting one's own life. Since it happens that one's view of the nature of things does influence his notions about how he ought to live, we have found occasion to refer to some of the metaphysical principles underlying the ethical philosophies which were discussed. Plato's view of things in general and the state in particular led him to the conclusion that the *summum bonum* for man was a life ordered by the ruling principle of reason. Man's varied nature with its undeniable sense elements was perfectly blended when the individual subordinated his instincts to his reason and himself to his state. For Aristotle, the *summum bonum* for man was "self-realization." Since he was quite sure that the self's proper nature was that of a rational and social being, his ethics, in the end, were not unlike Plato's, even if the goal of life was differently defined. Both emphasized the rational and social character of life, and both believed in subordinating pleasure to other ends. Stoicism sought the good life through the cultivation of Spartan virtues and the exercise of complete rationality. All this involved the attainment of a detached attitude toward the things and occurrences of daily experience. The Epicureans developed a negative pleasure philosophy which set out in a direction quite different from that of the Stoics but like them found the good life to consist essentially in self-sufficiency, the attaining of a calm indifference to the favors of fortune. Both of the last two philosophies were more individualistic than either Platonism or Aristotelianism.

Questions for Study

1. How was Plato influenced by his predecessors? Be specific.
2. How are Plato's Ideas to be understood? What does he mean by the Real, and why does he reject physical objects as real? Why are the Ideas real for him? Do they occupy space? Does he mean that *everyone's* ideas are real in his sense of the word? Explain.
3. Since reality is rational, how is true knowledge found? What is the position of sense experience and of objects known to the senses? What does Plato mean by the Idea of the Good? Is this God?
4. What does Plato say about metempsychosis and recollecting?
5. What relationship is there between metaphysics and ethics? Why does Plato deal centrally with the question of justice, and why in his discussion does he study the state before the individual? How would you have defined justice before you began this study?
6. In the ideal state, what three classes of people does Plato think essential, and what are the characteristics and what the virtues of each class? How does he define the virtues? What then is justice? Evaluate this definition.
7. In the individual, what three characteristics are found, and what virtues? How is justice in the individual defined?
8. Exactly why does Plato believe that the good life is the life in which reason is in control? How would you evaluate this system of ethics? Compare and contrast it with Christian or Hebrew ethical ideals and show why the differences between them appear.
9. At what principal points does Aristotle differ from Plato? What does he mean by form and matter? What four causes are required in order to explain change (or motion)? Explain each. Why is the final cause the most important one?

10. Where does God fit into Aristotle's system? Why is God needed, and what is God's relation to man and the world? What is the highest development any creature can reach?
11. Show how Aristotle's ethics grows out of his metaphysics, with its emphasis upon the final cause. What is the entelechy? What is the goal of life, and how is this reached by man? What is the nature of the two forms of virtue man may practice, and why is intellectual virtue the higher?
12. What was the origin of the Stoics? How did Stoicism change the ideas from which it arose? How did it see the nature of reality, and why did it say man should be rational? What is the chief enemy of reason for man? What is the highest virtue? Why did a Stoic maintain an attitude of indifference to external events, and how did he look at death? Why are all men brothers?
13. What was the origin of the Epicureans, and how did this movement differ from its predecessors? What did Epicurus mean when he said man should live for pleasure? What place did reason hold in his system? Why should man not fear the gods and death?
14. Which system of Greek metaphysics would you prefer, and which school of ethics? Defend. Show the place of reason in the systems of Plato, Aristotle, the Stoics, and the Epicureans. Compare with Christian ideas.

Selected Readings

Cushman, Robert E., *Therapeia,* Chapel Hill, University of North Carolina Press, 1958.

Festugière, A. J., *Epicurus and His Gods,* tr. C. W. Chilton, Cambridge, Harvard University Press, 1956.

Fuller, B. A. G., *A History of Ancient and Medieval Philosophy,* New York, Henry Holt & Co., 1938.

Hicks, R. D., *Stoic and Epicurean,* New York, Charles Scribner's Sons, 1910.

Jaeger, Werner, *Paideia: the Ideals of Greek Culture,* New York, Oxford University Press, 1943, vol. II.

Jaeger, Werner, *The Theology of the Early Greek Philosophers,* Oxford, Clarendon Press, 1948.

Kroner, Richard, *Speculation in Pre-Christian Philosophy,* Philadelphia, The Westminster Press, 1956.

McKeon, Richard (ed.), *The Basic Works of Aristotle,* New York, Random House, Inc., 1941.

Plato, *The Dialogues of Plato,* tr. Benjamin Jowett, New York, Random House, Inc., 1937, 2 vols.

Russell, Bertrand, *A History of Western Philosophy,* New York, Simon and Schuster, Inc., 1945.

IV. Philosophy and Religion in the Greco-Roman World

CHRONOLOGICAL FRAMEWORK OF PART IV

ca. 180-111 B.C.	Panaetius, Roman Stoic.
ca. 130-50 B.C.	Posidonius, Roman Stoic.
27 B.C.-A.D. 14	Caesar Augustus rules Rome.
14-37[1]	Tiberius rules.
ca. 25 B.C.-A.D. 40	Philo the Jew lives in Alexandria.
26-36	Pontius Pilate is procurator of Judaea.
Between 30-33 (?)	Jesus dies.
Between 33-35 (?)	Paul (Saul of Tarsus) converted to Christianity.
41-311	Persecutions of the Christians.
41-44	By Herod Agrippa, grandson of Herod the Great. The apostle James is killed.
64	Under Nero.
ca. 95	Under Domitian.
250-260	Under Decius and Successors.
303-311	Under Diocletian and Galerius.
ca. 47-56	Paul's missionary journeys.
54-68	Nero rules.
ca. 60	Paul in Rome.
135-160	Valentinus, the Christian Gnostic, in Rome.
139-144	Marcion writes in Rome.
ca. 153	Justin Martyr, the apologist, writes.
ca. 185	Irenaeus (*ca.* 130-200) writes.
ca. 204-270	Plotinus, the Neo-Platonist.
312-337	Constantine the Great rules.
313	Edict of Milan of Constantine places Christianity on a basis of religious equality in the Empire.
325	Council of Nicaea.
330	Constantinople dedicated by Constantine as the capital of the Eastern Roman Empire.
354-430	Augustine.
361-363	Julian, called the Apostate, rules.
380	Christianity made the official religion of the Roman Empire.
476	The Western Roman Empire falls.
529	Justinian I closes Plato's Academy.

[1] Dates are A.D. unless otherwise indicated.

10. The Situation at the Beginning of the Christian Era

"Marriage of East and West"

Socrates, Plato, and Aristotle are among the philosophical immortals. From the fourth century B.C. to the first century A.D. there arose no constructive genius of comparable greatness. This period has accordingly been referred to as one of intellectual decadence. Historically, however, these centuries were highly significant, witnessing as they did the intimate contact of Greek and Eastern cultures and the ultimate unification of the ancient Western world under the political guidance of Rome. If the historian finds little new in the way of creative ideas, he is nevertheless impressed by the extent to which the heritage of Greece mingled with that of the Eastern nations and later with Rome, preparing the way for the Christianity which eventually became the heir of all these cultures. Although never complete, this fusion inevitably wrought profound changes in the various cultures, producing interesting combinations of philosophies and religions, and gradually replaced the older provincialisms with a new cosmopolitanism.

The empire of Alexander the Great, whose military conquests laid the foundations for a unified world, is usually referred to as a Greek empire, and with considerable justification, for it is true that the Macedonians had a high regard for Greek literature, philosophy, and art, and consciously became thoroughly Hellenized before Alexander's time. Hence the culture which Alexander was responsible for carrying into his conquered lands was Greek. But it is equally true that the rise of Macedonia to world power brought about great changes in Greece proper. These changes centered around the fall of the Greek city-state, where the citizens had been able to participate actively in their government and had found their life's meaning. The civilization which arose as a consequence of Alexander's exploits is usually called Hellenistic, as we said, to distinguish it from the earlier Hellenic culture within Greece.

Alexander's career was brief but brilliant. In the 11 years between 334 B.C. and his death in 323, he made himself master of Greece, Asia Minor, Persia, Babylonia, Syria, and Egypt, and even penetrated into India. He proved to be a new kind of conqueror, for he showed respect for the local customs and religions of conquered nations and consciously tried to bring about the "marriage" of East and West. Egypt, for example, seemed to look upon him as a deliverer rather than as a conqueror, and, indeed, he must have appeared so in contrast to the less sympathetic Persians who had previously controlled that land. Here he founded the city of Alexandria which became an important intellectual and commercial center and fostered in later years the cosmopolitanism so typical of the Hellenistic age.

Following the death of Alexander, the empire soon fell apart. The Antigonids eventually became rulers over Macedonia, claiming Greece and Thrace as well, and continued in power until the appearance of the Romans in the second century B.C. The Asiatic territory fell to the Macedonian Seleucus, who, upon gaining control of Syria, founded the city of Antioch and made it his capital. Ptolemy, the son of a Macedonian nobleman, was the founder of the ruling dynasty in Egypt. The tiny country of Judaea was sometimes controlled by the Ptolemies and sometimes by the Seleucids.[1]

During these years the Greek cities on the European mainland became less important than Antioch, Alexandria, and other newly founded cities in the Orient. There was a series of revolutions in Greece, as a result of which many of the most talented citizens eventually migrated to the Hellenistic monarchies of the East. The majority of these "foreigners" became influential leaders and were thus instrumental in further Hellenizing Eastern civilizations. Although there was progress toward cultural mingling and unification, there was neither peace nor political stability in the Hellenistic world until the time of the Roman Empire. The Roman Republic had gained control of Italy by the middle of the third century B.C., and, at the time of the birth of Christ, Rome had increased its territory until it possessed the whole Mediter-

[1] See pp. 113-117.

ranean world. The addition of so many provinces had made the republican form of rule impracticable, so that political power now rested in the hands of an emperor. After the many years of civil wars and wars between the various Hellenistic monarchies, the peace achieved during the reign of Augustus (27 B.C.-14 A.D.) was heartily appreciated throughout the Empire. The rise of Rome to world domination added little to the philosophical and religious mixture. The dominant cultural elements remained primarily Greek and secondarily Oriental, while Rome's contribution was chiefly that of providing a measure of political stability and governmental efficiency which the people of the ancient world had never before experienced.

It might have been expected that the religion of Rome would become the religion of the neighboring states she conquered, just as the Greek culture of Alexander carried the worship of the Olympian gods with it; but such was not the case. The original Roman religion was a primitive form of animism in which festivals were held in honor of the spirits associated with the seasons of the agricultural year and families worshiped the spirits of the household like Vesta, spirit of the hearth, and the Penates, spirits of the storeroom. The religion that became the formal religion of Rome was that of Greece, which was taken over completely: Roman spirits were identified with the Greek gods, and all the ancient Greek legends were now associated with their Roman counterparts. Thus Jupiter was identified with Zeus, Juno with Hera, Mars with Ares, Minerva with Athena. This attempt to take over a complex polytheism was not successful. Greco-Roman Olympianism carried with it no power or religious enthusiasm. The Roman people themselves were skeptical about these "manufactured" gods, and the common people turned back to the old Roman spirits while the educated turned to philosophy and newer forms of religion to find spiritual nurture. Hence, no one distinct philosophic system or religious institution characterized the world culture of this period. Inevitably, the large cities became melting pots in which men with one type of background came in contact with other ways of thinking. Thus, the philosophies and religions tended to become *eclectic* or *syncretistic*, that is, blends of ideas drawn from various philosophies and religions without the development of a consistent system.

Within these amalgams it is possible to discover at least two dominant spiritual needs of men which philosophy and religion tried to meet, both of which arose partly because of the sheer size of the Empire. The Greek, as we have pointed out, had been accustomed to a very small political unit which was now swallowed up completely. The Oriental was accustomed to a larger but still culturally homogeneous kingdom. The Empire was anything but homogeneous, and there was a felt need for something besides the presence of the army to unify the whole. The first need, therefore, which philosophy and religion sought to meet was that of a spiritual and intellectual basis of unity. Men wanted to feel at home in the Roman world.

It was impossible, however, for individuals really to feel the unity of the Empire in any sense comparable to the way in which they had formerly felt themselves functional elements within smaller political units. No attempt at unity was entirely successful in conquering the sense of loneliness and insecurity. Thus individualism, economic and religious, became a marked characteristic of the period. Never before in history had the concept of the *individual* become so clear, the individual as a distinct human atom within society, the individual with his own private inner life. The older religions with their national gods could not supply the demands of this new individualism. The city dwellers, in particular, had lost the sense of nationality and thus were little interested in gods whose function it was to protect one nation against another. These cosmopolitan people were interested rather in a god with whom they could have communion, who would bring them salvation as individuals, who would guarantee them personal immortality. The second need, then, which philosophy and religion tried to meet was that of spiritual, intellectual, and emotional support for individuals trying to make their way in a world society. So great was this need that even the philosophies of the period took on the characteristics of religion, emphasizing ethical instruction, consolation, and ways of salvation. Nothing was more typical of this age than the increasing importance of religion and religious institutions in men's lives.

Emperor Worship

The varieties of philosophy and religion which at the time of the appearance of Christianity were prominent in meeting the needs of the age were the imperial religion or emperor worship, Roman Stoicism, religious versions of Platonism, Hellenistic Judaism, a number of mystery religions, and a syncretistic religio-philosophical movement known as Gnosticism. Among these, it was the practice of worshiping the emperor which furnished the emotional basis and Stoicism which furnished the intellectual basis for the unifying process. It is obvious that in a world of many nationalities and traditional national religions, the worship of the emperor as the personification of the entire Empire would become a conspicuous force in bringing about a spiritual unity and would serve in the various provinces as a pledge of their loyalty to the whole. Emperor worship was not an artificial ritual consciously created and promoted by the emperors themselves; on the contrary, Augustus tried to curb the tendency to deify him during his own lifetime. This practice was rather a result of certain tendencies already present in the Hellenistic world.

For centuries such nations as Egypt and Babylonia had endowed their political affairs with a religious significance. Kings were always special agents of the gods and enjoyed a peculiar relationship with them. The Egyptian rulers, although in ancient times not objects of worship, were nevertheless regarded as the incarnation of gods, and were thought not to suffer the fate of ordinary mortals at death. The Babylonian kings were not actually deified, but it is certain that they were looked upon as definitely set apart from the rest of mankind and as enjoying a unique relation with the gods. Although the political tradition of Greece had been democratic, the practice of hero worship was widespread, and some of the more distinguished of these heroes were elevated to the rank of divinity. Even the philosopher Empedocles was so honored by his followers. Within this background it is not surprising that in many quarters there should have been a spontaneous according of divine honors to a man like Alexander. During the Hellenistic age the Ptolemies in Egypt and the Seleucids in Syria, being foreign kings, found the practice of worshiping the ruler helpful in maintaining their positions. In both of these monarchies it was not long before even the living kings were deified. Thus the transition to the worship of the Roman emperor was an easy one and had its origin in the Eastern provinces rather than in Rome itself.

When Julius Caesar returned to Rome from his wars in the East, the unusual honors he was given marked the beginning of emperor worship in that city. Upon his death he was deified and given the name *Divus Julius*, and an official cult of Caesar was established in 42 B.C. The reign of Augustus was marked by the termination of the civil wars and the restoration of prosperity; in view of these achievements, it was natural that he should enjoy great popularity throughout the Empire. He was looked upon by the masses literally as a higher being than man: as a savior, benefactor, and restorer of peace on earth. The worship of Augustus was an act of genuine appreciation. In the East, even during his lifetime, numerous temples were erected in his honor and supplied with their priests and rituals. Upon his death in 14 A.D., the Senate at Rome made him one of the gods of the state. Thus emperor worship became firmly established in the West.

This imperial cult was not intended to be the exclusive religion of the Empire. The syncretism of the times made it possible for other cults to flourish so long as there was obedience to the state. Furthermore, the influence of traditional Greek polytheism made it possible for one to be devoted to more than one god without contradiction. Again, it was not the emperor as a person who was thought of as a god but the emperor as the personification of the state. In reality it was the Roman state which was deified, and the head of that state was accorded divine honors on condition that he served well, not merely because he held the title of emperor. Among those who were thus honored there were some whose worship was merely perfunctory, while for others the masses felt a genuine religious awe.

Thus the practice of worshiping the emperor served as an emotional force binding the people of various cultures together. That this practice became so easily established indicates also a general religious characteristic of the time—an almost universal hope of salvation from present ills, a salvation to be brought about with the aid of a messenger, helper, or agent possessing divine power. In the case of the imperial religion this hope took the form of a heaven-sent emperor who would deliver the people from such collective evils as war and economic distress and would usher in a golden age of peace and prosperity.

Roman Stoicism

Of all the philosophies of Greece, Stoicism was the one whose influence became most widely diffused in the Greco-Roman world. In a very real sense, however, this philosophy ought properly to be classified not as Greek but as Hellenistic since its originator, Zeno, was a Phoenician who lived after the Golden Age of Athens and during the lifetime of Alexander. Along with Epicureanism, Stoicism reflected the spiritual needs of the Hellenistic world. They were both practical philosophies whose purpose was to furnish a plan of life for the individual, a plan which would enable him to become self-sufficient and secure in his own peace of mind despite the vast problems and evils in the world about him. With slight modification, Epicureanism entered the Roman world and attracted a considerable number of followers, but its influence, compared with that of Stoicism, was limited. The message of Epicureanism was one that appealed only to that minority of intellectuals who felt that all striving was vanity and that the good life consisted in withdrawing from the outer world and enjoying such pleasures as could be readily obtained.

Stoicism, by contrast, offered individual consolation and a good deal more. Had it been merely an ethical teaching of self-sufficiency and withdrawal from the world, its influence would probably have been as limited as that of Epicureanism, but strains of thought existed within Stoicism which made it peculiarly suitable to the needs of a world society and fitted to become the primary philosophy of the Empire.

Like Epicureanism, Stoicism did have an individual ethic which taught men to be independent of their environment. One is unhappy only if he allows events in the outer world to make him so. His peace of mind is upset when his reaction to objective facts is of the emotional sort. The wise man will forever keep reason in control and will suppress his emotions with uncompromising consistency. Self-sufficiency is achieved by a strengthening of the will, devotion to duty, and indifference to both pleasures and pains. In this way does a man become captain of his soul. He builds a citadel within himself which nothing can destroy.

This much of the Stoic teaching would seem to be serving the same purpose as Epicureanism, but the individual ethic was supported by a quite different view of nature. Stoic metaphysics offered two reasons which reinforced the resolution of man not to rebel against the events of the outer world. In the first place, the universe is run according to inexorable law; what happens *must* happen. Therefore, the wise man realizes that to complain is futile and only adds to his misery. In the second place, it is not only futile but immoral to rebel, because the law of nature is providential. Not only are all things determined, but they are so determined that ultimately they all work for good. The beneficent universal law, called Providence, God, *Logos,* or Divine Fire, is itself rational. This divine fire which pervades the universe is of the same stuff as the sparks which light the rational souls of men. Both the *Logos* and man are rational, and the good man, sensitive to the call of duty to become godlike, interprets this call as the duty to become completely rational and thus to recognize the working of Providence in all that happens.

The universe is a moral order. Human beings are not alien creatures living in a morally indifferent nature. Unlike the lower animals, they are endowed with divinity since in their souls is a spark of that same divine fire which animates the world. Just as all things fit into a unified nature, so all men are parts of a single society or unified nature of human beings. This is why the Stoic talks of a world city or world state, and says that a man is not merely a citizen of Athens or Sparta but a citizen of the world as well. Above and beyond the local cities there is a worldwide human brotherhood, and this means that equality among men is more fundamental than social and racial distinctions.

This part of Stoic philosophy had important consequences for social and political theory in both the Hellenistic and the Greco-Roman world. The notion of equality provided a philosophic basis for minimizing the importance of social classes and race distinctions. After the time of Alexander, the Greek was forced by circumstances to abandon his disdain for barbarians and to recognize the positive values in cultures other than his own. Stoicism provided him with an intellectual justification for doing so. Politically, the idea of a world state was particularly well suited to an age which saw the breakdown of independent cities. Every man belongs to two political units —the local city which his body inhabits, and the world city which is ruled by reason. The first has its laws and customs which are different from those of other cities; the second is under one divine law, the law of reason, binding together all people as citizens, not by force but (insofar as men have attained rationality) by willing consent. Since the laws of cities are local and derived from custom while the law of the Great City is one and derived from reason, the latter should be used as the norm. Behind the variety of local customs there is one set of principles for human relationships. This fact offers a point of view from which the value of particular customs can be intelligently estimated. The one law of reason forms the basis for settling disputes between regions and for criticizing the justice of particular laws. The influence of this concept on the development of Roman law has been universally recognized.

It should now be clear that Stoicism was a philosophy which met *both* the needs of the age which we are discussing. It provided an ethic for the individual and at the same time had a cosmopolitan social and political philosophy. However, the early version of Stoicism, as held by Zeno, had to be revised before it could become generally effective. Two features of this earlier version were severely attacked by rival schools of thought and were modified before this philosophy had a marked influence in Rome. In the first place, the Stoic description of the ideal wise man made him a completely emotionless rational being. He had destroyed his capacity both for sorrow and for joy, for hate and for love. It is certain that no living person has ever completely attained this ideal, and it is even questionable whether such an ideal is desirable. And yet the Stoic maintained that either a man was virtuous and wise and entirely emotionless or he was evil and foolish. No provision was made for stages of development between these two extremes. In the second place, early Stoicism did not make clear any meaningful relation between the universal law of reason or the world city and actual social relationships which men knew in the world of experience. The ideal community of wise men was so ideal that it seemed to have no bearing upon actual communities.

In respect to both of these features important modifications were made by

Panaetius (*ca.* 180-111 B.C.) and his pupil *Posidonius* (*ca.* 130-50 B.C.), the former being responsible for bringing Stoicism to the Romans. These men were not averse to introducing ideas drawn from Plato and Aristotle, emphasizing, for example, the Aristotelian Golden Mean and the virtue of temperance. They also helped Stoicism gain acceptance by appealing to the native Roman virtues of courage, self-control, and devotion to duty in daily life. Gradually the ideal of the austere and emotionless wise man gave way to the ideal of a public-spirited, urbane, humanitarian citizen of the Empire. In this way there was a bridging of the gulf between the perfect virtue which none could attain and the virtues actually practiced by the better men in ordinary life. A large number of intellectuals for whom the traditional religions had lost their meaning found in Stoicism not only a helpful philosophy but an adequate substitute for religion as well. Panaetius was also instrumental in ridding Stoicism of the sharp opposition between the ideal community and everyday social relationships. Although he always had Stoic theory as the background of his thinking, he talked less about it as a philosophic system than about its application to specific cases of conduct and to actual social practices. His ethic was thus made applicable to the real world.

No changes in the development of Stoicism dimmed the clarity of its central ideas—the individual virtues of fortitude, devotion to duty, and inner strength of the soul; the ideal of the equality of all men and a worldwide human brotherhood; the notion that even a world state can have ethical foundations and impose a moral demand of obedience upon all its citizens. Consequently, Stoicism not only formed the basis of a political theory adequate for the Greco-Roman world in which there was, in fact, one world empire, but also helped idealize the results of the Roman conquest by showing the possibility of making the Empire a partial fulfillment on earth of the ideal world state.

Mystery Religions

In this chapter we have been examining two great needs which philosophy and religion sought to meet in the Roman Empire and have noted how, in different ways and with varying degrees of success, these two needs were met by emperor worship and Roman Stoicism. We look next at a third powerful movement, religious rather than philosophical, which met both these needs but in particular the second one—the need of spiritual and emotional support by individuals making their way in a world society. This movement is that of the mystery religions. No religious influence was greater at the beginning and in the early years of the Christian era than that of the mystery cults. We have become acquainted with the Orphic and the Eleusinian mysteries in our study of Greek religion. Similar to these were the mysteries of the East, especially the Phrygian cult of Cybele and Attis, the Egyptian mystery of Isis and Osiris, and the religion of Mithra, which was of Persian origin. Even in their earliest stages of development, these mysteries had so many similarities that it seems reasonable to suppose they all met a common psychological need. The similarities also made it possible, whenever there was contact between two mysteries, to identify the gods of one with those of the other. The Greeks, for example, at a comparatively early date identified the Egyptian Osiris and Isis with their own Dionysus and Demeter. After the time of Alexander the mysteries showed an amazing ability to adapt themselves to the needs of the period, and there was such interaction and mutual borrowing that by the Christian era they had become indistinguishable in many respects.

There were several reasons for the growing popularity of the mysteries during this period. In the first place, unlike Hellenistic Judaism, they had lost all national and racial affiliations. A person did not become a member of a mystery cult by being born into it or by becoming a naturalized citizen of a particular country. Membership was both voluntary and international. In this way the needs of a cosmopolitan society were met. Second, the mysteries reached the masses to a far greater extent than the religious philosophies of Stoicism or Platonism ever could. Their appeal was based not on intellectual concepts but on drama and ritual. In the third place, they offered their votaries assurance of personal salvation and individual immortality, thus appealing to the individualism of the day.

Certain features of the mysteries made them not unlike a modern college fraternity. Ordinarily a student is not immediately initiated into a fraternity after he has been accepted by the brothers. There may be several months during which he is a "pledge," undergoing a training which is designed as a preparation for full membership. Then comes the ceremony of initiation in which he is first sworn to secrecy and then witnesses the revelation of the meaning of the various symbols of the fraternity. So the mystery religions were characterized by a period of preparation and initiation. If a person wished to avail himself of the advantages of a mystery cult, he presented himself to the priests of the religion. It was a matter of personal choice and personal responsibility. The priests admitted him only if he proved himself sincere and capable of becoming fit for membership. He was examined and underwent a period of disciplinary preparation.

There were undoubtedly many motives which sent people to the mysteries, not all of which were of a particularly high moral or spiritual nature. Some people were attracted for the same reasons that men today like to join secret fraternal organizations. Some found an emotional outlet and an opportunity for self-indulgence in the ritualistic orgies. The superstitious looked for magical protection from evil spirits. But the predominant religious motive was the desire to be at one with the divine. It was connected with a feeling of loneliness on the part of individuals living in a world society, and also with a feeling that sins on their part had created huge barriers between them and the deity. During the period of preparation, therefore, the neophyte submitted to certain processes through which his unworthiness and uncleanness were removed and expiation was made for his sins. Such preparation consisted of a variety of practices; confession was fairly common. Also there were ceremonial washings and baptism by immersion. These were symbolic both of spiritual cleansing and of regeneration, that is, of the death of the old sinful self and the birth of the new man. Among the disciplines to which one was subjected during his probationary period were such ascetic preparations as long fasts, periods of continence, and bodily mutilations.

In Mithraism, a mystery which attained immense popularity by the second century A.D., largely through its appeal to the members of the Roman army, there were definite grades or degrees of spiritual progress of which three preceded actual initiation. At each stage of development the candidate was tested by certain ordeals such as passing through fire, swimming rivers, or leaping off a precipice. These ordeals may have been real at one time, but probably in the later refinements of the religion they were feigned in a way similar to the techniques employed by a modern secret fraternity. In any case, there was meant to be a serious testing of the candidate's courage, fidelity, and sincerity of purpose.

Historians have found it impossible to discover exactly what happened in the actual initiation ceremonies because the vow of secrecy was conscientiously kept. A number of researchers, however, have given us some information. It is certain, for example, that there were sacred objects which the candidate was allowed to see for the first time. Among these may have been holy books which were used as the basis for instruction. Theology and ethical teaching were not entirely missing, but they had little prominence compared with visible symbols and drama.

One of the more famous of the initiation ceremonies which was employed by at least two cults, those of the Cappadocian goddess Ma and of Cybele (*Magna Mater*), was the *taurobolium* (not found in the West before the second century A.D.). The person who was to receive the benefits of this rite

Mithra Slaying the Bull

The bull was the first of all created beings. At the command of the god Ahuramazda, Mithra captured and killed it. From its body came forth useful herbs and plants; from its blood came the vine; out of its spinal cord sprang wheat and out of its seed came all the species of useful animals. The snake and the scorpion represent the powers of darkness and destruction which try unsuccessfully to halt the process of creation by consuming the genital parts and drinking the blood. By his act, Mithra becomes the creator of all beneficient beings on earth, the god of light and civilization. (From Huart's Ancient Persia and Iranian Civilization, *Kegan Paul, Trench, Trubner & Co., Ltd.)*

descended into a large pit over which a perforated platform had been built. On the platform a bull was killed, and his blood dripped into the pit below. The person in the pit allowed himself to be covered with the blood, being particularly careful to allow it to touch all parts of his face and even to take some of it into his mouth. The origin of this practice is obscure, but its symbolism by the second century A.D. is fairly apparent. The bull was consecrated, and the initiate was thus bathed in divine blood which washed away his past sins. When he emerged from the pit drenched with sacred blood, he was a new man, born again for eternity.

The taurobolium, a vivid symbol of the process of redemption, illustrates one of the most important features of the mysteries. Initiation meant, above everything else, the death of the former self and birth into the life of the spirit. This perhaps explains the fact that the ceremonies often took place at midnight. Just as midnight is both the death of the former day and the birth of a new one, so the initiate experienced both death and rebirth. His former life, in which he was subject to the domination of evils of the flesh, was gone, and he now entered into a life of spiritual emancipation. Rebirth was accompanied by a feeling on the part of the individual that he had achieved intimate communion with the deity through whom his transformation had taken place. Frequently there were ecstatic experiences in which the normal functions of personality were lost and a feeling of emotional exhilaration was gained.

Salvation meant not only the purification of one's life in this world but, as also in the Greek mysteries, assurance of personal immortality as well. Usually there were myths concerning the mystery god to the effect that he had died and had risen from the grave, thus demonstrating his power over death and his ability to confer immortality on those who worshiped him. The stories concerning such gods as Attis and Osiris are instructive on this point. In the Phrygian mystery, Attis was a youth associated with Cybele, the Great Mother. In a state of fury, according to one account, he emasculated himself and died of his wounds beneath a pine tree, violets growing where his blood touched the earth. Then he was raised from the dead by the Great Mother. All of this was dramatized by the members of the mystery religion each year at the time of the vernal equinox. A pine tree was cut down, decorated with violets, and carried to the temple. The worshipers entered and mourned for the suffering of Attis, sharing his tragedy. The mourning was followed by rejoicing over his resurrection, while the worshipers identified themselves with him as a risen god, partaking of his immortal life.

The Isis-Osiris myth has much the same meaning. The Egyptian god Osiris had been a beneficent king, universally loved for his goodness and the benefits he bestowed on mankind. He was killed by his evil brother Set, and his body was placed in a chest and thrown into the Nile. Isis, sister and also wife of Osiris, wandered about in search of the body. After a long search, during which she suffered many persecutions, she was successful in recovering the body of Osiris. But again Set obtained possession of it and this time dismembered it, scattering its various parts about Egypt. In the meantime Isis had given birth to Horus, whom she reared secretly. Again she went in search of the dismembered Osiris, eventually recovering all the parts of his body. This time Osiris was miraculously restored to life and became the god of the dead. His son Horus was able to take vengeance upon Set and eventually received the crown and throne of his father. In this myth is symbolized the struggle between good and evil in the world, the suffering of the good god, and the eventual victory over death.

It is interesting to note the ideas which lay behind the process by which a human being took on immortality. Undoubtedly these ideas were for the most part of Greek origin. To be a human being was to be mortal, while the essence of divinity was immortality. Thus, if mortal man was to become immortal his very essence had to be changed. To put it in philosophic terms, man took on a different metaphysical status. In entering into the sufferings and ultimate resurrection of the god whom he worshiped, a man actually became divine, or the divine took possession of him in such a way as to alter his essential nature. Another version of this belief was that the spirits of both men and gods had originally been the same. The spirits of men, however, dwelling in physical bodies, had been contaminated and thus had lost their right to immortal life. Salvation both in this world and in the future life, therefore, meant the recovery by the soul of man of its original nature. In any case, salvation in the mystery cults was generally associated with the idea of a metaphysical change occurring in man.

Philo and Religious Platonism

In addition to the movements of thought in the Roman Empire at the time of the rise of Christianity which met great spiritual and emotional needs, there were other intellectual developments that did not meet these needs so clearly as the ones we have just examined but that were important in later thought, particularly within the developing Christian movement. We turn to look briefly at three of these: religious Platonism, Hellenistic Judaism, and Gnosticism.

The complex of religions and philosophies of the century preceding the beginning of the Christian era produced many curious combinations. An interesting and important example of the fusion of East and West is found in the work of Philo (*ca.* 25 B.C.-A.D. 40), a Jew who lived in Alexandria, Egypt, and was a contemporary of Jesus. Philo was loyal to the religion of his race and believed thoroughly in the divine origin of the Hebrew Scriptures, but he was also at home in Greek philosophy. He used the Greek language and read widely in Greek literature, particularly the dialogues of Plato. Just as his own spiritual life was nourished by both the Jewish religion and Platonic philosophy, so his writings not only reflect these same influences but are designed to show that there is no fundamental conflict between the two. This attempt to fuse Greek philosophy and Hebrew revelation was not unique; Philo is but the most conspicuous figure in a process which was typical of the intellectual and religious environment in which he lived.

In order to understand Philo it is necessary to know something of the Platonic influence of the first century B.C. and also to review some of the more important features of the Judaism which was familiar to the Jew who lived in Alexandria and other cities of the Greco-Roman world. First, let us see what had happened to the Platonic tradition. During his own lifetime, as we know, Plato had founded the Academy which had a continuous existence until A.D. 529 when it was closed by Justinian I. This explains how Plato's dialogues were preserved and why the Platonic influence was never completely eclipsed by other philosophies. Stoicism, as we have said, enjoyed a greater vogue than Platonism, and for a time (from 241 to 129 B.C.) the leaders of the Academy concentrated their attention upon criticizing certain features of the Stoic philosophy, especially its theory of knowledge. By the first century B.C. the rivalry between these schools had been replaced by an eclecticism which brought the two together. Not only were Panaetius and Posidonius rendering a Platonic version of Stoicism, but there were also attempts to read Stoicism into Plato. The reappearance of the philosophy of Plato as a pre-eminent influence did not take place until the third century A.D., when Plotinus in Rome became the outstanding leader of the school of Neo-Platonism. We shall discuss that in a later chapter. But there is abundant evidence that even in the first century B.C. a popular Platonism had reached many parts of the Empire.

Two factors influenced the course of the Platonic tradition. The first was the separation of science and philosophy. When the intellectual center of the ancient world shifted from Athens to Alexandria, the sciences were developed independently of philosophic schools. Plato himself had been devoted to mathematics and cosmology, but his successors in the Academy confined their speculations to technical and often barren work on the theory of knowledge. The second factor was the dominant religious interest of the Hellenistic world. There was an emphasis on moral idealism and religious aspiration in Plato, and this emphasis found its way into the religious syncretism of the times.

We have seen that central in Plato's metaphysics was his theory of Ideas. Although the world of experience presents itself as a constant flux, reason perceives that more fundamental than change is a world of eternal and changeless Forms or Ideas. This intelligible world of Ideas was given unity by making the Good the highest Idea of all. Just as all beautiful things are subsumed under the Idea of Beauty, so are all the Ideas subsumed under the Idea of the Good. The Good came about as near as anything to what for Plato was ultimate reality; yet there is no evidence that Plato himself consistently identified the Good with God. This identification was made, however, in later religious versions of Platonism.

Religious Platonism transformed the Idea of the Good into a God who, unlike the Stoic *Logos* which pervaded the world and thus was completely immanent, was distinctly and wholly other than the world and thus transcended it. One analogy which Plato used in *The Republic* in describing the Good was later employed, in a slightly different fashion, to make clear the relation of God to the world. The Good, he said, serves the same purpose in the intelligible world as the sun does in the sensible world. The sun is the very condition of our seeing anything. We can open our eyes, but if all is dark it is impossible to perceive any objects whatever. Only when rays of light are thrown upon these objects can we distinguish them. And it is almost impossible, indeed it is blinding and dazzling, to look upon the sun itself. So in the intelligible world the Idea of the Good is the very condition of our understanding, although it is difficult to climb to that place where we can know the Good itself. This same analogy was used later to describe the nature of God. God is like the sun. The sun remains what it is and is not diminished in any way by giving off heat and light. Furthermore, all we know of the sun is what it does. It is not a part of the earth, and yet, by means of its rays, it is the source of life, light, and energy on the earth. In like manner, God himself is not intellectually comprehended, although the effects of his reality—his power and divine rule—are experienced in the world.

Another analogy suggested by religious Platonism was that of likening God to a mind. The only way in which the mind of one person is known by another is through bodily behavior or through language. The mind itself always eludes the attempt of others to know it directly, but it can express itself through gestures, actions, and words. Thus the contact between God and the world is through his utterance, his expressed wisdom, his word (*logos*).

There are three things in this point of view which must be clearly seen if we are to understand the religious Platonism of Philo and the Christians. The first is the sharp distinction between God and the world. God is spirit and God is good, while the world, insofar as it is material, is evil. The dualism of spirit and matter becomes a dualism of good and evil. In the second place, there is no direct contact between God and the world. Such relation as there is between the two is effected by intermediary powers, which are described as streams of light, God's ideas, or God's word. Third, God can be known only through mystical intuition. There is some precedent for this in Plato's own writings—in *The Republic*, for example, where he pictures the ascent of the mind from the perception of shadows to perfect knowledge. The knowledge of the Idea of the Good is really of the nature of a mystic vision. These were among the interpretations of Plato which Philo and others elaborated. Let us turn our attention now to Philo's other main spiritual font.

Philo and Hellenistic Judaism

We have seen that from the time of the Babylonian Exile many Jews had had to learn to live away from their homeland and to carry on their traditions in the midst of other peoples. By the first century B.C., there were Jewish colonies in most of the important cities of the Greco-Roman world. Estimates place the total number of Jews in the Roman Empire at over 4,000,000, which was about 7 percent of the total population of the Empire. Every town and city in the Empire which had 10 or more adult male Jews had at least one synagogue. Many of these Jews were very wealthy, and because of their strong organization they were able to exercise great influence throughout the Roman Empire. Special laws were passed in their favor, particularly under Julius Caesar and Augustus, and the various Roman parties vied with each other to hold Jewish favor. Jews were excused from participation in emperor worship and from military service.[2]

Egypt at the time of Christ is credited with a Jewish population of about 1,000,000; hundreds of thousands lived in Alexandria alone, where two-fifths of the city was Jewish. These Jews of the Dispersion were determined to remain loyal to their religion and customs, but they inevitably felt the influence of their new environment, particularly the Greek element. The Greek language came to be commonly spoken even by the Jews, so that eventually, beginning probably in the third century B.C. with the Pentateuch and continuing sporadically during the next three centuries with the remainder of the books of the Jewish Scriptures, all of these sacred writings were translated from Hebrew into Greek, forming the Greek version, the *Septuagint*, so named because of the tradition that 70 scholars had shared in the work of translating it.

[2] S. Angus, *The Environment of Early Christianity*, New York, Charles Scribner's Sons, 1914, chap. 5; Morton Scott Enslin, *Christian Beginnings*, New York, Harper & Brothers, 1938, chap. 5.

Hellenistic Judaism was a complex structure within which we are able to distinguish clearly three general characteristics important to our study. The first was its exclusiveness. We know how strongly nationalistic the historic religion of the Jews was. Yahweh was Israel's God and Israel was Yahweh's nation. Hellenistic Jews could not consistently share the earlier nationalistic hopes, but they could think of themselves as a special race of people having a special relationship with their God. The emphasis was shifted from nation to race, so that in the Hellenistic cities the Jews lived together in the same sections, built synagogues, and carried on the traditional customs and teaching of the Law. This exclusiveness, as we have seen, allowed the Jews to maintain their religious and cultural integrity, but it was also one of the reasons for the anti-Semitism of that day. Their strict monotheism prevented them from participating in the public festivals where gods other than Yahweh were shown respect. Even worse, they could not take part in the imperial cult, which sometimes caused them to be suspected of political disloyalty. They were strict in their observance of the Sabbath, the regulations concerning diet, and the time-honored rite of circumcision.

It may seem strange, in view of its exclusiveness, that a second characteristic of the Judaism of this period was its extensive and successful missionary effort. This does not mean that there were professional Jewish missionaries who went to Gentile lands in order to make converts; that was not necessary, for the communities of Jews living in cosmopolitan centers throughout the Empire had merely to exert their influence upon the Gentiles through the local synagogues. That Judaism should become a missionary religion is logically understandable. The development of this religion had reached the point where the God of Israel was definitely regarded as the one God of all mankind. Along with the traditional nationalism or racialism, there was also the claim to universality which held that the children of Israel alone knew the true religion and worshiped the one God, but one day, through Israel as his instrument, Yahweh would be recognized throughout the world.

Many Gentiles were attracted by the teaching of the synagogues. To some, accustomed as they were to the variety of philosophic systems of the day, Judaism appeared to be one more philosophy possessing an admirable ethic. They probably found it difficult to understand the strange customs of the Jews, and in an age of religious syncretism they may have been puzzled by the authoritarian character of Judaism in claiming exclusive possession of the truth revealed in a sacred literature. Others were impressed by this very authoritarianism and the version it gave of the coming golden age. They wanted to become members of the group which served the one true God. Many converts were made, but Judaism, unlike Christianity at a later date, did not become an international church. Conversion meant not only accepting the tenets of a religious faith; it meant also becoming naturalized in the Jewish nation or race. The converts or proselytes, after being circumcised and baptized in water, had a sacrifice offered for them at the Temple in Jerusalem. In addition to the proselytes there was another group known as God-fearers, who were not circumcised and thus never became Jews in the full sense. But they received instruction in the Law, believed in its religious principles, and observed some of the Jewish rites. Many from this class of people turned later to Christianity.

In spite of its exclusiveness and authoritarianism, it is also true, in the third place, that Judaism could not avoid Greek influence. It was not long, for example, before Alexandrian Jews knew only the Greek language. Since words have subtle connotations, Jews who read their Scriptures in the Greek language necessarily imbibed something of the Greek spirit as well. No matter how carefully they observed their Law, they could not avoid becoming partly Greek in a cultural sense. And indeed, there were many things about the Hellenistic intellectual heritage which attracted them. Chief among these was the Platonic notion of an immaterial reality with which the souls of men could mystically commune.

Philo was one of those who were culturally both Jew and Greek. He wrote extensive commentaries on the Bible in which he tried to show the Greeks that all the values of their philosophical wisdom were already present in the Law and the prophets, and he also tried to show the Jews that Greek ideas were not always in sharp opposition to the Mosaic Law. In other words, he tried to fuse his revealed religion and his Greek philosophy. In order to make this plausible he resorted to the technique of interpreting the Bible as an allegory in which a great parable of the way of salvation is set forth. The use of allegory made it possible to retain the belief in the divine authorship of the Bible and at the same time read into it certain philosophical ideas. The familiar stories of the Old Testament were interpreted as descriptions of the process of mystical salvation. The call of Abraham to leave Ur of the Chaldees and to set out in search of the Promised Land was explained as the call to leave the world of physical things and sensory experience in order to rise to the spiritual realm of God. In like manner, Jacob's flight from his brother Esau was interpreted to mean that Jacob was turning away from the evils of the flesh in order that he might attain a mystical vision of God. The philosophy of religion which resulted from this fusion of Old Testament belief and Greek philosophy was both interesting and influential.

Philo's discussion of God sometimes suggests the Yahweh of Israel—a personal, living God. At other times Philo seems to have in mind the transcendent Being of religious Platonism; and again he gives the impression of insisting on the Stoic doctrine of a completely immanent God. At one and the same time God is both the personal God of the Hebrews and is completely transcendent, out of contact with the world and quite incomprehensible; this transcendent God is too pure and holy to have direct relationship with the world, which by contrast to him is deficient and even evil. The Biblical references to God, said Philo, are not meant to be philosophical descriptions of his nature but are rather helpful myths. The real Yahweh is this unchanging, perfect Being for which Greek philosophy is searching.

Since the good God so completely transcends the evil world, how does Philo find he influences it or relates himself to it? Aristotle, we recall, taught that the Unmoved Mover is not even aware of the world but that the world is attracted to him by his perfection. Philo is not willing to accept this view. On the opposite side, the Stoics said that God is completely immanent within the world, being actually the world mind or soul. Philo moves between this view and that of Aristotle by suggesting an idea which had vast influence on later thinkers: He wrote that the *Logos* is the bridge that unites God and the world. This *Logos* is not God himself, nor is he a creature—he is a spiritual being. Sometimes Philo refers to the *Logos* as impersonal and sometimes as a personal second God through whom God exercises his control of the universe. The *Logos* is not in any sense equal to God—in fact, the *Logos* is definitely inferior and subordinate. Called sometimes the firstborn of God or the first Idea of God, he is the means of creation of the world, the channel for God's revelation to man, and the instrument through whom God now exercises his control over events. By using this concept of the *Logos*, Philo was able to bring together God's transcendence and his immanent activity.

Still other ancient philosophical understandings are drawn into the net of Philo's thought. We recall that the Ideas which Plato regarded as the ultimately real seemed disconnected from anything that might explain them. God did not create them; they subsist in a quite rootless way. Philo took these Platonic Ideas and taught that they are the ideas *of God*, having their reality because God thinks them. They exist within the one *Logos* as many *logoi* or intermediary powers; the *Logos* is the Idea of all Ideas. Even here Philo does not call a halt, but goes on to say that these *logoi* are what the Old Testament called the angels of Yahweh. Whether Philo thought of the *logoi* as independent beings or as aspects of the *Logos* is uncertain, but it is readily seen that with his understanding of the *Logos* and the *logoi* he was able to provide a kind of unity, uneasy as it was, for Hebrew, Stoic, and

Platonic thought. His *Logos* differs from the Stoic *Logos* by being not God himself but an inferior being, standing between the transcendent God and the universe, and, further, by being purely spiritual while the Stoic *Logos* was "material."

Finally, Philo's great influence is seen in the impetus he gave to mysticism. The dualism of God and the world is reflected in man as a duality of spirit and flesh. Man's soul, derived from God, is held captive in the body; the goal of human life is to escape the chains of the flesh. There is only one means by which this can be accomplished: by the mystical path of meditation and contemplation. Philo believed, of course, that the Jewish Law was the perfect guide to life in the material world, and with the Stoics he believed also that since man lives in the world he should bear social and political responsibilities dutifully and cheerfully. But the ultimate good for Philo is the mystical ecstasy in which the soul turns its back on matter and reaches at last the beatific vision of God. In his essay entitled "Who is the Heir," he writes:

> Therefore, my soul, if thou feelest any yearning to inherit the good things of God, leave not only thy land, that is the body, thy kinsfolk, that is the senses, thy father's house (Gen. xii.1), that is speech, but be a fugitive from thyself also and issue forth from thyself. . . , be filled with inspired frenzy, even as the prophets are inspired. For it is the mind which is under the divine afflatus, and no longer in its own keeping, but is stirred to its depths and maddened by heavenward yearning, drawn by the truly existent and pulled upward thereto, with truth to lead the way and remove all obstacles before its feet . . .—such is the mind, which has this for inheritance.[3]

The influence of Philo, the syncretist, upon the developing Neo-Platonism and the thought of early Christianity can scarcely be overestimated. Possibly just because of rather than in spite of his looseness of logic and his attempt to hold irreconcilables together, his thinking was especially stimulating to the minds of his successors. In any case, his influence upon Neo-Platonism can be seen most clearly in his emphasis upon the transcendence of God, the activity of intermediary beings between God and the world, and the mystical, ecstatic vision as the goal of the soul's search. His influence was possibly greatest upon Christian thought in his use of analogy to interpret Scripture and in his making the *Logos* a second God, creator of the universe. While not itself the Christian concept, it pointed toward the later use in the Gospel of John of the term *Logos*, where the *Logos* is presented as

[3] *Philo*, 69, 70, tr. F. H. Colson and G. H. Whitaker, Cambridge, Harvard University Press, The Loeb Classical Library, 1949, vol. IV, p. 317.

incarnate in the man Jesus (John 1). It can be truly stated that Philo more than any other single thinker provided the bridge between Greek philosophy and the Biblical revelation over which Christian theology was later to pass.[4]

Gnosticism

Gnosticism was a typical product of the Hellenistic world. It appears to have belonged to the development of thought we have called religious Platonism. In many ways it resembled the mystery religions, and it is quite possible that the revival of Orphic and Neo-Pythagorean ideas and practices paved the way for its appearance. It was an eclectic way of thinking par excellence, containing elements of Greek philosophy, Babylonian mythology, Persian dualism, Egyptian mysticism, and Jewish theology. It managed to make its way into both Hebrew and Christian thought, and from the latter we have our best knowledge of it as it developed during the second and third centuries A.D. In a way it was philosophical in nature, though not in the sense of promoting a disinterested quest for truth. Its philosophy and religion, like those of practically all the thought of the period, were fused in a practical and serious search for a means of personal salvation. It was more eager to receive ideas from diverse religions and systems of thought than it was to work out a consistent system of its own.

Since Gnosticism was typical of the religious and philosophic quests of the Greco-Roman world and since it had a marked influence upon the development of early Christianity, we shall point out what seem to have been some of its more important features, although it is impossible to give a completely accurate summary. It was not a cult but was rather a name for a general way of thinking which was found in many cults. This is why it easily attached itself to a particular religion like Christianity. The word *gnosis* means knowledge. By connotation, the term had some affiliation with the Greek reverence for knowledge. The Socratic dictum, "Know thyself," was interpreted to mean that if one really did know himself and his place in the scheme of the cosmos he could attain salvation. Grafted to this Hellenic notion was the Oriental distrust of merely human knowing. Knowledge which was to be efficacious in bringing about salvation had to be of a higher order—it had to be divinely revealed. The purpose of Gnosticism was both

[4] Discussions of Philo can be found in Enslin, *op. cit.*, pp. 87 ff.; Richard Kroner, *Speculation in Pre-Christian Philosophy*, Philadelphia, The Westminster Press, 1956, pp. 237-240; and Frederick Copleston, *A History of Philosophy*, Westminster, The Newman Bookshop, 1946, vol. I, pp. 457-462.

metaphysical and ethical. It had the same dualistic philosophy which we have discussed in connection with Philo. As in the mysteries, salvation meant gaining freedom from the body, but contrary to the mysteries, salvation came through the possession of a higher order of knowledge, a hidden, esoteric knowledge which led one to a higher order of being.

The Gnostic metaphysics can best be seen in mythological form. One belief held that at the head of the universe is God, an impersonal and indescribable being. From him proceed a number of lesser beings who as a group constitute the Pleroma. Over against the Pleroma, or world of spirit, is Chaos. Ialdabaoth, the rebellious son of Sophia (heavenly wisdom), is the cause of creative work being done in the realm of Chaos, which results in the creation of the physical world containing both matter and spirit. Man's vocation is that of rising to the realm of spirit, an achievement which can be the privilege of only a part of mankind, the elect. Man cannot by his own unaided efforts reach salvation; it can be obtained only as the saving God imparts saving esoteric knowledge (*gnosis*). It is easy to see how the Gnostics, when they came in contact with Christianity, found in Christ the God who brought into the world his saving truth.

Conclusion

Judged from the standpoint of philosophy and religion, the Greco-Roman world was a world of restless seeking. Almost every conceivable idea of God and his relation to the universe found its place in this world, but no one system of thought was capable of dominating the scene. Even magic was widely practiced as still another way of delivering man from the hold of Fate upon him, thus freeing him for "salvation." In sum, it can be said that the dominant philosophic attitude was that of seeking for salvation for human life. Stoicism, possibly the noblest of the thought systems of the period, gradually lost its high position because it did not sufficiently meet man's desire for emotional satisfactions. Judaism was religiously satisfying to many, but it was associated very closely with a racial group and its particular laws. What was needed was a religion that would be deeply satisfying emotionally and religiously with a promise that met the individual needs of men, undergirded by the best thought of the day, and capable of drawing men of all cultures and races into a new social community which would practice the highest ethical living. Christianity eventually proved itself the one religion capable of this tremendous task, and it thus became the universal religion of late Roman and subsequent European culture. In its development, Christianity absorbed many elements from those movements we have been describing. To this topic we turn in the next chapter.

Questions for Study

1. How did Alexander help bring about a "marriage of East and West"? How did Rome gain power over Greece, and when? What two great needs do we find in the Roman Empire, and why?
2. How did emperor worship get established; what need did it fill?
3. How did Roman Stoicism differ from the Greek variety? How did it meet the great needs of the day?
4. What were the forms of the Roman mystery religions, and why did people join them?
5. What changes did religious Platonism bring into original Platonism?
6. Who was Philo, where did he live, and why did he feel the need to develop his thought? What were the characteristics of Hellenistic Judaism?
7. At what points did Philo hold to Jewish ideas, and where to Greek? How successful was his synthesis? Do you find syncretism taking place in the world today? Does your own thinking illustrate this process?
8. Show the points of Philo's greatest influence.
9. What are the central emphases of Gnosticism? What kind of knowledge did it believe brings salvation?
10. What did Christianity have to offer to the world of its day which brought about its rapid spread?

Selected Readings

Angus, S., *The Religious Quests of the Graeco-Roman World*, New York, Charles Scribner's Sons, 1929.

Bailey, Cyril (ed.), *The Legacy of Rome*, Oxford, Clarendon Press, 1928.

Case, S. J., *The Evolution of Early Christianity*, Chicago, University of Chicago Press, 1914.

Copleston, Frederick, *A History of Philosophy*, Westminster, The Newman Bookshop, 1946, vol. I.

Enslin, Morton Scott, *Christian Beginnings*, New York, Harper & Brothers, 1938.

Goodenough, E. R., *Religious Tradition and Myth*, New Haven, Yale University Press, 1937.

Moore, George Foot, *Judaism*, Cambridge, Harvard University Press, 1927, vol. I.

Rostovtzeff, M., *A History of the Ancient World*, Oxford, Clarendon Press, 1927, vol. II.

Tarn, W. W., *Hellenistic Civilization*, London, Edward Arnold and Co., 1936.

11. The Early Development of Christian Thought

Relation of First-Century Christianity to Judaism

Among the many surprises that history holds, one of the most astonishing is the fact that the tiny country of Judaea as it was in the eighth century B.C. should have made contributions to world civilization unparalleled by any of the great powers of its day, like Assyria, Babylonia, and Egypt. A still greater surprise is the fact that out of that same tiny, mountainous land should have developed a second world religion whose central figure was a carpenter who was executed by the Romans. Everything about that event seemed a failure; even the disciples themselves fled, disheartened by the death of Jesus, seemingly convinced that their high hopes in him as prophet or Messiah were proved unfounded by his shameful death. Here the story should have ended, lost among the seemingly far more important events taking place in the Roman Empire. Instead, the spark which seemed completely extinguished started a conflagration which spread throughout the Empire. Christianity became in time the dominant religion of Europe and the Near East, and is today the foundation upon which dominant features of Western culture have been erected. This chapter will sketch something of how what appeared to be a small and insignificant cult of Judaism changed the Roman Empire even while it was in turn adapted to it.

The Resurrection

The account begins with the reported resurrection of the crucified Jesus. In an earlier chapter it was seen that Jesus taught the coming of God's kingdom and attracted to himself and his message a group of Palestinian Jews, chiefly Galileans, who came to look upon him as leader and master and probably as the fulfillment in some way of that messianic prophecy which was so prominent a part of the thinking of the Jews of that day. He failed, however, to fulfill that expectation in its popular form, for instead of becoming a victorious king who would rule in justice and lead the Jews to political independence and greatness he permitted himself to be arrested and crucified. To his followers this seemed to be the end of all their hopes, and as Jesus died and was buried they scattered, returning to their homes. Yet within a short time—a few days or weeks—they reassembled with regained faith and certainty. The end of the story turned out to be the beginning of a vastly greater claim and message, for the disciples asserted that Jesus was other and far greater than the Messiah popularly expected. This claim they based upon their experience that he who had died and been buried had appeared to them, that he was not dead but was resurrected and was still their Lord and Master, yet in a fuller sense than when he had been physically present with them. For a period of 40 days, it was reported, he appeared to various of them. They were convinced that God had raised him from the dead, and that the time was not far off when he would appear publicly in a victorious return to establish the kingdom of God in its fullness.

Exactly what did happen in the resurrection is one of the most difficult of historical problems, but that it *had* occurred was for the disciples not to be questioned; and the Christian church arose because of their faith in it. In the Biblical accounts of the resurrection there is disagreement on details, but all agree on the central fact that the Jesus who had died had returned and made himself known. There are many remarkable aspects to these stories, as any student can discover for himself by reading the concluding chapters of the four Gospels. The earliest written account is not any of these, however, but that given by Paul, writing about A.D. 55 in his first letter to the Corinthians. He writes:

> For I delivered to you as of first importance what I also received, that Christ died for our sins in accordance with the scriptures, that he was buried, that he was raised on the third day in accordance with the scriptures, and that he appeared to Cephas [Peter], then to the twelve. Then he appeared to more than five hundred brethren at one time, most of whom are still alive, though some have

The Church of the Holy Sepulchre

The entrance to the church, which marks the traditional site of the burial of Christ and the site of the Crucifixion. The present structure, erected in 1810, is built upon the remains of a church constructed in the fourteenth century.

fallen asleep. Then he appeared to James, then to all the apostles. Last of all, as to one untimely born, he appeared also to me [15:3-8].

As treated in the accounts, the form in which Jesus appeared in the resurrection was highly mysterious. According to some of them, the same physical body which died on the cross was the body seen in the resurrection. The apostle Thomas, for instance, was told to touch the wounds in Jesus' hands and side (John 20:26-29). Yet for Paul, Jesus' resurrection was in the form of a "spiritual body," and as such of a very different nature from that of the resuscitation of a corpse, instances of which had already been reported in the Bible as having happened in earlier times. The prophet Elijah, for instance, is reported to have brought back to life the dead son of a widow (I Kings 17), and Elisha is reported to have done the same for the son of a

Shunammite woman (II Kings 4). The New Testament reports that Jesus restored a widow's son to life (Luke 7:11 ff.), the daughter of Jairus (Mark 5:35 ff.), and also his friend Lazarus (John 11). Jesus' resurrection was thought of as more remarkable than any of these; it was seemingly different and unique. According to Paul, he was the first to be resurrected and appear in the "spiritual body."

However the disciples themselves understood this event, it is clear that they believed it demonstrated the lordship and messiahship of Jesus. In this faith they returned to Jerusalem and formed a tightly knit community of their own, teaching and preaching that Jesus had truly been the Messiah and that he would soon return. To them came many other Jews, some from Palestine and others from throughout the Roman Empire. Even some Jewish priests joined them. They obeyed the Jewish Law in all its details, went often to the Temple, and showed themselves loyal Jews in every respect. As yet they did not think of themselves as the founders of a new religion such as later developed. They were waiting for the kingdom to appear, and were trying to convince others that they should prepare for its coming while there was still time. They reasoned that Jesus' death was the result of Jewish "hardness of heart" and refusal to recognize in Jesus the true Messiah who had been so long awaited. But soon the time would be fulfilled, they believed; Jesus would return to usher in the New Era, and God would reign.

The New Community as Fulfillment

Drawn together again by faith in the resurrection, the disciples spoke openly with power and conviction. They now saw in Jesus the fulfillment of the Old Testament prophecies, and as time passed they reminded their fellow Jews just what those expectations were and tried to show how Jesus was their fulfillment. They referred back to the expected Messiah of Isaiah, whose name was described by such terms as "Wonderful Counselor, Mighty God, Everlasting Father, Prince of Peace" (9:6); he would be a second David, descended from Jesse, David's ancestor, upon whom the Spirit of God would rest. Some saw in the crucified, suffering Jesus the Suffering Servant of Deutero-Isaiah of whom it was said, "He was despised and rejected by men; a man of sorrows, and acquainted with grief; and as one from whom men hide their faces he was despised, and we esteemed him not" (Isaiah 53:3). Then, too, had not Jeremiah spoken of a New Covenant that would be established at some future time? We recall that he had written:

> . . . this is the covenant which I will make with the house of Israel after those days, says the Lord: I will put my law within them, and I will write

it upon their hearts; and I will be their God, and they shall be my people. And no longer shall each man teach his neighbor and each his brother, saying, "Know the Lord," for they shall all know me, from the least of them to the greatest . . . [Jeremiah 31:33-34].

This prophecy had not been fulfilled before the time of Jesus; it was Jesus at the Last Supper, Paul stated, who had established it (I Corinthians 11:25). Hence the old Law and the old Covenant had been replaced by the new inward, individual relation to God, established through Christ.

The last book of the Old Testament stated that God would send Elijah the prophet before the great and terrible day of the Lord came (Malachi 4:5)—John the Baptist was claimed to have been Elijah come back again (Mark 9:13). Further, the book of Zechariah stated (9:9): "Lo, your king comes to you; triumphant and victorious is he, humble and riding on an ass, on a colt the foal of an ass." Did not Jesus ride thus into Jerusalem before the crucifixion, and was he not hailed with cries of "Blessed be the King who comes in the name of the Lord!" (Luke 19:38)?

All of these ancient hopes were adopted by the early Christians as pointing to Jesus as the awaited one, whose expectation had kept the faith of Israel alive for centuries. He certainly was therefore also the one who would bring these expectations to wonderful fulfillment through his glorious return in the near future.

In later centuries Christians looking back on this early period of their religion believed that even these early adherents understood Jesus in too narrow terms, much as they accused their fellow Jews of failure to see the full significance of the Messiah when he did finally appear. What this religion was to become in its universal, all-embracing aspects they had as yet no notion, for they still thought that Jesus' mission had been directed to the Hebrew nation alone. Within a generation this was reinterpreted in terms of a world mission, freed of its involvements with the narrower nationalistic and cultic Jewish religion.

The convictions of the early disciples as they met together frequently were further strengthened by happenings on the Jewish day of Pentecost, 50 days after Passover. Although again it is not possible to evaluate with certainty what happened on that day, as the account stands the event was interpreted as the pouring out again of the Spirit of God—after long centuries of almost complete silence during which prophecy had largely ceased. As recorded in the second chapter of Acts, this was interpreted by Peter as the long-awaited appearance of the Spirit expected to come just before the last days, now understood as the imminent return of Jesus, and as the fulfillment of a prediction by the prophet Joel (2:28-29). It strengthened the conviction arising from the resurrection that Jesus had truly been the expected one, the Messiah, and that through him came forgiveness of sins.

The disciples, we have seen, continued to think of themselves as loyal Jews, following the usual Jewish customs and not breaking with their traditions. Yet at the same time they considered themselves the ones who were to announce something new which had happened through the crucified Jesus. They thought of their new community with its faith in Jesus as the fulfillment of the old: it was actually the true Israel. The old Israel had for the moment failed God's plans for her by her failure to recognize—indeed, by crucifying—the Messiah. Hence, the message of the Christians immediately after the crucifixion and resurrection was a message intended to convince the Jews that Jesus was the Messiah and to bring them into the new community of which Jesus was the center. Many were indeed convinced and the spread of the message was amazingly rapid. It is reported that on the day of Pentecost alone, within two months of Jesus' death, 3000 new members were added to their numbers (Acts 2:41).

Early Persecution

As the cult grew, its existence became a matter of serious concern to those Jews, especially the leaders in Jerusalem, who refused to accept its message. Even though its members continued to follow the Jewish traditions, their message was one that reflected unfavorably upon the Jewish authorities, for if the disciples were correct then they themselves had been wrong in handing Jesus over for execution. The growing tension reached a first climax in the outbreak of Jewish persecution against the new cult. A Jew of the Dispersion named Stephen was the first to lose his life, on the charge of subversion. Others of the new group were driven out of Jerusalem, with the result that they carried the message afield. Peter was one of the original apostles who embarked on missionary activities, along with various Hellenist converts.

A second persecution, following a short period of peace, broke out under Herod Agrippa, grandson of Herod the Great, who governed Judaea from A.D. 41 to 44. In this persecution the apostle James lost his life and Peter barely escaped with his. The effect was that the message spread far more rapidly than if it had not been attacked, moving increasingly out of Palestine into the Roman Empire. Jerusalem continued for a period to be venerated by these Christians (as they were first called in Antioch), and in Jerusalem James, "the Lord's brother," became the head of the church.

Conflict Within the Community

As the centers of developing Christian life moved outside Palestine to Roman cities, converts were made increasingly from among the Gentiles rather than the Jews. Paul, an early Jewish convert who had been a very strict Pharisee in his relation to the Law, became the foremost of the Christian missionaries, carrying the message throughout the Empire. As more and more Gentiles became Christians, the question arose early for Peter and later for Paul and others of what it was that made a Christian and what requirements should be established for Christians who were not Jewish in background. Should they first become Jews and then add Christianity to their Judaism, or might they be Christians without being Jews? This problem brought about the first conflict within the Christian community.

Since the apostles, disciples, and early converts were Jewish, it was first assumed that Christians were a special kind of Jew. The first converts, loyal Jews, were accepted into Christian fellowship by expressing their faith in Jesus as the Messiah, by being baptized, and then by receiving certain "spiritual gifts." But shortly after the day of Pentecost some Gentiles, before being baptized, received "the Holy Spirit" upon hearing about Jesus and on that basis were baptized as members of the fellowship (Acts 10). This suggested that becoming a Jew was not essential to becoming a Christian, so that in Jerusalem itself even from the early days Gentile converts were not required to undergo circumcision and to undertake entire obedience to the Jewish Law.

As Paul traveled outside Palestine in Syria, Asia Minor, and Greece in his missionary work, he invariably went first to the Jewish synagogue in each town or city visited. There he was able to meet the attenders at the services, and at times was permitted to speak. A considerable number of Gentiles attended the services, but probably not many of these became actual converts to Judaism itself since to be a convert required that one be circumcised, receive a ceremonial washing, make an offering to the Temple, and, of course, agree to follow the rules and regulations of the Jews. This meant, in fact, that one became an actual member of the Jewish community, leaving behind his old life as a Gentile. A far larger number of Gentiles made up the group spoken of earlier called the God-fearers—earnest, spiritually seeking persons who found in Jewish worship and beliefs something profoundly satisfying, but who for various reasons were unwilling to be bound by the laws and customs of Judaism by joining the community fully. It was chiefly this group, rather than the Jews themselves or their converts, to which the

The Roman Theatre and Marble Street in Ephesus

St. Paul lived for a time in Ephesus. Because of the loss in trade occasioned by the preaching of the Christians, the silversmiths who made silver statuettes of the goddess Diana started a riot in this theater, coming up the marble walk from the sea on which their shops stood (Acts 19:23-40). At the present time the sea can be barely seen in the distance but in Paul's time a harbor whose outlines can still be distinguished made it possible for ships to come to the end of the marble walk.

Christian message made the greatest appeal, for in this message these persons found the same understanding of God and the same high ethics as in Judaism along with the added ingredient of Jesus Christ as the Messiah and without the full demands of the Law.

When the Jews in their various synagogues opposed Paul out of unwillingness to accept Jesus as the Messiah Paul turned to the God-fearers, many of whom joined his movement. He taught them that as Christians they were not required to follow the Law because the Spirit of Christ made that unnecessary. Hence Christian communities grew up outside Palestine made up primarily of Gentiles who had not been circumcised and who did not observe the Jewish Law. Even in Jerusalem, where of course the Gentile converts were a small minority group, James, "brother of the Lord," at this period the recognized head of the fellowship, was favorably inclined toward not making Gentile converts obey the Law. The issue became a serious one, partly because the so-called Judaizers among the Jewish Christians unsettled Paul's converts by their teaching, insisting upon circumcision and obedience to the Law as a requirement for all Christians. Probably about A.D. 49 Paul, accompanied by his companion Barnabas, went to Jerusalem and there met with the local Christian leaders, James, Peter, and John, and probably others. After these heard of the spiritual experiences and the great works taking place among Gentile converts who had not been required to obey the Law, they accepted Paul as the "apostle to the Gentiles," and gave him and Barnabas their blessing (Galatians 2:1-10).[1] Although the conflict was not entirely settled—it continued until the destruction of Jerusalem in A.D. 70—practically speaking it left the church outside Palestine free to expand in independence of Judaism and its regulations. This step was decisive in converting Christianity into a new religion from what would otherwise have remained the Jewish cult it had at first appeared to be.

It is difficult to overestimate the importance for later Christianity of this separation from Judaism. Had Paul and the other missionaries required their converts to become Jews, the Christian movement would have remained a small segment of Judaism. The church in Jerusalem is clear indication of this fact, for it did not show any great development between its beginnings and its disappearance when the city fell. Given this separation, Christianity was free to develop according to its own genius in its relations to the people of the Empire, becoming a universal religion for persons of any and all racial, national, and religious backgrounds. It should be added, however, that turning away from Jewish regulations and customs was not without serious

[1] A somewhat different account of what was probably this same meeting, referred to at times as the Jerusalem Conference, is found in Acts 15:1-29.

dangers, for many times in the succeeding years Christians were able to take up a life of extreme freedom or even license by appealing to Paul's defense of freedom from the Law for their justification.

Just before Jerusalem fell to Titus, the Christian community fled the city and so escaped the fate of the Jews who were slaughtered by the Romans when they captured the city. The date A.D. 70 marks the end of the first period of Christianity, during which Jerusalem was its parent center. It now left its old home and moved entirely out into the Roman world, finding its centers in such cities as Antioch, Ephesus, and Rome. It became a universal religion, opposed to Judaism and bitterly opposed by it as heretic. Evidences of this anti-Judaism are clearly seen in the Gospels; the daughter religion fought its mother. It is true to say that early Christianity was a modification and transformation of the Jewish heritage in ways not acceptable to Judaism itself, brought about by the thought and the practices of the Greco-Roman world.

As Christianity became increasingly Gentile (although it never lost its Jewish characteristics entirely), devotion to Christ continued to be its central element. The Jewish notion of a Messiah who would restore Israel was both strange and uninviting to its Gentile members. How, then, were they to understand him who was their Lord? Formulating answers to this question, the field of Christology grew up, and occupied the major portion of Christian thought for centuries to come.

Paul's Interpretation of Christianity

In the letters of Paul as they appear in the New Testament are found the earliest interpretations of Jesus, some of them written 10 or 15 years before the first of the Gospels. A Jew of the Dispersion, Paul (whose name was Saul before his conversion) came from Tarsus in Asia Minor, and had possibly studied in his younger days in Jerusalem. He had been devoted to the Jewish Law in its most strict form, and for a time had been so convinced of the evils and laxity of the Christian sect that he had become a leading persecutor of the followers of Jesus. The ninth chapter of the book of Acts tells the story of his sudden conversion to Christianity, and much of the remainder of that same book deals with Paul's work as a Christian missionary to the Gentiles. The understanding of who Jesus was and what he had done was based for Paul upon his own experience of the Jesus who had appeared to him as he journeyed to Damascus. As a result of this experience, he was prepared to reject the interpretations of Jesus as the Messiah of popular

Jewish expectation and to maintain instead that Jesus was a far greater being than had been understood during his own lifetime.

As he attempted to explain Jesus to the members of the churches he had established, Paul drew upon ideas and words common to the thought of his day. Sometimes he seemed to be echoing ideas of the mystery religions, and at other times of Stoicism or other philosophies; yet always the heart of his message and his real interests were thoroughly Christian, rooted in Judaism, and not to be identified with these other ways of thinking. His central principle may be said to be this—that through Jesus Christ one has access to God and his power, and as he meets God his sinful human nature is changed, bringing him salvation, which he is incapable of reaching by his own efforts. We have already seen that according to Paul the convert from paganism to Christianity did not need to be circumcised or to obey the Jewish Law and customs. Salvation, he wrote, was to be obtained not "by works of the law but through faith in Jesus Christ, . . . because by works of the law shall no one be justified" (Galatians 2:16).

What lay behind Paul's new understanding? The beginning of Paul's Christian loyalty came as he was going to Damascus from Jerusalem to arrest Jews who had become members of the Christian cult. As told in Acts 9:3-6, when he approached Damascus,

> . . . suddenly a light from heaven flashed about him. And he fell to the ground and heard a voice saying to him, "Saul, Saul, why do you persecute me?" And he said, "Who are you, Lord?" And he said, "I am Jesus, whom you are persecuting; but rise and enter the city, and you will be told what you are to do."

Temporarily blinded, he was led into the city and was there visited by a Christian named Ananias, who baptized him. He began to proclaim that Jesus was "the Son of God," and in time became one of the most powerful leaders of the new religion.

Who was Jesus Christ?

The letters of Paul were written over a period of some dozen years —probably between the years 50 and A.D. 62—to the new churches outside Palestine and to individuals concerning their faith and the Christian life. They do not always form a single pattern of thought, but basic ideas remain fairly constant throughout. Paul taught that Jesus was the Christ, the Son of God. Through his writing he contributed considerably to the developing discussion about the nature of Christ which continued for the best part of half a millennium beyond Paul himself. Titles for Jesus which he used continued to be used during the succeeding centuries, sometimes in ways different from his meaning. Thus, he calls Jesus Christ the Son of God, and yet he seems not to have meant by that what later was meant by calling Christ the Second Person in the Trinity. While he appears never to call Jesus actually God, yet at places he comes very close to doing so. Jewish apocalyptic thought just before the time of Jesus said much about divine, superhuman beings. That Paul thought of Jesus as divine in this sense there can be little question, but a divine being did not need to be thought of as God himself. A monotheistic Jew, Paul could not identify Jesus with God, and the concept of the Trinity had not yet been philosophically developed as a way of solving the problem of this relationship.

In his own experience of Jesus Christ on the way to Damascus, Paul had met not the human Jesus but the "exalted" and "glorified" Christ who had been raised by God from the dead. This Christ was God's chosen Son, appointed by God to perform a special work and to usher in the new world. Christ was therefore far more than a man. In fact, Paul writes that Christ had existed before he was born a man and continues now since his resurrection to exist. Philippians 2:5-11 advances this thought:

> Have this mind among yourselves, which you have in Christ Jesus, who, though he was in the form of God, did not count equality with God a thing to be grasped, but emptied himself, taking the form of a servant, being born in the likeness of men. And being found in human form he humbled himself and became obedient unto death, even death on a cross. Therefore God has highly exalted him and bestowed on him the name which is above every name, that at the name of Jesus every knee should bow, . . . and every tongue confess that Jesus Christ is Lord, to the glory of God the Father.

In this statement Paul is declaring that although not God, Christ was originally in the "form of God," and by "emptying" himself he had become a human being. By his self-humbling and obedience, he received God's favor and was exalted, receiving the name of Lord. Nor is this all, for Paul believed also that through the agency of this pre-existent Christ the entire world had come originally into being. He wrote in Colossians 1:15-20:

> He is the image of the invisible God, the first-born of all creation; for in him all things were created, in heaven and on earth, visible and invisible . . . —all things were created through him and for him. He is before all things, and in him all things hold together. He is the head of the body, the church; he is the beginning, the first-born from the dead, that in everything he might be pre-eminent. For in him all the fulness of God was pleased to dwell, and through him to reconcile to himself all things, whether on earth or in heaven, making peace by the blood of his cross.

Difficult as it may be to understand completely the thought Paul is expressing here, it is certainly clear that for him Jesus was no mere prophet nor a mere man appointed by God for a particular task, but a divine being who acted for God. Hence such titles as *Son of God* and *Lord* were appropriate for him, Paul believed. In the Old Testament the phrase *Son of God* had been used to refer to an ideal king chosen by God to rule. Paul used it in a stronger sense than this, to connote the intimacy of relationship between God and Christ. The word *Lord* (*Kurios* in the Greek) carried with it the thought of divinity. Still other terms were used, all implying the special, unique relationship of Christ to God.

The Work of Christ

The way in which Paul thought of the nature of Christ was always secondary for him to what Christ had *done* in and through his life, death, and resurrection. For, as he most succinctly expressed it, "God was in Christ reconciling the world unto himself" (II Corinthians 5:19). Paul breaks with the requirements of the Jewish Law and finds a new way of salvation because of what Christ did. He sees all men bound to evil powers and forces. Jesus was God's means of freeing them from the bondage. Man's sin and guilt before God, which could not be removed through the Law and its requirements, was removed not by man but by God himself who, through the obedience of his Son, Jesus Christ, broke the strength of the evil powers. He brought forgiveness and "justification" to men, placing them in the relation to himself which Paul calls faith but might better be called trust or self-commitment to God. God did this out of his love and undeserved kindness for men (his *grace*, as Paul calls it), and man's part is to accept in gratitude and humble self-giving what God has done for him. Paul believed that men and God come together in this way rather than through the fulfillment of a legal and moral code. Through his obedience and death, Christ has opened the way to God, making this direct relationship between God and man possible. Those who commit themselves to following the way of faith, which is the way of grace, forgiveness, and "reconciliation," are the people of the New Covenant; they form the true church of God, and are to establish a newer, greater, and more obedient community than the old Jewish community.

Paul said little about Christ as the Messiah for a particular race of people and much about him as savior of men without regard to race or nationality.

Now before faith came, we were confined under the law, kept under restraint until faith should be revealed. So that the law was our custodian until Christ came, that we might be justified by faith. But now that faith has come, we are no longer under a custodian; for in Christ Jesus you are all sons of God, through faith. For as many of you as were baptized into Christ have put on Christ. There is neither Jew nor Greek, there is neither slave nor free, there is neither male nor female; for you are all one in Christ Jesus [Galatians 3:23-28].

The Spirit

What welded all these divergent individuals into a single community was the Spirit of God or, as Paul often calls it, the Spirit of Christ. This Spirit, he said, continues to be the actual spiritual head of the Christian community, the church. Various members of this church have different functions, just as the human body has members with varying functions; and the church is a unity, as the body is a unity. Paul's religion was not merely a historical religion, centered in someone past and gone; it was a spiritual religion of the most vivid and living kind, for the Spirit of Christ was believed by Paul to be the ground of all the church was and did. It was therefore not a legalistic community like Judaism, obeying an ancient Law, but a church in most intimate unity with the living God himself in and through his Spirit. This Spirit made some members of the community into teachers, some into preachers, some into visitors of the sick, and so on, assigning each to his proper position within the body of those having faith.

In Paul's own experience, which began on the Damascus road, he was aware of such a deep, inner change in himself that he was able to write, "I have been crucified with Christ; it is no longer I who live, but Christ who lives in me; . . ." (Galatians 2:20). He was conscious that he was in some way mystically in union with Christ, and believed that at many points in his lifetime the Spirit of Christ instructed him in what he should do, directly and practically. He understood that this was the same Christ who had appeared and spoken to him at the beginning of his Christian life. In his letters, he made no attempt to separate the Spirit of Christ from the Spirit of God. Those who live according to the Spirit and its direction are "in Christ."

As the convert entered the Christian community and discovered how the powers of the Spirit guided and strengthened his life, he found that he was turned away from his old, sinful way of living. Paul made a strong distinction between living "in the flesh," which means living according to the usual demands of the unrestrained body and personal will, and living "in the Spirit." The former is a life of sin, violence, and dissension, while the latter is a life of intimacy with God, characterized by joy and peace. Paul described these two ways of living—the way of the world and that of the true Christian—as follows:

But I say, walk by the Spirit, and do not gratify the desires of the flesh. For the desires of the flesh are against the Spirit, and the desires of the Spirit are against the flesh. . . . Now the works of the flesh are plain: immorality, impurity, licentiousness, idolatry, sorcery, enmity, strife, jealousy, anger, selfishness, dissension, party spirit, envy, drunkenness, carousing, and the like. I warn you, as I warned you before, that those who do such things shall not inherit the kingdom of God. But the fruit of the Spirit is love, joy, peace, patience, kindness, goodness, faithfulness, gentleness, self-control; against such there is no law. And those who belong to Christ Jesus have crucified the flesh with its passions and desires [Galatians 5:16-24].

The person who lived the Christ life as inspired by the Spirit of Christ was a new creature, free of the law of the flesh which is the inevitable way of those who live in the flesh. The Christians live by a higher and more complete law than do these: the law of love and faith, for they have died to the flesh and now live in Christ as slaves to him, yoked to him and living the Christlike life. Paul himself illustrated this situation by his own "slavery" to Christ.

Paul believed that eventually God's purposes not only for men but also for the whole of creation would come to fulfillment in a new world which would appear. Paul expected that in the near future Christ would return visibly, in glorious power and victory.

The Sacraments

Mention has already been made of Paul's understanding of the resurrection from the dead in which the physical body would die and an immortal, spiritual body be resurrected. One further point of special importance in Paul's writing remains to be discussed. His letters indicate the growth in early Christianity of sacramental practices in regard to baptism and the Lord's Supper. Jesus himself had been baptized by John the Baptist; and a last meal had been eaten with the disciples before the crucifixion. Paul appears to teach that in baptism the faithful share directly in the death and resurrection of Jesus. Hence, baptism is more than merely a symbolic act; rather, in it a genuine victory over death takes place. Likewise, Paul's treatment of the Lord's Supper considers this rite to be more than simply a memorial meal, for he associates powers with it which may be dangerous if misused. He says, "For any one who eats and drinks [in the Lord's Supper] without discerning the body eats and drinks judgment upon himself. That is why many of you are weak and ill, and some have died" (I Corinthians 11:29-30). Thus we see that within a score of years after Jesus' death sacramentalism, which treats certain practices as carrying sacred powers and effects within themselves, appears.

Summary

This discussion of Paul's contribution to the Christian thought of the first century of the Christian era indicates that at all essential points Paul stood firmly within the early Christian tradition. He was Christ's apostle to the Gentiles and spoke truly as such an apostle. Yet it should be remarked, finally, that Paul's thought was not the most formative influence in the development of the church of his day. His greatest influence was exerted not so markedly upon the institution which developed as it was upon certain key individuals within Christianity, among them Augustine, three centuries later; Luther, in the Protestant Reformation; and many Protestant thinkers today.

The Interpretation of the Fourth Gospel

The Gospel of John differs markedly from the Synoptic Gospels in many respects. Although containing biographical elements concerning Jesus, it was written primarily as a theological interpretation of him and his work. It is therefore proper to consider it here as a prime example of the development of early Christian thinking. The author of this Gospel brings into it ideas drawn from many sources. We will glance briefly at these and then indicate how these concepts were changed as they were brought into a Christian context and used to interpret Jesus.

The Background of the Fourth Gospel

The author of this Gospel, commonly thought of as the apostle John but not identified with certainty, seems to have been familiar with the Synoptic Gospels and the letters and thought of Paul. Some scholars think that he wrote his Gospel as a supplement to the Synoptics, assuming that his readers would be familiar with their message. He had much in common with the thinking of Paul, understanding Jesus not as a Jewish Messiah but rather as a savior making salvation available to individual human beings. As did Paul also, he emphasized the importance of the two sacraments of baptism and the Lord's Supper in the process of salvation, and he had a similar understanding of God. But the content of this Gospel shows a similarity in form and approach to the thinking of the Gnostics and Philo of Alexandria, while in Paul little of these are to be found. The author of the Fourth Gospel draws also upon ideas found in rabbinic Judaism and, of course, upon the Old Testament.

Looking first at the Jewish background, we remark that in later Jewish teaching reference was made to wisdom not only as an attribute of God but personified as having its own separate status. In the book of Proverbs (8:22-27, 30) it is written:

> The Lord created me [wisdom] at the beginning of his work, the first of his acts of old. Ages ago I was set up, at the first, before the beginning of the earth . . . . Before the mountains had been shaped, before the hills, I was brought forth; before he had made the earth with its fields, or the first of the dust of the world. When he established the heavens, I was there . . . I was beside him, like a master workman; and I was daily his delight, rejoicing before him always. . . .

In the later, rabbinic Judaism, there is a similar idea, applied not to wisdom but to the Torah. In Jewish thought, the word *Torah* may mean many things, but it refers chiefly to teaching, instruction, or knowledge, and is used specifically of the first five books of the Old Testament, taken as revelation from God through Moses. Since the Torah brought the truth by which men live, it came to be itself personified. It was said by various rabbis to have been pre-existent, the agent of creation of the world. It was also called *light* and *life*, words which appear frequently in the Fourth Gospel in reference to Jesus. Further, rabbinic Judaism had much to say about the Messiah, as also did John, although he reinterpreted the Jewish messianic expectation.

The most important Hellenistic source for this Gospel was the thought of Philo with his emphasis upon the *Logos*. Philo used this word in ways different from his predecessors, possibly having in mind as he wrote the Old Testament references to wisdom referred to above. The *Logos*, he said, is God's divine agent in the work of creation. Transcendent in God's mind, he is also creator and governor of the world. In and through the *Logos*, God is revealed and comes to be known. We note from this discussion that Philo's *Logos* was an intermediary between God and the world, the agent of revelation and creation. Many of the specific statements made by Philo concerning the *Logos* are almost identical with statements appearing in the Fourth Gospel concerning Jesus. Both use similar symbols, among them light, wisdom, fountain, and shepherd.

The Interpretation of Jesus

Coming to the Fourth Gospel itself, we find that while it was written upon the varied background of Hebrew, Gnostic, and Philonic thought and has points of similarity with each, it is fundamentally different from them all. The author understands his world, in terms going back to Plato, as consisting of a spiritual reality of the highest being and a lower realm of reality which is the world in which men live. Out of love for men, God, who lives in the spiritual world, sent his Son, the *Logos*, himself also the Messiah, who "took on flesh" and became a man, the man Jesus, sharing in man's birth, suffering, and death and bringing "eternal life" to those who "believe in him." The author of this Gospel expressed his fundamental view in the striking and unique Prologue to his book:

> In the beginning was the Word [*Logos*], and the Word [*Logos*] was with God, and the Word [*Logos*] was God. He was in the beginning with God; all things were made through him, and without him was not anything made that was made. In him was life, and the life was the light of men. The light shines in the darkness, and the darkness has not overcome it. . . .
>
> The true light that enlightens every man was coming into the world. He was in the world, and the world was made through him, yet the world knew him not. He came to his own home, and his own people received him not. But to all who received him, who believed in his name, he gave power to become children of God; who were born, not of blood nor of the will of the flesh nor of the will of man, but of God.
>
> And the Word [*Logos*] became flesh and dwelt among us, full of grace and truth; we have beheld his glory, glory as of the only Son from the Father. . . . And from his fulness have we all received, grace upon grace. For the law was given through Moses; grace and truth came through Jesus Christ. No one has ever seen God; the only Son, who is in the bosom of the Father, he has made him known [1:1-5, 9-18].

At once we note the word *Logos*, used by the Stoics, Philo, and sometimes by the Gnostics, here applied by the author to Jesus himself. This Gospel was written to tell the story of Jesus, but a Jesus who was in fact the *Logos* in human form. The question of early Christians, "Who was Jesus?" was thus given an answer by the Gospel writer which was unique and vastly important for later Christian thought when it becomes known as *Logos* Christology. Jesus Christ was certainly a human being, but those who really understood recognized in him the divine, the incarnation of the *Logos*, the Son of God. He appeared as a genuine man, but his true nature was understood as something far different—that of the only Son of God. The *Logos* has existed eternally, has always been "with God," and is in some sense God himself.

As in Philo, the *Logos* is spoken of both as separate from God and as one with God. The *Logos* as an intermediary power is suggested by the statement that through him the world was created. Like Philo, again, the author refers to the *Logos* as light, suggesting that whatever light and goodness exist in the world are there because of the *Logos*. But because men had failed to recognize the *Logos*, he "became flesh," a human being. Some men (the Christians) now recognize him while others do not. To those who do, he gives the power to become God's children.

This Gospel intended to show that Jesus was actually the Messiah, the incarnation of the *Logos*, the true revelation of God. Indeed, for its writer, becoming a Christian meant essentially the recognition of Christ as the *Logos*. The goal of salvation was the knowledge of God which came to man as a heavenly illumination through the work of Christ. This is quite a different kind of knowledge from that which results from accepting an idea as intellectually valid. It is a grasping by one's deepest self which results in an inner "rebirth," out of which one comes to live a new life different in quality from the old one—a spiritual or "eternal life," as it is called. Throughout the Gospel, Jesus is portrayed as the bringer of new life, a real life that replaces the lesser life of unspiritual men. The one to whom this life comes finds that Father and Son now "abide" in him as does also that Holy Spirit which Jesus bestowed upon his disciples after his resurrection.

The newborn person who has found salvation now lives a life of high ethical quality (as Paul also insisted), demonstrating in his own life the love which God expressed in sending his own Son to men for their salvation. When men believe in Christ, they live ethically and show love in their lives. "A new commandment I give to you, that you love one another; even as I have loved you, that you also love one another. By this all men will know that you are my disciples, if you have love for one another" (John 13:34-35). "If you love me, you will keep my commandments" (John 14:15). Knowledge of God implies obedience to God.

The Fourth Gospel and Hellenistic Thought

In spite of the strong resemblances in vocabulary and ideas between the Gospel of John and Hellenistic thought at points, their differences are even more strongly marked. Philo's *Logos*, although intermediary between God and man, was never personal or in any sense human. He remained for Philo a supernatural reality. The Johannine *Logos* as incarnate, living and dying as a human being out of love for man, is the very heart of the Fourth Gospel. Personal piety enters into man's relation with the *Logos* for Christians—they love Christ even as they are loved by Christ. Philo showed none of this.

Even greater dissimilarity with Gnostic thought is found in this Gospel. The Gnostic "aeons" and saviors were never themselves the creator of the world; on the contrary, their task was to save men from the world which was created out of ignorance or ill will. These saviors never became human. Indeed, if they had become men and had taken on flesh, they would thereby have become contaminated. They were spiritual beings and only spiritual beings, sharing in no way in human life. Further, the saving knowledge which the Gnostic claimed to provide was the understanding of the nature of man and of higher reality—a matter primarily of intellectual illumination. But, said the writer of the Gospel, Jesus revealed God by obeying him in becoming man and in doing his will. Saving knowledge in Christianity results in ethical living, obedience to God, and love. Thus, in spite of the seeming similarity between this Gospel and Gnostic thought, they are in fact so different that the Fourth Gospel was the one used most successfully in opposing Gnosticism in later church controversies.

The Interpretation of Christianity as the New Law

The understandings of Christianity set forth by Paul and the author of the Fourth Gospel and those held by Gnostics who claimed to be Christians were by no means the only interpretations. They were in fact minority views, not held generally by church leaders or members. The main line of Christian thought followed the Synoptic Gospels, the Acts, the Revelation to John, the epistles to Timothy, Titus, Philemon, and the Hebrews, and the short books of James, Peter, and Jude. In addition, there exist writings by other men living at the close of the first and beginning of the second centuries. The names of some of these letters and tracts are First and Second Clement, the Shepherd of Hermas, Polycarp's letter to the Philippians, the Epistle of Barnabas, and the Didache or Teaching of the Twelve Apostles. The type of Christianity represented by these *Apostolic Fathers*, as they are called, drew almost exclusively upon Jewish thought for its basic concepts, not upon Hellenistic thought. In it appears nothing of the mystery religions, of mysticism, or of the *Logos*. Christianity was for these writers a new law from God; by obeying this law one might escape eternal punishment and be granted eternal reward.

On one point the Apostolic Fathers agreed with Paul and John. They had all moved away from the early Jewish interpretation of Christ as a national Messiah, and looked on him rather as a personal savior. But the Fathers did not share either the Pauline antipathy toward the Jewish Law or the Gnostic hostility toward the Old Testament. Their God was the same as the God of Israel, partially revealed to the writers of the Old Testament and fully revealed by Jesus. It followed that the Jewish Scriptures were of value to Christians. Those parts of the Law which were the particular objects of Pauline attack were disregarded by the Fathers—regulations concerning meats, the rite of circumcision, and the like. The Fathers agreed with Paul that salvation did not depend upon one's becoming a citizen of the Jewish nation and obeying all the Jewish customs, but they found much of value in both the ethical teachings of the Old Testament and the prophecies concerning the coming of Christ. Thus the God of Israel was the Christian God, and the Jewish Scriptures were Christian Scriptures.

The Fathers accepted Yahweh *because* he was a lawgiver. God had given a moral law which all men were to obey, meting out rewards and punishments on the basis of obedience and disobedience. The Jews had not taken advantage of their privileged relationship, so God had sent Jesus Christ to reveal the new law and to summon a loyalty from Jews and Gentiles alike. The Christians were the new and true heirs of the promises formerly given to Israel. In common with other interpretations, the Fathers thought of Christ as a divine being who had existed prior to his appearance on earth (although unlike the author of the Fourth Gospel they believed that God had created the heavens and the earth directly, not through the *Logos*), but primarily he was the revealer of the true morality which was divinely sanctioned. To be a Christian was to obey the will of God as this was revealed in Jesus Christ.

Although Christ was a unique being and his words the most important medium through which the will of God was revealed to men, there were other ways of making the divine law known. Before the earthly existence of Christ there was the Old Testament in which eternal ethical truths could be found. After the time of Jesus the apostles were authentic interpreters of the Christian law, and the Holy Spirit, present in the church, often inspired Christian prophets to declare the will of God. The Jews had always had their prophets as special mouthpieces for divine instruction, and undoubtedly the Christian prophets of the early church were their spiritual descendants. This sort of prophecy soon died out in Christianity because of abuses and the consequent difficulty of distinguishing between true and false prophets, but the authority of the apostles and the idea of the Holy Spirit remained as important parts of the Christian tradition.

The idea of salvation for the Apostolic Fathers showed the influence of neither the mystery religions nor Gnosticism. The means of being saved included repentance for failure to lead the good life, baptism as the rite of being inducted into the Christian fellowship, and faith—which meant not what Paul meant by it, but rather accepting and guarding a tradition once delivered. Most important of all was living a life of obedience to the divine moral law. Salvation meant neither a mystical knowledge of God nor a union with Christ. One of the requirements for attaining it was living a good life in this world, but the most explicit statements on the subject refer to the future, in which salvation meant being spared the eternal punishment accorded to sinners and obtaining the positive enjoyment of a reward. Eternal life was explicitly defined as the resurrection of the flesh. This line of thought made the Christian church the substitute for Israel in God's affections. At first the hope was present that Christ would return to set up his earthly kingdom, at which time people who had lived ethically would be brought back to life to enjoy their reward and the wicked to suffer their punishment. As the years passed we find less reference to the second coming of Christ (although the expectation was not given up), but the belief in the resurrection of the flesh persisted strongly.

The Christian Apologists

Thus far we have been telling the story of the various responses made to the Christian message in the first two centuries A.D. Different individuals and groups holding a common devotion to Christ formulated different explanations of his significance. We come now to another motive for speculation concerning the nature of Christ and the Christian religion, a motive arising from the attacks on the religion by its critics and enemies. As Christianity became widely known throughout the Empire, it was natural that it should be criticized. By the end of the first century, when it had become clear to all that Christianity was a separate religion and not a cult of Judaism, Christians were viewed by the state as criminals, and during the second century it was illegal for anyone to be a member of the religion. Being a Christian meant that one stood in imminent danger of arrest and possible death, although there were actually few martyrs at this time and no general persecution until A.D. 250. Various accusations were lodged against members of the religion, the two principal official charges being atheism and anarchy —the first because they refused to worship the gods of the Empire and the second because they could not join in the emperor worship which, as we have seen, was closely linked to political loyalty. Popularly, they were sometimes accused of cannibalism as a result of misunderstanding of the Lord's Supper, in which it was thought they literally ate their God; and because they frequently met secretly and in the evenings in order to avoid arrest, they were charged with gross licentiousness.

By the early part of the second century a number of able philosophers had joined the Christian religion. In the face of the criticisms brought against it, they set out to make an intellectual defense of Christian beliefs and understandings. It must be emphasized that these men did not attempt to set forth mystical or other strictly religious theories; their appeal was to the reason of those who would read their works. They set themselves to the task of making Christianity intellectually respectable and of explaining its worthiness both to pagan philosophers and to public officials. The interest of these literary defenders of the faith was not so much in interpreting Christianity to Christians, although their fellow Christians did value highly their writings, as in showing non-Christians its meaning and its right to exist.

These Christian philosophers were known as *Apologists*, by which is meant men who explain and clarify what they represent. Typical of the group and outstanding among them was *Justin Martyr*, who wrote, probably in Rome, about 153. Before his conversion to Christianity he had studied with the Stoics and was well trained in the Platonism of his day. His motive in studying philosophy was to gain knowledge of ultimate reality, or God, and to discover correct ethical and moral principles by which men should live. Upon careful consideration of the Christian religion, Justin concluded that here was not only a philosophy but the final answer to the philosophical quest.

The Christians, he wrote, have the answer to the question of ultimate reality, for their God is the one true God, the moral ruler of the universe who demands righteous living from all men. His moral order is such that virtue is ultimately rewarded and vice punished. The philosophical quest is that of knowing God and the divine moral law of God. Since God demands ethical and moral obedience from man, Justin believed, man is not hopelessly fallen, incapable of putting forth moral effort. On the contrary, all men have free will and are capable of righteous living if they but choose it. They fail to choose properly not as a consequence of original sin, as Paul said, but rather because they are ignorant. They need revelation to correct and enlarge their knowledge of God. Human reason is capable, it is true, of going far toward knowing God and his law, but it cannot gain full knowledge by itself. Even when intentions are good, ignorance leads men astray. Revelation shows them that God is indeed an ethical God, punishing sin and rewarding virtue. Knowing this and the true nature of God, men must repent for their sins, receive God's forgiveness, and make a new start, living now in love for God and fellow men, even enemies, and practicing kindness and purity. Justin agreed with the Apostolic Fathers that with Christ came God's new law, and it must be obeyed.

The superiority of Christianity over any other philosophy lies in the fact that God and his divine law are clearly revealed in Jesus Christ. Justin attempted to prove to skeptical intellectuals that Christ was the one full revelation of the divine. In order to do this, he pointed to the fulfillment of prophecy. He avoided the circular argument of assuming the Bible to be the revealed word of God and concluding that Christ was God's messenger because the Bible said so. Rather, he pointed to statements in the Old Testament concerning the coming of a Messiah and showed that Jesus had done the things predicted, thus fulfilling the prophecies. Since the predictions and Jesus' acts agreed, it was evident that both the book which contained the predictions and Jesus who fulfilled them were of divine origin.

Jesus Christ came from God. The Platonists had conceived of God as a transcendent being whose relations with the world had to be mediated through a secondary power. The philosophers had speculated concerning God and the *Logos* or intermediary power, but the Christians claimed to have knowledge and not just speculative ideas, since the *Logos* had become incarnate in Jesus, leaving no doubt as to the character of the *Logos* and providing an explicit revelation of God and God's will. Christ, the *Logos*, was for Justin, as in the Fourth Gospel, a pre-existent, divine being not identical with God but having the same divine nature and purposes. He was the Son of God, the only Son, both in his pre-existent state and in his earthly existence as the man Jesus. When Justin refers to him as the *Logos*, he has in mind much the same concept as did the non-Christian philosophers of his time, that is, as divine reason, the wisdom of God. Yet Justin also thought of the *Logos* in personal terms, because the *Logos* became man. The *Logos* was begotten of God before the creation of the world and was the agent through whom creation was accomplished. The *Logos* was also the source of rationality in human beings. This implies that Hebrew prophets like Moses and Abraham and Greek philosophers like Socrates and Heraclitus were vehicles for the voice of the *Logos* before the time of Jesus. Insofar as these men possessed reason and truth they possessed the *Logos*, and insofar as they possessed the *Logos* they possessed Christ. Thus, in a very real sense, the remarkable statement could be made that there were Christians *before* Christ, and Christianity was justified in having a high regard for both Hebrew prophets and Greek philosophers.

In spite of the fact that the *Logos* had been present partially in prophets and philosophers, there was still such a lack of understanding of truth that the world needed a full and complete revelation. This was effected when the *Logos* became the man Jesus. As evidence for the uniqueness and *Logos* nature of Jesus, Justin appealed to the account of the virgin birth of Jesus, a tradition current in the second century which had appeared in the first century in the Gospels of Matthew and Luke. Justin, however, was the only one of the Apologists who brought it into his Apology, using it to account for Jesus' being divine and not just a man (*First Apology*, 33).

Justin's final and practical justification for Christianity lay in his appeal to its moral fruits in the lives of the worshipers. He stressed both the superior ethical teachings of Jesus and the lofty moral practices of his followers. In particular, he emphasized the unique steadfastness found in Christians because of which on occasion they were willing and even anxious to die for Christ.

The Christian Gnostics

Several times in this chapter and the preceding one we have had occasion to mention Gnosticism, which brought about the chief problems of thought and organization faced by the Christian church in the second century. Eventually, because of the decisions the church was forced to make in opposing it, it was largely responsible for the formation by the end of the second century of what is called the Ancient Catholic Church.

Until recently, practically everything known about the Gnostics was derived from Christian documents attacking them as heretics within Christianity. However, in 1945, a very remarkable find of Gnostic documents was made in a cemetery near the Egyptian village of Nag Hammadi, comprising some 48 writings containing 800 or more pages out of 1000 pages of original material, all of which are thought to be Gnostic, derived from originals of the first and second centuries A.D. Although not as yet studied exhaustively, these will without doubt add greatly to our knowledge of this remarkable philosophical-religious type of thought.[2]

The Gnostics were highly eclectic in their thinking, bringing together into loose unity ideas from all the known traditions of the time, and uniting these in patterns of great complexity. As Christianity appeared on the scene,

[2] For information on the Nag Hammadi writings, see Hans Jonas, *The Gnostic Religion*, Boston, Beacon Press, 1958; Robert M. Grant, *Gnosticism and Early Christianity*, New York, Columbia University Press, 1959, and *The Secret Sayings of Jesus*, Garden City, Doubleday & Company, Inc., 1960; and F. L. Cross (ed.), *The Jung Codex*, London, A. R. Mowbray and Co., Ltd., 1955.

many Gnostics adopted elements of Christian thought, particularly the figure of Jesus. By the second century, questions they raised in regard to their interpretation of Christianity as more basically Gnostic than Christian made them a most formidable peril to the early church. The difficulty of the problem was increased by the fact that among the Gnostics were to be found some of the best minds of the period, a number of whom considered themselves Christians. Outstanding among these was *Valentinus*, a teacher in Rome from A.D. 135 until 160, whose prestige in the church was so high that he even aspired to become a bishop.

Philosophically, all Gnostics accepted the strongly dualistic notion that spirit alone is good and matter is evil. On this point their view is similar to that held in religious Platonism. They believed also in a savior, one who revealed to spiritual men the knowledge (*gnosis*) needed for salvation from matter, which would carry one into the spiritual world. As Gnostics came to know Christianity, they readily identified Jesus as the savior, but in doing so they changed the understanding generally held of the nature of Jesus. In accordance with their basic principle, they insisted that Jesus must have been a purely spiritual being in order to perform the work of the Gnostic savior.

As we think back over the variety of interpretations given Jesus and early Christian concepts in general (and we have touched only some of the more prominent), we are faced with the question of whether such various ideas could be united, or whether some would have to be eliminated from the Christian tradition. Was it possible, for example, to bring Pauline Christianity —with its dualism of flesh and spirit, its emphasis upon spiritual union with Christ, its idea of salvation through faith and spiritual rebirth which bring freedom from the Jewish Law—into harmonious synthesis with the legalistic conception of Christianity which characterized the Apostolic Fathers? Whether or not such a fusion resulted in a consistent philosophy, it is a historic fact that both of these interpretations of Christianity as well as others were able to remain within the Christian tradition. One reason was that there was little in Paul's writings which was definitely contradictory of other points of view. In the case of Gnosticism, however, the situation was different, for it was logically impossible to affirm both the generally held beliefs of Christians and the teachings of the Gnostics. Granted that many of the Gnostics were sincere Christians and could find some sort of support in tradition for most of their doctrines, the general trend of Gnostic Christianity was nonetheless so antithetical to the main line of development that the two could not live in harmony. Among the ideas of the Gnostics which caused the greatest difficulty, the five discussed below could not be accepted by Christianity without destroying most of Christianity's historic meaning.

In the first place, the implication of the dualistic concept of flesh and spirit was that it was impossible to find any place for the salvation of the flesh. Only man as spirit was to be saved. But this ran directly counter to a line of Christian thought which had incorporated into itself the Jewish view of man: that man is not merely a loose, temporary combination of body and soul, but in his wholeness is a close unity of body and soul in which both are necessary to his full being. Plato and other Greeks had suggested the thought that the soul temporarily inhabits the body and is quite independent of it for its being, but the Hebrews refused to accept such an understanding. It was for this reason that the later Jews, and Christians after them (in spite of Paul's teaching on the resurrection of a spiritual body), maintained that eternal life includes resurrection of the flesh.

In the second place, early Christian thought had not developed a distinctive idea of God but had taken over the God of Israel by and large, emphasizing his universality and his interest in all men. Yet Yahweh was the creator God, and the Gnostics had assigned the work of creation not to the supreme God himself but to an inferior spiritual being, often identified as the demiurge. Did this not mean that the God whom the Jews worshiped and about whom their Scriptures, the Old Testament, were written was not the true God after all, but an inferior divinity? Such a conclusion seemed almost inevitable and was openly preached by *Marcion*, a wealthy shipmaster who lived in Rome from 139 to 144. He counted himself a Christian, but had much in common with the Gnostics and is often classified as one in spite of the fact that he differed from them in important ways. He thought of himself as the interpreter of true Christianity, which for him had its essence in the teaching of Paul. Paul had said a good deal about salvation through Christ bringing freedom from the Jewish Law, so central to the Old Testament, and Marcion feared that Christianity was developing its own form of legalism in opposition to Pauline teaching. The Jewish influence within Christianity was responsible for this development, Marcion thought, so he set about the task of purifying Christianity by destroying and removing this influence. He began with an explicit argument that the God of the Old Testament was not the God revealed by Jesus Christ. The former was the God of the Jews, creator of this evil world, possessing characteristics directly antithetical to the true God of love and mercy. Yahweh was a warrior God, often cruel and even unreliable. Essentially he was a lawgiver, the author of that very legalism which characterized Judaism and was threatening to corrupt Christianity. Consequently, Marcion rejected the Old Testament as divine truth. His generally hostile attitude toward Judaism was shared by the Gnostics, even though there were some Jews among them.

The third difficulty also arose from the Gnostic dualism of flesh and spirit, and consisted specifically in its great influence upon the Gnostic interpretation of the nature of Jesus Christ. Having such a low regard for the body, the Gnostics thought it inconceivable that their savior was truly born of woman, had actual flesh and blood, genuinely suffered on the cross, and died. They therefore rejected the true humanity of Jesus, standing at the opposite pole from the Fourth Gospel which states that the *Logos* became flesh. Some of the Gnostics said that Christ had a heavenly, spiritual body, others that the spiritual Christ temporarily inhabited the body of the man Jesus, and still others that what Jesus' disciples thought to be a human body was really only an appearance. These last were called *Docetists,* from the Greek word for appearance. All agreed that Jesus Christ did not participate as a man in human experience.

Fourth, the salvation offered by Gnosticism was not universal, but was available only to those men whom the Gnostics called "spiritual." Others *could not* be saved, and all attempts to teach them Gnostic knowledge would be without value. By contrast, Christians taught that salvation is made available to all men through Jesus Christ, and refused to consider any men by nature incapable of receiving it.

Finally, Christian Gnosticism in common with the earlier Gnosticism from which it sprang was without any consciousness of cult or church. It was a speculative system and a practical program of individual salvation which included as one element within it the person and work of Christ. The salvation it offered was quite individual, requiring help from neither priest nor sacrament. This was one of its great weaknesses, since a religion must have its cult structure to survive.

Gnosticism raised a host of new and important issues for Christian thought to face and resolve: what literature was divinely inspired, the nature of God, the humanity of Jesus, the resurrection of the body, and the function of the church as an organization.

Irenaeus and the Apostles' Creed

The most influential person in bringing to a head the problem posed by the Gnostics within the Christian church was Irenaeus. Reared in Smyrna, he was bishop of Lyons in Gaul and wrote toward the end of the second century, about A.D. 185. He was one of the greatest thinkers produced by the early church and one of the most significant figures in its history. Irenaeus was the first man to call the Christian church by the name *Catholic* (universal), a term that suggests the gradual development from a loosely organized Christianity to a closely knit body with official leaders, capable both of defining the faith and of excommunicating those who did not accept the creed of the church. No one person was more influential than Irenaeus himself in bringing this church into existence. Against the Gnostics he wrote a lengthy work entitled *Against Heresies* in which he attempted to demonstrate their errors and to set down a method for discovering and guarding true Christianity. The Gnostics and other thinkers suspected of heresy often claimed to be guided by the Spirit which Jesus had promised to his followers as a guide to all truth (John 16:13). But those who made claim to such guidance by the Spirit did not always agree with each other, and, even more seriously, they frequently failed to agree with what were taken by most Christians to be the basic beliefs of Christians. In short, in a period of a century and a half, Christianity had reached the stage of development where a distinction had to be drawn between orthodox belief and heresy. This in turn created the necessity of determining a standard or standards of truth beyond individual thinking and personal experience.

The first criterion explicitly laid down by Irenaeus, and one which had already been generally assumed, was that true Christianity must be in agreement with apostolic teaching. That which was in harmony with what one of the twelve disciples or Paul had taught was orthodox, and anything to the contrary was heretical. This principle had some interesting consequences. In the first place, it led ultimately to the formation of an authoritative Christian literature, the New Testament, to supplement the Old Testament.[3] Marcion had arranged his own Christian Bible, consisting of an expurgated edition of Luke's Gospel and 10 of the letters of Paul, along with a book by Marcion himself entitled the *Antitheses;* but Irenaeus criticized this for its incompleteness, maintaining that there were four Gospels of apostolic origin. Matthew and John, he said, were themselves apostles; Mark's gospel presented the views of Peter; and Luke was a follower of Paul. In addition to these, there were other letters written by apostles which should be included in the Christian Scriptures.

But the solution of the problem of heresy was a difficult one. Not only did Irenaeus have to prove the authentic apostolic origin of all the books he wished to include in the New Testament; he also had the problem of determining the correct interpretation of the various points of view which they contained. The Gnostics could accept his Bible and still interpret certain pas-

[3] It should be noted, however, that the development of the New Testament canon was not completed until about A.D. 400.

sages in such a way as to substantiate their doctrines. Thus was Irenaeus forced to discover an authoritative interpretation of an authoritative literature. He was sincere in his belief that all the Christian churches except the Gnostic ones were agreed on the genuine apostolic tradition or central meaning of the New Testament. This tradition, he said, was briefly expressed in a "rule of truth." What he probably had in mind was the baptismal formula used by the church of Rome, which was the formula from which the *Apostles' Creed* later developed. In its present form the creed contains more phrases than were used in the Roman baptismal ritual, but the latter probably included the following familiar items:

> I believe in God [the] Father Almighty;
> and in Christ Jesus his Son,
> who was born of Mary the Virgin,
> was crucified under Pontius Pilate and buried,
> on the third day arose from the dead,
> ascended into heaven,
> sitteth on the right hand of the Father,
> whence he cometh to judge living and dead;
> and in [the] Holy Spirit,
> resurrection of the flesh.[4]

The purpose of appealing to this creed as the statement of true Christian belief was obviously that of demonstrating the falsity of Gnosticism. "God the Father Almighty" leaves no doubt that the Christian God is the same as him who exercises absolute control over the universe; also, this and not some other God was the father of Jesus and was revealed in him. Jesus was actually born of woman and was crucified. It is stated unambiguously that there is resurrection of the flesh. It is not strange that this formula should be so apt a refutation of Gnosticism. To be sure, Irenaeus claimed apostolic origin for it, but in fact it was probably a creation of the Roman church of the middle of the second century as a safeguard against the doctrines which the Gnostics were preaching in Rome. However, the idea became firmly entrenched that this creed came directly from the apostles and consequently was authoritative. In this way there developed not only an official New Testament but also an official creed or brief statement of belief.

Irenaeus contrived still a third way of meeting the problem of heresy, a way which would provide for situations where the Apostles' Creed might prove ineffective and where contradictory interpretations of the New Testament might threaten the unity of the Christian church. He maintained that

[4] A. C. McGiffert, *A History of Christian Thought*, New York, Charles Scribner's Sons, 1932, I, 157.

the tradition which came from the apostles was guarded by successive generations of the bishops of the various churches. His theory was that the apostles themselves had appointed the first bishops as their official representatives, and that the authority vested in them had been passed on by them in turn to their successors. In each generation, therefore, an authority resided in the bishops of the church which could be traced back directly to the apostles and which preserved the genuine apostolic teaching.

This meant two very important things as far as the future of the church was concerned. First, the teachings of the churches in Rome, Ephesus, Smyrna, and other centers could be known to be valid because of their bishops' descent by apostolic succession—and these teachings were contradictory to Gnostic thought and proved it wrong. Second, it meant that for the future, matters at issue could be decided by these same bishops, since they inherited the authority of the original apostles themselves. They were the true guardians of the Christian tradition, able to make official pronouncements upon heresy and other matters.

The peril of Gnosticism was finally overcome and the Gnostics were eliminated from the Christian church by means of the threefold apostolic authority—Scriptures, creed, and succession of bishops. Through this crisis the church learned valuable lessons. Christian thinkers saw the need to develop more clearly the philosophic basis of their faith and the true function of their ecclesiastical organization.

The Christian Concept of God

One of the consequences of the Gnostic controversy was the development of a theory of the nature of God. Christianity had been essentially a religion of salvation, and intellectual speculation had concentrated on the nature of the Savior or Christ. But we find that Origen, an Alexandrian theologian of the third century, introduced his systematic work with a discussion of the nature of God. This indicates that the question was coming to occupy a place of importance in Christian thinking equal to that of the nature of Christ.

The theological issue between orthodox and Gnostic Christians had concerned the God of the Old Testament. The victory of orthodoxy established the sole reality of the divine being worshiped by Jesus and the early Christians, but the problem was not closed. The increasing influence of philosophically trained theologians as champions of Christianity led to metaphysical descriptions of the nature of God. The Old Testament God was a manlike king, judge, friend, or father. There had never been reasoned arguments designed to prove that God exists; there had been merely prophetic pronouncements concerning his superiority to the gods in whom other people had faith. But Christian theologians created a philosophic literature concerning both the existence and the nature of God. The framework for these discussions was mainly Platonic, and the arguments uniformly stressed the transcendence, spirituality, and oneness of God. His transcendence and spirituality were maintained in opposition to Stoicism, and his oneness as a refutation of Greek polytheism and in substantiation of the universal appeal of Christianity.

The God of Stoicism was a kind of material which pervaded the universe. The God of the theologians was absolutely incorporeal and "wholly other" than the world. This is not to say that the theologians contrasted God and the world after the fashion of the Gnostic pessimism concerning evil matter. The contrast was of a different sort: on the one hand stood inert matter, which could not move unless acted upon and which was created and divisible, and on the other hand was God as spirit—infinite, incorporeal, indivisible, incomprehensible, and creative. Although this God may seem to us much more like a metaphysical abstraction than a loving father, he was meant to be the same as the object of simple Christian faith.

If the essence of God is spirit, he must be one. Unlike matter, spirit cannot be divided into separate parts, and thus to say that God is spirit is to say that he is one. Furthermore, it is necessary that such a spirit should exist. We can observe the regular and orderly motions of material in the physical world, and since matter cannot move itself there must be an eternal and immaterial reality more powerful than matter which is the ultimate cause of the orderly activity of the universe.

Such was the general pattern of the contributions of Greek philosophy to Christian thinking about God. But logical minds eventually saw difficulties in the practice of worshiping both God and the *Logos* or Son of God as though they were equals. God was one, and yet he was referred to as God the Father, as a deified Christ, and as the Holy Spirit. What precisely was the relation among these three? It was an established part of the Christian tradition that Jesus Christ had existed prior to his human life and that he was in some sense divine. That God could be one spiritual reality in which both the Father and the Son shared was comprehensible to Christian Platonists on the basis of that same Platonic principle which affirmed the oneness of the Idea of beauty in which, nevertheless, a number of beautiful things participate. But it was also a part of Christian tradition that somehow the Son was subordinate to the Father. The identification of the Son with the *Logos* had helped make the latter notion clear because of the general conception of the *Logos* as an intermediary power. However, the question remained of whether the *Logos* was fully God or a spiritual being less than God.

The Arian Controversy and the Nicene Creed

The controversy with the Gnostics settled once and for all the fact that Jesus Christ had been a genuine human being and not just an appearance of one. It did not settle the exact degree of that humanity, nor did it define the relation of Christ to God. Many controversies appeared during the third Christian century for which we have no place here. The most famous and the one usually considered the most important of all the theological controversies occurred during the fourth century: the Arian controversy, named after Arius, who most fully represented the losing side. But before we look at the issues of this dispute and the solution brought to them we will pause for a brief survey of the history leading up to it.

Throughout the third century, Christianity remained a minority movement, and Christians continued to stand in peril of their lives. Various persecutions broke out against this condemned religion and its followers, but it nonetheless continued to grow. A universal and systematic attack upon Christians broke out in the year 250 and lasted, with many deaths and lapses among the Christians, for 10 years. An even more cruel period of persecution with destruction of churches, torture, and numbers of deaths broke out in 303 under the emperor Diocletian, but upon his retirement a few years later the tide again changed, and in 311 an edict of toleration was issued. Constantine, one of four contestants for the Empire in 312, won a decisive victory over his chief rival the day after he had a dream in which he saw the Greek letters *chi rho*, which form the Christian emblem for the name of Christ, and taking this as an omen he painted the monogram on his soldiers' helmets. From that time on he was considered a Christian, although he had not as yet been baptized. In 313 he proclaimed complete freedom of conscience for Christians in the Edict of Milan, thus placing Christianity on a basis of absolute equality with the other religions of the Empire. In 323 Constantine became the sole emperor of the Roman world, and at last the church was free of persecution. Yet at the same time it moved under a very large measure of control by the Roman emperor.

One of the first problems faced by Constantine in regard to the Christian church was the long-smoldering controversy concerning the nature of Christ, which separated the Christians in the Empire and consequently weakened the Empire itself. Although Constantine did manage to bring the controversy to a decision, it did not actually reach a final conclusion for another three centuries. Even the immediate dispute continued in heated form for more than half a century after Constantine thought he had settled it at Nicaea.

The two names principally connected with the controversy were those of *Arius*, a presbyter of the church in Alexandria, and *Athanasius*, also from the Alexandrian church and its deacon, later its bishop. The question was the one posed above: was Christ, the *Logos*, fully God or was he less than God? In approaching this problem, Arius, as a theologian whose motivation was primarily philosophical (placing great emphasis upon correct logic), insisted that God is one, a unity, to such an extent that the essential divine nature is indivisible and cannot be shared by any other being. He and he alone is eternal and uncreated; all other beings were created by God out of nothing. The Son of God is no exception—he too was a created being, although, as the first of all created beings, he belongs to a higher order than the others and was the power through whom the world was made. He became incarnate in Jesus Christ, who, because of his supreme devotion to the will of God, is worthy of worship and may be called God. Yet he is not actually God, for he does not fully share the nature or essence of God.

As incarnate in Jesus Christ, the *Logos* had a human body but not a human soul. In other words, the *Logos* had an essence, a nature, that was unique. He was not fully God, nor was he fully man; he was for Arius, in fact, a kind of demigod, less than God and yet greater than man. Here was a logical and consistent system, but it caused a bitter doctrinal battle. Opposition to Arianism arose, not so much on the logical grounds where Arius was prepared to fight but rather for religious reasons. As a religion of salvation, Christianity needed the belief that Jesus Christ was both really God and really man at the same time. This does not mean that he was to be understood as identical with God, the same individual, but that God and he were of the same nature or essence. Though it was difficult to make this position logically consistent, it seemed a necessary stand because of practical considerations deriving from the manner in which man's sin before God and the demands of salvation were understood at that time. These arose largely from the work of Irenaeus.

Irenaeus had been the first Christian thinker to emphasize what proved to be the important doctrine of the Fall. Salvation was necessary, he said, because of Adam's fall, which was the result of disobedience. Through this fall mankind lost its original likeness to God, becoming enslaved to Satan. Salvation, which meant gaining freedom from the prison in which Satan held men captive and being reunited with God, was brought into the world by Jesus Christ, who undid the mischief created by the Fall. Christ had been consistently obedient, had resisted the temptations of Satan, and had been faithful even unto death. The temptation experience had demonstrated Christ's supremacy over Satan, and his death was a ransom paid to Satan for the release of the rest of men. This implied that Jesus must have been both man and God. He had to be a man in order to bring about a just victory of mankind over Satan, since none other than a human being could atone for the sins of men and break the power which Satan had exercised since the fatal disobedience of Adam. But in order to be able to accomplish his saving work, Christ had to be God. He was able to overcome Satan only because he was more powerful than Satan, and therefore he was divine. Furthermore, salvation meant the transformation of human into divine nature, and only if the real Godhead was united with full manhood in Christ could such a transformation take place. Therefore, Christ was not only more than man; he was actually God in man. If one does not have this doctrine of salvation in mind, he cannot appreciate the significance of the Arian controversy. The meaning of Christianity as a redemptive religion had as its focus the meeting of divine and human natures in Jesus Christ, and Arianism made of the *Logos* an essence neither completely divine nor completely human.

The leader of the opposition was Athanasius, a man noted not so much for his philosophical and theological ability as for his deep religious convictions and great character. He did, however, have considerable intellectual ability and was able to brush aside technical problems to get to the main point, which was the issue of Christ as the bringer of salvation. He was convinced that the idea of the incarnation of God in Christ was central to Christianity and its distinctive element, a fundamental doctrine which he recognized Arianism was attacking and threatening to undermine. Because of his able writings, in which he argued for the necessity of believing that the Son was truly God and that he really became man, Athanasius was early recognized as the leader of the anti-Arian party. The dispute spread far beyond the Alexandrian church, involving a large part of the Christian church and threatening its unity.

The emperor Constantine, courting the support of Christians and wishing to have the church as powerful as possible and therefore united, called a council of all the bishops at Nicaea in Asia Minor in 325. This is generally recognized as the most important of the church councils and is referred to as the First General or Ecumenical Council. Here was an issue which could be decided neither by Scripture, since the opposing sides could each quote

Scripture favorable to itself, nor by the Apostles' Creed. Only through a decision of the bishops themselves in general council could a solution be reached.

It appears likely that Constantine was not fully aware of the theological issues or greatly concerned about them. His was a practical interest—that of settling the matter and averting a division of the church. Only a minority of the bishops who attended this assembly were extreme Arians or extreme anti-Arians, so it was the large middle group who took the leadership. The Arians were first asked to present a statement of their beliefs. This was found unacceptable by the great majority of the bishops, who rejected it. Then the baptismal formula of the church in Caesarea was set forth as a possible solution. As it stood, it was silent on the principal issues and hence was acceptable to all parties. At this point the anti-Arians, who apparently had no creed of their own, indicated their willingness to accept this statement but shrewdly suggested a few alterations and changes which changed it into a completely anti-Arian document. As thus revised, the formula, which was the original (but not the final) form of the Nicene Creed, read as follows:

> We believe in one God, Father Almighty, maker of all things visible and invisible; and in one Lord Jesus Christ the Son of God, begotten of the Father, only-begotten, that is from the substance of the Father, God from God, Light from Light, true God from true God, begotten, not made, of one substance with the Father, through whom all things were made, both the things in heaven and the things on earth; who for us men and for our salvation came down and was made flesh, was made man, suffered, and rose again on the third day, ascended into heaven, and cometh to judge quick and dead; and in the Holy Spirit. But those who say, "There was once when he was not," and "Before his generation he was not," and "He was made out of nothing"; or pretend that the Son of God is of another subsistence or substance, or created or alterable or mutable, the Catholic church anathematizes.[5]

This was a clear-cut defeat of Arianism. The test word in it is the word *homoousion*, which means consubstantial or of the same substance (*homo* and *ousia*) with the Father. Another anti-Arian phrase is "begotten, not made." The point was that one who is begotten, such as a child begotten of its mother, is of the same nature or substance as the one who begets it, while something made, like a desk, is less than the one who makes it. The Arians preferred the word *made* of Christ, thus showing his difference in nature from the Creator, while their opponents for this very reason preferred *begotten* in order to emphasize the sameness of nature. The anathemas which end the Creed were directed against favorite Arian phrases. Constantine

[5] *Ibid.*, I, 262 f.

thus obtained the decision he wished and for the moment the problem seemed solved; yet it was not long before controversy broke out again. Many of the moderates as well as the Arians thought that the word *homoousios* suggested too close an identity between Son and Father. Some preferred the word *homoiousios*—the addition of the *iota* makes it mean, of a similar or like substance rather than of the same or equal substance. For a short period Arianism actually came back into official favor, but by the end of half a century orthodoxy in terms of the Nicene Creed returned and was secure in the hands of the opponents of Arianism.

The Doctrine of the Trinity

A religious doctrine unique to Christianity is that God is triune, a trinity. This means that there is, in truth, only one God, but that this one God is known under the form of three "Persons": Father, Son, and Holy Spirit. This is not strict unitarianism, nor is it a polytheism of three gods. The view as it developed attempted to walk a very narrow line, if indeed there is one, between these two extremes. It attempted to hold at the same moment to a oneness and to a threeness. The result has always been logically unsatisfying (and in truth this doctrine is always mentioned as one of the great mysteries of Christian thought), but it has been adhered to and regarded as necessary by conservative or orthodox Christianity.

The origin of the doctrine is found in the New Testament, although the doctrine itself is not to be found there. In II Corinthians 13:14 Paul wrote, "The grace of the Lord Jesus Christ and the love of God and the fellowship of the Holy Spirit be with you all." And in the Gospel of Matthew the statement is made (28:19) that after the resurrection Jesus sent out his disciples, telling them to make disciples of all nations, "baptizing them in the name of the Father and of the Son and of the Holy Spirit." The origins of Christianity were in Judaism, which was strongly monotheistic. God is one, and there can be no second God for Jews. But the question of the nature of Jesus Christ, as we have just seen, was one which could not be solved easily. Early Christians called him Lord, prayed to him after his death, and thought of him as God's Son or as the *Logos*. After the Council of Nicaea it was said that he was of the same "substance" as the Father, himself Son of God, a divine being.

During these same centuries a parallel thought regarding the Holy Spirit had been developing. The problem arose of the relation of the Spirit to the Father and the Son. Both the book of Acts and the letters of Paul are full of accounts of the work of the Spirit in the early church. How then is the Spirit to be understood?

The controversy had to do with giving intellectual formulation, so far as possible, to beliefs commonly held in the church. Jesus Christ was thought of as divine, the Son of God. The Holy Spirit also was believed to be divine by nature, sharing in the Godhead. Through centuries of discussion, during which all the resources of contemporary philosophy were called upon to find ways and illustrations to retain the unity of God while emphasizing the threeness, a council at Constantinople in 381 made decisions concerning the nature of the Holy Spirit which brought about the doctrine of the Trinity in its classic form. This formula states that there is one God, but this one God exists in the three Persons of Father, Son, and Holy Spirit. These three are all equal, all alike fully divine, and eternal within the Godhead; yet there are genuine distinctions between them. The Son is begotten of the Father and the Father begets the Son, and the Holy Spirit proceeds from both Father and Son.

All the ancient writers on this most difficult topic admit that the mystery of the Trinity is too great for the human mind to solve, but some of them have attempted analogies. The analogies of Augustine, written in the fifth century, are possibly the best known. He suggested that Father, Son, and Holy Spirit might be thought of as analogous to the unity of the individual soul in which memory, understanding, and will (which unites the two others) are three genuine distinctions, though all appear within one soul and are equal to each other within the soul. He also suggested the analogy of love. In it are the lover, the beloved, and the love itself which unites lover and beloved. Augustine stated that these analogies do not really make clear what the facts are in regard to God, but he believed they suggest a single, harmonious, spiritual being with a threefold center, the three being equivalent to one.

For practical understanding, the symbol below formulates the essential statement concerning the Trinity without actually helping us conceive his nature with any clarity. The three Persons on the outer circle are *Pater* (Father), *Filius* (Son), and *Spiritus Sanctus* (Holy Spirit). Connecting the outer circles are found the words *non est*, meaning "is not." The outer portion is to be read thus: the Father is not the Son, the Son is not the Holy Spirit, and the Holy Spirit is not the Father—this maintains the distinction between the three Persons. In the center of the circle is the word *Deus* (God), connected to the outer Persons and to be read: the Father is God, the Son is God, the Holy Spirit is God.

Finally, incomprehensible as the concept is, it is clearly intended to fall

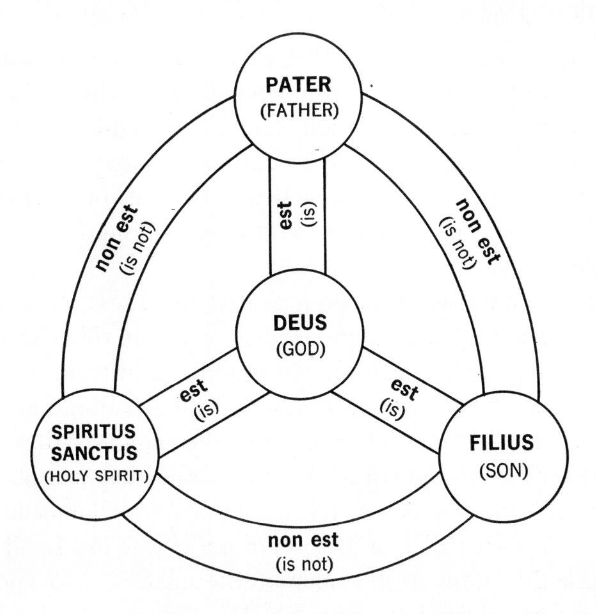

Emblem of the Holy Trinity

between the simple oneness of God of Jewish thought and plurality of God of Greek thought. Its proponents claim for it a richness of content and yet a basic unity which they find lacking in both Jewish and Greek ideas. Those who affirm it maintain that it encompasses somehow the Christian experience and faith that both Jesus Christ and the Holy Spirit are divine.

The Church Universal

The principle of apostolic authority had proved effective in defeating the Gnostics but showed weaknesses in the face of the Arian controversy. Arian Christianity persisted, and carried on successful missionary activity for years. This showed the need of a definitive doctrine of the church as a universal and united organization. Irenaeus' principle of the apostolic succession of bishops had given the individual officers of the church an authority independent of the congregations they served, but apparently there was unwarranted optimism concerning the ability of the several bishops to agree on matters of doctrine and practice, the Arian controversy being a case in point. Even though each bishop was an authoritative guardian of the true Christian tradition, it was demonstrated in the councils that there could be disagreement among them. Yet there could obviously be only one truth. A further principle was laid down, therefore, that a council of bishops had precedence over the individuals who attended the council. The will of the council expressed the true apostolic teaching and had to be recognized by all. For practical application this principle needed a central authority to enforce the will of the council and, although the papacy was a matter of later development, we can see that there was a need for a "bishop of bishops" in order to centralize authority.

Several factors contributed to the idea that there was a church universal beyond and above the local congregations, and that this church was in a peculiar sense both the guardian of truth and the instrument of salvation. For one thing, the efficacy of the sacraments for salvation had long been a part of Christian tradition. At the same time, the administration of the sacraments was controlled by the church, and thus salvation was impossible outside the church. Further, in our review of the early development of Christian thought, we have seen that one important strain was the legalistic conception of Christianity. God as the ruler of the universe had one moral law which all men were obliged to obey. The law was revealed by Jesus Christ, who had established the church as his official earthly representative. This type of thinking was strong in North Africa, Spain, Gaul, Italy, and especially Rome, where important contributions were being made to secular legal thinking. There might be differences of opinion and practice within the Christian brotherhood, but above these there were one truth and one church discipline. Christ had revealed the moral law and appointed his apostles and through them the present officers of the church, and it was sinful for there to be permanent division. To have factions in the church universal was like having civil war in the empire. The divine moral law and the means of salvation were everywhere the same. Therefore, the church, as God's own institution and instrument of salvation, had to be united.

Historic events helped make these ideas applicable. Legalized during the reign of Constantine, Christianity was made the official and only religion of the Empire in 380 by Theodosius, ruling as emperor of the East, and Gratian, emperor of the Western Roman Empire. In 392 heavy penalties were imposed on persons practicing pagan worship, but paganism died out only slowly. The Christian God was installed as the official guardian of the affairs of the Empire; thus church and state shared a common responsibility. The emperors were of practical help in enforcing church discipline because it was to their advantage to have a united empire. But this started to change at the close of the fourth century as the Roman Empire in the West began to disintegrate and barbarians from the north migrated into Italy. The foundations of the church were shaken by these events, but so efficient an organization had been established that the church's claim to superiority over the state was partially justified in fact as well as in theory. It was the church which was able to bring something of Greco-Roman culture and a civilizing influence to Western Europe.

Questions for Study

1. What was the reason that the disciples of Jesus reassembled after his death? In what form was Jesus seen? What did this mean to the disciples? How did they now interpret Jesus? What expectation concerning the future did they hold?
2. How did the early Christians think of themselves as a community? Why did the Jews who were not sympathetic start persecutions? What were the effects?
3. What was the cause of conflict within the Christian community? To what people outside Palestine did the Christian message primarily appeal? What issue arose as a consequence, and how was it settled? Why then did the followers of Jesus form a religion separate from Judaism? What importance did this hold?
4. What was Paul's central message; what did he mean by faith? How did he think of Jesus? What did he say God had done through Christ? What were the importance and meaning of the Spirit for Paul? What sacramental emphases did he make?
5. What emphases appeared in the Apostolic Fathers, and how did these emphases differ from those of Paul and John? Sum up the different ways in which Christians explained the significance of Jesus.
6. Why were the Apologists needed, and what did they do? Outline the chief ideas of Justin Martyr.
7. What was the basic idea of the Christian Gnostics; what attitudes did they take toward Christian ideas? Why could their ideas not be accepted within Christianity?
8. Why is Irenaeus a great figure in Christian history? What tests did he lay down for true Christians? Why was something like this unavoidable? How did the Apostles' Creed get rid of the Gnostics in the church?
9. How did Christians understand God? How did the belief that Jesus was the *Logos* incarnate raise a problem for Christian thought?
10. What was the issue in the Nicene controversy? What views were held respectively by Arius and Athanasius, and why did each hold the view he did? What decision was ultimately reached, and what was its significance?
11. Why did the question of the Trinity arise in Christianity and not in other religions? What formulation came to be accepted, and what does this mean?

Selected Readings

Angus, S., *The Religious Quests of the Graeco-Roman World*, New York, Charles Scribner's Sons, 1929.

Barnes, Earnest William, *The Rise of Christianity*, London, Longmans, Green and Co., Ltd., 1947.

Carrington, Philip, *The Early Christian Church*, Cambridge, Cambridge University Press, 1957, vols. I and II.

Dodd, C. H., *The Interpretation of the Fourth Gospel*, Cambridge, Cambridge University Press, 1955.

Enslin, Morton Scott, *Christian Beginnings*, New York, Harper & Brothers, 1938.

Kee, Howard C., and Franklin W. Young, *Understanding the New Testament*, Englewood Cliffs, N. J., Prentice-Hall, Inc., 1957.

McGiffert, A. C., *A History of Christian Thought*, New York, Charles Scribner's Sons, 1932, vol. I.

Neve, J. L., *A History of Christian Thought*, Philadelphia, Muhlenberg Press, 1946, vol. I.

Porter, F. C., *The Mind of Christ in Paul*, New York, Charles Scribner's Sons, 1930.

Walker, Williston, *A History of the Christian Church*, rev. ed., New York, Charles Scribner's Sons, 1959.

Weiss, Johannes, *The History of Primitive Christianity*, tr. and ed. Frederick C. Grant, New York, Wilson-Erickson, Inc., 1937, vols. I and II.

12. Toward a Christian Philosophy

Christianity had entered the Roman world as a new religion in an ancient culture; it entered the world of Western Europe as a well-established religion in an infant culture. The Christianity Europe inherited from the ancient world was for the most part a version which had passed through the temperament and intellect of Augustine and had emerged equipped with a relatively complete philosophy.

The Life of Augustine

Augustine (354-430) was a native of the town of Tagaste in that part of North Africa which is today called Algeria, then a colony of the Roman Empire. His mother, Monica, was a Christian who made a Christian catechumen of her infant son and gave him the best religious instruction of which her limited understanding was capable. His father, Patricius, one of the Roman administrators of Tagaste, did not become a Christian until shortly before his death. In keeping with a general custom of the time, since there was as yet no developed method of penance to remove sin committed after baptism, Augustine was not baptized as a child. His mother felt it better for him to pass through the "fiery years of youth" before he availed himself of the cleansing power of the sacrament, believed to remove original and all prebaptismal sin. As Augustine grew up he found himself divided strongly between an irresistible urge toward sensuality and a deep religious interest of a philosophical variety. Torn between his desire for virtue and his uncontrollable sexual desire, he later wrote, "Wretched youth that I was . . . I had entreated chastity of thee [God] and had prayed, 'Grant me chastity and continence, but not yet.' For I was afraid lest thou shouldest hear me too soon, and too soon cure me of my disease of lust which I desired to have satisfied rather than extinguished."[1]

He became convinced that the meaning and goal of life was the attainment of knowledge of God. Both during his training and later in teaching rhetoric he had as his avocation the contemplative search for truth; yet this search was always threatened by his sensual inclinations and practices. Again, he wrote about the struggles of this period:

> I was bound by the iron chain of my own will. . . . Out of the perverse will came lust, and the service of lust ended in habit, and habit, not resisted, became necessity. . . . Thus my two wills—the old and the new, the carnal and the spiritual—were in conflict within me; and by their discord they tore my soul apart. . . . I loathed myself . . . I was mad for health, and dying for life; knowing what evil thing I was, . . .[2]

Intellectually restless, religiously and morally starved and at war with himself, Augustine was attracted by societies and systems of thought which he felt might offer peace to his mind and sustenance to his soul. The Christian church, as he understood it at that time, seemed to him full of superstition and not intellectually acceptable, while its Scriptures, which he knew in crude Latin translations, offended his literary tastes. Hence he formed his associations elsewhere. While still in Africa he became attached to *Manichaeanism*, a form of Persian Gnosticism named after its third-century founder, Mani, which included in its system the person and work of Christ. It seemed more rationalistic and intellectually respectable than orthodox Christianity, and it claimed Augustine's loyalty for a period of nine years.

Augustine's temporary attachment to Manichaeanism did not deter him from the individualistic path toward the goal of knowledge. His professional interests led him from North Africa to Rome, where he fell under the influence of skepticism. The skeptics were busily arguing that it was impossible to attain certain knowledge concerning matters of experience; not knowl-

[1] Augustine, *Confessions*, book VIII, chap. 7, in Albert C. Outler (ed. and tr.) *Augustine: Confessions and Enchiridion*, Philadelphia, The Westminster Press, 1955, p. 169.

[2] *Ibid.*, book VIII, chaps. 5-8, pp. 164-170, *passim*.

edge but opinion was the best that the physical sciences could give us. But, Augustine must have wondered, if such doubt clouds the most persistent efforts of the human mind to try to understand the physical world, what hope is there that we can determine the true causes which lie behind the world of appearance, and how can we possibly ascend to the knowledge of God and the moral principles inherent in the nature of things? Such considerations led him toward agnosticism.

While wrestling with the doubts which his acquaintance with skepticism had awakened in him, Augustine happily came upon a way to truth furnished by Neo-Platonism. The ultimate reality or Being which formed the apex of Neo-Platonic thought seemed to Augustine the true object of his philosophic and religious quest. His studying Neo-Platonism at just this period of his life brought about two important decisions. First, he felt that the God of Neo-Platonism was in essence the same as the Christian God, the Being whose will was revealed in the Scriptures and by the church. There appeared to be no reason, therefore, for him to postpone baptism any longer. Second, soon after this discovery he experienced religious conversion. He had reached a crisis in his moral and intellectual life which was solved when, upon hearing a child's voice from a neighboring garden saying, "Pick it up, read it," he reached for a copy of Paul's epistles and read, ". . . not in reveling and drunkenness, not in debauchery and licentiousness, not in quarreling and jealousy. But put on the Lord Jesus Christ, and make no provision for the flesh, to gratify its desires" (Roman 13:13-14). His sensual inclinations at that point lost their power over him, and he was filled with certainty of the truth of Christianity.[3] He forsook his concern for earthly fame by abandoning his profession and devoted himself thenceforth exclusively to philosophic and religious meditation. This took place in 386; the following year he was baptized into full membership in the Christian church. Thus Christianity and Neo-Platonic philosophy were intimately united in his personal experience, and through him the results of this union passed into the mainstream of Christian thought in the West.

Some time after this experience, Augustine retired to his native town of Tagaste with a few congenial friends to cultivate a life of personal piety and philosophic speculation. But in 391, almost against his will it seems, he was made a priest in the church of the nearby city of Hippo, and in 396 he became its bishop. His work as an administrator forced him to consider the nature of the Christian church and its teachings. Through controversies like the Donatist and the Pelagian he sharpened his own insights, developing in

[3] *Ibid.*, book VIII, chap. 12, 175 ff.

the process the basic structure of Christian thought that dominated the Western church for almost a thousand years. Our concern here is not with the intricate development of his thought so much as with the seminal ideas he furnished which formed the framework of Christian philosophy and theology during succeeding centuries and still continue to exert powerful influence. First it is necessary to learn something of the nature of that Neo-Platonism which so strongly conditioned his ideas and those of all later Christian mysticism.

Neo-Platonism

This philosophy grew out of the same soil which had nourished the mystery religions, Gnosticism, and the other philosophies and religions of the late Roman period. It is therefore not strange that Neo-Platonism should have had certain features in common with them, but the verdict of history is that this philosophy as set forth by *Plotinus* (204-270), its greatest exponent, was a more carefully developed system of thought than the others, and, unlike them, was quite free of an undigested eclecticism. There is little question that it grew out of a scholarly reading of Plato's own works and a true appreciation of one aspect of the Platonic spirit. Plotinus, designated by Bertrand Russell the last of the great philosophers of antiquity, could not of course escape the spirit of his time any more than a modern philosopher can free himself from the scientific spirit which characterizes our day. The Platonic teachings that appealed to Plotinus and received his attention were quite naturally those which concerned ideas attractive to this same third century—on religion, myth, and imaginative flights and allegory rather than on science.

One way to understand the philosophy of Plotinus is to interpret his metaphysics in terms of his theory of human nature. Like Plato, who had said that the state is the individual writ large, Plotinus saw in the universe as a whole the same elements that compose the human individual. Therefore, as we know the nature of the self we have a good start in understanding the nature of reality. In his analysis of the self, Plotinus discovered three factors. First there is the physical part of one's nature, or the body. The second factor is the soul; this term refers to the life function, the principle which accounts for such processes as nutrition and breathing, for sensation, and for practical reasoning. Third is the *nous*, the intellectual principle or mind. In addition to his sensory capacities and his practical reason, then, man possesses this higher faculty of theoretical reason called the mind, with which he is able to understand the eternal principles, forms, or Platonic Ideas which constitute the structure of reality. Body, soul, and mind are the three constituents of the human being.

Plotinus built his philosophy on this psychology and also on mysticism. In a mystical experience one tries to overcome his sense of individuality and to go beyond mere knowledge to an immediate experience or intuition of that which lies at the very heart of reality. The climax of the mystical experience is the feeling of being absorbed in the Whole, of being united with the source of all existing things. The steps through which the mystic passes are three. First, he loses his awareness of his body, of the physical part of his nature. Next, he passes beyond any sense of his individual personality, his life functions, or soul. What is now left is the impersonal and universal realm of ideas. Finally, the ideas vanish, and the mystic is united with the ultimate source of all things. This experience suggests the ascending order of importance of the four factors involved. The lowest in the scale is body. Above body is soul, and above soul is mind. That which has absolute being lies *beyond* mind; Plotinus calls it the One. If we think of the One as ultimate reality, and if we universalize the other three factors, we have a picture of Plotinus' world view. There is the One, the World Mind, the World Soul, and, least "real" of all, the physical world.

Let us consider this picture a little more in detail. The ultimate reality is neither the world of things of which we have sensations nor the world of Platonic Ideas. It is more like the Aristotelian pure form, or the Platonic Idea of the Good. It is beyond any of the Ideas of which we can conceive or to which we can assign names, such as number, equality, beauty, or justice. It is pure Being in which is contained all the possibilities which, when they are realized, make up the variety of things which we experience in our universe. Such a reality is so rich in possibility and yet so definitely a unit that the only term Plotinus is willing to use in referring to it is the One.

The One is the ultimate reality and the source of all else. The next problem is that of deriving the universe from it. This is solved by pointing out that the One, being what it is, cannot help pouring out its essence any more than the sun, being what it is, can help sending out its heat and light. Just as the sun pours out its light until all the corners of the solar system are illumined, so from the One reality emanates until all possible forms and types of existence are actualized. Following the analogy of the sun a little further, we can see that although close to the sun the heat is almost as intense and the light almost as brilliant as the sun itself, this area is nevertheless different from the sun. In like manner, as reality emanates from the One, it is separated from its source, is different and slightly less fully real than the One. The first emanation, although close to the source of all reality, becomes aware of its independence and experiences a yearning to turn back to the One. It becomes a subject seeking its object. This first emanation is the Intellectual Principle or World Mind, because the meaning of *mind* is to be a knowing subject seeking the object of knowledge. The World Mind is merely a generalization of that type of intellectual activity which goes beyond the multiplicity of things to a contemplation of the Platonic Ideas, desiring to come to rest in an apprehension of the unity of the universe.

The World Mind is only the first emanation. Reality is, as we know, much more than a system of timeless patterns or ideas. In man himself comtemplative reason is only a small part of his conscious life. He also has emotional drives and appetites, ears that hear and eyes that see, and an imagination which brings up memories of sights and sounds experienced in the past. What accounts for all these familiar attributes of the self is a second emanation. Just as the World Mind is an emanation from the One, so the Mind cannot help pouring itself out also and having its emanation, and this is the World Soul. When the Soul realizes its separation from Mind it wishes to return to its source, just as the Mind wishes to return to the One. But the best it can do in the realm of thought is to carry on the problem-solving sort of activity which we study in our courses in logic. It is not in its province to arrive at self-evident truths. As those rays of light, removed by a considerable distance from the sun, are still brilliant but quite different from the sun itself, so the Soul, as a second emanation, is a vehicle of reality different from the Mind. The Soul, in addition to being the principle of reflective thinking, is also the principle of sensation and life which men and animals have in common. In the Soul emanation there is both a unity and a division into many individual souls. The Mind is a unity forming a single system of Ideas, but the Soul (although from one point of view a unified and single World Soul) is also divided into the particular souls of individual beings. Furthermore, the souls of individuals are not merely parts of a general soul but are quite separate and distinct from one another. The individual souls are also immortal.

But we still have not accounted for the existence of the physical universe and the presence there of living bodies. The universe is one more emanation. The Soul, like the One and the Mind, necessarily generates something beyond itself, and the result is the physical world and its law-abiding structure. Another phase of the Soul's emanation is its descent into individual bodies. The One, Mind, and Soul, although different from each other, have in common their nature as spiritual, but the universe of experience is material. This means that by the time the light of reality has gone so far from its original source as to result in the physical world, it has lost its brilliance and has grown dim. Whatever natural harmony the universe displays is an indication of its success in approximating the likeness of the World Soul, but in the process of actualizing the many forms of existence, reality approaches at last the exhaustion of logical possibilities. As it approaches this end, the light of reality (speaking analogically) fades more and more until it comes at last to nothingness or complete darkness.

Although this result reminds us of that dualism of spirit and matter, good and evil, which we have found in Philo, the Gnostics, and Paul, we must note that there are nevertheless no eternally opposed positive powers of good and evil. The material world is an emanation whose ultimate source is the good God. It is simply so far removed from ultimate reality that the clear light has become crossed with shadows and finally fades into darkness. Thus, evil is not a positive power, but merely the absence of good. In the darkness which is matter, the universe loses its absolute harmony and gives way to operations which involve conflict between the various beings of the world, bringing suffering to men, frustration of desires, limitation, strife, and destruction. The individual soul, having generated a material body, becomes involved in the lesser being or evil of that body and often yields to the temptation to serve rather than to master its passions. Plotinus taught that the individual soul is a free moral agent, capable of avoiding the choice of evil. But for some obscure reason, the individual may decide to choose individual independence instead of oneness with God, and by this personal choice he falls away from his original state, bringing sin into the world.

Like the other religions and religious philosophies of the Roman world, Neo-Platonism had its theory of salvation, for which indeed all the rest of its notions existed. This theory called for a long and extremely arduous process of redemption in contrast to the easy salvation promised by some of the other movements of the day. It had no belief in a dying and rising Savior God with whom one could identify himself and thus become deified, and it avoided the initiation rites of some of the mysteries. Plotinus taught that for the soul to extricate itself from attachment to matter, the evil result of its fall from the spiritual realm, it must pass through a long period of self-discipline. Man as a human being is triune. His physical body is the lowest aspect of his make-up. He is an individual soul, and, most significant, his soul is capable of rising to the world of the Mind and the universal Ideas. The fall attached him to his lowest aspect; salvation must take him in the opposite direction, breaking the ties of the physical which bind him. Like Plato and the Orphics, Plotinus taught that the soul is immortal, having existed many times before this life and returning to life again through metempsychosis as long as it fails to find salvation.

Broadly speaking, the stages leading to salvation are three, and it may require aeons before they are fully realized. In the first place, the soul seeking for salvation must learn to control its relation to the physical world through self-discipline, learning the value of self-sufficiency and accepting cheerfully its social obligations, discharging them honestly and unselfishly. It must cease to look for pleasure or the meaning of life in the events which take place in the world of sense. Recalling that for Plotinus this material world is next to nothingness, the least real of the four levels of reality, we can understand why the first step toward salvation must be that of emancipating oneself from attachment to this largely unreal world. Second, the soul must direct its mind toward the difficult intellectual task of understanding the unchanging Ideas which lie behind this world of appearance. In this stage there is no short cut—reason must be used to the fullest and at its highest in the pursuance of hard metaphysical thought. The individual, in short, must become a philosopher. Finally, and most important since it reaches the goal which is sought, the seeking soul is ready to contemplate Truth itself. No longer does it regard the details of the world or the many Ideas in the World Mind, for it is now prepared to glimpse the ultimate, the One behind all the apparent multiplicities. The discipline of thoughts and emotions must be continued, and now, at this stage, the soul becomes aware not only of Truth but also of its own true self, seeing itself not as a part of the world among other parts but as the "whole of being" with the same center as that of the One. At last, in a moment of ecstasy, the soul comes to the end of its search in the direct apprehension of the One and achieves unity with the One. Here all words fail. The supreme goal of life has been reached. The final goal of salvation is achieved in the indescribable "mystical vision," in the "flight of the alone to the Alone."

Neo-Platonism and Christianity

The relations between Neo-Platonism and Christianity were alternately friendly and antagonistic. *Ammonius Saccas,* the reputed founder of Neo-Platonism who taught in Alexandria during the early part of the third century A.D., himself had been reared a Christian, and Origen, the Christian theologian, had once been a student of his and continued in his Christian teaching to hold much in common with Neo-Platonism. The attitude of Plotinus himself toward Christianity was one of disdain rather than hostility, but some of his followers attacked it openly and directly. In the fourth century, Neo-Platonism became the center of a united pagan effort to prevent the triumph of Christianity in the Roman world.

From the beginning of its history, Christianity displayed an amazing talent for absorbing the ideas and practices of its rivals and at the same time treating them intolerantly. There is no doubt that by the fourth century Christianity was indebted not only to Judaism but also to the mysteries, Greek philosophy, and Gnosticism for much of its intellectual content and many of its ritualistic forms. Unlike Judaism, it had become an international church, but it did not share the attitude of mutual tolerance which characterized the pagan religions. It stood firm in its conviction that it had the one and only truth, refusing to allow itself to be classed as one of many valid ways to salvation. Jesus Christ was not to be added to a list of deities all of whom were worthy of worship, for he alone was the true Savior. Its ability to draw the best of paganism into itself made Christianity a strong contender for the religious yearnings of a large number of people. Although its intolerance led it into many difficulties, this same intolerance was also one of the chief causes of its ultimate triumph.

The growth of the church resulted in its becoming a kind of religious nation within the Empire, an organization which even dared defy the supreme secular authority by refusing to worship the emperor. Official persecutions only served to strengthen the internal ecclesiastic organization. The struggle between church and state took a new turn after Constantine's Edict of Milan in 313, which was the beginning of Christianity's ascent to the position of official religion of the Empire.

But this political victory did not mean that the church was as yet victorious over pagan culture. Oriental, Greek, and Roman religions came to look upon Christianity as their common foe, and regarded Neo-Platonism as an intellectual basis for unifying a divided paganism. If the universe is a series of emanations from the one absolute Being, and if it is the nature of the One to overflow until all possible types of existence are realized, then all the deities known to the Roman world had their places in "the great chain of being." Each pagan cult was one of many ways of realizing the divine presence in the world and of giving men a partial understanding of ultimate reality. In becoming a Neo-Platonic philosopher one became a cultivated gentleman-scholar, urbane and tolerant. He did not have to be "converted" or to forsake the religious cult to which he had formerly belonged. The more enlightened realized that the official beliefs of old Greek and Roman religions were quite meaningless to them, but in turning to Neo-Platonic metaphysics they did not set out to destroy whatever of value these ancient beliefs had for the less cultivated part of the population. This doctrine became more than mere theory, for the Oriental gods did come to take their places at the Empire's capital along with the old Roman gods. Only Christianity with its intolerance was despised by the others, and only Christianity appeared to be on the way to becoming *the* religion of the Empire.

Persecutions of the church had uniformly failed to impair its strength, as Constantine himself had realized when he took the attitude of toleration toward Christianity as well as toward the other religions. But Constantine's sons, themselves professing to be Christians, moved on toward a position just the reverse of the policy pursued before their father's time: they made Christianity official, and set out to destroy paganism by legislation. It was now paganism's turn to resist persecution by becoming unified and taking on new life. Its opportunity for official support arrived in the person of Julian, Constantine's nephew, who became emperor in 361. Like all members of the royal household, he was nominally Christian and received instruction from Christian teachers, but at heart he had contempt for Christianity with its quarrelsome bishops, its attacks on the other religions of the Empire, and its lack of that peace, brotherly love, and charity which it preached so constantly but did not practice toward those who differed with it. Even morality in the court did not seem greatly improved when Christianity became the official religion. On the other hand, Julian admired everything that was Greek. He professed Christianity until he became emperor, and then publicly announced his adherence to the ancient religion of Greece. Although he did not persecute the Christians, he did open the pagan temples again, issued an edict of toleration for all religions, and did what he could to discourage Christianity, going so far as to forbid Christians to teach their doctrines in schools and universities.

Most important in his attempt to supplant Christianity, Julian (now called the Apostate by Christians) needed to find some center around which to unify the old religions. For this purpose he used Neo-Platonism as the intellectual foundation of his religion of Hellenism. But the attempt failed. Julian died just two years after he became emperor, but he would probably have failed even if he had ruled much longer, for Christianity was not a barbarian religion standing at the opposite pole from Hellenism, but was a system that had incorporated into its theology much of the wisdom of Greece. Julian had tried to restore life to a dying religion, and this proved to be no match for the young, vital, well-organized, influential Christian church. The final blow was dealt when Neo-Platonism itself, which was to have constituted the intellectual center of the new Hellenism, was instead made an ally to Christianity. This brings us back to Augustine.

Augustine and Neo-Platonism

Plotinus' Neo-Platonism gave Augustine practically all the knowledge he had of Plato. As we have already noted, the influence of Plotinus on Augustine's thought was very great, both preparing him for the step into full membership in the Christian church and providing him with many of the insights which informed his later theological writing. This philosophy alone played a significant part in his mature thinking, and it has even been claimed that "To Plotinus he [Augustine] is indebted for almost all the matter and for the whole technique of his philosophy."[4] Yet this influence must not be over-exaggerated, for Augustine differed from Plotinus at many junctures, in particular on all the essential points which stressed the unique elements of Christian teaching—the Son of God's becoming man, the creation instead of the emanation of the universe, the resurrection of the dead instead of metempsychosis. Neo-Platonism was of special significance to the thought of Augustine in its insistence upon the spiritual nature of God and of the human soul and in the interpretation of evil as absence of being rather than as a positive reality, as the Manichaeans had claimed. These three elements will appear in the general discussion which follows of the principal constituents of Augustine's thought. We will begin with still another point—the question of what one can know. The elements in this discussion which remind the reader of Plato's teaching are also, of course, drawn from Plotinus.

The Question of Knowledge

Augustine's first contact with Neo-Platonism followed upon the period of doubt brought on by his association with the skeptics. He was an apt pupil in the lesson of doubting everything, and upon this strange foundation he started to build his theory of knowledge. He came to feel that one could remain a complete skeptic only if he does not carry his doubting far enough. It may be the case that certainty concerning matters of sense experience is impossible, but of one thing there is certainty: the fact of one's own existence. Doubting is thinking, and therefore one's very doubting is a demonstration of his own self-conscious reality. "I doubt, therefore *I am*" sums up the point, for there can be no doubt unless there is one doing the doubting.

[4] Étienne Gilson, *The Christian Philosophy of Saint Augustine*, New York, Random House, Inc., 1960, p. 234. See also Eugène Portalié, *A Guide to the Thought of St. Augustine*, tr. Ralph J. Bastian, Chicago, Henry Regnery Co., 1960, chap. 6.

The stronger the doubt the more certainty one has of his own existence as a doubter. Hence, the more skeptical one is, the more certain he becomes of an indubitable fact—that *he* exists. Carry skepticism to its conclusions and it results in at least one certainty. In this argument Augustine develops a point which we will find reproduced 12 centuries later in the work of the French philosopher Descartes.

As we turn our attention to this self whose existence we have discovered cannot be doubted, we find that it possesses many ideas. Some of them, to be sure, have come to us by way of the senses, and about these there can be no certainty. Such experiences as sweet and sour or cold and hot are not reliable and tell us nothing about the permanent nature of things. However, in true Platonic fashion, Augustine goes on to show that there are ideas of a different kind, arrived at as necessary conclusions of logical processes. These are not dependent upon shifting sense experience, but are the product of intellectual activity. Two and two are always four, and the sum of the angles of any triangle must be equal to two right angles. About such ideas there is no uncertainty. The intellect also perceives the difference between good and bad or beautiful and ugly, distinctions which are eternally valid and independent of changing circumstances.

In sum, real knowledge can be found in the intellectual sphere. But how can we account for the fact that our intellects do reveal the unchanging realities? It must be because the light of eternal truth illumines the inner eye of reason, and this truth can be none other than God himself. It is God who makes known to men the eternal verities and in so doing makes himself known. Thus, if one starts out by doubting everything, he comes first to the certainty of his own self-consciousness, then to a knowledge of the eternal ideas, and finally to a knowledge of God, the source of truth.

The Idea of God

In no part of his philosophy is Augustine's Neo-Platonism more apparent than in his idea of God. God is above all Spirit, the one eternal Being. He alone is absolutely good and real; he is the source of all other things, and without him there is nothing. Everything depends upon God for its existence and would lapse into nothingness were it not for the constant and creative divine energy. The world is essentially good inasmuch as it has its source in God. Evil is not a positive power; it is simply the absence of the creative activity of God. So far as the world is truly real, it is good, but the actual world is neither completely real nor perfect. God alone possesses these characteristics because he is the one eternal Being. He is above time; his consciousness is an eternal present; he is changeless. Time and change belong to the created world—and this accounts for the imperfection of existence, for only the changeless is completely good. And yet because God's creative activity is continuous, there is some reality even in the changing world.

The World

These notions of the sole reality of the spiritual God and of the utter dependence of man and nature on him for their very existence were central in Augustine's philosophy. Since God alone has true being, Augustine (in opposition to Plato, who said that creation is done with materials already existing) formulated the doctrine that God created the world out of nothing (*ex nihilo*). The only opposition to God is nonbeing, and therefore the only opposition to goodness is the lack of goodness. Like Plotinus, Augustine gave a negative definition of evil. It follows that the only worthy goal of the intellectual quest is the knowledge of God. In and of itself nature is nothing. Its only reality consists in its reflection of the divine will. Augustine was no more interested than were the Neo-Platonists in studying the physical world as an independent reality. The object of his quest was true reality, God, and the physical world meant nothing beyond being an expression of God's creative activity and eternal providence. Providence was seen in all that truly has existence. This attitude and dominant set of interests account for the fact that the Augustinian Christian philosophy seems other-worldly.

Divergence from Neo-Platonism

On all these points Augustine's thinking is indebted to Neo-Platonism. Yet though his central emphases show the Neo-Platonic cast of thought, they find their true home in the historic Christian tradition. His God, for instance, is far less removed from the actual world than is the impersonal One of Plotinus. God, he believed, is conscious of those beings he has created and loves them so greatly that he sent his own Son to redeem them from sin. Again, the Christian Trinity found a central place in his thought, although in his discussion of this doctrine it was probably his Neo-Platonic background which led him to stress the unity of God as a single "substance" and to employ psychological analogies in his explanation of the mutual relations of "subsistence" among the three "Persons" (a word he himself recognized as improper, yet could think of no better). These three are, of course, Father, Son, and Holy Spirit. In this connection Augustine used the analogy of mind which has the three attributes or functions of memory, understanding, and will: "Since, then, these three, memory, understanding, will, are not three lives, but one life; not three minds, but one mind; it follows certainly that neither are they three substances, but one substance."[5]

Reason and Faith

As a Christian theologian, Augustine faced a problem of knowledge which carried him beyond the philosophical speculations referred to at the beginning of this section. For Christianity is a revealed religion, and Augustine had to take up the question of the relation between the truths derived from reason and those alleged to be revealed, which are the truths of faith. This is one of the great problems of theology. Augustine's solution found a place for both reason and faith but emphasized the latter.

Concerning reason itself, he held a rather unusual doctrine, one quite different from that generally accepted in modern times. The truths of reason he believed to be the general truths about reality such as Plato referred to in his notion of Ideas. He did not mean truths derived from scientific study of changing nature. These general truths, he taught, are reached as a result of a "mysterious influence" of God upon the mind, operating to produce a kind of image of the truths which stand behind all genuine knowledge. Even man's reason, therefore, functions properly as a result of God's activity, with God acting as teacher and guiding him into the discovery of truth.

Augustine believed religious knowledge has two origins: reason, and faith based upon authority. By faith he does not mean trust and self-commitment to God, as did St. Paul, but the intellectual acceptance of truths taught on the basis of authority. With this concept of faith, Augustine laid down the principle that faith *precedes* knowledge, that is, that one must have faith in Christian teachings in order to understand them. As the modern student comes upon this principle he may be inclined to smile at its seeming naïveté. Reason, the modern thinker believes, should be allowed to come to its own conclusions even though they may be contrary to the content of faith. All this principle seems to do is limit intellectual activity to the task of demonstrating the truth of what is already accepted on faith. But if we look a little further we can see that Augustine had a valid psychological insight. Reason is not merely a machine which grinds out impersonal truths but is always associated with purposeful activity and follows acts of the will. The whole line of modern physicists had faith in the intelligibility of the physical

[5] *On the Trinity (De Trinitate)*, book X, chap. 11, in *The Works of Aurelius Augustine*, tr. and ed., Marcus Dods, Edinburgh, T. and T. Clark, 1873, vol. VIII, p. 259.

world *prior* to their discovery of specific physical laws. Men are attached to the ideals of democracy by faith *before* they offer rational justification for that political philosophy. A man standing outside the Christian tradition can no more understand the real content of Christian doctrine than he can see if he keeps his eyes closed. Faith in God must precede the perceiving of divine instruction. In Augustine, the dictum "I believe in order that I may understand" had real vitality. It becomes artificial when the "I believe" does not issue from a genuine act of will but is merely a perfunctory intellectual assent to the authority of the past.

When, then, a person accepts the faith which the church presents to him on its own authority, he can proceed to reason about it. This faith appeals to his reason, and if he were not a rational person he could not accept it; in this sense reason comes first. But since the truths of the faith go beyond what he is able to discover for himself through his own reason, he accepts them on authority, using them as starting points for his reasoning. The authority of the church which teaches the faith is based on four "proofs" for Augustine: the miracles of Christ, the fulfillment of prophecy, the multitude of the faithful, and, most important for him, the moral transformation of the world by the church.[6] It can be seen from this discussion that for Augustine faith and reason stand in very close relationship, *both* requiring God for their truth; that each has its own part to play; and that the faith to be accepted is that of the authoritative church, and that it must be assented to on grounds other than those of reason alone.

Three of Augustine's theological teachings command our special attention because of their influence on later Christian thought. One of these is his doctrine of man, including the ideas of the fall and original sin, and of salvation through the grace of God. The other two teachings are his philosophy of history and his doctrine of the church. His thinking on both these questions was influenced by the practical tasks he faced as a bishop of the Catholic church.

The Doctrine of Man

Among the beings created by God *ex nihilo* are men. Like all other created beings, they are dependent upon their Creator, and their true vocation is to attend to the divine voice and live according to the divine will. To turn from God to one's own personal ambitions is to turn from reality to what is in its own nature nothingness.

[6] Portalié, *op. cit.*, chap. 7.

Augustine had a doctrine of the Fall of man, as did the Neo-Platonists, but he meant something quite different by it, for he denied the eternality of immaterial souls which descended into material bodies. On the contrary, man —spiritual soul and material body—is a creature who had a beginning in time; thus, there is no eternal pre-existence of the soul. We find in Augustine the same two views of the nature of man which were a part of earlier Christian thought. On the one hand is the Platonic view that there is only a temporary and loose connection between man's soul and his body, and the former is his real self, the only worthy part of his nature. Immortality and salvation are explained, from this viewpoint, as the soul's gaining its freedom from bondage to the body. On the other hand, we find also in Augustine the second view, that man is a unity of body and soul. Death or separation of soul from body is not looked upon by Augustine as desirable but as punitive. The final good is postponed until the day of resurrection when soul and body will be reunited and will share in the bliss of Paradise.

Although apparently incompatible, these two views have been a part of Christian tradition since very early days. The former furnished a philosophic foundation for belief in immortality, but the latter better served the idea that the *whole* man was to be saved and that the body was not to be despised. In retaining the latter view, Christianity has always had a doctrine of man which by implication leads to a recognition of the value and dignity of the human body. That Augustine was himself puzzled by the problem of harmonizing these views is shown in the fact that he asks more questions than he answers.

> What is man? Is he both of these [body and soul]? Or is he the body only, or the soul only? For although the things are two, soul and body, and although neither without the other could be called man (for the body would not be man without the soul, nor again would the soul be man if there were not a body animated by it), still it is possible that one of these may be held to be man and may be called so . . . . This dispute is not easy to settle . . . .[7]

A good deal of Augustine's teaching about man centers around the problem of human freedom. When what he had to say on the subject is compared with his doctrines on original sin and the need for grace, it gives his philosophy the appearance of a mass of contradictions. And yet any attempt to think clearly on this problem is fraught with difficulties. Let us first state in a purely modern setting some of the assumptions which most of us make on this question. In the first place, we all assume that we are to some extent free

[7] *On the Morals of the Catholic Church*, chap. 4, tr. R. Stothert in *Basic Writings of Saint Augustine*, ed. Whitney J. Oates, New York, Random House, Inc., 1948, vol. I, pp. 321 f.

to act as we will. Our whole system of justice rests upon the idea that any man who has not been officially diagnosed as insane is morally responsible for what he does, and deserves to be punished for criminal acts. To be a human being is to have moral responsibility. But we also assume that there are many determining factors over which the individual has no control and yet which influence his behavior. For example, he cannot help having been born of his parents. He had no choice in that matter, and yet our biological studies make a strong case for the argument that one's heredity plays a decisive role in determining the kind of person he becomes and consequently the acts which he performs. Again, the individual does not choose the sort of neighborhood, social class, or economic status of which he is a member. However, sociological investigations leave no doubt that more criminals come from one type of social background than from another, and that in general one's social environment is added to one's heredity in determining his behavior. Analytical psychology, too, has revealed the fact that each of us has a mental and emotional life which rarely reaches the level of consciousness and yet which accounts for many of our choices. Thus, we assume both that we are free and that we are compelled by factors beyond our control in choosing among alternatives which lie before us. Third, we are painfully aware of the inability of men to extricate themselves completely from the evils that beset them. In a period of economic distress it is impossible to know with certainty the cause of unemployment or an industrial slowdown, and no plan has ever been put into effect which has resulted in permanent prosperity for all men. When someone paints a utopian picture we immediately grow skeptical and say it won't work—that human beings are too selfish—and so we affirm a permanent moral weakness in human nature as such.

These same assumptions, elaborated from a theological point of view, run through Augustine's philosophy. Man has been created by God, is dependent upon him for his very existence, and yet has been created with free will. He can choose the greater or the lesser good, and his acts are his own. Still, men habitually choose the lesser good. They turn to a concern for themselves rather than to living for God. Indeed, mankind as a whole is so depraved and so bound by evil that the only way to account for man's present condition is to assume that he has become infected with a moral disease. In other words, there has been a fall, and that occurred in the life of the first man, Adam.

Augustine gives a detailed description of the nature of Adam's fall. He pictures the Garden of Eden as endowed with everything needed to satisfy all good human desires. Adam was created with free will, and in the beginning he possessed the highest imaginable righteousness and perfection. He was endowed with immortal youth and health—he was immune to sickness and even to death. He had superb mental powers, and both because of his innate character and because of his intelligence he was able to choose not to sin. Eve was given to him as a companion in the lovely garden, and they were to have children, but only according to the dictates of high morality and superior wisdom, not accompanied by the disturbing emotions of sex which are experienced by people in their fallen state. But Adam ate of the forbidden fruit, and in so doing became the leading character in a cosmic tragedy. There was more than enough food in the garden, and Adam had fullness of knowledge. Yet in spite of the perfection of his state of being, Adam deliberately went out of his way to eat the fruit of the tree of the knowledge of good and evil, wantonly disobeying the precise command of God. Since there was really nothing Adam lacked or needed, this act of disobedience had a depth of significance beyond anything a man can do today. It was, in fact, an attempt by Adam to put himself in the place of God, to serve himself alone (who was of himself nothing) in place of serving the God who had created him and is the source of all. Created a perfect being, Adam willfully turned from God and life and reality to self and death and nothingness. This was the essence of this evil deed, this original sin, which has corrupted the whole of the human family since his time—that one made from nothing deliberately preferred himself and his own will to God and his will.

Two tragic results followed upon Adam's fall. First, the man created perfect in morality became morally diseased and weakened. At the same time he lost his immortality, becoming subject to death, and lost the fullness of his knowledge, becoming ignorant and uncertain about truth as men have been ever since. Instead of controlling his actions through his good will and knowledge, he became subject to personal interests and ambitions, the victim of ignorance and of that conquering of the soul by bodily desires (of which lust is the worst) which Augustine calls concupiscence. His moral degeneracy showed itself in the tendency to turn from God, the supreme and immutable good, and seek his satisfactions in what is less than God, that is, in created things. The arousing of sexual passion and the desire to make of its satisfaction an end in itself is an example of this. The very act of begetting children is tainted with original sin. Furthermore, since Adam became morally diseased and weakened before he had any children, he passed on this disease to all his progeny, which means, of course, to the entire human race. All of us, therefore, find that our freedom to choose the good life is limited by the sinful nature we have inherited, just as we are also subject to ignorance and death. We are still endowed with the measure of morality that remains from God's original endowment. This makes it possible for us to choose lesser rather than greater evils. None can be perfect, however, capable of choosing to do *only* the will of God; yet we need not be scoundrels.

There is a second result of original sin. We have inherited not only the moral weakness of Adam but also the *guilt* of his disobedience, and so are subject to his punishment. The best way to explain the notion that all men are guilty of Adam's fall is to resort to Platonism. The Idea of man is the eternal reality in which all individual men participate. According to this view, Adam was not merely the *first* man; he was Man. Adam is a name standing for the entire human race, and in his fall the whole of mankind fell from its perfect state. As men ourselves, we participate in this fallen condition and are subject to punishment because we are involved in the original guilt.

Up to this point, Augustine's philosophy of man is decidedly pessimistic. All of us are depraved and cannot avoid sin, either in its original form, as we are born with it, or in the form of those sins we ourselves commit out of ignorance and moral weakness. But a degree of optimism is admitted into the picture when we remember that what man cannot do for himself God can and does do for him. Because of the condition of moral and spiritual degeneracy in which he finds himself, man cannot save himself; his best efforts toward moral living leave the fundamental weakness and guilt of original sin untouched. But the grace of God can lift him from the level of disobedience and self-seeking to a life of devotion to God, restoring him to godliness and immortality. This grace comes as a free gift from God and not as a reward for man's goodness. Man cannot *earn* salvation, no one *deserves* it; it issues only from God's mercy and love. The greatest example of divine grace is the incarnation of God in Christ, through whom and through whose church we receive salvation. This does not mean that everyone receives salvation; only those who will to receive it may receive it. But these are already elected (chosen) by God; the rest of mankind suffers the punishment which all men deserve. Hence God cannot be accused of injustice to those not chosen.

The idea that God chooses some men to be saved and allows others to remain in their condition of depravity is known as *predestination*. However, this belief formed only one aspect of Augustine's philosophy. He also emphasized individual responsibility and endeavor, even though, considered superficially, these seem logically inconsistent with the doctrine of predestination. The notion that God saves some and allows others to be damned suggests an arbitrariness on the part of the ruler of the universe, whereas Augustine's feeling for God was warmly devotional; he emphasized the love and kindness of the Supreme Being. It was in the heat of the so-called Pelagian controversy, which began in the year 412, that the idea of predestination was brought to the fore.

Pelagius was a contemporary of Augustine, a British monk highly respected as a Christian teacher in Rome. He was convinced that man actually does have a completely free will, that he did not lose it in the fall. He therefore denied Augustine's doctrine of original sin, believing instead that every man has the same start in life which Adam had, except that all men since Adam have had the unfortunate example of the wickedness of others before them. Adam was created a mortal being, so death was no punishment. Each of us is free to live the Christian life or to choose the life of moral wickedness. Most people do sin because they do not use their freedom properly. Pelagius felt, then, that although the will is free it still sins, while Augustine taught that the will itself is the problem and it sins because it is corrupted and only partially free. Pelagius called for a reformation of man's conduct; Augustine taught that men needed the grace of God to reform them at the very roots of their wills. Pelagius thought that as men believe in an inherited sinful nature they are deterred from making their best efforts. He wished to raise the standard of moral living. Yet strangely enough, in spite of its optimism about human nature, the position of Pelagius reaches a conclusion far more pessimistic than Augustine's. Precisely because one's freedom of will is total, one is condemned for any sin whatever he may commit. Only those who live perfect moral lives can enter the kingdom of God. This rigorism, reminding one of the most extreme forms of Pharisaism, gave men far less hope than did Augustine with his emphasis on God's grace for sinners.

Augustine's views prevailed and Pelagius' were condemned. Augustine's position emphasized the seriousness of sin as rooted in the very will of man, as he himself had known it in his long struggle for freedom from lust; it also confirmed for him the need for a Savior and the necessity of the church. Whatever freedom men possess is decidedly limited, and self-centeredness *is* a deeply rooted characteristic of all human beings. It therefore seemed reasonable to hold that a miracle of divine grace is necessary to make a man godlike.

Philosophy of History: *The City of God*

In 410 Rome was sacked by the Goths under Alaric. Plunder and destruction, exile and murder, were a part of this event which shook the very foundation of the world. Rome, for centuries the capital of a great empire, had fallen prey to barbarians. This seemed to be the end of the order which civilized Christians and pagans had known. Paganism as a concerted movement to combat Christianity was long since dead, but there were still many individual pagans who felt a deep resentment toward the Empire's official religion. The sack of Rome brought forth from these pagans a literature of criticism in which it was argued that Rome's disaster was a direct result of its abandoning the old gods and turning to the impotent God of the Christians. Rome had grown to a mighty power under the protecting care of the pagan gods, but under the banner of Christianity it had seen its armies defeated and its empire crumble.

Men seldom reflect on the meaning and destiny of the historic process when there is a well-established social order. There is recognition of time and change, to be sure, and there is a vague awareness of the rise and fall of political powers in the past. But there is also the feeling that the social order to which they and their fathers and grandfathers have been accustomed cannot possibly give way to something entirely new. Certainly the Romans had good reason for feeling this way; their city had been the first to create a genuine world empire, and to Rome had come poets and philosophers and merchants from the far corners of what was thought to be the entire inhabited world. And yet the mighty Rome had fallen. No wonder reflective pagans pondered this extraordinary event and looked for an explanation of history.

Christians did not allow the pagan interpretation to go unchallenged. Augustine was in a particularly favorable position to refute the charge that Christianity was responsible for Rome's misfortunes. His diocese of Hippo was comparatively free of the devastating results of the sack of Rome. North Africa, as a matter of fact, was a refuge for many whose property had been confiscated but who had themselves escaped death. Also, in North Africa, where the heavy hand of the Roman government had aroused considerable resentment, Augustine had never felt the pride in Rome which many Christians as well as pagans had known, and did not experience the same grief in its misfortunes. The renewed pagan attack on Christianity did not escape him, however, and in answer to it he produced *The City of God,* a monumental philosophy of history.

The first 10 books of *The City of God* are devoted to refutation. Historical evidence is produced to show that the pagan gods did not, in fact, save Rome from perils in the past. They were not reliable in guaranteeing worldly success to those who worshiped them, and they were utterly useless in bringing men salvation in eternity. Augustine does not claim that the acceptance of Christianity by a nation necessarily means that the nation as such will be preserved. Christianity is not a religion which guarantees happiness on earth. The salvation which it brings is other-worldly. Still, one is better off, even in this life, if he is a Christian. On the one hand, then, pagans falsely claim for their gods the power to lead a nation to greatness, while these gods do nothing whatever to bring other-worldly salvation. On the other hand, the Christians correctly believe their God capable of bestowing eternal bliss on his worshipers, and, while their religion is not particularly concerned with earthly happiness, it nevertheless follows that Christians are better off even here than are pagans. Augustine offers the following summary of the argument of the first 10 books:

> And therefore, in these ten books, though not meeting, I dare say, the expectation of some, yet I have, as the true God and Lord has vouchsafed to aid me, satisfied the desire of certain persons, by refuting the objections of the ungodly, who prefer their own gods to the Founder of the holy city, about which we undertook to speak. Of these ten books, the first five were directed against those who think we should worship the gods for the sake of the blessings of this life, and the second five against those who think we should worship them for the sake of the life which is to be after death. And now, in fulfilment of the promise I made in the first book, I shall go on to say, as God shall aid me, what I think needs to be said regarding the origin, history, and deserved ends of the two cities, which, as already remarked, are in this world commingled and implicated with one another.[8]

In the eleventh book Augustine begins his constructive philosophy of history. He finds the meaning of the historic process in an opposition of two cities—the City of God and the City of Satan. Men cannot clearly distinguish the outlines of these because in this world they are fused together. The origins of the two cities lie in a prehistoric event. God had created angels, all of whom were originally good. One of these angels committed the sin of pride, and tried to set himself up to be equal to God himself. Having ceased to abide by his true vocation of cleaving unto God, he became the founder of an evil city opposed to the City of God. To the former belong Satan and all those angels who, though created good, nevertheless suffered a defect of the will and put personal pride before the glory of God; to the latter belong those angels who have persevered in their loyalty to God and who will remain eternally blessed.

History proper began, Augustine says, less than 6000 years ago with the creation of the world and of man. Adam, too, as we have seen, fell from his original condition of righteousness and passed on his evil nature and his guilt to successive generations of mankind. And yet the City of God was

[8] *The City of God,* book X, chap. 32, tr. and ed., Marcus Dods, New York, Hafner Publishing Co., 1948, vol. I, p. 435.

not completely lost in the affairs of the world, because God promised to redeem some of Adam's descendants and restore them to eternal bliss. The meaning of history between the fall of Adam and the coming of Christ centers in the progress of the two cities, the City of God claiming for its membership those who somehow have not entirely lost the ability to be loyal to God. Thus Noah and his family were saved from the universal punishment at the time of the flood. The earth was repopulated through Noah's sons, from whom developed 72 nations and 72 languages, but the original language and people were Hebrew. The Hebrews as a group lived closer to God than the others, and thus their history is the only significant history. All other ancient peoples were of the City of Satan. Only among the Hebrews do we find an appreciable number of individuals who clove unto God before Christ, and only among the Hebrews do we find events which foreshadowed the great revelation in Christ.

The all-important historic event was the Incarnation. The full and complete revelation appeared in Jesus Christ, the God-man; following his time, those who receive salvation through him are members of the City of God. After the time of Christ the outlines of the two cities are somewhat more easily distinguished. Christian revelation is opposed to pagan knowledge, Christian supernatural morality to natural morality, the Christian church to worldly institutions. All those whose fortune it is to belong to the City of God are also members of the Christian church. This does not mean that all members of the visible church are also members of the elect, for a person may belong to the church who has not received the grace of God.

> We must understand in one sense the kingdom of heaven in which exist together both he who breaks what he teaches and he who does it, the one being least, the other great, and in another sense the kingdom of heaven into which only he who does what he teaches shall enter. Consequently, where both classes exist, it is the Church as it now is, but where only the one shall exist, it is the Church as it is destined to be when no wicked person shall be in her.[9]

The consummation of the historical process is to be an event "beyond history," the end of the present order and the complete separation of the two cities in the Final Judgment. In that day, all members of the City of God will experience a resurrection of their bodies, which are to be reunited with their souls, and will enter into their perfectly blessed existence. All members of the City of Satan will arise only to endure their eternal punishment.

In the light of such an exalted view of the meaning and destiny of human

[9] *Ibid.*, book XX, chap. 9, vol. II, pp. 364 f.

history, Augustine saw the fall of Rome to be a relatively minor event. Rome had possessed some real virtues which enabled it to enjoy a measure of temporal greatness, but its downfall was inevitable because it did not see its true function as service of the one God. Rome, like all earthly powers, was ultimately a representative of the City of Satan. Only the Holy Catholic Church is permanent because this is the one earthly institution of the City of God.

The Holy Catholic Church

After his conversion to Catholicism, Augustine was consistently loyal to the institution of the church. His *City of God* was a philosophical justification of the importance of the church in human history and of its superiority to worldly institutions. But his ideas on the practical problems of ecclesiastic organization came out of his experience as an administrator trying to maintain a united Christendom. The defender of the Catholic church had to do more than answer the pagan criticism of Christianity. It was all very well to talk of the church against the world, but the fact was that there were divisions within Christianity itself. Arian churches still existed and had succeeded in gaining the patronage of barbarian princes. Manichaeanism was still alive, and in spite of Augustine's refutation of Pelagius, the latter's influence continued to make itself felt. As a philosopher, Augustine could turn his criticism upon these because they were heretical; they all had doctrines which were at variance with orthodox Catholic belief. But his most pressing problem in North Africa was the Donatist church, which had been in existence for a century and which had the very same doctrines as Catholicism. It was in his conflict with the Donatists that Augustine worked out his ideas on the church and the sacraments.

The Donatist church arose as a result of the persecutions of the Christians under Diocletian in 303. At that time government officials demanded that the Christian clergy turn over their Scriptures to be destroyed. Those who refused were killed. Mensurius, bishop of Carthage, and Caecilian, his archdeacon, presented a collection of heretical writings instead of the Scriptures. By doing this they were able to escape the death penalty and at the same time, so they hoped, avoid the stigma of being thought traitors, as those members of the clergy were called who actually turned over the Scriptures to save their own lives. Several years later, when Caecilian became bishop, other bishops of North Africa raised serious objections to his appointment, insisting that he was actually a traitor and in addition that he was morally lax. They encouraged a group to leave the Catholic church, be rebaptized, and elect a bishop of their own.

So began a new movement that lodged chiefly in North Africa but that spread even to Rome and continued to be powerful for well over a century. It took its name from its dominant figure, *Donatus* the Great. It had been in existence for a century when Augustine turned his attention to it, and at that time the Donatist church is said to have had a larger membership in Hippo itself than did the Catholic church. The important point of this church's claim, which made it a special threat to the Catholic church, was that it insisted that it was the true Christian church, preserving the high moral qualities of genuine Christianity. This claim led Augustine to define with great care the nature of both the church and the sacraments.

The chief theoretical issue between Donatists and Catholics was the matter of the purity of the clergy. An older tenet related the efficacy of the sacraments to the quality of life of the clergy who administered them: to carry holiness, the sacraments had to be administered by holy men. But as the church developed organizationally and in power it developed the theory, which had come to wide acceptance, that the office of the bishop was holy in itself, not necessarily the man who held that office, and the sacraments were holy, not necessarily the men who administered them. The Donatists, therefore, were appealing to the older, more primitive view. It is important to note that, unlike the Gnostic and Arian controversies, there were no differences of theology in the Donatist controversy; the two churches accepted the same doctrines. That the Donatists succeeded in gaining so many adherents was probably due to two reasons. In the first place, the movement became popular with the many Christians who believed that the call of their religion was to holiness and that a holy church should have a holy clergy. In the second place, it became a national church in North Africa, representing for many there who felt antipathy to the power of Rome a way of expressing their own distinctive identity by opposing the Catholic church which had come to be the religious side of the Roman government.

In his controversy with the Donatists, Augustine was led to state more clearly than ever before the nature and function of the Christian church. On this question he was not original; he merely clarified the Christian tradition. He designated unity, sanctity, apostolicity, and catholicity as the four marks of the true church. Taking these in order, he said that there is only one true church, which is a unity in doctrine and organization. Heretics are to be condemned because they have wandered from true doctrine, while schismatics like the Donatists are to be condemned because they have seceded from the true organization. The Catholic church shows the second mark, sanctity, because it controls the sacraments. Third, it is apostolic, for the Roman bishops are able to trace their offices back to Peter and the apostles, while there has not been a single Donatist bishop in this series. Finally, it is catholic (universal) in the sense of its geographic distribution, being literally worldwide in its influence, while the Donatist church is almost entirely limited to North Africa.

On the central issue, Augustine reaffirmed the doctrine that the efficacy of the sacraments is independent of the personal worth of the clergy, that is, even when the sacraments are administered by a priest who is not holy or by a bishop who is a traitor they are still efficacious. It is obvious that if the Donatist view were to be taken as the valid one, it would follow that the worshiper could have no assurance of receiving the genuine sacrament since he could never be entirely certain of the quality of the priest's life; hence, he could not be certain of receiving the grace which the sacraments mediate to man.

Augustine brought out two arguments to support his view. First, he accused the Donatists of destroying the real meaning of the sacraments by making their validity depend upon human beings. In truth, the sacraments are "sacred signs," "visible signs of divine things," instruments of divine grace, and thus receive their power and importance from God, not men. No matter how reprehensible the personal lives of members of the clergy might be, the holiness of that which God has consecrated cannot be destroyed as long as the sacrament is properly administered by a properly appointed person. Second, the philosophy of *The City of God* made it clear that the company of the elect is not identical with the membership of the church, although all those who are of the elect become members of the church. Thus, there are in fact two churches, the one invisible, including only those elected for salvation, and the other visible, which has among its members both the saved and the damned. It follows that in both its membership and its clergy the visible church is composed of the evil and the good, those who have received saving grace and those who have not. Even bishops may be members of the City of Satan. But the sacraments are consistently holy.

Since members of the invisible City of God are to be found only in the visible church, it is clear that there is no salvation outside the church (*extra ecclesiam nulla salus*). Augustine is also fond of repeating a phrase of Cyprian that he will not have God as his father who does not wish to have the church as his mother. Furthermore, since grace is so important in Augustine's philosophy, the sacraments too, as the means through which grace is conferred, are magnified. Baptism, for example, is the sacrament through which the forgiveness of original sin takes place, but it does not automatically produce a fully disciplined life. When one has been very ill with a fever, says Augustine, he cannot regain health until the cause of the sickness has been removed. Baptism removes the cause of moral infirmity. On the other hand, there is the long process of growing well and regaining strength after the fever has been removed. These "two things are plainly shown in the Psalm where we read, 'who forgiveth all thine iniquities,' which takes place in baptism; and then follows, 'and healeth all thine infirmities' and this takes place by daily additions, while this image is being renewed."[10]

In the Donatist controversy Augustine had the further problem of deciding whether or not the sacraments were valid even when administered by a schismatic or heretical bishop. We should expect that he would have to admit their validity since the personal life of the bishop was supposed to be irrelevant. As a matter of fact, he does say that the benefits of baptism and of ordination remain even when conferred by a schismatic:

> For the sacrament of baptism is what the person possesses who is baptized; and the sacrament of conferring baptism is what he possesses who is ordained. And as the baptized person, if he depart from the unity of the Church, does not thereby lose the sacrament of baptism, so also he who is ordained, if he depart from the unity of the Church, does not lose the sacrament of conferring baptism.[11]

On the other hand, grace does not follow until one returns to the Catholic fold; there is still no salvation unless one is a member of the one church: "But as, by reconciliation to unity, that begins to be profitably possessed which was possessed to no profit in exclusion from unity, so, by the same reconciliation, that begins to be profitable which without it was given to no profit."[12]

Here was an ecclesiastical theory which affirmed the infallibility and the unity of the church, the superiority of the church to worldly institutions, and the church as the exclusive means to salvation. But the theory still lacked one thing. There could be no complete unity and no practical application of the idea of infallibility until there was a single recognized central authority. This difficulty was later removed when Rome came to general acceptance as the chief bishopric of the Western church.

In conclusion, Augustine stood at the turning point from the late Roman

[10] *On the Trinity*, book XIV, chap. 17, *op. cit.*, p. 372.

[11] *On Baptism, Against the Donatists*, book I, chap. 1, in *The Works of Aurelius Augustine*, tr. and ed., Marcus Dods, Edinburgh, T. and T. Clark, 1872, vol. III, p. 2.

[12] *Ibid.*

period into the Middle Ages. Great as he was as a theologian, philosopher, and church administrator, he was greatest of all as a man of religion who loved God and sought to bring other men to the Christian life. He left as a legacy to succeeding generations many unsolved problems and seeming contradictions which even a casual reading of what has been written here will make evident. His own personal experience centering upon his sexual sins and his conversion, the thought of historic Christianity and Neo-Platonism, and the necessities of being a church administrator and as such of taking sides on controversial issues are all woven into his writings in differing patterns over his long lifetime. Like Plato, he failed to develop a thoroughly unified and harmonious system of thought, and for this very reason, again like Plato, he provided inspiration for many later movements, including even the Protestant Reformation.

Questions for Study

1. When and where did Augustine live? Describe his spiritual pilgrimage through Manichaeanism, skepticism, and Neo-Platonism to Christianity.
2. Into what four terms does Plotinus analyze reality, and what does he mean by each? How does our complex world arise? In what sense is creation different from emanation? What is the status of matter for Plotinus?
3. What is the nature and cause of sin for Plotinus? What is the nature of salvation, and how is it reached? Describe the ultimate state of union with the One.
4. Why was Neo-Platonism capable of being used by the pagan religions against Christianity? Why did Julian fail in his attempt so to use it?
5. At what point did Augustine use Neo-Platonism in his own thinking? How did Augustine move from skepticism to God? How does his view of God and evil reflect Neo-Platonism? Where does he differ from Neo-Platonism?
6. What relation does Augustine see between reason and faith? What justification might you see for his view of this relationship?
7. How does Augustine understand man as unity of soul and body, as free, as originally perfect, as fallen, as morally diseased and weakened, as guilty of original sin, as guilty before God, as one to whom God extends grace for salvation, and as predestined?
8. What was the issue of Augustine's controversy with Pelagius, and what the result?
9. Why did Augustine write *The City of God*? In this book, what is the relation between the City of God and the City of Satan in his time? Who belongs to each city, and why does each so belong? Why was the incarnation the central historical fact? What will the consummation of history be, and what will happen at that time? Within how great a time span did Augustine see all this happening? Why does his view give individual life great significance?

10. What occasioned the rise of the Donatist church? In answer to the Donatists, what four points did Augustine emphasize as marks of the true Christian church? What did he say about the efficacy of the sacraments? What would have been the effect if the Donatist view on this matter had come to general acceptance? How did Augustine defend his view, and what was that view?
11. Why did Augustine state that there is "no salvation outside the church"?
12. How would you evaluate Augustine as a man and as a theologian? To your mind, what was his greatest contribution?

Selected Readings

Battenhouse, Roy W. (ed.), *A Companion to the Study of St. Augustine*, New York, Oxford University Press, 1955.

Copleston, Frederick, *A History of Philosophy*, Westminster, The Newman Press, 1952, vol. II.

Fuller, B. A. G., *A History of Ancient and Medieval Philosophy*, New York, Henry Holt & Co., 1938.

Gilson, Étienne, *The Christian Philosophy of Saint Augustine*, New York, Random House, Inc., 1960.

McGiffert, A. C., *A History of Christian Thought*, New York, Charles Scribner's Sons, 1933, vol. II.

Oates, Whitney J. (ed.), *Basic Writings of Saint Augustine*, New York, Random House, Inc., 1948, 2 vols.

Outler, Albert C. (ed. and tr.), *Augustine: Confessions and Enchiridion*, Philadelphia, The Westminster Press, 1955.

Portalié, Eugène, *A Guide to the Thought of St. Augustine*, tr. Ralph J. Bastian, Chicago, Henry Regnery Co., 1960.

Walker, Williston, *A History of the Christian Church*, rev. ed., New York, Charles Scribner's Sons, 1959.

West, Rebecca, *St. Augustine*, New York, D. Appleton & Co., 1933.

Whittaker, T., *Neo-Platonists*, New York, The Macmillan Company, 1928.

Williams, N. P., *The Ideas of the Fall and of Original Sin*, London, Longmans, Green & Co., 1927.

V. Medieval Philosophy and Theology

CHRONOLOGICAL FRAMEWORK OF PART V

135	Jerusalem destroyed.
330	Constantinople dedicated the capital of the Eastern Roman Empire.
476	Western Roman Empire comes to an end.
527-565	Justinian I emperor of Eastern Roman Empire. Built St. Sophia.
768-814	Charlemagne king of the Franks. Crowned Holy Roman emperor in 800.
1054	Schism between East and West churches.
1453	Constantinople falls to the Turks. End of Byzantium.

ca. 150-225	Tertullian.
354-430	Augustine.
440-461	Leo I, called the Great, pope.
494	Gelasius I pronounces doctrine of the two spheres.
590-604	Gregory I, called the Great, pope.
1073-1085	Gregory VII pope. Conflict with Henry IV of Germany.
1198-1216	Innocent III pope. Deposes Otto IV.
1294-1303	Boniface VIII pope. Encyclical *Unam Sanctum* and the two-swords doctrine.
1545-1563	Council of Trent.

MEDIEVAL THEOLOGIANS

Johannes Scotus Erigena, *ca.* 810-877.

Anselm, archbishop of Canterbury, 1033-1109. The *ontological* argument.

Roscellinus, *ca.* 1050-1122.

William of Champeaux, 1070-1121.

Peter Abelard, 1079-1142.

Albertus Magnus, *ca.* 1198-1280. Master of Thomas Aquinas.

Thomas Aquinas, *ca.* 1225-1274.

John Duns Scotus, *ca.* 1264-1308.

William of Ockham, died *ca.* 1349.

ARAB THINKERS

Avicenna, 980-1037.

Algazel, 1058-1111.

Averroës, 1126-1198.

13. The Development of the Medieval Church

The death of Augustine in 430 marked the end of an epoch, for in him the elements which combined to form Christianity had been blended into a fairly harmonious whole. His work was the last great creative product of philosophers, Christian or pagan, in the Roman period. In 476, less than half a century after his death, Rome, which had been attacked and overrun several times before and yet had retained enough vitality to expel the invaders, was conquered by the Goths. The old order was exhausted and the Western Roman Empire came to an end. The barbarians, able to conquer but incapable of creating or governing an empire, left the Roman world in chaos. The early Middle Ages had begun.

Rome and the Eastern Empire

The account of the fate of Roman culture in the centuries following the fall of Rome is too involved and extensive for us to do more than merely glance at it, but that much is necessary. We first notice that almost two centuries before the final destruction of the Western Roman Empire, the Empire had been divided into two parts by Diocletian, who ruled from 285 until 305—a most important development for later Christian history. Realizing that the Empire was far too large for one man to control efficiently, he placed Maximian over the western section and he himself governed the East. Both shared in the title of Augustus or emperor. Constantine the Great later reunited the Empire under his own control but made arrangements for the joint rulership of his sons upon his death. Believing it highly desirable to have an Eastern capital as a counterbalance to Rome in the West, he constructed Constantinople on the site of an older town named Byzantium, dedicating it in A.D. 330. He thought of it as a city that would preserve the great Greek tradition, just as Rome preserved the Roman, and erected great buildings and public works. Here he himself preferred to live, and from this city he exercised his rule. So it happened that after 330 the Roman Empire had two capitals and, for much of its remaining history, two emperors who shared the power.

Increasingly the East felt its difference from the West since it found its cultural roots in Greece rather than Rome. In fact, by the sixth century, following the death of Justinian I, the Latin language ceased to be used by the Eastern emperor. Contrary to the usual view that the West was the carrier of culture, the East was urbane, cultured, wealthy, and powerful long after the Western Empire had entered the Dark Ages.

After 476 Rome was the name of a city only. During the centuries which followed this date, various Germanic and other peoples moved through the reaches of the fallen empire, carving out units of power for themselves. We will soon see what was happening to the church of Rome during this period, but for the moment let us turn our attention to the Eastern Empire, which continued in existence for another thousand years.

In the sixth century one of the greatest Eastern rulers appeared in the person of *Justinian I* (ruled 527-565), who set himself the task of restoring the unity of the Roman Empire. He sent his armies into Italy and North Africa and managed to reconquer considerable lost territory, including much of Italy. In one way this was desirable, since it restored these sections to the Empire, but in another way it was not, for the city of Rome and its church came under the political domination of Constantinople. Since the Eastern emperors took the attitude that they exercised power over the church even to the point of interpreting doctrine, many conflicts developed between East and West on religious matters. One of Justinian's outstanding cultural achievements was the erection of the magnificent church of St. Sophia (Holy Wisdom) which still stands in Constantinople, now Istanbul, as a monument to its builder and his people.

As a consequence of his wars and great building enterprises, Justinian left his Empire bankrupt. Within a generation of his death the Lombards, a Germanic tribe, pressed down into Italy and conquered most of it except for Rome and some other cities. Many parts of the Eastern Empire were also lost, particularly to the Moslems, who conquered North Africa, much of Asia Minor, and parts of Europe in the seventh century. By 700 only a small part of the great empire of Justinian was left.

Political relations between East and West deteriorated as a result of the Iconoclastic Controversy. When Emperor Leo III of Constantinople passed a law in 725 that no images or icons (sacred pictures) could henceforth be used in any Christian church, Italy revolted against him. The Lombards, by now converted to Christianity, took the opportunity of increasing their hold upon Italy still further, threatening to take even Rome itself. In desperation the bishop of Rome, Pope Stephen II, formed an alliance with the Germanic Franks and anointed Pepin king. Pepin responded by attacking the threatening Lombards and gaining much of Italy from them. This large territory, in what is called the Donation of Pepin, he turned over to the pope, who made it an independent principality under his own control and called it the Papal States. Charles the Great or *Charlemagne* (ruled 768-814) became king upon the death of Pepin, his father. Since the Lombards had reconquered the lands given to the pope, Charlemagne first attacked them, regained the territory, and turned it back again to the pope. He then went on to conquer much of Western Europe not already under the Franks. In 800 the pope, claiming for himself the power to do so, crowned Charlemagne emperor of the Holy Roman Empire, so called, an empire more German than Roman that was to last 1000 years, until 1806, when it was dissolved by Napoleon Bonaparte.

East and West moved ever farther apart. All control of the East over Rome had come to an end with the ascendancy of Pepin and the Franks. In the period beginning just before 900 the papacy reached the lowest point in its history, and the following 150 years are properly referred to as the Dark Ages. Within 8 years 10 popes reigned, one for only 20 days and another for a month. The period of 60 years following 904 is called the Pornocracy because of the great power exercised, even over the popes, by the unprincipled Theodora and her two infamous daughters. When the illegitimate son of the younger of these, Marozia, became pope, she plotted to have herself made empress. In startling contrast, this same period was one of great wealth, culture, power, and brilliance in the Eastern Empire. It was said that at this time the glory of ancient Athens had truly come to Constantinople. The Eastern church spread rapidly, bringing Russia as well as other lands into the Christian fold.

East and West increasingly recognized their deep-lying differences. Temporary schisms separated the two churches several times, and there were periods when they were out of communion with each other because of doctrinal differences. In the year 1054 the final break took place. The Roman pope had his envoy lay a sentence of anathema on the altar of St. Sophia against the patriarch of Constantinople, who a few days later retaliated by excommunicating the Roman pope. The break remains unto this day. The Eastern or Byzantine Empire itself continued to exist, much of the time as a very prosperous, cultured world, until the Ottoman Turks captured the city of Constantinople in 1453.

From time to time Christians in both East and West wished to end the schism between the two churches. To this end two major efforts were made, one of which actually reached the stage of ratification at the Council of Lyons in 1274, but when the Eastern emperor, Michael Palaeologus, attempted to put the reunion into effect in the East he was strongly opposed, and upon his death in 1282 the union collapsed. Again, in 1439, when the Turks were threatening Constantinople, a new decree of union was accepted as a last desperate means of obtaining help from the West, and again the people refused it. When the city fell in 1453, the attempt to end the schism between the two great branches of Christianity fell with it.

Christianity in the Eastern Empire

Since Christianity arose in Palestine, it appears strange on first thought that Jerusalem did not remain the center of Christianity and the first church of Christendom. How the church at Rome became the principal Western church and that at Constantinople the head of the Eastern churches needs brief attention.

We recall that the Herodian temple in Jerusalem was destroyed in A.D. 70, and that as a result of a revolt under the Jewish revolutionary Bar-Cochba in 132 Jerusalem was totally destroyed by the Romans in 135. Hadrian rebuilt it as a small Roman city, renamed it Aelia Capitolina, and prohibited all Jews (but not Christians) from living in it. Because of these events, the Jerusalem church was greatly disturbed and unable to develop as it might otherwise have done. Further, because Jerusalem was not a city of great influence in the Empire, the church established there also lacked size and influence, although it was regarded with veneration and honor. When Constantine came to the throne he beautified Jerusalem, and in association with his mother, Helena, strengthened the Jerusalem church by building the Church of the Holy Sepulchre.

The relative importance of the churches to each other was linked to the importance of the cities in which they were located. Since the Roman church was in the very capital of the Empire, it naturally considered itself the principal church and claimed pre-eminence from early times. It and three other churches—those in Alexandria in Egypt, Antioch in Syria, and Ephesus in Asia Minor—held special importance after the first century. The bishop of the church in Rome was called father or pope, this being derived from the Greek word *papas* or *pappas*, meaning father. At first the title held none of the associations of power and primacy later associated with it but was simply the way of referring to this bishop. Rome was the only outstanding church in the West; the other three churches were all Eastern.

At a church council held in 381 in Constantinople, then the most powerful city in the Empire, it was declared that along with Rome, Alexandria, and Antioch, Constantinople was also a patriarchate, taking precedence over Alexandria and Antioch and ranking next to Rome. This claim was made on the basis of Constantinople's being the "New Rome." Ephesus, Antioch, and Alexandria immediately protested on the ground that they and Rome had been founded by apostles while Constantinople could scarcely claim that honor. However, because of the power and position of Constantinople, nothing could stand in the way of the declaration. After that time Constantinople generally claimed primacy in the East under its patriarch, and Rome claimed supremacy in the West under its pope.

Accordingly, in the late fourth century there were four recognized patriarchates, each governed by a patriarch (or pope) under whom served metropolitans or archbishops, bishops, priests, deacons, and subdeacons. A fifth patriarchate was formed later: Jerusalem, so designated at the great council held at Chalcedon, near Constantinople. It was then, however, and it remained the smallest and weakest of the five. Rome continued to claim primacy over all the churches. It is a fact that in the fifth century Eastern bishops did ask the pope at Rome for his decision on questions of orthodoxy, but the Eastern churches never fully admitted the jurisdiction of Rome over them. Even in the West the Roman church was not yet granted full authority.

The Iconoclastic Controversy was the great issue in the eighth century. Leo III of Constantinople was opposed by both East and West when he ordered that all images and icons be removed from the churches. In 787 at a second council held at Nicaea it was declared that statues and icons might remain in the churches but were to receive reverential respect, not worship. This is the position still maintained in both the Eastern and Western churches.

Since the final break in 1054, the two great churches of the East and West, which have come to be called the Orthodox and the Catholic respectively, have regarded each other as schismatic; each considers itself as the true church of Christ. Because we will have no occasion to deal with the Eastern church again in this volume, we will conclude this section by noting its present situation.

Unlike the Roman Catholic church with its single head, the pope, now considered infallible in his pronouncements, the Orthodox churches form a rather loose confederation. They use the Byzantine rite, accept the decisions of the first seven Ecumenical Councils (the seventh was held in 787), are in union with the patriarch of Constantinople, and are out of communion with the Roman pope. Constantinople is considered not an authoritarian head of these churches but rather as the "first among equals" (*primus inter pares*). At the present time the Orthodox churches consist of the four ancient patriarchates of Antioch, Alexandria, Jerusalem, and Constantinople; a variety of national churches, among them the Russian and Greek; and a number of independent churches. None of these acknowledges the pope's claim to either primacy or infallibility. Their priests may marry but not their bishops, who are chosen from among celibate monks. Some Eastern churches, called the Uniate, are in communion with Rome although they still follow the Eastern or Byzantine rite and allow their priests to marry.

The Ideal of a Theocracy

Although the early Middle Ages did not inherit a stable government from the Roman Empire, the period did inherit the idea of a world state. This inheritance was transmitted by the church and idealized in St. Augustine's *City of God*. The form of this world state was conceived as an absolute monarchy ruling through a centralized hierarchy of officials. The bishops of Rome, the former capital of the Empire, were especially devoted to this ideal, and lost no opportunity to impose their spiritual supremacy over other bishops, both Western and Eastern, as far as that was possible. As the only probable successors of the Roman emperors in the West, they also began to entertain notions of political as well as religious supremacy. In this way the church transformed the Roman idea of world government into the religious ideal of a *theocracy*, or rulership of God, a governing of the world both religiously and politically through an ecclesiastic hierarchy with the Roman pope at its head as God's representative. The ideal of a theocracy was not a new one, for the Jews had held it in ancient times, believing themselves the ones chosen by God to be the human leaders of God's kingdom. But since Palestine was politically weak this ideal remained unrealized, while for the popes it at times approached—without ever actually reaching—fulfillment.

Following the destruction of the Roman Empire in 476, the only agency capable of introducing law and order on a wide scale was the church. Divorced from political life, she was generally spared by the victors over the empire. Impressive in her magnificence, she aroused feelings of awe and respect in the minds of the conquerors, some of whom were already partially Christianized. Thus it came about that the church was able to stand as a defense against anarchy. Here was a highly disciplined institution claiming supreme authority on earth in spiritual matters, with an organization reaching throughout what had been the empire, impressing men of all ranks and stations with its stability, dignity, and power. Hence the church was in a position to begin the remarkable career which was to make her not only the sole dispenser of salvation and the arbiter of the intellect but a great and at times supreme authority in civil affairs also, thus approaching the theocratic ideal.

The Extension of Spiritual Power

The leaders of the church were not slow to rise to their opportunity and responsibility. The popes of Rome rapidly extended their ecclesiastic as well as their political and economic power in the West. The extension of ecclesiastic authority began even before the final overthrow of the Empire. *Leo I*, called Leo the Great, who was the Roman pope from 440 to 461, insisted upon the supremacy of the bishop of Rome over the entire church of Christ, Eastern as well as Western. In claiming primacy over the Western church he was following the lead of Innocent I (pope from 402 to 417), but Leo extended the claim to cover all of Christendom. Leo himself was a remarkably able man who carried out negotiations with both the Huns and, later, the Vandals when they threatened Rome. He supported his claim by the tradition that the church at Rome had been founded by Peter. Peter was the prince of the apostles; to him Jesus had said, ". . . you are Peter, and on this rock I will build my church. . . . I will give you the keys of the kingdom of heaven, and whatever you bind on earth shall be bound in heaven, and whatever you loose on earth shall be loosed in heaven" (Matthew 16:18, 19). Thus, the Roman bishops were successors to Peter. This claim was endorsed by the Roman Emperor Valentinian III in an edict issued in 445 in his own name and that of the Eastern Emperor Theodosius. Although the legitimacy of this edict was questioned for a time, it was generally accepted in the West. Leo's scriptural support of the papal claim proved to be of capital importance; it remains the principal substantiation of papal authority among Catholics to this day. Moreover, the successful establishment of papal authority over the ecclesiastical organization was quite logically extended to the announcement of papal infallibility, but this came much later, in 1870.

The ultimate support of Leo's claim for the supremacy of Rome was due not alone to his appeal to Scripture and the imperial endorsement but also to the practical achievement of another pope, *Gregory I*, also called the Great. Pope from 590 to 604, he was so competent a statesman and administrator that he was able to convert the theoretical power of Rome over distant churches into actual influence. Leader against the Lombards and politically the strongest man in Italy, he protested claims to supremacy of Constantinople and reached out into France and Spain with his own claim to supremacy. He insisted that by the authority of Christ himself the care of the whole church was committed to Peter, the prince of the apostles, thus repeating the declaration of Leo I a century and a half earlier.

The Growth of Temporal Power

After the time of Gregory the Great, the claim of the bishops of Rome to the position of supreme head of the church in the West was not seriously questioned, but exactly what this primacy involved was disputed. There were some who would have restricted it to religious and churchly matters, while others held that it included authority over civil states and their rulers as well.

The popes did not at first compete for civil power; they received it by default. Thus, when the Vandals sacked Rome in 445, Pope Leo I represented the city in treating with the conquerors. Again, Gregory the Great conducted the defense of the city against the Lombards and negotiated the peace with them. These popes assumed temporal functions because there was no competent civil power remaining for these necessary tasks. Since they had assumed command in the dark days of confusion during and after the barbarian invasions, it was only natural that they should continue to claim temporal power even after kings and emperors once more asserted their own prerogatives. Except under Charlemagne, whose rule was absolute, even over the church as its "protector," the popes claimed and exercised various degrees of authority over medieval rulers and thus over their states until the end of the thirteenth century. During and after the eighth century, they exercised direct civil authority over the city of Rome, which was then a duchy, and over the Papal States.

Theory regarding the proper jurisdiction of church and state, pope and king or emperor underwent various changes in response to the actual power any given pope had or hoped to gain. All versions of papal claims did, however, trace back to Augustine's assertion, in general terms, of the supremacy of the church over the state. As early as 494, Pope *Gelasius I* gave the classic formulation of the doctrine of the two spheres—the spiritual and the civil or political—known as the Gelasian theory. It asserts the supremacy of the church and the duty of the temporal sovereign to submit to the pope in religious matters. While the papacy thus claimed spiritual jurisdiction over the persons of rulers as well as their subjects, its claims did not at this time extend to political authority. The emperor was recognized as having complete control over political matters. This significant recognition of the mutual independence of the two spheres, the spiritual and the temporal, long remained normative.[1] It found Biblical support in Jesus' own words, "Render . . . to Caesar the things that are Caesar's, and to God the things that are God's" (Matthew 22:21).

This nice theoretical distinction between the two powers or spheres was difficult to maintain in practice, however. As the actual power of the papacy over temporal rulers grew, the theoretical defense of extending this power kept pace with existing fact. Thus there appeared during the pontificate of Nicholas I (858-867) a most remarkable set of documents which were generally accepted as valid but six centuries later were shown to be forgeries. These documents have come to be called the Pseudo-Isidorian or False Decretals. Most important of the various documents making up these Decretals was one called the Donation of Constantine which purported to be an official decree made by Constantine the Great in the fourth century when he was emperor of the Roman Empire, declaring that the Roman church should be supreme over all the other churches of the earth and that its power should be exalted over all other power, even Constantine's. Further, it conveyed to the bishop of Rome, Sylvester I, and his successors the city of Rome and other cities of Italy, the Western Roman Empire, and even Constantine's own Lateran Palace in Rome. The fact is that Constantine himself paid little attention to the pope of Rome, preferring the Eastern patriarchs over him, but this was not known in the ninth century, with the result that for 500 years this "Donation" was appealed to again and again

[1] It was adopted by St. Thomas Aquinas and remains the authoritative Catholic formula for the division of spiritual and temporal jurisdictions at the present time.

by the Roman authorities as the charter for the temporal power of the Roman pontiff, paralleling the appeal to the words of Christ to Peter as the charter for the spiritual power of the church at Rome.[2]

In later centuries the popes came to believe that only as the spiritual power controlled the political could the church free itself from being controlled by the rulers. It seemed impossible to discover and maintain a workable equality. This idea was taken up by a most remarkable pope, *Gregory VII,* who took office in 1073. Filled with the ideal of establishing a theocracy, Gregory asserted in his *Dictatus Papae* that the Roman church had never erred and never would. He claimed the right for the pope and the pope alone of exercising power over all other governments, of deposing emperors, of absolving subjects from their oath of allegiance to political rulers, and of judging everyone without himself being judged. Had he been able to put his ideal into effect, the pope would have ruled as God's vice-regent, and kings would have held their power under his authority.

Nor was this only an ideal. Faced with refusal by the German king, Henry IV, to obey certain papal measures of reform, Gregory excommunicated and deposed him, releasing his subjects from their oath of allegiance and forbidding anyone to serve him as king. Deprived of all religious functions, the populace stood with the pope. There was only one thing for Henry to do, and that was to seek Gregory's forgiveness. Acting the role of a penitent, he stood for three days barefoot in the snow before the hostel of the pope in Tuscany, begging for mercy. Henry was pardoned, regained his power, invaded Italy and captured Rome, and forced Gregory to flee. He then deposed Gregory and placed another pope in his place, under whom Henry was crowned Holy Roman emperor.

The control over political power which Gregory had claimed but had been unable to put into effect was carried further by *Innocent III* (1198-1216), one of the greatest of the popes. He enlarged the Papal States by conquest, decided between candidates for the imperial throne, and undercut the support of the German throne by "freeing" German churches from royal control. When the German Otto IV, who had become emperor by Innocent's decision in 1201, turned against papal policies, the pope did not hesitate to foment civil wars that brought about Otto's undoing. The pope then replaced him with his own ward. He forced Philip Augustus of France to comply with his wishes concerning that king's personal life, and even brought England's king to his knees by use of the interdict. He encouraged Crusaders to attack the Moslems, and persecuted Christian heretics in France.

[2] See A. C. McGiffert, *A History of Christian Thought,* New York, Charles Scribner's Sons, 1933, II, 336 f.

On every side we see this powerful pope participating vigorously in temporal affairs.

Innocent justified his political activities by the theory that the pope as the vicar of Christ is lord of earthly states as well as of the church. He held that princes, like bishops, are the pope's agents since the successor of Peter "has been placed in the middle between God and man, below God but above man, . . . and he judges concerning all and is judged by no one."[3] Specifically, Innocent held that the papal function of crowning emperors implied the function of examining and, if need be, rejecting them. Unlike Gregory, he was able to substantiate his claims to universal sovereignty by his actual achievements.

The theocratic ideal and the accompanying claims to papal sovereignty reached their apex with *Boniface VIII* (pope from 1294 to 1303), who in the bull *Unam Sanctum* held that in the power granted to Peter

> . . . there are two swords, the spiritual and the temporal . . . . Both the spiritual and material swords are in the power of the church, but the latter is wielded for the church, the former by the church; the one by priests, the other by kings and soldiers but at the command or with the approval of the priest. Moreover one sword ought to be under the other and the temporal power ought to be subject to the spiritual. . . .

He went on to make subjection to papal authority an article of faith and therefore necessary for salvation, saying that "to be subject to the Roman pontiff is altogether necessary to salvation for every human creature."[4]

But while Boniface made the strongest claims of any pope to supremacy over political rulers, he failed even worse than did Gregory to make good these claims. Involved in a dispute with Philip IV of France over the king's power to tax the clergy, the pope announced the old principle that the clergy were not to contribute to the support of the state without the consent of Rome. Philip replied by forbidding, on pain of death, the export from France to Rome of any money and negotiable paper whatever. The financial structure of the papacy was thus threatened, and the pope had to retract his statement. The resulting peace was brief, however; a few years later the contest was renewed over the question of whether a member of the clergy could be tried in secular courts. When the pope denied the secular courts this power and reasserted his supremacy over the king, the latter worked up public opinion against the pope. The quarrel flourished. Philip planned a general council which would try to depose the pope. Part of this scheme

[3] As quoted in *ibid.*, II, 339.

[4] As quoted in *ibid.*, II, 340 f.

was to seize Boniface and make him a prisoner; a new papal election was to determine Boniface's successor. In retaliation, Boniface threatened Philip with excommunication.

While Philip's plans partly miscarried, the shocking turn of events probably hastened the pope's death, which took place within a month; the aftermath demonstrated the complete victory of the French king. The papacy, with its seat removed to the French town of Avignon for nearly 70 years after 1309 and its incumbent elected by a French college of cardinals, became subordinate to the royal power in all matters under dispute.

The results of the conflict between Boniface and Philip illustrate how the papacy, trying to carry out the theocratic ideal, met with an opposition in fact and in theory that it could not overcome. The temporal power, represented by the young and vigorous monarchies of Western Europe, grew too strong for continued subordination to papal domination. The opponents of the theocratic claims of the popes did not lack theory to support the growing independence of rulers, for they could call on the doctrine of the divine right of kings. Like the papal party, nationalists also could quote Scripture to buttress their position. Had not Peter and Paul both stated that kings rule by divine right? As it turned out, the doctrine of civil independence from the church had to wait for its practical victory until the rise of nationalism which gave monarchs the actual power to withstand the encroachments of the papacy. The triumph of Philip the Fair over Boniface VIII was a sign of the decline of papal power, and a sign as well of the end of the Middle Ages.[5]

The full development of the doctrine of authority, which lies at the root of the Catholic system, does indeed involve the superiority of church over state. This is the medieval version of the ancient conception that priests as divine agents are to exercise control over the whole of life and administer God's rule directly. Under this theory, the state is subordinated to the church as an organ that governs temporal things, bringing temporal relations and values under the absolute spiritual purpose of life which the priestly hierarchy guards and promotes. "The dogma of the universal episcopate required as its complement the dogma of theocracy."[6] Thus regarded, the church is the divine empire; the pope is God's vice-regent, a terrestrial governor general; and all the machinery of civil government is subject to

[5] In our time the church adheres in general to the Gelasian formula with its division of jurisdiction between church and state; but there are areas of conflict, since it is not always possible to draw a line between matters of faith and morals on one side and matters of state on the other.

[6] Ernst Troeltsch, *The Social Teachings of the Christian Churches,* New York, The Macmillan Company, 1931, I, 229.

ecclesiastic control. Any challenge or disobedience to this control becomes heresy and idolatry, and because it questions the principle of authority, it is treason against the divinely established order. Since the salvation of souls was believed to depend upon that order and upon the authority behind it, the opponent of theocracy was regarded as a traitor to the church and a rebel against God. As such, he was held to deserve the usual penalties of excommunication or death.

This extravagant claim to authority by the church over the lives of men rested upon theory that was not, in the end, very far removed from practical concerns. The theocratic ideal, indeed, had considerable practical justification and reason for being. In the first place, temporal power came to the church by default in the Middle Ages. We have already seen how, after the fall of Rome, the church alone stood against anarchy and possessed the machinery to maintain law and order. Moreover, the church as a central authority, universal in scope, actually served as the equivalent of a powerful league of nations. While herself not above crass interests which she sometimes pursued with military weapons, the fact remains that the church in the early Middle Ages did mitigate strife between petty principalities and was able many times to force peace upon European civilization.

The beneficent effects of the medieval attempts at theocracy extended also to economic and commercial life. The church subordinated commercial considerations to the religious goal of life and held that economic activities were just one phase of personal conduct to which the rules of morality fully applied. Hence, there was no radical separation between "religion" and business in the Middle Ages. All of life's activities were held to be subject to religious interpretation and regulation. Speculation, profiteering, and taking interest were effectively condemned on religious grounds.

As the church claimed and seized power, she defended her authority in theory and partially, at least, justified it by her works. Although her power might be challenged, its rationale disputed, and her good works annulled by simony and abuse, the foundation of the church's authority was solidly set is the unquestioned belief that the church was the "ark of salvation"; that outside the church there was no possibility of eternal life. To challenge her authority meant to jeopardize one's hope of heaven.

The Church as the Sole Ark of Salvation

The church's claim to a virtual monopoly of the means of salvation had its roots in the early Christian view that although man was made in the image of God he had fallen into disobedience and pride. Sometimes this duality between man as he ideally ought to be and originally was and as he now actually is was made into a dualism of flesh and spirit. This we found in Gnosticism, religious Platonism, and the Orphic belief. More generally in Christian theology, man was understood to have been made by God to live in unity of will with his Creator, but to have turned away from God to follow his own interests. Paul and Augustine developed this understanding of man. As fallen away from God, man is at present in a most regrettable condition from which he is incapable of saving himself. The only hope for salvation lies in receiving supernatural help. To gain salvation one must be born again: he must indeed be *re-created* spiritually through God's grace. As St. Paul said, Christ must be born in him. Man's unaided efforts were held to be in vain. It was upon this sense of man's corruption and consequent state of needing God's grace that the Catholic system (as later Protestantism also) was erected, although Augustine's extreme doctrine of original sin and predestination did not command popular belief (it had to wait for Calvinism for that). While there was always some emphasis upon human effort, stemming back possibly to the Jewish strain in the Christian heritage, this never came to mean more than that man must make right use of the divine help that grace brings to him. Without God's grace man could not even begin to find salvation; without regeneration he was thought doomed to eternal destruction.

In the medieval view, man is not only presently corrupt but has fallen from a higher state of being. Unlike the modern theory of evolution which, when applied to ethics, regards man as having ascended from lower to higher moral levels, the Christian belief was that man was created in a condition of perfection from which he has fallen; having offended against the divine law, he is doomed to eternal punishment. God in his righteousness cannot allow sin to go unpunished; yet God is also merciful and loving, and therefore has provided guilty men with a way to escape from the consequences of their sin. This way is Christianity, with its salvation through the savior, Christ. His sacrifice on the cross, according to one theory, atoned for man's sin and satisfied the divine justice. Moreover, Christ may come to take possession of man's soul by grace, transforming his nature and liberating him from bondage to the lower impulses into the freedom of the spirit.

The view of the church as the exclusive ark of salvation, then, was based on the belief in the essentially sinful character of human nature and in man's consequent need for salvation. To be saved, one had to be a member of the church since the power of conferring saving grace was assumed to have been given by Christ to his apostles and by these in turn on their successors, the bishops. To be out of communion with the bishop meant, therefore, to be out of communion with Christ. The priests, ordained to their tasks by the bishops, became the mediators of saving grace. But even as the laity were dependent upon the priest, so the priest was dependent upon the bishop. Thus we can see how important in the medieval scheme of salvation the bishops were. Where they were, there was Christ's church, there was the font of grace, the source of salvation.

The importance of being in communion with the church, as this presented itself to the medieval mind, can be made most clear in connection with the sacraments. The sacraments are the means of grace, by which the church mediates salvation to the faithful. Once it is believed that there is no salvation without grace, that the sacraments are the means of grace, and that the church alone has power to administer the sacraments, we have sufficient basis for the acceptance of the authority of the church. She who controls the "medicine of immortality," the sacraments, can effectively command obedience in all things. McGiffert has summarized the point well:

> Upon one thing there was general agreement. If a person is to be saved he must have the divine grace which is imparted through the sacraments alone. As the authorized dispenser of these sacraments the Catholic church seemed to most men indispensable. This it was above all else that gave it its hold upon them and kept them loyal to it even when they might, as was often the case, chafe under its restrictions, or feel impatient with its failures, or deplore the frequent worldliness of its rulers and the unworthiness of its priests. Not only devout believers but even the most indifferent and least religious-minded men might well hesitate to cut themselves off from its ministrations, or die outside its pale, when to do so meant possibly if not certainly to forfeit the hope of eternal life and incur the risk of everlasting punishment.[7]

Therefore, we may with reason say the church was regarded as the supreme authority on earth *because* she dispenses sacramental grace. Once this point is grasped, it will be clear why Luther could leave the fold of the church after he had enunciated his doctrine of salvation by faith alone; this made the sacraments unnecessary as a means of grace and consequently undercut the authority of the church.

The Sacramental System

From the beginning of our survey of philosophy and religion, we have seen that religion is intimately connected with man's quest for well-being.

[7] McGiffert, *op. cit.*, pp. 357 f.

All the religions we have encountered provided their adherents not only with a body of beliefs about the supernatural world which was supposed to control the destiny of men and to prescribe the nature and condition of salvation. These religions, whether Hebrew, Greek, or Christian, have also formulated more or less elaborate methods for coming to terms with the divine and for receiving supernatural powers for the fulfillment of life's meaning. Medieval Christianity, being essentially an other-worldly religion, was concerned chiefly with performances or ceremonies designed to keep men out of the clutches of Satan and to forward their progress toward eternal life. The Catholic sacraments constitute the system of ceremonies that surrounds the Christian with the means of divine help, that is, with grace, from birth to the grave.

In the very early church the word *sacrament* stood for any act or rite thought to be holy and able to transmit divine grace. Certain of these acts, like baptism and the eucharist (the Lord's Supper), stood out as having a special sacramental character, but many other rituals were also considered sacred, so that the word *sacrament* was given a very general meaning during the first centuries of the church's life. The tendency was to enlarge the number of sacraments, but since it was obvious that not all were of equal importance, some being thought necessary to salvation and others not, theologians came to give more specific definition to the nature of a sacrament and to distinguish between sacraments and sacramentals. St. Augustine recognized many sacraments, but he emphasized three as holding special importance—baptism, the eucharist, and ordination. He defined them as "sacred signs" or as "visible signs of divine things"; yet he believed that they were more than signs, for he was convinced that in and through them God's grace is actually bestowed.

Abelard and others who followed him recognized five sacraments: baptism, confirmation, the eucharist, extreme unction, and marriage. To these his disciples added penance and ordination, making a total of seven. These were adopted by Peter Lombard (1100-1160) and popularized through his great work, the *Sentences,* and they were accepted by Thomas Aquinas and officially sanctioned by the Council of Florence in 1439. Since that date both the Eastern and Western churches have accepted seven sacraments as the proper number.

Following Augustine, some scholars said that the sacraments were signs only while others said they were effective signs, actually conveying grace. Opinion wavered for a time between symbolic and realistic interpretations until the debate was settled, first by a papal bull and then by the Council of

Trent, with the official declaration (1563) that the sacraments both contain and convey saving grace; they both signify and sanctify. Moreover, they convey grace *ex opere operato*, that is, by virtue of what they are in themselves independent of the character of the priest or bishop who administers them (as long as he is duly ordained and in good standing and intends to perform the rite) and independent also of the faith of the recipient. Yet it was believed that if they are to be effective something must be required of the recipient, although exactly what was not made clear. The conclusion reached in the fifteenth century was that they convey grace upon those who "receive them worthily" or "do not oppose an obstacle," and this still remains the formal statement. When the recipient receives them with a good disposition of faith and penitence, he receives additional grace from them. Three things go to make up a sacrament, according to official pronouncement: the matter of the sacrament, such as the water of baptism or the wine and wafers of the eucharist; the words of institution; and the priest, or agent. In the absence of any one of these there is no sacrament. Except for baptism, which may be performed by any adult Christian in an emergency, the minister must be an ordained priest or, in the case of confirmation and ordination, a bishop. (Under certain rare and extreme circumstances, today marriage and penance may not require the presence of an officiating minister.)

In the sacraments, then, the medieval church had a mantle of ceremony with which to cloak every significant stage of life. Baptism removes the stain of original sin and of sins committed before the sacrament is received. Confirmation establishes the adolescent in his faith. Ordination brings the special benediction of God upon the young priest assuming holy orders. Marriage redeems sexual relations from their sinful character and blesses the union of man and wife. Penance provides absolution from the guilt of sins committed after baptism, while extreme unction restores to health a person in the presence of death or tides him over safely into eternity. The chief of the sacraments is the holy eucharist, which lost its significance as a memorial meal and became the repetition of the sacrificial death of Christ with its attendant renewal of divine grace. This involves the doctrine of transubstantiation, according to which the bread and wine are miraculously transformed into the very body and blood of Christ. Although the appearance remains that of bread and wine, faith knows that the substance has been transformed. As the focal point of the ritual known as the mass, this sacrament remains the central act of Catholic worship. Here, it was taught, the sacrifice of Christ on the cross is repeated with every celebration, bringing a renewed outpouring of its gracious benefits to the faithful communicant.

Medieval Other-Worldliness

The view of human nature which held that man, although made in God's image, is fallen and a sinner dominated medieval thought and determined its scheme of salvation. It also influenced medieval man to regard the world in which he lived as sharing in his corruption and doom; it was not something inherently and essentially good, but was something from which to be saved. One must not conclude from this that medieval men did not enjoy life, for they did—they participated in the usual human pleasures; but they never saw the world as a reality in and for itself, to be enjoyed as if it alone were real and of importance. Rather, it was a very temporary condition, a prelude of brief duration before eternal reward or punishment in heaven or hell. It is God's world, yet fallen, and God, not the world, is the final reality toward whom all men should move and in whom all find their goal. Salvation *from* the world *to* heaven was the basic ideal in Christendom. Hence the dominant note in the medieval outlook was other-worldliness, in the sense that the goal of life lies beyond this existence and this world.

That there is a goal for life was accepted with almost no question—a very great difference between the medieval period and the modern which, with its emphasis upon the world and its goodness, has for many people today lost the sense that there is any meaning or purpose beyond the world. The man who attempted to reach the Christian goal regarded himself as belonging already to the other world and thought of his life in this "vale of tears" as a kind of pilgrimage, important only for the fate to which it took him after death. His interest was directed to spiritual things; his goal was the future life. In order to reach this goal, he had to forego many of the enjoyments of this life. Indeed, the restraint of worldly desire and the denial of worldly pleasure which would attach him to this fleeting mundane existence were regarded as aids and conditions to the attainment of heaven. In a very real sense, this life with all its pleasures and good things is significant chiefly as a period of probation before the true life of eternity. Quite logically, therefore, the monastic life with its vows of poverty, chastity, and obedience was regarded as the ideal for the religious person who loved God deeply.

This concentration upon the next world was reflected also in the prevailing social attitude. To love one's neighbor did not entail responsibilities for changing radically the social conditions under which men suffered. Earthly conditions were of secondary importance; what really mattered was salvation of men for eternity. Salvation was thought to be of such transcendent importance that it might even be considered a kindness to place a heretic (whose soul was endangered by his heresy) upon the rack or burn his body in the flames of the Holy Inquisition, for the erring person might repent and so be saved.

Finally, medieval other-worldliness was reflected in the attitude toward nature. The natural environment lost all independent interest, and the sciences which had been studied by the Greeks—biology, physics, chemistry—now disappeared almost entirely from human interest. Any importance natural science might have was as an aid to theology. Like ourselves, medieval man did desire to understand nature, yet not for itself but as a clue to life's eternal meaning and as evidence of God's purposes. His ready faith in miracles was consistent with this attitude. Every sacrament was a special miracle, bearing witness to the intervening power of God, but in addition exceptional miracles might appear at any moment, showing God's hand in any aspect of life. The unseen world was very near, with good and evil spirits all about; this faith in the supernatural ranged all the way from the credulity of the ignorant peasant to the basic assumptions of the scholar. It was simply part of medieval man's outlook to view the world as a stage where one act of the cosmic drama was being performed. He accordingly sought an explanation of every detail in terms of the ideas and intentions of God, the cosmic playwright and director. Nothing that happened was either too great or too small to be explained in terms of God's purposes in his providential control of the world.

Contrary to the modern scientific attitude which seeks to find out *how* things happen, the medieval attitude sought to know *why*, and always in terms of God's purposes. Hence, it came about that the queen of medieval "science" (or knowledge) was theology, which concerned itself with God and his purposes for the world. Instead of interpreting nature and human experience in material and mechanical terms, the medieval thinker sought to explain what he saw in personal and moral terms. He had the same motive as we, namely, to understand, but since his primary concern was not to control the world but to reach heaven his speculative efforts were directed to the ways of God. The result was a science of divine purposes, which is theology, rather than of natural law. This leads us to our next chapter, in which we will investigate the kind of thinking that took place during the high Middle Ages.

Questions for Study

1. How did it happen, and when, that the Roman Empire had two capitals, and which was the second? What was the relation of the Eastern emperors to the

Eastern church? What factors and events helped drive the Eastern and Western churches apart? While the Western world was declining, what was the situation in the Eastern Empire? When did the final break between them occur? What was the fate of Byzantium?

2. Trace briefly the relations between the Western and Eastern Christian churches, and indicate the present position of the two.
3. Why did the political power of the Roman church increase so greatly after the fall of the Roman Empire? On the basis of what claims did Leo the Great urge the supremacy of the church at Rome over the other churches? What did Gregory the Great do to strengthen Leo's claim?
4. What is meant by a theocracy? What was the Gelasian theory of the two spheres? What problem might this theory face in practical matters? What was the Donation of Constantine, and how was it used?
5. Why did later popes feel it necessary to claim supremacy over the rulers? How did Innocent III justify his active participation in political activities? What was Boniface's theory of the two swords? What was the result of his attempting to put this theory into effect? What values can you see in the theocratic ideal during the Middle Ages?
6. What view is accepted by the Roman Catholic church today on the matter of the relation of church and state? Under what conditions can you imagine conflict arising today on this issue?
7. Discuss the statement in the text, ". . . we may with reason say the church was regarded as the supreme authority on earth *because* she dispenses sacramental grace." What relation has this to calling the church the sole "ark of salvation"?
8. What interpretation was eventually given to the sacraments?
9. How did medieval man understand his world, and what was his primary interest? What bearing had this upon his study of the sciences?

Selected Readings

Cannon, William R., *History of Christianity in the Middle Ages*, Nashville, Abingdon Press, 1960.

Ferguson, Wallace K., and Geoffrey Bruun, *A Survey of European Civilization*, Boston, Houghton Mifflin Company, 1936.

Hughes, Philip, *A History of the Church*, New York, Sheed & Ward, 1934, vol. I.

McGiffert, A. C., *A History of Christian Thought*, New York, Charles Scribner's Sons, 1933, vol. II.

Sabine, G. H., *A History of Political Theory*, New York, Henry Holt & Co., 1937.

Troeltsch, Ernst, *The Social Teachings of the Christian Churches*, New York, The Macmillan Company, 1931, vol. I.

Walker, Williston, *A History of the Christian Church*, rev. ed., New York. Charles Scribner's Sons, 1959.

14. Christian Scholasticism

One of the great developments of Western thought is that of Scholasticism, so named from the *scholasticus* or master of the *schola* or school during the late Middle Ages. Disinherited by the Enlightenment, it was for centuries largely disregarded and sometimes misunderstood by non-Catholic philosophers. Only recently has the contribution to thought made by the Schoolmen come to more general appreciation.

Scholasticism must be understood as an awakening of the mind, especially in the eleventh through the thirteenth centuries, under the stimulus of the rediscovery of the thought of Aristotle. In its origins it was a radical and rationalistic development considered dangerous by its opponents. We will examine first something of its background and early period and then the system of thought of the greatest of the Scholastics, Thomas Aquinas.

The Degradation of Philosophy and Secular Learning

The political decline of Rome was quite understandably accompanied by intellectual decadence. As early as the second Christian century intellectual activity had begun with the Christian Apologists, who attempted to provide philosophic support of a kind to Christian understandings. Great figures like Origen and Clement of Alexandria developed theological thinking in the late second and third centuries. Augustine carried his theological achievement to a very high point with his works in the fifth century. But as the Roman Empire drew to an end in the final quarter of that same century, philosophical and theological thought also went into a decline. Philosophy in any fresh and creative sense disappeared entirely, and in theology Augustine's work was accepted in an authoritative way which discouraged new thought. Occupied as the church was during the fifth and succeeding centuries with preserving itself and increasing its religious and political power, it was quite willing to accept Augustine's intuitive approach to religion without making any serious attempts to develop philosophic concepts. The Scriptures as interpreted by church councils were authoritative, providing everything truly essential in the realm of knowledge for this life and the next. Some Christian leaders regarded it as a waste of effort if not positively dangerous to occupy oneself with intellectual endeavors that had no direct religious application. The ultimate degradation of the kind of philosophic learning we found among the Greeks and Romans is illustrated in the famous rebuke which Gregory the Great administered to the bishop of Vienne:

> A report has reached us which we cannot mention without a blush, that thou expoundest grammar [which included literature] to thy friends. Whereat we are so offended and filled with scorn that our former opinion of thee is turned to mourning. The same mouth singeth not the praises of Jove and the praises of Christ.[1]

Given the political situation of the times and attitudes like Gregory's toward philosophy and science, we can understand the decadence of philosophy which characterized the more than three centuries from the fall of Rome to the time of Charlemagne, when, rather feebly to be sure, creditable scholarship began to revive. What scholarly activity there was during this period was devoted largely to developing aids to Christian instruction aimed at promoting the faith. One writer has said that the dominating feature of medieval civilization from the fifth to the ninth centuries was a "passive receptivity," marked by repetition of Greek and Roman ideas.[2]

Charlemagne revived the Roman Empire when he was crowned emperor in the year 800. His rule had more than political significance; it also marked the revival of a measure of scholarly activity which is sometimes called, with a degree of exaggeration, the Carolingian Renaissance. When Charles, struck by the illiteracy of the clergy and the lack of teachers in France itself,

[1] As quoted in A. K. Rogers, *A Student's History of Philosophy*, 3rd ed., New York, The Macmillan Company, 1932, p. 191.

[2] Maurice de Wulf, *History of Medieval Philosophy*, 3rd ed., London, Longmans, Green & Co., 1935, I, 21 f.

looked about for scholars to aid him in the development of education, he found qualified men chiefly in England and Italy. Outstanding among these was an Englishman named *Alcuin* (735-804), often considered the first of the medievalists, who became chief counselor to Charlemagne in educational matters. In 789, even prior to his being crowned emperor, Charles required every parish to provide a school open to all children, of freemen and serfs alike. Many—though not all—parishes developed excellent schools, and almost all provided some form of educational possibilities for their children. At a church council in 802, at Aachen, the emperor entrusted higher education for both clerical and lay students to the cathedrals and monasteries. Education within these schools consisted in studying the manuscripts possessed by the school under the guidance of a qualified teacher.

The greatest single figure in ninth-century scholarship was Johannes Scotus Erigena (*ca.* 810-877), an Irishman who taught in the developing university at Paris. He knew Latin and, remarkable in his day, also Greek and possibly even Arabic. He was well acquainted with the writings of the Greek church Fathers and the Neo-Platonists. He himself was strongly influenced by the philosophy of Neo-Platonism. With his death, philosophy was once again eclipsed for nearly two additional centuries.

The Birth of Scholasticism

From Augustine until the thirteenth century the thought of the Western church was dominated by Platonic emphases as these had been interpreted through Plotinus and Neo-Platonism. We recall in Plato the emphasis upon the real world of forms or Ideas. The world of experience known to the senses was for him unreal or less real than the ideal world knowable to reason. We recall also that both Plato and Plotinus believed that man's soul is his real self, separable from the body at death, and that salvation consists in this separation and the attainment of a higher, spiritual state of being with no further return into physical stuff. In Platonic thought generally there is a degree of depreciation of physical experience and an emphasis upon the invisible spiritual world. Illumination of the mind by God was one of the ideas taken from later Platonism by Augustine, and this, combined with a mysticism separated from rational thought, made reason and philosophy for Augustine and his followers an inferior approach to reality (which, incidentally, it was not for Plato, although he too taught that one had to pass beyond reason to find ultimate truth). The thinkers who appear in the medieval period before the twelfth and thirteenth centuries, influenced as they were by Platonic thought, stand together in their basic views, drawn largely from Augustine.

The thinkers of medieval Christendom understood life as a *via*, a way, leading to a definite goal beyond life itself in a blessed immortality. The way of life is laid out in the Scriptures, God's revelations to men; and the blessedness to be reached in heaven far exceeds anything human life itself has to offer. It is important to understand this underlying view since apart from it nothing of medieval thought is comprehensible. This means that theology continued to hold the center of interest throughout all the centuries after the second, for theology finds its basic principles in revelation. Reason was the handmaid of theology and had the task of ordering and attempting to understand that which was accepted as truth from God. The Scholastics brought a new emphasis into their times with their increased recognition of the importance of reason, although, of course, reason did not oppose revelation. It was for them a relatively independent discipline, with great powers of its own for discovering truth, even though the higher truths were available only through revelation. The goal set by the Scholastics in their use of reason was to elucidate and defend the truths of religion.

To define Scholasticism properly is no simple task, for the word covers many different aspects of culture. We have said that its greatest development took place during the eleventh, twelfth, and thirteenth centuries, and yet it may be traced back as far as the ninth century. The term covers a multitude of men, ideas, and schools of thought. It can be divided into a *method*, called the scholastic method, and a *content*, or the principal emphases appearing within it.

As a method, Scholasticism took its approach to thinking from Aristotle and his logic, called in the Middle Ages *dialectic*. It was a way of conducting intellectual research which all the Scholastics followed. First, the idea which the scholar felt prepared to develop and defend, call the *thesis*, was stated. Then all the rational support that could be given to this thesis was brought to its defense. Next, objections to the thesis were stated, and each in turn was examined for its possible effect upon the thesis. Finally, the objections were answered and the thesis reasserted. This obviously was a rationalistic procedure based on the strict application of reason, with nothing in it of feeling, intuition, or mysticism.

This type of thinking was largely deductive in form, meaning in this context that ideas taken as true on the basis of revelation and authority or as demonstrated by reason were examined by means of the logic derived from Aristotle, and the deductions drawn from these general truths were made obvious. The movement of thought was thus from general to particular. In some respects this is the opposite movement from scientific, inductive thinking which starts from particulars, derived from sense experience, and moves to general truths, the hypotheses and laws of science. Yet the Scholastics also used induction, for in his philosophy Thomas Aquinas started from what his senses showed him and moved from these particulars to general truths, established by reason. He insisted that all ideas in the final analysis are derived from sense experience. As the mind acts upon the reports of the senses, it develops intellectual knowledge, different in kind and degree from the simple sensory impressions from which it starts.

We see then that Scholasticism used both induction and deduction but that the latter was its principal approach to knowledge. The Scholastics denied that men are born with "innate" ideas, already present in the mind of the child before his sensory experiences begin. The Augustinians and Platonists, who had represented the dominant theological emphasis before Scholasticism appeared, opposed the method and its conclusions just because it seemed to them to place far too much reliance upon reason at the expense of intuition and mysticism.

Philosophy was reborn at the hands of Scholasticism, though as a servant to theology, which continued to be "Queen of the Sciences," and not as an independent discipline. In other words, theology provided men with wisdom about eternal things, and philosophy assisted it by providing rational and natural grounds for theological truth. The content of Scholasticism can be best described by examining the thought of St. Thomas, which we will do soon. In brief, it combined Christian understandings with ideas drawn from Aristotle. We turn now to examine two great issues which appeared during the early Middle Ages. The former is that of faith and reason and their relationship; the latter is the controversy over the Universals.

The Problem of Faith and Reason

The first problem to engage the attention of medieval thinkers, beginning with Augustine, was that of faith and reason. Granted that faith comes first and that the ancient body of Christian truth as set down in Scripture, defined in the Creeds, interpreted in the writings of the Fathers, and taught by the church was on no account to be questioned, had not the Fathers themselves invoked reason to defend dogma and make it acceptable to the understanding? What, then, is the true relation between faith and reason, between natural knowledge and revealed truth? This question is one with which every religious philosopher must deal, and medieval philosophers were no exception.

The word *faith* is a difficult one to deal with since it is given a variety of meanings. For those like St. Paul who stress the emotional and volitional approach to life, it means commitment, trust, and self-giving. For those who emphasize reason, it means the intellectual acceptance on the basis of authority of certain ideas that are beyond intellectual demonstration. In the Middle Ages the word *faith* was generally used in the latter sense, but at times it was used with connotations of the former meaning as well, carrying overtones of commitment and trust in addition to intellectual belief. Likewise, the meaning of *reason* is somewhat problematic. At one time it refers to logical demonstration which seems irrefutable and at another to rational insight into the deep truths of reality.[3] With this comment and warning, we will look at several representatives of differing views on the relationship of faith to reason.

In the days of the church Fathers, we find an extreme view, best illustrated by *Tertullian* (*ca.* 150-225), who held that everything one needs to know is to be found in revelation and its truths and that consequently reason is unnecessary. As Gilson expresses it, "Since God has spoken to us, it is no longer necessary for us to think."[4] All that is needful is to be found in the Scriptures—we should read, meditate upon, and live by them. Without philosophy man is far better off, for philosophy is the father of heresy. Hence Tertullian cries, "What indeed has Athens [philosophy] to do with Jerusalem [Christianity]? . . . We want no curious disputation after possessing Christ Jesus, no inquisition after enjoying the Gospel! With our faith, we desire no further belief."[5] He went even further, stating that the more unreasonable the articles of faith may appear to be, the more opportunity they provide for faith to develop. The phrase "I believe because it is absurd" is used to characterize this approach, which appeared frequently during the Middle Ages and is still to be found among Christians—faith is all and reason is a threat to faith. As thus understood, the true Christian is the one who avoids reason and holds blindly to revelation.

Other thinkers turned away from this extreme denial of reason to point out that reason itself is a gift of God to man and is therefore to be used. They believed that all wisdom was due to God's inspiration, so it was impossible that there be any contradictions between God's revelation in the

[3] Étienne Gilson, *Reason and Revelation in the Middle Ages,* New York, Charles Scribner's Sons, 1938, pp. 18 ff., 24 ff.

[4] *Ibid.*, p. 6.

[5] As quoted in *ibid.*, pp. 9 f.

Scriptures and those truths open to reason. Natural and revealed knowledge, they claimed, are in fundamental agreement, not opposed, as Tertullian thought. Augustine, as a representative of this view, stated that faith comes first, and without this preliminary faith true understanding is impossible. "We believe that we may know," he wrote, "we do not know that we may believe."[6] But unlike Tertullian he did not stop with faith, for he brought in reason to support and clarify it. After believing, the man of faith looks for explanations of his faith. Thus, "Faith seeks understanding." Augustine did not reject the Greek ideal of seeking knowledge; he transformed it by teaching that it is faith which guides one toward rational understanding. He himself devoted his chief intellectual effort toward the understanding of Christian faith.

Another thinker who represents much the same position as that of Augustine was *Anselm*, archbishop of Canterbury (1033-1109). Echoing his master, he wrote,

> I do not endeavor, O Lord, to penetrate thy sublimity, for in no wise do I compare my understanding with that; but I long to understand in some degree thy truth, which my heart believes and loves. For I do not seek to understand that I may believe, but I believe in order to understand. For this also I believe—that unless I believed, I should not understand.[7]

He wrote also,

> No Christian ought in any way to dispute the truth of what the Catholic church believes in its heart and confesses with its mouth. But always holding the same faith unquestioningly, loving it and living it, he ought himself as far as he is able to seek the reason for it. If he can understand it let him thank God. If he cannot let him not raise his head in opposition but bow in reverence.[8]

In short, it is fitting and proper that reason should try to understand dogma, but in the event this cannot be done, reason must yield gladly to authority.

Anselm proclaimed publicly and with confidence that *all* the accepted doctrines of the church could be understood by reason, and that it was the duty of the Christian to apply his reason to this understanding. Not to put faith first in our understanding, he said, is presumption, but not to use one's reason upon one's faith is negligence; the Christian must avoid the second as well as the first fault. Anselm did not claim that if revelation had not been

[6] As quoted in Eugène Portalié, *A Guide to the Thought of St. Augustine*, Chicago, Henry Regnery Co., 1960, p. 116.

[7] St. Anselm, *Proslogium*, c. 2, tr. S. N. Deane, LaSalle, Open Court Publishing Co., 1939, pp. 6 f.

[8] As quoted in A. C. McGiffert, *A History of Christian Thought*, New York, Charles Scribner's Sons, 1933, II, 186.

given man's reason could have discovered its truths, but he did believe that, given the revelation, man's reason is practically without limit in its ability to interpret the given revelation. The method of proof Anselm used was one later used by Thomas Aquinas, called dialectics, derived as we said from Aristotle. Used thus, reason supports and clarifies dogma, he believed. For Anselm, then, as for Augustine, reason enters as an aid to faith, vital and important but in no way challenging the authority of church teaching.

The position that faith precedes knowledge was first strongly challenged by *Johannes Scotus Erigena*, the first original thinker of the Middle Ages. His native country of Ireland had escaped the ravages of barbarian invasion, and its ancient culture had accordingly been preserved to a higher degree than on the Continent. In the discussion of the relation of faith to reason, he asserted the primacy of reason over faith; yet he did this indirectly, verbally upholding the primacy of faith! He started his discussion by stating that since philosophy and religion have the same source in the divine wisdom, there can be no genuine contradiction between them. He declared that the chief source of our knowledge of God is the Scriptures; hence, he starts with faith in God's revelation in the Bible. In its own way, faith grasps truth before the intellect does, he said, and in this he stood in agreement with Augustine; but now he raised the question of the *meaning* of the Scriptures. At this point reason enters on its own, for if reason fails to discern the proper meaning mistakes will arise. Hence the source of authority is actually reason discovering truth from the revealed Scriptures. He agreed that when God speaks, as he does in the Scriptures, one must believe him whether or not he understands him; but when men speak as interpreters of the Scriptures, what they say is true only if reason approves it. This view led Erigena to question interpretations by the church Fathers. He was of a mind to treat the Fathers with respect, but at the same time he insisted that their authority is that of the rational truth which they have discovered concerning the object of faith. This suggests that the Christian is not bound by their authority if reason indicates otherwise, for reason must in such instances have the final word. True reason and true authority cannot stand in contradition, but the latter is to be followed only as it is reasonable.[9] We see that in effect Erigena makes reason the judge of all authority, thus giving it preference over faith. By considering the thought of the Fathers as merely probable and not authoritative and by interpreting the authoritative Scriptures allegorically, he adapted dogma to his own ideas and ended by creating a system of thought that was repeatedly condemned by the later church.

[9] Étienne Gilson, *History of Christian Philosophy in the Middle Ages*, New York, Random House, Inc., 1955, pp. 114 and 610, n. 12.

The question of the respective claims of reason and faith was brought to a head by *Peter Abelard* (1079-1142), one of the principals of the famous and tragic romance of Abelard and Heloise and the most famous professor of philosophy and theology of the twelfth century. On the question under discussion, he quoted with approval the words of a skeptical apocryphal writing, *Ecclesiasticus:* "He who believes quickly is light minded." A man of dialectic temper, Abelard was as admirably fitted to teach of logic as he was unsuited for getting on with his colleagues. In one of his books, *Sic et Non* (*Yes and No*), he set down a large number of doctrines under the heading of 158 propositions, and opposite each he placed quotations from the church Fathers both for and against the propositions. He explained that in many instances the apparent contradiction which resulted was the result of using words in different senses, and yet, after making all allowances, contradictions do remain, which must be the result of the ignorance of the Fathers! That the Fathers were not infallible need occasion no great alarm, he taught, for there is no obligation to follow them as there is to accept the authority of the Scriptures. He presented his book, he said, as an illustration in dialectic, using contradictory statements to sharpen the mind, in this way preparing the student to search out the truth for himself. By doubting, he claimed, one comes to inquiry, and through inquiry truth is discovered. This may well be a fine educational principle, but it was received with something less than complete approval by Abelard's ecclesiastical superiors. Yet the method he set forth in this famous book of dealing with issues by presenting both an idea and its opposite proved of great value in later scholastic thought, for Abelard was the first man to apply dialectic to theology itself.

Like all his predecessors, Abelard did not reject the Scriptures, revelation, or faith, but accepted them, teaching that what is *plainly* written in the Bible is true. However, he disliked and roundly criticized the way in which commentators and theologians read their own opinions into the Scriptures, and felt free to criticize the Fathers generally, frequently with devastating effect. In dealing with theological issues he, like Erigena, gave the primary position to reason in its investigation and understanding of the bare deliverances of faith. He championed man's right to free rational inquiry, and yet he did so as an apologist for Christianity and in no intended sense its opponent. To his mind, Christianity's greatest enemies were those who refused to think clearly.

In Abelard's principle that it is impossible to believe what is not understood in the first place, we appear to have a reversal of the accepted Augustinian position that it is necessary to believe in order to understand. Although

Abelard's teaching on the Trinity was condemned at a church council held in 1141 and the condemnation was upheld by the pope, his thought continued to exert great influence. The question of faith and reason, in the meantime, persisted until it reached its definitive form, as far as Catholic teaching is concerned, in the solution provided by Thomas Aquinas a century later. In summary, we can state that Augustine and Anselm said, "I believe in order to understand," while Erigena and Abelard preferred to say, "I understand in order to believe." In essentials they are in agreement, differing only in emphasis, but the emphasis makes for considerable difference in attitudes and conclusions.

The Debate over the Question of Universals

Much of the thought of the Middle Ages, it has been remarked, goes back to Plato directly or indirectly. One of the greatest philosophic problems which occupied the thinkers of this period, particularly in the earlier Middle Ages, was one arising from Plato's doctrine of Ideas, known as the problem of Universals. The immediate question had been inherited by medieval thinkers from Porphyry (*ca.* 232-304), whose essay entitled *Isagoge,* an Introduction to the *Categories*, one of Aristotle's writings on logic, had been transmitted to medieval scholars along with the logic itself. Porphyry had asked three questions (without answering them himself) which stimulated the thought of half a dozen and more centuries. He had inquired whether *genera* and *species* actually exist in some way in nature, or are merely mental constructions, and whether their existence is separate from sensible things or only in and through them. Perhaps the beginning student will agree with Porphyry's own opinion that "this is a lofty business, unsuited to an elementary work," but to this consideration many medieval thinkers gave their energies.

Let us stop and make clear just what the problem actually is. We are all aware of having two different sorts of knowledge of objects, which we believe to exist beyond our own minds. One kind is the sort that arises from our senses and so is called sensory—our impressions of sight, touch, sound, taste, and smell. This kind of knowledge we generally believe presents to us the individual and concrete aspects of the objects themselves. We see this book in all its individuality of color, size, and shape. We hear that bird song with its own tones and trills of sound. The second kind of knowledge we have of objects is intellectual. We have ideas or concepts formed from seeing many books and hearing many bird songs which are generalized or abstract forms of thought true of bird songs as such or books as such, but omitting the particularities of this individual book or song. The remarkable thing about these generalized or abstracted concepts, without which we would be incapable of thought, is that although through them we lose the particular, at the same time we gain knowledge of all objects of the species or genera. A true concept of book, for example, gives us knowledge about every book, no matter what size or color, even while it fails to tell us the particular characteristics of this book before us. It presumably gives us some reliable knowledge of the Universal, *book*, and we arrange such universal terms generally into species and genera on the basis of observed similarities. We have, for instance, the species *white oak tree* as a universal term referring to all white oak trees everywhere. Even more inclusive is the genus *oak tree* which refers to all oak trees. The reader will recall that we are here touching upon a point raised by Plato when he developed his theory of Ideas, for his Ideas are these same Universals.

Plato himself took the extreme position that only these Ideas, existing in a state of being quite other than the sensory, are genuinely and fully real, and that the particulars are endowed with a lesser degree of reality since they come into momentary being and pass out of it again, owing whatever degree of reality they have to their participation in the Ideas. Aristotle disagreed with this position, holding by contrast that the forms, as he called them, exist only in the individual beings and have no existence apart from or in independence of them. From Plato through Aristotle and Porphyry, then, this problem reached the Middle Ages, but even if there had been no Plato or Aristotle, the problem would still be a genuine one for the probing intellect. This is the problem: as we consider such a universal concept, what is the actual relation between the *concept* of tree and the actual trees of our experience? And, since the nature of the concept is different from the particular in detail, does it actually give us genuine knowledge about the world of particulars? Simple as this problem may appear at first sight, careful consideration will show something of its difficulty and subtlety.

In the Middle Ages the issue implied in this discussion was not merely an intellectual one, indulged in for the sake of philosophical discussion. It was in fact a matter of great theological importance, for in several instances doctrines of the church were at stake. The significance of such terms as *Trinity*, *universal church*, and *original sin* depends upon whether one takes a Realistic or a Nominalistic view.

The earliest important view on the question, derived from Plato and Plotinus, is designated exaggerated Realism. It must be first noted that the word *realism* is used differently in varying philosophies. In our own day the term is often used for the thought that objects are in some sense real as we perceive them, having an existence of their own in an external world independent of our thought of them, whereas in the Middle Ages the Universals were thought of as real according to this doctrine—they were believed to have a being of their own independent of particular things. The medieval usage, exaggerated Realism, stated that a universal concept such as humanity reflects a genuine reality of its own existing extramentally, in objects themselves, corresponding adequately to the way it exists in thought. A given particular man, according to the Realism of the early Middle Ages, shares in or is a modification of the universal idea of man or humanity.[10]

One of the consequences of this view is that since these concepts are the materials of logical thought, what is true *logically* is considered also true *in fact;* what is most real in thought is also most real in actuality, and the Universal is more significant than the particular. This idea was used by at least one theologian (Odo of Tournai) to explain how original sin is carried from one generation to the next. Since humanity is infected by sin from Adam, he taught, every individual exemplification of humanity, every particular man, is also infected.

In the eleventh and twelfth centuries, representatives of three particular views of the relation of concept (what is thought) to percept (what is experienced through the senses) came to the fore. They are commonly designated as Nominalist, Realist, and Conceptualist. The most important representative of Nominalism is *Roscellinus* (*ca.* 1050-1122), who, influenced by Aristotle and his emphasis upon the individual objects of experience, said in effect that only the particular, the individual, is actually real. What then are the universal terms? His answer appears to be (for his works are lost) that the Universal is merely a word or name (*nomen*)—hence his view is called Nominalism. It is only a sound, a "breathing of the voice" (*flatus vocis*), entirely mental and subjective, which serves simply as a *sign* for common objects. Exactly how Roscellinus is to be understood is not clear, but it is certain that he stood in opposition to the prevailing Realism of his day. He was severely criticized by his contemporaries, largely because of the consequences his thought had for the doctrine of the Trinity. He seems to have taught that, since only the particulars are real, the Trinity is only a *name* given to the common attributes of what are in effect three

[10] See De Wulf, *op. cit.*, pp. 143 ff.

distinct gods. This led him apparently to a theological tritheism (three gods), for he is said to have stated that if theological usage were to make it permissible he would actually speak of three gods, the Father, Son, and Holy Spirit. He added, however, that they have only one will and power, but this sop to orthodoxy was not enough to save him from being condemned and having to retract his theory at a church council (Soissons, in 1092).

The Realists, as represented by *William of Champeaux* (1070-1121), sought to combat this heresy by attacking its philosophical root. Declaring that the Universal alone has real existence, William held that individuality (*this* man, *that* dog) is only an accidental variation or modification of the universal essence. But this theory also had distressing theological implications, for it reduced the three Persons of the Trinity to unessential and accidental modifications of God. This denies that Christ was a real person and leaves the Incarnation a mere appearance. Further, as Abelard was quick to point out, the logical implication of such an extreme form of Realism is pantheism.

We diverge here briefly to indicate another development from a realistic doctrine, this one propounded by *Anselm* of Canterbury who, along with William, is to be classified as an extreme Realist. He developed the famous ontological argument for the existence of God from his realist premises. He supposed, along with Realists generally, that the more universal anything is, the more real it is. Reality, therefore, was associated less with particulars and more with Universals. The most universal of all terms, God, would then be the most real of all beings. Also, Anselm used the idea of perfection of being, according to which he thought that the more truly anything *is*, that is, real, the more nearly perfect it is. The word *perfect* can accordingly be used as synonymous with fullness of reality or being. On the basis of these assumptions, he developed his famous argument for God in his work called the *Proslogium*. In brief, Anselm reminds his reader that even the fool who denies God "is convinced that something exists in the understanding . . . than which nothing greater can be conceived." Since this is the case, Anselm argues, then this something "than which nothing greater can be conceived [God], cannot exist in the understanding alone. For, suppose it exists in the understanding alone: then it can be conceived to exist in reality; which is greater." That is to say, if God were to exist *only* in the understanding and not in reality, then it would be logically possible to conceive of a still greater being, namely, one that exists in reality also. But this, he states, is impossible, according to the original statement which says that nothing greater can be conceived. He concludes, "Hence, there is no doubt that there exists a being, than which nothing greater can be conceived, and it exists both in the understanding and in reality."[11] Anselm believed that in these few words he proved God's existence by appealing to the nature or being (*ontos*) of God.

This argument was attacked by a monk named Guanilo. Granting, he wrote, that Anselm's arguments do lead to the *idea* of a single, complete, and perfect being, this does not establish the conclusion that this idea has a counterpart in objective reality, apart from the idea as such.[12] He argued that the idea of a perfect island does not guarantee that there is in actuality such an island. It appears that the theological basis of Guanilo's criticism was one opposed to the underlying Realism of Anselm; hence, he was willing to reject the identification of the necessities of logical thought with objective reality.

In a lengthy reply, Anselm pointed out that Guanilo's illustration of a perfect island merely served to demonstrate his misunderstanding of the point at issue, for no object in nature, no thing (which is always changing into something else) can be properly referred to as perfect in Anselm's sense, meaning having every possible positive attribute of being.[13] Such a statement or idea cannot be applied to islands or, as in the later argument against Anselm of the philosopher Kant, to dollars in the pocket. In the sense implied by Anselm it can be used as an argument *only* for the being of God. Taken on its own realistic basis, the argument seemed to Anselm irrefutable. It is interesting to notice that Descartes in a later century adopted the argument and that Leibniz defended it. St. Thomas rejected it, with the result that modern Catholic theology does little with it. Generally speaking, since the modern mind is largely Nominalist, it tends to reject the argument, frequently without investigating its cogency with any degree of care.

Returning now to the debate over Universals, the third point of view is known as Conceptualism, perhaps best described as a moderate form of Realism. Its chief representative was Peter Abelard, who studied with both Roscellinus and Champeaux and then, as students frequently will, rejected the conclusions of both his teachers, seeking to work out a compromise position. He held that the universal concepts which the mind entertains are more than empty names for surface resemblances of things. They are actually abstractions from the objects of general characteristics they genuinely possess in common. These natures or characters that are implied in the

[11] St. Anselm, *op. cit.*, p. 8.
[12] *Ibid.*, pp. 14 f.
[13] *Ibid.*, pp. 153 ff.

universal terms do actually exist, but only in the objects which possess them. For example, the abstraction *tree*, again, is not merely a sound or a name loosely applied by the mind to a lot of objects which have certain superficial resemblances to each other (the view of Nominalism) but is an "isolation by the mind" of common features actually present in all trees.[14] Yet this must not be taken to imply, as extreme Realists might say, that the idea of a tree has a separate, real being of its own. The Universal *is* only in the objects from which it is abstracted. They are the indispensable forms of knowledge needed by man to know his universe, for they point to the similarity of essential characteristics in particular and individual substances. The Universal exists in nature as "a multiplicity with like qualities" making possible prediction if and as it is apprehended by human thought.[15] This solution, it will be noticed, rejects both extreme Nominalism and extreme Realism. Abelard's position in effect destroyed the influence of Plato insofar as the notion that Universals have some sort of reality of their own apart from nature is concerned, and it prepared the way for the ascendancy of Aristotle and, eventually, the rise of modern science. His Conceptualism foreshadowed the view finally accepted as the philosophy of the Catholic church, but the ultimate formulation of this view had to await the advent of Aquinas.

As we see, the "battle over Universals," appearing on the surface to be a philosopher's debate of a technical issue unrelated to practical concerns, bristled with theological implications. Remembering that medieval thinkers considered theology a vitally practical subject since it dealt with the central concern of eternal salvation, we can understand how the issue of Universals should have generated so much interest.

Between the two extremes of Realism and Nominalism, the church naturally inclined generally toward Realism. The *Church Universal*, not individual congregations, was held to be the depository of faith and the source of sacramental grace. *Mankind* must come before individual men, else how could meaning be found in the notion of original sin incurred by Adam's fall or the notion of the redemption of man through Christ's sacrifice? Nominalism would make of the Holy Catholic Church little more than the name for a collection of congregations and would free the individual from the taint of Adam's sin and remove him from the reach of Christ's redemption.

Moreover, Nominalism, finding reality in individual things alone, gives significance to observation, repudiates the theory of knowledge upon which

[14] B. A. G. Fuller, *A History of Ancient and Medieval Philosophy*, New York, Henry Holt & Co., 1938, p. 358.

[15] W. Windelband, *A History of Philosophy*, New York, The Macmillan Company, 1935, p. 299.

Neo-Platonism rested, and thus becomes an ally to the naturalistic spirit which later developed in opposition to dogma founded on revelation. To direct attention to particular facts may lead to new generalizations in conflict with traditional generalizations crystallized in dogma. Nominalism, accordingly, encourages the principle of private judgment, which in modern times challenged the principle of authority.

On the other hand, there are hidden dangers for Christian belief in extreme Realism also, and for this reason the church came to favor a moderate Realism. The exaltation of the Universal which allows the individual merely accidental status as an instance of the Universal is at heart inconsistent with the Christian belief in the worth and dignity of every person; moreover, it makes the theoretical possibility of personal immortality unlikely.

Modern thought tends to regard itself as primarily Nominalistic, but investigation shows that it includes a good deal of Realism, hidden or expressed. When we speak of the law, the church, the state, society, the laws of planetary motion, the periodic table of the elements, and the second law of thermodynamics, do we mean that these Universals actually exist or that they are merely names? Are they separate from sensible things or are they in them? And if we believe that Universals are *only* ideas in the minds of thinkers, with no relevance to any reality outside the mind (in objects) corresponding to them, then we have the problem of explaining how it is that scientific *thought* is able to discover actual truth about our factual universe. Like Porphyry, we shall probably withhold our answer to these questions; at least we must admit that medieval thinkers grappled with an issue which still has lively significance today.

The Resurgence of Aristotle

Little of the great thought of the ancient Greek philosophers came down directly to the church in the eighth and ninth centuries. Knowledge of the Greek language itself had almost disappeared, and what Greek writings were possessed had to be read in Latin translation. Plato's *Timaeus* and fragments of others of his dialogues were known. A commentary by Chalcidius gave some knowledge of pre-Socratic teaching, Aristotle, the Stoics, and Neo-Platonism. The only works of Aristotle known at that time were his treatments on logic, supplemented by Porphyry's famous book on the *Categories* which played so large a part in medieval thought generally. Little was known of the Latin classics. Augustine and Dionysius the Areopagite, a Neo-Platonist writer of the late fifth century, were well known and exercised great influence. The dominant intellectual influence of these centuries was, of course, the Platonic.

In the eleventh and twelfth centuries, however, a new temper in intellectual life appeared. Reason obtained its defenders, and the independent spirit represented by a man like Abelard continued to flourish. This new rationalism was encouraged by a growing acquaintance with the main body of Aristotelian philosophy. It was from the Arabs, and partly as a result of the learning brought back from the Crusades, that this new stimulus came to full birth. Through the Syrian Christians the Arabs came into contact with Greek thought, translated into Syriac. As the Arabs conquered the Middle East and Persia they were put in touch with this entire tradition and developed their own philosophy in large part through the stimulus thus received. In the court of Baghdad, Syrians translated these ancient documents into Arabic, and in this way the Arabs obtained in translation the works of Aristotle, some important commentaries, and various Greek treatises on medicine and mathematics. They had little of Plato, but one of the works they attributed to Aristotle under the title of *Theology* was in fact a compilation of sections iv-vi of the famous Neo-Platonic work of Plotinus, the *Enneads*.[16] It was the Arabs, then, who carried the torch of philosophy during the Middle Ages of Europe.

Arab thinkers wove these materials and ideas derived from their own Moslem tradition and other Eastern sources into systems of philosophy. The greatest of their philosophers were three: *Avicenna* (ibn-Sina, 980-1037), a Persian physician; *Algazel* (al-Ghazzali, 1058-1111), a Moslem mystic and a powerful influence among the Moslem Sufis, who lectured in the University at Baghdad; and the great *Averroës* (ibn-Rushd, 1126-1198), who lived in Seville and Cordova, Spain, and was both a physician and a judge. An outstanding Jewish philosopher, Moses *Maimonides* (Moses ben Maimon, 1135-1204), was a contemporary of Averroës and held similar views. His thought was of special importance for its influence upon Jews of his own day and later. All of these philosophers showed great indebtedness to Greek thought, particularly to Neo-Platonism on the one hand and Aristotle's teachings on science, metaphysics, and ethics on the other.

The close proximity of Cordova to the schools of France and Italy and the growing intellectual interests of Christian scholars combined to bring Aristotle's wider thought to those countries. The first acquaintance Christian scholars had with Aristotle's metaphysics, physics, psychology, and ethics consisted of Latin translations of Arabic translations of Syriac translations of the Greek originals! Various centers for translation were established,

[16] De Wulf, *op. cit.*, pp. 290 ff.

most of these working from the Arabic but some also from Greek sources directly. One was on the island of Sicily; others were in Spain, with the chief center in Toledo. This new material flooding into Europe was a source of great stimulation to the minds of European thinkers, who found in it a veritable mine of knowledge already arranged, classified, and interpreted by a set of first principles—in short, a full-grown philosophy. Keen intellects began to make this find their own.

The ecclesiastical authorities at first condemned and prohibited these new materials from the Arabs. The advent of the complete Aristotelian philosophy in the twelfth century shocked medieval Christendom no less than the doctrine of evolution did religious orthodoxy in the nineteenth. The University of Paris (formally established in 1200), where these works were first studied, interdicted the teaching of Aristotle's scientific treatises in 1210, and in 1215 forbade also the teaching of his *Metaphysics*. His *Logic* was, however, still permitted. Yet at the very same time, Aristotle was freely taught in England and Toulouse. And though teaching of the forbidden books stopped at Paris, reading them did not.

The opposition to Aristotle arose from various causes. One was simply his strangeness and newness, which inclined the authorities to hold him at arm's length. More importantly, he held ideas not in agreement with Christian teaching. Possibly the principal reasons were that certain writings, such as the *Theology*, later discovered not to be his own, were at first attributed to Aristotle, and that Arab commentaries were assumed to give correct interpretations of Aristotle's thought. The interpretation of Averroës, for example, was especially opposed to Christian teaching. Some of these works gave Aristotle a Neo-Platonic cast of an extreme sort, and others emphasized concepts like the eternity of the world which Christian theology could not approve.

In spite of the condemnations, interest in these works continued, and their influence spread. In 1231 Pope Gregory IX renewed the interdict, but by adding that the *Physics* could not be taught *until* its errors were removed, he suggested that the attitude had softened somewhat. By 1255 all the works of Aristotle were openly and officially lectured upon at the University of Paris, and in 1366 this same university actually required all its candidates for the licentiate of arts to have a knowledge of them all. Earlier than this it had become clear which works were genuinely Aristotle's and how far the commentaries could be taken as accurate interpretations of his thought.

When all has been said that can be said to explain the misinterpretations of Aristotle, it must still be recognized, however, that from the standpoint of Christian orthodoxy several elements in his thought were particularly unacceptable, chiefly his teachings that the universe is eternal and hence there was no creation, that God is an Unmoved Mover without knowledge of man or interest in him, and that there is no personal immortality. We recall that on the first point Aristotle had said that the universe with its forms and matter has always been. On the final point he said that men are essentially one, all sharing in the form of man, and that individuality results from the union of particular matter with this form. Such individual differences as men possess are due not to their essential natures but to the accidents of the matter in which that form is embodied in each particular instance. The form of man never ceases to be, but this particular man perishes with the body which gave him his individuality. Such ideas as these, which the church considered to be errors, were to be condemned.

In still another aspect Aristotelianism was even more dangerous to the Catholic position, although this was not at first evident. This was Aristotle's interest in natural science, expressed in his observation, collection, and analysis of natural phenomena. Believing that reality is to be found in the world of experienced things, he had confidence in the worth of natural knowledge based upon sense perception. Given this confidence, men may probe the secrets of the world by observing it, and by reflection upon what they observe may reach conclusions that are true—although possibly not in harmony with authoritative dogma. In Aristotle's science are found a principle of knowledge and a method of gaining truth which accept no authority except their own results.

Moreover, under the guidance of Neo-Platonic thought Christian theology had allowed for the possibility of a direct vision of God. This possibility Aristotle implicitly denied. For him, knowledge consisted of sense experience and the logical conclusions based upon it, and nothing more. While he held that man can know God, the Unmoved Mover, he held likewise that this was not the direct knowledge of acquaintance but a knowledge attained by thought. There was for him no such thing as a special form of religious knowledge which brought immediate apprehension of divinity.

Finally, the Aristotelian interest in the natural world was alien in quite another way, for medievalism concentrated attention upon the next world and regarded this world as merely a passing scene in the drama of salvation whose fulfillment is found in heaven. The Aristotelian study of nature and of man as part of nature might easily direct attention to earthly matters and might even suggest that the meaning and destiny of human life could find fulfillment against the background of nature without reference to the supernatural. In short, the study of nature might lead to naturalism which would find the world sufficient and man's powers adequate to make the best of it. This is, of course, the very antithesis of Catholicism.

Since the study of Aristotle could not be halted, the church gradually adapted his teaching to orthodoxy, and in this form made him an ally instead of an enemy of faith. The intellectual interests of the time demanded a knowledge of the sciences—physics, biology, astronomy, and psychology—so it was only natural to adopt the work already done so magnificently by Aristotle in these fields rather than start afresh or at a lower point. Aristotle had been able to build a metaphysics upon his natural science, and with changes, few but fundamental, his God might be rendered acceptable to Christian belief and his argument for the existence of God used as a philosophic defense of the faith.

The result in science was that gradually Aristotle's teaching itself became authoritative, a kind of scientific dogma questioned as little in its field as theological dogma was in its place. It thus came about that in matters of science as in matters of faith authority was the court of final appeal—in the former case, the authority of Aristotle; in the latter, that of the church. The question in science was no longer what it had been for Aristotle himself—what nature revealed, freshly and experientially—but what Aristotle had said. This state of affairs is illustrated by an anecdote of a student who thought he had discovered spots in the sun. "My son," replied his teacher, "I have read Aristotle many times, and I assure you that there is nothing of the kind mentioned by him. Be certain therefore that the spots which you have seen are in your eyes and not in the sun."[17] Thus it was that the *spirit* of Aristotle was smothered and his results embalmed. When the new science began to emerge in the sixteenth and seventeenth centuries, one of its first tasks was to destroy this mummy of what had been a living body of science 20 centuries earlier. Aristotelianism had become a synonym for reaction and a barrier to progress.

With the weakening of her condemnation of Aristotle, the church began the process of harmonizing the new philosophy with the theology of the church, an undertaking that reached its highest point in the work of Thomas Aquinas, in whose hands a remarkable synthesis of Christianity and Aristotelianism was molded.

The Thomistic System: Mature Scholasticism

Thomas Aquinas, (*ca.* 1225-1274) was born of a noble family in its fortress castle at Roccasecca, close by the town of Aquino and not far from Naples, in southern Italy. His family was illustrious on both sides; his mother was of

[17] As quoted in Rogers, *op. cit.*, p. 202.

high Norman stock and his father of the Lombard nobility, a nephew of Frederick Barbarossa. When only 5 years old Thomas was sent to nearby Monte Cassino, a Benedictine monastery, to begin his schooling. At the age of 14 or 15 he went to Naples to study liberal arts where, to the great chagrin of his ambitious parents, he became a begging friar of the newly formed Dominican Order. His parents and brothers attempted to turn him aside from this life, and even the pope was brought to interfere. At the age of 20 he was offered the position of abbot of the Monte Cassino monastery. But against all these attempts to dissuade him he continued steadfast in his determination to be a friar, with no ambition except that of scholarship. For a year or two his family kept him a prisoner in the family fortress. His chronicler tells us that while he was there an effort was made to break his determination by introducing an alluring young woman into his chamber. In great anger, he drove her away with a burning stick, which he then used to scratch the sign of the cross on the door. In this determined, self-contained young man one meets a temperament entirely different from that of another great saint, Augustine.

Eventually he was allowed to escape, and he traveled to Paris to study with the noted scholar *Albertus Magnus* (Albert the Great, *ca.* 1198-1280), an Aristotelian and an enthusiastic teacher who became Thomas' close friend. Several years later Thomas accompanied him to Cologne, returning to Paris after four years to teach in the University at the age of 27. He early gained an international reputation. In great demand as a teacher, he acted also as advisor to the pope, and spent his last days in reorganizing the University of Naples. He was a very pious, simple-living, deeply religious man. His life was one of daily worship and prayer, of writing, dictating, lecturing, and disputing with those who attacked the Aristotelianism of his master Albertus Magnus and himself. Rather surprisingly, in view of his controlled rationalism, he was an ecstatic of whom a number of well-authenticated instances of mystical experience are recorded.

Thomas was noted for his reserved manner, and when occupied with an especially difficult point he could readily be entirely abstracted, unaware of his surroundings. The following is a delightful account of one such experience. In Paris, he was a good friend of the king, Louis IX of France (later canonized), who frequently invited him to dine. The story continues:

> He had been taken by the prior to dine with the King, on a day when he was busy with the *Summa Theologica*. In the course of the meal he forgot where he was and grew lost in thought. The others were in the midst of conversation when suddenly he struck the table with his great hand, crying, "Ha! that settles the Manichees." There was consternation; the prior jerked him by the shoulder, but

Louis, who knew him, with royal courtesy called for a secretary to take down the thought lest it escape.[18]

Some years after Thomas' death several of his teachings were condemned, but eventually his system came to general acceptance and his opponents were silenced entirely. Within 50 years of his death, in 1323, he was canonized. In 1567 he was proclaimed a *doctor ecclesiae* (doctor of the church) and in 1879 his work was made the basis of Roman Catholic theological instruction. Much of his later popularity was the result of his great good fortune in having his basic theological ideas woven into one of the world's greatest pieces of literature, the *Commedia* or *Divine Comedy* of Dante.

Although he died before he was 50, during the course of his fairly brief life Thomas produced 30 large volumes on abstruse subjects which together form a comprehensive synthesis of Aristotelian philosophy and Christian thought. This work in theology is a monumental achievement, but Thomas was more than a theologian; his intellectual interests had a very wide range. He left a manuscript on mechanical engineering and was the moving spirit behind the translation of Aristotle into Latin directly from the Greek. His place in medieval scholarship may be compared to that of Innocent III in medieval politics, with the qualification that the scholar's work and influence outlasted that of the politician.

The two works in which Thomas most fully elaborated his system are the *Summa contra Gentiles* (*Summary against the Gentiles*) and the *Summa Theologica* (*Summary of Theology*). In the first and third parts of the *Summa Theologica*, Thomas treats of the whole Christian drama of salvation, while in the second part he presents the most elaborate treatment of Christian ethics ever produced. Popular in its own time, this *Summa* remains an authoritative statement of Roman Catholic doctrine to this day. In the *Summa contra Gentiles*, Thomas worked out the relationship between revealed theology and philosophy. As the title suggests, this work is a defense of the Christian faith against the attacks of those who relied on Aristotelian teachings to challenge Christian belief. Thomas' teacher, Albertus Magnus, had already laid the groundwork for the huge task of harmonizing natural knowledge as represented by Aristotle with revealed knowledge as represented by church dogmas. This task, needed to effect the defeat of unbelief, was brought to a brilliant conclusion by Thomas in the *Summa contra Gentiles*, a work scientific in arrangement and magnificent in scope.

We have mentioned that Thomas' thought brought Aristotelian and Christian ideas together. It also included much of Augustine and Plotinus and,

[18] M. C. D'Arcy, *St. Thomas Aquinas*, Dublin, Clonmore & Reynolds, Ltd., 1953, pp. 29 f.

consequently, of medieval Platonism, but these are minor themes compared to the major place given Aristotle. Like Aristotle, Thomas started his thought from sense experience instead of from the inner mystical experience so much emphasized in the Middle Ages. He exalted the powers of reason against those who would have depreciated reason in order to glorify faith or dogma. He united the physical and the mental worlds. His dialectic and his use of the concepts of form and matter and act and potency he derived directly from Aristotle. Everywhere that one touches Thomas' thought, he senses the shadow of the great Greek philosopher, his guide and inspiration in philosophy. Nevertheless, Thomas is at the same time a typical Christian thinker in that he holds as certain the deliverances of faith and the teaching of the Scriptures and the church. Nothing is allowed to contradict or bring into question these truths.

The most difficult problem Thomas faced in his work of synthesis was that of dealing with those elements in Aristotle's thought which appeared to be in conflict with Christian thought. He did not hesitate to adopt Aristotelian views against views held by his contemporaries when convinced that they were true in themselves and not contrary to Christian revelation. When what seemed to be a clear-cut contradiction between Aristotle and Christianity appeared, even then he was at times able to avoid the radical step of rejecting Aristotle by explaining either that the supposed position of Aristotle was not really his own but was that of a later interpreter, like Averroës, or else that the words of Aristotle did not require the usual interpretation but could be interpreted in ways congenial to Christian thought. Sometimes he overcame such difficulties by interpreting Aristotle in ways now felt to be unjustified.[19]

For Thomas, theology gave the philosophy he derived from Aristotle a deeper dimension than it had in its original form, for Aristotle saw human life and its purposes for any individual entirely within the limits of a lifetime while Thomas added the future life in which man's true end lies. At every point, Aristotle's philosophy was one limited for the individual by nature, of which he is a part, while Thomas added the superstructure of supernaturalism provided by his theology. For example, he added supernatural ethics to natural ethics and the vision of God to the highest possibilities of human knowledge, and asserted that the church is superior to the state.

With this as an introduction to Aquinas and his work, we will now examine some of the principal issues of his thought, looking first at his solution to one of the great problems of the early Middle Ages.

[19] See Frederick Copleston, *A History of Philosophy*, Westminster, The Newman Press, 1952, II, 426 and the whole of chap. 41, on this relationship.

The Harmony of Faith and Reason

Some of Thomas' predecessors had been certain that all church dogmas could be shown to be reasonable, but this optimistic view had been challenged by Abelard. A little later, when Aristotle's teachings were accepted as the conclusions of reason, it was plain to all that theological and philosophic beliefs did not coincide, and that it was by no means certain that reason and revelation did not stand in actual contradiction to each other at vital points. Before Albertus Magnus and Thomas, some theologians, influenced by the interpretations of Aristotle arising from Averroës, had taken refuge in the ancient (and oft-discredited) doctrine of the double truth, according to which it is possible for statements to be true for reason and false for faith and vice versa. Following the lead of Albertus Magnus, Thomas adopted the distinction between philosophy with its truths arising from natural reason and theology with its truths arising from revelation, though he divested this distinction of any suggestion of opposition. The two forms of truth are not opposed but supplement each other, he insisted. Both forms are needed if man is to possess the full actuality of truth.

With this formula, Thomas attempted to bring reason and faith, philosophy and theology, into a harmonious unity by assigning each a proper sphere of its own. Some truths fall properly within the province of philosophy, others within that of theology. Each sphere has its place and cannot contradict the other, since all truth is one and comes from God. Thomas is very definite in not committing himself to two opposing species of truth; like any careful thinker, he abhorred this solution. There are two sources of truth, not two different varieties or species. Philosophy through reason starts from the world and ascends to God. Theology, based on God's revelation, originates in God and descends to man.

Thomas regarded philosophy as valid in itself and yet incomplete. Theology by itself he regarded as also incomplete, not offering specific knowledge about the natural world. The supernatural completes and fulfills the natural, as the natural in a sense completes and fulfills the supernatural. Opposed to those theologians before him who stated that all the articles of faith could be demonstrated by reason, Thomas argued, on the contrary, that if reason were able to demonstrate them they would no longer be articles of faith but would be matters of reason, and faith would not be needed. The articles of faith, he said, rest upon divine authority alone, not upon any rational demonstration. Faith is certain that God has spoken and that what he has said is true, even though the full meaning of that message is not comprehended. But why should one believe that God has spoken?

Thomas replied that history offers proofs to this belief even if reason cannot, for in history we find records of God's miracles, the most impressive and certain of which is the existence of his church in its origins (the birth, death, and resurrection of Christ, its head, who is God's Son), its growth and preservation, and the continuing divine presence within it for man's salvation. So the Christian can know that God has spoken and that his word contained in Scripture and interpreted by the church is true. It tells men about God, themselves, their destiny, and what God has established for their salvation.

Within the field of theology itself, which deals with the being and nature of God, Thomas drew a distinction between what he called *natural* theology and *revealed* theology. According to this distinction, the former uses reason alone and deals with the question of God's existence, some of his essential attributes, the immortality of the soul, and other matters. All of these Thomas claimed can be demonstrated by reason and are, consequently, not properly matters of faith. God would not have needed to reveal such matters as these since unaided reason is quite capable in itself of discovering and demonstrating them, but because few men are philosophers and because most men are too occupied with everyday activities to make the intellectual effort required to discover them, God does reveal them through his word. However, since reason is able to discover such truths as these, it is proper to consider them the necessary *presuppositions* of faith rather than articles of faith themselves.

Revealed theology offers men truths which surpass the powers of the human reason to find unaided, coming from God himself in his revelation. These truths are not, of course, irrational, but since they come from God he and not reason is their foundation and guarantee. The Christian believer is usually prepared by reason to accept the truths of faith, but reason is actually irrelevant in demonstrating them, since divine authority is their foundation.

We may sum up the point by saying that for Thomas reason is not by itself a sufficient guide for man's life since it needs revelation to complete it, and that reason and revelation, while distinct, are not opposed to each other, for faith preserves reason from error and reason is the handmaid or bodyguard of faith. Reason serves faith by preparing the mind to receive it through its proofs of those truths which are the basic presuppositions of faith, by explaining as far as possible and developing the truths of faith, and by defending (though not demonstrating) these truths.[20]

Thus far we have mentioned the two forms of knowledge available to

[20] Article on "Thomas Aquinas" in *The Catholic Encyclopedia*, New York, Robert Appleton Co., 1912, vol. XIV.

man during his lifetime. No matter how much we may learn from faith and reason, knowledge is not fulfilled within this world. There is a still higher form of knowledge to be reached, the direct knowledge of God himself, obtained in and through the vision of God. This *beatific vision,* which the Platonists thought might be obtained mystically within a lifetime, can be realized only after death, according to Thomas. In the hierarchy of knowledge it is supreme. It is reached when saving truth becomes invested with a higher form to become the reality of the vision of God himself, which constitutes man's greatest good and the end of life. In reference to these three forms of knowledge, Thomas wrote:

> Man may have a threefold knowledge of divine things. The first is what he gains by the natural light of reason when he ascends through creatures to God. The second is when divine truth exceeding human understanding descends to us by way of revelation, not as it were proved to sight but offered for belief. The third is when the human mind is raised to a perfect insight into the things that are revealed.[21]

In this way Thomas was able to reconcile and bring into a synthesis Aristotle's thesis of natural knowledge and the Neo-Platonic teaching that God can be known directly through mystical experience and that man has a faculty of direct vision by means of which he may attain the vision of God. At this point the issue between Aristotle and Neo-Platonism was sharply drawn, the former insisting that all knowledge is rooted in the evidence of the senses and the latter claiming there is a special way of religious knowledge. The former is naturalistic, the latter mystical. Thomas' problem as synthesizer was to show, on the supposition that all knowledge is derived from the senses, how the Christian can yet know God and come into direct communion with him. His solution was to draw a distinction between the conditions of knowledge in this world and the next. Reason and faith, he said, are the only modes of knowledge in *this* world, but in the *next* the mystic vision is possible. In this world the highest knowledge available to man, even through revelation, is knowledge *about* God; in the next world we shall be freed from our human limitations and by God's grace may look upon him directly in a knowledge *of* him as he is in himself.

Natural Knowledge and Supernatural Knowledge

Let us observe what sort of knowledge man may gain, in Thomas' first way, "by the natural light of reason when he ascends through creatures to God." To begin with, by means of reason we may prove the existence of

[21] *Summa contra Gentiles,* IV, 1, as quoted in McGiffert, *op. cit.,* pp. 272 f.

God. In accordance with his Aristotelian theory of knowledge, Thomas rejected Anselm's ontological proof, stating:

> Granted that everyone understands that by this name *God* is signified something than which nothing greater can be thought, nevertheless, it does not therefore follow that he understands that what the name signifies exists actually, but only that it exists mentally. Nor can it be argued that it actually exists, unless it be admitted that there actually exists something than which nothing greater can be thought; and this precisely is not admitted by those who hold that God does not exist."[22]

He likewise disposed of the argument that God is self-evident, an inborn knowledge within every man.

The way the existence of God can be demonstrated is to start by observing the world about us, in which we can perceive the effects of God's activity. Motion, growth, and change are the most evident of facts, and since objects do not move or change themselves but remain at rest until moved from without, philosophy must account for the fact of change. At this point Thomas developed five arguments for God's existence, three of which are drawn from the fact of change or motion. We will look only at the first, generally considered the most important and basic one, which is derived from Aristotle. Since the argument starts with an examination of the world about us and ascends from the world to God, it is intended to be an inductive, not deductive, argument. It is sometimes referred to as the argument from motion, but the word *motion* must be understood in a way not common to modern usage. Thomas meant by it not merely movement in space, as we ordinarily do, but any change of condition within an object or in its relation to another. Thus, the process of growth in living ceatures, a change from hot to cold or cold to hot, the development of man's intellect, are all motion in his sense. Anything moved (or changed, as we would say) must be moved by another object or being which already has the quality or character imparted by the motion. A cold object, for example, does not become hot unless heat already present in something else is brought into contact with it. In Thomas' language, whatever is changed or moved is done so by another being or object in which that which is potential in the former is already actual and changes or moves this potentiality into actuality.

It is basic for the argument to notice this dependence of the present upon the past, the fact that all change is the result of previously existing causes, without which the change could not happen since nothing changes itself. Change, in other words, is dependent and contingent upon previous actions

[22] *Summa Theologica,* I, q. 2, art. 1, in Anton C. Pegis (ed.), *Basic Writings of Saint Thomas Aquinas,* New York, Random House, Inc., 1945, p. 20.

for its being and becoming, and these previous actions are likewise contingent and dependent upon others preceding them, and so on back in time. We human beings, for example, did not bring ourselves into being but in our existence are entirely contingent (we might not have been) and dependent upon our parents for our having arrived in this world; they in their turn are likewise dependent upon their parents, and so back into the past. There are no exceptions in the world of nature to this fact. No action or change is necessary or inevitable by reason of an object's own nature, for it might not have happened if circumstances had been otherwise. Nothing that happens is explained by itself in its existence and changes; it is explained, so far as explanation is possible, by other dependent beings which, because dependent, are in turn explained by those upon which *they* depend.

It therefore follows that no matter how far back in time we go within the events of natural happenings, we never find a *sufficient* explanation, that is, an explanation which does not require explanation in its own turn. Until such an explanation is found, the mind of the philosopher is unsatisfied, for he believes that this universe is not irrational. But the best that the mind seems capable of concluding in the face of this seemingly endless series of contingent activities, if it remains within the series, is that there is simply an infinite regress, an endless series of causes going back infinitely in time. Yet such a solution is not really a solution at all for the rational mind seeking for a truth upon which it can rest as a final answer to the problem. How can it be solved in an intellectually satisfying way?

Thomas now comes to his conclusion, which is, quite simply, that the only possible solution is one that steps outside the endless series of contingent, dependent events and recognizes that there *must* be a cause or mover that is not itself contingent or dependent. Such a cause is quite properly called a First Mover or First Cause. It is fundamental to notice that this First Cause must then be of a different order of being from all other causes if it is to solve the problem. It must be *necessary* and *independent*, the opposites of contingent and dependent. It must be of a nature that, instead of existing only because of previous causes, it could not *not* be. It must be dependent upon nothing else than itself alone. Such a cause and only such a cause can be a sufficient explanation for our world, he believes; any other leaves it finally unexplained.

Thomas states the argument, which we have amplified, in the following words:

Whatever is moved must be moved by another. If that by which it is moved be itself moved, then this also must needs be moved by another, and that by another again. But this cannot go on to infinity, because then there would be no first mover, and, consequently, no other mover, seeing that subsequent movers move only inasmuch as they are moved by the first mover; as the staff moves only because it is moved by the hand. Therefore it is necessary to arrive at a first mover, moved by no other; and this everyone understands to be God.[23]

Before commenting on the final phrase, we need to explain that by the term *First Mover* Thomas does not mean simply the first beginning of the world of nature, millions of years ago, thus providing a scientific explanation for the physical universal. Rather, he is saying that we have here a *metaphysical* explanation, one that provides a rational understanding for there being a world of contingent nature. The argument in its conclusion takes us out of the world of nature entirely (which is everywhere dependent and contingent) and leads us to a totally different kind of reality, needing no explanation of its own just because it is not dependent and contingent. If one should ask where God comes from, he would thereby show his failure to understand the argument, since that question, both appropriate and necessary for dependent being, is irrelevant for the First Cause.

If there were no such First Cause, the only possible explanation for our dependent world would disappear, Thomas wrote, and under such circumstances there would be no world. That which makes the world of today possible would not then have been produced by the world of yesterday from which it came, because that world would not have been since the conditions of its being would not have existed.

The conclusion, that this First Mover "everyone understands to be God," is made meaningful only in the light of the immediately succeeding sections of the *Summa Theologica*, since on the surface there is no reason for asserting that everyone understands this to be the fact. Having proved to his satisfaction that the First Cause or First Mover must exist, Thomas proceeds to use the philosophic method of dialectic, or logical deduction, to show what the nature of such a First Cause must be. Without attempting to develop his argument, we can mention some of the conclusions of this reasoning. As the First Cause, this being must be pure actuality, since it depends upon nothing else for its being. Having all perfection within itself, it must be good. Being infinite, it must be possessed of infinite intelligence, freedom, and power. It must also be simple, one, and unchangeable. All such qualities as these belong to God and God alone, so the First Cause must be God.

Other arguments, including the teleological, are used by Thomas for God, but the cornerstone of his natural theology is the argument from motion to the First Mover.

[23] *Ibid.*, I, q. 2, art. 3, p. 22.

Two of the most pressing problems raised for the Christian mind by Aristotle in his philosophy were his teaching that the world is eternal and that the soul of man is mortal. Concerning the former point, Aquinas said that from the standpoint of philosophy the honors are about even for and against the belief in creation, which opposes the idea of the eternity of the world. As a matter of Christian faith, he accepted creation as a fact. To conform Aristotelian philosophy to the Christian belief in personal immortality was somewhat more difficult. The former, with its doctrine that matter is the principle which differentiates all individuals of a class or species, denies the possibility of personal immortality. Thomas loyally follows Aristotle in asserting that man is a body-soul, not simply a soul which temporarily inhabits a body, but he holds that personal immortality is not only possible but can be demonstrated philosophically, in the following way. When Aristotle spoke of the soul of man he meant the rational principle in man. Thomas, enlarging the concept, thought of the soul as that which gives man his determinations; it controls his body and provides him with his vegetative and sensory operations in addition to the intellectual. At death, said Thomas in opposition to Aristotle, the soul does not perish but leaves the body, which disintegrates and ceases all its functions. The soul finds it desirable to have a body, for although it has in itself the vegetative, sensory, and intellectual functions, it can exercise these only through a body. Even the powers of the intellect function and form their ideas in dependence upon sense experience, which of course requires a body. It is a *good* thing, therefore, to have a body, and in the union of soul and body the soul is made capable of acting fully according to its nature. At these points Thomas is quite opposed to forms of Platonism which hold that the soul is somehow imprisoned in the body and is better off free of it.

The nature of the soul of man is unique, said Thomas, for the soul can know all corporeal things and must therefore not itself be corporeal, since if it were itself some kind of body this fact would prevent it from knowing all other bodies. Also, if knowledge were achieved through a particular bodily organ, this organ would distort the knowledge made available through it by its nature. But this is not the case, for the intellect knows reality truly, not in distorted fashion. Further, the intellect obtains abstract knowledge of objects, which means that in the act of knowing them it removes them from their physical characteristics and knows them in their essential being (the nature of "treeness" instead of this physical maple tree). Finally, the intellect has a most remarkable ability called self-consciousness by which it is able to be aware of and examine its own self, an ability which a material being cannot possess. We must conclude in view of these characteristics that the soul is not itself a body, corporeal in nature, but is spiritual, in essence independent of the body and self-subsistent.[24] It has a life of its own and is not merely the reflection of a common form of man. Each soul is a spiritual entity with its own individual life.

The nature of the spiritual is such that it is not made up of parts and therefore cannot be destroyed, since destruction results from breaking up the parts of which a thing is made. Nothing from within itself or from without can make the soul cease to exist. It follows that it is by nature immortal. After the death of the body, the soul remains a substance with its act of being. A minor argument added by Thomas to his principal one was that since it is natural for the intellect to apprehend existence absolutely and for all time, it has a natural desire always to exist. Because this is part of its very nature, it cannot be mistaken, and the soul is immortal.

Thomas is careful to point out that because man's soul is created by God it is not immortal in the same sense as God is. Conceivably, since he made the soul, God could destroy it again, but because of his goodness this will not happen. In this way Thomas reminds men that they are always subordinate to God even though endowed with immortality.[25]

Thomas believes he has demonstrated the soul's immortality by philosophy. A further point, taken from faith rather than reason, is needed to complete his thought. Although the soul is in a sense complete and immortal, it does not carry in itself the *full* essence of man, which appears only in the union of soul and body. For this reason the fullness of man is not realized when his soul leaves his body but when, in the resurrection of the body, soul and body join once again. That there is a resurrection of the body (like the fact of the creation of the world) is not a matter that can be proved philosophically, hence belongs properly to the next topic, but to complete the discussion we need to mention it at this point. In the resurrection the body is transformed. It is made incorruptible and is spiritualized, sharing the soul's own perfection and having no further need for material goods. In this way, Thomas carries the natural into the supernatural, and finds that man's fullness is achieved beyond life in another kind of existence.

Supernatural Knowledge

With all his emphasis upon philosophy and the powers of reason, as a Christian theologian Thomas insisted that revelation is a higher source of

[24] H. D. Gardeil, *Introduction to the Philosophy of St. Thomas Aquinas,* tr. John A. Otto, St. Louis, B. Herder Book Co., 1956, III, 224 ff.

[25] *Ibid.*, pp. 227 f.

truth than reason. Man needs revelation, for without it he cannot know his supernatural end or how it is to be received. God's deepest nature and the ways in which he deals with men are not clear to reason itself. We have seen that Thomas accepted the doctrine of creation on faith alone and that the teaching of the resurrection of the body rested on revelation. Other important truths known only through revelation are the triune nature of God; the incarnation of Christ, the Son of God; man's original sin; the nature of the sacraments; redemption through Christ and his church; and rewards and punishments in the postmortal state. These are examples of the second body of knowledge which results "when divine truth exceeding human understanding descends to us by way of revelation, not as it were proved to sight but offered for belief."

The Sacraments. The Status of Universals

In his theory of the sacraments, Thomas used the Aristotelian principle of the union of matter and form to constitute reality. We recall that according to this scheme matter is the seat of potentiality (boards have the potentiality of becoming a chair, table, bench, etc.). Matter's capacity to become something can be made actual only when it is combined with a form proper to it. Neither form nor matter can exist in isolation, since form without matter would be empty and matter without form would be bare, unrealized possibility. This thought is now applied to the seven sacraments of the church. Each of these sacraments, Thomas held, consists of two principal elements: a material portion and a formula, a set of words, conveying the sacred usage to the material. When united in authorized fashion by a properly qualified administrant who intends to do what the church has appointed and a recipient not in a state of mortal sin and desirous of receiving the benefit of the sacrament, they constitute a true sacrament. If either of these elements is absent it is not a sacrament. Applying this principle to the eucharist, Thomas was enabled to explain the difficult doctrine of transubstantiation, that is, that the bread and the wine of the sacrament are actually changed into the flesh and blood of Christ. The bread and wine, natural substances, are the matter of the sacrament, which becomes the sacred substances of Christ's body and blood when informed by the priestly words of institution. When this is done, the entire substance (or underlying reality) of the bread is changed into the body of Christ and the substance of the wine into his blood. Nothing is left of bread and wine except their form or appearance. Why this is not also changed with the substance Thomas explained as follows:

> First, because it is not customary but horrible for men to eat the flesh of a man and drink his blood the flesh and blood of Christ are offered to us under the form of things which are more frequently used, namely bread and wine. Secondly, lest this sacrament might be ridiculed by unbelievers if we ate our Lord in his own form. Thirdly, that while we receive the body and blood of our Lord invisibly this may contribute to the merit of our faith.[26]

The Status of Universals

Thomas' work in philosophy inevitably brought him to the second great problem of the earlier Scholastics, namely, the status of Universals. For Thomas, this was a question as to how forms exist. Aristotle had held that forms exist only in sensible things. Aquinas was willing to accept the forms as being in objects of sense, but he refused to say that they are *only* in things. He added that forms also exist as ideas and archetypes in the mind of God (not, as in Plato, having independent existence or subsistence apart from God), and, in a third way, they exist as concepts in human thought which abstracts them from the particulars of experience. Thomas is to be classified as a moderate Realist on this problem, holding a position not far different from that of Abelard. As a synthesizer and harmonizer, he felt the forces motivating Realists, Nominalists, and Conceptualists alike and sought to give each due justice in his catholic solution. Santayana formulates the point admirably:

> This solution is that universal terms or natures exist before the particulars, *and* in the particulars, *and* after the particulars: for God, before he made the world, knew how he intended to make it, and had eternally in his mind the notions of a perfect man, horse, etc., after which the particulars were to be modelled, or to which, in case of accident, they were to be restored, either by the healing and recuperative force of nature, or by the ministrations of grace. But universal terms or natures existed also *in* the particulars, since the particulars illustrated them, shared in them and were what they were by virtue of that participation. Nevertheless, the universals existed also after the particulars: for the discursive mind of man, surveying the variety of natural things, could not help noticing and abstracting the common types that often recur in them; and this *ex post facto* idea, in the human mind, is a universal term also. To deny any of these three theories, and

[26] *Summa Theologica*, III, q. 75, art. 5, as quoted in McGiffert, *op. cit.*, p. 323.

not to see their consistency, is to miss the mediaeval point of view, which, in every sense of the word, was Catholic.[27]

Ethics and Social Philosophy

Thomas continued his synthesis of Aristotle and Christianity in the field of ethics also. He agreed with Aristotle that the goal or end of life is to find happiness, which for Aristotle is achieved in the contemplation of the highest objects and in particular of God, the Unmoved Mover. Thomas accepted this as far as it goes, but again added another dimension to it. This sort of contemplation, he taught, yields only imperfect happiness, such as might be found within a lifetime. The particular acts of man's life do not and cannot bring perfect happiness. Only as the universal, supreme, and infinite good is reached and known can such happiness be found. The greatest happiness of all, and the true goal of human life, is found in the vision of God. As God becomes its goal, life becomes fully and truly virtuous and good in every sense.

The virtues by which one lives best and ultimately most happily, are of two distinct kinds—the natural and the supernatural. The natural virtues are the familiar "cardinal virtues" of Greek antiquity: prudence or wisdom, justice, fortitude or courage, and temperance or self-control. They are within man's own power of achievement. Through them as a result of the exercise of his own strength and reason man may realize a genuine measure of happiness, even though it will be imperfect since God is not its goal. The higher degree of happiness is realized through the supernatural or theological virtues. They are supernatural because they are beyond the ability of natural man to reach by his own unaided efforts (who, for instance, is able to love God by making an effort of the will?), and they are theological because they have God as their object and are revealed and communicated by him as a result of his grace. There are three such virtues, as taught by St. Paul (I Corinthians 13): faith, hope, and charity or love. By the third of these, Thomas meant primarily love or friendship for God for his own sake and secondarily love of neighbor for God's sake. One is commanded also to love himself properly for the sake of God, which he does when he avoids all sin. Even enemies and sinners are to be loved, but not demons and animals. A degree of love is possible as the result of making an effort to love, but its fuller development

[27] George Santayana, *Three Philosophical Poets*, Cambridge, Harvard University Press, 1910, pp. 99 f.

depends upon God's grace being given, and this is something man cannot control.

These two forms of virtue do not stand in contradiction to each other, for just as revealed theology complements natural theology, so does theological virtue complement natural virtue. God's grace does not destroy our human nature, but strengthens and perfects it. It is clear from this treatment that a person having only the natural virtues or only the theological virtues (if that were possible) would not be fully virtuous. The virtuous Greek, for example, would lack the grace of God and therefore the faith, hope, and love which make life most significant. It is thinkable that one might have the theological virtues and lack the natural; in that situation he would lack rational control over his life. Complete and perfect virtue combines in human life the rational and God's works of grace.

Thomas also rewrote Christian social philosophy using Aristotelian principles as a foundation. Before this time, Augustine's distinction between the City of God and the City of Satan had been applied to the church and to the state and other strictly human institutions respectively. The conditions of this world were something to be saved *from;* therefore, the highest Christian ideal was the monastic life, withdrawn from all natural human relations. This dualism and actual opposition between church and state, earth and heaven, is opposed to the Aristotelian world view. Thomas, accepting the latter outlook at this point, finds in nature the *possibility* of the supernatural instead of opposition, and in human society the possibility of the kingdom of God. According to this understanding, society, like the natural order of which it is a part, is a system of ends and purposes in which the lower strives to become the higher. The ultimate goal, of course, transcends nature since the ultimate society is that of the redeemed in heaven, but orderly political life is a contributing cause to this ultimate goal. This contribution of Thomas' was a most significant one in terms of the church's attitude toward human life and society, although practically it was often forgotten in the espousal of otherworldliness.

Thomas' social theory contains a rationalization of the feudal society of his time, but his description of the ideal social organization follows that of Aristotle also. The fact is that Thomas appeared to believe that the social order of the thirteenth century was the more or less perfect embodiment of the Christian conception of society, and sought in his philosophy to justify that existing order. In his attempt to give a place to all its parts in a rational scheme, he found the Aristotelian social philosophy well adapted to his purpose. Accordingly, society is compared to an organism in which each of the many members contributes his part for the good of the whole. The farmer and the craftsman supply material goods; the priest supplies prayer and religious observance; and, even as God rules the world or the soul rules the body, so the civil ruler must govern and maintain the social order.

The power of the ruler is, according to this scheme, derived directly from God. This is not an expression of the somewhat later doctrine of the divine right of kings. For Thomas, the social and political order is divinely ordained just as is the church. Both are part of the providential order and each has its charter directly from God. Since the state must have a ruler, the latter derives his authority from the divine ordination of the social structure. This is the ground for both the independence of the civil ruler's authority from the church and the restrictions and limitations upon it by law and morals. Thus, in purely political affairs, the ruler, while independent of the church, is subject to human law which is itself divinely ordained; the ruler's authority, while derived from God, is part of the divinely instituted political order and subject to the demands of that order. The divinely granted authority of the ruler is therefore not a license to tyranny but a commission to just statesmanship.

As to the relations of church and state or pope and temporal ruler, Thomas took a moderate position. He accepted the traditional Gelasian doctrine of the division of jurisdiction between the spiritual and civil powers, and rejected the tendency to elevate the admitted supremacy of the spiritual power to legal supremacy. The fact that the church represented to him a higher form of organization than the state did not lead him to question the power and authority of the state in its own sphere. Nor did he emphasize any theoretical difficulty over the division of jurisdiction. Thomas, it should be remembered, regarded the actual situation as divinely ordained in its basic structure. He therefore did not set before himself the task of social reform but accepted his society by and large as he found it. However, it is significant that he held to the Gelasian doctrine of the relation of church and state in the very period when Popes Innocent III and Boniface VIII, who lived shortly before and after him, made their strongest claims to church control over the state.

The Disintegration of Scholasticism

The thirteenth was the greatest century of Roman Catholic culture. The flowering in Thomas and others of philosophic and theological thought was only a part of this greatness, for during the same century many other cultural achievements reached their highest expression. The greatest of the Gothic cathedrals were erected; the guilds of workmen organized in towns and cities poured out a wealth of remarkable sculpture in wood and stone; literature reached a new development, culminating in Dante Alighieri (1265-1321) and his *Divine Comedy*. Mystery and morality plays appeared in considerable numbers. Hospitals were founded and many great universities appeared, including Paris, Oxford, Cambridge, Bologna, and Toledo. A golden century it was, indeed; but the flowering of a golden age is always followed by disintegration, and to this rule the thirteenth century was no exception.

New movements and attitudes began to appear in this same century, carrying with them new ways of understanding and of looking at the nature and purposes of human life. Cities grew up, trade developed, and a host of new interests stirred into life. But in philosophy and theology themselves many factors existed which were bound to make the future of such a synthesis as that created by Thomas precarious. The Arab philosopher Averroës continued to draw the attention of Christian thinkers, who challenged Thomas and his interpretations of Aristotle. The teachings of these theologians were condemned by the church in 1277, but their influence continued to be felt so strongly that it is fair to say they were largely responsible for ending the "honeymoon" between philosophy and theology which Thomas had labored so hard to promote. The path which led away from his synthesis was a double one, seemingly going in opposite directions. One led toward the independent use of reason (the point emphasized by Averroës), including new respect for sense experience as a reliable mode of knowledge—with the corollary that observation is a fruitful method of procedure. Eventually reason and observation asserted themselves in new explorations and investigations, like those of Columbus, Tycho Brahe, and Galileo. The discoveries made by these and like men and the theories following from them entailed revolutionary consequences, particularly when several centuries later faith and theology were themselves questioned in the name of science and eventually of naturalism. The second direction taken away from Thomas' synthesis was a distrust in reason and its powers, leading to a return to the older views arising from Augustine and the Platonists, with emphasis upon mysticism and an inner approach to God. As a result of this trend, mysticism reached its highest development in Christian history during the century following Thomas, the fourteenth, with such great figures arising as Thomas à Kempis (*Imitation of Christ*), Meister Eckhart, Jan van Ruysbroeck, Johannes Tauler, Heinrich Suso, Gerhard Groote, and the unknown author of the *German Theology*.

Even within Thomas' system itself tensions existed between philosophy and religion which eventually became obvious. It is not possible to unite two such different approaches to truth as those of an ancient Greek philosopher and a medieval Christian theologian and forge them into an entirely harmonious system. Erecting Christian supernaturalism upon the base of Aristotelian naturalism was a remarkable attempt to relate the two to each other. But to accept Aristotle's system of philosophy, arrived at without benefit of revelation and entirely by the use of human reason, was dangerous to faith, even though Thomas insisted that reason is not autonomous but remains under the norm of theology. When the time came to deny the supremacy of theology, philosophy was able readily to assert its independence and could look to Thomas himself for its charter of greatness. It has been said by a modern Catholic philosopher,

> The acceptance of a great system of philosophy known to have been thought out without the aid of revelation was almost certain sooner or later to lead to philosophy going her own way independently of theology. . . . the synthesis achieved by St. Thomas was intrinsically precarious. . . . St. Thomas' baptism of philosophy in the person of Aristotle could not, historically speaking, arrest the development of philosophy, and in that sense his synthesis contained a latent tension.[28]

To illustrate the way in which reason and faith did move apart once again after Thomas, we will look very briefly at two great thinkers who complete the Scholastic period and at the same time begin to move into the new period of the Renaissance. *John Duns Scotus* (*ca.* 1264-1308), a follower of Thomas called the Subtle Doctor because of his critical mind, was not convinced that there is no real disagreement between philosophy and theology. He criticized some of Thomas' rational arguments, including his famous argument for the existence of God, and taught that there is much in theology which is philosophically improbable and much that Thomas thought he had demonstrated which Scotus thought not provable. For instance, Scotus thought that Thomas had failed in his attempts to prove philosophically the omnipotence, immensity, omnipresence, providence, justice, and mercy of God, and either Scotus himself or a follower added to this list his oneness and his preservation of the world.[29] This meant that much of Thomas' philosophy was rejected. To balance his philosophical criticism, Scotus placed great emphasis upon the authority of the church and the necessity to accept what it teaches on faith. In Scotus we see a marked beginning of the developing tendency to split the synthesis of Aquinas apart.

[28] Copleston, *op. cit.*, p. 430.
[29] Gilson, *Reason and Revelation in the Middle Ages*, pp. 85 f.

This tendency was carried much further by *William of Ockham* (died *ca.* 1349), who taught that only individuals exist and opposed all forms of Realism accordingly, even of the moderate sort held by Thomas. Universals have no objective reality, he maintained; they are only symbolic terms. Hence he is called a *Terminist*. It might be well to point out here that with Ockham the controversy over Universals came to the end of its creative discussion, even though it was not finally solved and still remains a pressing philosophic problem with us.

Ockham denied the possibility of any genuine philosophic knowledge of reality. Men, he said, do not know things in themselves, as they truly are, but know only their own ideas or concepts of things. Consequently, no theological doctrines can be proved by philosophy! At best they must be considered merely probable. However, they are to be accepted, not because proved or unproved, but on the authority of the church. Like Scotus and all the Schoolmen, we find no rebellion in Ockham against this authority. He did attack the pope, however, by saying that neither popes nor councils are basic authority for Christians, who must look only to the Scriptures and the church herself as interpreter of the Scriptures. Ockham took a step in the direction later taken by Protestantism under Luther at the point where Luther declared that the Scriptures are authoritative, but then Luther added that the Christian individual, not the church, interprets them.

The Nominalism of Ockham (for that is what his Terminism was) dominated the fourteenth century. It was called the modern way in contrast to the position of Thomas and Scotus, called now the ancient way. Philosophy and theology were entirely separated, and some thinkers again went to the extreme of holding a double theory of truth. Ockham's position allowed the freest possible inquiry in philosophy while claiming that complete authority lay in theology. As long as the authority of the church was not seriously questioned, this uneasy relation might continue, but when the time came for that authority itself to be questioned, skepticism toward theology was one of the consequences.

Scholasticism disappeared under a series of changes in the life of Europe. Its social philosophy ceased to be fully relevant with the breakdown of the Holy Roman Empire and the rise of nationalism; the medieval theory of spiritual supremacy gave way to the doctrine of the divine right of kings. With its emphasis upon salvation by faith alone, the Protestant Reformation held the sacramental system of the Catholic church to be superfluous, thus undercutting the doctrine of ecclesiastic authority in the sphere of religion. The interest of the Renaissance Humanists in the values of this world and in the individual who could enjoy them meant the repudiation of the emphasis on other-worldliness and asceticism in medieval ethics. Discoveries in astronomy and physics discredited certain scriptural teachings and raised science to a place of supreme interest, replacing theology in that position for many people.

In the next two chapters we shall undertake a brief survey of these movements, disruptive of medievalism and transitional to the modern world.

Questions for Study

1. What happened to education and philosophic thought during the Middle Ages?
2. What was the dominant slant of thought in the Western church from Augustine until the thirteenth century? What ideas were prominent in this period? What new emphasis did the Scholastics bring into the twelfth and thirteenth centuries?
3. What was the method of Scholasticism? What place did Aristotle hold within it?
4. Precisely why was there a problem for medieval Christians of faith and reason, and what was its nature? On the question of faith and reason, what views were held by Tertullian, Augustine, and Anselm on the one hand and by Johannes Scotus Erigena and Abelard on the other hand?
5. Explain what is meant by Universals and why there was a "debate" over them. What issue of great concern to the church was at stake in this debate? What are the views on this problem called extreme Realism, Nominalism, and Conceptualism? Which of these would you prefer to defend, and why?
6. What is Anselm's ontological argument for the existence of God? Explain why it is said that this argument is based on Anselm's realism.
7. Why did the church at first oppose the thought of Aristotle? Be specific. What place did Arab scholars hold in transmitting this thought to Europe? How did the church deal with Aristotle's science so as to make him an ally of the church?
8. Contrast the life of Thomas Aquinas with that of Augustine. What are Thomas' greatest works, and of what do they treat? What is meant by saying that he synthesized the thought of Aristotle with Christian thought?
9. How did Thomas deal with the question of the relation of faith and reason? How does each serve the other? What is the third and highest form of knowledge, and when may it be reached?
10. Outline Thomas' cosmological argument for the existence of God, including the terms *dependent, contingent*, and *sufficient explanation.* What is the nature of the First Cause? Why did Thomas consider this an inductive argument?
11. How did Thomas argue for personal immortality? Why did he believe that the soul needs a body?

12. What truths come from revelation alone?
13. How did Thomas understand the nature of the sacraments? How did he deal with the problem of the universals?
14. How did Thomas deal with the relation of the natural and the supernatural virtues, and what are these, respectively? How did his social teachings turn away from Augustine and include something of Aristotle?
15. What factors—political, economic, and theoretical—contributed to the disintegration of Scholasticism?

Selected Readings

Cannon, William R., *History of Christianity in the Middle Ages*, New York, Abingdon Press, 1960.

Carré, Meyrick H., *Realists and Nominalists*, London, Oxford University Press, 1950.

Copleston, Frederick, *A History of Philosophy*, Westminster, The Newman Press, 1952, vol. II.

D'Arcy, M. C., *St. Thomas Aquinas*, Dublin, Clonmore & Reynolds, Ltd., 1953.

de Wulf, Maurice, *History of Medieval Philosophy*, 3rd ed., London, Longmans, Green & Co., 1935, vol. I.

Fuller, B. A. G., *A History of Ancient and Medieval Philosophy*, New York, Henry Holt & Co., 1938.

Gardeil, H. D., *Introduction to the Philosophy of St. Thomas Aquinas*, tr. John A. Otto, St. Louis, B. Herder Book Co., 1956, 4 vols.

Gilson, Étienne, *History of Christian Philosophy in the Middle Ages*, New York, Random House, Inc., 1955.

Gilson, Étienne, *The Philosophy of Thomas Aquinas*, 2nd rev. ed., St. Louis, B. Herder Book Co., 1941.

Gilson, Étienne, *Reason and Revelation in the Middle Ages*, New York, Charles Scribner's Sons, 1938.

Gilson, Étienne, *The Spirit of Mediaeval Philosophy*, New York, Charles Scribner's Sons, 1936.

McGiffert, A. C., *A History of Christian Thought*, New York, Charles Scribner's Sons, 1933, vol. II.

Pegis, Anton C. (ed.), *Basic Writings of Saint Thomas Aquinas*, New York, Random House, Inc., 1945, 2 vols.

VI. Mind and Spirit in Transition from the Medieval to the Modern World

CHRONOLOGICAL FRAMEWORK OF PART VI

1300/1350-1600/1650	The Renaissance.
1309-1377	"Babylonian Captivity" in Avignon.
1378-1417	Church schism.
Before 1450	Printing invented.
1545-1563	Council of Trent.

RENAISSANCE HUMANISTS AND SCIENTISTS

Roger Bacon, *ca.* 1214-1294.

Petrarch, 1304-1374.

François Rabelais, 1494-1553.

Desiderius Erasmus, 1466-1536.

Nicolaus Copernicus, 1473-1543.

Tycho Brahe, 1546-1601.

Johannes Kepler, 1571-1630.

Galileo Galilei, 1564-1642.

René Descartes, 1596-1650.

REFORMATION AND PRE-REFORMATION FIGURES

Meister Eckhart, 1260-1327.

Johannes Tauler, *ca.* 1300-1361.

John Wycliffe, *ca.* 1328-1384.

John Huss, *ca.* 1373-1415.

Martin Luther, 1483-1546.

Huldreich Zwingli, 1484-1531.

John Calvin, 1509-1564.

Henry VIII of England, rules 1509-1547. Act of Supremacy, 1534.

Menno Simons, 1492-1559.

Fausto Sozzini (Socinus), 1539-1604.

Jacobus Arminius, 1560-1609.

Ignatius of Loyola, founder of the Jesuits, 1491-1556.

15. Emancipation from Other-Worldliness and Authority

The Nature of the Renaissance

To the period of European history which followed directly after the high Middle Ages is given the name of the *Renaissance*. This word, meaning re-birth, refers to the surge of new interest in the spirit of classical antiquity and especially in the ancient Greek and Latin classics which characterized the first phase of the period. Before reaching its conclusion, the Renaissance led European thought away from many of the attitudes considered fundamental during the Middle Ages, particularly other-worldliness and authority. Like all great historic periods, it was composed of many aspects—philosophical, religious, cultural, political, and economic. Its roots extended back into the Middle Ages; its influence continues in our modern world. Unlike a specific historic event, such as Columbus' discovery of the new world, it cannot be given precise dates. Certain figures like Petrarch and Boccaccio are Renaissance rather than medieval men, while other later luminaries like Locke, Berkeley, and Hume just as definitely belong to a still later period. Generally speaking, and with some reservations, it may be said that the Renaissance started in Italy in the early or middle fourteenth century, came into full development there by the middle of the succeeding century, and by the beginning or middle of the seventeenth century was largely at its ebb. From this standpoint, its life was about three centuries, with overlappings at both ends. Such men as Newton, Descartes, Leibniz, and Spinoza are sometimes included within the Renaissance and at other times are treated as the originators of the modern period. The problem of classifying them illustrates how difficult it is to date the period with precision.

The Renaissance was a transitional period. It saw many noteworthy achievements in architecture, literature, and the arts which are so magnificently memorialized in the city of Florence, but basically it was a bridge between the Middle Ages and our own times. Its great figures all considered themselves Christians, no matter what their theories in science and philosophy, expressing their faith in the fundamental Christian teachings and, prior to the Reformation, in the religious authority of the Catholic church. Yet at the same time that its religious foundations were grounded in the Middle Ages, the Renaissance contained elements of philosophic, political, and scientific thought that engendered the development of the world of the eighteenth century and later. It represents a slow process of turning away from medieval attitudes to a new reliance on reason and science.

The Renaissance was transitional also in that it moved toward both the past and the future. In its cultural, humanistic phase it turned back 11 and more centuries to the ancient classics for inspiration; in its religious aspect, especially in the Protestant Reformation, it returned to the Scriptures of original Christianity. As the prophets of the eighth century B.C. sought their roots in Moses and early Hebrew history and thereby justified a new ethical movement in the Hebrew religion, so by turning back to antiquity did the Renaissance thinkers develop what became a new cultural pattern.

As a vivid illustration of the transitional nature of the period we can take the work of the famous Italian poet *Petrarch* (1304-1374), who, as he climbed Mt. Ventoux near Avignon in southern France, carried with him a copy of St. Augustine's *Confessions* to read at the top. He took great delight in the marvelous scenery that lay spread before him from the peak, and then as he opened the book his eye fell upon this passage: "And men go to admire the high mountains, the vast floods of the sea, the huge streams of the rivers, . . . and desert themselves." He closed the book, "angry with myself that I still admired earthly things," and as he descended the mountain he saw no more the beauties of nature but, he wrote, "turned my inner eye toward myself."[1] To ascend a mountain for the enjoyment of the panoramic landscape showed a modern regard for nature as something valuable, to be appreciated by man, but to let this enjoyment be overshadowed by the thought of the soul and its search for God and self marks Petrarch as still a medieval man.

[1] Quoted in Ernst Cassirer, Paul O. Kristeller, and John Herman Randall, Jr. (eds.), *The Renaissance Philosophy of Man*, Chicago, University of Chicago Press, 1948, p. 44.

During this period human curiosity concerning the world in which man lived broke out explosively after a thousand years of relative quiescence. The secular spirit came to a position of dominance, even among church leaders and at times in the popes themselves. Individualism developed, for now for the first time in a millennium it was possible to find new ways of making a living and to move about with a large degree of freedom, not entirely restricted by guild membership and rank in a feudal system. A tremendous urge grew among men to let human nature express itself in every way, whether it led them into forms of cruelty and criminality or raised them to the heights of human creativity. The fifteenth and sixteenth centuries, for example, were marked by both great criminals and most remarkable artists. They produced a Lorenzo the Magnificent on the one hand and a savage and unprincipled murderer like Cesare Borgia, illegitimate son of Pope Alexander VI, on the other. Some of the greatest Western artists appeared during this same period—men like Leonardo da Vinci, Raphael, Michelangelo, Ghiberti, and Donatello. It was a time of great violence, passion, and excitement, with assassination, torture, witchcraft, bribery, war, and disease on every hand.

Originating Forces of the Renaissance

The Renaissance did not burst unannounced upon the Western world but represented rather the slow maturing of forces that had existed for centuries. Among these forces may be mentioned the Crusades, which brought Europeans into contact with Moslem culture. Before the Crusades, Christian theologians could readily claim ultimacy for their ideas since no competitor to them existed. But as Arabs with their superior culture were encountered, this provincialism began to disappear. It was replaced by a wider viewpoint and a willingness to broaden intellectual interests. The revival of learning in the eleventh and twelfth centuries, which culminated in Thomas Aquinas, was in itself a kind of renaissance of Christian knowledge and thought, although quite different from the one we are now considering. Yet by gaining knowledge of Aristotle and Moslem science and by developing an interest in ancient texts it left seeds which later came to flower in Humanism and modern science.

Chief among the external causes of the Renaissance was the growth of cities and their increasing prosperity. Trade and commerce brought a concentration of material riches, opening up the possibility of luxury to an expanding merchant class. An economy of goods based on barter was gradually replaced by a money economy, and money can be stored, placed at interest, and used in many ways that goods cannot. The discovery of Amer-

The Crusader Castle of Krak des Chevaliers

For 150 years, until 1271, the Christians held this vast castle, large enough to hold 2000 men, in the heart of the Moslem lands in western Syria.

ica and India opened up vast areas for exploration and trade. The feudal system and the guilds began to break down as men became more independent and able to exercise greater freedom of movement. Manors lost their importance as the cities became centers for industry and trade, and eventually many of the nobility moved into them. Comforts in living began to appear in the luxurious city houses, frequently quite in contrast to the harshness of life in the fortress castles. In Italy the cities early achieved independence from both pope and emperor, eventually becoming kingdoms or states in their own right. Economically and politically life in the cities was vigorous and dynamic, and the growth of urban centers effected a profound transformation in the character of European civilization.

New nationalistic sentiments began to appear with these other changes. It is difficult for us today to realize that the sense of country we call patriotism did not always exist and that it emerged during a particular period in Western history. It is interesting to speculate on the influences that created nationalism. People always have a sentimental attachment for the spot in the world they call home. They usually share this with members of their own family, tribe, or race, with whom economic prosperity and security against attack are a common concern. Living together in the same geographic setting, with rivers and mountains as natural boundaries, members of the same family or race, speaking a common language and having common economic and military interests, accumulate a set of memories of the past and a traditional pattern to govern the conduct of life in the present. Geography, language, economic and military interests, common memories and traditions —these are the ingredients of national sentiment.

In the Middle Ages, the centers of loyalty were small and numerous. Each feudal manor and each town was itself the object of fidelity. Concentrating for a moment on the influences that transformed this local sentiment into national patriotism, we may list several factors. First, the Crusades brought men from all parts of Europe together and made them conscious of group similarities as well as differences. Wars, transcending the limits of feudal struggles between one baron and another, also united men from diverse groups, amalgamating custom and tradition into more inclusive units. Exhausted by long civil wars between feudal powers, the common people were ready to turn to the centralized power of a king for peace and order. Second, the invention of printing sometime before 1450 made it possible to distribute books widely, which tended at once to remove the medieval differences between the dialects of a given language in different towns and to make the language more permanent and stable than a merely spoken tongue can be. Once put into printed form, the common languages replaced Latin as the means of communication between manor and manor and between town and town. While Latin had been the language of the learned, the common people now had a means of communication that was uniform over areas wider than feudal divisions, though it was less universal than the language of the church.

Coupled with the rise of patriotic sentiment were other factors making for nationalism and its consequent disruptive effect on the medieval hegemony of the church. Chief among these was the growth of commerce. The guild organization of manufacture and trade proved inadequate and gradually gave way to other systems. Banks and bankers, prepared to extend credit, appeared in the towns. Great commercial companies used their cash and credit in promoting far-flung enterprises that involved risk and the prospect of large profit. Since towns proved too small as units of commerce, it was seen that trade must be at least national in scope to satisfy the new capitalism.

The disorders of feudal strife and Catholic restrictions on the taking of interest and profiteering interfered with business. Quite naturally, then, the merchant class turned to the kings to police the barons and restrain the church. The economic support which the commercial class could give the kings, chiefly through taxes, enabled the latter to cut loose from feudal levies and to establish strong professional armies. It was thus possible to consolidate the national domain and to establish the "king's peace." "If the consequence of this was an increase in royal power," says Preserved Smith, "the kings were among those who had greatness thrust upon them, rather than achieving it for themselves. They were but the symbols of the new, proudly conscious nation, and the police commissioners of the large bankers and traders."[2]

In the rising of the Renaissance spirit religious and political factors also appeared which played a highly important part in making the period possible. During the very century in which the Renaissance began, the power of both emperor and pope were at their lowest, leaving a power vacuum into which the national kings and the princes of the city-states could step. We recall that the Holy Roman Empire began with the crowning of Charlemagne in 800. In the fourteenth century the ruling emperors were able to exercise very little real power, particularly in Italy. As for the popes, a series of very severe misadventures brought their power to its nadir. Just how this happened is worth our brief examination.

We recall that in the problem of the relation of the church to the state the greatest claim to the church's power was made by Boniface VIII, who in his bull *Unam Sanctum*, issued in 1302, claimed that the political "sword" is to be used under the command of and for the church. Boniface died the following year, largely as a result of his violent conflict with Philip IV of France, who refused to bow to him. His successor, Benedict XI, was forced to leave Rome, and the next pope, Clement V, a Frenchman, moved the seat of the papacy to Avignon on the Rhone River, where it remained for 68 years. The period from 1309 until 1377 is called the Babylonian Captivity of the papacy. Precisely speaking, it was in no sense a captivity, for the popes remained in Avignon partly because of the comfortable, worldly life in the papal court there and partly to escape the turbulent and dangerous life of Rome. The people of Europe were bitterly critical of the popes for having deserted Rome, the city of the martyrs, and also for the worldly and often immoral lives they and members of their court displayed in Avignon. The Holy See stood in danger of losing all its prestige, but matters became still worse. In 1378, as a result of the attempt to return the papacy to Rome, two

[2] Preserved Smith, *The Age of the Reformation,* New York, Henry Holt & Co., 1920, pp. 5 f.

popes appeared, each claiming to be the vicar of Christ, one in Rome and one in Avignon. This schism in the papacy continued until 1417, shortly after a church council held in Constance finally settled the issue and a single pope reigned again from Rome.

All this long and unsavory difficulty at the very heart of the church was important for the Renaissance because it left the papacy weakest and most open to criticism at the very time, 1309 until 1417, that the Renaissance was coming into full flower. Developments that might well have been checked under stronger popes were able to continue under these circumstances.

Philosophically, movements of thought prominent in previous centuries continued into the Renaissance period. No one thinker was more influential than William of Ockham, both philosophically and scientifically, with his individualism and Nominalism. Scholasticism in the fourteenth century was much criticized on the charge that its method of dialectic was barren and worthless. Yet by the sixteenth century it was making a very strong comeback. Aristotle's thought continued to be influential in both its philosophic concepts and its scientific content, the latter acting as a brake upon the development of scientific investigation and new discovery. Plato's influence, through Neo-Platonism and Augustine, continued to be very strong. The thought of the Arab Averroës exerted great stimulation both in religion, where it was considered heretical, and in science.

It remains to state that the rebirth of interest in the classical period and its writings did not cross the Alps into Central and Northern Europe for a century after it arrived in Italy. When it did filter into the North, however, it found a less volatile and more sober spirit than among the Italians. Many of those most strongly affected by it chose to give more attention to the Christian Scriptures than to the pagan classical writings, with the result that among them the Renaissance took the form of a new and deepened concern for vital religion rather than the sensuality and disorder that Italy experienced. Its most prominent result was, of course, the Protestant Reformation.

Three principal movements of thought within the Renaissance demand our special consideration. These are Humanism, with which the period began, the rise of science, and the Protestant Reformation. The third will be reserved for a special chapter; the first two will now be examined.

Humanism

Humanism was the opening phase of the Renaissance in Italy. The word itself has many different meanings, but in this context it refers to the state of mind of men who have achieved genuine humanity through the development provided by cultural studies like literature and philosophy. It carries with it a certain depreciation of the thought of the Middle Ages and a great emphasis upon those aspects of antiquity neglected by the church. Scholars and literary men like Petrarch and Boccaccio who cultivated a knowledge of the classics were called Humanists. At its heart, then, was zeal for the pagan classics—for Cicero, especially, and Lucretius, Homer, and Plato. Yet this enthusiasm was itself the reflection of a new spirit that was abroad, for many of the classics had always been in the libraries of Europe but had been largely unread. A new interest arose in the kind of *ideas* set forth by classical authors which brought men to read the works themselves and led to an avid search for these books. The Humanists examined libraries, rejoiced when they found a previously unknown work of one of the classical writers, and made these available to others through the use of the new printing presses. The new learning that resulted was aided greatly by Greeks and a flood of Greek manuscripts brought to the Italian universities from the city of Constantinople when it fell in 1453. A Platonic academy was set up by the Medici family in Florence. Lectures were given on Greek literature, and the language itself was widely studied.

The primary interest of the Humanists was man—the enjoyment and expansion of his life, the best forms of political organization, and knowledge of the world about him as that knowledge directly enriched his life. Pagan literature provided much material for the break with the spirit of medievalism. In it Humanists found more than simply freedom from authority, which often became license; they found also much wise counsel for the exercise of that freedom.

The natural appetites and passions were regarded by classical writers as the material from which man as a rational animal could fashion a good life. The conduct of life was regarded as an art, and its successful ordering according to temperance and moderation constituted true virtue. The ideal of excellence was the harmonious and complete functioning of the natural man in a rich world. How different from the medieval ideal of asceticism and obedience! Although ardent spirits forgot the principle of moderation in their new-found freedom to taste the joys of life and nature and burned their candle at both ends, many others remembered it and were able to show that freedom does not mean baseness and violence. While intoxication with the possibilities and delights of a free life brought forth the brutality of a Cesare Borgia and the sensuality of a Benvenuto Cellini, the spirit of Humanism produced also the magnificence of a Leonardo da Vinci and a Michelangelo, examples of what genius may become when freedom is subjected to rational control. If the characters of Leonardo and Michelangelo fulfill the humanistic ideal, they also dramatize its sharp divergence from the monastic and ascetic pattern idealized by medieval Christianity and enforced by the fear of hell and the hope of heaven.

In glorifying the possibilities of this life, Humanism was in effect a revolution against medieval Christian ethics, repudiating both the monastic ideals of poverty, chastity, and obedience and the religious reasons for being virtuous. Christian ethics appealed to supernatural sanctions for a life of virtue, but Humanists insisted that morality should be divorced from the expectation of punishments and rewards. "The reward of virtue is virtue itself, while the punishment of the vicious is vice," declared Pietro Pomponazzi (1462-1525). This is the sentiment of Plato's *Republic* rather than of St. Paul's epistles. The rebellion against the medieval ideal, as well as against the churchmen who failed to live up to it, was carried on in vigorous fashion by the Frenchman *François Rabelais* (1494-1553). His *Pantagruel* and his *Gargantua* give riotous expression to his delight in the full range of human animality and his scorn for the hypocrisy, vice, and intolerance of the clergy. By means of lewd and obscene stories he pillories monks and nuns, their ideals as well as their vices.

Perhaps the greatest of the Humanists was *Desiderius Erasmus* (1466-1536). Born in Holland, he became virtually a citizen of the world, equally at home in Florence, Cambridge, and Basle. His reputation was so great that John Colet, the great English Humanist, on hearing him converse, was prompted to say, "You are either Erasmus or the devil." Keenly aware of the abuses within the church, he sought to reform it from within. His *In Praise of Folly* heaped satiric ridicule on church dignitaries in the hope of instructing and improving them. In the *Enchiridion*, he denounced religious rites and ceremonies as worthless apart from inward spiritual qualities. He believed that through education, attacks on religious abuses, and a return to the original sources of Christianity, the church would be restored to purity. Although he lived at the time of the Protestant Reformation, he did not give up his allegiance to the Catholic church, in spite of the ways in which he attacked it. He was also a positive influence in Christianity, producing with the help of others the first Greek text of the New Testament and a series of translations of the Fathers. As much opposed to the excesses of a pleasure-bent life as to the evils of ecclesiasticism, Erasmus conceived his mission as that of Christianizing the Renaissance and humanizing Christianity. The result was a religion of simple morality, a universal ethical theism, more philosophical than religious in nature, which included the Greek philosophers along with the Christian gospel in his "philosophy of Christ."

Central to the Humanist movement was a new emphasis on the individual, characteristic of the entire Renaissance as we have seen. In the medieval world neither the social structure nor the church left much room for genuine individual expression. Society demanded that each person take the place provided for him in its structure, whether serf, vassal, or noble, each with the duties of his station. The church in the course of its long development had evolved a structure which allowed for a degree of individual initiative, but it closely circumscribed the area of acceptable activity. The hierarchy of the church was paralleled by that of feudal society. Men in medieval society were accordingly doubly assigned to their stations in life, by society and by the church, and were bound by fidelity and perfect obedience to their superiors. Against this kind of formalized life individualism rebelled.

As individualism came to the fore it expressed itself in every direction—in investigation of man's world, in the development of observation and thought, and in delighted self-expression in literature, art, and religion. Men began to emphasize their own idiosyncrasies in dress, so that the time came in the city of Florence, for instance, when there was no prevailing fashion in clothes for men and brilliant and novel "creations" were the order of the day. In literature, Petrarch, sometimes called the first modern man, was ready to declare that the highest conditions of culture could be realized only by the free development and interaction of intellects. Art, sculpture, and painting departed from the stereotyped artistic forms of the Middle Ages and became mediums for individual expression, each artist stamping his own personality upon his work to give it a character of its own. Curiosity drove men to exploration and discovery, sent Columbus across the Atlantic and Galileo to focus his telescope upon the moons of Jupiter. Even in religion, men began to appeal to their own reason and conscience against the dictates of the church, thus claiming the right of private judgment and inaugurating reforms. In almost every area of human interest, the individual burst his bonds, asserted himself, and sought in his own way to realize his possibilities. The achievements of the Renaissance, more than of most periods, were the products of unfettered individuality seeking to taste and express fully what it means to be human.

Let us endeavor now to assess Humanism as a bridge between medievalism and modernity. In the first place, the contribution of the Humanists to the future was not all positive. In its attitude toward science, Humanism was actually harmful, delaying the development of scientific knowledge considerably by its opposition. It aided science indirectly, however, because in its search for ancient manuscripts it brought to light early scientific documents of great importance. Yet Humanism sought to discredit science, although some Humanists, Leonardo da Vinci for one, were exceptions. The hostility sprang from the belief that scientific interests turned men's attention away from the human problems of morality and ethics. In those days when science was only laying its foundations it appeared to have very little direct significance for the improvement of human life; it seemed rather to be a dilettante concern for matters that had little real significance, like the movement of stars and descriptions of animals. It was against this sort of science that Petrarch was declaiming when he wrote, "Even if all these things were true, they help in no way toward a happy life, for what does it advantage us to be familiar with the nature of animals, birds, fishes, and reptiles, while we are ignorant of the nature of the race of man to which we belong, and do not know or care whence we come or whither we go?"[3] Even Erasmus, with his great interest in ethics and morality, actively opposed the science of his day.

Another unfortunate legacy from Humanism, one quite surprising to us, arose from the nature of the Humanist movement itself. As it turned its attention to the past and its classics, its scholars were forced to master the tools of research: criticism of texts and rules of grammar. The time came when the tools of scholarship were studied not for what could be done with them but for their own sake. People began to study Latin or Greek as languages, with little appreciation for or understanding of the classical thought that the use of these tools was intended to convey. This classical pedantry came finally to dominate the curriculum of secondary schools and universities to the neglect of other matters. The very names of secondary schools founded even in America during the age of the Renaissance reveal its educational preoccupation—witness the Boston *Latin* School (1635) and the Hopkins *Grammar* School (1666) in New Haven.

Indeed, it is just to say that Humanism, starting as a revolt against Christian Scholasticism, substituted for the latter not modern intellectual independence but a different kind of scholasticism. Like medieval Christianity, it was rooted in a literature of other times and other peoples. While the Christians found an authoritative philosophy of life in the Old and New Testaments, the Humanists sought their guidance for life in the literature of Greece and Rome. In their revolt against the monastic and ascetic ethics of medieval Christianity, the Humanists foreshadowed and laid the foundations for modern humanitarianism, but, being concerned with the best of the past, they were not oriented to the oncoming future.

The individualism which animated Humanism produced much that has found a place in the modern outlook and promised much more than it actually produced. Modern theories of education reflect the Humanist

[3] Petrarch, *Opera* (1581 ed.), 1038, quoted in John Herman Randall, Jr., *The Making of the Modern Mind*, rev. ed., Boston, Houghton Mifflin Co., 1940, p. 213.

emphasis on the worth of the individual, while the Humanists' confidence in reason and private judgment has been preserved in liberalism in religion as well as in politics. It is probably not too much to say that the principles of democracy have their root in Humanist ideals.

The Rise of Science

The second main aspect of the Renaissance was the rise and development of physical science, primarily in the sixteenth and seventeenth centuries. In the direction of their interests Humanism and science are both similar and different: similar in that both are in revolt against asceticism and other-worldliness, different in that the interest of Humanism is directed toward self-expression and enjoyment while that of science is directed toward understanding and control. The former represents the spirit of the artist, and the latter the combined interests of the metaphysician and the engineer. One is interested in individual man, the other in his world.

The revolutionary character of science is shown by its bearing on the old issue of reason against revelation, only now in a stronger form than during the Middle Ages. Reason as it appeared in science was completely disconnected from revelation, which it never was in the earlier centuries. While medievalism, with its interest in the supernatural, assigned the supreme position to revelation, the founders of science gave first place to reason and experience. The goal of medieval knowledge was God and his control of human life, but that of science was the understanding of natural causes and the control of nature to serve human ends. We may speak of modern science as having its beginning in the sixteenth and seventeenth centuries if we remember that this beginning was not without roots. We have already noted in the previous chapter how the complete works of Aristotle, introduced to the Western world in the eleventh and twelfth centuries, might have meant the beginning of a scientific movement in the modern sense. Aristotle's trust in observation and his insistence that theory must have a logical basis in experienced fact contained the seeds of naturalism and a revolt against theological authority. It was the unfortunate fate of Aristotelian science that the church adopted its conclusions as a body of scientific dogma and repudiated its method.

Although Aristotle was thus fairly well removed from exercising any vital influence upon medieval scientific thought, the same Arabs through whom the West came to learn about him did make a considerable contribution. During the centuries that Western thought was occupied fully with theology, the Arab universities had kept the torch of secular learning, particularly mathematics and science, burning brightly. In the thirteenth century the West adopted Arabic numerals to replace the clumsy Roman numerals used until that time.[4] Algebra (an Arabic word), trigonometry, and astronomy had all been well developed by the Arabs, along with advanced astronomical instruments for making observations and computations.

The first European to stand out as a forerunner of modern science, providing many ideas which were later developed into highly significant contributions, was the Franciscan friar *Roger Bacon* (*ca.* 1214-1294). He and his associates were Augustinians rather than Aristotelians, a fact that finds its significance in their not believing that Aristotle had all the solutions to the problems of nature and in their thinking with Augustine (but not with Aristotle) that God may work freshly in his universe and consequently that original occurrences might take place.[5] Bacon seems to us today to be a man born centuries before his time (in the century of Thomas Aquinas) who suffered for his error in timing by spending 14 years in prison. As a Franciscan friar, he shared the chief medieval convictions: the truth of Scripture, the absolute validity of revealed religion, and the divine sanction of its dogmatic formulations. Concerned with the study of nature, he yet believed that the purpose of science was to serve theology, for, said he, the more one learns about God's activity (in nature) the better able he is to serve God. He stood opposed, however, to those who proceed on blind faith and custom, relying on hearsay and untested authority in intellectual matters. He held that "the example of frail and unworthy authority, long-established custom, the sense of the ignorant crowd, and the hiding of one's own ignorance under the show of wisdom" are the four great stumbling blocks to comprehending truth. The three worst arguments, accordingly, are, "This was the way of our ancestors, this is the custom, this is the common view."[6] These points may seem harmless enough in our day, but in his they were considered highly suspect.

He condemned pretentious systems spun out of deductive logic without content of experienced fact. He considered Scholasticism (which was opposed by many Franciscans) such a system, and charged St. Thomas with having manufactured his theology out of dialectic, that is to say, by mere argumentation. Against such proceedings he advocated another method, namely,

[4] Imagine the difficulty of multiplying MDCCCLIX times itself in Roman numerals as compared with squaring 1859!

[5] William R. Cannon, *History of Christianity in the Middle Ages,* New York, Abingdon Press, 1960, pp. 261 f.

[6] Roger Bacon, *Opus Tertium,* quoted in Henry Osborne Taylor, *The Mediaeval Mind,* 3rd ed., New York, The Macmillan Company, 1919, II, 524.

the method of experience. This most perfect of all approaches to truth he called experimental science, which he said "neglects arguments, since they do not make certain, however strong they may be, unless at the same time there is present the *experientia* of the conclusion. Experimental science teaches *experiri*, that is, to test by observation or experiment the lofty conclusions of all sciences."[7] Mathematics was the chief key for investigating all matters of scientific knowledge, and experiment took the place that logic held for the Scholastics and Aristotle.

In his appeal to experience and his principle of deriving knowledge by generalization from many experienced instances (induction), Bacon sounded a modern note. The method of induction was to have a large place in modern science, and the reference to experience was to become one pole of scientific method. But induction and observation alone do not constitute the method by which some of the most spectacular advances of science have been made. Nature, after all, is reticent about her secrets. Like a cooperative witness in court, she answers only yes or no to proper questions addressed to her. The questions which the scientist must ask, the *hypotheses* which he must subject to proof, are themselves rarely derived from observation. They flow rather from antecedent theory in the scientist's mind, suggested either by some prior writer or by some general theory of things, that is, a metaphysics, held by the scientist. The truth of this view is dramatically illustrated by both aspects of modern scientific development which we shall here consider. The first is the change in astronomy known as the Copernican revolution; the second is the creation of a new physics by Galileo Galilei, known as the Cartesian revolution.

The Copernican Revolution

We have already noted that the Humanist revival of Latin and Greek literature produced as a by-product the rediscovery of classical science through the ancient scientific documents uncovered. Scholars here and there made the acquaintance of Alexandrian physics and mathematics. Moreover, in their revolt against the Aristotle of the Scholastics, the Humanists turned avidly to Plato for intellectual ammunition. The Neo-Platonic writings eagerly studied were full of the Pythagorean faith that the truth about reality is somehow wrapped up in numbers. Both of these factors, the acquaintance with Hellenistic science and the revival of Platonism, had tremendous effect. The knowledge of particular Alexandrian scientific writings provided specific

[7] *Ibid.*, p. 532.

suggestions for hypotheses; thus Copernicus was helped to his momentous discovery not by observing the stars—he made few observations and added very little to the known facts—but by reading Cicero, who reported an ancient theory that the earth turns upon its axis daily. The notion that the earth not only rotates but also revolves around the sun he derived from Aristarchus (third century B.C.). On the other hand, the Platonic faith that the secrets of the world were to be discovered by tracing out the mathematical relations among observed facts gave to the founders of modern science their fundamental assumption: that the key to the interpretation of nature is mathematics.

Indeed, Copernicus did not have to go to classical science for the faith that the world is an orderly system. This faith had been shared by the Scholastics who, in following Aristotle, had held that the order of nature was essentially teleological, dominated by final causes. Things were what they were and did what they did in fulfillment of a cosmic purpose that permeated everything. In Christian terms, nature was regarded as the scene of a divine drama whose every act and event expressed the purpose of God. From this point of view, the key to the interpretation of nature is theology. Plato and the Renaissance Platonists, however, held that mathematics was the dominant science. Had not Plato placed above the entrance to his Academy the words, "Let no one ignorant of geometry enter here"? His theory of Ideas is an elaboration of the doctrine that number, quantity, and mathematically fixed relations and proportions lie at the base of reality. Thus it was that the rediscovery of Plato gave form to the scientific revolt against medievalism. Influenced by Platonism, Copernicus' faith that the world is orderly was formulated in the conviction that this order is mathematical. If this is the case, then theology must give way to mathematics as the key which will unlock the mysteries of nature.

Part of the Platonic philosophy of nature was to regard astronomy as the geometry of the heavens, a branch of mathematical science. Geometry is the science of space relations in which the starting point of reference is of no consequence so long as the relations—for instance, the size of angles and the length of lines—remain constant. Thus, in surveying, which is a form of applied geometry, it does not matter at which part of a plot of land one begins, whether at the northeast corner or at the southwest, so long as one observes the field notes carefully. Astronomy has always been concerned with the survey of the heavens—an attempt to set down the field notes of the positions and motions of the heavenly bodies with reference to each other and to the earth. The point of observation being the earth, it was only natural that in the growth of astronomy the earth should be taken as the stationary, fixed point with reference to which the positions and motions of the stars and planets were measured.

This assumption, called the geocentric theory of the universe, was the basis of the entire medieval system of astronomy which bears the name of *Ptolemy*, who developed it in its basic outlines in the second century A.D. It was an elaboration of the early Greek theory that around the earth as a center a number of transparent spheres move, each carrying its respective planet. These spheres were conceived of as being like great hollow glass balls, one each taken in order for the moon, Mercury, Venus, the sun, Mars, Jupiter, and Saturn. Beyond these planets (wandering stars) was the sphere of the fixed stars, and beyond all these was the outermost sphere of the *primum mobile*. However, this simple system failed to explain adequately the observed facts that Mercury, Venus, Mars, Jupiter, and Saturn do not move directly across the heavens as do the moon and the sun. When their positions are plotted at the same hour on successive nights they seem to move at times backward and at other times (and generally) forward. This backward motion is known as retrograde motion.

To explain in reasonable terms why there is retrograde motion while holding to the common belief that all motion in the heavens is circular (because the circle was considered the perfect curve), Ptolemy was forced to modify the ancient Greek system outlined above by treating the spheres as hypothetical and by adding more spheres as well as epicycles. Some of these additional spheres were supposed to be concentric with the original ones but moving in opposite directions, while the epicycles described the paths of planets supposed to revolve around centers which in turn revolved with one or another of the concentric spheres. As astronomical knowledge increased, chiefly through the work of Arab students of the subject, the picture of planetary motion became ever more complicated as astronomers tried to account for observed motions, until by the time of Copernicus almost 80 epicycles were required to give a reasonable account of the data then known. It is a remarkable fact that on the basis of such immensely intricate theoretical structures it was still possible to predict eclipses and other phenomena with a considerable degree of accuracy; yet the work was most cumbersome and complicated.

The revolutionary achievement of *Nicolaus Copernicus* (1473-1543), a Polish churchman and astronomer, was simply the successful attempt to rewrite the geometry of the heavens with the assumption of a different point of reference from the earth. He saw that by treating the sun as stationary and the earth as one of the movable planets about it he could simplify astronomy, reducing the complex movements of the heavenly bodies to a

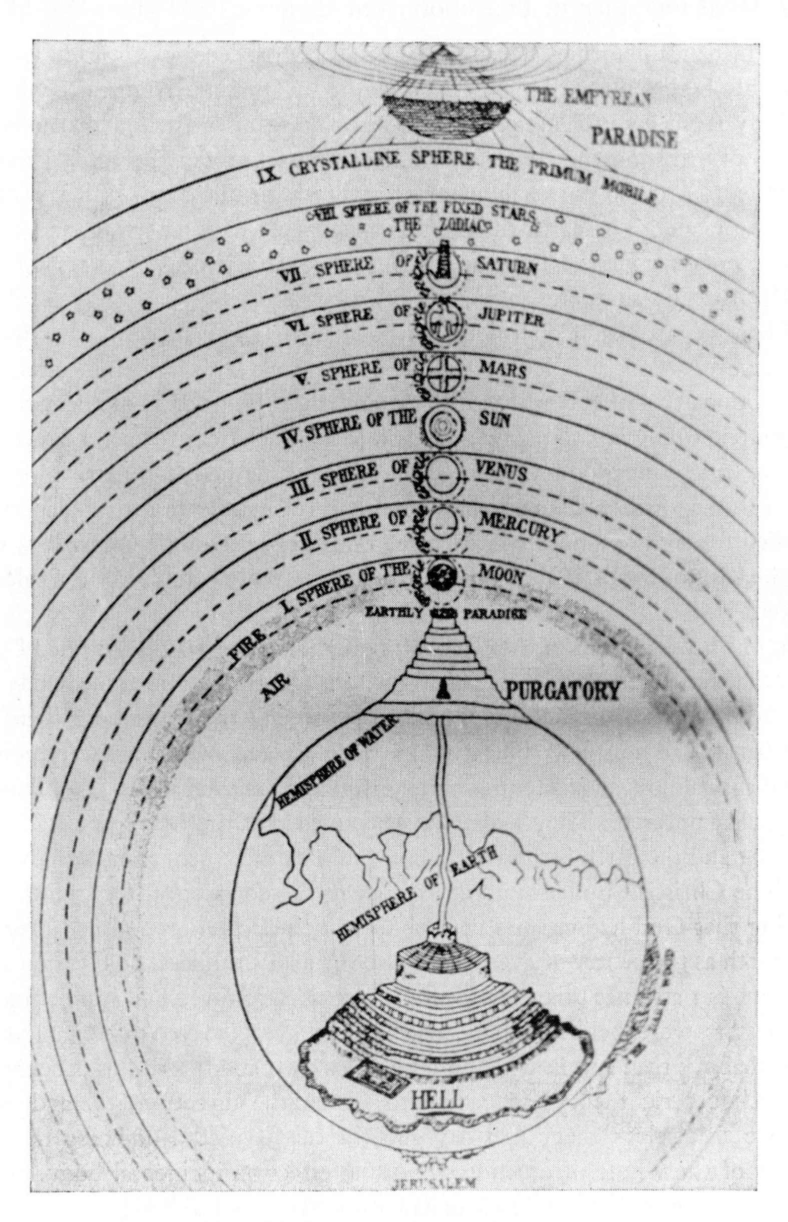

The Universe as Pictured by Dante

The medieval conception of the universe was well summed up by Dante (1265-1321) in his great work, The Divine Comedy. *This picture illustrates Dante's understanding of the world; an understanding generally shared by the people of his time. (Charles Singer,* Studies in the History and Method of Science, *Oxford University Press)* more manageable order. Because he like all his predecessors insisted that the heavenly bodies must all move in circles, he was not able to dismiss epicycles entirely from his explanation, but he was able to discard about half of them by simply shifting the center of planetary motion from the earth (geocentric theory) to the sun (heliocentric) and treating the earth rather than the sun as a planet. The earth turns on its axis once a day, he wrote, and circles the sun once a year. His theory was a great gain because the results were mathematically simpler.

Thus we see that Copernicus, without any significant new data derived from observation, was led to the heliocentric view through his antecedent convictions that the world is orderly and that its order is mathematical in character, following the simplest possible mathematical forms. This emphasis, we have noticed, goes back to Plato and his mathematics, derived largely from Pythagoras. It is interesting to note in this connection that Copernicus studied for six years in Italy with a Platonist named Dominicus Novara who, on the basis of his Platonic-Pythagorean views, freely criticized the Ptolemaic system.[8]

In our investigation of the work of Copernicus, we may be puzzled by the fact that his theory, which seems so obvious to us, was not immediately embraced by his fellow scientists. Let us note some of the reasons for their feeling that he had not proved his case. In the first place, his theory went counter to all that almost all sixteenth-century thinkers believed about the nature of the stellar universe. They had always assumed that the heavens are airy and moving and the earth is solid and immovable, as the senses seem to show it to be. The Christian understanding had taken this conception for granted, believing that God had created man as his principal creation and had prepared the earth as the center of everything else for man's abode. The creation story in Genesis 1 assumes this, as does all the rest of Scripture. The wandering and fixed stars were believed to be part of the great heaven which God had placed above man and in which God had his own abode. All this is denied by the heliocentric theory, according to which the directions *up* and *down* reverse themselves every half-day and the earth, instead of being the very center of the whole of creation, is now in effect an incidental body. Such a view both contradicted what man had always believed, relying upon what his senses told him, and dealt his pride a blow that he was unwilling to accept. Furthermore, the authority of the Scriptures as revelation of God was the basic point of Christian belief, and this new theory seemed to imply that the Scriptures were in error.

[8] Edwin A. Burtt, *The Metaphysical Foundations of Modern Physical Science*, rev. ed., London, Routledge & Kegan Paul, Ltd., 1932, p. 42.

But even more important than ancient opinion and the Scriptures was the fact that Copernican astronomy was unable to account for any astronomical motions or make any predictions that could not be adequately handled by the Ptolemaic system, and in addition it left unsolved a number of very serious problems which it raised. One of these was that if the earth in six months moved to the opposite end of its cycle from the sun, then the fixed stars should show a parallax due to this difference in position. With the instruments known in that day no such parallax was discoverable. Further, if an object is projected straight up in the air, since the earth is turning rapidly on its axis and moving in its supposed orbit the object should fall some distance to the west of its starting point. This does not happen, of course. It remained for Newton to reply to the point, but at the time this and the former objections seemed sufficient to discount the Copernican theory on its own basis.[9]

Why, in the face of these difficulties, should Copernicus have come to the conclusion which he reached, seeing that his view was opposed to Scripture and common observation, did not get rid of the epicycles entirely, gave no more accurate results than the Ptolemaic system, and left special problems of its own unsolved? The reason is simply that he held certain metaphysical views on faith, we might say, which convinced him that in spite of all these objections mathematics will yield unchanging truth and that the explanation which provides the simplest mathematical description of a process is the truth.

Johannes Kepler (1571-1630), a German mathematician and astronomer and the first Protestant scientist of note, shares with Copernicus the honor of founding the new astronomy. His work illustrates further how the Platonic faith that the universe consists of harmonious mathematical relations was foundational to the new theory. The Danish astronomer *Tycho Brahe* (1546-1601) was unsympathetic to the view of Copernicus and developed a theory of his own in opposition. According to this theory, the earth remains the center of planetary motion. Around it move the sun, moon, and fixed stars. But the other planets—Mercury, Venus, Mars, Jupiter, and Saturn—move around the sun as their immediate center, carried along with it as it revolves around the earth. This system could account for observed astronomical phenomena while saving the geocentric theory. The great importance of Brahe for future astronomy was not his theory, however, but the accurate observations he made of the heavenly bodies, adding greatly to what was known in Copernicus' day. His charts showed beyond doubt that the orbits of the planets cannot be interpreted as circular, as everyone had previously supposed. It remained for Kepler to make these observations fruitful by bringing

[9] *Ibid.*, pp. 23 ff.

Platonic mathematical philosophy to his consideration of them. Kepler was greatly disturbed by the fact that he could not express the planet's orbit in the "perfect" geometrical figure, the circle. Still convinced that in some way all these relations could be reduced to geometric form, he finally discovered his first law, that the planetary orbit is an ellipse of which the sun is one focus. The planets' departure from pure circular motion did not, after all, destroy the geometric constitution of the heavens!

Kepler was puzzled also by the fact, shown in Brahe's calculations, that the planets move with irregular speed; that is, the speed of any planet is greater when it is nearer the sun and less when it is further away. It seemed that the theory of the harmony of the spheres might after all be a romantic illusion not supported by fact. Not knowing the amount of variation in a planet's speed, Kepler calculated the orbit and velocity of Mars 70 times and found that its velocity in all parts of its orbit is such that the areas of all segments swept in equal times by a line drawn from the sun to the planet are equal. This may be made clear by reference to the accompanying diagram, in which the ellipse represents the planet's orbit, with the sun at a focus.

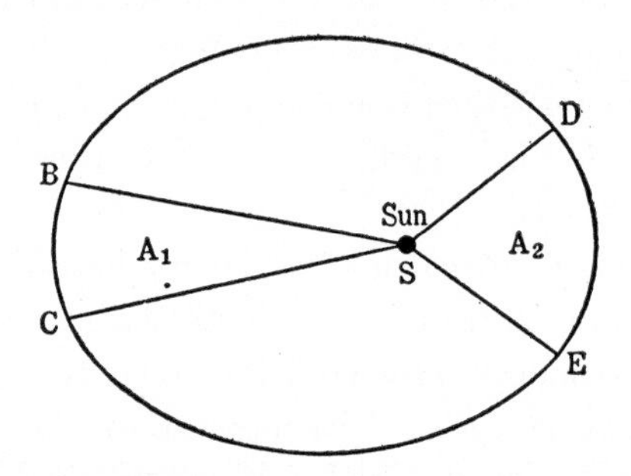

Although BC is a shorter distance than DE, it takes the planet the same length of time to travel the one as the other. But if we draw the lines BS, CS, DS, and ES and measure the area BSC, comparing it with the area DSE, we find these *areas*, A_1 and A_2, to be the same. Thus, although the velocity varies, the geometric harmony is saved by the equality of the areas. This gives us Kepler's second law: The planet-vector sweeps out equal areas in equal times.

Following out the principles underlying the second law, Kepler discovered also a mathematical relation between the times of revolution of the various planets—the planetary "years"—and their distance from the sun. For example, the planet Saturn, with an orbit about 9 times that of the earth, has a year about 27 times as long—actually 29 and a fraction years. As formulated by Kepler, this third law reads that the squares of the periods of revolution around the sun are proportional to the cubes of the mean distances of the planets from the sun. As a way of explaining the motion of the planets, he supposed a moving force in the sun, which he thought emits the rays of force that account for planetary motion. This idea also awaited Newton and his theory of universal gravitation for its correction.

The role played by philosophy in the Copernican revolution was great. Not only was it the inspiration for a new synthesis of the empirical knowledge already available; it also (and more importantly) supplied astronomers with a set of general ideas from which to proceed. Platonic mathematical philosophy helped the scientist of the time by suggesting the sort of questions to ask of nature.

The ascendancy of Copernican astronomy sealed the triumph of Platonism over Scholastic thought for the time being and consequently established the independence of philosophy from theology. The philosophers of the early modern period were no longer theologians seeking to reconcile reason with revelation but were rather mathematicians like Descartes, who invented analytical geometry, and Leibniz, who discovered the calculus.

The mathematical interpretation of nature, so basic to the Copernican revolution, involves the four following principles, brought out clearly in Kepler's writing.

1. The mathematical harmony discoverable in observed facts is the cause or the reason that things are as they are. As Kepler put it, God created the world in accordance with the principle of perfect numbers; thus, the mathematical harmonies in the mind of the Creator determine the size, number, and motions of the heavenly bodies. It is noteworthy that Kepler's ultimate explanation is God, but for practical purposes mathematics gives the answers.

2. Of a number of variant hypotheses about the same set of facts, that one is true which shows why the facts are what they are, that is, which demonstrates their orderly and mathematical connection. Thus, the Ptolemaic theory of the heavens had been forced to rest content with the simple statement that the completion of certain planetary epicycles *happens* to coincide with the time of the sun's apparent revolution around the earth. According to the mathematical interpretation of nature, the Copernican theory is true since it shows mathematically why astronomic events *must* be as they are.

3. The real world has quantitative characteristics only. Sensory qualities are not real qualities of things, but only signs of them; and real differences are quantitative only.

4. All certain knowledge must be knowledge of the quantitative character of objects. Perfect knowledge is always mathematical. Sensory experiences lack mathematical clarity and consistency, and therefore do not yield certain

knowledge. This principle is reflected in the aim of contemporary scientists to express their results in mathematical formulas.[10]

The new discoveries were scientific in nature, but they were accompanied by great changes in man's view of his universe and his own place within it. The revolution in astronomy, we can say, involved a revolution in man's whole picture of his world. Preserved Smith has admirably described this upsetting situation:

> The Copernican astronomy changed the whole picture of the world as it had been viewed by all generations. Hitherto the universe had been a snug little place, and the earth occupied its center both in space and in importance. Around a globe not too big to make one feel comfortably at home the concentric spheres of the heavens curtained off the scene on which was enacted the drama of the universe. Like convenient coulisses, hell, purgatory, and heaven were at hand to receive the several actors after their exits, while on the stage of the world men played that absorbing melodrama, conceived and put on by God, half spoiled by Satan as impresario and villain, and viewed with rapt attention by a large audience of supernatural beings. And as a guarantee that this idea of the universe was correct, man had the witness of his own senses, which could see the sun and the planets rise and set, and he had also the testimony of . . . prophets inspired by God to write the first acts of the divine comedy . . . .
>
> And now, at one blow from an infatuated star-gazer, the world, which had stood so fast on its foundations for six thousand years, began to twirl giddily on its axis and spin like a fretful midge around a candle. Though the implications of the new science were not worked out immediately, it began even from the first to be suspected that, if the theories advanced were true, man had lost his birthright as the creature for whose sake all else existed, and had been reduced to the position of a puny and local spectator of infinite forces unresponsive to his wishes and unmindful of his purposes. . . . With the possible exception of Darwinism, there has never been such a blow to man's pride, nor one involving such a complete subversion of all his most cherished prejudices. The war between the old and the new beliefs was long and bitter.[11]

Catholic and Protestant alike arose to do battle against the new theory. John Calvin quoted Psalm 93:1, ". . . the world is established; it shall never be moved," in refutation, while a Catholic cardinal appealed to the story of Joshua (in Joshua 10:12-14) commanding the sun to stand still. Even Francis Bacon, who might have known better, argued that the earth must be the center of the universe because of its weight. Galileo Galilei, who developed the telescope and popularized the new astronomy, was called before the bar

[10] *Ibid.*, pp. 53 ff.

[11] Preserved Smith, *A History of Modern Culture*, New York, Henry Holt & Co., 1930, I, 39 f.

of the Inquisition, forced to deny his true opinions, and sentenced to prison. But all opposition was in vain. Neither ponderous quotations from Scripture nor Catholic decrees of condemnation could prove that the earth remains stationary or refute the testimony of Galileo's telescope. Eventually, both Catholics and Protestants came to accept the new astronomy. Since 1835 the works even of Copernicus, Kepler, and Galileo no longer appear on the Catholic *Index of Prohibited Books*, although the church has not admitted that the older views were in error.

In spite of the Copernican challenge to the medieval world view and the resultant struggle that could end only in the defeat of theology, theologians might very well have been able to reconcile their religious beliefs with the new science. The Platonic philosophy on which the revolutionary theory rested was no stranger to Christianity. Until the time of Aquinas, Christian philosophy had been almost entirely Platonic; it might have been shifted back again with the aid of proper theological statesmanship. But such statesmanship was lacking, and before it could arise the Copernican was followed by the Cartesian revolution, which proved to be even more radical. Its mechanistic interpretation of the world was so inimical to the theological view that the church withdrew more positively and dogmatically into its stronghold of Scholastic Aristotelianism. Theology accordingly fell to the position of one rival philosophy among others, a position which it has held to this day. In the thirteenth century, thanks to the genius of Albertus Magnus and Thomas Aquinas, theology had been able to absorb the science of the newly discovered Aristotle; but in the sixteenth century the changes came so rapidly and in such varied form that the possibilities of reconciliation were dissipated in a futile theological attack on the new science, with the consequent hardening of dogma and the perpetuation in Catholic thought of the medieval outlook. Philosophy and science turned away in independence from the conservative church and hurried along the road of secularization.

The Cartesian Revolution

The next great figure in the account of Western science's development is that of *Galileo Galilei* (1564-1642), an Italian scientist. The period of scientific discovery he ushered in receives its name not from him, however, but from the French philosopher *René Descartes* (1596-1650), who expressed the wider philosophic significance of his achievement. We will look first at the scientist and then at the philosopher-mathematician.

Galileo was popularly known as the champion of the new astronomy, for it was he more than any other single man who gave experimental verification to the ideas of Copernicus. Until his time, the many theories which various thinkers developed in astronomy could in no way be demonstrated; the most that could be hoped for any theories, even those of Copernicus and Kepler, was general agreement between them and the known facts of astronomical observation. But as Galileo was able to show through observation the errors of Aristotle, he popularized Copernican astronomy, bringing the significance of Copernicus' ideas to thinking people in large numbers. In so doing he made those ideas dangerous to church teaching in a way they had not been previously, when they were known to only a few astronomers and even then only as interesting hypotheses. Because of Galileo's popularization, Copernicus' principal work, his *De Revolutionibus Orbium Celestium* published in the year of his death (1543) and earlier unnoted by any large numbers of people, was placed on the church's *Index* in 1616, over 70 years later.

The discoveries which showed some of the errors in previous thought were made possible by the telescope, which Galileo had developed into a usable instrument. (Its actual invention was the work of a Dutchman, Hans Lippershey, in 1608.) Galileo saw the mountains on the moon, a discovery which led him to say that the moon is of the same substance as the earth and is not a perfect sphere, as Aristotle had taught. He followed the phases of Venus, which proved its rotation around the sun, and was able to see and follow the movements of some of the moons of Jupiter, showing that they revolve around the planet as their center and not around the earth, which Aristotle had taught is the center of all heavenly motion. Here for the first time anyone who cared to look and examine the implications of what he saw with his own eyes could know that Aristotle was mistaken in at least some of his ideas concerning astronomy, and that everything discovered favored Copernicus. These discoveries themselves did not bring condemnation to Galileo, for Jesuit scholars of his day were willing to agree with him that Ptolemy was quite mistaken and went as far as accepting the views of Brahe. But through a variety of circumstances and Galileo's own indiscretion, he was hailed before the Inquisition and forced to state in recantation that he was mistaken in thinking with Copernicus that the earth moved. Galileo was then an old man. He was allowed, with unusual leniency, to retire to his home in Florence, where he wrote his most significant work, a thesis on mechanics entitled *Dialogues Concerning Two New Sciences* which he completed when he was 72 years old.[12]

Great as were Galileo's contributions in the field of astronomy, his dis-

[12] For an account of this episode see Arthur Koestler, *The Sleep Walkers,* The Macmillan Company, 1959, part 5, chaps. 1 and 2.

coveries in the field of physics were still more significant. Aristotelians of Galileo's day assumed that every object seeks its "natural place," the place of heavy objects being below, that of light bodies above. Such physics as they had was a science of purposes and hence ultimately a branch of metaphysics and theology. But Galileo repudiated this probing into the purposes of things and sought instead the laws of their *behavior*. Accepting the principle of Leonardo da Vinci that "proportions are found not only in numbers and measures, but also in sounds, weights, times and places, and in every force,"[13] Galileo no longer asked *why* bodies fall but *how* they fall. What mathematical formulation describes the motion of a freely falling body? It appears to ordinary sense experience that Aristotle was correct in believing that heavy objects fall at a greater rate of speed than do lighter ones, for sheets of paper do not fall so rapidly as do pencils, for example. Galileo conducted a number of experiments with freely falling bodies, and after announcing these from his professorial chair in the University of Pisa in 1591, he is said to have conducted the experiment of dropping two iron objects of different weights from the platform of the Leaning Tower of Pisa, ideally suited to such purposes. He was not the first to conduct experiments with freely falling objects, for five years earlier a man named Simon Stevin had demonstrated through experiments with leaden balls Aristotle's error in believing that the velocity of falling bodies is proportional to their weight.[14] According to the tradition, which is denied in some quarters, Galileo dropped his weights from the Leaning Tower, and they struck the ground at the same instant. Whether or not he actually held such a public demonstration, Galileo did disprove Aristotle by dropping weights and showed that any person could in turn disprove him to his own satisfaction by a very simple experiment. Aristotle was thereby shown mistaken not only in astronomy but also in physics. Once one bit of authority is destroyed it is possible to challenge all the rest, with the result that the authoritative position assigned Aristotle in the thirteenth century was now undermined and the realm of knowledge through experimentation opened up in a new way.

Galileo went further with his discoveries. It had been observed that the free motion of a falling body is continuously accelerated, and he demonstrated that the distances traversed during equal intervals of time by a body falling from rest stand to one another in the same ratio as the odd numbers beginning with unity. He thus answered his question of how bodies fall with a mathematical formulation, a proportion between units of time and

[13] John Herman Randall, Jr., *op. cit.*, p. 236. See footnote 3, p. 497.

[14] Frederick Copleston, *A History of Philosophy*, Westminster, The Newman Press, 1953, III, 280 f.

degrees of velocity. By means of his investigations, Galileo achieved liberation from Aristotelian physics and, along with Copernicus and Kepler, freed science from Ptolemaic astronomy.

Basic to Galileo's method were certain fundamental assumptions, three of which we may mention. The first was his belief, shared with Copernicus, Kepler, and others, that nature is a simple, orderly system whose every proceeding is regular and necessary, governed by "immutable laws which she never transgresses." Moreover, he shared the faith that the order of nature is fundamentally mathematical in character. As he himself wrote,

> Philosophy is written in that great book which ever lies before our eyes—I mean the universe—but we cannot understand it if we do not first learn the language and grasp the symbols, in which it is written. This book is written in the mathematical language, and the symbols are triangles, circles, and other geometrical figures, without whose help it is impossible to comprehend a single word of it; without which one wanders in vain through a dark labyrinth.[15]

But Galileo's originality lies in the combination of the mathematical faith with the Baconian emphasis on experimental verification. The confidence in the validity of controlled sense experience marks the second of Galileo's fundamental assumptions. He continually stressed the need of direct appeal to nature, of observation and empirical verification. He implemented the new astronomy by the development of the telescope and verified his theories in physics by experiment. He once wrote to Kepler, inviting him to share a hearty laugh at some professors of philosophy, one at Padua who refused to look through the telescope, another at Pisa who sought "with logical arguments, as if with magical incantations, to charm the new planets out of the sky." Galileo thus illustrated his contempt for the pretensions of knowledge that ignores facts and refuses to be corrected by observation. For him, knowledge was the mathematical *interpretation* of the sensible facts of the world about us. Ignore the facts and knowledge is left without content. This does not mean, however, that naive sense experience is to be given priority over scientific conclusions. The reasoned conclusion of Copernicus is to be trusted above the uninterpreted experience of the peasant who sees the sun rise and set. Accordingly, Galileo could not sufficiently admire those scientists who, like Aristarchus of Greece and Copernicus of Poland, had the courage to base their opinions on the dictates of reason even when these seemed a manifest "rape on their senses." The tempered combination of faith in the mathematical order of nature with the appeal to experiment, first achieved in the Western world by Galileo, brings us close to the assumptions and methods that have dominated modern science to this day.

[15] As quoted in Burtt, *op. cit.*, p. 64.

The third basic assumption of Galileo was the atomic theory of matter. First developed by Leucippus and Democritus and put into poetry by the Roman Lucretius in his famous *De Rerum Natura,* this theory was known to Galileo and employed by him. The astronomers had not needed this philosophy. The mathematical harmonies which they were so eager to discover were vast geometric relations among celestial bodies. But Galileo, extending the mathematical interpretation to the motions and relations of objects on the earth, found the atomic theory a convenient one. The changes of solids into fluids and gases and the phenomena of cohesion, expansion, and contraction could be explained by the atomic theory without admitting the existence of empty spaces within solid bodies or the penetrability of matter. The theory of atoms, which were regarded as alike in quality and as differing only in the quantitative characteristics of size, shape, and motion, could readily be incorporated with most of the principles of the mathematical philosophy. The conjunction of atomism, the mathematical philosophy, and the appeal to experience marks Galileo as a modern scientist; the materialism of Democritus, the mathematical faith of the Platonists, and the experimentalism of Roger Bacon are the working principles of modern science. Having merged these in his work, Galileo left the medieval world of revelation and authority behind and stepped over the threshold of the modern era.

The philosophical effects of Galileo's work were tremendous. Mechanical force—the tugs and thrusts of moving bodies—replaced divine purpose as the immediate cause of natural events. The real world was henceforth held to consist of physical bodies moving in space and time according to laws susceptible of mathematical formulation. The qualitative aspects of things—their odors, colors, tastes, and sounds—were accordingly regarded merely as effects in the minds of men caused by the motions of atoms, which in themselves are odorless, colorless, tasteless, and without sound. The distinction was therefore drawn between *primary* and *secondary* qualities. Primary qualities are said to be the absolute, immutable, objective qualities which belong to the world independent of human knowledge. These are the qualities of number, figure, magnitude, position, and motion. The secondary qualities are the relative, fleeting, and unstable characteristics which depend upon the mind of the perceiver—taste, odor, sound, and color. Since real knowledge consists of mathematical formulations, the primary or measurable qualities alone constitute its subject matter. The secondary qualities, subjective and beyond the reach of mathematical description, constitute the realm of opinion and illusion. Such is the logic of Galileo's philosophy of science.

Primarily a scientist, Galileo did not generalize his methods and principles. It remained for his contemporary René Descartes, the French philosopher, to express the philosophical implications of Galileo's achievement. Believing that mathematics is the most powerful instrument of knowledge, he set to work on the twofold task of perfecting this instrument and applying it to the mysteries of nature. He accordingly combined geometric analysis and algebra, producing analytical geometry, and then proceeded to employ this as the tool of philosophy. Faced with the problem of primary and secondary qualities, he believed that the geometric quality of matter, extension, is alone really primary. The resultant Cartesian revolution has been eloquently described by Randall:

> To Descartes thenceforth space or extension became the fundamental reality in the world, motion the source of all change, and mathematics the only relation between its parts. . . . He had made of nature a machine and nothing but a machine; purposes and spiritual significance had alike been banished. . . . He had reached the notion of seeking an explanation of all things in the world in purely mechanical terms. Intoxicated by his vision and by his success, he boasted, "Give me extension and motion, and I will construct the universe." The whole working-out of mechanical physics in the next two centuries is but the development of this idea. All energy is reduced to kinetic energy, the energy of motion; all qualitative differences in the world to quantitative differences of the size, shape, and speed of motion of particles of matter. Living beings form no exception; life becomes a mere matter of chemical and physical changes, all animals are mere automata, even the body of man is a purely physical machine. The world of the Middle Ages has been explicitly and entirely rejected for the world of modern physics.[16]

How different is this Cartesian world from that of Aquinas! In the latter's conception, God exists as the final cause of all that is, with man occupying a place just a little lower than the angels but superior to the rest of nature. In Descartes' world, the function of God is reduced to that of an engineer who brought the world machine into being. Since the machine is able to go on its mechanically determined way without further divine assistance, the work of God appears to be finished. Even the body of man is a part of this machine, although his soul, indeed, is held to be in some mysterious fashion independent of it.

But the independence which Descartes allowed for the soul did not alter the emphasis of his total picture. In the first place, the soul was theoretically useless in the world. If only physical forces are effective causes and the soul is by definition not physical, how can it influence human behavior? In the second place, the really important world continued to be quantitative, mechanical, and mathematically computable—the world of primary qualities.

[16] Randall, *op. cit.*, pp. 241 f.

The soul is merely the ineffective spectator of secondary qualities which depend for their existence on being perceived.

The Cartesian division of the world into primary and secondary qualities and the designation of body and soul (or mind) as separate entities have given modern thought its most persistent problems. How, if at all, can this divided world be brought together again? Or how are the independent sets of things—primary and secondary qualities, body and mind—related, since they are in one world, after all? Or yet again, if they really belong together, what blunder of speculation separated them? These questions continue to be a bone of contention among modern psychologists, theologians, and philosophers.

Questions for Study

1. To what "rebirth" does the name *Renaissance* refer? In what sense was this a transitional period, and from what to what?
2. What were some of the originating forces of the Renaissance, and specifically how did they effect this change? What effect did the Babylonian Captivity of the papacy have on the rise of this period?
3. What were the interests of Humanism? What were its forward-looking features, and what its harmful aspects? Compare it with Scholasticism.
4. What contributions did Roger Bacon make to the rise of science? How did Humanism make contributions in this same direction? What basic assumption lay behind Copernicus' heliocentric theory, and where did he obtain it? What gains were made by his theory, and what scientific shortcomings did it have? What were the contributions of Brahe and Kepler to the growing astronomy?
5. What four basic principles are involved in the mathematical interpretation of nature? How does this interpretation differ from the theological interpretation of the Middle Ages? What attitude toward the new astronomical theories was taken by the church? Why?
6. What did Galileo do for the ideas of Copernicus? In his investigations into physics, what was he looking for, in contrast to the Aristotelians? How does mathematics play into this? Specifically how did he disprove Aristotle? What three assumptions underlay his method? Why did he use the atomic theory?
7. What were the philosophical effects of Galileo's work? How did Descartes picture the world as a result of Galileo's work? What place has man with his values in this world?
8. How would you describe the basic changes that took place during this period? What of the Middle Ages was pushed aside as relatively unimportant, and what new elements were given great importance? What will the effects of this transition be in the succeeding period?

Selected Readings

Barnes, H. E., *An Intellectual and Cultural History of the Western World*, New York, Random House, Inc., 1937.

Burckhardt, Jacob, *The Civilization of the Renaissance in Italy*, Vienna, Phaidon Press, Ltd., 1937.

Burtt, Edwin A., *The Metaphysical Foundations of Modern Physical Science*, rev. ed., London, Routledge & Kegan Paul, Ltd., 1932.

Cassirer, Ernst, Paul O. Kristeller, and John Herman Randall, Jr. (eds.), *The Renaissance Philosophy of Man*, Chicago, University of Chicago Press, 1948.

Clagett, Marshall, *The Science of Mechanics in the Middle Ages*, Madison, University of Wisconsin Press, 1959.

Copleston, Frederick, *A History of Philosophy*, Westminster, The Newman Press, 1953, vol. III.

Ferguson, Wallace K., *The Renaissance in Historical Thought*, Boston, Houghton Mifflin Company, 1948.

Huizinga, J., *The Waning of the Middle Ages*, New York, Doubleday & Company, Inc., 1954.

Hulme, Edward M., *The Renaissance, the Protestant Reformation, and the Catholic Reformation in Continental Europe*, New York, The Century Co., 1923.

Lucas, Henry S., *The Renaissance and the Reformation*, 2nd ed., New York, Harper & Brothers, 1960.

Pirenne, Henri, *Medieval Cities, Their Origins and the Revival of Trade*, Princeton, Princeton University Press, 1925.

Randall, John Herman, Jr., *The Making of the Modern Mind*, rev. ed., Boston, Houghton Mifflin Company, 1940.

Singer, Charles, *A Short History of Science*, Oxford, Clarendon Press, 1941.

Smith, Preserved, *A History of Modern Culture*, New York, Henry Holt & Co., 1930, vol. I.

Symonds, John A., *A Short History of the Renaissance in Italy*, New York, Henry Holt & Co., 1894.

Taylor, Henry Osborne, *Thought and Expression in the Sixteenth Century*, New York, The Macmillan Company, 1920, vol. I.

16. The Protestant Reformation

Two of the great developments of the Renaissance were Humanism and the beginnings of modern science. With these must now be examined a third development which in its effects was of equal if not greater importance. The Protestant Reformation also was a bridge from the ancient to the modern world. It was medieval in many of its basic views, and yet departed from medievalism in fundamental ways. It destroyed the authority of the Roman Catholic church in much of Europe in the name of a larger Christianity. It returned to the ancient Christian classics (the Old and New Testaments) for its inspirations, while at the same time inheriting much that 15 centuries of Christian thought and experience had developed. The individualism which was a feature of the entire Renaissance is clearly manifest in the Protestant emphasis upon the relation of the individual soul to God which requires no church or pope as mediator. In short, the Protestant Reformation was the religious aspect of the whole movement of rebellion against medievalism. Where the Humanists attacked other-worldliness and self-denial and the scientists rejected the sanctified Aristotelian astronomy and physics, the reformers repudiated the Catholic claim to exclusive control over the means of salvation and the authority of the church that rested on it.

Like Humanism and the rise of modern science, this transitional religious movement was but the maturing of forces that had their roots in the past. Especially important in the background of the Reformation were medieval mysticism and the teachings of the so-called pre-reformers.

Major Factors in the Appearance of the Protestant Reformation

Mysticism

Mysticism represents personal religion at its most intense level. The mystic believes that the goal of religion is the experience of God and the finding of unity with him. By a process of self-purification and contemplation, by meditation and waiting for light, the mystic frees himself from all things that separate him from God—the lusts and passions of the flesh and the distractions of sense experience. Finally, if the mystic's quest is successful, he has an experience which he calls indescribable because it is like no other experience. It is for him the apprehension of divinity with his inner spiritual vision, the reflection of God in his own soul. Mysticism had been present in the church from the time of St. Paul. As long as Catholic thought was patterned after the Neo-Platonism of Augustine, mysticism had a logical place in the Christian scheme. When Augustine gave way to Aquinas, with his stress upon reason, mysticism continued as a sort of minority tradition, always making its appeal to certain temperaments and frequently associated with the piety of saints. But in the thirteenth and fourteenth centuries, when the sacramental system seemed to have become an external ceremonialism and the careful calculation of merit acquired by "good works," often with no moral significance, had made religion seem like trading for eternal life, a school of mystics sought once more to bring health and integrity to Christianity. They deplored the substitution of formal religious observances, mechanically performed, for personal spiritual experience. The interposition of a mediating priesthood seemed to them a hindrance to the essence of religion, which was the union of the soul with God. They did not reject the church with its priests, its sacraments, and its ceremonies, but they sought to restore these things to their proper place as simply aids to the spiritual life.

Two of the greatest of the mystics were Meister Eckhardt (1260-1327) and Johannes Tauler (*ca.* 1300-1361), both Dominican monks. Eckhardt emphasized the philosophical and speculative side of mysticism; Tauler, his disciple, emphasized its practical side. Tauler spent his life preaching in the common language the necessity for a pure life and the possibility of communion with God through meditation and prayer. Stressing conversion from an evil to a good life, he held simple trust in God as better than theological learning or monkish exercises, and taught that all honest labor, whether shoemaking or preaching, might be a divine calling.

Martin Luther, father of the Reformation, was influenced by Tauler's sermons, published in 1498, but acknowledged even greater indebtedness to *The German Theology*, a mystical book of anonymous authorship whose central message was man's sinful state and the necessity for absolute self-surrender as the condition of reconciliation with God. *The German Theology* was translated from Latin into German in 1516 by Luther himself, who said that apart from the Bible and the works of St. Augustine, he had never met with a book that taught his so much about "God, Christ, man and all things."

Although the mystics were not rebels against the church, their piety embodied at least one of the principles of the Reformation. Their rejection of all ceremony and formal ritual as in themselves inadequate for salvation foreshadowed the Lutheran emphasis on justification by faith alone. But mystical piety alone did not lead to revolution against the established order. Dissatisfaction with the ecclesiastic scheme of salvation had to be coupled with other powerful forces, economic and political, before a full-fledged revolution could be generated.

The Pre-Reformers

Throughout the long history of the Roman Catholic church many criticisms had been voiced against her, directed particularly against her claims to authority and against corruption involving the officers of the church themselves, from priests to pope. Among these critics were William of Ockham, Rabelais, Dante, Abelard, Erasmus, and others. Two men stand out above the rest as forerunners of the Reformation in a very special sense. Not all the principles of that momentous development are to be found in them, for the central doctrinal principle came from Luther alone, but various of the elements entering into it were already present in their teaching.

These two influential men whom we may well call pre-reformers were the Englishman John Wycliffe (*ca.* 1328-1384) and the Bohemian John Huss (*ca.* 1373-1415). Wycliffe was primarily concerned with abolishing the temporal power of the church and reforming the character of its priesthood. He attacked the laziness, luxury, and dishonesty of the clergy, denied the effectiveness of sacraments administered by sinful priests, and characterized the sale of indulgences as robbery. When the church declined to reform, he referred the matter to Parliament. He judged the church and its teachings by appeal to the Scriptures, which, with the help of friends, he translated for the first time into English in 1384. With Augustine, he defined the true church as those chosen by God for salvation, not as the Roman organization with its hierarchy of priests. He was thus prepared to say that membership in the visible church and participation in its sacraments were not necessary to salvation.

By training "poor priests" to go about preaching this new gospel among the people, he attained some success, but the power of the church was great enough finally to force Wycliffe's personal followers to recant. Thus stripped of its leadership, the Lollard movement (as it was named) all but disappeared. But Wycliffe's attempt to link religious reformation with national sentiments, his rejection of sacramentalism, and above all his appeal to the authority of Scripture pointed the way for later reformers and provided a platform of revolt.

Some Czech students at Oxford carried Wycliffe's doctrine to Bohemia. Thus the University of Prague became the center of reformation and John Huss, a professor there, its leader. His advocacy of Wycliffe's doctrines got Huss into difficulties with his superiors, and papal bulls were issued against him. He burned the bulls and withdrew from Prague. But he was summoned to the Council of Constance where he went with the safe-conduct of the Emperor Sigismund. Refusing to recant, Huss was burned alive. Sigismund had failed to make good his safe-conduct, and the princes of the church adopted a resolution that no pledge like Sigismund's that was prejudicial to the Catholic faith was binding.

In Bohemia, national consciousness was growing strong and came to the support of religious rebellion. The Bohemian Diet remonstrated against the betrayal of Huss. The principles which he had espoused left their mark in certain reforms in the church in Bohemia and became the animating force behind a separate religious body known as the Bohemian Brethren. These held to the supremacy of the Bible literally interpreted, and rejected the primacy of the pope, the validity of indulgences, masses for the dead, and all ceremonies not authorized in Scripture. The Bohemian Brethren continue to this day as the *Moravians*, a Protestant sect whose piety influenced John Wesley in the eighteenth century.

Wycliffe and Huss are properly termed pre-reformers for although Luther himself seems not to have known of Wycliffe, he recognized his indebtedness to Huss. Given a more favorable political and cultural situation and his positive doctrinal principle of salvation through faith, Luther was able to put the program of reform into effect. We shall now consider some of the cultural factors that helped him succeed where his predecessors had failed.

Nationalism

In the discussion of the Renaissance we have already mentioned the large part played in that general development by the rise of nationalism. Here we shall add to that discussion, confining ourselves to a consideration of the growing national consciousness and power as these were related to the success of Luther's revolt. Some writers have gone so far as to state that the causes of the Reformation were largely secular rather than spiritual. We must reject this estimate of the religious motive as a causal factor, though at the same time we must recognize that the Reformation did have a secular side and that it was a phase of the clash between the secular national state and the international ecclesiastical state—between the modern nation and the medieval church with its claims to superiority over temporal power. The spirit of religious rebellion did not find embodiment in an effective movement of reform until it was allied with nationalistic political sentiments and power.

National sentiment, we have said, developed through the consciousness of larger group loyalties than just the local communities, through the unity of those using a common language, strengthened by the invention of printing, and through the growth of commerce and exploration. This growth of national sentiment and power had repercussions for the church. Before 1500, there was a strong movement in the national states to subordinate the church to national laws—a movement inspired almost entirely by economic and political motives. For example, England forbade the practice of withdrawing land from civil taxation by deeding it to the church, and repealed the right of its subjects to appeal from the civil courts to Rome. In the Pragmatic Sanction of Bourges issued by Charles VII in 1438, France denied the papal right of taxation and threatened anyone bringing into the country a papal bull against this law with penalty of death. In Germany, where there was no central government but where pronounced national consciousness nonetheless existed, minor princes and free cities demanded from the papacy the same powers as those claimed by kings. The imperial diets in Germany got into a virtual habit of drawing up lists of grievances against the church. By 1520 it was an established principle that no German could be tried in Rome without being tried first in Germany—a ruling that probably saved Luther's life. Thus we see that before the outbreak of the Reformation national and secular rulers had challenged the papal claims of unlimited power, had asserted control over patronage and taxation, and had curtailed the jurisdiction of papal decrees. When Luther revolted against the church, strong national interests existed that were ready to capitalize on his religious motives for political purposes. The electors of Saxony, for example, protected and encouraged Luther because he offered religious justification for their political struggles with the church.

Corruption of the Church

Finally, in tracing out the causes of the Reformation, we must mention also the corruption in the church. While the significance of this for the Reformation may be easily overemphasized, the fact remains that the immorality of the clergy and abuses in connection with financial matters entered effectively into the total picture. The three most common forms of corruption were lechery (or venery), nepotism, and simony. Regarding the first, the Humanists Rabelais and Erasmus, along with many others, attacked the failure of monks and nuns to live up to their vows of celibacy. Even some of the popes, especially those of the Renaissance, were guilty of the same failure.[1] While it is true that there was a leaven of saintly priests like the one described by Chaucer,

> Who Christes lore and his apostles twelve
> He taught, but first he folwed it himselve,

a large proportion were both ignorant and immoral. Many were unable to understand the Latin of the service or to repeat the Lord's Prayer or the Creed in any language, and failed even to conform to decent standards of sobriety and temperance.

Historically of greater importance were the abuses connected with money. Church offices were frequently sold to those who could pay the highest price for them, which is the evil of simony. At other times those holding power practiced nepotism, granting privileges to nephews and other close relatives.[2] The papacy collected dues and percentages from the clergy, who passed on the taxes by charging high fees for their professional services. Through wars and extravagance the popes ran into debt and sought to repair their financial affairs by the sale of indulgences, distorting the sacrament of penance for the sake of financial profit.

The nature of indulgences needs to be understood. Penance is one of the seven sacraments of the church and involves four steps: contrition, confession, absolution, and satisfaction. Sin was held to involve two aspects—guilt

[1] See John A. Symonds, "The Popes of the Renaissance," in *A Short History of the Renaissance in Italy*, New York, Henry Holt & Co., 1894, pp. 52-84.

[2] *Ibid.*

and penalty. The guilt of sin is freely forgiven by God to the repentant sinner but the penalty still remains. When absolution is pronounced upon the contrite person who has confessed his sin, the eternal consequences of the sin are removed, but certain temporal penalties have still to be discharged. If this is not done within the lifetime it must be done in purgatory. Satisfaction, the fourth of the steps under penance, consists in performing certain penitential acts imposed by the priest for the removal of the temporal consequences of sin. Proper forms of satisfaction might be the saying of prayers, fasting, payment of money to charity, or making a pilgrimage (as in Chaucer's *Canterbury Tales*).

Theologians of the tenth century changed the early practices in this regard by teaching the doctrine that the church had at her disposal a treasury of "excess merit" of Christ and the saints, which could be applied to anyone by the pope, drawing upon this "treasury," in lieu of the temporal penalties for sin. An indulgence, then, was a papal excuse from the temporal consequences of sin. It might remove part or all of the penalty. A plenary (full) indulgence might be granted for making a pilgrimage to Rome or for fighting the Moslems in the Crusades, for instance.

Claiming the power to forgive sins, the church found it only logical to go on to the practice of granting indulgences. In their earlier forms these were generally a direct aid to the spiritual life; but by the fourteenth century an indulgence might be granted for money payment, and the sale of indulgences had thus become a means of papal income, leading to frequent abuses.[3] When in the fifteenth century the assumed power of the popes to free living men from purgatory was extended to include the dead, so that one might release one's dead parents or other loved ones from purgatory by the payment of money, this "holy trade" began to flourish. Bankers became the papal agents to organize the sale of indulgences on commission; civil rulers and bishops got a share for permitting sales in their jurisdictions; and the agents sent out to distribute these pardons—and to collect the money—participated in the profits in accordance with their zeal. Temporal rulers, who wanted the revenues for themselves, were incensed at the amount of money carried to Rome in connection with the sale of indulgences. Religious leaders like Wycliffe and Huss opposed these practices as a travesty on religion. It was this traffic in indulgences that aroused Luther. Attacking a patent abuse of the sacrament of penance, he came to deny the whole sacramental system. Thus we see that the financial abuses of the church brought on political opposition from the princes and religious rebellion from the reformers. The

[3] See article on "Indulgences" in *The Catholic Encyclopedia*, New York, Robert Appleton Co., 1910, VIII, 26-38.

one supported by the other meant ultimate success; the temporal power of the church was ultimately broken and its religious authority repudiated in half of Europe and in the British Isles.

The Lutheran Revolt

In *Martin Luther* (1483-1546) the forces of revolt became personified. He was at once the product and the leader of the seething discontent against Rome. The time was ripe, and Luther, with his gift of popular speech, his strong will, and his earnestness, dominated his age. He was born of peasant stock in the small village of Eisleben where his father was a miner. His childhood was one of poverty, but his father, a hardheaded, practical, ambitious, and pious man, managed to improve his income to the point where he was enabled to provide his son with an excellent education. Luther was sent away to school at the age of 13, first to Magdeburg, then to Eisenach, and finally, at the age of 18, to the University of Erfurt. This was a university of excellent reputation which followed traditional methods and ideas. Its philosophic approach was that of William of Ockham, a form of Nominalism. Luther, essentially a practical man, did not admire the philosophy taught him, but he seemed to have an even lower opinion of the thought of Thomas Aquinas, which he appears to have known only slightly. He referred to Thomas and the Scholastics as men of "stupid audacity and thickheadedness."[4] He received his master's degree and expected to enter law as a profession.

However, this was not to be, for suddenly he changed his mind and went into a monastery of Augustinian hermits in Erfurt in 1505. The immediate cause of this sudden decision was a thunderstorm, a few miles from Erfurt. Lightning struck a nearby tree and he was thrown down. In his fear he cried, "Help, St. Anne, I will become a monk." This incident does not stand alone, however. The death of a friend shortly before this time had filled his mind with thoughts of death. He was often moved by religious discontent and equally often by a sense of either severe depression or exaltation. Persons of such temperament have frequently become religious leaders. In spite of his father's disappointment, he was ordained a priest and celebrated his first mass in 1508. He hoped to find within the monastery the inner peace with God that he had not found in the world outside.

Like Paul and Augustine before him, Luther was a seeker. He sought for holiness according to the teaching of his order, following to extremes the practices recommended and prescribed. He fasted, kept vigils, prayed, and

[4] M. C. D'Arcy, *St. Thomas Aquinas*, Dublin, Clonmore & Reynolds, Ltd., 1953, p. 189.

practiced austerities, though not because he had particular sins or strong sexual temptations as was the case with Augustine. Rather, he could never be certain, regardless of how far he had gone in humility, prayer, and the practice of good deeds, that he had really pleased God. He wrote later about this period, "I was a good monk, and I kept the rule of my order so strictly that I may say that if ever a monk got to heaven by his monkery it was I. All my brothers in the monastery who knew me will bear me out. If I had kept on any longer, I should have killed myself with vigils, prayers, reading, and other work."[5] We are reminded of St. Paul and his attempt to please God by obedience to every detail of the Jewish Law.

Luther's problem was further complicated by a trip to Rome which he made in 1510. There he was disillusioned by the frivolity and ignorance of the priests, and was informed that if there was a hell Rome was built upon it. He returned to Erfurt, was transferred to the University of Wittenberg, became a doctor of theology the following year, and then began lecturing. A few years later he was appointed director of teaching and district vicar in charge of 11 monasteries of his order. His own studies of theology led him back from the later Scholastics like Ockham to Augustine and ultimately to St. Paul. From Augustine he learned that man cannot be saved by merit (a view opposed by the teaching of the church of his day as it affirmed its ability to make available the excess merit of Christ and his church) but only by the grace of God. The mystic Tauler impressed him with the necessity for complete surrender to God. Gradually, through his study of Paul's epistles and particularly the book of Romans he began to find the solution to his problem. By his own efforts and deeds, he discovered, he could not be just before God, but what he himself could not do had already been done for him through Jesus Christ. He wrote:

> My situation was that, although an impeccable monk, I stood before God as a sinner troubled in conscience, and I had no confidence that my merit would assuage him. Therefore I did not love a just and angry God, but rather hated and murmured against him. Yet I clung to the dear Paul and had a great yearning to know what he meant [by the "justice" of God].
>
> Night and day I pondered until I saw the connection between the justice of God and the statement that "the just shall live by faith." Then I grasped that the justice of God is that righteousness by which through grace and sheer mercy God justifies us through faith. Thereupon I felt myself to be reborn and to have gone through open doors into paradise. . . . This passage of Paul became to me a gate to heaven. . . .
>
> If you have a true faith that Christ is your Saviour, then at once you have a

[5] Quoted in Roland H. Bainton, *Here I Stand: A Life of Martin Luther*, Nashville, Abingdon-Cokesbury Press, 1950, p. 45.

gracious God, for faith leads you in and opens up God's heart and will, that you should see pure grace and overflowing love.[6]

This new understanding prepared him for the conviction that God had forgiven him his sins and accepted him. In this assurance his soul was filled with joy, peace, and complete trust in God. He had found saving faith. From this experience he came to believe that it is faith and faith alone that saves men, but not faith in the sense used by Aquinas, who meant intellectual acceptance of what cannot be demonstrated by reason. It was rather faith as a personal relationship to God, in which one trusts and gives himself completely and without reservation to the divine. A man cannot be justified by his works (of prayer, fastings, scourgings, good deeds) but only by the grace of God who through his love forgives and justifies. *This* is the gospel, the good news that Jesus brought and Paul preached. Man, on his part, need only have the faith to accept this gospel and to appropriate this grace. Thus was born Luther's revolutionary doctrine, which became the watchword of the Reformation, that man is justified by faith alone (*sola fide*). This doctrine makes the entire system of salvation by sacraments and "good works" irrelevant and superfluous. It follows that if the church's system of salvation is no longer to be considered necessary, her authority over men's lives, which rests upon that system, must also be rejected. Thus, in 1516 Luther had gained the positive principle which gave him the means to oppose the claim of the church to authority over the lives of men in a way more fundamental and drastic than that of any of the critics of the church before him, because he could now challenge its control of the means of salvation.

Armed with his conviction that man is justified before God by faith alone and not by good works, it was inevitable that Luther should come to grips with the most infamous of the "good works" of his day, the traffic in indulgences. He was particularly offended by the activities of *Johann Tetzel*, a Dominican prior, who preached in a popular vein that by purchasing an indulgence one could deliver the soul of his deceased loved ones from purgatory. Although the sale of indulgences was not allowed in Saxony, many people from Wittenberg, which lay close to the border, went out to buy these certificates. Incensed at this deception of the people, Luther posted his Ninety-Five Theses against the sale of indulgences on the door of the Castle Church at Wittenberg on October 31, 1517. These theses were brief statements in Latin presented for theological debate. Most of them were not heretical, although some challenged the pope's power to remit guilt. Little attention was given them at first until someone had them printed and dis-

[6] *Ibid.*, p. 65.

Luther's Ninety-Five Theses in Wittenberg

These bronze doors of the Castle Church in Wittenberg now carry the theses placed by Luther in 1517 upon the wooden doors which originally occupied this position.

tributed without Luther's knowledge. The effect was tremendous. Tetzel was mobbed and the market for his certificates vanished. Luther was ordered to retract his theses; he responded with a sermon that reiterated his position more strongly.

The papal lightning descended, and Luther was summoned to Rome for trial. The scene of the trial was changed to Augsburg, and Luther was provided with a safe-conduct by Frederick the Wise, elector of Saxony. Ordered to retract his statements about indulgences, Luther refused and appealed "from the pope badly informed to the pope to be better informed."[7] He had not yet challenged papal authority, but he was soon to be drawn into a debate with the theologian Johann Eck. The latter declared that the Theses challenged the authority of the papacy. Luther admitted as much and supported his denial of the superiority of the church by appeal to history, the Bible, and the Council of Nicaea. Pressed further by Eck, Luther declared that the Council of Constance had erred in condemning Huss. Not only the pope but even a general council of the church was held possible of error!

Starting with an attack on an obvious abuse of a sacrament, Luther was led to deny first the whole sacramental scheme of salvation and then the authority of the church which rested upon it. He had appealed from indulgence sellers to the pope, from the pope to a church council, from council to Scripture. In place of salvation through sacraments and good works he put salvation by faith; in place of the authority of the church he put the authority of Scripture. The basic principles of the Reformation were now complete.

Luther, continuing his attack upon the established order, found himself at the head of a lively movement. Humanists and political leaders as well as many deeply religious people were looking to him for leadership. The pope, urged on by Eck, sent a papal bull of condemnation in 1520, but this only served to stimulate Luther to a further formulation of his ideas. The bull itself he burned publicly six months later, along with a copy of the canon law of the church, while students and townspeople applauded him. The following month, in January, 1521, the pope issued a bull of excommunication, and it now became the duty of the emperor, Charles V, to put the two bulls into effect. When the imperial diet met at Worms in 1521, the question of what to do with Luther had a prominent place on the agenda. After stormy debate he was summoned before the diet. With the safe-conduct of both Frederick of Saxony and the emperor, Luther appeared. He heard the titles of his books read and was asked whether they were his and

[7] Quoted in Preserved Smith, *The Age of the Reformation,* New York, Henry Holt & Co., 1920, p. 68.

whether he would recant the heresy they contained. He asked for time and was granted a delay until the next day. Having had the night to think over the matter—his life was at stake—he made a great oration before the august

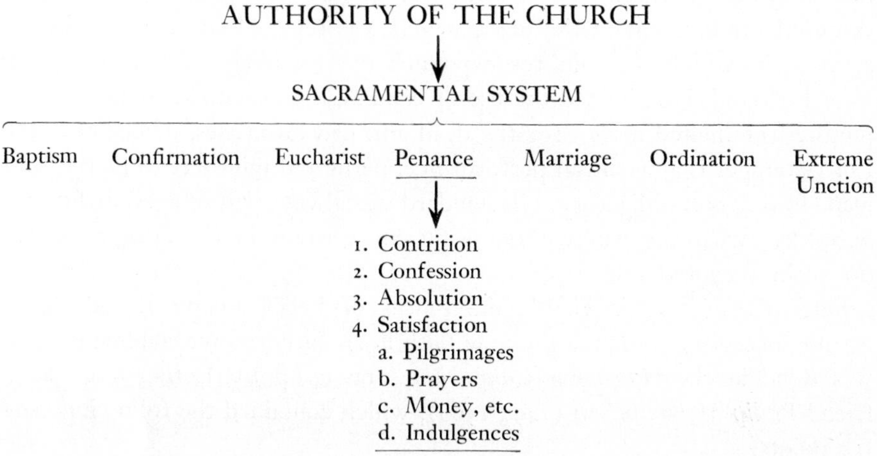

AUTHORITY OF THE CHURCH

↓

SACRAMENTAL SYSTEM

Baptism | Confirmation | Eucharist | Penance | Marriage | Ordination | Extreme Unction

↓ (Penance)

1. Contrition
2. Confession
3. Absolution
4. Satisfaction
   a. Pilgrimages
   b. Prayers
   c. Money, etc.
   d. Indulgences

Luther and the Church

Challenging the abuse of the sacrament of penance through the sale of indulgences, Luther went on to deny the whole principle of sacraments and, finally, the authority of the church which depended on it.

assembly the following morning. Admitting that the books were his, Luther closed with the famous words, "Unless I am convinced by Scripture or by right reason (for I trust neither popes nor councils since they have often erred and contradicted themselves) . . . I neither can nor will recant anything since it would be neither safe nor right to act against conscience. God help me. Amen."[8]

This bold declaration brought forth the Edict of Worms that put Luther under an imperial ban, commanded his surrender, and forbade anyone to give him shelter or to read his books. Once again he was saved only by the intervention of his prince, Frederick, who hid Luther in Wartburg Castle near Eisenach. With this open alliance of political independence and religious rebellion, the Reformation came to maturity and the Lutheran Protestant church was established in open defiance of Catholicism. By the time of Luther's death in 1546, Lutheranism had spread over all of central and northern Germany, to a part of southern Germany, to Sweden, Norway, and Denmark, and to the Baltic provinces.

Luther himself was essentially a conservative in most respects and conse-

[8] *Ibid.*, p. 80.

quently desired to retain as many of the Catholic forms and principles as possible. His fundamental theological beliefs were largely those of the Roman church except for his rejection of the primacy of the pope and of the sacramental system as the means of salvation. The service of Christian worship centered for him not in the mass, which was rejected as such, but in the sermon, in which the minister expounds the teachings of Scripture, the Word of God. He retained the use of candles, the crucifix, and images and pictures. He halted masses for the dead and private masses, denied that the Lord's Supper is a sacrificial performance, permitted ministers to marry, and made fasting non-obligatory. His standard was always that of agreement with Scripture; whatever was without sufficient warrant in the Scriptures was not to be accepted.

Since there were inevitable differences of belief among Lutherans, it became necessary to define the new faith in an authoritative statement. This was done in the *Augsburg Confession*, drawn up by Luther's scholarly friend *Philip Melanchthon* (1497-1560), which contained the following central points:

1. The only final authority for either conduct or belief is the Scriptures. In them the will of God and the love of God as exhibited in Jesus Christ are revealed to such as have power through the Holy Spirit to understand.
2. The one condition of salvation is faith or trust in the divine love thus revealed.
3. Faith itself is a gift of God, not an achievement of man. God in his mercy grants to whom he will the power freely to trust him, leaving the rest to their own evil devices.
4. The community of the faithful constitutes the true church, whose only head is Christ. The growth and unity of the church are fostered by preaching the Gospel and the observance of just two sacraments—baptism and the Lord's Supper (in its commemorative aspect), the only ones clearly authorized in Scripture.

Calvinism

Just as Luther was the outstanding figure in the German revolt against the Catholic church, so the leading figure in the Swiss revolt was *Huldreich (Ulrich) Zwingli* (1484-1531), founder of the Reformed church. He was a highly educated priest, basically a Humanist holding close connections with Erasmus. Zwingli had studied in Vienna, Paris, and Basel. In his early days he thought of Christianity as essentially an ethical code and consequently criticized such practices as pilgrimages, showing a spirit critical of his church even before he had heard of Luther. In 1519 he was appointed to Zurich as people's priest and there read Luther's writings. They influenced him deeply, leading him eventually away from Catholicism. Many similarities appear in the teachings of Luther and Zwingli. Both preached the doctrine of justification by faith alone; both erased the distinction between priest and layman by declaring the "priesthood of all believers"; both rejected the authority of the church in favor of the authority of the Bible. Zwingli, however, was more intellectual in temper and radical in reform than was his German colleague, conditions that made for friction between them. In his intellectualism he drew out logical implications of man's absolute dependence on the grace of God for salvation, and arrived at an extreme form of the Augustinian doctrine of predestination and a definition of the church as those both within and without the visible church who are predestined to salvation. His radicalism led him to change the forms of worship, to eliminate musical instruments from the service, to abolish the mass entirely, and to establish the sermon as the central element in worship.

The Zwinglian Reformation brought about civil war in Switzerland between Catholic and Protestant armies, and Zwingli fell in battle in 1531. The monument on the Sonnenquai in Zurich, presenting Zwingli with an uplifted sword in the right hand and the Bible in the left, serves both to commemorate his role in the Reformation and to remind us of the two weapons with which Protestants severed the bonds of the medieval Church.

The spiritual successor of Zwingli in the work of reform was *John Calvin* (Jean Chauvin or Cauvin, 1509-1564), born in the small French town of Noyon, about 60 miles from Paris. His parents, of the middle class, had a high regard for education and sent their son to the University of Paris to study theology, which he later abandoned for the study of law at Orléans. Strongly influenced by Humanist interests, he learned Greek and later studied in the Humanist Collège de France, seemingly uninterested in any strong way in religion. About 1533 he experienced a conversion which resulted in an intense religious concern. He was convinced that God had spoken to him through the Scriptures and that the will of God must be obeyed. Caught up in the swelling tide of the Protestant Reformation, he fled France and in 1535 reached Basel. From that year until his death the Reformation claimed his time and energy and gave him a place of outstanding influence in Western history.

By temperament unemotional, cold, calculating, and rationalistic, Calvin lacked the warm temperament and full religious experience which had given Luther his humanity and sympathy. For Calvin, religion was something to be analyzed and defined with the logic of the theologian and put into practice with the unbending rigor of a lawyer executing a court decree. The result was a doctrinal system of uncompromising intellectual rigor and a form of life modeled more on the legalism of the Old Testament than on the gospel in the New.

Calvin's theology was set down in the greatest of his works, his *Institutes of the Christian Religion*, published in its earliest form in 1536 when he was only 26 years old. A monumental work, its very title suggests the logician's interest in first principles and the lawyer's concern with authoritative precepts and rules. Most of its principles are implicit in Luther's doctrines also, but the tone and emphases are different. In Luther's teaching the warm, enthusiastic appropriation of the gospel of a forgiving God was made the touchstone of everything else. All for Luther sprang from this. But in Calvin this warmth is replaced by logic unhindered by emotion. The most characteristic passages of the *Institutes* affirm the following points of belief.

1. The unconditional sovereignty (kingship) of God is revealed in the Holy Scriptures, in which the "elect," guided by the Holy Spirit, find God declared to be triune, the source of all goodness, a just Creator and all-powerful Governor whose purposeful providence is all-embracing. Whatever happens happens because God wills it so.

2. Man's total depravity (inner corruption) and abject helplessness, following from his original sin of disobedience, make the help of a superhuman savior indispensable to man's salvation. To extricate man from this condition it was necessary, because of the love of God and according to his will, that the eternal Son of God should become man and suffer in man's stead, paying the penalty that guilt carries with it.

3. By rigorous predestination, the divine mercy and love show themselves in the election (choice) of some men to salvation. The work of the Holy Spirit within those thus chosen brings about repentance and, through faith, a living union between believer and Christ. All those who are not elected by God for salvation receive eternal punishment in hell, and justly, says Calvin, because of their guilt before the majestic glory of God. For Calvin as for Luther, there is no purgatory, since Scripture does not clearly teach the doctrine. Those chosen by God are chosen not because of anything they have done or can do but simply by his own inscrutable will. Being of the elect, however, they will do good works, as Christ did good works.

4. Those chosen by God for salvation (the elect) constitute the church. To preserve true religion pure and unmutilated is the concern of civil as well as ecclesiastic rulers. God's law is over all, and every rebellion against divine law demands punishment, temporal as well as spiritual. Civil officials,

therefore, are called upon to act under the direction of the ecclesiastic authorities in the service of God. Carried to its full implications, this principle logically leads to a theocratic government no less complete than that claimed by Pope Boniface VIII for the Catholic church.

Calvin's temperament was reflected also in his ethics. The form of life which he advocated had little place for emotion or spontaneous joys. Life for him was a serious business, requiring a concentration of effort and strict discipline. Emphasizing the absolute sovereignty of God, he held that the meaning of human life is to glorify God by obedience to his will. Sobriety, industriousness, and thrift he regarded as divinely ordained virtues; frivolity and the enjoyment of luxuries were vices to be shunned.

Calvin eventually became a virtual dictator of Geneva, where he spent most of his life, and was able to put his ideas of how the life of a Christian city should be conducted into effect. Everything was to be done for the glory of God. Overfondness of the gay pleasures of dancing, music, and masquerades was curbed. Women must dress soberly. Penalties were established for fortune telling, inability to recite prayers, and laughing during preaching. All citizens were required to attend two sermons on Sunday. All those who showed open opposition to Calvin's control were excluded from the city, and those who did not belong to the church also left. From the standpoint of those who enjoy the innocent pleasures of life the result was that Geneva became a very dull place indeed; from the standpoint of high ideals, law, and order it became a model that other Protestant communities envied and tried to emulate, notably in Scotland and later in New England. Also, by founding the Genevan Academy in 1559, Calvin established the greatest center of theological instruction within the Reformed church, as the Protestantism he represented was called. Ministers went from there to other countries on the Continent and to England, with the result that Calvin's influence through this university as well as through his very extensive writings was remarkably far-reaching.

From Geneva his teachings spread to France, where the Huguenots, mainly bourgeois, were his followers. Here the movement was significant not only religiously but socially and politically as well, resulting ultimately in the establishment of a kind of "Protestant state" within France. Calvinism became important also in the Netherlands, where it played a significant role in bringing about Dutch independence from the Spanish. The chief exponent of Calvinism in Scotland, where it came to be called Presbyterianism, was John Knox, who led the Protestant nobles in revolt against the Catholic queen, Mary Stuart. Knox's influence led to the downfall of the queen and committed Scotland to Calvinism. A large number of the middle class in England also became followers of Calvinistic teaching in the forms of Presbyterianism, Separatism, and Puritanism.

With this brief sketch of Calvinism, we may now profitably go on to a comparison of the two original systems of Protestantism, the Lutheran and the Calvinistic.

Comparison of the Two Forms of Protestantism

While the teachings of Luther and Calvin obviously have much in common, they are marked also by important differences. Some of these are explicit while others appear only as implications are examined. Still other differences are a matter of emphasis, reflecting the temperaments and personal experiences of the great reformers.

Lutheranism

The principal point of divergence between Lutheranism and Calvinism is in the differing concepts of God. The central emphasis of Luther is the love and mercy of God who in his graciousness forgives man's sin and guilt and reinstates him in divine favor. This divine grace cannot be bought by human merit; its only prerequisite is faith—faith in God, the loving father, revealed in Jesus. This has its consequences for ethics. If faith brings freedom from the fear of punishment, man becomes free also from time-serving religious duties, and thus free to devote himself to the spontaneous service of man in the confidence of God's love. Such freedom is, of course, far removed from license. It is rather the freedom of life that knows no master but love, that recognizes no rules but those of tenderness. In conformity with this principle, Lutheran piety has always found a place for the amenities of life. German *Gemutlichkeit* could be cultivated without conflict with the religious ideal. Luther himself was full of fun, liked his beer, and was famous for his conversation. How different from the comparative austerity of life under Calvinistic regulations!

The Lutheran appropriation of the gospel of salvation by faith alone is reflected also in the conception of the church. If the means of salvation is faith in the gospel, then the chief business of the church—the association of those having faith—is to teach and evangelize. The church became primarily a society for the spread of the gospel and the administration of the sacraments.

This conception of the church and its function is responsible for the almost total divorce of religion and secular affairs in Lutheran cultures. Since the primary business of the church is to preach the gospel, that is, to bring to men the message of divine grace, which may be appropriated by the experience of faith, religion becomes a personal and subjective matter. Coupled with the Lutheran dependence upon and regard for the rulers of the secular state, this conception of religion as an affair of the individual's inner life has left churches of this denomination with little to say about the ethics of either business or politics. A vivid illustration of this point is seen in the conflict between the German National Socialist government and the Lutheran church in Germany. In this struggle the Lutheran pastors claimed primarily the right to conduct the internal affairs of the church, free from interference by the state. They did not emphasize the duty of the church to make critical pronouncements on National Socialist policies from the standpoint of Christian ethics. For Lutherans, the church is concerned principally with religion; it has nothing directly to do with secular affairs. Besides questions of internal organization, all that it claims for its province is the personal life of individuals. It is ready even to draw distinctions between the duties of a man as Christian and as an officer of the state; to defend a double standard of morality, the one religious, the other secular.

Calvinism

Examining the Calvinistic position on these several points, we find ourselves in a rather different atmosphere. For Calvin and his followers, the starting point is the conviction of God's absolute sovereignty, his dominating will and power. God is the celestial king to whom man owes absolute obedience. Being all-powerful, he will save those whom he so predestines. That he saves some shows his mercy; that he condemns others shows his justice; that he does both enhances his glory. The supreme test of religious devotion is the willingness to be damned for the glory of God—the religious counterpart to the patriotic willingness to die for the glory of one's country.

Since God's glory demands absolute obedience, man must know and perform the divine law. The pious man, accordingly, obeys God's commands not primarily because they are good but because God has given them. The criterion of the Christian life, then, is the strict and literal performance of religious regulations. Obeying the religious law and living for the glory of God leave little or no place for foolishness and the lighter pleasures of life; these make men of firm and unyielding character, fellow workers with God.

The Calvinistic conception of the business of the church follows from this attitude. It is not primarily, as with Luther, to teach the gospel, but to train its members in holiness, to enforce upon them the divine rules. The church is thus given a practical regulatory function, which we have seen illustrated by Calvin's work in Geneva. To exercise this duty, ministers must be men of superior learning and holiness, dependent not like the priests upon the authority of their holy orders but upon their own personal superiority in the accepted virtues.

Nothing distinguishes the Calvinistic churches more sharply from their Lutheran neighbors than their social teachings. Since it is believed that God regulates human life according to his standards and that it is the business of the church to enforce these standards, Calvinists recognize no separation between religion and secular affairs. On the contrary, the church is regarded as supreme in all things. Not only must it place its regulations upon the private life of men; it must also order state and society, politics and commerce. Education, law, and industry fall under its control. Although a reformer, Calvin here reasserted the medieval doctrine of theocracy, the supremacy of the church over secular powers. This theocratic principle was actually employed by the Calvinistic founders of certain New England colonies; in New Haven the distinction between ecclesiastical and civil powers all but vanished and church membership was a prerequisite to the right to vote, and in colonial Boston those found guilty of profiteering were expelled from church membership. Calvinism, then, has within itself the ideal of religious regulation of all of life.

That the churches professing this principle have not done more to soften the brutalities of modern industrial life is probably due to the fact that their conception of God's will was too narrow. Turning for its standards to the laws of the Old Testament rather than to the message of Jesus in the New, the church had often nothing constructive to say. The very men who from the standpoint of Jesus' teaching are the worst sinners—violators of Christian principles of love, brotherhood, and cooperation—might successfully exemplify the Calvinistic virtues of thrift, industry, and sobriety.

While Lutheranism washed its hands of secular problems, the tragedy of Calvinism was that, claiming responsibility for them, it had insufficient ideals. It frittered away its marvelous moral energies in condemning petty vices, and was indeed often unable to distinguish between the vital and the trivial: since gambling is wrong, all card playing must be wrong; since some dancing might lead to improprieties, all dancing is sin. This was the logic of Calvinistic Puritanism. Its moral fervor undirected by discrimination and unilluminated by social ideals, it missed much of its opportunity in the modern world. For example, it is sometimes said that because its spectrum of human values was so narrow, Calvinism failed to understand the social significance of the growing capitalism which needed the guidance of humanitarian ideals. This charge has some justification but it can be overdrawn. The industrial revolution and the factory system lay far ahead, and no one foresaw how the industrial leviathan would feed upon human well-being. The time would come, however, when the Calvinistic principle that religious ideals must govern the whole of life would be recognized as applicable to social conditions.

While it is to be regretted that Calvinism in the past has conceived religious ideals too narrowly, we can be grateful that it did preserve the principle that religion and social affairs belong together. When in the last generation Protestant churches turned once more to the teaching of Jesus for their social ideals, they found Calvinism far more congenial than Lutheranism to their attempt to apply these ideals to economic and international affairs.

Consequences of the Protestant Reformation

One of the most obvious results of the Protestant Reformation was the creation of a number of relatively independent churches. The division of Protestantism into followers of Luther and Calvin respectively represents only the most general line of distinction. Within each of these groups appeared many separate churches, usually coordinate with political divisions. Thus, in Germany there were about as many Lutheran churches as there were Lutheran princes and free cities, while the Lutheran churches in Scandinavian countries were divided on national lines. There were in the end some 200 separate churches subscribing to the Augsburg Confession but actually being dominated by the rulers. This was the result of two factors: the principle of compromise between Lutherans and Catholics according to which the religion of the ruler should be the religion of the land, and Luther's practice, to be discussed later, of appealing to the prince for the settlement of disputes over the interpretation of Scripture and for the enforcement of orthodoxy. The nationalization of Protestant churches operated among Calvinists also, as in Switzerland, the Netherlands, and Scotland, with some variety of doctrine and discipline. The Lutheran church in Sweden and the Reformed (Calvinistic) church in Holland are the established churches of these lands today, enjoying special favors from and subjected to some control by the civil government.

The Anglican Church

The most familiar example of an established church outside of Catholic lands is the Church of England. While England had witnessed the same national sentiment and criticism of abuses in the Catholic church as those we have encountered in Germany and Switzerland, the Reformation in

England arose not from the people but from the king of England himself, and therefore exhibits a very different character. The political and social factors were dominant over the religious interest, while on the Continent the religious and theological issues were primary in initiating reform. England resented the controls exercised by the pope in national affairs, the need to send sums of money to Rome, and the fact that a tenth of the property in England was owned by the church. The incident which led to revolt from Rome (yet not by intention from the Catholic church) was both political and personal. King Henry VIII (ruled 1509-1547) was a strongly orthodox Catholic; in recognition of a reply he had written to some tracts of Luther in 1521, the pope had conferred upon him the title of Defender of the Faith —hence he was theologically no heretic! But when the pope refused to annul his marriage to Catherine of Aragon in order that he could marry Anne Boleyn, Henry ordered Thomas Cranmer, whom he had appointed archbishop of Canterbury, to do what the pope had refused. This was followed in 1534, in reply to the pope's threat of excommunication, by the Act of Supremacy in which Parliament declared the king to be the sole and supreme head of the Church of England, not as regards spiritual rights but in practically every other area formerly under the pope's jurisdiction in the English church.

Even now Henry did not think of himself as a Protestant in the German or Swiss sense. Except for the matter of authority, he regarded himself as in every way a Catholic. In 1539 he had Parliament pass the Six Articles, according to which such thoroughly Catholic beliefs and practices as transubstantiation, aurical confession, private masses, and the celibacy of priests were affirmed. It was under his son and successor, Edward VI (ruled 1547-1553), that Protestant ideas began to be officially accepted. The Six Articles were repealed and the *Book of Common Prayer*, combining at first both Catholic and Protestant beliefs, was put into general use. When Mary, daughter of Henry VIII and Catherine, came to the throne in 1553, she rejected the Protestant elements in the church and in the following year restored Catholicism (including papal authority). It remained for Elizabeth, daughter of Henry VIII and Anne Boleyn, to bring the movement away from Rome to completion, which was done in the Act of Supremacy of 1559.

Since the revolt in England was so largely the work of the political ruler, no Protestant theology was worked out to replace Catholic dogma. Consequently, many Catholic ideas and practices survived in the Anglican church which disappeared in the Lutheran and Reformed. Principally, this church retained the Catholic principles of unity and authority, vesting the ultimate authority in the king instead of the pope. The Anglican church provides us with an excellent illustration of the way a genuine desire for reform can play into the hands of powers intent on political and personal gain. In England, the political forces wanted independence from Roman interference and control of church property. One result was that many of the new Protestant churches became essentially state institutions, supported, controlled, and directed by the secular political rulers.

The Sects

In addition to the Lutheran, Calvinist, and Anglican forms of Protestantism, usually incorporated in nationally established churches, there arose from the Reformation a large number of sects as well. The causes were social as well as theological. One social factor was that the reformed churches soon proved themselves to be the expression of the religion of the middle class and the nobility more than of the poorer classes. Appealing rather to Paul's theology than to Jesus' ethics, the churches of the Reformation gave scant satisfaction to the religious needs of the poor, and exhorted them to obey their masters and to rest content in their economic misery. As a result, some religious outlet was needed for the socially submerged classes. This necessity gave rise to "the churches of the disinherited," among them the Anabaptists and later the Quakers and the Methodists.[9] The theological factors making for the rise of sects were rooted in disagreements over the interpretation of God's word. All the reformers substituted the Bible for the church as the repository of divine truth. That the Bible really was God's word was held to be guaranteed by the witness of the Holy Spirit in the minds of the faithful. The Holy Spirit was also expected to guarantee correct reading and interpretation of Scripture. The reformers apparently did not foresee the different interpretations that could be given scriptural teachings. But differences were inevitable, and each group naturally believed that it had been led by the Holy Spirit to its particular interpretation. The underprivileged classes thus formed their own churches and justified themselves by appeal to Scripture and religious experience. Among these additional Protestant movements we shall note three—the Anabaptists, the Arminians, and the Socinians.

The *Anabaptists* ("rebaptizers") were so called because of their belief that a person must be baptized in adult life after he has understood the meaning of the Christian life and submitted voluntarily to its sacraments. They discarded infant baptism as unscriptural, and baptized many adults who had

[9] See H. R. Niebuhr, *The Social Sources of Denominationalism*, New York, Henry Holt & Co., 1929, chap. 2.

been previously baptized as infants. They placed great emphasis upon the Holy Spirit, and taught that the church should be composed only of those who had undergone a genuine spiritual experience of conversion and had been "born again." They accepted the Bible literally: they believed that in accordance with Jesus' teaching it was wrong to take oaths, bear arms, or take any part in civil government. The movement attracted more than its rightful share of fanatics, some of whom emulated Old Testament figures by practicing polygamy; others looked for the end of the world after the present governments had been destroyed. They were extremely unpopular among both Catholics and other Protestants. Some of the bloodiest chapters of the Reformation are those dealing with the destruction of Anabaptists, who were forced to submit to the most terrible forms of torture. Luther was outspoken in his opposition in order to protect his movement from being identified with them. The outstanding figure among the Anabaptists was *Menno Simons* (1492-1559), who purged it of its extreme elements. The modern *Mennonites* preserve his name and teachings. The *Baptists* continue the emphasis upon baptism of adults.

The *Arminians* developed in Holland as a movement within Calvinism. They take their name from *Jacobus Arminius* (1560-1609), their greatest exponent, who came to doubt the doctrine of unconditional predestination and believed that man does have some control over his salvation through repentance and faith. His successors taught that salvation depends upon the use men make of the means of grace provided by God. They thus found a significant place for human choice, softening the rationalistic rigor of the doctrine of predestination. Arminianism gave moral courage and strength to those Christians who were not certain that they were of the elect. Its greatest historic importance is the influence it exerted upon Anglican thought and particularly upon John Wesley and the *Methodist* movement.

Protestantism appeared also in Italy, making inroads in various cities, particularly Venice. Many were influenced by Reformation ideas, but as the Catholic Inquisition became adroit at identifying heretics, liberals had either to suffer martyrdom or to flee Italy. Some went to Switzerland, but more to Poland. *Socinianism,* the most radical movement appearing in the Reformation era, arose from and is named after two of these Italian Protestants, *Lelio Sozzini* (1525-1562) and his nephew *Fausto Sozzini* (or *Socinus,* 1539-1604). They were influenced by Erasmus and his ethical Christianity, and were strongly rationalistic in their approach to religion even while they were also strongly supernaturalistic. They rejected the doctrines of predestination and total depravity, and thus diminished the dramatic role accorded the saving work of Christ by traditional Catholic and Protestant teaching alike. If man is not totally corrupted, he has within himself powers of goodness and freedom of will which can be developed and used for his salvation. The sole mission of Christ, then, was that of guide and teacher. He was not divine, but was a man adopted by God who showed men through his life and teaching the way to God and to salvation. There is no resurrection of the body and no eternal punishment in hell, for the wicked are annihilated. The Holy Spirit is not a divine "person" but is a power or attribute of God. The Socinians denied the doctrine of the Trinity, the very center of Christian orthodoxy.[10] They were vigorously opposed by orthodox Christians, both Catholic and Protestant, and their movement in Poland was later stamped out by the Jesuits.

In these sects as well as in the great national Protestant churches can be found the spiritual ancestry of many of the denominations with which we are familiar today. The Lutheran church is important today, as is the Church of England and its daughter church, the Episcopal church in America. Calvinism has become a part of many denominations, particularly the Presbyterian. The Methodist church shows the same evangelical fervor as the Arminians did, while both the Friends and the Baptists clearly reflect certain teachings of the Anabaptists. The Socinians were the spiritual ancestors of the liberal movement in Protestantism, especially of our modern Unitarians.

Protestant Orthodoxy

A direct consequence of the rise of sects like the Anabaptist was the crystallization of thought in the established churches into what is known as Protestant orthodoxy. This process is well illustrated by the development of Luther's own views, especially in regard to the authority of the Bible. What changed Martin Luther from a devout and believing monk into the arch-rebel of the church were not primarily intellectual or moral factors; it was rather that in his experience he discovered a new gospel, an experience of faith and assurance in the fellowship and love of God *not* mediated by the church and its works. With this new principle, further dependence upon the ministrations of the church was unnecessary. Luther broke first not with the church's claim to authority, then, but with its conception of salvation. Not until after he was sure that every Christian could go immediately to the source of grace did Luther take the next step of repudiating the church's claim to authority.

[10] E. H. Klotsche, *Christian Symbolics,* Burlington, Lutheran Literary Board, 1929, pp. 264-266.

Once driven to break with the authority of the church, Luther substituted the word of God for it at first. This was not the literal word of Scripture, but rather Scripture as it mediated the good news of God's forgiving love in Christ. That part of the Bible which brought men knowledge of this gospel, roused in them the response of faith, and brought them the assurance of forgiveness—that part was God's word. The actual authority for Luther was a kind of spiritual experience, and the various parts of the Bible were evaluated in terms of their power to produce this experience regardless of their authorship. Luther was in fact quite willing to discard certain books like Revelation from the sacred canon, and he thought St. James' Epistle "a mere letter of straw." In short, his authority was inward, not external.

But Luther's principle of looking to Scripture illuminated by faith as the supreme authority had in it the seeds of disagreement and disunity. If the authority of the Bible replaces the authority of the church, it follows that every believer can claim the right to interpret Scripture for himself; moreover, the inner light of faith may shine differently for different people, which means that the Bible might be interpreted in divergent ways. This possibility became an actuality in the rise of the sects, like the Anabaptists and the Arminians, who justified their "heretical" beliefs and practices by Luther's own principle of private judgment. While Luther had found the principles of scriptural authority and faith useful and even necessary weapons with which to fight Rome, they proved worse than useless for bringing heretics to the mark. These too could quote from the diverse riches of Scripture and appeal to the indwelling spirit. But Luther could not tolerate heresy, since this threatened to bring the religious confusion which his Catholic opponents had predicted and contained a threat to political stability also, since the heretics showed an alarming tendency to draw their members from among the poor and the politically rebellious. Feeling that he had to combat heresy in the interests of unity and order, he sought to undercut the ground on which his adversaries stood. In doing this, he virtually repudiated his own elastic and subjective principle of authority. He was thus led, as McGiffert has said,

> ... to substitute the Bible for the gospel, and to put ... the Scriptures of the Old and New Testament in place of ... the indwelling Spirit or inner light to which his radical adversaries were appealing. ... The Bible to which he then appealed as his authority, often reading it in the most slavishly literal fashion, had long been the favorite resort of all critics of the principles or practices of the Church, and his use of it gave it permanent and supreme authority within Protestantism.[11]

[11] A. C. McGiffert, *The Rise of Modern Religious Ideas*, New York, The Macmillan Company, 1915, pp. 282 f.

With the establishment of the letter of Scripture as the authority of Protestantism, the Bible became a textbook of doctrine and ethics and of the whole Christian revelation. This emphasis was accompanied by a most significant change in the meaning of *faith*. For Luther, faith was trust, a personal relationship with Christ and God. But now the meaning of the word was gradually transformed to simple *belief*—to the acceptance of certain Christian ideas as true. Since faith (now understood as belief) was held to be the only condition of salvation, correct *belief* as to what Christian revelation contains became of prime importance. It is not surprising, therefore, to find Protestant churches anxious about the soundness of their belief and intolerant of beliefs differing from their own. The consequence was that intellectual agreement in matters of doctrine became the basis of fellowship. Instead of securing unity, Biblical literalism bred division. Every doctrinal disagreement gave rise to a new sect, each with its own set of "fundamental" beliefs that formed the limits of thought for its members. Instead of there being one body of dogmatic Protestant thought to rival the inclusive unity of thirteenth-century Scholasticism, there were now as many "orthodoxies" as there were denominations and sects. Not only did this new *Protestant Scholasticism* suffer from lack of unity, but it was more narrow and sterile than its Catholic predecessor. Where Aquinas had approached his task with great breadth of knowledge, understanding, and vision, orthodox Protestant theologians ignored philosophic, scientific, and political thought. Grubbing around for scriptural proof-texts, they were untouched by the vitalizing influences of the science and philosophy of their time. Thus isolated from other intellectual concerns, theology became justly regarded by the best minds as reactionary and possibly irrelevant to the main concerns of the growing age.

Yet despite their bitter disagreements over details, the various sects and denominations shared a common core of Protestant theology; and apart from the questions of authority and the means of salvation, this common body of belief was not different from the historic tenets of the Catholic church. The doctrines of the Trinity, of Adam's fall and man's consequent original sin, the need for supernatural salvation and its provision through the work of Christ, the divine inspiration and authority of the Bible—these are some of the traditional Christian beliefs common to Protestants and Catholics. Their acceptance among Protestants became a general test for Christian orthodoxy which, as thus constituted, still survives. The clearest example of Protestant orthodoxy is now usually known as fundamentalism, so called because of the insistence of its advocates that they alone adhere to the fundamentals of the faith.

The Catholic Counter-Reformation

The Protestant revolt against the authority of the Catholic church naturally caused a strong reaction within that church. Many Catholics were by no means indifferent to the abuses which were criticized by the reformers, and there had indeed been reform efforts within the Catholic church even before Luther. Some attempts were made to bring about reconciliation with the Protestants after the Reformation had begun, but then it was too late; the composite movement which resulted from the union of political and religious interests could not be reversed.

Three steps stand out as especially important in the Catholic reaction once reconciliation was found impossible. First, the Inquisition, used against Jews and heretics in Spain from the middle of the thirteenth century, was now used wherever there was sufficient Catholic power to support it. Through this means Protestantism was largely destroyed in Italy and Poland. Second, Ignatius of Loyola (1491-1556) formed the Society of Jesus (Jesuits). Its members bound themselves to complete obedience to their superior or general and to the sacrifice of their own wills in the service of Christ. Their influence throughout Europe and the wider Christian world became enormous. Their chief agencies were preaching, teaching through excellent schools, and the use of the confessional. Bound together very closely on a pattern drawn basically from the military, the Society became international in character and wielded great power politically as well as religiously. The Jesuits were successful in overcoming much of the influence of Protestantism. Third, the Council of Trent, held sporadically from 1545 to 1563, carried forward a wide-reaching program of reforms within Catholicism begun under Paul III, pope from 1534 to 1549. The Council made provision for further regeneration of the morals of the clergy, emphasized the education of both laymen and clergy, affirmed the authority of the pope, reaffirmed the Scholastic theology of Thomas Aquinas as the true interpretation of Catholic dogma, and decided to allow no compromise with Protestantism. This Council marked a turning point in Roman Catholic life and led to a true renaissance of Catholicism, particularly in its spiritual character.

The Reformation as a Transitional Movement

We began this chapter with the statement that the Protestant Reformation was the religious aspect of the transition from the medieval to the modern outlook. Perhaps we can most profitably conclude with an attempt to evaluate the Reformation from this standpoint.

In the political sphere, the religious revolt against Rome strengthened and aided the development of modern nationalism; Protestant principles gave religious sanction for the political movement away from the medieval ecclesiastic state. Likewise, Protestantism proved to be more congenial to the growing capitalism than the medieval church had been with its prohibition of interest on loans and its attempts to regulate prices and restrict profit. The Lutheran conception of its function denied the church any right to legislate business ethics. While Calvinism claimed the regulation of all life as the duty of the church, it early permitted interest and profit—the essence of the capitalist economy. The Puritan ethic, emphasizing the moral quality of work, frugality, and self-restraint, gave religious reinforcement to those qualities in men that make for business success and the accumulation of capital as its reward. Moreover, both Lutheranism and Calvinism taught that *any* life work may be a religious vocation, so that a man in business might feel that he was fulfilling God's will. In respect to both nationalism and capitalism, it can be said that Protestantism hastened the transition to the modern world.

In regard to education, the Reformation both helped and hindered progress. By emphasizing the worth of the common man, it gave theoretical justification for the education of the masses. While it took a long time for this principle to find practical application, popular and public education in Protestant countries bears witness to its influence. On the other hand, the reformers feared and opposed secular learning. The triumph of the Lutherans, said Erasmus, is the death of good learning. Luther damned the intellect as the bride of Satan, and Calvin declared natural science to be godless and harmful. Modern science and philosophy had to move forward against the opposition of both Protestantism and Catholicism.

In theology, the Reformation was a step on the way toward modern Protestantism. Luther himself, essentially conservative, was not so much seeking for a new development as he was attempting to recover a Biblical faith. But whatever his intentions, the result of what he taught and did favored much that has appeared in the modern outlook. The central principles of the Reformation—salvation by faith alone without priestly mediation and the authority of the Scriptures privately interpreted—are the foundation stones of religious individualism. While these principles were somewhat submerged in Protestant orthodoxy which, like Catholicism, was also quite ready to destroy heretics—witness Luther's outcry against them and the burning of Servetus in Calvin's Geneva—they yet contained the seeds of the modern assertion of the right of private judgment in religion. On the other hand, the appeal to Scripture was not fundamentally a break with the medieval reliance upon authority and revelation. The Roman Catholic church also held to the authority of Scripture but believed that the church was its authoritative interpreter. It was this latter belief that the Reformation rejected, not the basic idea of authority. In this respect, then, the reformers were oriented toward the past, not toward the discovery of new truth, which was the trend in the developing sciences and the more radical philosophic approaches. The element of medievalism in Reformation theology is emphatically illustrated by the theology of Protestant orthodoxy, which, as we have seen, is in most essentials not different from the Catholic.

In spite of all that has been said, however, it is true that toleration and freedom and the recognition of the right of private judgment and opinion did spring from the Reformation. Many people, inspired by the Protestant teaching concerning the rights of the individual conscience, were willing to die—and did die—for what they believed. Minority groups like the Anabaptists consistently stood for individualism and tolerance and were able, little by little, to cause those in power to recognize their claims. In Holland, for example, where persecution had been as bitter as anywhere, toleration became so fully established by the seventeenth century that that country was the refuge for such individualists as the Pilgrims and such advanced thinkers as Spinoza and Descartes.

The Reformation, then, was a movement of transition. Like the Humanism of the Renaissance, it contained within itself principles both reactionary and progressive, both medieval and modern. It represented a movement of religious change which was later to be greatly influenced by eighteenth-century rationalism and nineteenth-century romanticism and science to become a liberal form of religion in the early twentieth century.

Questions for Study

1. What was the part played by the Protestant Reformation in the revolt against authority? In what way was mysticism, so prominent in the Middle Ages, a factor in bringing about the Reformation?
2. What attacks were made by the pre-reformers upon the church? Who were two of these, and what did they do?
3. How did nationalism become a very important factor in the rise of the Reformation?
4. What forms of corruption were common in the fourteenth and fifteenth centuries in the church? What is an indulgence, and how was it misused?

5. Indicate the stages in the development of the Reformation. What was the central problem for Luther, and how did his principle of justification by faith solve this problem for him? At what points do you find agreement between the thought of Luther and that of the Catholic church, and at what points disagreement? What are the basic tenets contained in the Augsburg Confession?
6. What are the fundamental principles of Calvin? Show where he is similar to and where different from Luther in temperament and teaching.
7. What differences does it make between Calvin and Luther that the former emphasized the sovereignty of God and the latter the love of God? Why did Calvin reach the ideal of a theocracy, as the popes had reached it earlier?
8. How did the Anglican church come into being, and in what respects is it different from the other Protestant churches? What gave rise to the sects? What emphases appear in Arminianism and Socinianism?
9. What led Luther, against his own principles, to make the Bible the authority in Protestantism? How did this change the meaning of faith? What is meant by Protestant Scholasticism, and how can it be evaluated? What core of common beliefs do orthodox Protestants generally share?
10. What was the Catholic response to the Protestant Reformation? Discuss the three steps taken by the Catholic church.
11. Show in what respects the Reformation was, like the Renaissance generally, a transitional movement.

Selected Readings

Bainton, Roland H., *Here I Stand: A Life of Martin Luther*, Nashville, Abingdon-Cokesbury Press, 1950.

Bainton, Roland H., *The Reformation of the Sixteenth Century*, Boston, Beacon Press, 1952.

Ferguson, Wallace K., and Geoffrey Bruun, *A Survey of European Civilization*, Boston, Houghton Mifflin Company, 1936.

Grimm, Harold J., *The Reformation Era*, New York, The Macmillan Company, 1954.

Lucas, Henry S., *The Renaissance and the Reformation*, 2nd ed., New York, Harper & Brothers, 1960.

McGiffert, Arthur Cushman, *Protestant Thought Before Kant*, New York, Charles Scribner's Sons, 1912.

Neve, J. L., *A History of Christian Thought*, Philadelphia, Muhlenberg Press, 1946.

Randall, John Herman, Jr., *The Making of the Modern Mind*, rev. ed., Boston, Houghton Mifflin Company, 1940.

Smith, Preserved, *The Age of the Reformation*, New York, Henry Holt & Co., 1920.

Smith, Preserved, *A History of Modern Culture,* New York, Henry Holt & Co., 1930, vol. I.

Taylor, Henry Osborn, *Thought and Expression in the Sixteenth Century,* New York, The Macmillan Company, 1920, 2 vols.

Walker, Williston, *A History of the Christian Church,* rev. ed., New York, Charles Scribner's Sons, 1959.

VII. Philosophy, Religion, and Science in the Modern World

Chronological Framework of Part VII

René Descartes, 1596-1650.

Benedict Spinoza, 1632-1677.

Gottfried Leibniz, 1646-1716.

John Locke, 1632-1704.

Isaac Newton, 1642-1727.

George Berkeley, 1685-1753.

David Hume, 1711-1776.

Condorcet, 1743-1794.

Auguste Comte, 1798-1857.

IMPORTANT EVENTS AND PERSONS IN EVOLUTION

Lamarck, 1744-1829.

T. R. Malthus, 1766-1834.

Principles of Geology, by Charles Lyell, 1830-1833.

Charles Darwin, 1809-1882. *Origin of Species*, 1859.

Gregor Mendel, 1822-1884.

IMPORTANT FIGURES IN RECENT PHYSICS AND PSYCHOLOGY

Pierre de Laplace, 1749-1827.

Albert Einstein, 1879-1955.

Sigmund Freud, 1856-1939.

John B. Watson, 1878-1958.

Carl G. Jung, 1875-1961.

Alfred Adler, 1870-1937.

TWENTIETH-CENTURY THINKERS AND THEIR PREDECESSORS

Søren Kierkegaard, 1813-1855.

Karl Marx, 1818-1883.

Friedrich Nietzsche, 1844-1900.

Bertrand Russell, 1872———.

Karl Jaspers, 1883———.

Ludwig Wittgenstein, 1889-1951.

Rudolph Bultmann, 1884———.

Karl Barth, 1886———.

Paul Tillich, 1886———.

Emil Brunner, 1889———.

Reinhold Niebuhr, 1892———.

17. The Enlightenment

❧❧❧❧❧❧❧❧❧❧❧❧❧❧❧❧❧❧❧❧❧❧❧❧❧❧❧❧❧❧

The term *modern world* is open to a variety of interpretations. It may be used to differentiate some limited segment of time, as from the end of World War I to the present, or the entire twentieth century, but a common historic usage is to designate as *modern* the whole of history since the Renaissance. Any dividing line drawn between what is modern and what is not modern is necessarily somewhat arbitrary.

From one point of view, our entire survey of philosophy and religion has been modern. Thus, the Old Testament is a contemporary document in the sense that it is read today as part of the worship service in Christian churches and Jewish synagogues. Similarly, the New Testament continues to exert great influence upon our thinking. The relevance of Greek thought to our present outlook has been clearly demonstrated. On the other hand, we are aware of the fact that what was a commonplace to the man living in ancient Israel or Greece, in the Roman world, or in medieval civilization is unfamiliar to us. The setting in which early religious and philosophical ideas were produced was radically different in many respects from our own.

The Meaning of Enlightenment

We tend to believe that those ideas are modern which we take for granted and which to a large degree control our thoughts and actions. From this standpoint, the Enlightenment is the beginning of the modern period. It started in the middle of the seventeenth century and continued through the eighteenth century. It no longer exists in the form in which it appeared in those years, yet because we continue to live under the control of a large proportion of the ideas which it produced we may take the Enlightenment as the point of departure in our discussion of philosophy and religion in the modern world. Americans are particularly indebted to the Enlightenment because their democratic ideas and ideals were formed during that period. When Thomas Jefferson wrote the second paragraph of the Declaration of Independence, he was not writing as an individual divorced from the intellectual atmosphere in which he lived; he was giving expression to the tenets of a political philosophy which was widespread in the eighteenth century. To Jefferson it seemed axiomatic that "all men are created equal, that they are endowed by their creator with certain unalienable rights, that among these are life, liberty and the pursuit of happiness; that to secure these rights governments are instituted among men, deriving their just powers from the consent of the governed. . . ." We still live on the assumption that men are equal politically and before the law, and that governments are instituted by the people and are responsible to them. It was the age of Enlightenment which undermined the belief in the supernatural origin of the power of government (the divine right of kings) and laid the foundations of democracy. The eighteenth century also witnessed the rise of popular enthusiasm for science, the beginning of the process of secularizing education, the breaking of the bonds of tradition and authority in many areas, including religion, and a number of other cultural movements which are definitely a part of the world in which we live today.

The Enlightenment was not, of course, an entirely new movement. In it tendencies that had already showed themselves in the Renaissance came to full development, and as they did so they changed the basic attitudes of the people of Northern and Central Europe. The whole world of thought and culture was transformed as a result of the Enlightenment. This does not mean, however, that it had universal effect; the great majority of Europeans continued to live by ideas and values common to the Middle Ages and the Reformation. Yet gradually its emphases made their impact, often indirectly, upon culture. The full effects of some of the ideas, especially in science, have had to wait until our own day to receive general acceptance. The period as a whole was one in which the older elements of European culture came to be criticized and often rejected, and new understandings took their place. McGiffert has well expressed the two sides of the impact of the Enlightenment in the following quotation:

The humility, the self-distrust, the dependence upon supernatural powers, the submission to external authority, the subordination of time to eternity and of fact to symbol, the conviction of the insignificance and meanness of the present life, the somber sense of the sin of man and the evil of the world, the static interpretation of reality, the passive acceptance of existing conditions and the belief that amelioration can come only in another world beyond the grave, the dualism between God and man, heaven and earth, spirit and flesh, the ascetic renunciation of the world and its pleasures—all of which characterized the Middle Ages—were widely overcome, and men faced life with a new confidence in themselves, with a new recognition of human power and achievement, with a new appreciation of present values, and with a new conviction of the onward progress of the race in past and future.[1]

The development of science in the sixteenth and seventeenth centuries was particularly significant in creating attitudes in philosophy and religion which were moving forces in men's lives by the time of the Enlightenment. The success of astronomy and physics in investigations of nature through the use of mathematics suggested the possibility of applying the concepts and methods employed by these sciences universally. Because ancient problems long thought to be beyond solution had yielded solutions to scientific approaches, the attitude of thinkers toward their world went through a transformation. Instead of being resigned toward nature, they now believed it was within their power to change it, and they set about doing just that. Criticism, discontent, efforts to destroy the old and to create the new were the order of the day, not only in religion and philosophy but also in political situations and in the economic order. The Middle Ages had valued the passive virtues; the Enlightenment valued the active ones.[2]

Of particular importance during the Enlightenment were the concepts of reason, experience, and nature—and the greatest of these was reason. Indeed, the eighteenth century is frequently called the Age of Reason. Yet reason does not stand alone, for along with it we find a parallel interest in experience (which sometimes stands in opposition to it), and underlying both is a deep concern with nature and the science which exposes its secrets. It was often assumed that the rational and the natural were so much at one with each other that natural religion and rational religion meant the same thing.

The emphasis upon reason exhibits itself in philosophy as *rationalism* and that upon experience as *empiricism*. These two types of philosophy with their respective methods replaced the theological method, basing itself upon

[1] A. C. McGiffert, *The Rise of Modern Religious Ideas,* New York, The Macmillan Company, 1915, pp. 11-12.
[2] *Ibid.*, pp. 12 f.

revelation, which dominated the Middle Ages. Since mathematics played so large a part in the thinking of the Enlightenment, we might consider this period, particularly in science but also in philosophy, as the time in which the mathematics which had appeared so tentatively (yet so fruitfully) in Copernicus and Kepler came to full triumph.

We will now examine briefly the work of the great rationalists of this period, being concerned not so much with details of their thought as with their emphases upon the powers of reason. The three outstanding men are Descartes, Spinoza, and Leibniz.

The Rationalist Emphasis

To say that the Enlightenment was the age of reason does not mean that this was the only period in which men resolutely employed their rational faculties in dealing with human problems. Thomas Aquinas, for example, and others of the great medieval theologians undoubtedly had as much respect for reason as any eighteenth-century thinker. The difference lay in the interpretation of reason and its function. During the Middle Ages reason was generally considered the handmaid of faith; faith was certain, while reason might err. Revelation and the authority of the church were the foundations of certainty. Reason did not criticize religion, but was used instead to support it and elaborate its statements. During the fourteenth and fifteenth centuries reason and faith moved apart, but the truths of faith still were received on the basis of authority without serious question. Later, however, the belief that there could be two *areas* of truth—one for faith and one for reason—which might stand in opposition to each other and yet both be true, was accepted by a number of thinkers. As long as authority was accepted, particularly the authority of the church, faith maintained itself over against reason and often at its expense. But when the Reformation removed the church as the basis of authority, all of this was changed. Reason now was not satisfied to deny the authority of the church or the pope; it attacked the fundamental concepts of Christianity, like the Trinity, incarnation, and the sinfulness of man. Reason, in short, became critical, standing apart from faith in certainty of its own powers and criticizing even those beliefs once most dear to men but now out of harmony with the dominant interests of the new age. The eighteenth-century philosophers believed that reason was the judge of all things, including even the value of church or Bible, which had formerly been considered authoritative. Almighty reason became the unrivaled judge of truth.

In its relation to custom, tradition, and religious authority, reason may be used for one of two purposes. It may provide an intellectual foundation in support of these things, just as Aquinas had tried to demonstrate the reasonableness of Christian doctrine; or it may become a destructive critic, and it was in this role that reason appeared in the Enlightenment. Rationalism, allied with empiricism, set out consciously to destroy whatever was left of the medieval spirit. Undoubtedly there was a widespread feeling that the essence of medievalism was, as Goethe believed, the view that nature is sin and the intellect the devil. This view was to be destroyed in order that nature might be deified and reason enthroned.

We shall find that the eighteenth century developed a rational religion which openly opposed the idea of special revelation and unpredictable interference with the orderly processes of nature on the part of God. In the political sphere rationalism served to undermine the myth of the divine right of kings and to make the actions of rulers subject to rational criticism. In economics there was a critical appraisal of the established privileges of the ruling classes. All of this was based on the rationalist philosophy which had been formulated in the previous century and which was most closely associated with the method pursued in physical science, a method which sought to banish magic and mystery from the world.

The method which was bringing success to astronomy and physics involved, as we have seen, both empirical and rationalist elements. It included direct observation of the behavior of natural phenomena and the development of experimental techniques. But the science of mathematics had proved to be particularly valuable in furnishing clues for the interpretation of the data collected. Mathematics is a rationalistic science in that it can be pursued by the mind without observing the behavior of things. Starting with certain axioms, one may sit in his study and work out all the inferences. The remarkable thing was that this rationalistic science did prove to be not only applicable to the real world in which we live but also absolutely essential in giving meaning to men's observations. No wonder the idea developed that the language of nature was the language of mathematics. And no wonder that it occurred to the alert mind of Descartes that this method might be made the basis of a universal method, a way of dealing with all problems.

Descartes

René Descartes (1596-1650) was the first modern philosopher to affirm unambiguously the supremacy of reason. This is what is meant by his famous method of critical doubt, a method reminiscent of St. Augustine but used for different purposes. Descartes had come to distrust the validity of all his beliefs, and like Augustine he doubted everything until he arrived at the one certainty that, since he was doubting, it followed that at least he, the doubter and thinker, existed. Thus, he boldly set *himself* against every accepted authority and resolved to accept no belief as true until it passed the test of reason. And what was reason? Descartes, mathematician and philosopher, had for some time been working on a theory which, when perfected, became that branch of science known as analytical geometry, which is a unification of algebra and geometry. Then it occurred to him that the same principles which he had used in inventing a science which provided so great a gain in simplicity and generality, and which had demonstrated the complete correspondence between algebra and the realm of space, could be used in handling any problem. In his *Discourse on Method* (written at age 23) he enumerated four principles which he resolved to follow as constituting the method of reason.

The first of these was to accept nothing as true which I did not clearly recognize to be so: that is to say, carefully to avoid precipitation and prejudice in judgments, and to accept in them nothing more than what was presented to my mind so *clearly and distinctly that I could have no occasion to doubt it.*

The second was to divide up each of the difficulties which I examined into as many parts as possible, and as seemed requisite in order that it might be resolved in the best manner possible.

The third was to carry on my reflections in due order, commencing with objects that were the most simple and easy to understand, in order to rise little by little, or by degrees, to knowledge of the most complex, assuming an order, even if a fictitious one, among those which do not follow a natural sequence relatively to one another.

The last was in all cases to make enumerations so complete and reviews so general that I should be certain of having omitted nothing.

Those long chains of reasoning, simple and easy as they are, of which geometricians make use in order to arrive at the most difficult demonstrations, had caused me to imagine that all those things which fall under the cognisance of man might very likely be mutually related in the same fashion; and that, provided only that we abstain from receiving anything as true which is not so, and always retain the order which is necessary in order to deduce the one conclusion from the other, there can be nothing so remote that we cannot reach to it, nor so recondite that we cannot discover it. . . . Considering also that of all those who have hitherto sought for the truth in the Sciences, it has been the mathematicians alone who have been able to succeed in making any demonstrations, that is to say producing reasons that are evident and certain, I did not doubt that it had been by means of a similar kind that they carried on their investigations.[3]

[3] *Discourse on Method*, in R. M. Eaton (ed.), *Descartes Selections*, New York, Charles Scribner's Sons, 1927, pp. 16 ff. [Emphasis supplied.]

This is a striking statement, particularly when one recalls that Descartes was a contemporary of Galileo and lived at the time of the Inquisition. Here there is no slightest dependence upon any kind of authority, church, or philosopher. It was his own sense of certainty alone that he was willing to make his final authority, and that for the subjective reason that it was clear and distinct to his mind.

The method which he so clearly formulated proved to be highly useful, particularly in mathematics. But when he attempted to give it the universal application he believed it was fitted to provide, he found it was not fully satisfactory. His emphasis upon accepting ideas as true if they seemed clear and distinct to him proved to be an insufficient basis for the study of nature itself. In other words, geometry, with its axioms and principles, to which Descartes' method ideally lends itself, is an unsatisfactory method for studying the physical world.[4] It remained for Newton to take those steps which led to modern physical investigation. The scientist must begin not with general assumptions, however clear and distinct they may seem to be, but with direct observations from which he moves to general statements as conclusions. Analysis of phenomena, not Descartes' method of deduction, is basic to modern thought.

To this negative conclusion concerning Descartes' approach to knowledge it must be added, however, that although his only permanent contribution to scientific knowledge was his brilliant work in analytical geometry, his ambitious hope of universalizing the mathematical approach in solving problems of nature was the beginning of that faith in the supremacy of reason which became fundamental for eighteenth-century philosophers. This rationalism provided one of the most potent instruments in the attacks upon authority and tradition.

Spinoza

Like Descartes, his greatest disciple, the Dutch Jew Benedict Spinoza (1632-1677), based his philosophic system of thought upon mathematics. In his primary work, the *Ethics,* he developed his rationalist system by the geometric method, believing that the greatest problems of philosophy and religion could be solved in this way. He proceeded exactly as one does in Euclidian geometry, beginning with axioms and principles which he considered self-evident and indubitable. From these he developed step-by-step demonstrations, erecting each upon the truths established by the previous

[4] See Ernst Cassirer, *The Philosophy of the Enlightenment,* Princeton, Princeton University Press, 1951, pp. 51 f.

ones. His starting point was God, defined as the one substance, of whom thought (the mental) and extension (the physical) were known attributes. By strict logical deduction everything was then derived, with the result that the conclusions appeared to be as certain as are the conclusions in Euclidian geometry. No appeal to experience is necessary for Spinoza's thought. This is rationalism in its purest form.

Leibniz

The third of the great seventeenth-century rationalists is the German philosopher, mathematician, and courtier Gottfried Leibniz (1646-1716). His underlying concept, from which he derived the remainder of his system, was that ultimately reality is made up of an infinite number of centers of conscious force, designated *monads*, arranged in a hierarchy of being with God at the top as the Monad of monads. Each monad is itself an individual universe, unextended (not occupying space) and with a degree of consciousness. Each represents in its own degree the entire universe. By the pre-established harmony of God, all are aware of the same universe at the same time. In terms of possibility, many worlds might have come into being, but because God is good he has created the best of all possible worlds—a doctrine made sport of by Voltaire in his *Candide*.

Leibniz' philosophic concepts are not as significant for our purposes as is his method. Influenced by Spinoza's geometric method, he also derived knowledge from that which is intuitively certain, self-evident, and clear and distinct in itself. He too proceeded from principles derived from what reason finds certain in itself. Once more we find a great rationalist system with mathematics setting its dominant character. We might add that Leibniz' mathematical interests were not directed wholly toward philosophy, since he shares with Sir Isaac Newton the honor of having invented the calculus, a most important discovery for future thought since it made possible the measurement of curves.

Empiricism: Locke's Theory of Knowledge

In addition to the mathematical side of scientific method there is also the empirical side, which concerns direct experience and observation. From the perspective of our own day we can understand that the two approaches are equally important, but it was natural in an earlier day, when scientific method was in the process of developing, that a philosophy should tend to emphasize one of these more than the other. Descartes stressed the rationalist or mathematical phase, as we have seen; it was the Englishman John Locke (1632-1704) who laid the foundations of an empirical philosophy. In some respects Locke was just as rationalistic as was Descartes, but certain new emphases in his work served to place him in the empirical tradition. Locke was neither a mathematician nor a particularly learned philosopher. His chief claim to fame is that he had an amazing amount of common sense and knowledge of his world which together enabled him to understand and state clearly the ideas which the more advanced minds of his generation shared. He managed to write so persuasively on the enlightened view in philosophy, religion, morals, politics, and education that his philosophy became one of the chief gospels of the eighteenth century.

Locke was above all a champion of toleration, of freedom of thought and speech, and thus was opposed to both political and ecclesiastical control of man's beliefs. He wished to remove all artificial and arbitrary restrictions on human thinking, but he came to see that there are certain *natural* restrictions which hinder man's discovery of truth. It was this insight which led him to write his famous *Essay Concerning Human Understanding*. In "The Epistle to the Reader" on this work, Locke says:

> Were it fit to trouble thee with the history of this Essay, I should tell thee, that five or six friends meeting at my chamber, and discoursing on a subject very remote from this, found themselves quickly at a stand, by the difficulties that rose on every side. After we had a while puzzled ourselves, without coming any nearer a resolution of those doubts which perplexed us, it came into my thoughts, that we took a wrong course; and that before we set ourselves upon inquiries of that nature, it was necessary to examine our own abilities, and see what objects our understandings were, or were not, fitted to deal with.[5]

And so he set about the task of examining the natural powers and limitations of the human mind.

The first thing which Locke attacked was the notion of innate ideas, so dear to Descartes. He could find no reason for believing that the mind, apart from experience, has any ideas whatever. On the contrary, the mind at birth, he wrote, is like a blank writing slate, a *tabula rasa,* upon which are written ideas that one gains through experience of the outside world. Many people seem to believe, said Locke, that there are certain general principles which

[5] Sterling P. Lamprecht (ed.), *Locke Selections,* New York, Charles Scribner's Sons, 1928, pp. 84 f.

are universally subscribed to and which must therefore be known independently of experience. That is, they believe that certain ideas are always found among men, whether they be Europeans or Asiatics, ancients or moderns, and that such ideas must be innate. Locke pointed out that even if there were universal beliefs, the fact of their universality would not prove them to be innate, but that as a matter of fact he could not discover any ideas which were universally believed. Moral principles, for example, vary from age to age and from place to place. Our ideas of right and wrong are demonstrably based on experience.

Experience, then, is the sole origin of the furnishings of our minds, and by experience is meant sensation and reflection upon sensation. Knowledge is not present at birth, but the process of learning begins as soon as one has sense experience. Thus one sees and feels things, and these sensations make their marks on the blank tablet which is the mind. These marks do not fade immediately but remain as items of memory upon which there is reflection. A person may compare one idea with another, make distinctions between them, give them names, find qualities which are present in several things, and so build up a complex mental content. But the origin of it all is experience.

This point of view is very different from rationalism. Mathematics taken as a model for thinking suggests the notion that there are axioms which the mind intuits independently of experience. Leibniz wrote that Locke did not "sufficiently distinguish . . . the origin of the necessary truths, whose source is in the understanding, from that of the truths of facts drawn from the experience of the senses, and even from those confused perceptions which are in us."[6] This rationalism had offered the hope that axioms could be intuited in physics, ethics, politics, and religion as well as in mathematics. We saw that Spinoza actually worked out a system of ethics on the geometric plan. But Locke's analysis of human understanding seemed to undermine this even though Locke himself retained something of the rationalist spirit, but in a different form. To the rationalists of the seventeenth century, reason was the realm of the *eternal truths* through which one participates in the divine nature and enters into the intelligible world; but to Locke and his followers, reason was an intellectual *force* which had the task and capability of acquiring knowledge. Reason was a kind of energy instead of a body of principles and truths.[7] It was in this sense that Locke used reason and retained the rationalist spirit.

The eighteenth-century philosophers were able to make effective use of

[6] *New Essays Concerning Human Understanding*, tr. A. G. Langley, New York, The Macmillan Company, 1896, p. 71.

[7] See Cassirer, *op. cit.*, p. 13.

both early rationalism and empiricism. Following Descartes and his fellow systematizers, they asserted the supremacy of human reason. Following Locke, they were able to show the influence of experience in the formation of ideas. But their interests were not so much theoretical as practical, for they were intent on destroying what they considered the falsities and evils of the past and on establishing new ways of understanding and living. In Locke's footsteps, they attempted to condemn ideas they disliked by showing that such beliefs were merely written on the mind by an objectionable social environment which ought to be replaced by a better one. Professor Carl Becker has described the influence of empiricism in this respect:

> [Locke's *Essay Concerning Human Understanding*] became the psychological gospel of the eighteenth century. Its great service to the men of that time was to demonstrate that the mind owed nothing to inheritance, to "innate ideas"; everything to environment, to the sensations that flowed in upon it from the outer world. . . . What Locke aimed at no doubt, what the eighteenth century acclaimed him for having demolished, was the Christian doctrine of total depravity, a black, spreading cloud which for centuries had depressed the human spirit. For if, as Locke maintained, the mind at birth was devoid of implanted and ineradicable ideas and dispositions, was in fact no more than a blank white sheet of paper upon which the outer world of nature and human association was to write whatever of good or ill repute might be found recorded there, why, then, the mind of man was a record made by that outer world: jazzed and discordant now that the outer world was so; a satisfying and ordered symphony when that outer world should become, as it might, what men had conceived it ought to be. This was Locke's great title to glory, that he made it possible for the eighteenth century to believe with a clear conscience what it wanted to believe, namely, that since man and the mind of man were shaped by that nature which God had created, it was possible for men, "barely by the use of their natural faculties," to bring their ideas and their conduct, and hence the institutions by which they lived, into harmony with the universal natural order.[8]

Empiricism and rationalism satisfied the eighteenth-century philosophers' zeal for reform by offering an effective intellectual instrument for attacking existing beliefs and institutions. Beyond this was their faith in nature as offering the pattern according to which the new ideas, relationships, and human institutions were to be constructed. Physical nature, as described by Newtonian mechanics, was a harmonious system, and human nature, if freed from the artificial and harmful bonds of custom, would also develop a harmonious social system.

[8] Carl L. Becker, *The Heavenly City of the Eighteenth-Century Philosophers*, New Haven, Yale University Press, 1932, pp. 64 f.

Newtonian Natural Philosophy

In Isaac Newton (1642-1727), born the same year that Galileo died, we reach the consummation of that scientific development which Galileo and Kepler had labored so hard to bring into being. He it was who drew together the central emphases of the revolutionary period in which he lived. His discovery of the principle of universal gravitation was his greatest scientific discovery, but, his importance is not so much indicated by the discovery itself as it is illustrated by it. The *method* by means of which he came to the principle was vastly important and influential, continuing still as the basic method in modern science.

The rationalists of the seventeenth century attempted to approach the study of nature through methods based upon strict deduction. Ideally, they hoped eventually to be able to understand the entire universe by starting from self-evident truths which seemed to them indubitable (such as the statement that the whole is equal to the sum of its parts), and from these truths to derive all knowledge by means of logical deduction.[9] This, we saw, was the method and hope of Descartes, for example, which worked remarkably well in mathematics but failed to be of value in physics. These men felt that in clear ideas one had certainty while in experimentation one was exposed to the uncertain and the fallible. Newton treated this method with suspicion, believing that when one starts his study of nature with self-evident, clear, and distinct ideas he finds that there is no good reason for preferring one of these ideas above another, and that there is no way to determine what their actual relation to the facts of nature is. He believed it essential to check one's reasoning constantly by repeated experimentation and observation in order to be certain that the processes of abstract thought relate immediately to the world itself. The goal of scientific study is to reach mathematical formulations of natural processes; yet the final test of truth must always be agreement with observed fact.

Newton's famous method, used with such great success during the more than 250 years since his day, was this. Start by analyzing observed facts, like the motion of the moon, for instance. Attempt to find some fundamental principle (later called the hypothesis) by which the item being studied can be understood. In the instance of the moon, the theory Newton came to

[9] It is of interest to note that the method of these rationalists was the same as that of the thirteenth-century theologians, namely, that of logical deduction. The difference came at the starting point: the theologian began with the truths of his faith and the rationalist with those truths which his own mind found to be certain.

was the theory of universal gravitation. Deduce the mathematical consequences of this principle—that is, place it in the form of a mathematical formula, if possible. Finally, by further observation and experimentation, show that the consequences which must logically follow from the principle are in entire agreement with experience.[10] This method combines the rational and the empirical, insisting always that the rational is valid for physical reality only when complemented by the empirical. The rational alone is uncontrolled by fact; the empirical alone is blind, incapable of discovering general truths.

Newton rejected the so-called hypotheses with which the rationalists of his century began their investigations since he felt them incapable of demonstration, but he himself came to a new sort of hypothesis which he used constantly in his studies; his hypotheses being not the starting points but the generalizations derived from observation and experimentation. It has been stated that "The successful invention of hypotheses is . . . the mark of his scientific eminence."[11]

Let us examine his work briefly and then point to some of the consequences for thought of his discoveries.

It seems almost incredible that a generation should ever have become really excited over Newton's work in astronomy, mechanics, mathematics, and optics. His greatest work, *Mathematical Principles of Natural Philosophy*, published in 1687 and usually referred to as the *Principia*, was hardly written for popular consumption and was indeed understood by few. It contained not only a great deal of mathematics but new and difficult mathematics, for Newton, along with Leibniz, had invented the calculus. No interesting illustrations, literary gems, or amusing stories relieved the detailed statement of his scientific method and achievements. Nevertheless, those who were capable of understanding it were highly enthusiastic, and in a short time a large number of popular expositions of the new science were published. Voltaire, who introduced Newton to the French and who did more than any other writer to popularize the basic concepts and make them understandable, made the remark, "Very few people read Newton because it is necessary to be learned to understand him. But everybody talks about him."[12]

The world of the late seventeenth and early eighteenth centuries came to the point where something called nature was virtually the object of worship.

[10] See John Herman Randall, Jr., *The Making of the Modern Mind*, rev. ed., Boston, Houghton Mifflin Company, 1940, pp. 262 f.

[11] Charles Singer, *A Short History of Science to the Nineteenth Century*, Oxford, Clarendon Press, 1941, p. 255.

[12] *Oeuvres Complètes de Voltaire*, Louis Molaud, ed., Paris, Garnier Frères, 1879, XXII, 130.

Newton, it seemed, was its high priest, having revealed what this nature was. A good insight into one type of popular acclaim which he received is found in the humorous lines of Byron who, in referring to the story, popularized by Voltaire, that Newton had come upon the idea of universal gravitation as he watched an apple fall to the ground, wrote that Newton was

> The sole man who could grapple
> Since Adam, with a fall, or with an apple.[13]

Humor frequently contains profound truth, and it is probable that these lines provide an accurate index of public opinion during the Enlightenment. The story of Adam's disobedience in eating the fruit of the tree of knowledge had occupied a central place in the Christian view of man and history. The result of that disobedience had been to plunge the whole of mankind into a state of original sin and its accompanying moral weakness which could be relieved only by the grace of God. The Age of Reason was trying to replace this traditional Christian outlook with a more optimistic view of human nature and a different morality. Thus, Newton's observations seemed to symbolize the realization of a new era. Using the method of rationalism in conjunction with his study of nature in order to think God's thoughts after him, he said, he truly discovered what God's world of nature was like. And so men of this age rejoiced with Pope:

> Nature and Nature's laws lay hid in night:
> God said, Let Newton be! and all was Light.[14]

The history of Newton's discovery of universal gravitation and of the writing of his *Principia* takes us back, as L. T. More says,

> . . . to the time when he spent the greater part of the years 1665 and 1666 quietly at Woolsthorpe to escape the plague. He had just been graduated from college and had been successful enough to be appointed to a scholarship. As a boy, he had spent his days on the farm, meditating on the childish problems which interested him, and now as he comes back, a man, he takes up again his former life; but his mind is now full of profound ideas, and his meditations are to change the course of all future thought. In the long summer afternoons, he sits in the orchard which still stands near the old gray stone house; on one memorable day, an apple falls with a slight thud at his feet. It was a trifling incident which has been idly noticed thousands of times; but now, like the click of some small switch which starts a great machine in operation, it proved to be the jog which awoke his mind to action. As in a vision, he saw that if the mysterious pull of the earth can act

[13] *Don Juan*, canto X, I in T. G. Steffan and W. W. Pratt, eds., *Byron's Don Juan*, Austin, University of Texas Press, 1953, III, 225.

[14] Randall, *op. cit.*, p. 275.

through space as far as the top of a tree, of a mountain, and even to a bird soaring high in the air, or to the clouds, so it might even reach so far as the moon. If such were the case, then the moon would be like a stone thrown horizontally, always falling toward the earth, but never reaching the ground, because its swift motion carried it far beyond the horizon. Always falling toward the earth and always passing beyond it, the moon would follow its eliptical path if these two motions were equally balanced. How simple the idea seems to us now as we look backward, but how difficult it was to foresee can be gathered from the fact that even a Galileo, who had solved the problem of the projectile, did not have sufficient imagination to guess that the moon was only a projectile moving swiftly enough to pass beyond the earth. . . . Perhaps even more significant of Newton's genius, was the fact that he not only guessed the law of attraction, but he immediately set himself the task of calculating what would be the law of the force which could hold the moon in her orbit.[15]

The law of gravitation or the universal attraction of matter was central in Newton's natural philosophy. With it he believed he could account for both the motions of the heavenly bodies and the movements of objects on the earth. In other words, he brought together the work which had been done in astronomy and physics. Primarily, he successfully completed what Galileo had begun—the formulation of a science of mechanics by which the motion of matter could be measured. Again, his discovery of the calculus made this possible, for it provided a method to measure the processes of change in the world. Since any regular change, not only of motion but also of such processes as cooling, expanding, and contracting, can be represented by a curve, the calculus provided a tool that was used in dealing with phenomena of light, heat, electricity, and magnetism.

The universe in Newton's conception is a vast and harmonious machine, referred to since his time as the "Newtonian world-machine." The same principles which govern the movement of matter on the earth govern such movement everywhere, and the heavens are to be thought of as like the earth. Law was believed to be the same everywhere. Newton believed in the existence of God, but the physical universe was to his mind entirely independent of the spiritual order. His was the most complete break yet made with everything the Middle Ages had represented.

With Newton began the age of *scientific determinism.* As he visualized it, his world-machine consists of particles of matter possessing measurable masses. These bits of matter move in empty space, and any variations in their motions are due to forces whose laws can be determined. This means that if one could know the positions, velocities, and masses of the various

[15] L. T. More, *Isaac Newton,* New York, Charles Scribner's Sons, 1934, pp. 288 f.

particles of matter at any one moment, he could calculate with mathematical precision all the positions and velocities of masses in the future. This means also that the entire present was determined by the motion of particles in the past, and that the future is being determined by the present. Such a universe as this has little to do with men and their joys, sorrows, hopes, and aspirations. In it there is no development or purpose. During the Middle Ages there had been weaknesses in science, but men had believed that the world was made for them, and they were at home in it. But in Newton's world men as persons were not actually parts of the universe at all; they were merely its observers and interpreters.

Furthermore, the fact that Newton demonstrated the harmony and intelligibility of physical nature suggested that the "natural" could be discovered in other fields as well. As compared with Newtonian nature, for example, the realm of politics was decidedly chaotic. This chaos, eighteenth-century thinkers believed, was the result of the blunders of men. Undoubtedly a true social system in which men can live together in a well-ordered society was discoverable. A scientist of human nature could do for this area what Newton had done for physical nature. Religion, too, had become loaded with crude superstitions and had often led to cruel persecution. But the philosophers of this age were confident that in contrast to the objectionable forms of Christianity among which they lived reason could discover a *natural religion.* They believed that the original religion was natural and reasonable, but that this had been corrupted by priests who deliberately cultivated religious magic and superstition in order to keep people under their power. Intelligent reform would mean revolt against existing states and a return to the natural harmony of society; it would mean revolt against current religious superstitions and a return to natural religion.

Locke and Political Concepts

It may be that no thinker achieved a success in the science of human nature comparable to that of Newton in the science of physical nature, but in the eyes of the eighteenth century John Locke came very close to enjoying this distinction. John H. Randall, Jr., illustrates this by referring to an engraving in the front of an old edition of the works of Jean-Jacques Rousseau.

> Rousseau is seated at his writing-table, facing a pleasant pastoral landscape of green fields, sheep, and graceful willows—that rationally ordered Nature which he and his contemporaries accorded so respectful an admiration. On his desk are

two volumes, which, in the absence of any other books, seem designed to sum up the learning of the age–the *Principia Mathematica* of Isaac Newton, and the *Essay Concerning Human Understanding* of John Locke.[16]

Certainly, as applied to the political realm, Locke's philosophy was tremendously influential. It provided the intellectual defense of the English revolution of 1688, the theoretical foundation for a radical attack on vested interests in France, and the basis of the principles that guided the American colonists.

Seventeenth-century England had been the scene of political, religious, and social strife. There had been the struggle between Parliament and a succession of Stuart kings, each of whom had sought to gain absolute power. The Anglicans had aimed to impose their religion upon all people in the British Isles, and this was met by the attempt of the Scottish Presbyterians, who had dominated the so-called Long Parliament, to have religious uniformity on the pattern of their brand of Calvinism. The middle classes, who on the whole leaned toward Calvinism, were at odds with the upper classes, who were high churchmen and Catholics. These struggles took shape in the revolution under the leadership of Cromwell, the beheading of Charles I, the restoration of the monarchy under Charles II, and the deposing of James II in 1688. Parliamentary government, religious toleration, and recognition of the middle class became secure in the so-called Glorious Revolution which followed James' flight. William of Orange—the husband of Mary, Protestant daughter of James II—was made king. The principles which William and Mary accepted led to religious toleration, Whig leadership, and the decline of royal power.

Locke's political writings belong to the period immediately following the Glorious Revolution and apparently were designed to oppose the theory of the divine right of kings and to give theoretical justification to constitutional government and other principles which had emerged victorious from the civil wars, in which he had taken an active part. The starting point of Locke's social and political philosophy was, strangely enough, not society or the state but the individual. We will remember that in his theory of knowledge Locke compared the mind of man to a blank writing tablet: there are no innate ideas, and the whole of one's mental content comes from environment by way of experience. But now we find that there *is* something innate in individual human beings after all, something which they have not received from their environment. Each individual is born with certain indefeasible rights, which are "life, liberty, and estate [property]." The individual and his

[16] Randall, *op. cit.*, p. 253.

rights are the basic principles of Locke's political philosophy. To introduce this notion of innate rights, the existence of which cannot be empirically verified, seems inconsistent with other portions of his philosophy. However, Locke never did achieve a consistent system, and in his political philosophy he merely gave expression to the growing emphasis upon individualism. The state exists only to preserve the rights of individuals, and the sanctity of these rights imposes a natural limitation on the power of any government.

In order to make this clear, let us imagine with Locke the "natural" condition of mankind, that is, the mode of life which he thought men followed before they had organized themselves into political units. Thomas Hobbes, a seventeenth-century English philosopher, had described the pre-political condition of mankind as one of warfare, every man against every other man. But Locke insisted that men have always lived under a moral law in which the rights of others were respected. As he described this situation, "Men living together according to reason, without a common superior on earth, with authority to judge between them, is properly the state of nature."[17] Not only does a man have his own rights; he recognizes those of others as well. The right to property, for example, is examined in some detail. The general principle upon which Locke defended this is that when a person "mixes" his own labor with some natural object he has, in fact, projected his own personality upon it and has a natural right to it. If a man comes upon some uninhabited land, places a fence around a portion of it, tills the soil, and constructs some buildings, he has a natural right to the land. Therefore, the right of individuals to property is prior to the existence of society or of the state.

The natural condition of mankind, then, is a situation in which men, endowed with certain natural rights, live under a moral law in peace and mutual respect. But if this is the case, how did civil society come into being? The answer is that the state exists only because individuals created it for their own convenience. In the state of nature each man had to take personal responsibility for defending his property against those who, on occasion, failed to obey the moral law. So, by mutual consent or *social contract*, a whole group of men decided to give up their own natural power of defending their property and to put this power in the hands of the community or public as a whole. The state, then, is something created by a group of individuals that exists for the purpose of protecting private property and "the execution of . . . laws . . . for the public good."[18] This, in brief, was a philosophy which gave priority to the individual and his rights, and which

[17] As quoted in Bertrand Russell, *A History of Western Philosophy*, New York, Simon and Schuster, Inc., 1945, p. 625.

[18] *Of Civil Government*, book II, chap. 1, London, J. M. Dent & Sons, Ltd., 1955, p. 118.

measured the value of government by its success in serving the interests of individual men.

Such a philosophy was particularly popular among the American colonists. For them, the social contract was more than fiction because they actually witnessed this process in the formulation of their governments. By the time of the Revolution, the ideas of Locke were taken as self-evident truths. Jefferson had read Locke so much that he used not only his ideas but his very phrases. Reference has already been made to the second paragraph of the Declaration of Independence which so clearly reflects the political philosophy we have been discussing. A letter in which Jefferson discusses his writing of the Declaration points out that he was trying

> . . . not to find out new principles, or new arguments, never before thought of, not merely to say things which had never been said before; but to place before mankind the common sense of the subject, in terms so plain and firm as to command their assent. . . . Neither aiming at originality of principle or sentiments, nor yet copied from any particular and previous writing, it was intended to be an expression of the American mind. . . . All its authority rests then on the harmonizing sentiments of the day, whether expressed in conversation, in letters, printed essays, or the elementary books of public right, as Aristotle, Cicero, Locke, Sidney, etc.[19]

In America Locke's political philosophy clarified the common sense of the subject, but in France it was the basis of revolt. Absolutism in France reached a higher degree and lasted longer than in England. At the beginning of the eighteenth century there were criticisms of the government of Louis XIV from time to time but these were aimed at specific and obvious abuses. There was no philosophical basis for making a fundamental attack on absolutism as such. Voltaire, whose residence in England gave him the opportunity to learn Newtonian science, learned also the principles of Locke's philosophy and was in large measure responsible for introducing both of these to the French; there the idea that governments exist only for the purpose of serving the rights of individuals was revolutionizing in its effect. This was largely due, as Professor Sabine points out, to the peculiar social conditions in France.

> French society was a tissue of privilege which made the cleavage between classes more conscious and more irritating, if not more real, than in England. . . . To the middle class both clergy and nobility seemed parasites decked out with social privilege and with substantial exemptions from the burdens of taxation. . . . In French political writing there was a class-consciousness and a sense of exploita-

[19] *The Writings of Thomas Jefferson*, Washington, Taylor & Mawry, 1854, VII, 407.

tion such as had appeared only sporadically in English political writing. And in fact the French Revolution was a social revolution as the English Revolution was not; it compressed into three or four years an expropriation of church lands, crown lands, and lands of *émigré* nobles comparable to that spread through the reigns of Henry VII and Henry VIII. It is hardly an exaggeration to say that Locke's philosophy in France before the Revolution was an attack on vested interests and in England after the Reformation a defense of them.[20]

Natural Religion and Deism

Just as the political philosophy of the Enlightenment was based upon an allegedly natural condition of mankind, so religious thought also turned to the notion of natural religion. This was inevitable in the light of the current deification of nature and the unbounded trust in the capacity of human reason. If magic could be banished from the physical world and all material motions be explained in a rational science of mechanics, and if the myth of the divine right of kings could be destroyed and replaced by rational political principles, so also might religion be freed from superstitions and made completely rational.

The eighteenth-century philosophers were opposed to the idea that religion is an affair of the heart. It does not issue from subjective human needs, but is as objective as physical science, consisting of a system of rational propositions which is to be tested as any other system is tested. The utility of religion lies in the fact that by providing a divine sanction it promotes virtuous living. Anything going under the name of religion which either is contrary to reason or fails to stimulate ethical activity is to be rejected as bad. There is and always has been a religion which is perfect and which all men can know solely through the activity of their rational faculties. The content of this perfect religion can be summarized in three propositions: first, there is one supreme and omnipotent God; second, God demands virtuous living on the part of men; and third, there are rewards for the virtuous and punishments for the wicked in both this existence and the future life.

But if this is the rational and perfect religion, what place has Christianity, which claims a divine origin and the possession of truths which come through special revelation? There were two types of answer which the defenders of natural religion gave to this question. One group, the supernatural rationalists of whom John Locke was typical, did not reject the idea

[20] G. H. Sabine, *A History of Political Theory*, New York, Henry Holt & Co., 1937, p. 549.

of revelation completely. Locke argued that revelation is necessary, not because it adds anything to our knowledge but because men sometimes lose their awareness of God even though they are naturally endowed with the ability to know him. They also become lax in their obedience to the moral law and thus need a special revelation to bring them back to God and virtue. Reason is still superior to revelation, and those parts of revelation which are particularly valuable can also be discovered by natural reason. Revelation may contain certain items which are above reason, but anything found in revelation which is contrary to reason must be rejected. On the whole, then, revelation adds nothing to natural religion, but, in the opinion of certain philosophers, it does serve to make religion more effective in promoting the good life.

But if we take this position, how are we to know whether the claims of a religion to be divinely revealed are genuine? Locke replied that there are two tests which we can apply, one negative and one positive. The first is to determine whether a so-called revealed religion contradicts any of the tenets of natural religion. If it does, we may be certain that its claim to divine origin is false. In the second place, there must be positive reasons for supposing a religion to be revealed. In the case of Christianity two such reasons can be advanced: Jesus Christ fulfilled the prophecies of the Old Testament, thus proving that he was the Messiah; and he demonstrated his divine nature by his ability to perform miracles. A great deal of emphasis was placed on this latter point. Locke defined a miracle as "a sensible operation, which being above the comprehension of the spectator and in his opinion contrary to the established course of nature, is taken by him to be divine."[21] The main points in this definition are that (1) a miracle is an event actually observed by somebody, (2) it is thought to be contrary to the laws of nature, and (3) this supernatural event is a sign proving the divine origin of him who performs it.

There were other religious philosophers, known as deists, who went further than did Locke and his associates in assessing the place of Christianity, rejecting the idea of revelation entirely. The most famous deists in England were Matthew Tindal (1657-1733) and John Toland (1670-1722). Alexander Pope and Voltaire are also to be so classified. Their understanding of God is different from that of theists, who hold that God is in some sense personal, responds to prayer, and although not to be identified with the universe is nevertheless immanent within it. The deists, on the contrary, believe in God's existence as the creator of the "Newtonian world-machine," and argue that

[21] *Discourse of Miracles,* as quoted in Arthur Cushman McGiffert, *Protestant Thought Before Kant,* New York, Charles Scribner's Sons, 1912, p. 205.

having created this world he has now withdrawn from it and allows it to run on forever according to the laws of mechanics which are basic to it, as a perfect clockmaker might conceivably make a clock which requires no further attention. In such a universe men cannot pray to God, for he will not interfere with his perfect creation; nor has he shown any interest since the beginning in it or the human beings who inhabit it. In other words, God is presently without importance to men. He is needed solely to explain how this world came to be.

Deists argued that reason is able to demonstrate the existence of the God of the universe, and that every man can discover the way of salvation, which is achieved by rational and moral living. It would be quite irrational, they maintained, to suppose that God actually made the truths of religion known through a special revelation, for this would mean that only the portion of mankind to whom the revelation came has access to the means of salvation. A particular religion like Christianity with its claim to revelation has added unneccessary and even harmful items to the perfect natural religion. The sacramental ceremonies and other features are the work of cunning priests who, playing upon the superstitions of people, have tried to increase their personal power and prestige. Such practices have weakened the true religion and obscured fundamental religious truths.

That the deists voiced such protests does not mean, however, that they were uniformly opposed to the whole of Christianity. Most of them remained in the church and thought of themselves as holding the true religion of Christ. Voltaire denied that Jesus was himself a "Christian," in the institutional sense, picturing him instead as a deist. These critics of the church carried their judgments much further than did their spiritual predecessors in the sixteenth century with their attack on the authority of the Roman Catholic church; they were convinced that much of organized Christianity was evil.

Since the deists did not accept revelation, they attacked the arguments used by Christianity to support its claim to revelation. They made careful Biblical studies to show that there are disagreements between the prophetic statements in the Old Testament and the actual deeds of Jesus as recorded in the New Testament, and came to the conclusion that there is no basis for believing Jesus the fulfillment of prophecy. Also, they examined the reported miracles of Jesus carefully and concluded that it is doubtful whether he really did perform miracles and, even if he did, whether these are evidence that he was a messenger sent from God. Whatever value Christianity has, the deists claimed, is due to those features in it (such as its teaching on ethics and morals) which are the same as the tenets of natural religion.

Just when deism seemed to be victorious in its battle with revealed religion, a critical attack was launched against the principal beliefs of natural religion itself which led in the direction of skepticism. The attack came from two camps: from orthodox Christians and from skeptical philosophers who had themselves abandoned the halfway house of deism for agnosticism or even complete atheism. Representative of the former group was Anglican Bishop Joseph Butler (1692-1752), who argued that natural religion was on no surer rational grounds than was revealed religion. His purpose, of course, was to use this argument as a support for Christian revelation, but from the point of view of logic what he actually accomplished was to show that since neither natural nor revealed religion rested on a sure *rational* foundation, there was no coercive reason why men should not reject both from this standpoint. Of the skeptical philosophers, the most outstanding was David Hume, whose criticism was directed against both the orthodox and the deist thinkers of his day. We will discuss his very important work at length.

Hume's Criticism of Rationalism

Locke, as we have seen, laid the foundations of an empirical philosophy by asserting that none of our ideas are innate; that our whole system of ideas comes from experience. This was in opposition to the rationalist claim that the source of necessary and universal truths lies in the understanding. But Locke did not carry out the implications of his theory of knowledge. We have discovered that when he came to his political and religious philosophy he made use of ideas which are to be taken as self-evident truths and which are not derived from experience.

It remained for David Hume (1711-1776) to develop a complete and consistent empiricism, which had important consequences for science, political theory, and religion. Let us examine the implications of holding that all knowledge comes from experience. In the first place, this means that we have impressions, such as awareness of a patch of color if our eyes are turned in a given direction or an emotional feeling like anger or joy. In the second place, what we call an idea is nothing more than a copy of one of these impressions. Now, among our ideas are those complex ones which form part of a system of science or theology. When we begin to wonder whether these ideas are true, the only thing we can do, says Hume, is to see if they really do correspond to or resemble any impressions we have had.

When we employ this method we find that doubt is cast upon many important notions. Newtonian science, for example, contained the idea that a necessary system of relations obtains among particles of matter. The very meaning of physical science, in other words, was tied up with the notion of rigid causality. A natural law, most people felt, expresses a relation which simply *must* take place. But now Hume asks, how have we arrived at this idea of necessary causality? To what actual experiences or impressions does this idea correspond? The ideas of cause and effect, he replied, are derived from nothing more than our experience of linking two events, one of which immediately precedes the other in time. That which comes first is known as the cause and that which follows is called the effect. Thus, I go to the wall, push a button, and lights go on in the room. The total impressions I have are, first, of pushing a button, second, seeing lights, and, finally, noticing that the one follows the other. Nowhere do I find the *impression* of a *necessary relation* between the two. Where, then, does the idea of causal necessity come from? The answer is that it is based upon psychological habit. That is, after I have pushed the button on the wall a large number of times and on each occasion observed that the light goes on in the room, I come to expect the light whenever I push the button. There is no *observable* necessary connection between events in the world of nature—there is only the psychological awareness of the repeated association of events which leads me to expect, when I see the former of these events, that the other will follow. A scientific "law," then, does not describe a necessary and universal relation in the objective world; it is rather a summary of certain regularities which have been observed up to the present time and which are expected, yet without certainty, to hold in the future.

Hume's radical empiricism had important consequences for political philosophy. In the first place, it was not difficult to show that Locke's notion of the innate rights of individuals has no basis in experience but is merely a dogmatic expression. In the second place, it is by no means empirically demonstrated that the social contract is the origin of states, and even if it were, there is no indication that political loyalty is based upon the obligation of contracts. It seems that habits have developed among people empirically which lead them to a feeling of loyalty to their nation. There are no necessary and universal moral or political principles. Through the years certain conventions or "rules of the game" have been built up, and people habitually obey these on the whole because by so doing they maintain an orderly society. Only when oppression becomes too great to bear do they rebel against the rules and attempt to change them.

It is difficult to estimate Hume's influence in the field of social philosophy, for while it is true that social science has become increasingly empirical and that the concept of natural law has received decreasing use, it is also true that the philosophy of individualism which the theory of natural rights sought to justify has continued to exert great influence in England, France, and America.

Finally, Hume's critical work had very significant implications in the field of religion. We have seen that a crucial point in the deist controversy was whether or not one could use miracles as a basis for believing in the divine origin of Christianity. Further, all the defenders of natural religion, deists included, were confident that the existence of an omnipotent God and the fact of a future life could be rationally demonstrated. Let us see what Hume has to say about miracles, God, and immortality.

We note that the definition of a miracle during this period always involved the belief that it was an event contrary to the laws of nature. But according to Hume a law of nature is nothing more than a summary of observed regularities; hence, it is impossible to observe any act which is "contrary to a law of nature." At most, one merely observes something happening which is different from what had formerly been observed. Having witnessed this exception to usual happenings, the observer must simply realize that he was mistaken in what he thought to be the order of occurrences in this particular regard. It is therefore impossible to have a direct experience of a miracle in the accepted sense of the word.

As regards the so-called miracles which are supposed to demonstrate the divine origin of Christianity, we ourselves have had no direct experience of these, having merely read the reports of others. Can they then legitimately be used as *proofs* of the divine origin of Christianity? These reports inform us that certain events happened (such as Jesus' walking on water, the virgin birth, and miracles of healing and multiplication of food) which were different from the regularities to which we ourselves have experienced no such exceptions. What can be said about these, from Hume's standpoint? Obviously, it is impossible to return to that time in history to which the reports refer and have a personal experience of the events; we must decide in the present whether or not to believe the testimony of others. On the one hand, we have the uniform experience that such things do not happen; on the other, we have the statement that they did happen during one period of history, 2,000 years ago. How shall we weigh these, one against the other?

Hume replies that on the basis of our own experience it seems improbable, though not impossible, that such exceptional and seemingly unique experiences did take place. Over against this, however, the report of others must be placed. Yet when we reflect upon the frequent unreliability of testimony we know that much of it turns out to be merely idle gossip. Thus, it is not reasonable always to accept as true the reports of others when these run counter to the observed regularities of human experience! Yet again, we are reminded that there *are* times when testimony that seems unlikely is reliable —when, for example, a number of independent and competent witnesses agree in all important details. In the light of these considerations, how may one then evaluate the reports of miracles supposed to establish the truth of a particular religion? On the whole, Hume concludes, "no testimony is sufficient to establish a miracle, unless the testimony be of such a kind, that its falsehood would be more miraculous than the fact which it endeavors to establish."[22] Hume's argument is not intended to demonstrate the impossibility of miracles, for on the basis of his empiricism this would itself be impossible. Rather, his argument shows that "a miracle can never be proved, so as to be the foundation of religion."[23] Since Hume's time theologians who have understood his argument have been slow to appeal to miracles in their defense of religion.

Hume also examined the assumption of those, including the deists, who believed that the existence of God could be demonstrated rationally. It must be understood that Hume was not trying to prove that there is no God or immortality; he simply tried to show that the arguments employed by eighteenth-century thinkers were not logically coercive. One argument for God which seemed irrefutable to all the rationalists was that of the necessity of a First Cause of the world as a whole. Believing as they did that the universe is a scene of necessary cause-and-effect relationships, they took it for granted that nothing exists merely by itself—everything which is observed is the effect of a sufficient cause. Since the universe as a whole exists, it must be an effect for which the only conceivable cause is God.

Let us see what happens to this argument when we apply Hume's analysis of the meaning of causality derived from his extreme empiricism. The terms *cause* and *effect*, we have discovered, are completely relative, meaningless except in relation to each other. Together they make sense only when we observe two events which are contiguous in time. Any event observed alone can properly be called neither a cause nor an effect. Now, no one has had the experience of witnessing a world coming into being; this is the one and only world any men have ever seen. To say, therefore, that this world as a whole is the effect of a cause (God) is to make a statement which is logically indefensible. More generally, since Hume denies that there is in nature any necessary relation between cause and effect, we cannot argue for a necessary cause for the universe's existence. All we can say is that here is an existent—

[22] *An Enquiry Concerning Human Understanding*, sec. X, part 1, L. A. Selby-Bigge, ed., *Hume's Enquiries*, Oxford, Clarendon Press, 1927, p. 116.

[23] *Ibid.*, sec. X, part 2, p. 127.

the universe—but we can make no statement about what preceded it, if anything.

Even if we were to suppose that there is a cause of the universe, we could have no idea whatever of the nature of that cause. There is nothing in the nature of the effect itself to give a clue to the characteristics of what produced it. Such knowledge is always based upon experience of both cause *and* effect, and in this case such experience is not available. The rationalists supposed that an examination of the world suggests without doubt that its author is an omnipotent, just, and intelligent being. But Hume counsels them to look again

> . . . round this universe. What an immense profusion of beings, animated and organized, sensible and active! You admire this prodigious variety and fecundity. But inspect a little more narrowly these living existences, the only beings worth regarding. How hostile and destructive to each other! How insufficient all of them for their own happiness! How contemptible or odious to the spectator! The whole presents nothing but the idea of a blind Nature, impregnated by a great vivifying principle, and pouring forth from her lap, without discernment or parental care, her maimed and abortive children![24]

Finally, the purpose of natural religion was to promote virtue. Motivation for the good life is furnished by the belief that God demands righteousness and will reward the good and punish the wicked in the future life. But, of course, according to Hume's empiricism there is no possible way of demonstrating the reality of a future life. All arguments for immortality drawn from morality are shot through with fallacious reasoning. If justice, that is, reward of virtue, is observable in this world, then there is no need of looking to another life where justice may be found. But if we cannot find justice here, we have no reason to suppose that there is another world where it does exist. All the justice we can *reasonably* believe to exist is that which we can experience in our world.

Hume's attack on natural religion was forceful, but we should not make the error of supposing that he destroyed religion. One result, to be sure, was a period of skepticism, but Hume did not destroy religion any more than he destroyed science by undermining the notion of causal necessity. In both science and religion the method employed since Hume's time has become more empirical. That is, theologians began to study more carefully the psychological experiences which are distinctively religious in character. Instead of making religion a series of rational propositions, they talked about religious experience. We find that Friedrich Schleiermacher (1768-1834),

[24] *Dialogues Concerning Natural Religion,* part XI, in Norman Kemp Smith, ed., *Hume's Dialogues Concerning Natural Religion,* Oxford, Clarendon Press, 1935, pp. 259 f.

often called the father of recent theology, defined the essence of religion not as belief in a God as final cause of the universe but as "the feeling of absolute dependence." More to the point, perhaps, we can now see that Hume's radical empiricism is itself suspect, for in effect it denies the validity of all inductive reasoning since such reasoning proceeds from what has been experienced to generalizations derived by the mind from a study of these experiences. The effect of his thought, if taken seriously, would be to make *all* knowledge, both religious and scientific, impossible. While we may agree that we do not have a final knowledge, we do believe that we have a degree of reliable comprehension in both fields.

Natural religion made a permanent contribution to Western thought by showing clearly the relation between reason and experience, on the one hand, and revelation on the other. It made the mistake of supposing that religion is entirely an intellectual affair of accepting a system of rational propositions, thereby missing the very heart of religion. Hume rendered the great service of showing the limits of reason when applied to religion and opened the way to reinterpreting religion upon a much wider perspective, with typical experiences of its own.

The Idea of Progress

The philosophy of the Enlightenment, we have discovered, was built around the three notions of reason, experience, and nature. The rational method as formulated by Descartes and the empirical approach as suggested by Locke were the intellectual tools of the eighteenth century, instrumental in forming that still greater tool of Newton, the scientific method, which he used to bring his natural philosophy into being. Carried to its farthest point in Hume, empiricism became in turn a useful critical instrument against some of the faiths which the Enlightenment itself had developed.

The ideas of the Enlightenment were also highly effective in the field of philosophy of history, which raises the question of what meaning if any there is to the movement of human history. Our last explicit reference to the philosophy of history was in connection with Augustine. His theory, we recall, was based upon two principles. First, he said that at the beginning of history mankind was perfect, but immediately after being created suffered a fall from perfection into sin. The past, according to this view, was the golden age when man was perfect; the present is a period of degeneration. This principle had produced in Western man the habit of supposing that all good lay in remote ancient times. In the second place, Augustine's theory assumed that fallen men are incapable of doing anything to improve the present state of affairs through their own unaided efforts. Only in God and his providence is any basis for hope to be found, and the help he extends through grace provides no human progress within this life. It determines simply who will be saved and who condemned at the end of historic time.

Eighteenth-century philosophers, particularly in France, questioned and indeed denied both of these premises. Aware of the great intellectual achievements of their own day, they compared these with the knowledge possessed by the ancients and came to the conclusion that men had made very considerable intellectual and scientific progress through use of their own natural abilities. History recorded not an original perfection from which there had been a falling away but, on the contrary, a gradual and progressive development from ancient ignorance to modern knowledge! Continuing the thought, men came to believe that in the future reason would be increasingly successful in conquering superstition and ignorance. This same progress could be discovered in social and political relations; hence the world could confidently expect a better and more harmonious society in the future.

This confidence in the greatness of the future is no stranger to modern thought, and at this point certainly we see clearly why the Enlightenment is called the beginning of the modern world. The scientific developments begun only two centuries ago have been carried to a height of development undreamed of even by Newton. Whether they have brought with them the expected better and more harmonious society is by no means so certain. In any case, the Enlightenment was marked by a tendency unknown in any earlier period of the world to anything like the same extent to look to the *future* for the best of life rather than to the past. Optimism was the keynote: the future would see the golden age of human achievement. And since man's own rationality was responsible for the great developments of the period, it was believed that this same reason would lead also into a wonderful future. The enemy of progress was not original sin which had corrupted man at the very roots of his being, but ignorance—and ignorance could be removed through education. Progress through education accordingly became a great theme of the eighteenth century. It was thought that once men of great intellectual quality got behind the movement toward man's "Heavenly City" on earth, it would take only a few generations to reach that state in which all men would find happiness and in which all evil, especially that of war, would be destroyed. The Marquis de Condorcet (1743-1794), the good friend of Voltaire, summed up this optimism at its height in his book *The History of the Progress of the Human Spirit*, designated "the most sublimely confident book that has ever been written."[25] He wrote at the beginning of his book,

[25] Randall, *op. cit.*, p. 383.

The result of my work will be to show, by reasoning and by facts, that there is no limit set to the perfecting of the powers of man; that human perfectibility is in reality indefinite; that the progress of this perfectibility, henceforth independent of any power that might wish to stop it, has no other limit than the duration of the globe upon which nature has placed us. Doubtless this progress can proceed at a pace more or less rapid, but it will never go backward; at least, so long as the earth occupies the same place in the system of the universe, and as the general laws of this system do not produce upon the globe a general destruction, or changes which will no longer permit the human race to preserve itself, to employ the same powers, and to find the same resources.[26]

Most of the men of this period continued to believe in God, either theistically or deistically, but the philosophers did not find it necessary to depend upon God for salvation in any sense. Man was to place his trust rather in human reason and human experience, through the use of which the ideal world was to be ushered in.

From the standpoint of traditional Christianity such views as these are downright heretical. The center of error, Christian apologists could readily point out, lay in the belief in the goodness and perfectibility of man and in the thought that God is either nonexistent or unimportant in man's history. Yet objections like these were brushed aside by the philosophers and considered insignificant before the great successes the newer ideals could claim for themselves. During the next century Darwin's theory of evolution provided what appeared to be a firm scientific foundation for optimistic confidence in man and his future. It remained for the twentieth century to question both the optimism regarding man and the confidence in reason.

In reviewing the attacks made upon religion, let us not overlook the fact that even at the height of the Enlightenment's achievement,

. . . many groups of Christians continued along the old ways, sometimes actively counterattacking in press and pulpit, sometimes quietly living out lives untouched by the new ways. . . . the established churches continued to educate and to carry on their usual services. The masses and a good number of the middle classes and of the aristocracy continued all during these years to observe the ways of traditional Christianity.[27]

Christianity not only continued, but it found new approaches to religion and developed new emphases which made a positive contribution of their own. Those elements in human nature and human experience which were submerged in the Enlightenment's emphasis upon reason, nature, and experience—for example, the aesthetic, ethical, and religious—broke out in reaction

[26] *Ibid.* Condorcet's optimism about man would not permit him to consider the possibility that man might destroy himself.

[27] Crane Brinton, *Ideas and Men,* New York, Prentice-Hall, Inc., 1950, p. 403.

against the dominant thought. Romanticism appeared in philosophy and literature; Schleiermacher provided a new support for theology with his claim that religion belong primarily to the realm of feeling, not to intellectual ideas. John Wesley began a religious movement in England in 1738 which emphasized faith instead of reason. His movement swept England and America, revitalizing Christianity even in the centers of intellectualism. Christianity survived the eighteenth century, but the old unquestioned confidence in the truths of Christian dogma was severely shaken, particularly in Protestantism. Since that period, Christian theologians have faced the problem of interpreting the ancient truths in forms consistent with the best of current thought.

Idealism's Reply to Naturalism

The preceding discussion of the Enlightenment has pointed out that the chief ideas of the eighteenth century were reason, experience, and nature. The dominant emphasis fell upon reason—a fact indicated by references to this century as the Age of Reason. Men had supreme confidence in the power of the human mind, unaided by revelation, to think out the truths of nature, to trace out the meaning of nature's laws, and then to employ the knowledge of these laws to human advantage. This attitude assumed both that reason has the *power* to find the truth about the world and that nature is in some sense rational—that it contains within itself an order that exemplifies the principles of reason. If this were not the case, then the secrets of nature would have no logical connection with the clues that we have, and reason would be unable to uncover them.

In the works of Isaac Newton we have the generally accepted picture of nature in the eighteenth century. Nature is both rational and material. As such, its existence is quite independent of man and his knowledge. This conception has been very influential in the modern world. Materialistic naturalism, as Newton's view is called, provided the theoretical background for nineteenth-century science. The naturalistic approach to the study of man himself ranges all the way from the eighteenth-century doctrine of natural rights to those contemporary psychologists who in the interest of exact prediction interpret thought in terms of brain mechanics. Thus, naturalism seeks to find the basic principles of the interpretation of reality solely in the external world, the world of nature, and attempts to interpret humankind as a part of that world. We may call this the *outside-in* view, a view that starts with the outside world and its laws and seeks to include man, the knower of that world, and his mind as products of nature. It tends to interpret the conscious life of man, his emotions and his knowledge, in terms of the outer world, as though the garment of his humanity were cut out of the cloth of nature, spun with matter as its warp and with mathematical law as its woof.

However, this naturalism, powerful as was and is its influence, was not to be the only philosophy or the most acceptable one to professional philosophers of the nineteenth and early twentieth centuries. Its most important rival, but one that at the moment has largely lost its power over the minds of men, was the type of philosophy called idealism. Idealism inverts the approach of naturalism—it may be termed as *inside-out* philosophy. It starts by asking the question, what do we *truly* know, the *objects* of the world about us or our *ideas?* It answers that we undoubtedly know our ideas, and that this is the very meaning of knowledge. Ideas, then, are certain; the outer world is not. Experience shows the thinker that it is the mind and its ideas which cannot be doubted and the outer world that is uncertain and problematic. The basic conviction of idealism, then, is that reality is ultimately of the nature of mind—that the ultimate substance of things is *mental.*

Idealism, the inside-out approach to truth, may be regarded as a product of the romantic rebellion against the rationalistic-materialistic view of the world which dominated the eighteenth century. This outlook seemed to do less than justice to a large part of human experience. It denied significance to feeling and had little place for creative spontaneity and artistic impulse. Impatient with this hard and barren view of things, a great many men in the latter part of the eighteenth and the first part of the nineteenth centuries once more turned inward for their inspiration, elevating feeling above reason and instinct above law. These men were known as Romantics. But this return to the inner world was already presaged in the eighteenth-century concern with experience. While engaged in rationalistic speculations, some of the early empiricists came to feel that before knowledge could advance, men had better ask some questions about how we know and how much we can know. In short, they turned from the study of nature to the study of the mind. Hence, it is quite proper to say that modern idealism has its roots in eighteenth-century empiricism with its emphasis on experience as the source of knowledge.

John Locke, it will be remembered, had taught that all we know comes from experience. While Locke was primarily interested in refuting the doctrine of innate ideas, his own theory that we get ideas from experience alone has interesting implications. Knowledge, he taught, consists of ideas of sensation and of reflection. Ideas of sensation provide the raw materials of knowledge, as it were, while reflection provides their orderly arrangement and combination. But in the last analysis sensations give the mind its sole contact with the material world. Sensations give us ideas of external things.

For Locke, the ideas themselves are, of course, not the things; they only stand for external things, acting as messengers between the outside world and the mind. Ideas thus have representative character only. When a blue thing is brought before the eye, a stimulus is transmitted to the brain. The resultant brain action produces in the mind the idea of blue. What the mind knows, then, is not the blue *thing* but the *idea* of blue, which by reflection it joins to other representative ideas to construct the world of experience. But the mind does not know the world of real things—it knows only ideas which copy and represent things.

Locke indeed did not doubt that there *are* external things which somehow generate in us ideas which copy their qualities. He found it necessary, however, to draw a distinction between secondary qualities like heat, color, taste, and smell on the one hand, and primary qualities like extension in space, motion, solidity, and number on the other. The secondary qualities, he held, do not belong to things in themselves. Do they not vary with circumstances and the bodily condition of the receiver? Without light there is no color; the same water will feel warm and cool depending on the temperature of our hands; food and drink lose their flavor when our senses of taste and smell are impaired through illness. These considerations led Locke to declare that these secondary qualities were simply effects in us, mental or subjective, as we would now say. They are ideas without exact counterpart in the world of nature. Primary qualities, on the other hand, are not so variable as secondary ones, so Locke believed that these really do belong to substantial things quite independently of our experience of them. Extension, solidity, motion—in short, the qualities which the physicists can measure—these Locke left standing as the properties of external things.

The distinction between primary and secondary qualities, employed by Locke to save the independent existence of external things, proved hard to defend. *George Berkeley* (1685-1753), Locke's successor in studying the nature of knowledge, had a fairly easy time showing that primary qualities are really on the same footing as secondary ones. If the mind knows only its own ideas, then the supposed external things with their primary qualities are themselves ideas. Berkeley showed, in brief, that primary qualities are just as subjective or mental as secondary ones, and that the independent substances of things cannot be known—we can know only ideas, not things! This being so, there is no justification for postulating material substance, which for Berkeley has no reality in itself and is merely a notion or an empty concept of reason. He had a variety of arguments for rejecting Locke's primary qualities and his independent substance, arguments which deserve review.[28]

[28] See George Berkeley's *Three Dialogues Between Hylas and Philonous* (1713).

Accepting Locke's analysis of *how* we know, then, Berkeley drew the logical conclusion that we can never get outside our own ideas. We are confined to the world of our experience. This world, of course, is the same world we have always known, filled with things, from men and houses to trees and sunsets. These things all exist—they have being—but they exist as ideas, as images of our perception. What does it then mean to say that anything is? The answer, for Berkeley, is that to be is to be perceived—*esse est percipi.*

In this way, as a result of his empiricism, Berkeley attacked the theory of the independent existence of material substances having primary qualities. Locke had begun the process of destruction. His inquiry into the limits of human knowledge led him to a dualism between the world of ideas and the world of things: he was left with two of everything, the one mental, the other independent substance. Thus he had, for example, the perceived tree and the substantial tree. Berkeley, with a smooth argument that appears at once sophistical and unanswerable, shows that there is really only one of everything. The tree that we experience is the only tree there is. It is an object of our experience, a composite of ideas.

If this seems artificial, it is worth noting that Berkeley's tree is much nearer the tree of common sense, the tree of the farmer and the woodsman, than is the materialist's duality of trees, the tree of experience and the "real" tree of "matter." Berkeley gives us back one tree; the real tree is the perceived tree. Of course, it is still made of wood, but wood now is seen to be a name for some of the ideas of our experience. We have ideas of hardness, extension, roughness, and so on which taken all together we call *wood.* So when we speak of any thing, we mean that it is a combination of ideas. The reality of things consists just in their perception. To be is to be perceived! The world of the mind and the real world are one. This is Berkeley's contribution to modern idealism.

Berkeley's idealism was not a finished system. It raised important questions, some of which we need neither name nor answer. We must note one difficulty, however, since recognition of this problem and the attempt to answer it constitute an important phase of later idealism: how could Berkeley escape subjectivism? If we know only our own ideas, the content of our own minds, how can we know other selves and the existence of a common world? Are we not caught in the "egocentric predicament," unable to escape from the prison house of our own fantasies? Are we not driven to *solipsism,* the view that my ideas alone exist?

In facing these and similar questions, Berkeley claimed that the real world is a world of many minds and ideas, and that within this world of minds there exists one supreme, infinite Mind "in whose eternal and all-comprehensive experience all finite minds share in varying degrees."[29] To the question concerning the origin of our experiences and therefore of our ideas (since there is no material substance present to "cause" them), he replies that the origin is to be found in God's experience, in which all human minds participate. This is the reason that objects have continuance, for even when we do not perceive them, they are still contents of God's mind and therefore exist. Conceptions which are not that, are mere fantasies, imaginary ideas of the human mind. The Englishman Ronald Knox, summed up this thought in a well-known limerick:

There was a young man who said, "God
Must think it exceedingly odd
If he finds that this tree
Continues to be
When there's no one about in the Quad."

Reply

Dear Sir:
Your astonishment's odd:
I am always about in the Quad.
And that's why the tree
Will continue to be,
Since observed by
Yours faithfully,
GOD.

In spite of the difficulties which Berkeley's critics found in his idealism, his belief in the unity of experience and nature and his teaching that the mental world is the real world gave modern idealism two of its basic convictions. His system is a philosophic outpost which other explorers in the things of the mind and its world have used as a base of operations, a point of departure in their attempts to penetrate and chart the unexplored realm lying beyond. And here our own investigation of idealism and its effects must come to an end. The interested student of these matters will wish to examine the challenge of the rational element in nature brought by the skeptic Hume, the dualism developed by the great German thinker, Immanuel Kant, and the vast system of G. W. Hegel termed absolute idealism. Many lesser figures appear in this account, and many opponents also, among them Arthur Schopenhauer. Religion was deeply affected by idealism, particularly by the absolute idealism of Hegel. Hegel also influenced political

[29] R. A. Tsanoff, *The Great Philosophers*, New York, Harper & Brothers, 1953, p. 369.

thought very greatly, although indirectly and in ways opposed to his own principles, for the method he used, called the dialectical method, was taken over by *Karl Marx* (1818-1883) and used to provide a philosophic foundation for communism. As Marx himself wrote, he turned Hegel's dialectic upside down, believing that Hegel had stood it "on its head." In place of an idealistic use of dialectic, Marx used it materialistically, with the result that his philosophy became *dialectical materialism.* Marx understood what he had done in these terms:

> My dialectic method is not only different from the Hegelian, but is its direct opposite. To Hegel, the life-process of the human brain, i.e., the process of thinking, which, under the name of "the Idea," he even transforms into an independent subject, is the demiurgos of the real world, and the real world is only the external, phenomenal form of "the Idea." With me, on the contrary, the ideal is nothing else than the material world reflected by the human mind, and translated into forms of thought.
>
> . . . The mystification which dialectic suffers in Hegel's hands, by no means prevents him from being the first to present its general form of working in a comprehensive and conscious manner. With him it is standing on its head. It must be turned right side up again, if you would discover the rational kernel within the mystical shell.[30]

In one sense at least, and insofar as one can hold Hegel responsible for a method used in inverted form by Marx, it can be truly said that the contemporary struggle between the great power centers of East and West is at bottom a difference of two philosophical approaches to life. Western democracy springs from the thought of John Locke who, in his doctrines of the natural rights of men and the social contract theory of government, laid down the theoretical foundations of democracy. The close relationship between philosophical thought and political systems brings sobering thoughts —philosophy bakes no bread, as the old saying has it, but it helps determine the movement of world history. ! ! !

Questions for Study

1. In what sense is the Enlightenment modern? What basic concepts of the Enlightenment continue to be prominent today, and by contrast what were the chief concepts in the Middle Ages?
2. How is reason used differently in this period than in the Scholastic period? What in Christian belief did it now attack? What in the approaches of Descartes makes him a rationalist, and why is mathematics so important for ration-

[30] Karl Marx, Preface to *Capital,* 2nd ed., Chicago, Charles H. Kerr & Co., 1906, I, 25.

alist thinking? What four principles did Descartes lay down as basic to his method? What limitations does this method have?

3. How do Spinoza and Leibniz illustrate rationalism?
4. What is meant by empiricism? How did Locke attack the doctrine of innate ideas? How did he think knowledge is achieved? How was he different from the rationalists?
5. What was the great method developed by Newton which made him so successful as a scientist? What did he believe to be the goal of scientific studies? What is his principle of universal gravitation? How would you describe his "world-machine"? Where might you disagree with his conclusions?
6. What are Locke's doctrines of innate rights and the contract theory of government? What effect had these on the American colonists?
7. What is meant by natural religion, and how would you distinguish it from orthodox Christianity? What did eighteenth-century philosophers believe reason could prove of religious belief? How were the deists attacked?
8. How does Hume, as an empiricist, attack the idea of causality? How was the effect of his theories felt in political philosophy and religion?
9. What beliefs stood behind the idea of progress? How would you criticize these?
10. What is meant by saying that idealism is an inside-out philosophy and materialism an outside-in philosophy? How would you defend the idealist's view?
11. How would you reply to Berkeley's arguments?
12. How did Karl Marx use the dialectic of Hegel?

Selected Readings

Becker, Carl L., *The Heavenly City of the Eighteenth-Century Philosophers*, New Haven, Yale University Press, 1932.

Berlin, Isaiah, *The Age of Enlightenment*, Boston, Houghton Mifflin Company, 1956.

Brinton, Crane, *Ideas and Men*, New York, Prentice-Hall, Inc., 1950.

Bury, J. B., *The Idea of Progress*, New York, Dover Publications, Inc., 1955.

Cassirer, Ernst, *The Philosophy of the Enlightenment*, Princeton, Princeton University Press, 1951.

Ewing, A. C., *Idealism: A Critical Study*, London, Methuen & Co., Ltd., 1934.

Hibben, John G., *The Philosophy of the Enlightenment*, New York, Charles Scribner's Sons, 1910.

McGiffert, Arthur Cushman, *Protestant Thought Before Kent*, New York, Charles Scribner's Sons, 1912.

McGiffert, A. C., *The Rise of Modern Religious Ideas*, New York, The Macmillan Company, 1915.

Manuel, Frank E., *The Eighteenth Century Confronts the Gods*, Cambridge, Harvard University Press, 1959.

Mowat, R. B., *The Age of Reason*, Boston, Houghton Mifflin Company, 1934.

Nicholson, Harold, *The Age of Reason*, Constable & Co., Ltd., 1960.

Randall, John Herman, Jr., *The Making of the Modern Mind*, rev. ed., Boston, Houghton Mifflin Company, 1940.

Rockwood, Raymond O. (ed.), *Carl Becker's Heavenly City Revisited*, Ithaca, Cornell University Press, 1958.

Sabine, G. H., *A History of Political Theory*, New York, Henry Holt & Co., 1937.

Singer, Charles, *A Short History of Science to the Nineteenth Century*, Oxford, Clarendon Press, 1941.

Tsanoff, R. A., *The Great Philosophers*, New York, Harper & Brothers, 1953.

18. The Influence of Evolution on Philosophy and Religion

The advent of Darwin's theory of evolution was even more revolutionary in its effects than the upheaval caused by Copernicus and Galileo. The impact of this concept has made profound changes in the intellectual and religious temper of the modern world. We will sketch here an account of the theory itself in both its original and its more recent forms and point out some of the changes it has brought about in modern thought.

We have already discussed the work of some of the outstanding Western scientists and philosophers. Through these men, science and philosophy had made many advances, but their discoveries and theories were remote from the interests of the average man. Orthodox Christian theology had been only slightly affected by them. Although the deistic movement was an attempt to make theological ideas compatible with the Cartesian and Newtonian conceptions of the universe, the great majority of Westerners followed a conventional pattern of belief—a pattern largely unaffected by either the philosophy or the science that had been developing in the modern world. The mode of creation by divine fiat, the crowning presence of man in the Garden of Eden, his fall and subsequent suffering and depravity, the plan of salvation through the atoning blood of Christ, the revelation of God within the Bible, the short period of time since the creation of the earth—all these beliefs were left essentially untouched by the science and philosophy of pre-Darwinian days. But after Darwin, none of these could be held as unquestioningly again. The consequent changes are by no means complete, and the biological theory of evolution itself contains many points which need further elucidation and clarification. Nevertheless, among scientists themselves and increasingly among Christian people it is being accepted as the valid description of how life has developed.

Organic Evolution

The term *organic evolution,* in its most general sense, means "a natural process of irreversible change, which generates novelty, variety, and increase of organization: and all reality can be regarded in one aspect as evolution."[1] The evidence for this theory is so impressive that for the past 50 years students of biology have not doubted the fact of evolution, even though there remain many unsolved problems regarding the process by which evolution takes place. It was *Charles Darwin* (1809-1882), called by Julian Huxley the Newton of biology, who first suggested the basic mechanism of evolution and at the same time presented convincing evidence for the evolutionary process.

Pre-Darwinian Theories of Evolution

The idea of evolution, however, was not at all new with Darwin. Philosophers among the early Greeks entertained the general possibility of some sort of origin of developed creatures from simpler and more homogeneous stuff. As early as the sixth century B.C. Anaximander proposed a theory of organic evolution. He taught that there was a progressive adaptation of organisms to the environment by means of a survival of the fittest. With marvelous astuteness, he argued that the ancestors of man must have been simpler organic beings with different physiological habits and a different environment. He thought this because it appeared to him that the human species could not have survived if the long period of infancy had originally been as protracted as it now is. From his observations of marine life, he concluded that early life came from the sea, and that some forms adapted themselves to the land. Other philosophers besides Anaximander suggested theories of evolution also, but after Plato and Aristotle, with the notable exception of Lucretius, the Roman poet and philosopher, the notion of evolution was discarded until modern times. We shall presently see what Aristotle had to do with shelving this idea.

[1] Julian Huxley, "The Emergence of Darwinism," in Sol Tax (ed.), *Evolution After Darwin,* Chicago, University of Chicago Press, 1960, I, 18.

The scientific development of the modern period created a new interest among philosophers and scientists in developmental theories, in place of the study of static, unchanging "reality." The renewed interest arose first not from biology but from efforts to understand some of the implications of physical theory. By the time the nineteenth century was well under way, a great deal of accumulated data on animals and plants and on the geological structure of the earth which could not be fully explained on any known basis aroused much speculation about the possibility of an organic as well as a physical evolution. The ancient view generally held in Christian thought, that the earth had come into existence about 4000 B.C. by God's act of direct creation, was challenged by the discovery of fossils and by evidences for erosion on the earth's surface. Immense periods of time were required to account for both of these. Even prior to 1800, geologists were claiming that the beginning of the earth was aeons rather than thousands of years ago. The most influential work on geology in developing this view was Charles Lyell's *Principles of Geology* (written 1830-1833). Through these geological theories, the minds of men were prepared to accept the thought that millions of years were required for the development of living forms as well. Not the least important discovery was that of fossilized bones of creatures long dead, belonging to types no longer in existence.

In recent centuries Charles Darwin was not alone in making specific suggestions concerning the evolution of the species, nor was he the first. His own grandfather, Erasmus Darwin (1731-1802), wrote prolifically on biology and other subjects. He in turn relied for many of his ideas upon Count Georges Louis Leclerc de Buffon (1707-1788), the first modern naturalist to develop in scientific ways a theory of the evolution of living forms. Erasmus Darwin turned his attention to the problem of how living beings could acquire naturally (rather than through acts of God) their varied adaptations to the environment. In his *Zoonomia: or the Laws of Organic Life* (written 1794-1796), he pointed to environmental influences which much later Charles Darwin also was to find impressive, and reached the conclusion that all living creatures, man included, "have alike been produced from a similar living filament."[2]

A brilliant predecessor of Charles Darwin was Jean-Baptiste de Monet, Chevalier de Lamarck (1744-1829), a great systematizer who developed his own theory of the mechanism of evolution. He supposed that biological variations are the result of use or lack of use of a characteristic, and that the consequent effects on the organisms are inherited. Thus, he thought that giraffes, by stretching to obtain the leaves high up on a tree, developed longer

[2] Charles Singer, *A Short History of Science to the Nineteenth Century*, Oxford, Clarendon Press, 1941, p. 376.

necks which were inherited by their descendants. This is the theory of the inheritance of acquired character, generally rejected today.

Another prominent pre-Darwin figure was *T. R. Malthus* (1766-1834), a clergyman. The end of the eighteenth century was a time when great optimism was being expressed concerning the future of man, who was expected to reach entire liberty and equality in the near future. In contradiction to these hopes, Malthus wrote a history-making paper entitled *An Essay on the Principle of Population* (1798), which reached the pessimistic conclusion that populations tend to increase beyond the available food supply since population growth proceeds by geometric ratio while food supply increases only arithmetically.

The Darwinian Theory

Charles Darwin profited by the thought of all these predecessors. His grandfather's observations and theories were part of his own thinking. In 1838 he read the *Essay* of Malthus, and even earlier, in 1831, the *Principles* of Lyell. It was Lyell who suggested to Darwin the general theory of evolution of living beings. In his *Autobiography*, Darwin wrote that after he had read the Malthus essay he came suddenly one day to perceive that the joint effects of overpopulation and insufficient food supply as pictured by Malthus would result in a struggle for survival. He added, ". . . it at once struck me that under these circumstances favourable variations would tend to be preserved, and unfavourable ones to be destroyed. The result of this would be the formation of new species."[3]

The theory of evolution by natural selection was announced jointly by Charles Darwin and Alfred Russel Wallace in a paper dated July 1, 1858. Wallace had arrived independently at the theory of natural selection as the explanation for the operation of evolution, also after reading the Malthus essay. By publishing their findings jointly, the two scientists shared the honor of the discovery. The laurels go to Darwin, however, for he amassed a vast quantity of evidence in support of the theory, which Wallace was unable to do. In 1859 Darwin published the first edition of his classic, *On the Origin of Species by Means of Natural Selection,* in which he presented the evidence he had accumulated. Much of it had been collected during his voyage around the world in the years 1831-1836 on H.M.S. *Beagle*, during which he stopped at the Galapagos Archipelago off the Pacific coast of South America. As he had set sail on this trip, he had still intended to become a

[3] Francis Darwin (ed.), *Charles Darwin's Autobiography*, New York, Henry Schuman, Inc., 1950, p. 54.

clergyman, for which profession he had prepared himself, and had accepted uncritically the creation of species by divine fiat. But during the voyage he read Lyell's work on geology. This, combined with his observations of the varied species of bird and animal life and fossils in the Archipelago, led him to his radical theory of evolution by natural selection.

Not only did Darwin show that variations within species occur, but he also presented a theory to account for the origin of new species by entirely natural processes without any recourse to God as explanation. It was this aspect of his theory which made Darwinism so shocking to the people of his day, and yet it was this same feature which made species development available to the study and understanding of scientists. Because Darwin believed the process to be an entirely natural one, he gave to it the name *natural selection.* This process was the chief discovery of both Wallace and Darwin.

When biologists speak of *species* they are referring, in the words of Ernst Mayr, to "groups of actually or potentially interbreeding natural populations, which are reproductively isolated from other such groups."[4] Species are the least inclusive major classification into which, for the sake of convenience and study, living beings and fossils are divided. In ascending order of inclusiveness, above a species are genus, family, order, class, phylum, and finally kingdom. It was the species which Darwin observed. Some of his observations were made of certain closely related species of finches he found in the Galapagos. All of these, though similar, were sufficiently differentiated to justify placing them in separate categories. Another example of species and genus can be taken from oak trees. All oaks together form the genus *Quercus.* Within the genus are a number of species, among them black, white, and pin oaks. The specific problem with which Darwin dealt was that of how one species within a genus became a different one—how one species of finch, for instance, became in the course of time another. The evidence he presented in his *Origin* for the development of new species out of older ones is highly persuasive.

Darwin's explanation, natural selection, includes several factors. Darwin assumed that life has existed for an enormous period of time, an idea derived from the geologists. He supposed also that in reproduction the characteristics of the parent stock are carried on. The elements of the theory as erected upon these assumptions are very simple, seemingly almost self-evident. First, there is a struggle for existence. More members of a species appear than the environment is capable of supporting in terms of food sup-

[4] Ernst Mayr, *Systematics and the Origin of Species,* New York, Columbia University Press, 1942, p. 120.

ply; hence, the struggle to exist is inevitable. Second, a point for which he provided much evidence, within a species slight variations occur. Why they do so he could not say, but he studied their appearance. Some of these variations are heritable, capable of being transmitted from one generation to the next. Third, those creatures best fitted by their characteristics to survive in a given environment will be the ones generally that do survive and propagate themselves. This is the process called the survival of the fittest.

At points in Darwin's writings it appears that he thought of nature as a great battlefield, "red in tooth and claw," in which the strongest creatures survive. Yet according to his general theory what makes for survival may be something quite other than sheer physical strength. Those of the species best qualified to survive by reason of any of many qualities do normally survive and propagate their kind to a greater degree than do those less well fitted. A continuation of this process in the course of millennia accumulates the changes appearing from slight variations to such a degree that a distant descendant may be different enough from its early ancestor to constitute a new species. Of course, when a variation is not favorable to survival, as usually happens, the descendants of its possessor will survive in lesser numbers and eventually disappear. But in Darwin's theory, it is the piling up of the many slight variations favoring survival in the particular environment which in the course of time accounts for the appearances of new species. Summed up in brief form, the principal may be stated thus: favorable variations within a species when tested by the struggle for existence eventually result in that adaptation which becomes a new species.

Although the evidence produced by Darwin was used to argue for an evolution of species, it was and is supposed that what is true of species development is equally true in the development of the more inclusive categories, from the genera through the phyla. Like the species, they too have "emerged" through the process of natural selection. All that was needed for this view was to assume still more vast periods of time. Biological discoveries during Darwin's life provided no evidence for this extension of the theory, but it appeared to be (as it still does) both a natural and a proper elaboration of the basic view. Also, evidence for it was adduced from geology, which exhibited forms of life now extinct but presumed to be ancestral to some present forms.

Darwin developed his belief that man also is the product of the same process of natural selection as are all other living beings in his *Descent of Man* (1871). To support his contention, he gave various evidences still familiar today: the unity of anatomical design between man and the subhuman creatures; evidences from embryology which illustrate the amazing similarity of embryonic forms of various types of life, man included; and the possession by man of rudimentary organs, such as the appendix, of little or no use to man himself but of great importance to some animals and presumably to man's ancestors.[5]

Darwinism Today

Darwin's descriptive explanation is generally accepted currently as sound in its major outlines. Since Darwin's death, and especially since 1900, a great amount of scientific observation and investigation has thrown new light on the process of evolution. The Mendelian data on heredity, the mutation theory of De Vries, and the unabating research on genes and chromosomes are illustrations of the intensive effort put forth by biologists to discover how heredity and evolution function. As an example of the problems unsolved by Darwin himself, let us look at his inability to explain how heritable variations occur. That they happen he was able to demonstrate by a wealth of evidence, but what the mechanism was he could not say. It was generally supposed that in sexual reproduction each parent made a contribution carrying its specific characteristics, but this view would seem to require that all the descendants of the same pair of parents be alike. Critics of Darwin were not slow in pointing out the weakness of the theory at this point.

It was not until 1900 that the theory currently accepted was discovered in the work of a poor peasant, a monk of the Augustinian order, *Gregor Mendel* (1822-1884), whose consuming interest was science. Working with the common pea, he formulated the concept of hereditary units which led to the theory of genes. Although he had presented his findings in a paper read in 1865 before a natural science society and the paper had been distributed to 100 important libraries in Europe and the United States, its significance was entirely overlooked until it was discovered independently by three biologists from as many countries in 1900. Genes are now believed to be the determinants of traits in an individual during its development, and variation within the genes is thought to cause the mutations (heritable variations) from which variations within species primarily arise. These, then, may eventually develop a new species if they are favorable in terms of the environment. Natural selection will favor some variations over others; these will survive and produce a larger number of descendants than the others. According to modern views, the effect of the process of natural selection is "to alter the frequency with which particular genes are present in the

[5] Wilfred Le Gros Clark, "The Study of Man's Descent," in S. A. Barnett (ed.), *A Century of Darwin*, London, William Heinemann, Ltd., 1958, pp. 186-205.

population of animals or plants which is being considered."[6]

It is now thought also that the genes are carried by what are called chromosomes. Mutations are due both to changes within the genes (gene mutation) and to changes of the chromosomes (chromosomal mutation) such as the arrangement on the chromosomes of the order in which the genes appear. The causes of mutation are not fully understood, but it is known that the rate of occurrence of mutations can be increased by certain chemicals and by high-energy radiations like X-rays. Although some biologists uphold the theory of macro-evolution, according to which great changes may take place between one generation and the next, the more general belief is that the changes undergone are very slight. Variations which are not an aid to survival tend to disappear, but those beneficial to a species in the struggle for existence are passed on to numerous progeny and are accumulated over a long period of time by fortuitous natural selection.

Much more could profitably be said about Darwin's theory, the criticisms of that theory, and the various forms of neo-Darwinism, but this account must limit itself to suggesting the general outlines of this contribution to modern thought and then turn to the implications of the theory for religion and philosophy. However, it is interesting to note that these theories are not completely satisfactory to biologists themselves, and that new discoveries will change them in the future. Modern gene theory leads to the conclusion that gene mutation is "essentially a 'random' process," as C. H. Waddington writes, so that the time when it will happen and the nature of the change cannot be predicted. He continues,

> To a tidy mind, this is not a very satisfying way of filling the gap in Darwin's theory concerning the origin of variation. One would like to have a coherent, logical connection between new variation and something else in the organism's world— . . . Instead, we are offered two signs saying "Road Closed."[7]

It is difficult for the modern student, accustomed to the idea of evolution, to gain any clear conception of the furor occasioned by Darwin's discovery. Very few there were who welcomed it at first, apart from a small number of philosophers and scientists. For the most part the reception the theory received was one of alarm. Again man's world and the system of nature were turned upside down—there is not a single field of scientific and academic study which has not been greatly modified by the concept of evolution. It provided a new approach to astronomy, geology, philosophy, ethics, religion, and the history of social institutions. Now, with one clarifying word, the

[6] C. H. Waddington, "Theories of Evolution," in Barnett, *op. cit.*, p. 10.
[7] *Ibid.*, p. 14.

whole course of nature and man was illuminated. It made possible a clear view of what had taken place—one continuous evolving history to be traced from modern civilization back to primitive man, and from early man on through an evolution of species, and before that to the formation of the solar system. This was a staggering panorama which gave tremendous momentum to scientific research. Eager men set forth like prospectors to stake out the seemingly limitless terrain.

The Influence of Evolution on Philosophy

Nothing seems to be more certain than the fixity of nature's forms; yet even among the early Greek philosophers there was a controversy over the problem of permanence and change. Heraclitus insisted that everything was in the process of change as sense observation testifies. Therefore, he argued, nothing is permanent, and nothing is fixed except the fact of change itself. On the other hand, Parmenides stressed the need for permanence. How can we have knowledge if there are no fixed properties? The possibility of knowledge requires permanence in that which is to be known. So Parmenides and his followers said that the changing world of sense experience is illusory, and that the "real" world can only be known by the mind through the use of reason. One solution of the problem was provided by the materialistic atomism of Democritus. He declared that invisible atoms are the permanent elements of the world, and that their combinations make the various things of the experienced world. These combinations change, but the atoms do not. It will be remembered that some philosophers were not satisfied with this solution, for materialism seemed to leave out very important aspects of experience, especially the non-quantitative phases like ideas, mathematical relations, feelings, personality, and human relations. Plato in particular was mentioned as the chief exemplar of this view. We learned of his emphasis on immaterial reality which he called forms or Ideas and which only the mind could discern. Aristotle also made great use of the concept of form in his process philosophy. As we followed the course of this book, we saw much use made of the notion of form by early Christian thinkers, Neo-Platonists, Augustine, and St. Thomas. The philosophy and political structure of the medieval world grew out of the mode of thought which held forms to be the permanent and the real.

Oddly enough, it was Aristotle, the founder of biological science, who fastened the notion of fixed forms upon Western thought. Aristotle collected biological specimens and classified them according to types. The organisms with the simplest structures he classified as lower forms. Increasing complexity of organization and function determined the status of a given organic object as a higher form. Furthermore, Aristotle was well aware of the many stages of development from a seed or an egg to full maturity, but he found no reason in his biological studies for supposing that the forms—or species—themselves were also evolving. He grasped the basic distinction between lower and higher forms, but he understood actual organic development as limited to growth within the species itself.

The failure to discover that species evolve meant that philosophic conclusions were drawn from a belief in the fixity of natural categories. The influence of Aristotle and Plato merges in the notion that behind the world of sense appearance there is a realm or rational order of forms or universals that are permanent and real. All observed changes are subject to order and form. In other words, philosophic generalizations were made on the basis of Aristotle's scientific assumptions that form is imbedded in the processes of nature and that all changes are subservient to a fixed and established order. The mind of man was believed capable of grasping the pattern of the created world. As this concept was absorbed and applied down the centuries, men created a religious and political structure based on the philosophy that the natural order is the counterpart of a fixed and immutable heavenly order, existing as Idea or Form in the mind of God. They were confident they knew what that order was. Both politics and religion divided people into classes, like the order of Ideas, and fixity of place became a virtue. The established order in the church and in society consequently became an end to be maintained, and scientific or philosophic ideas which threatened that order had to be stifled.

The influence of Darwin, or rather the extension of the idea of evolution, brought the idea of unchanging order in the universe into question. Nature, it seemed, is not as we thought it to be. Even the forms apparently are not immutable, but undergo modification. At first many hasty conclusions were drawn regarding the philosophical significance of the theory. Herbert Spencer (1820-1903), for example, attempted to work out a "synthetic philosophy" which would include within one system the "first principles" of everything from biology and psychology to sociology and ethics. The materialists, with Ernst Haeckel (1834-1919) as their leading representative, interpreted the theory to fit their own ideas. But it was too early to lay down as confidently as Haeckel did a 12-point program for nature's unfolding. There were many other philosophical efforts, some of which adapted older systems of philosophy to newer ways of thinking. A number of philosophies of evolution are more recent still, bearing the names of such men as C. Lloyd Morgan, Samuel Alexander, and Henri Bergson. It is apparent that the influence of evolution on philosophy has been and continues to be great, and the end of this influence has not yet been reached.

Most of the philosophers of the past assumed that there is some key by which the mind can grasp the structure of reality—its direction and innermost meaning. But more recently there have appeared other philosophers, deeply influenced by evolutionary ideas, who have rejected system-building as the proper work of philosophy on the ground that we do not know enough to construct comprehensive philosophies as though we were cosmic giants of the intellect. Rather, they held that the mind is a tool or instrument whose function is to assist the human organism in adapting itself to the world in which it lives. Let us consider the meaning of the conception of the mind as an instrument.

In a sense the mind has always been viewed as an instrument, but before Darwin's time it was never considered a tool developed in the process of organic evolution or one that would aid man in survival and development. The newer philosophical view maintained that the total organism, of which the mind is one part, finds itself in an environment in which it must learn to live. This was true of primitive man; he used his mind as an instrument of survival within his natural surroundings, and thus developed skills and customs which he passed on as a heritage. From an evolutionary standpoint the mind is not therefore primarily a window through which we have access to ultimate reality. These more recent philosophers insisted that men had overestimated the function of the mind when they thought a succession of logical ideas was a disclosure of the pattern of nature.

The expression of this new viewpoint opened up a line of philosophical inquiry which was bound to affect philosophy in the direction of practical interests and turn its attention away from the speculations and system-building which had earlier been dominant. William James, one of our own American philosophers, may be taken as representative of the new spirit which was sufficiently distinctive that a new label was required for it. The name *pragmatism* was coined, suggesting the practical phase of this philosophy. Following James, a further development was made by John Dewey, another American, who called his position *instrumentalism* to emphasize the main point of the philosophy, that the mind is an instrument. From the viewpoint of instrumentalism, all theoretical problems, if they are really problems, must be statable in practical terms, that is, in relation to some life situation, whether scientific, political, social, or ethical. This evolutionary philosophy contended that we will actually learn more about the universe we live in if we learn about particular processes and particular truths and forgo all efforts to affirm what is the absolute reality, the absolute truth, and the absolute goodness. Let us see what turn this recent philosophy has taken with reference to these three absolutes—reality, truth, and goodness.

Reality

Whereas under the concept of fixed forms the nature of reality was believed to be disclosed by a knowledge of these forms, it becomes less certain what the nature of reality is if the forms are not absolutely fixed. Development and change introduce a doubt which arises out of the same considerations that produced the problem faced by the early Greeks regarding permanence and change. If all is change, then we cannot have any real knowledge since nothing maintains fixed characteristics. The Greek skeptics believed that we are doomed to hold this conclusion and therefore considered all knowledge relative.

According to modern evolutionary theory, we are presented with the fact that new and unpredictable forms appear, though we do not know precisely how they appear, much less why. There is at first inorganic stuff, and "life" emerges. Life proceeds to run its course, and evolutionary theory tries to account for its manner of operation, although why the process is what it is or why it runs its course at all is not completely revealed in the process. From life "mind" emerges as a new form out of the womb of nature.

There are two points connected with the problem of reality which seemed to some philosophers, especially in the nineteenth century, to follow from the emergence of new levels in the organic process. First, the fact that the new level appears to be much more than the former level and so is to be classified as a higher form suggested that effects are greater than their causes! This point seemed especially strong as one assumed that the process of evolution was self-explanatory. Second, despite the fact that there are new forms or change, one is not left without some degree of permanence. Some stability and some order are found, else how could the various forms be classified into genera and species? That degree of order, even if not permanently fixed, has sufficient permanence for practical purposes. It is relatively permanent, like the "everlasting" hills which are not everlasting but which last long enough to be called permanent. Reality is not beyond experience; it is the great variety of forms of our experience. It discloses itself in a great variety of ways—in the inorganic forms of atoms, rocks, and galaxies; in the organic forms of amoebae, trees, and babies; in the psychic forms of animal intelligence, morons, and geniuses. What is reality? It is all these things, and a good deal else besides. We have reason to suppose it is still laden with potentialities. Because reality is always changing, to ask what is the absolute nature of reality is to ask an unanswerable question.

Truth and Knowledge

Regarding the effect of evolution on the conception of absolute knowledge or truth, we can see at once that if the approach described above is valid, then the older mode of thinking must be modified. What takes place in this instance is but a corollary of what we have just been saying. Our knowledge of reality can never be absolutely fixed, but only relatively so. There is little point in talking about Absolute Knowledge and Absolute Truth in capital letters. There is, however, a great need to talk about knowledge and truth without the capitals, for one can discover particular facts which are very useful and more immediately important for daily living than some vague absolute which he could never feel sure he knew absolutely anyway.

So there arose a tendency in philosophy as a consequence of evolutionary theory to redefine knowledge and truth, divorcing them from the word *absolute*. Instead, it was agreed to call knowledge whatever could be tested or verified in some way. It was pointed out that man lives and learns by discovering and using facts. Facts always involve some particular object, process, condition, or state of this or that aspect of nature. Observation may cause us to speculate about some condition of nature, but the speculation is not knowledge. We cannot reasonably assert that the speculation as such is true. We must test or verify it, and it may turn out that what we guessed to be the case is the case. From this standpoint, knowledge is not a priori (prior to experience) but a posteriori (after experience).

For example, a number of people speculated or guessed that mosquitoes were carriers of the yellow fever germ. That was not yet knowledge. But experiments or tests were undertaken to determine whether mosquitoes did infect people, what kind of mosquitoes might be responsible, and under what conditions, and the speculations were thus verified. This particular fact is now known. It is a particular truth or item of knowledge. But if we guess that there is a vast cosmic plan or purpose working itself out through nature, we still have the task of verification before we can say whether it is certainly true or not. So far as our present ability to carry out tests is concerned, we can neither affirm nor deny the existence of a cosmic plan. We may believe or have faith that there is a purpose, but belief is not knowledge. We may let our speculations roam whither they will, but knowledge, as that word has come to be used in recent times, must humbly plod a painstaking course of fact-finding and testing.

Note, however, that according to this approach we may take the particular facts or knowledge in our possession and theorize *beyond* them. This is exactly what happened in the case of the theory of evolution. Many scientific men believed or had faith in evolution before they had verified it. At first, theorizing went beyond the facts. In other words, a tentative proposal was offered in explanation of known facts. Observe that it was not a fantastic theory—on the contrary, Darwin's theory had a high degree of probability. So in recent philosophy, as well as in science, such phrases as *degree of probability* and *degree of truth* are used. These terms suggest tentative standpoints, experimental attitudes, and the implication that more verification will be sought and a higher degree of probability, or possibly a lesser degree, will be obtained. Recent reflective thinking makes a clear distinction between faith and knowledge in science. Faith may go beyond knowledge in the acceptance of a theory about the nature of the universe or in the acceptance of theological ideas. However valuable it may be to hold some things on faith, that faith should have some reasonable grounds, that is, there should be some basis of probability. If the accepted faith has a very low degree of probability, then its foundation is weak. But in any case, faith must be distinguished from knowledge. Even in the case of knowledge, there should be an open end for possible revision, for knowledge has a tentative aspect, only a relative permanence. A new fact may require modification of even accepted knowledge all along the line.

If an illustration were needed, it would only be necessary to point to the fact that by 1895 many physicists believed that all the fundamental principles of physical science had been discovered and that only practical application of these principles remained to be worked out. But that very year the X-rays were discovered, marking the beginning of a far-reaching revision of the body of knowledge which had been accepted up to 1895. And this is precisely what happened when Darwin announced the results of his work—it caused a revision of the knowledge of that day in biology, geology, and many other fields.

One of the philosophical effects of the theory of evolution, then, was the redefinition of the words *knowledge* and *truth*. As redefined, neither word carries the idea of absolute certainty with it. Certainty came to be regarded as merely practical and tentative; knowledge was restricted to that accumulation of data which could be verified. As said above, experience has also taught that it is well to keep a door open for modification. This is the best that can be done in regard to knowledge as so defined. Many ideas and theories are still candidates for election to the academy of knowledge; and that election is a genuine distinction, even though permanent tenure is not guaranteed.

The Good, or Ethics

The third effect of the evolutionary theory on philosophy which we have selected for discussion is its influence on ethics. This is a very long story indeed, but it will suffice to indicate a few aspects of the thinking in this area.

Darwinian theory was almost as startling in its implications for moral philosophy as it was for theology. The recognition that man had an organic descent—or ascent, if we prefer—from lower animal forms was a very unpalatable pill for the human ego to swallow. Many people opposed the theory lock, stock, and barrel. But numerous thinkers jumped to the opposite extreme and concluded that the system derived from the course of organic evolution should be rigorously applied to the sphere of moral relations. Such terms as *survival of the fittest* and *adjustment to the environment* became the catchwords of a new theory of ethics.

A representative of this approach who was deeply affected by evolutionary thought was the German philosopher-poet Friedrich Wilhelm Nietzsche (1844-1900). He believed that as a result of the process of survival of the fittest in evolutionary development a higher type of being would appear, which he called the superman. Nietzsche thought that the survival of the weak and the delay of the appearance of this more-than-man was primarily due to Christian ethics and morals.

But this leads to the now-familiar problem of the meaning of the term *fittest*. As it is used in the strictly biological sense of organic fitness to the environment, it may not be applicable on the higher level of human relations. Furthermore, both the word *fittest* and the word *environment* are ambiguous. Note the difficulty which the words create. Whatever is "fittest" is regarded as good by the moralist who bases himself upon evolutionary theory. What then is fittest? Is it brute strength, which certainly is sometimes a factor in survival? Is it fleetness of foot, which is no doubt sometimes a factor in survival? Is it thickness of skin, or cunning? Clams and oysters are remarkably well fitted to their environment. In fact, some forms of marine life have survived without much change through ages of time. Are they fittest? What is fittest for a clam is not necessarily fittest for a man. In the terrestrial environment groups of men have survived by overcoming other groups by force and numbers. Does it necessarily follow that the stronger is the better? We demur somewhat at this point, for we hesitate to endow all instances of survival with the quality of good.

The reader perhaps shares the feeling that the terms *fitness*, *survival*, and *the good* are not exactly synonymous. We have the impression that some falsification occurs by such identity. Good as a human term must be studied in relation to human affairs, and must not be equated indiscriminately with factors operative on the biological level. From the standpoint of the evolutionary approach, moral experience appears in the course of evolution as one of the phenomena characteristic of human beings. It is a new or emergent form. Therefore, what it is and does must be learned from the level where we find it, for obviously it cannot be known in terms derived from an entirely different level. If we have occasion in ethics to use such words as *survival* and *fittest*, we use them in a moral context, not a biological one. This realization is important, for it was the recognition of this point which turned many philosophers away from the expectation of explaining ethics solely in biological terms. Instead, they began to look at the actual nature of moral development, which is different from organic evolution in many respects.

Ethics, as we know, is concerned with such questions as the nature of the good life, the best life to live, and what is good. Morality in Western culture has been essentially an adjunct of Christianity. By that we mean that the culture and hence the dominant morality, at least the moral ideal, of the Western world have been molded by that heritage of ideas which have been derived from Hebrew, Greek, and Roman sources through the medium of the Christian church. Obedience to the Ten Commandments, Christian virtues like altruism in the form of alms to the poor and care for the sick, occupation or work, thrift, marital fidelity—all these have long been emphasized as meritorious. In general, we may say that morality has been a primary concern of all branches of the Christian church. A common ground of morality has underlain the differences in religion and been made part of each theological position. Prior to Darwin's time, men believed that the moral demands made on them were laid down and were almost as "fixed" as the form or species *man* was "fixed" by the Creator in the Garden of Eden. The Ten Commandments, for example, were thought of not as the compact result of long years of experience in social living upon which Moses had been able to draw but as literally revealed by God to Moses in their set form as something altogether new. There was nothing debatable about the Commandments because they were divine ordinations.

As the evolutionary concept was adopted, however, it came to be believed that there was a history or evolution of morals through the course of long ages of human living. Thinkers concluded that this long history needed to be studied in order to understand the growth and development of moral ideas among different peoples widely separated by time and location. They found that what was judged to be good in one place was judged to be bad elsewhere—a disturbing discovery, because some had expected to find a fundamental moral sense analogous almost to the sense of sight or smell. It soon became evident that there was nothing quite like that. Extremists then concluded that *moral* is just a name used by modern civilized man for whatever people agree to call good, that it is just another word for custom and convention.

This started a debate on ethics over the very same issue that was at stake between Socrates and the Sophists described earlier. Is there something permanent about ethics in the way of discoverable principles which *ought* to be binding on all men, or is ethics entirely relative, that is, entirely a matter of custom which may change and is not binding outside the given society which happens to approve of this way of doing things? The reader should be able to observe at once that he is confronted by a familiar actor in this unfolding drama of philosophy and religion: this member of the cast is the issue of permanence and change again, but now in different dress. This time the problem of permanence and change is in the realm of morals, but it is the old problem just the same. Perhaps, as before, the choice need not be between absolute permanence and absolute change.

The early impression of scholars investigating moral history was that the variation in moral habits was so great that no common basis of morality disclosed itself. But further study indicated that this was only a superficial observation. As a distinguished writer in this field says, the great variety of customs which confronts the student bewilders him at first but

> . . . ends rather by impressing him with a more fundamental and far-reaching uniformity. Through the greatest extent of time and space over which we have records, we find a recurrence of the common features of ordinary morality which, to my mind at least, is not less impressive than the variations which also appear.[8]

These statements, based on wide acquaintance with the actual findings, show us that the course of morals has not been one either of absolute change or of absolute permanence. Change does seem at first to be the most constant feature of morals when we take a long look across the years. Yet we also find that there are certain moral features which repeat themselves over and over again, indicating some aspects of human nature which remain

[8] L. T. Hobhouse, *Morals in Evolution*, New York, Henry Holt & Co., 1923, p. 28.

more or less constant. Virtues like courage, sincerity, and kindliness within the group life are regularly found. Both relative permanence and change work together in moral evolution.

We know that man is a moral being, that is, he judges some actions to be valuable or good and others to be worthless or evil. This bare statement of fact applies to primitive man as well as to ourselves. As we examine the life of early man and his judgments of what is good and what is not good, we make an interesting discovery. Primitive man assumed, without conscious reflection, that whatever made the group prosper was good. This is still the permanent element in morals. But change comes in because men differ on what will preserve or benefit the group. Because of differing social conditions, limitations of knowledge, and occasionally wrong decisions, variations in group morals have appeared.

The theory of evolution influenced men to study morals as a natural phenomenon regardless of existing religious-moral patterns, and encouraged them to approach morals naturalistically. It influenced morals by loosening the hold of ecclesiastical authority. That is, the evolutionary idea applied to the development of morals caused men to question the finality or absolute permanence of moral requirements laid down by religious bodies. The sanction of a church or any other body is not considered sufficient from this standpoint to establish any code or moral doctrine permanently.

Evolutionary theory thus influenced moral philosophy in the direction of flexibility. No moral patterns are considered absolutely fixed, and yet neither are they entirely relative. What is found is both change and stability in a moving equilibrium. There is sufficient stability for the practical needs of organized social living in communities and nations, but all the while there is an open end, so that movement can be made from present goods to possible better goods that lie ahead. Imbedded in this approach is the idea of progress as a possibility for mankind.

The Influence of Evolution on Religion

We are well aware by this time that the recurring issue raised by evolution in all the areas discussed so far is that of permanence and change. It is no less important with regard to religion. If we approach the effect of evolution on religion from the standpoint of this issue, we can appreciate the larger significance of the influence of Darwin's theory instead of giving much space to the more immediate alarm it occasioned. That is the reason why it is more profitable to consider the religious effect after the philosophical.

The doctrine of evolution was one more blow to man's sense of his own importance and significance in his world. Before the time of Copernicus he could believe that his earth was the stationary center about which all motion of the heavenly bodies took place. The sun, moon, planets, and all the stars were believed to revolve about this earth, having been placed there by God for man. Copernicus dealt the first great blow to this belief with the heliocentric theory. Shortly afterwards the discovery of the immense spaces in which the earth moves gave men a sense of their own physical smallness. Newton with his mechanical model of the universe found no real place for man and his most important values. Still, religious people had been able to cling to the belief that God had made man a special creation different from all other beings in nature and majesty. Darwin attacked this last shred of man's pride in his significance within the universe, for he saw man as only one of multitudes of emergent biological forms, and asserted that his appearance in the world came about no differently from the way in which all other species had appeared. This was the Enlightenment's greatest blow to man, for it threatened to rob him of his last dignity. Reaction against the theory was understandably vigorous and often violent.

In order better to understand how great an effect this theory had in the religious field, it is well to look at the state of mind of a well-educated religious man in 1859, the year following Darwin and Wallace's presentation of their paper on evolution. In a volume of essays on evolution, one contributor, a clergyman of the Church of England, stated that even prior to Darwin he and a number of his contemporaries had come to believe that an evolutionary process had taken place, that this world not only is but has become what it is by a process of change. He wrote:

We were, as I have said, evolutionists at heart. We had begun to realize the immense extent of the Sidereal Universe. It was incomparably more to us than it was to the writer of the first chapter of Genesis, who added incidentally that God "made the stars also". Lyell and others had also familiarized us with the age of the earth, its slow and gradual formation, and the long succession of forms of life on it. We were becoming reconciled even to the thought of pre-Adamite man, and an undefined but possibly very great antiquity of man. And the effect of such extension of time as well as of space was, with the generation brought up as I had been, finally to dissolve the traditional theology we had inherited of Creation and the Creator, and we could form no conception to replace them. But simultaneously the fact that there should be this amazing Cosmos, and not only that, but also beings like ourselves, to whom the details and processes were at least partly intelligible, convinced us more than ever that there was some Purpose and Mind, in some way akin to us, who had created and was creating all things, but whose nature and method were hopelessly beyond our power to understand. Upon us, when in this state of mind, burst Darwin's *Origin of Species*.[9]

The writer of the above passage went on to describe how he had read and reread Darwin and had become convinced that the idea of evolution was not only confirmed as a reality but that the process of evolution was explained with at least partial accuracy. This left him with the recognition that he could see no direct action of God in this process. A state of religious perplexity followed.

I did without the thought of God for a time; and strange to say I did not think my life deteriorated in any way, nor did I miss it much. I hoped, though scarcely expected, that the eclipse was only for a time, and retained all the old habits of religion, even prayer, in the darkness.[10]

Then followed a period of further reflection. The writer wondered whether possibly the current conception of God was immature and should be enlarged.

The primitive conception of God as a Being, with faculties resembling but surpassing human faculties, was, it appeared to me, inevitable as the "first thought", when man's spiritual and speculative powers first developed, because man was the chief and highest visible agent possessing creative faculties. Hence anthropomorphism and mythologies were the inevitable mould in which primitive theology was formed; they provided the framework and symbols and language of early theology. These mythologies and symbols and words, when venerable and established by age, became hardened into solid facts, and were regarded as supernatural revelations; as facts from which equally solid inferences could be drawn. To use another metaphor, I came to regard our orthodox theology as a superstructure logically built up in the past on what were thought to be known facts, but were really metaphors, analogies, symbols, men's "first thoughts". These were naturally expressed in forms drawn from material nature, and had thus got far away from the spiritual facts, unexpressed and often inexpressible in words, which had been and are the real and permanent suggestion and ground for belief in God. I began to think that a time was at hand when men's first thoughts of God, however logically worked out into a system, would

[9] James M. Wilson, "The Religious Effect of the Idea of Evolution," in *Evolution in the Light of Modern Knowledge—a Collective Work*, London, Blackie and Son Limited, 1925, p. 488. This and the following quotations from this source by permission of the publishers.

[10] *Ibid.*, p. 489.

share the fate of first thoughts in every other science, and be superseded by "second thoughts" of a wholly different nature.[11]

How well the above passages indicate the intellectual and emotional upheaval taking place! Many men and women were suffering under the impact of these new ideas and were endeavoring to adjust themselves to a new conception of the creative process and of the Creator. One more passage will suffice to show how the mind could courageously move forward.

Think of the orthodoxy of creation a century ago. There is in the Worcester Cathedral Library, among our early printed books, a copy of the *Nuremberg Chronicle*, a History of the world from the creation downwards. The primaeval void is represented by concentric blank circles, with a Hand stretched over them. In the next page the Creator is shown as an old man modelling Adam out of clay, with animals standing round. Adam is finished down to his waist, and alive; the rest of his body is a formless lump of clay. I show this book sometimes to visitors, as Boswell tells us it was shown to Dr. Johnson, and they smile. But let us remember that this represented both the orthodoxy of the whole Church and the science of naturalists till the lifetime of some of us. Can we in the same breath admit that the orthodoxy of seventy or eighty years ago was temporary and mistaken on so great a matter, and still hold that the orthodoxy of today is final and correct? The retrospect of the past in which I am indulging is valuable if it forces this question on us, and demands an answer. *The orthodoxy of the past was based on the science of the past; and if the science alters and expands, so also must the orthodoxy.*[12]

There is a degree of dramatic effect and impressiveness which strikes us in reading autobiographical passages from one who felt at first hand the impact of evolution on religious thinking. How well he brings out the apparent necessity of accepting the fact of change as a permanent feature of our environment, paradoxical as that sounds. We should not regard change as an enemy to our best interests, but as a friend, though we may be startled by the form in which it appears.

Accepting the thought that reality and truth are in a process of constant change is extremely difficult if not impossible for formal religion to do, for fairly obvious reasons. Organized religions hold that the God worshiped is an unchanging God and that this God has revealed himself to their founders. These revelations, in turn, are given permanence in theological forms and religious practices, and the body of accepted belief constitutes orthodoxy. The thought that God and the truths believed revealed through him are

[11] *Ibid.*, pp. 489 f.
[12] *Ibid.*, p. 486.

temporary and changing, to be replaced in the future, is directly contradictory to everything formal religion stands for. The question faced by the religious person as he first comes to the theory of evolution is how far he is willing to accept change. As the quotations given above indicate, it is possible to accept it up to a point. Beyond that point the believer cannot go without destroying the very foundation of his faith.

What now are some of the effects of the idea of evolution on the Christian tradition? We select as specific features for consideration the changed conception of the Bible, the modifications of the idea of God and the nature of man, and the new approach to the study of non-Christian religions.

The Bible

In regard to the Bible, we need to recall that the Protestant reformers substituted the authority of Scripture for the authority of the Roman Catholic church. The Bible was understood to be the account of God's revelation to man of infallible truth, written in the glow of divine inspiration. In contrast to this approach, those who applied evolutionary principles in full force to religion and the Bible held that the earlier written sections of the Bible were simply primitive documents that were of little religious value; they felt that the later sections, presumably developed in the course of the centuries, were of greater value. The Bible came to be considered a record of man's evolving ideas; the thought of revelation and inspiration was largely discarded. Though the majority of Christian thinkers were unwilling to carry their position to such an extreme as this, many now approached the study of the Bible in a new spirit: they attempted to understand it as a literary creation in its own right, to be studied by the critical methods generally applicable to historical literary materials. To this new approach was given the name of historical analysis.

Historical analysis is a process of careful study that starts from the fact that the Bible is a collection of many books, written at different times and places by many authors whose various human qualities are reflected in the writings. Under this minute examination, various details emerge. For instance, the Bible records man's enlarging insights about God and God's relation to men. This method demands that the Bible be studied in the light of contemporary conditions, and that it be subjected to critical analysis of the kind that is properly used upon any ancient document. Through historical analysis and the related field of archaeology, the vast knowledge of the Hebrew past available today has been obtained. Without this knowledge to draw upon, even the brief history of Hebrew development and the composition of the Gospels given earlier in this volume could not have been written.

Valuable as this work has proved to be, it was subject to bitter attacks. The new conception of the Bible was upsetting; it left men without the ground of absolute certainty which the older view had seemingly provided. This struggle still continues; it is more noticeable in Protestant circles than in Catholic, largely because for Catholics the authority of the Bible is secondary to that of the church itself. However, in the Catholic church too historical analysis was opposed. The loosely knit organization and lack of central authority among Protestant denominations made it impossible to stifle the new studies entirely, as they largely were in Catholicism.[13]

Ideas of God and Man

The changed outlook which evolutionary theory brought upon conceptions of God and man has not as yet run its entire course. Ideas about God and his method of producing the universe have a long history, and have gone through many modifications. It has been one of the important tasks of this volume to convey that fact. The theory of evolution required theologians to reconsider their conception of God as Creator. Some of them were quite willing to drop their initial antagonism to evolution and to accept it fully. Their way was eased by Darwin himself, who presented evolution as the method used by God to bring the many and varied forms of life into being. In the final chapter of his *Origin of Species*, he wrote,

> I see no good reasons why the views given in this volume should shock the religious feelings of any one. . . . A celebrated author and divine has written to me that "he has gradually learned to see that it is just as noble a conception of the Deity to believe that He created a few original forms capable of self-development into other and needful forms, as to believe that He required a fresh act of creation to supply the voids caused by the action of His laws."[14]

Darwin's concluding sentences are:

> Thus, from the war of nature, from famine and death, the most exalted object which we are capable of conceiving, namely, the production of the higher animals, directly follows. There is grandeur in this view of life, with its several powers, having been originally breathed by the Creator into a few forms or into

[13] See Alfred Loisy, *My Duel with the Vatican*, New York, E. P. Dutton and Co., Inc., 1924, for an account of a distinguished Roman Catholic scholar who was excommunicated because of his research and publications in historical criticism.

[14] *The Origin of Species by Means of Natural Selection*, New York, Merrill and Baker, n.d., p. 496.

one; and that, while this planet has gone circling on according to the fixed law of gravity, from so simple a beginning endless forms most beautiful and most wonderful have been, and are being evolved.[15]

Those who accepted this new view felt that it showed a process far more subtle and wonderful than the older view of creation which hitherto had been accepted. How much greater then must be the Creator, and how much greater the intelligence which could generate such an unfolding! The old argument from special design which evolution had destroyed was replaced by a newer teleological argument. One still found it possible to argue that God has a purpose which is being worked out, and that evolution is his method for achieving it. Those who were able to make such modifications in their belief about God found themselves quite satisfied with it, and discovered too that it led them to great optimism concerning the future of mankind. For they believed that contained in the evolutionary process is the divine purpose moving toward ever higher levels of being. Man himself was created by God through this means and is undergoing moral, religious, and social evolution. The religious attitude arising from this view encouraged men to cooperate with the evolutionary process and in this manner become coworkers with God and his purposes. For many, the evolutionary theory not only modified the conception of God's relation to the world but gave them also a new religious enthusiasm.

This change in religious belief concerning God's creation was for some accompanied by a change also in the traditional doctrines of man and his salvation. Those who embraced the new views were led to deny that there ever was a Garden of Eden in which man at one time lived in perfect innocence and then by disobedience fell. Rather, they pictured man as descending (or ascending) from a tremendously long organic past. He has had to learn through pain and pleasure, joy and sorrow. He is not a totally depraved being but a mixture of many elements and impulses derived from his animal ancestry. He needs to develop discipline and follow ideals. Human waywardness should be regarded with sympathy and tolerance, but without condoning behavior harmful to a man himself or to his fellows. The work of Christ would also be re-evaluated from this point of view, for it would be thought of primarily as providing precept and example, inspiring reverence and imitation. One would be said to be saved from his lower impulses and led to his higher ideals through Jesus' teaching and example.

Furthermore, the evolutionary modernist, if we may so designate him, laid stress on the humanitarian side of Jesus' life and tended to express religious sincerity and devotion in terms of social good will and practice. He aligned himself with all those forces which promoted the educational, moral, and

[15] *Ibid.*, p. 505.

economic well-being of man. The church came to be thought of as a fellowship of those committed to this view. The kingdom of God came to be interpreted as the kingdom of man's increasing and inevitable development and achievement. The progress theory of history, rooted as it was also in evolutionary faith, helped to bolster the religious view at this point.

Attitude Toward Non-Christian Religions

Finally, the theory of evolution brought about a change in attitude toward non-Christian religions. Protestant churches enthusiastically engaged in missionary activity during the early part of the nineteenth century. In the New Testament is the saying, "Go therefore and make disciples of all nations, baptizing them in the name of the Father and of the Son and of the Holy Spirit" (Matthew 28:19). This "commission" was believed to have come directly from Jesus and therefore was understood to be authoritative. There came to be a feeling of responsibility for the "heathen"—the non-Christians—and the effort had to be made to save them. This meant that they should receive and accept the Christian message. The Protestant missionary movement got under way in all parts of the world. All the major religious denominations and many of the small ones sent out their emissaries. The Roman Catholic church also took on fresh missionary motivation. The assumption behind the Christian effort was that in Jesus Christ the Christian representatives had the truth, while the "heathen" were in spiritual darkness.

The effect of the evolutionary theory in this regard was to suggest the attitude that all religions were to be looked upon as products of evolution, developed in all instances from primitive beginnings and existing as means of adjustment to the environment. The living religions of the world were considered to be simply a number of forms or species which had come into separate existence in independence of each other. They were not regarded as either necessarily false or true but rather as useful, and it was because of their usefulness that they had survived. The value and truth of each religion was considered in the light of its historical antecedents, its evolution and contemporary ideas, and its merits in terms of the ethical consequences on its adherents. It was denied that Christianity was the final religion.

Evolution and Religion Today

The easy optimism with which some theologians embraced evolutionary thought is now found by many to have been naïve. Although Darwin himself wrote of God's creation of an original form or, at most, four or five original forms, his successors were not so willing to think in theological terms. From the standpoint of science generally, any claim at all to God's activity is in effect a way of moving that area out of the realm of possible scientific investigation. For this reason, and quite properly so we may judge, scientists have resolutely resisted the use of the divine as an explanation for any phenomenon. In the studies of evolution also this practice has been followed. Therefore, theologians who felt prepared to accept the general theory of evolution but wished to insist that God in some way stood behind the process and accounted for the changes, bringing into being new species and orders, have found themselves now abandoned by the theory itself. Let us see what modern scientists themselves have to say upon this matter, and then how writers on religion have responded.

We start with a quotation from Hermann J. Muller in a paper read during the Darwin Centennial celebration at the University of Chicago. He emphasized the purposelessness and unknowingness of the process of evolution by stating, "Through billions of years of blind mutations, pressing against the shifting walls of their environment, microbes finally emerged as men."[16]

We recall, furthermore, that the optimism exhibited by theologians and other thinkers as well arose from the belief that evolution inevitably promises a better future. There was thought to be an inevitable drive or movement toward a better world. But today, we are told, evolution knows nothing of progress at all. It signifies simply changes of forms arising from natural selection. Whether these new forms are in any way higher or better than the old is a moot question; the words *better* and *higher* here seem meaningless. That a new species or order appeared shows simply that it had high survival value in its environment, but little more than that can safely be said—from the standpoint of biology. Garrett Hardin writes, "There may be a sense in which it is useful to say that progress has occurred [in biological evolution]; but we have not yet discovered it."[17] Such a view, rather generally held today, undermines all religious and secular faith in the future as a time of development and purpose. Evolution is now said to be purely a chance process knowing nothing of progress. Purely natural adaptations to environment of the changes that appear occur through mutations in the genes and other causes. The biologist who speaks and writes in this fashion —and many do—finds no place whatever for religion within the framework of his science. There would seem also to be no place for meaning.

Julian Huxley has probably dealt with the place of religion in relation to

[16] "Guidance of Human Evolution," in Tax, *op. cit.*, II, 460.

[17] Garrett Hardin, *Nature and Man's Fate*, New York, Rinehart & Co., 1959, p. 71. See the whole of chap. 4.

science and evolution more extensively than any other great contemporary biologist. In a paper presented at the Darwin Centenary, he began by making the statement that

> This is one of the first public occasions on which it has been frankly faced that all aspects of reality are subject to evolution, from atoms and stars to fish and flowers, from fish and flowers to human societies and values–indeed, that all reality is a single process of evolution.[18]

One notes in this statement that not only are biological forms a product of evolution but human societies and values as well.

Concerning man and his destiny, Huxley of course sees no place or need for God. That same process of evolution which has brought man into the position of being the highest type of life to appear in two and a half billion years of biological improvement "effected by the blind opportunistic works of natural selection" has made him the only agent for the future evolution of the planet. If he does not destroy himself, he may look forward to an equally long stretch of time to "exercise his agency." But this he must do without false hopes of outside help from God. "In the evolutionary pattern of thought there is no longer either need or room for the supernatural." Everything came into being by evolution (a purely natural process), including religions themselves, for they are "organs of psychosocial man concerned with human destiny and with experiences of sacredness and transcendence." Some religions, Huxley writes, have given rise to the idea of gods who might intervene in nature. These supernatural religions are "destined to disappear in competition with other, truer, and more embracing thought organizations . . . with the new religions which are surely destined to emerge on this world's scene."[19]

Mr. Huxley, it appears, believes that religion is a necessity to man, and that in the future a new religion will appear, freed of all entanglements with the supernatural—a religion, in short, cut to fit the measure of naturalistic evolution. How might one describe such a religion—one without supernature and yet containing "experiences of sacredness and transcendence"? To this question, Mr. Huxley replies as follows:

> The emergent religion of the near future . . . will believe in knowledge. . . . it should be able, with our increased knowledge of mind, to define our sense of right and wrong more clearly so as to provide a better moral support; it should be able to focus the feeling of sacredness onto fitter objects, instead of worshiping

[18] "The Evolutionary Vision," in Sol Tax and Charles Callender (eds.), *Evolution After Darwin*, Chicago, University of Chicago Press, 1960, III, 249.

[19] *Ibid.*, pp. 252 f.

supernatural rulers, so as to provide truer spiritual support, to sanctify the higher manifestations of human nature in art and love, in intellectual comprehension and aspiring adoration, and to emphasize the fuller realization of life's possibilities as a sacred trust.[20]

These remarkable statements clearly do not share in the early optimism that first appeared when evolution was greeted as God's way of doing things. God disappears entirely from the scene as unnecessary before that dependable natural process which has made all the wonders of the world and man himself, and which has given him a "potent incentive" for carrying out his own role in the process as he contemplates the glories of the future. Theologians might well feel that although Huxley speaks easily of sacredness and transcendence and of obtaining spiritual support without God, it would be very difficult for him to give such words persuasive meaning within the naturalistic framework of his thought.

The attitude of the majority of Protestant theological writers upon the topic of evolution is to accept it as a scientific fact—as a description of the method by which higher forms of life have come into being. So much might well be granted, but the more extreme claims of evolutionists, for example, Huxley's, would generally be rejected. His denial of purpose in the process and his reduction of all to chance, his treating religion as merely a means of adjustment to environment, and his facile rejection of God would all be opposed. The basis of the opposition would be that Huxley and like-minded evolutionists have left the areas of proper scientific description and have entered areas of interpretation for which their science gives them no competence. The underlying factor in such explanations is the assumption of *naturalism*, itself a philosophical viewpoint not at all derived from biological studies. Naturalists begin with the thought that nature alone is; they interpret their findings in terms of this assumption, and then, not at all remarkably, reach the conclusion that nature alone is. Such would be the most basic criticism by modern theologians of views like those of Mr. Huxley. It is pointed out that science deals with secondary causes and God's activity is primary cause. The natural process itself may be automatic, but the production of higher forms of being (and the theologian insists there are such, culminating in man) shows the existence of a primary purpose behind the entire process. God and regularized nature are for theologians dual explanations, each on its proper level.[21]

In earlier chapters, attention was directed to the reception given the first

[20] *Ibid.*, p. 260.

[21] See Langdon B. Gilkey, "Darwin and Christian Thought," *The Christian Century*, January 6, 1960, pp. 7-11.

developments of science by religion, both Protestant and Catholic. It will be recalled that the principal work of Copernicus was placed on the Catholic *Index of Prohibited Books.* Modern Catholic scholars are far more cautious in their treatment of evolution than they were of the heliocentric theory of the universe. There appears still to be a greater degree of reserve among Roman Catholics in accepting the theory than there is among Protestants. Indeed, Catholics are warned not to assume it is a proved fact. Yet increasingly it is moving toward general acceptance, and a Catholic anthropologist can declare it a "valid scientific theory." However, such acceptance as it is given is always within the theological framework of the assertion that God is creator of both the body and the soul of man. The human spiritual soul, Catholics insist, is immediately created by God, and even if man's body did evolve from animal ancestors, still God made "changes in the already organized body" of a subtle sort which raised it to the human plane.[22]

The issue between religion and the doctrine of evolution is, in fact, the issue existing between religious and scientific thought at every level. Religious thinkers insist that explanations which leave out God and primary causes are at best incomplete; scientists in many instances, moving within the circle of natural phenomena, have felt it sufficient to find explanations appropriate to that framework of interest. In this issue is found one of the greatest of contemporary problems. It is claimed that "truth is one" and that there can be no genuine conflict between true science and true religion, and yet the discovery of the underlying relations which draw them into unity has yet to be made.

Questions for Study

1. Trace the "evolution" of the theory of evolution. Show what factors brought Darwin to the theory, and what his own fundamental principles were. What changes have come into the field since the time of Darwin?
2. What does the evolutionary approach to life suggest about the nature of knowledge and truth? Compare Plato's teachings on the same points. What is meant by calling the mind an instrument? How is the concept of reality affected by this same approach? What effect was felt in the field of ethics?
3. Show how evolutionary thinking opposed fixity and yet did not favor complete relativity in reference to reality, truth, and ethics.
4. Why was the doctrine of evolution such a great blow to religious belief? What did it appear to do to the approach to the Bible, to the ideas of God and man, and to the attitude toward non-Christian religions?

[22] J. Franklin Ewing, "Current Roman Catholic Thought on Evolution," in Tax and Callender, *op. cit.,* pp. 23-28.

5. What views concerning human life are held by evolutionists who deny the validity of religious views of life? Define the area of genuine conflict between religious and evolutionary views, and indicate how you think this might be solved.

Selected Readings

Barnett, S. A. (ed.), *A Century of Darwin*, London, William Heinemann, Ltd., 1958.

Carter, G. S., *A Hundred Years of Evolution*, London, Sidgwick and Jackson, 1957.

Conger, G. P., *New Views of Evolution*, New York, The Macmillan Company, 1929.

Darwin, Charles R., *The Descent of Man*, New York, D. Appleton Co., 1871.

Darwin, Charles R., *The Origin of Species*, New York, D. Appleton Co., 1870.

Dewey, John, *The Influence of Darwin on Philosophy*, New York, Henry Holt & Co., 1910.

Dillenberger, John, *Protestant Thought and Natural Science*, Doubleday & Company, Inc., 1960, chap. 8.

Greene, John C., *Darwin and the Modern World View*, Baton Rouge, Louisiana State University Press, 1961.

Hardin, Garrett, *Nature and Man's Fate*, New York, Rinehart & Co., 1959.

Mascall, E. L., *Christian Theology and Natural Science*, New York, The Ronald Press Company, 1956, chap. 7.

Morgan, C. Lloyd, *Emergent Evolution*, New York, Henry Holt & Co., 1923.

Simpson, G. G., *The Meaning of Evolution*, New Haven, Yale University Press, 1949.

Tax, Sol (ed), *Evolution After Darwin*, Chicago, University of Chicago Press, 1960, 3 vols. (vol. III ed. Sol Tax and Charles Callender).

19. The Influence of Twentieth-Century Science on Philosophy and Religion

The influence of the science of biology in the form of evolutionary theory continued into the twentieth century, as we have just seen. The twentieth century also, in its turn, has produced highly important contributions from other sciences which have made and are making further profound changes in our philosophical and religious outlooks. The sciences which are particularly pertinent in this respect are physics and psychology.

The Influence of Modern Physics

Twentieth-century science has nowhere been more far-reaching in its reconstruction than in the field of physics. Indeed, it is true that "The present transformation of physics is far more radical than the famous 'Copernican revolution' of the sixteenth century."[1] Ideas which were accepted with certainty at the end of the nineteenth century have been called into question, and the world view which was based upon these earlier ideas is no longer considered adequate.

Throughout this survey we have seen how first one and then another science has influenced religious and philosophical speculation. With Plato,

[1] Milič Čapek, *The Philosophical Impact of Contemporary Physics*, Princeton, D. Van Nostrand Co., Inc., 1961, p. 378.

mathematics was the dominant science, and Platonic philosophy bore eloquent testimony to its influence. With Aristotle, biology provided the fundamental concepts for understanding nature. During the Middle Ages, theological considerations were of paramount importance, and philosophy was preoccupied with religious problems. This attitude yielded very slowly to the world view dictated by the development of modern science, which issued in a naturalistic philosophy based upon Newtonian physics. New notions have now arisen in physics which are destined to play a major role in forging future philosophies. Before examining some of these new concepts, let us refresh our minds on the characteristic philosophical outlook which had arisen under the stimulus of the older physics.

Newton and his successors had come to think of nature as a gigantic machine run according to certain immutable laws, like the law of universal gravitation. The fundamental concepts by means of which men sought to understand their world were mass, space, and time. Masses moving through absolute space in an absolute time were thought to be reality par excellence; all else was merely phenomenal, to be ultimately explained in terms of the redistribution of mass particles. Man was a spectator whose task it was to discover the laws according to which matter redistributed itself.

Because physics had made remarkable strides and seemed such a thoroughly complete science while operating with very few fundamental concepts, it became the model of what science ought to be. Men dreamed of the time when all sciences might conceivably be reduced to physics and all physics reduced to mechanics, the science of moving masses. Some hoped that biology, chemistry, and even psychology would be reconstructed along purely automatic lines, without any need for such concepts as purpose, design, or final causation. The doctrine of organic evolution seemed to suggest that mechanical laws operated no less in the realm of biology than in physics, and behaviorism came as a belated expression of the quest for purely physical and mechanical explanations in psychology.

All these scientific tendencies affected philosophy and provided the framework for a modern materialism not unlike the view which was held by Democritus in the classical Greek period. The modern development seemed far more convincing than the older variety, however, primarily because it had the backing of modern scientific notions. Certain materialistic tenets seemed indubitable. Three of these deserve special attention.

First, only material things were considered real. By *matter* was meant a fundamentally inert or inanimate space-occupying substance, as understood in the science of mechanics. Second, everything happened according to strict necessity in conformity with the laws of mechanics. As Edward Fitzgerald translated Omar Khayyám, so too the materialists thought that "The first Morning of Creation wrote what the Last Dawn of Reckoning shall read." If a man only knew enough of physics he might predict every item of behavior in the universe. No one expressed this belief more clearly than *Pierre de Laplace* (1749-1827), father of the nebular hypothesis and famous for his statement that he had no need of the "hypothesis of the deity." Laplace wrote,

> An intelligent being who at a given instant knew all the forces animating Nature and the relative positions of the beings within it would, if his intelligence were sufficiently capacious to analyze these data, include in a single formula the movements of the largest bodies of the universe and those of its lightest atom. Nothing would be uncertain for him: the future as well as the past would be present to his eyes.[2]

The third of the apparently unshakable notions was that matter moved in absolute time and space.

For every one of these notions philosophy could find good scientific support; hence the chief criticism of materialism came from nonscientific sources. There were those who wished that materialism were not true because it ran counter to a religious interpretation of things; and because they wished it to be untrue they believed it to be so. There were others who were quite willing to concede that nineteenth-century physics was perfectly correct so far as it went, but who believed that it was improper to expand its findings into a complete metaphysics. To such people it did not follow that because the world could be described in terms of physical laws, it could not be described in any other terms. Science might be correct and still be incomplete. The materialist philosophers themselves probably looked on these two types of criticism as essentially the same. Both groups were considered merely wishful thinkers who were unwilling to follow the best knowledge available. But then something happened: nearly all the basic assumptions of nineteenth-century physics were called into question by the physicists themselves! Criticism from this quarter could hardly be neglected. Let us examine the three main dogmas we said were characteristic of the natural philosophy which drew its inspiration from Newtonian physics, and see what has happened to them in the light of recent research. The first of these had to do with the notion of matter.

[2] Quoted from Laplace's *Complete Works* in E. L. Mascall, *Christian Theology and Natural Science*, New York, The Ronald Press Company, 1956, p. 178.

Revision of the Concepts of Matter and Necessity

Prior to the middle of the nineteenth century an atom was supposed to be a "particle of matter," a sort of tiny billiard ball, of irreducible size and permanent structure. Our outer world was thought to consist solely of these particles with simple forces acting between them. Then it came to be realized that the particle was surrounded by a field which was something more than a mere void. In electromagnetics the old mechanical view proved inadequate, and scientists were made to realize that "not the behavior of bodies but the behavior of something between them, that is, the field, may be essential for ordering and understanding events."[3] Soon the billiard ball theory had to be abandoned altogether. Atoms were found to be divisible into much smaller units composed of electrically charged particles.

Different physicists have drawn up various models of what an atom may be like. In 1911, Ernest Rutherford pictured the atom as having a central nucleus which carries almost all the mass and yet has a diameter only one ten-thousandth that of the atom. Later physicists discovered that this nucleus, made up of protons and neutrons, is electrically positive. Around it circle the electrons, negatively charged particles. This description suggests that an atom is similar to a miniature solar system, with the central nucleus holding the position of the sun and the electrons the positions of the planets. So great are the relative distances between the nucleus and the electrons and so tiny these particles (if they are particles) in proportion to the size of the atom that a solar system is not a bad analogy. But styles have changed rapidly in modern physics, and newer models are available; all agree, however, in breaking with traditional conceptions. The break consists chiefly in regarding the atom, previously thought to be solid and indivisible, as an electrical structure of considerable complexity in which positively and negatively charged particles are fundamental and relatively empty space makes up the vast bulk of its extension. Finally, the elementary particles are reducible to energy, currently regarded as primal substance, which can be transformed into matter, heat, or light.[4]

The behavior of electrons does not seem to fit the time-honored concept of absolute determinism in the way nineteenth-century physics had come to think of it, thus bringing up the second of the dogmas to which we have

[3] Albert Einstein and Leopold Infeld, *The Evolution of Physics,* New York, Simon and Schuster, Inc., 1938, p. 312.

[4] Werner Heisenberg, *Physics and Philosophy,* London, George Allen & Unwin, Ltd., 1959, p. 67.

made reference. Earlier mechanics had insisted that every physical action is entirely determined by previous physical action. It was assumed that what was true of the very large (the macroscopic)—the masses of matter with which mechanics deals—was also true of the very small (the microscopic), and indeed it was claimed that determinism was true of the macroscopic just because it was true of the microscopic. Werner Heisenberg, a contemporary physicist, challenged this assumption as it applied to the microscopic with his *principle of indeterminacy*. Starting with the idea that electrons have the properties of waves as well as those of particles (quantum mechanics), he proposed that it must be impossible to obtain precise information about *both* the velocity and the position of an electron or any other particle. "The knowledge of the position of a particle is complementary to the knowledge of its velocity or momentum. If we know the one with high accuracy we cannot know the other with high accuracy. . . ."[5] The overall precision of the information we can obtain is limited, so that the more precisely we know one of the two (say, the position) the less precisely we know the other (the velocity, in this instance); or the more nearly accurate either of these measurements becomes, the less accurate is the other. In any physical process for obtaining information, energy is transferred to the object being measured and, consequently, the information obtained is limited. No way to avoid this occurrence seems to be possible. The element of indeterminacy therefore enters into the situation.

Heisenberg's principle may be interpreted as suggesting that the stranglehold of fate, or absolute determinism, is broken by microscopic particles—that even if we knew their habits on the Morning of Creation we should still be unable to reckon their behavior at the Last Dawn. Their behavior cannot be described in terms of *necessary laws* but only in terms of *probability*. Other physicists, like Albert Einstein, who said that "God does not play dice" (but it is doubtful that he is referring to God), opposed the view derived from quantum physics. He believed instead in absolute determinism and maintained that there is no indeterminacy ("playing dice") in nature. To his mind the seeming indeterminacy results from our present inability to make accurate measurements. Heisenberg and those who agree with him do not accept this view. They are convinced that there *is* a basic indeterminacy or probability in nature itself.

This concept must not be interpreted, however, as suggesting that dependable regularities cease to exist in the field of mechanics. The observations of Heisenberg and others in this regard deal with the individual electron or other particle. But when one shifts his examination to the larger masses

[5] *Ibid.*, p. 50.

which mechanics studies, he still finds dependable causality, for the indeterminism becomes negligibly small. The causality resulting from the principle of indeterminacy appears to be somewhat less stringent than the old nineteenth-century determinism, yet it is all the same causality. "Whereas causality in Newton's and Einstein's physics is of the stronger type and, hence, both mechanical and deterministic, in quantum mechanics it is of the weaker causal type and, hence, mechanical but not deterministic."[6]

The behavior of individual electrons can be described only in terms of probability, but when great numbers of such electrons act together, the probabilities reach a result that is dependable and predictable. Instead of being a statement of what absolutely must and does happen all along the line from the smallest quanta of energy to what we call physical objects, law is *statistical* in nature. Accurate prediction cannot be made of the behavior of the individual particle, but the actions of large numbers of particles can be predicted accurately.

Perhaps the meaning of this can be made clear by the use of a commonplace analogy. An insurance company predicts with great accuracy the number of people per thousand in any given classification who will die within a given period of time. It cannot tell which individuals in the group will die and which will not, but by dealing in large numbers it can provide a statistical treatment which describes the behavior of the whole group. The behavior of the individuals eludes exact prediction. In like manner, the physicist can deal with electrons only in a statistical fashion. He can know for certain how a large group of them will behave, but he can predict their individual behavior only within the limits of such probability as can be inferred from the group. This involves quite a breach with traditional notions and has removed contemporary physics from the mechanistic model of the last century. Quantum physics, of which this recent development is an aspect, is so called because it deals with electricity and light as constituted of discrete particles, or quanta, rather than as thoroughly continuous waves which might be infinitely divisible. Research in the subatomic field is still only in its early stages, but it is significant that already it has found the old categories inadequate.

Einstein's Theory of Relativity

We examine next the third of the tenets held by classical nineteenth-century physics: that of absolute time and space. To add insult to the injury

[6] *Ibid.*, Introduction by F. S. C. Northrup, p. 22.

inflicted upon Newtonian physics, *Albert Einstein* (1879-1955) has indicated that space and time must not be thought of as absolute and separable. The older notion has given way to the idea that space and time, when taken individually, are relative for all purposes of science to the point of reference from which they are measured. Perhaps the meaning of this can be made clear if we first try experimentally to determine the meaning of simultaneity.

We are all conscious of the fact that some things happen at the same time, or simultaneously. Moreover, intuition tells us that there is a meaning to absolute simultaneity—that while I am writing this sentence there are things going on in various other parts of the universe of which all observers might say, "All these things are happening at the same time." While this seems indubitable to common sense, yet it happens that if we set up experiments to determine which things are exactly simultaneous, we shall discover that different observers will disagree about the simultaneity of some spatially separated events. What will appear simultaneous to observers moving at a certain velocity relative to the event will not appear so to others moving at a different velocity. As d'Abro has put it, "There is no meaning in speaking of the same instant of time in different places until we have objectivised time, as it were, by specifying our frame of reference."[7] Since science operates with measured times and distances rather than with intuited ones, it follows that the relativity of time is a cardinal principle of the new physics. In just a moment we shall try to clarify further the meaning involved in this principle by recourse to a commonplace example.

Before doing so it is necessary to have in mind two modern principles of science, both of which rest on good experimental evidence, and which taken together imply the special principle of relativity which we want to illustrate. In the popularly written book *The Evolution of Physics*, Einstein has stated these principles as follows:

> 1. The velocity of light in empty space always has its standard value, independent of the motion of the source or receiver of light.
> 2. In two coordinate systems moving uniformly, relative to each other, all laws of nature are exactly identical and there is no way of distinguishing absolute uniform motion.[8]

Just a word in explanation of each of these and we will be ready for our illustration. Principle number 1 means merely that anyone wishing to determine the velocity of light will find it to be always a constant, approximately

[7] A. d'Abro, *The Evolution of Scientific Thought*, New York, Boni & Liveright, 1927, p. 171.

[8] Einstein and Infeld, *op. cit.*, p. 185.

186,000 miles per second, regardless of whether that person or the source of the light is moving or at rest (in case there were any meaning to being "at rest"). Principle number 2 means that two bodies which are moving relative to each other (for example, a train moves relative to the station which it passes) are equally good points from which to describe the events of nature, and that a description which holds for one of these places will be valid for the other—provided their relative motions are uniform, that is, that neither body is undergoing an accelerated motion. Now, in the light of these two principles we might perform the following experiment.

Imagine two towns, A and B, 10 miles apart. Suppose that you wish to determine whether two events happened simultaneously at these two places. How can you tell this? You might station an observer (call him X) at the precise midpoint between the two towns. Place a cannon in each of the towns and arrange to have both fired. If our observer X, midway between the two, observes the flashes from the cannons at exactly the same instant, he will declare that the cannons were fired simultaneously. He knows that light travels at a "standard value" and that he is precisely midway between the cannons.

But now let us imagine a railroad connecting the two towns, A and B, and a second observer (call him Y) riding on a train going from A to B and also watching for the flashes. At the exact moment that he reaches the point where X is doing his observing, midway between the two towns, he also observes the two flashes at precisely the same instant. But he, in contradiction of X, just *because* he has so observed the flashes, declares that the cannons could *not* have been fired simultaneously! How can one account for his claim? We do so by referring back to the two principles mentioned above. The velocity of light always has a standard value, regardless of the motion of an observer. And in coordinate systems "all laws of nature are exactly identical and there is no way of distinguishing absolute uniform motion." Y prefers to explain what happened by saying that, relative to observer X and the two towns A and B with their cannons, *he* was standing still and the towns and observer X were in motion. In order that the two flashes reach him precisely at the same moment—as they did—as the midpoint between the two towns was passing him, it must have happened that the light from B was emitted earlier than the light from A, for at the moment of emission (because light requires time to travel) B was *further away* than A. Hence it is clear to Y that the two cannons could *not* have been fired simultaneously!

No doubt you feel like saying that Y should correct his observations to fit X's description, since X was not so foolish as to move while making his calculations. Unfortunately, in a universe where light travels with an absolute velocity (and there is excellent experimental evidence for believing that this is such a universe) there is no reason for preferring X's measuring system to that of Y. The reason for this is obvious: since X and Y (who is moving uniformly in relation to X) both get the same measured velocity for light, either one has a right to consider his frame of reference as the "proper" one, for there is no possible way to distinguish which, if either, body is at rest relative to the other.

There remains one further question which will probably spring to mind. If light is such a strangely behaving phenomenon as to maintain a constant velocity, regardless of the speed with which it is approached, why use it for determining the meaning of simultaneity? If I travel 60 miles an hour in an automobile and pass another going at the rate of 40 miles an hour, my speed relative to the second automobile is 20 miles an hour, for I must subtract his speed from mine to find our relative velocities. Why not subtract velocities in the case of light rays? The only answer to this is that it does not work! Experimentally, the absolute velocity of light has been amply verified. Why not use some other medium than light for determining simultaneity? The answer to this is exactly the same. Intuitionally one can get a different meaning for simultaneity of spatially separated events, but practically such a meaning is less useful than the definition which is experimentally arrived at. To put this abstractly, the relativity of simultaneity is a principle which is pragmatically justified, which is merely another way of saying that it is a concept that works well. By assuming that simultaneity has an experimental meaning only in reference to some particularized frame of reference, physicists are able to dispense with a large number of other notions which are indispensable under Newtonian assumptions. In sum, relativistic explanations are simpler (scientists would say "more parsimonious") than non-relativistic ones.

The implications of the relativity of simultaneity go far beyond the mere fact that "same-timeness" has a different meaning for people in different frames of reference. If light has an absolute velocity for all observers, that must mean that if there were an observer who could move with a velocity approaching that of light, he and all his measuring apparatus would shrink in the direction of his motion. This can be inferred from the principle of the absolute velocity of light. If an observer traveling with the approximate speed of light gets the same results for the speed of a light ray approaching him as one who is not moving at all in reference to the first observer, surely the first observer must be using measuring devices which have shrunk in relation to those employed by the other.

This notion has the merit of making absolute velocity meaningful, and it has also proved highly successful in making physical predictions. The upshot of all this is that the old laws of mechanics are invalid when applied to velocities approaching that of light, although for more mundane matters they are still applicable. This means that the relativity theory can do all that classical theory could do and more, for it encompasses all the features of the classical theory as a limiting instance of its own principles. It does this with fewer basic assumptions (although the ones it does make seem more radical) and is therefore preferable for its theoretical symmetry as well as for its practical efficacy. If continued experimentation should force physicists to abandon the principle of the absolute velocity of light, physics would, of course, be headed for a post-Einsteinian revolution, but until then the relativity principle will continue to be justified by its fruits.

What we have discussed so far under the head of relativity is what is known as the special theory of relativity, since it is applicable only to inertial frames of reference, that is, to systems in which the law of inertia, as formulated by Newton, is valid. A further consequence of the special theory is that mass is found to be convertible into energy and energy into mass. Hence, the old laws of the conservation of mass and the conservation of energy are transformed into one law of the conservation of mass-energy. This constitutes a further step in simplification.

Further generalization of the principles implied in the special theory of relativity led Einstein to the formulation of what is called the general theory. This theory deals with problems of gravitation and has pointed the way for new structure laws for a gravitational field. As with the special theory, the general theory entails spectacular readjustments of some familiar notions. Among the consequences of the new theory is the idea that non-Euclidean geometries work better than Euclidean ones in dealing with the problems of cosmic space, and that space must be interpreted as being curved. Moreover, it has become more evident than ever that the concepts of space and time as absolute and separable entities must be discarded. In their stead there has arisen the notion of a four-dimensional space-time continuum having non-Euclidean properties. In his *History of Science*, Dampier-Whetham has summarized this as follows:

> Physically space and time, considered individually, are relative quantities depending on the position of the observer. . . . The space of which we are accustomed to think has three dimensions—length, breadth and thickness, and . . . we must look on time as a fourth dimension in this combination of space and time, one second corresponding to the 186,000 miles which light travels in that time. Just as the distance between two points in the continuous space of Euclidean geometry is the same however measured, so in the new continuum of space-time, two events

may be said to be separated by an "interval," involving both space and time, which has a true absolute value whoever measures it.[9]

In other words, events in nature must be described in terms of combined spatial *and* temporal dimensions, such dimensions being interpreted as internally rather than merely externally related. The old notion of a particular body moving through an absolute space in an absolute time has been supplanted by a view which finds that the whole field, rather than abstract elements within the field, is the proper object of physical study. The concept of space-time gives us a more objective picture of reality than the dualistic space and time of the older view. Paradoxical as it sounds, relativity is an instrument for introducing us to the non-relative aspects of nature. The third dogma of traditional theory has thus been challenged as thoroughly as the first two which we have discussed.

The Implications of the New Theories

In the light of all the changes which we have mentioned as having taken place in modern physics, what is left of the scientific foundation on which the nineteenth-century form of materialism was based? The obvious answer is that scarcely anything is left by way of support from physics. What are the implications of the new views which have supplanted the older ones? It is far too early to risk very positive opinions on such a subject, but several things seem fairly evident.

In the first place, dogmatic materialism of the old type is no longer in style. The universe has proved itself to be complex beyond the wildest imaginings of the nineteenth-century philosophers. If a new materialism is to arise, it must certainly be vastly different from its philosophic forerunner. The new analysis of matter had led some of the more speculative minds of the present century to shift clear over to a "mentalistic" conception of things. Because materialism in the old sense has been found inadequate, the highly speculative conclusion has once more been drawn by some philosophers that the ultimate explanation of things must be in terms of mental categories. Even among some modern theoretical physicists, one sometimes meets the notion that physics is entirely a mental construct, its structure reflecting the structure of the human mind rather than that of reality, although this is by no means the dominant view. Such an approach, of course, raises once more

[9] W. C. Dampier-Whetham, *A History of Science*, New York, The Macmillan Company, 1929, p. 422.

all the ancient problems concerning the relation between thought and the universe.

Heisenberg's principle of indeterminacy (or uncertainty) has been employed by a number of recent philosophers to support the doctrine of freedom of man's will, although with what degree of success is open to question. Since that aspect of physics which provided the chief basis for a rigorous determinism in philosophy has been challenged, the adherents of indeterminism have been provided with a new argument for their position. Another use has been made of the principle of indeterminacy by some recent pragmatists in philosophy. John Dewey used the idea to defend his position that knowledge is never a mere mental picture of reality, but is rather an end product which involves experimental rearrangement of antecedently existing things. Just as any conceivable experiment with electrons is destined to change their behavior, so all knowledge entails rearrangement of antecedent material which is employed in the process of getting knowledge. This provides the basis for a radical "nonspectator" theory of knowledge which has been influential in recent philosophy.

In conclusion, it can be said that modern physics presents for our knowing an infinitely more complex and mysterious world than that of nineteenth-century physics. Just because of its complexity and mystery, dogmatic assertions concerning materialistic and deterministic qualities of our physical world cannot be so confidently made. By this we do not mean to imply that modern physics has destroyed determinism and naturalism; it has rather reopened the questions within a far wider framework than that of the nineteenth century.[10] Ultimately, as the truths of physics meet with the claims of religion and some forms of philosophy, they must be approached—as must the truths of evolution under the same circumstances—from a standpoint wider than that of the science alone. They must be approached from the standpoint of one's ultimate philosophy of life, whether it is that of naturalism or of a religious or philosophic faith. Scientific discovery does not determine these basic viewpoints.

Modern Psychologies and Their Effects

It is evident from the preceding chapters of this survey of our intellectual and spiritual heritage that psychology has frequently been very influential in

[10] A timely and valid warning is sounded by John Dillenberger against "the bland assumption that contemporary science has destroyed the notion of materialism . . ." (*Protestant Thought and Natural Science,* Garden City, Doubleday & Company, Inc., 1960, p. 284).

the related fields of philosophy and religion. Consider some examples. Plato's psychological theory of the three faculties of the soul (reason, spirit, and appetite) was fundamental for his definition of virtue. Aristotle's doctrine of man and human good rested upon his psychological theory that reason is unique in man. The Neo-Platonists used their view of the human mind as a model for the conception of the universe, and Augustine explained the doctrine of the Trinity by psychological analogy. Modern psychology, beginning with Locke and Berkeley, has infected all our ideas with the suspicion of subjectivism. Influenced by the psychological analysis of our knowledge process and by the usual conclusion based on this analysis that we know only our own ideas, many have inclined toward skepticism about the possibility of knowledge of anything beyond those ideas. This has led them toward agnosticism in both religion and philosophy. If we know only our own ideas, how can we be sure that God is not merely an idea and independent reality a fiction? Since it is abundantly clear from these examples that psychology does affect theology and metaphysics, it follows that different types of psychology will have somewhat different effects.

In modern times, religious and philosophic thought have been much exercised by certain twentieth-century psychologies. We mention behaviorism and the psychology of the unconscious, giving a very brief statement of the significance of the former and a longer exposition of the latter because of its far-reaching effect on our understanding of human nature, with which both philosophy and religion are concerned.

Behaviorism

This type of psychology is connected with the name of *John B. Watson* (1878-1958), its chief exponent.[11] As the name implies, behaviorism sought to define psychology in terms of activity. From this standpoint the mind *is* what it *does*. Strictly speaking, behaviorism was a method for the study of the subject matter of psychology. Seeking to make psychology just as scientific as physics, behaviorists manifestly could not consider introspective material. Our private feelings and thoughts—the things that go on within consciousness—do not lend themselves to the public manipulation and control that exact science demands. So Watson and his followers attempted to study only behavior and to write psychology entirely in terms of stimulus and response, without even using the word *consciousness*. In approaching psychology in this way, Watson and his school performed a very great service.

[11] See his *The Ways of Behaviorism*, New York, Harper & Brothers, 1928.

They were able to introduce exact measurements into the study of the self, and they provided a stimulus to further research by their findings which was of tremendous value to their field.

In this text, we are interested not so much in scientific theories for their own sake as for their meaning in philosophy and religion. As we examine Watson's behaviorism we recognize the legitimacy of his approach as one method of investigation. But we discover that behaviorism became more than a method. Its exponents were not satisfied merely with describing how living organisms behave but extended their approach beyond the limits of its scientific capacities. They made it into a theory, more philosophic than scientific in nature, of the causes, the whys and the how, of behavior. Having ruled out all psychic causes as beyond the reach of scientific method, behaviorists were obliged to interpret mental activity in physical terms. Psychology thus became a branch of physiology, and ultimately of chemistry and physics! Thus, for the behaviorists, memory consisted merely of habits which were to be explained in terms of traces and tracks in the nervous system, much like the grooves on a phonograph record. They described thinking as "incipient verbalization," that is, the word-making behavior that does not get beyond twitches and contractions in the larynx. Behaviorists steadfastly refused to speak of purposeful ideas; what laymen ignorantly call planned activity they described as behavior dominated by "prepotent stimuli," or by the discharge of energy along a "predisposed neural arrangement," or by a "series of dated anticipatory responses." But whatever the language employed in the desperate attempts to avoid the use of terms associated with consciousness, the central idea of theoretical behaviorism was that all mental activity could be explained ultimately in terms of chemistry and physics. For this psychology, all mental activity is at bottom the result of neural and cerebral mechanics; the mind is like an infinitely complicated automatic telephone switchboard.

The implications of behaviorism for religion and philosophy are fairly obvious. Explaining the mind in terms of physical forces, it reverses the idealistic approach. The metaphysics of theoretical behaviorism is materialism. As far back as our study of Democritus, we learned the implications of atomic materialism for religious belief. Materialism requires no God in its theory; the ultimate reality consists of material stuff, not God. Likewise, there is no place for personal immortality; the mind or soul is only a combination of physical elements. The soul will disintegrate when death brings physical dissolution to the body.

Theoretical behaviorism was the center of debate among intellectuals from 1915 to about 1930, but it has lost its influence since then for two main reasons. One is the revolution that the science of physics has itself undergone. Another and more significant reason is that behaviorism left out too much important subject matter. Keenly bent on making psychology "scientific," it was forced to ignore a great deal of mental material. Psychology did become more scientific under behavioristic auspices, but it did so at the cost of irrelevance to many human problems that require knowledge of the mind for their solution.

The Psychology of the Unconscious

A second and far more important recent psychology is connected in its beginnings with the name of *Sigmund Freud* (1856-1939). Regardless of what we may come to believe about the final truth contained in his theories or about the value of psychoanalysis as a method of treatment, we shall have to recognize in Freud one of the makers of the modern mind. On a list of the men who have profoundly influenced contemporary thought, he should be included along with Darwin and Einstein, for the psychology of the unconscious takes its place beside the theory of evolution and the theory of relativity as influences that have revolutionized thought in the last century.

Discovered as a method of treating nervous diseases, psychoanalysis has outgrown its purely medical significance. It has become an influence extending to every area of human thought. Its effects appear in literature, art, religion, sociology, ethics, and education. Even our everyday language, employing words like *complex*, *inhibition*, *repression*, and *Freudian*, bears witness to Freud's influence. It therefore seems important to include in this survey a short account of the psychology of the unconscious and its implications for philosophy and religion.

In 1881 Sigmund Freud became a medical doctor whose interest was primarily in nervous diseases. The character and causes of nervous afflictions were not well understood, and consequently treatment was little more than a groping in the dark—a sad commentary on the ignorance that hung like a black shroud around all forms of mental derangement. A great deal of experimentation with hypnosis had been taking place. Freud had worked with the neurologist Jean-Martin Charcot in France, where the latter had demonstrated that the symptoms of certain nervous ailments could be artificially induced (and removed) by means of suggestion under hypnosis. When Freud returned to his practice in Vienna, he not only employed hypnosis in treating the symptoms of his patients but discovered from a colleague that under hypnosis patients could be induced to talk about their symptoms and to trace them back to certain unhappy past experiences. Moreover, the symptoms were cured when the situations out of which they had arisen were recalled and the emotion attached to them freely expressed. It was thus established that some mental disturbances have their seat in an area of the mind of which we are not ordinarily aware—an area below the level of consciousness. And on this level, he came to believe, the most general causes of mental illness were factors relating chiefly to sex, as that word was defined in broad and inclusive ways.

Repression

In the course of time, Freud, dissatisfied with hypnosis as a method of treatment, discovered a new way of probing into that hidden part of the mind, the unconscious. Simply by means of assurances and encouragements on the part of the physician, without hypnosis, patients could draw forgotten facts and their connection with present symptoms out of their place of burial, and a cure could be obtained. This raised the question of how and why patients had forgotten so many facts which could be recalled only by means of a particular technique. The kind of material that was thus uncovered supplied the answer.

> Everything that had been forgotten had in some way or other been painful; it had either been alarming or disagreeable or shameful by the standards of the subject's personality . . . that is precisely why it had been forgotten, i.e., why it had not remained conscious.[12]

Normally the struggle between our impulses and our ideals is resolved in the full light of consciousness, and the accompanying emotion is dissipated. But in neurosis[13] the offensive thoughts and impulses are merely silenced, and the conflict they set up is pressed down into the unconscious. In short, the objectionable thoughts, experiences, and impulses are repressed without having discharged their load of emotion.

According to psychoanalytic theory, these repressed impulses, maintaining their dynamic character, seek some means of expression, some substitute outlet. This usually comes in the form of a disguise that satisfies the standards of the personality. In the case of some of the neuroses, the repressed impulses

[12] Sigmund Freud, *Autobiography,* tr. James Strachey, New York, W. W. Norton & Company, 1935, pp. 52 f.

[13] Neuroses are functional nervous diseases, some of which, without demonstrable physical causes, are mental in origin. Neurotic symptoms include paralysis of the limbs, nausea, obsessions, fears, etc.

break through and produce symptoms. Such symptoms, then, are regarded as substitute expressions for repressed impulses. By way of example we may take the victim of shell-shock, who cannot walk and must creep like a baby as an expression of his unconscious wish to be a child who does not have to face the enemy's fire. Or consider the case of the destitute young man who had largely lost his memory. He had even forgotten who he was, except that his name was something like Bert Wilson. It turned out that the patient's name was Richard Albert Williams, and that he had failed in his attempt to support his young wife. Bert Wilson was an unmarried acquaintance who had gone to sea. Williams had forgotten the painful circumstances of his life and had unconsciously identified himself with another person whose name was somewhat like his own—a sailor who had no domestic responsibilities and hence could not fail in his duty toward them.[14]

The search for the experiences that led to repressions and thence to symptoms produced an important discovery: many of these damaging experiences occur in the early years of childhood. A fact formerly observed by poets and educators now found psychological verification. The impressions of that early and "forgotten" period of life leave deep traces in the individual's character and lay the foundation for nervous disorder which may later appear. The needs and fears, wishes and resentments of our childhood are thus held to be potent forces that shape our characters; they determine our biases and prejudices, our convictions and our beliefs.

The Interpretation of Dreams

In the course of his growing experience, Freud again modified his method of treatment. He gave up the practice of urging and encouraging the patient to say something upon the particular subject of his symptoms. Instead, he now asked the patient to practice free association—to repeat whatever thoughts and memories passed through his mind, without conscious direction or censorship. It happened that patients, while practicing free association, frequently reported dreams. Taking the various parts and items of a dream as starting points for further association, Freud discovered that dreams, too, have meanings which can be interpreted.[15] But the meaning is not to be found in the manifest dream. The dream that we remember turns out to be merely an abbreviated and somewhat distorted structure of mental activity.

[14] Reported by Ernest Jones, *Papers on Psycho-analysis*, 3rd ed., Baltimore, William Wood and Co., 1928, pp. 458-472.

[15] See Sigmund Freud's *Interpretation of Dreams*, in *The Basic Writings of Sigmund Freud*, New York, Modern Library, Inc., 1938.

The manifest dream is useful, however, as a starting point for free association, which leads to related ideas or latent dream-thoughts. These last contain the meaning of the dream. But what do dreams mean?

Freud's answer to this question is that the dream is the disguised fulfillment of a repressed wish. In the state of sleep the "censor"[16] is relaxed and off guard. The repressed impulse or unconscious wish takes advantage of this condition of relaxed vigilance to push its way into consciousness in the form of a dream. The impulse or wish

> . . . is the actual constructor of the dream: it provides the energy for its production and makes use of the day's residues as material; the dream which thus originates represents a situation in which the impulse is satisfied; it is the fulfillment of the wish which the impulse contains.[17]

But the dream is not a perfect fulfillment. The "censor" is merely off guard, not off duty. Even dreams are partly censored; some of the latent dream-thoughts are altered so that the forbidden meaning of the dream is acceptably disguised. Thus the dream takes its place alongside the neurotic symptom as a compromise between the demands of the repressed impulse and the censoring demands of the personality. Both have a meaning which analysis can disclose and turn to account in treatment.

We have now seen two ways in which repressed material in the unconscious intrudes itself into consciousness. The neurotic symptom is a substitute for a forbidden impulse, and the dream is a wish-fulfillment in disguise. The first of these means of compromise expression is, of course, found only in people who are mentally ill. If the only evidence of subconscious activity consisted of neurotic symptoms, we might conclude that psychoanalytic theory belonged only to abnormal psychology—that it had nothing to say about the mental activity of normal people. The dream, however, bridges the gap between the abnormal and the normal, for everybody has dreams.

The Unconscious in Normal Life

The dream is not the only way in which unconscious impulses and thoughts press through to consciousness in normal people. The many little slips of the tongue and mistakes that we all make are "symptomatic" too. They are not strictly accidental, but have a meaning which can be inter-

[16] Freud's term for the mind's sense of propriety which causes objectionable and disreputable impulses and wishes to be repressed.

[17] Freud, *Autobiography*, pp. 86 f.

preted in the same way that dreams are made to yield their secrets.[18] The meaning of mistakes is well illustrated by the classic story of the printer's error which caused a news item to refer to a certain general as "that bottle-scarred veteran." The next day the attempted correction read, "that battle-scared veteran." It is obvious what the printer thought of the general's sobriety and courage. He subconsciously found a way to express it. But such an illustration is really not needed, for it is well known to common sense that errors of forgetting often have a meaning. We need no psychoanalyst to tell us what it means when a young lady forgets an engagement with a certain man, or when a man forgets to meet the train bringing his mother-in-law who is coming for an extended visit.

If dreams are constructed like neurotic symptoms and the common errors of everyday life are witness to unconscious mental activity, then psychoanalysis has flown the nest of the physician's office and becomes the basis of a new psychology of the normal mind. Its evidence and its theories are then applicable to other spheres of mental life. It certainly seems a safe extension to view daydreams as fantasies in which impulses and desires, frustrated in real life, find substitute fulfillment. If this is the case, then it is at least suggestive to apply psychoanalytic theory to the interpretation of artistic creations, such as painting and literature. Thus regarded, the products of the poet's imagination seem "symptomatic" too; like dreams, they are substitute experiences for desires and wishes otherwise frustrated. The important difference between the artist and the neurotic, however, is that, unlike the neurotic, the artist produces something of social value and can find his way back from the imaginative "flight from reality."

It would take us too far afield to enter fully into Freud's theory of the structure of personality. For the purposes of this chapter we will add to the foregoing a very brief description of the self as he pictured it in his mature writings. The personality, as he understood it, is made up of three major systems, which he designated the *id*, the *ego*, and the *superego*. These interact very closely, although each has its own specific nature and functions. The original system of the personality is the id; it consists of everything of a psychological nature that is inherited by the child and is present at birth, including the instincts. It provides the psychic energy for the other systems. It is completely subjective in nature and operates according to the pleasure principle, which results from reduction of tension in the organism.

The ego comes into being because of the necessity for the organism to

[18] See Sigmund Freud's *Psychopathology of Everyday Life*, also included in *The Basic Writings*.

relate itself to the outer world. Its function is to find in the outer world objects which satisfy the needs of the id. It is the "executive of the personality," since it postpones action until it gives permission for it to take place. The superego is the system which represents the values and ideals taught to a child by his authorities. It acts in terms of right and wrong. The sense of guilt is the superego's punishment for performance of action considered wrong. It frequently operates in opposition to the instinctual drives of the id and tries also to direct the ego. These three systems work together in the personality under the guidance of the ego. This concept as well as the others we have discussed has had considerable influence on various fields of thought, as we shall see.

Psychoanalysis and Philosophy

The implications of Freudian psychoanalytic theory for philosophy have not received very much attention. Certainly there has not been as much systematic work here as in the field of religion, which will be examined below. However, we shall try to present two fairly obvious applications that the discovery of the unconscious and its activity has to philosophy. The first is that philosophic systems are the product of unconscious as well as rational factors. Metaphysical beliefs may be wish-fulfillments. The second is that the mental can no longer be equated with the conscious mind. Philosophers who conceive reality in terms of mind will have to revise their pictures of the universe.

While psychoanalysis did not discover that non-rational factors are at work in man's rational constructions, it has made us take this truth seriously. It has provided us with a psychology of philosophy, for it has demonstrated the connections that may exist between unconscious wishes and the particular intellectual systems with which we fulfill them. Thus, one philosopher describes himself as a skeptic. He can find no certain order in nature, no fixed arrangement of things that reason can fasten to in its search for truth. When he regards the stars, whose order has figured so largely in theology, philosophy, and science, he finds there no particular order at all. He declares that the order we find there we have put there—that we read it in, not off. Upon being questioned, he admits that as a small boy he felt very keenly the oppressive order that his parents imposed upon his life. Is it too much to say that his childhood rebellion against unbending order and discipline is now reflected in his philosophical doubt that the universe is orderly?

On the other hand, consider the thinker who simply "cannot conceive" the universe except in terms of perfect rationality and order, for whom every event must have some meaning even though he cannot say what this meaning is. He passionately opposes any suggestion of chaos in the metaphysical picture. The proposal to regard the universe as being made up of many elements which do not always harmonize makes him think of a mass of "crawling maggots." What shall we say of such a one? Perhaps he is motivated by the persistence of his childhood suffering of economic or social insecurity, or some other poignant uncertainty that pressed upon his mind when he was young. Of course we will not be popular or necessarily always correct if we seek to psychoanalyze our teachers' and colleagues' philosophic biases. We usually do not know enough about them for that. But the point of these illustrations, not wholly fictitious, is that philosophic beliefs are often if not always deeply affected by unconscious needs and wishes, stemming back in most instances to childhood experience. Here again we must be careful not to become victims of the fallacy that, since the type of one's philosophy is psychologically affected, all philosophies can be dismissed as mere wishful thinking. Psychology and biography can tell us something about the personal history of beliefs, but they are not competent to judge their truth. This, in philosophy as in theology, is a question of proof, to be decided by evidence and logic.

Perhaps the most obvious philosophical consequence of psychoanalysis is the new meaning it gives to the word *mental.* It has been almost a common assumption of traditional philosophy that by *mind* one meant *consciousness.* Mental life was equated with the processes of feeling, willing, and thinking of which we are aware. The new psychology manifestly invalidates this assumption. There are processes going on in our minds of which we are quite unconscious. Moreover, the mind can no longer be regarded as the fundamentally moral and rational entity that we supposed it to be. It is also the seat of confusion, of repressed impulses, of conflicts and complexes which are excluded from awareness. But, though excluded, these facts yet exist and exercise their power.

The philosophical implications of this new conception of the mind are several, but we shall confine ourselves to suggesting, by way of illustration, its implications for idealistic philosophy. Idealism, as we know, regards reality as at bottom mental. Idealists believe that reason and moral concerns are the basis of things, and that they have secured a spiritual interpretation of the universe. But with the new conception of the mental, idealism is forced to revise its picture of reality. Having committed itself to the use of the mind as a model for the conception of the universe, idealism now finds this model taking on those rather disagreeable features which analysis has discovered as present in all human minds—repressions, conflicts, and unacceptable and irrational material. The mind has a skeleton in the closet, and if reality is of the same nature, then it too must contain irrational and brutal elements. This view is quite the opposite of that of classical idealism, which thought of the mind as containing every moral and intellectual virtue.

Psychoanalysis and Ethics

Turning next to the application of psychoanalysis to ethics, we find that here a good beginning has been made. Erich Fromm's *Psychoanalysis and Religion*[19] and *Man for Himself*,[20] J. A. Hadfield's *Psychology and Morals*,[21] and Hans Schaer's *Religion and the Cure of Souls*[22] provide systematic discussions of the relation of psychoanalytic insights to moral questions. While recognizing the value of these works, we shall attempt an independent discussion of the subject.

In the early days of psychoanalysis, when people first heard of the dangers of repressed impulses and frustrated instincts, some hastened to the conclusion that the best way to avoid those unconscious conflicts which are the disagreeable results of repression was to give unrestrained expression to our instincts. Psychoanalysis was thus made into a justification for unconventional behavior and moral irresponsibility. But such a use of the new psychology was never justified. Psychoanalysis is not a charter for license; on the contrary, it shows very clearly that moral ideals are essential in the dynamic growth of character and personality. Doing violence to one's ideals is as dangerous to the integrity of one's personality and mental health as is the too-rigid suppression of instinctive wishes. The happy and creative personality, capable of living a good life, is not a creature of instinct alone, seeking to fulfill itself in a succession of instinctive satisfactions. It is rather a personality in which instinct and ideal have been properly integrated into a harmonious whole.

As psychoanalysis teaches that we must respect our ideals, it teaches with equal force that ethics must respect our instincts. These passions and tendencies are among the raw materials of life. If we repress them, they rule (and perhaps ruin) our lives in hidden ways. In religious terms, the repressed impulse makes one an unconscious sinner. While religion and the law attach a

[19] New Haven, Yale University Press, 1950.
[20] New York, Rinehart & Co., 1947.
[21] New York, Robert M. McBride & Co., 1928.
[22] New York, Pantheon Books, Inc., 1950.

great deal of importance to conscious intention, nature is not lenient with unconscious sinners. She punishes them just as severely as if they had committed a conscious offense. It was no psychoanalyst but a clergyman who once observed that highly "moral" people, unaware of their other side, develop a peculiar irritability and hellish moods from which they themselves as well as their relatives and associates suffer.[23] On the other hand, if we indulge these instincts, this "other side," at the cost of our ideals, we set up feelings of guilt that exact their price. In themselves, instincts are neither good nor bad; their energy, forever seeking discharge, makes them pregnant with the possibility of either good or evil.

Psychoanalysis did not discover the truth of these remarks; it was certainly known to Aristotle. But our new psychology sets forth with new clearness the need for proper handling of the instincts. What is even more important, it suggests the way in which instinctive energy may be redirected into channels in which it may run safely. Psychoanalysis teaches that the instincts' tendency to anarchy can be disciplined without repression. This is the way of *integration*.

By integration we mean the blending of different elements into a harmonious whole. Of course, our instincts are naturally discordant, for each is a desire toward its own satisfaction without regard for other consequences. According to the psychology of the unconscious, the ideal of an organized personality is not achieved by repression of these discordant instincts and impulses. "Repression," as Dr. Jung has described it, "is a sort of half-conscious and half-hearted letting go of things, a dropping of hot cakes or a reviling of grapes which hang too high, or a looking the other way in order not to be conscious of one's desire."[24] The integrated personality is not built by this method. The integrated harmony which psychoanalysis reveals as the "moral" ideal is built by the conscious process of deliberate selection, with one's eyes open. Some impulses have to be suppressed (not *re*pressed) or renounced, others sublimated. Sublimation is of particular importance, since this means that instinctive energies are directed into substitute ways of satisfaction—ways in harmony with the dominant theme of the personality. When this process of organization, consisting of conscious selection, suppression, and sublimation, is completed and the personality can operate as a harmonious whole, we may say that integration has been achieved.

We have just spoken of the dominant theme of the personality. Indeed, the whole process of integration presupposes some focal interest, some

[23] As reported in C. G. Jung, *Psychology and Religion*, New Haven, Yale University Press, 1938, p. 91.

[24] *Ibid.*

supreme value or ideal around which all other interests can be organized. Psychoanalysis recognizes clearly the need for such a supreme ideal, and in so doing gives a modern echo to Jesus' instructions, "Let your eye be single," and "Seek first his [God's] kingdom." The focal ideal of psychology is the supreme good in ethics. It must be noted, however, that our new psychology gives no warrant for grafting on an ideal. The central ideal of a personality must be found among the many purposes and interests already internal to it. It must also be an ideal of sufficient scope to build a life around. Once such an ideal appears, psychoanalysis declares, its supreme demands must be recognized. All other wants and desires must be judged with reference and in subordination to it. This may require painful renunciation. Thus psychological ethics demands discipline.

The psychological ideal does not just happen. Like other and lesser good things, it has to be achieved. But even as religious renunciation may bring joy in the possession of something more important, so psychology can offer the hope that the pain of disciplinary suppression and renunciation may be superseded by the joy of self-fulfillment. When this harmonious fulfillment is realized, it no longer matters whether we describe it as psychological integration or as moral achievement. Psychology and morals have here become identical.

Character does not mature in a vacuum; it has a social matrix. Hence, the ideal for personal development requires justice not only for instinctive and "selfish" needs but for social demands as well. Let us see how this places a degree of limitation upon and provides a certain direction to individual moral achievement, thus breaking down opposition between the individual and the social good.

We have long been familiar with the notion that character is a product of heredity and environment. A very important part of our environment is social. The traditions, customs, and ideals of the society in which we grow up are strong influences upon our lives. These influences work not only from without. Psychoanalysis has discovered abundant evidence to support the view that these social demands become internalized. The standards of society find a subjective counterpart in the individual conscience. In short, the codes and ideals of society become also *our* codes and ideals. They become a part of our private mental equipment along with the instincts. This complex of social demands, subjectively effective in the form of conscience or the "standards of the personality," is just as much a part of our personal make-up as is our biological inheritance. In fact, the problem of personal moral development is precisely that of lifting both our social and our biological demands to the level of consciousness. Ideally, here the various elements can be integrated around a dominant purpose, as was explained above. Thus the individual's integrated character must include social demands and ideals. Psychoanalysis then leads us to a conclusion like Plato's, that the individual cannot achieve virtue in himself except as a harmonious unit in society.

Analytic psychology is prepared to deal with the question, why be moral? Its answer is that the dynamic interests of our own nature, our instincts and our social heritage, demand it. He who really knows himself will not possibly want to be other than integrated—the psychological equivalent of moral. Our new psychology thus illuminates the Socratic dictum that knowledge is virtue, and provides significant support for empirical ethics.

Freud's Psychoanalysis and Religion

Religion is a very complex affair that includes codes of conduct, rituals, and ceremony as well as beliefs. Writers who have approached the study of religion from the standpoint of psychoanalytic theory have been quick to note analogies between the mental products of neurotics and primitive peoples. Thus the phenomena of magic, totem, and taboo seem to have parallels in certain symptomatic expressions of the mentally ill. Similarly, religious symbolism seems to have a counterpart in the symbols appearing in dreams. However interesting it might be to explore these fields, we shall confine ourselves here to the application of Freud's psychoanalytic theory to religious belief.

It has long been known that our wishes play a very prominent part in determining our beliefs. We tend to accept that account of things which we desire to believe. This is true in every field. The laboring man lends a more willing ear to the apostle of a socialist utopia than does the capitalist. The citizens of a war-weary land believe with pathetic eagerness the false report of peace. It is a commonplace in religious thought that faith is a product of the heart, that the beliefs of the religious man are the fulfillment of the deepest desires of the soul. The place of need and want, of wish and desire, of hope and will—all the non-rational factors of human nature—in the molding of belief is well established and widely accepted.

It is to this aspect of religious belief that Freud's psychology of the unconscious has made its most widely known contribution. It has given a detailed psychological account of the part that wishes play in our religious belief and has offered an explanation of the peculiar emotional satisfaction which such beliefs afford.

According to this psychology, our religious beliefs are the ideal satisfaction of unconscious wishes. Freud advanced the theory that the psychological basis of belief in God is the childhood sense of dependence upon the father. According to this view, the first love object of the child is the mother. She satisfies hunger and affords protection against anxiety. But the father soon replaces the mother as provider and protector. The father is also a danger, a threat to some of the child's instinctive satisfactions. He is the disciplinarian—he is sometimes filled with anger. In short, he is to be feared as well as loved. This situation lasts throughout childhood. When the child grows up, he finds that in his relation to nature he must remain a child forever, helpless against though dependent upon it. He thus interprets nature in terms of personal agency. More, he invests the agents of nature with the traits of the father figure: he projects upon the universe the fulfillment of his wishes, placing at its heart a God whom he both fears and loves, whose requirements he must satisfy, and upon whose care he must depend.

In its origins, religion is therefore actually an illusion, a belief based upon wish and not upon reality.[25] All religious ideas are illusions, for they do not lend themselves to proof. This does not necessarily mean that all these ideas are false, but Freud himself was convinced that the basic ones were. Prayer and the belief in providence he regarded as "infantile," and religion itself he considered a "collective neurosis" resulting from conditions not dissimilar from those which produce childhood neurosis. He regarded religion as definitely a danger, believing that it impoverished the intellect by halting critical thought. He insisted that it would be far better for men to reject religion and all other childish illusions, stand on their own feet, and become responsible men, developing their own inherent capacities.[26]

In his old age, Freud seems to have moderated his views somewhat, for in his last book, *Moses and Monotheism,* he wrote that the religious emotions attain greater sublimity and profundity than the other emotions. But he found no way to account for this fact.

Jung's Analytic Theory

In the course of a long and creative lifetime, Freud gained many disciples, most of whom as they developed moved away from the teaching of their master at one point or another. We have space to consider only one of these, *Carl G. Jung* (1875-1961), a Swiss, who for some years was very closely

[25] Sigmund Freud, *The Future of an Illusion,* New York, Liveright Publishing Corp., 1953.

[26] Fromm, *Psychoanalysis and Religion,* pp. 10 ff.

associated with Freud and was for a time considered Freud's successor. However, the relationship cooled and eventually came to an end, chiefly because Jung was unwilling to accept Freud's theory of sex. Jung's approach came to be known as analytical psychology.

While Jung, like Freud, found that the personality consists of a number of interacting though separate psychological systems, he identified these in quite different ways from his teacher. Reducing his highly complex analysis to utmost simplicity, we can describe the Jungian psyche as consisting chiefly of the *ego*, the *personal unconscious*, and the *collective unconscious*. The ego is what we usually think of as ourselves, the conscious mind, made up of conscious perceptions, thoughts, feelings, memories, and anticipations. It provides one with his feeling of identity and continuity. The personal unconscious consists of once-conscious experiences which have been forgotten but are accessible to consciousness. Some of these materials are repressed; others are forgotten or were too weak in the first place to leave a conscious impression. The personal unconscious contains the complexes.

The collective unconscious is a radically original aspect of Jung's psychology. He held that within the psyche the influence of this system is the most powerful of the three constituents. It is the "storehouse of latent memory traces inherited from man's ancestral past," included within which are latent memories from animal as well as human ancestry.[27] In the course of human evolutionary development, the collective unconscious assembled the psychic effects of experiences taking place over the ages. It is apparently not personal but universal. Moreover, it is not the racial memories directly that are inherited by each person but rather the possibility of recovering or reproducing experiences of the past. This collective unconscious is the very foundation of the personality structure, the experiences of the past upon which the present is erected. The components making up the collective unconscious are called the archetypes. Some of these, which contain great power capable of being used for good or for ill within the self, are archetypes of death, rebirth, the child, God, and the earth mother.

The goal of personal life is to bring the *self* to birth. The self is one of the archetypes, expressing itself in various symbolic forms. Before it can come to be, all the elements that make up the personality must become fully developed and individuated. The person who is well developed on one side of his personality but poorly on another may find that psychic disturbance appears as the result of an inner effort to bring about balance. Neurosis can be understood, therefore, as the attempt of the personality to reach selfhood.

[27] Calvin S. Hall and Gardner Lindzey, *Theories of Personality*, New York, John Wiley & Sons, Inc., 1957, pp. 79 ff.

The spiritual process by which the self is developed is called *individuation.* To develop the self requires utmost courage and honesty: a facing of oneself, a probing into the personal unconscious, and an immersion in the collective unconscious, generally through the help of an analyst. When the self is formed (which it rarely is), there is an experience of freedom and of inner unity of all that one is, described by Jung as the kingdom of God that is within one.

A very important aspect of Jung's analysis of personality is the emphasis he placed upon purpose or teleology. The individual is not to be understood entirely in terms of what the past has made of him, for he is also the product of the future in that something in his structure urges him toward fulfillment of himself. The ultimate goal is the actualization of his self. This reminds us very strongly of Aristotle with his emphasis upon the fulfillment of the entelechy as the goal of man's life. Both Aristotle and Jung saw in the life of every man an inner drive toward the goal of self-realization. Here, of course, the similarity ends, for Aristotle, it will be recalled, believed that the rational mind of man in its development brings about this realization, while Jung looked for a far more difficult and complicated inner process in which not primarily the rational mind but the unconscious processes are determinative.

Even this very brief statement of Jung's thought indicates how far his views moved away from those of Freud in essential matters. This same divergence is found in the attitudes the two men hold toward religion. As a psychologist, Jung attempted to refrain from discussions of the metaphysical truth of religious ideas, but, again as a psychologist, he found these ideas not only a part of man's psychic life but indispensable to psychic health. An oft-quoted statement sums up his view on this subject:

> Among all my patients in the second half of life—that is to say, over thirty-five—there has not been one whose problem in the last resort was not that of finding a religious outlook on life. It is safe to say that every one of them fell ill because he had lost that which the living religions of every age have given to their followers, and none of them has been really healed who did not regain his religious outlook. This, of course, has nothing whatever to do with a particular creed or membership of a church.[28]

Thus, in place of Freud's evaluation of religion as a dangerous illusion from which man would do well to be free, Jung takes a more friendly attitude to it, as a psychological need of man. The image of God is for man a spiritual fact, arising in his own personal experience. No intellectual proof

[28] Carl G. Jung, *Modern Man in Search of a Soul,* London, Kegan Paul, Trench, Trubner & Co., Ltd., 1936, p. 264.

need be offered for God because experience of him, like all experience, is self-validating. Psychology must deal with it. The image of God is a "psychic function" of tremendous significance. Another religious need of the individual which shows itself as a great psychological necessity is that of believing in life beyond death. Whatever the truth of immortality may be, psychic health, especially of those people beyond the middle of life, demands that one accept belief in immortality wholeheartedly. A life beyond death, like God, is one of the primordial ideas of the collective unconscious.

From this brief analysis, it is clear that Jung is no enemy of religion, but at the same time he is not defending religion as theology understands it. Whether or not its beliefs are metaphysically true, one's structure of personal being requires that he accept its basic concepts as valid, says Jung. The religious thinker finds in him no enemy, but only indirectly an ally.

Alfred Adler (1870-1937) also provided emphases in his teaching which are concordant with aspects of Christian thought, and particularly with Christian ethical teaching. He stated that lack of love for one's fellows is the greatest single cause of neurosis, and that it is a psychic necessity for every man to love his fellows. Yet he too, like Jung, refused to commit himself to the theological beliefs of Western religion.

New Directions in Recent Psychological Theories

Two recent approaches to the nature of the self and the problems of psychological health depart radically from classical psychoanalysis. One is represented by the psychologist O. Hobart Mowrer, and the other, termed existential analysis, is represented in this country by Rollo May.

In O. Hobart Mowrer's *The Crisis in Psychiatry and Religion*,[29] the point is made that the mysterious unconscious which we have been examining with Freud and Jung may in truth be a name simply for a conscience laden with the sense of guilt. Anxiety arises not from the acts which one would like to perform but dare not, but rather from those acts he has committed and wishes he had not. The aim of psychoanalysis is accordingly not to draw up the contents of the unconscious for examination, as Freud held, but to relieve the conscience of its guilt in order that it may subside and the self may once more become free and self-determining. The analyst's purpose should be not so much to reduce the superego of Freud to the level of actual conduct as to raise the level of conduct to high ideals. Mowrer writes,

[29] Princeton, D. Van Nostrand Company, Inc., 1961.

> . . . it is not nearly so much a question, as it was formerly, of how to pare down or reform the conscience; rather the question is, how to get the conscious self-system or ego of the individual to grow and mature, so that it is more responsible and more competent to deal with the manifold demands that impinge upon it.[30]

In line with this approach, Mowrer brings back into psychology the concept of sin. Psychic illness, as psychiatrists have often called the problems of their patients, must from this standpoint be reinterpreted. Mowrer quotes with approval the statement that "mental illness is a myth, whose function it is to disguise and thus render more palatable the bitter pill of moral conflicts in human relations."[31] Recovery from psychic disorders is achieved not by helping one reject his own sinfulness but rather by helping him to accept it in full responsibility. Not to acknowledge guilt, argues Mowrer, means that one continues to hate himself and consequently to suffer, for such self-hatred is realistic and justified until there are radically altered attitude and action. The problem of psychic disorder is the problem not of guilt feelings but of genuine guilt. This approach to mental problems will remind the student of Christian approaches to man. Augustine and others, it will be recalled, had much to say about man's sin, guilt, and responsibility.

Existential analysis is the name given to a new approach to the psyche which a number of psychologists in Europe initiated quite independently of each other. Instead of identifying any one detail of human life as the cause of mental disorder, these men, dissatisfied with the current techniques of psychoanalysis, developed the view that neurosis is existential in nature, arising "from the individual's inability to see meaning in life, so that he lives an inauthentic existential modality."[32] The problem arises out of discontent over the whole of one's life, and hence moves on a level quite other than that of repressed trauma. Crisis situations are in fact "deviations in the structure of that particular patient's existence."[33]

This form of analysis recognizes that modern man stands in a situation peculiar to his own day, which is that man has lost his essential dignity and humanness. He senses that he does not live out his real self, or, in other words, does not experience himself as real. He knows that nonbeing faces him, and before the threat of death he is filled with anxiety, which strikes at the core of his sense of value as a self. In the face of this anxiety, he is afraid to accept new possibilities for living since striving for the new means

[30] *Ibid.*, p. 34.

[31] *Ibid.*, p. 51. Quotation from Thomas S. Szasz, article entitled "The Myth of Mental Illness," 1960.

[32] Rollo May, E. Angel, and H. F. Ellenberger (eds.), *Existence: A New Dimension in Psychiatry and Psychology*, New York, Basic Books, Inc., 1958, p. 119.

[33] *Ibid.*, p. 5.

leaving the present relative security. But in his fear to reach out confidently to what might be, he is filled with guilt. This guilt is not the guilt of breaking moral codes, but the guilt of failure to fulfill potentialities—an existential matter since it deals with the very center of one's being. Rollo May agrees with Mowrer that guilt is not just guilt feelings but is genuine guilt. Other forms of guilt also are to be discovered: the guilt of not relating fully to one's fellow men and the guilt of separating oneself from nature. These forms of guilt, called together ontological guilt, are forms in which, faced by the threat of nonbeing and consequent anxiety, every human being participates. And they arise not from cultural prohibitions but from the deepest nature of self-awareness.[34]

The work of the analyst in existential analysis is to bring the patient to full acceptance of his existence as real. The individual must commit himself, decisively and responsibly. He must face the facts of his own being; look courageously at his anxiety, despair, and tragedy; and take his own being seriously, with full commitment to his future.

This approach tends to minimize the importance of the unconscious. It seeks to go below the surface of human fears and despair and to find in the basic nature of the self both the problems and the cure of psychic difficulties. Because it deals with ontological problems and analyses, it has much in common with the religious venture; at many points these two are able to agree and to support each other.

We bring this discussion of religion and modern psychologies to a close by making the observation that the first development of the theories of psychoanalysis under Freud were considered definitely hostile to religion. As time has gone on and more has been learned about the nature of the human psyche and its motivations, many of the emphases made in the past by religious thought are coming to be accepted as valid by at least some psychologists and analysts—such views as the reality of sin and guilt, the necessity for man to have goals beyond himself, the value for psychic health of faith in God and immortality, and the need of every individual to relate himself in love to other men. The gap between the two fields, in other words, has narrowed considerably in the past quarter-century.

Questions for Study

1. What were the characteristics of nineteenth-century materialism?
2. What revision concerning the nature of the atom has taken place within this century? How does this affect the concept of matter? What is meant by the

[34] *Ibid.*, pp. 50-55.

Heisenberg principle of indeterminacy? What does its effect upon older views seem to be? Does this destroy mechanical causality? What is meant by stating that law is statistical rather than absolute?

3. What was the meaning of Newton's principle of absolute time and space? How did Einstein demonstrate that the notion of simultaneity cannot be given actual content? What is the implication of the fact that whenever the velocity of light has been measured, it remains constant, regardless of the rate of speed of the measuring device? What is meant by relativity of time and space?
4. How has modern physics changed the views of nineteenth-century physics?
5. How did behaviorism attempt to make psychology scientific?
6. What are some of Freud's basic ideas concerning mental difficulties? What views did he come to regarding the unconscious and its place in human life? How did he understand the structure of personality?
7. What implications has psychoanalysis for philosophy?
8. What are the implications of psychoanalysis for ethics? By what methods may one avoid repression without giving full liberty to instinctual drives? How does this understanding lead to views similar to those of Plato and Socrates?
9. How did Freud understand religion? What would you say to this analysis?
10. Generally speaking, how did Jung differ from Freud, and what attitudes did he hold toward religion?
11. How do Mowrer and the school of existential analysis approach the problem of mental health and the causes of mental illness?

Selected Readings

PHYSICS

Čapek, Milič, *The Philosophical Impact of Contemporary Physics*, Princeton, D. Van Nostrand Co., Inc., 1961.

Cassirer, Ernst, *Substance and Function and Einstein's Theory of Relativity*, New York, Dover Publications, Inc., 1953.

d'Abro, A., *The Decline of Mechanism in Modern Physics*, New York, D. Van Nostrand Co., Inc., 1939.

d'Abro, A., *The Evolution of Scientific Thought*, New York, Boni & Liveright, 1927.

Dillenberger, John, *Protestant Thought and Natural Science*, Garden City, Doubleday & Company, Inc., 1960.

Einstein, Albert, and Leopold Infeld, *The Evolution of Physics*, New York, Simon and Schuster, Inc., 1938.

Heisenberg, Werner, *Physics and Philosophy*, London, George Allen & Unwin, Ltd., 1959.

Mascall, E. L., *Christian Theology and Natural Science*, New York, The Ronald Press Company, 1956, chap. 5.

Romer, Alfred, *The Restless Atom*, Garden City, Doubleday & Co., Inc., 1960.

PSYCHOLOGY

Freud, Sigmund, *Autobiography*, tr. James Strachey, New York, W. W. Norton & Company, 1935.

Freud, Sigmund, *The Future of an Illusion*, New York, Liveright Publishing Corp., 1949.

Fromm, Erich, *Psychoanalysis and Religion*, New Haven, Yale University Press, 1950.

Goldbrunner, Josef, *Individuation*, New York, Pantheon Books, Inc., 1956.

Hall, Calvin S., and Gardner Lindzey, *Theories of Personality*, New York, John Wiley & Sons, Inc., 1957.

Jung, Carl G., *Psychology and Religion*, New Haven, Yale University Press, 1938.

Jung, Carl G., *Psychology of the Unconscious*, New York, Moffat, Yard & Co., 1916.

May, Rollo, E. Angel, and H. F. Ellenberger (eds.), *Existence: A New Dimension in Psychiatry and Psychology*, New York, Basic Books, Inc., 1958.

Mowrer, O. Hobart, *The Crisis in Psychiatry and Religion*, Princeton, D. Van Nostrand Company, Inc., 1961.

Outler, Albert, *Psychotherapy and the Christian Message*, New York, Charles Scribner's Sons, 1954.

Roberts, David, *Psychotherapy and a Christian View of Man*, New York, Charles Scribner's Sons, 1951.

Schaer, Hans, *Religion and the Cure of Souls*, New York, Pantheon Books, Inc., 1950.

20. Faith and Reason in the Contemporary World

The final chapter of this book possibly can best serve its readers by outlining in a fairly simple way the situation in Western thought today, bringing up to the present the movements traced in the earlier sections. We are interested in faith, reason, and science; therefore, let us examine the impact of these three topics upon our culture in the second half of the twentieth century, first as they have affected our thinking generally and then more specifically.

People in every age generally regard their culture uncritically as the fulfillment of the past, considering earlier periods inferior to their own. And they suppose that the life of the future will continue to be much like that of the present. As a result of our study, we recognize our great debt to the past and the values of that same past in which every important understanding we hold had its origin. As we look ahead to the future, we can be certain that it too will be rooted in its past, but that as we are different from the Middle Ages so the future will differ from us. It is well to add also that in one sense the past is not dead but is drawn up into the present and reinterpreted and appropriated in living ways. Every philosophic and religious idea once vital in the past is still active in our own culture, actually or potentially. In the course of history nothing seems lost, and views of life that once showed great vigor may once again gain adherents who will accept and live by them, although in altered perspectives and with new emphases.

Heirs of the Enlightenment

In our attempt to gain understanding of where we in today's world stand, we find that our position may be roughly equated with the beginning of the Renaissance insofar as that period also witnessed the origin of a new way of looking at life and a slow turning away from an old way. But it took centuries before the new period, the Enlightenment, came into full flower. In our turn, we stand at the close of the Enlightenment, the fulfillment and the heirs of that great period of human self-confidence and optimism from which emerged science with all its wonders and perils. As persons in the late fourteenth century were unable to foresee what the eighteenth century (not to mention the twentieth) would bring forth, so we cannot see clearly what the twenty-first century will find characteristic in theology, philosophy, and science, although that century certainly will be grounded in the present.

Some contemporary thinkers are convinced that religious and philosophic beliefs of an earlier century will make a powerful impact once more. Others, like Sir Julian Huxley, to whom we referred in the discussion on evolution, believe that the older religious concepts are gone forever, having served their day, and will be replaced by a "religion" without the supernatural. Many thinkers suppose they can discern the shape of things to come, but there is little agreement among them as to what that shape will be. And there are many persons who continue to hold to the ancient Christian hope that the return of Christ, the end of the world, and the Last Judgment are near at hand. For them, history has just about run its course, and our period is the one destined to write *finis* to that largely unhappy account.

We recall that the three great words of the period of the Enlightenment were reason, experience, and nature, and that these three stood in marked contrast to the regnant words of the Middle Ages, some of which were God, faith, revelation, salvation, sin, grace, and immortality. We recall further the vast optimism with which the eighteenth century looked forward to the great achievements which men were about to perform, an optimism which reached its full expression in Condorcet. The Golden Age was felt to be within reach, and man believed it to be within his own power through the use of mighty reason to bring about that perfect period. God's existence was generally acknowledged, but the deity was felt to be secondary in importance to man's consuming interest in developing and using his own abilities and exploiting the world about him.

The scientific method, as it was developed and used in the seventeenth, eighteenth, and nineteenth centuries, combined experience and reason in experiment and hypothesis. It produced such astounding results that the early optimism regarding human ability seemed quite justified. Men actually appeared to hold it within their power to form the future as they wished, and nature through evolution guaranteed the greatness of that future. The philosopher Auguste Comte seemed to many in both the nineteenth and twentieth centuries quite correct in stating that in relation to the three successive stages of human development which he posited—the theological, the metaphysical, and the positive, which studies phenomena—Western thinkers had finally reached this last stage. Theology and metaphysics in the future would have no real relevance for men of wisdom.

The mood of optimism which for these more than two centuries had seemed so highly justified has gone through a radical change since the beginning of the current century, a change that was felt in Europe just after World War I and reached America a score or more of years later. It had its forerunners a century ago in men like Søren Kierkegaard, a Dane, and more recently in Friedrich Nietzsche. The new mood, now so much a part of our plays, art, literature, and general thought patterns that it is almost impossible for us to grasp imaginatively the extreme optimism of that earlier day, is characterized by deep-lying pessimism, anxiety, and despair. The genesis of this temper was not to be found, as might be expected, in the discovery that man's powers were insufficient to continue on the path of discovery through the use of science and reason; on the contrary, science had proved itself capable of successful discovery far beyond the greatest dreams of man. Yet in a way it was this very success, combined with a failure in science of a different nature, which constituted one important cause of the new mood. Let us examine how it was that this strange thing happened.

During the Middle Ages, man's confidence in himself and his reason was always subordinated to God's power and grace. Medieval man believed that in and by himself he was nothing. His very being was bestowed on him by God's creative act, and both his deeds and his eternal fate were held in the hands of God. This view had a double result: on the one hand, medieval man kept the ultimates of life in the center of his attention—life, death, salvation, and the meaning of life concerned him most deeply, and these were always related for him to the supernatural, the God who was beyond nature and man and all the powers of man. It meant also that he did not depend upon his own powers to achieve the meaning and value of his own life, nor did he attribute ultimacy of value to nature, which like himself depended for its being and its potentialities upon the Creator. It was believed that man did have very considerable ability—Thomas Aquinas, for instance, thought that reason was sufficient to demonstrate God's existence. But man's life found its setting and its meaning in its relation to and never apart from the Divine. It was taught also that God's will for man must be primary in his living, and that thinking too highly of oneself, called pride, was the greatest of all sins. Hence, in the Middle Ages man's understanding of himself and his powers, as well as his understanding of the purposes of his life, was always related to God. And in that relationship, under the protection of the church, he found life promising and hopeful, for God was good and was concerned with his creation. The great values of life—love, faith, beauty, joy, brotherhood—were all secure because they were founded in God. Such was the medieval view—a view considered pessimistic by thinkers of a later century because it did not seem to emphasize sufficiently man's native capacities of mind and qualities of goodness.

During the development of the Renaissance, and particularly as that period moved into the period of the Enlightenment, the medieval approach to life was vitiated for many thinkers. Reason freed itself from its former status as handmaid to revelation and theology, and in this freedom discovered its own vast capacities. Human life would henceforth be lived within its own framework alone, independent from God. And nature would be studied for its own sake as that which is of primary concern to man. In victory over nature man was to find his supreme purpose.

Close consideration of these two approaches to life discloses an interesting situation. The medieval approach seemed somewhat pessimistic about man's powers, in that it always made them secondary to God and his purposes; the Enlightenment had unlimited optimism about these same human capacities. The medieval scholar studied God and salvation, the ultimates of being; the Enlightenment found its chief interest in the spheres of man and nature with their limitations. During the Enlightenment it was generally assumed that the values of life could preserve themselves, that they somehow required no support to give them their value. But now, in our own century, we are discovering the limitations of human ability and what it might achieve at the very moment that we are seeing highly successful uses of human powers. The secrets of nature have been probed deeply, but what about man himself, it is now asked. Apart from faith in God, what purposes and what source of meaning can be discovered for the individual? What grounding can be pointed to in a world without God for the great human values of truth, goodness, beauty, sacrifice, and love? Such questions as these could be pushed aside for a time in the face of the seemingly more important discovery of nature's secrets. But if man did not know the meaning of his own life, of what importance for him was the knowledge of nature? Power and technical control had certainly been won, but meaning and significance seemed to have departed within the framework of the approach of the Enlightenment. Walter Lippmann stated this point some years ago when he wrote,

> The older fable [the religious story of the Christian gospel] may be incredible to-day, but when it was credible it bound together the whole of experience upon a stately and dignified theme. The modern man has ceased to believe in it but he has not ceased to be credulous, and the need to believe haunts him.[1]

Scientific discoveries have not satisfied this human need, nor have they lessened the enigma of being. On the contrary, they have immeasurably increased the sense of mystery, for each new discovery has served to expose the levels of the deeper unknown behind it. Yet this fact is only a part of what Joseph Wood Krutch has referred to as "the disillusion with the laboratory."

> Science has always promised two things not necessarily related—an increase first in our powers, second in our happiness or wisdom, and we have come to realize that it is the first and less important of the two promises which it has kept most abundantly.[2]

Approached from the standpoint of nineteenth-century optimism, this modern mood or temper is very difficult to understand precisely because the promise of great discovery has been so fully realized and the future continues to promise still greater advances. Approached from the religious way of viewing life, however, the new mood is found quite comprehensible and could have been anticipated. For the religious understanding insists that all of nature, man himself, *and* all his values find their being within God. When God is denied or overlooked, then nature and man lose their value; and values themselves, deprived of their foundations, cannot be given importance. Expressed in a different vocabulary, this means that man and nature are both finite and find their explanation and significance not in themselves but in the infinite, and that human values likewise depend upon the infinite for their foundation. When the infinite is disregarded it is to be expected that the worth of both man and his values is made very problematic or is denied. This is precisely what has taken place in the thinking of many sensitive people during the past half-century. Knowledge of and control over our world have increased immeasurably, but man's sense of his significance and purpose has diminished.

[1] Walter Lippmann, *A Preface to Morals,* New York, The Macmillan Company, 1929, pp. 8 f.

[2] Joseph Wood Krutch, *The Modern Temper,* New York, Harcourt, Brace & Co., 1929, p. 61.

Lippmann summed up the modern temper in a sentence from Aristophanes: "Whirl is king, having driven out Zeus." "Whirl"—the giddying search for values and meaning apart from God—has replaced the religious conviction that every human being is of value in the sight of God, and that it matters greatly what one does with his life. Anxiety has become the companion of many, and guilt feelings continue, now doubly difficult to deal with since there is thought to be no God who judges one guilty and is capable of offering forgiveness and reconciliation. The novels of a Franz Kafka, the plays of a Jean-Paul Sartre, much of modern painting, and the music of a Berg and a Schönberg all give expression to the unrelieved anxiety and meaninglessness of life which have resulted. Theologians say, in short, that when religious hope and faith are rejected, meaninglessness and anxiety occupy the place they have left vacant.

To this general sense of the problematic nature of human existence has been added the dreadful discovery not only that science has deepened the mystery of being but also that the powers of science can be used to blast as well as to bless. The billions of years of evolutionary development leading to the appearance of man may lead not to billions of years of marvelous development, as evolutionary optimists still hope, but simply to the annihilation of all life, human and subhuman. That same human reason of which the eighteenth century was so proud may possibly turn out to be its own destroyer. It should be recalled that this is not the first time in human history that the end of that history has been envisaged. For nearly two millennia orthodox Christian faith has expected the end of the world along with the return of Christ. The difference which makes the thought of destruction by atomic bombs so horrible to the modern mind is the purposelessness and senselessness of such destruction, while the Christian expectation of the end was and is related directly to divine purposes.

Still another grave threat faces this century which is, once again, a result of the successes of science. This threat is the opposite of the former and in certain respects appears to be even less avoidable. The population explosion threatens to overwhelm the world in the very near future, and there are indications that the growth of population will outrun every effort to develop new sources of food supply. Scientific discoveries in the field of medicine and public health and increased knowledge of agriculture have contributed to this problem, with which it is particularly difficult to deal just because in the past the bearing and rearing of numerous progeny and the preservation and extension of human life were considered highly desirable values. The economic, political, and ethical effects of this factor alone are quite beyond present imagination.

As both optimism and faith in reason have been shaken in our day, so also have the primary values of individualism and the desire for personal freedom been deeply affected. These too were marks of eighteenth-century Western man, triumphing in the great achievements of democratic government and individual self-fulfillment. But now men are generally by no means sure of their ability to direct their own lives satisfactorily, and many regard security as a more important value than freedom. As a result, there is in this second half of the twentieth century a turn to the voice of authority and the security it promises. This new state of mind, so marked in contrast to the attitudes of the Renaissance and the Enlightenment, is clearly observed both in the widespread willingness to have government take additional responsibility and authority and in the renewed interest in authoritarian forms of religion.

We have been discussing chiefly those who, as a result of the influence of the thought popularized by the Enlightenment, have departed from historic religious thought and practice. Now let us consider those who continue within formal religious bodies, as do the majority of contemporary Americans. Upon them too the successes of science and the changed picture of the universe it has created have made a deep impression. During ancient times and through the Middle Ages, religion and science were unified in their view of nature and the world, and religious concepts fitted easily into scientific understandings. For example, Hebrew religious faith in Yahweh was entirely at home within the Hebrew conception of the universe. God's presence "up there" in his heaven caused no intellectual discomfort to the views held of the physical universe. Sheol occupied a spatial location below the surface of the earth, and heaven was literally in the sky overhead. Concept and imagination were at one with each other. God's occasional intervention, his revelations and miracles, were not difficult to accept literally, nor was Jesus' ascension into heaven, up in the sky, and his expected return from the same place in space.

All this has changed, again largely as the result of scientific discoveries and theories. Now God is the God of innumerable universes, all directions are relative to the one judging them, miracles seem ruled out by invariable mechanical law, man himself is seemingly a chance product of a natural process of evolution, time appears to be endless, and all purpose seems to have disappeared before mechanism. How to picture God and his relation to this universe of ours is one of the modern believer's great problems. Instead of forming a single pattern, imagination and concept seem to stand often in contradiction to each other. In place of the comfortable harmony of medieval views, we find the uncomfortable realization that no *place* can be found for God or heaven or hell, and that God's purposes and intervention in human life, as well as his having a plan for man's salvation, are difficult to adjust to scientific thought. There is a tension in the minds of many men arising from the conflict between their inability to conceive of a God great enough to be God of known reality and their simultaneous unwillingness to believe in a God who is too small for our universe. The resultant inner division leads even a devoutly religious man away from the full-hearted faith that once characterized the Western believer to a faith that is full of uncertainties and qualifications, lacking the qualities of full commitment and conviction which in the past have made Western religion so potent an influence.

There are some important changes in both Judaism and Christianity of interest to the study we have been making, each related to elements from the past which have been previously examined. Three special topics now receive our special attention: the position of the Jews in the modern world, the ecumenical movement in Protestantism, and the meeting of Christianity with other world religions.

Significant Recent Religious Developments

The Restoration of Israel

During the current century the position of the Jews in the world has gone through great changes. Throughout the Middle Ages the Jews in Europe lived generally in ghettos or communities of their own, often under sets of laws especially designed for them, and were frequently persecuted by Christians. Many professions were closed to them and their rights were often denied or severely limited. In some countries they were entirely forbidden to settle or own land. The rise of the ideas of the Enlightenment, particularly the belief in the natural rights of men and in human equality, favored them and paved the way toward changes in their situation. A small number migrated to the United States in early colonial days. About 5000 were settled in this country by 1825. Between 1820 and 1870 some 200,000 to 400,000 arrived, mostly from Central Europe, many of them German; and an additional 2,000,000 or thereabouts came between 1870 and 1914, the majority from Russia.[3] Religiously, they formed three principal groups or sects, called the Reformed, Conservative, and American Orthodox. These reflected to a large degree the European origins of the peoples constituting them. Many

[3] Will Herberg, *Protestant–Catholic–Jew*, Garden City, Doubleday & Company, Inc., 1955, chap. 8.

second-generation Jews turned away completely from their historic religion to secularism. However, they usually continued to show great interest in social justice and in internationalism, an interest which was derived from their religious faith.

The more liberal Jews and those more favorably situated economically and socially during the nineteenth century, as were those in France, England, Germany, and the United States, favored a degree of amalgamation with their respective cultures, in numerous instances intermarrying with Gentiles and loosening their hold on their distinctive Jewish beliefs and customs. Some American Jewish leaders were outspoken in their fear that the Jews as a distinctive group might be entirely absorbed and disappear. On the other hand, European Jews who were harshly treated in their native countries, particularly in Eastern Europe, held tenaciously to their beliefs and traditions, upon which they were thrown back by repression. They longed for the day when God would again restore them to a homeland of their own. The first World War made this hope a possibility, to be realized in the creation of the state of Israel in 1948. Thus, for the first time since the destruction of Jerusalem by the Romans in A.D. 135 the Jews again had their own state, and for the first time since 63 B.C. independence within that state. It is a curious fact that almost at the same time that Israel once more appeared on the world scene as a modern power her ancient neighbors and frequent enemies, Syria and Egypt, after centuries of being ruled by foreign powers, also gained their independence, Egypt in 1922 and Syria in 1946.

The majority of Jews throughout the world support Zionism and the national homeland, although some have expressed their opposition on the basis of their conviction that Judaism has a universal message best served as it constitutes a continuous challenge and ferment in world society rather than when centralized in a separate state. In any case, the twentieth century has witnessed a coming full circle of events of over eighteen centuries ago.

The Growing Unity of Christianity

One of the effects of the Protestant Reformation was the creation of numerous bodies of Christians both as national churches and as sects. In our time also the direction taken during past centuries (in this instance, during the four centuries between the Reformation and the early part of this century) is being reversed. A movement directed toward increased unity between Christian churches is one of the most marked features of modern Protestantism—a movement which has reached out to accept Orthodox churches in membership also. Over the past centuries more than 200 Protestant denominations have appeared within the United States, although six or seven large denominations have included the majority of Protestant Christians.

The movement toward Christian unity has taken two forms. First, a number of Protestant denominations have merged organically with each other in the recent past and others are considering merging. That some have found it possible to unite indicates what is taking place in Protestantism. For one thing, factors which once divided the denominations are no longer felt to be vital. Against a world marked by strongly irreligious attitudes, the churches have discovered that they are more alike in what unites them than different in what separates them.

Second, on the local, national, and world scene a union of a less formal kind is now coming into existence. Many of the Protestant churches in the United States have joined activities in city councils of churches and in a national movement. In 1908 the Federal Council of Churches of Christ in America was founded, which in 1950 united with other like-minded groups to form the National Council of Churches of Christ in the United States of America. A smaller organization of Protestant churches, formed in 1944 by strongly fundamentalist denominations, is called the American Council of Christian Churches.

On the international level, the ecumenical (from the Greek word for the inhabited world) movement began with interdenominational meetings at Oxford, England, in 1937. The World Council of Churches, formed as a consequence of this and other meetings, has held several world assemblies—the first at Amsterdam, Holland, in 1948; a second at Evanston, Illinois, in 1954; and one in New Delhi, India, in 1961. Within this rather loose organization, Protestant churches and more recently Eastern Orthodox churches as well have been able to meet on an ecumenical basis. It remains for the future to disclose how this reaching out across the ancient lines of Christian division will develop. The Roman Catholic church, continuing to maintain its claim that it alone is the true ecumenical church of Christ, stands aloof from participation in the movement but has exhibited a degree of interest in it.

Christianity Confronts the World Religions

A third development in contemporary religion is only beginning to make its appearance. Unlike the two former changes, which move in the direction of re-forming the past, this development is something quite new. Christianity has been associated from its beginnings with Judaism, and in that relationship has come to a clear understanding of its position. The Christianity of the Orthodox churches since the seventh century and of Western Christianity since the Crusades has been keenly aware of the religion of Islam, and in this relation also has reached definite positions. But until recently Christianity has had little direct challenge from the Eastern religions—Hinduism, Buddhism, and Confucianism-Taoism. Christian missionaries have worked among the people of these religions, but under circumstances in which many Easterners felt themselves inferior because the Christian nations were in some instances their conquerors and were the possessors of the dominant Western civilization. But the relative position of these religions vis-à-vis Christianity is now changing radically, partly as a result of the recently gained independence of Eastern nations, like India, and the growing pride of these peoples in their own culture and religions. Opposition toward Western religion accompanies opposition to Western "imperialism." No longer is Christianity the ascendant religion in the Far East. As these ancient religions regain their self-confidence, they are beginning to send out missionaries, partly with the aim of making converts out of Christians. At this moment the long-range effects upon Christianity of confrontation with Eastern religions cannot be accurately assessed, but it seems likely that the mystical emphases of religions like Hinduism and Buddhism will make a marked impact upon future Christianity. The kind of complacency which Christianity exhibited when it was the dominant religion of the centers of world power seems certain to be shaken, and it may be expected that it will make way for more vital and inclusive attitudes.

Having noted some of the effects of science upon our modern world and some prominent changes which have occurred within this century in areas of religion previously studied, we are now prepared to examine changes in philosophic and religious thought themselves.

Twentieth-Century Philosophy

As so much of modern life, philosophic thought also has been radically altered during this present century, both in its methods and in the definition of the proper field and function of philosophy. Plato and Aristotle, Democritus and Parmenides set the patterns generally followed in former philosophical investigation. But in reaction to the period of idealistic thought during the latter half of the nineteenth century, new emphases have appeared which, though rooted in classical philosophy, are not typical of its main streams of development. Of these we will note two that have received special attention during our own century, existentialism and analytic philosophy, the latter to be examined under the two forms of logical positivism and linguistic analysis. It is questionable whether any one of these should be given the distinction of being called a *school* of philosophy. Possibly they are better referred to as expressions of contemporary moods—such moods as have been described in the first part of this chapter. Be this as it may, each has played an important part in recent thought, and each continues to receive a large share of attention.

Existentialism

In the rise of existentialism we discover a particular viewpoint or attitude toward life which expresses itself in numerous ways. Included within that viewpoint are found atheists like Jean-Paul Sartre and Martin Heidegger and Christians like Søren Kierkegaard, a Protestant, and Gabriel Marcel, a Catholic. The mood represented by existentialism is that of meaninglessness, anxiety, despair, and anguish. Although it was *Søren Kierkegaard* (1813-1855) who in recent times laid the groundwork for existential thought, he had no marked influence upon the people of his own day. Only in the twentieth century have his ideas struck fire, and that because the attitudes he represented have now become common ones and consequently many persons are prepared to listen to him.

The mood to which existentialism appeals is one that has become fairly general since the world wars have undermined much of man's optimism concerning himself and his future. It is probably true that existentialism stands at the opposite pole from the materialistic faiths of the past century—disillusioned and pessimistic in contrast to their rather naïve optimism. It has rejected vigorously the thought of idealism, particularly that of Hegel, and refuses to believe that knowledge of ultimates is possible. Its name is taken from the word *existence*, a word which expresses opposition to the essentialists and their emphasis on truth as knowledge of the essence of objects or beings of a certain class. Thinking back again to Plato in order to illustrate the point, we recall that knowledge for him meant understanding of the Ideas. The particulars, such as *this* chair, dog, or man, were real for Plato only insofar as they exemplified the Ideas. These Platonic Ideas are the essences, the "pure" nature of something apart from those particularities and qualities which accompany particular beings or existences. Contrary to such beliefs, existentialists hold that the essences or the Ideas are not real but are simply abstractions. The only real is this object here or that man there—the existing being rather than the essence. What is real of an individual man, for instance, is not his generalized, abstract human nature in which all men share but his own concrete being, that which makes him himself in all his uniqueness, concreteness, and individuality, and not another.

To express this meaning otherwise, existentialism approaches philosophy from the standpoint of the full man, the one who acts, the one who *is*, in all his variety and multiplicity, not the objective, unconcerned observer who attempts as far as possible to remove himself and his particularity from the scene of his acts of observation and rational consideration. Or again, existentialism sees the real not as an abstract, timeless universal term but as the particular within its period of time.

Applying this approach or viewpoint to man himself, we obtain emphases typical of existentialism, although there is wide variety among individual existentialists. They agree in teaching that each man is responsible for his own true self; only at his own peril does he attempt to fit himself into an idealized picture of what man as such should be. He himself should be just what he as a unique individual is. Existentialists assume that men have a degree of free will and freedom; by their choices they determine their lives. As they deliberately and consciously make their choices, they become what they previously were not. Yet by his peculiar endowments and nature, each individual man has a kind of becoming that is natural to himself and himself alone. As he chooses in the direction of his own nature, he achieves authenticity and becomes himself. The exercise of choice in courage and in full responsibility for the results marks the authentic human being. Because he determines for himself what he is to be, such a person will blame no one and nothing for the consequences.

Existentialists who believe in the reality of God stress the point that man becomes authentic only as he enters into personal relation with God himself. For the Christian existentialist like Kierkegaard, the very heart of Christianity is quite evidently not primarily the holding of specified intellectual beliefs or ideas about God, nor is it primarily a matter of moral practices, although both belief and practice are aspects of Christianity. Rather, Christianity is centrally the encounter with God in the individual's deepest experience. To this encounter Kierkegaard gives the name of *faith*, which is something very different from beliefs simply as reasoned conclusions. Faith is rather an "act of appropriation," something highly dynamic and vital. True faith always has intensity, for it arises out of despair, a despair which is the result of the discovery that one needs to believe in God and the truths of religion. Yet in Christianity he discovers the paradox, which is rationally insoluble, that God, the eternal truth, has entered into time as the man Jesus. Because of the paradoxical element in Christianity, Kierkegaard defines faith or truth as "an objective uncertainty held fast in an appropriation-process of the most passionate inwardness."[4] Truth is subjective, and one's appropriation of it

[4] Walter Lowrie, ed., *Kierkegaard's Concluding Unscientific Postscript*, tr. David F. Swenson, Princeton, Princeton University Press, 1941, p. 182.

is a subjective act. Hence, the truth for any individual is not abstract ideas which he has discovered through calm, rational analysis, but is on the contrary that which he as an individual has been able to "appropriate" in his "passionate earnestness."

Difficult to grasp as is Kierkegaard's thought on first acquaintance, it is clear from the above that his approach is individual, inward, and "passionate." It stands poles apart from the views generally characteristic of past philosophic thought, which emphasized calm, impersonal, detached, rational judgment. Truth *is* subjectivity, declares Kierkegaard.

Atheistic existentialists, in contrast to Kierkegaard, assume that there is no God and there are no ultimate principles. With Nietzsche they say that God is dead, a myth without reality. The old truths of religious philosophy are thoroughly rejected. Because there are no ultimates there are also no ultimate values for human beings to discover and to live by. *Jean-Paul Sartre* (1905——) may be taken as the most easily understood representative of this viewpoint. He has written:

> The existentialist . . . finds it extremely embarrassing that God does not exist, for there disappears with Him all possibility of finding values in an intelligible heaven. There can no longer be any good *à priori,* since there is no infinite and perfect consciousness to think it. . . . Everything is . . . permitted if God does not exist, and man is in consequence forlorn, for he cannot find anything to depend upon either within or outside himself. He discovers forthwith, that he is without excuse . . . we have neither behind us, nor before us in a luminous realm of values, any means of justification or excuse. We are left alone, without excuse. That is what I mean when I say that man is condemned to be free. Condemned, because he did not create himself, yet is nevertheless at liberty, and from the moment that he is thrown into this world he is responsible for everything he does. . . .[5]

There is no God, and consequently there are no absolutes or values to which men may turn. Yet men have freedom and are therefore responsible for all that they do with and make of themselves. Whatever meaning they find in life, they themselves have given to life. The result is terrifying and ends in anguish, for each man is totally responsible for himself. In one sense each man stands alone and is filled with dread before the emptiness of being. In another sense each man is responsible to both himself and mankind since in making choices he is acting as both an individual and a representative of humanity. The anguish arising from this great responsibility is the anguish of having to bear the fate of others through one's decisions without having

[5] Jean-Paul Sartre, *Existentialism and Humanism,* tr. Philip Mairet, London, Metheun & Co., Ltd., 1948, pp. 33 f.

any formal standards to guide oneself by—much like a ship's captain responsible for bringing his ship and its passengers safely into port without having any compass by which to steer. Sartre teaches that there are just two kinds of persons in this world—those who accept with courage the kind of responsibility we have just examined and those who avoid it. The latter are the cowards or the cads who blame their lives on God or external conditions. The supreme value is *integrity*—being what one truly is.

This form of existentialism is a direct and typical product of factors we have already recognized as arising in the thought of the Enlightenment and the nineteenth century; those which emphasize individualism, subjectivism, and atheism. Sartre wrote again,

> There is no other universe except the human universe, the universe of human subjectivity. . . . This is humanism, because we remind man that there is no legislator but himself; that he himself, thus abandoned, must decide for himself; also because we show that it is not by turning back upon himself, but always by seeking, beyond himself, an aim which is one of liberation or of some particular realisation, that man can realize himself as truly human.
> . . . Existentialism is nothing else but an attempt to draw the full conclusions from a consistently atheistic position. . . .[6]

A large number of persons, not primarily philosophers, find in Sartre a man who speaks to their condition. Agreeing with him in his atheism and belief in a meaningless universe, they find a certain nobility in his emphasis upon integrity, responsibility, avoidance of self-deception, authenticity, and courage. Others criticize him as having an incomplete or contradictory philosophy and ontology, while still others, like Abraham Kaplan, see in the emphasis upon anxiety, despair, anguish, and subjectivism not so much a philosophy as a psychology, a "sickness unto death," as Kierkegaard entitled one of his works—a looking into the void and enjoying the giddiness. Kaplan carries the point still further by stating that "what existentialism deals with is not so much a psychology as a psychopathology."[7] Kaplan's is not the final evaluation of this viewpoint, for particularly in its theistic forms (but also in Sartre himself) it has helped to restore a balance in thought, which had come to stress too exclusively the abstract and accordingly the nonhuman. It has served to remind us that man—the concrete, living individual in all his particularities—stands at the heart of the venture of being and knowledge.

[6] *Ibid.*, pp. 55 f.

[7] Abraham Kaplan, *The New World of Philosophy*, New York, Random House, Inc., 1961, p. 114.

Analytic Philosophy: Logical Positivism

The great development of the exact sciences and their remarkable success in dealing with the physical world quite understandably have gained them great prestige. It is at least partially true that philosophy, which in the Middle Ages had been the handmaiden to theology, has become the handmaiden to science in this twentieth century, and thereby has shared to a degree in that prestige. Since by its method science is unable to deal with the question of God, some forms of modern philosophy also separate themselves from belief in God, restricting their field of interest to what can be known and verified by the scientific method. The prophet of this approach, which generally goes by the name of positivism, was *Auguste Comte* (1798-1857). Not all positivists are atheists as far as personal faith is concerned, but all agree in denying that God can become a matter of knowledge.[8] Generally speaking, however, because of their almost exclusive interest in that with which science deals, they tend to disregard or deny God.

Those primarily associated with the first formulations of the modern form of philosophy termed inclusively analytic philosophy were Bertrand Russell and G. F. Moore of Cambridge University and Ludwig Wittgenstein, in his earlier days at the University of Vienna. It was primarily Russell who developed what he called *logical atomism*. Later, Wittgenstein carried this philosophic approach on to *logical positivism*. After World War II, analytic philosophy assumed still another form, termed *linguistic analysis*. Like the existentialists, the analytic philosophers also reacted strongly against the absolute idealism of Hegel in particular and against idealism in general, finding great vagueness of meaning in many idealist concepts. Like earlier common-sense British philosophers, they wished to clear aside esoteric statements and limit philosophical discussion to propositions capable of being given entire clarity of meaning. Metaphysics was that area of human thought which they found most lacking in precision. This they accordingly rejected on the ground that essentially metaphysics is quite devoid of genuine meaning. By this statement they meant that metaphysical propositions cannot be given meaning of the sort verifiable by scientific methods. They regarded only that which can be so verified as having meaning, as capable of being considered either true or false. Thus, in the interests of precision and certainty, they reduced the field of philosophy to positivism, rejecting as

[8] Frederick C. Copleston, *Contemporary Philosophy*, London, Burns, Oates and Washbourne, Ltd., 1956, pp. 30 ff.

meaningless all those problems, questions, and theories not susceptible of "positive" demonstration. The basic thesis of logical positivism is the verification principle, which states that the meaning of a statement is the method of its verification. Verification is always by observation and consequences, and proceeds by means of sense data.

It is clear that logical positivism is strongly empirical in nature, finding a basic kinship of approach with that of John Locke and David Hume. This empirical interest was combined with a new form of logic developed by Bertrand Russell and others. Positivists hold that the statement, "There is vegetation on Mars," has genuine meaning (it may be true or false), because if men ever reach Mars they can verify it by scientific means. But they deny that statements like "God is good" and "Ideas are the real" have meaning, for they cannot be verified in such ways. Hence, these latter propositions are considered neither true nor false but meaningless. Positivists hoped by their analysis to lop off the ancient problems of theology and metaphysics in one stroke and thus limit the field of philosophy to those questions which could be approached scientifically and therefore with some hope of reaching definite conclusions.

A crucial problem for logical positivism, recognized as such by positivists themselves, has been that of the status of ethical and moral statements or propositions. These cannot be verified by scientific procedures. Does it therefore follow that they are meaningless? To make such a claim would be disastrous in its effects upon human society. Positivists have replied that propositions concerned with ethical matters are not actually propositions at all but are "expressions of moral emotions or attitudes" which may be said to have "emotive meaning."[9]

Critics of logical positivism have been numerous, and many of its former defenders are no longer as enthusiastic about it as they once were. The exact meaning of *verification*, for instance, is not entirely clear. Further, it has been pointed out that the verification principle itself is not capable of being verified on its own grounds. More recent positivists find it desirable to call this principle not an empirical one but a "rule of scientific method." But if this is its real status, then it cannot be used to rule out metaphysics and theology as meaningless. Also, historical statements claim to be dealing with matters of truth and to have meaning, and yet they cannot be verified by the verification principle.

Logical positivism is by no means dead; its influence upon philosophic thought remains a very powerful one. Certainly it is true that some of the

[9] John M. Moore, "Analytical Philosophy and Its Bearing Upon Theology," *The Journal of Religious Thought*, XVII:2, p. 93.

issues raised by classical philosophy and theology appear to be meaningless or insoluble and that clarity of thought needs to be sought after. Yet it would seem also that the solution to this problem offered by logical positivism is far too radical. In its intense desire to obtain clarity and certainty, it has not only failed to gain certainty by the extreme method of reducing meaning in human experience to a very limited area, but it has shown itself unequipped to deal with the most significant problems human life faces, such as those concerned with ethics and values generally.

Analytic Philosophy: Linguistic Analysis

A recent development within the general field of analytic philosophy, linguistic analysis, owes most of its fundamental concepts to Wittgenstein. In the logical atomism which Russell had at first developed at Cambridge, he had assumed that all "complex propositions can be analyzed into simple or 'atomic' propositions of which the most important parts would be the names of the single elements or particulars of which reality is composed."[10] In a radical change of approach, Wittgenstein showed that meanings cannot be reduced to detailed, "atomic" statements without losing much of their *intention.* He was able to show that propositions and statements are determined in meaning by the use to which they are put. Language is fluid, and even when the identical words are used in a sentence spoken more than once, the meaning changes with change in accent or intonation. As a result, Wittgenstein's linguistic analysis turns away from attempts to discover precise meanings of propositions and concentrates instead upon discovering the different *functions* performed by propositions, utterances, and assertions. What is sought is the meaning of utterances in actual use, not as an abstract group of words. Language analysis attempts to discover what is happening in a whole situation when a particular expression is used.

Linguistic analysis, which "began as a kind of thinking about the use of language which relied for its proof on logical matters like self-contradiction or *reductio ad absurdum,*"[11] became through the effect of Wittgenstein's ideas as developed in his posthumous work, *Philosophical Investigations,* a matter largely of observation, an empirical investigation into the many functions performed by language. Accordingly, it is actually becoming a kind of science, developing a body of knowledge which consists of its discoveries about language uses.

[10] *Ibid.*, p. 95.
[11] John Holloway, "Analytical Philosophy," in Alan Pryce-Jones (ed.), *The New Outline of Modern Knowledge,* New York, Simon and Schuster, Inc., 1956, p. 42.

In this newest as well as in older forms, analytic philosophy remains quite consciously anti-metaphysical. Yet it is not unwilling to examine metaphysical and theological assertions in order to understand what functions they actually perform in human discourse. When so examined, even though the intended philosophical content of the theological phrase, such as "God is good," is not considered a valid proposition, still it indicates a way of seeing "life as a whole" and therefore carries a kind of meaning not found in more prosaic statements. Linguistic analysis is exhibiting an increasing interest in the use and meaning of language for religious purposes.

Much has been learned from linguistic analysis which has made modern scholars increasingly conscious of the need for accurate and precise use of words, and has drawn attention to the multitude of functions performed by language. The initial radicalism of philosophic analysis has been moderated in later developments. Still further movement in the same direction may well show the need for philosophy again to study metaphysical and theological issues, better prepared because of analysis to handle these issues.

Twentieth-Century Christian Thought

During the current century, the various strands of thought from the Enlightenment have appeared in Protestant religious thinking. Roman Catholics continue to hold officially to the theological approaches and formulations of Thomas Aquinas, yet the influence of Augustine and other medieval scholars has not been lost. In addition, the views of some modern Roman Catholic writers show their acquaintance with the thought of some non-Catholics. For example, logical positivism and linguistic analysis have been carefully examined and evaluated by Catholic philosophers and theologians, and Protestant theologians, among them Karl Barth and Paul Tillich, have received serious consideration. Because of the position held by the dominant Thomistic theology and philosophy it is not clear what influence non-Catholics have had upon Catholic thought, but it cannot be doubted that within the framework of Thomistic belief much creative work is being done in Catholic scholarship. With this statement we turn our attention to recent Protestant thought, in which changes are apparent.

Protestant Liberalism

Within Protestantism, this century has seen considerable intellectual activity. Because Protestant thought has not been crystallized through authoritative pronouncement, it has responded to the variety of influences in recent times in a way that Roman Catholic thought has not. Naturalism and scientism, with their denial of the ancient Christian beliefs and even of the fact of revelation itself, continue to be great issues. In recent decades a trend toward re-examining orthodox Christian formulations has been strongly felt.

Until the first World War, *liberalism* stood in the forefront of Protestant theological thought in the United States. It must be understood that most church members held generally to orthodox views, but in the books published and the theological discussions held liberalism was the center of interest. Liberalism can be characterized in several ways. Liberals felt it most important to make the Christian faith intelligible in the post-Enlightenment age and to bring it into harmony with the leading thought in the fields of science and philosophy. Contrasted with Catholic teaching during this same period, liberal Protestants showed great freedom from their orthodox past. Because of the vigorous claims of science and because idealism was felt to be sympathetic to religious concepts in a way that empiricism was not, Protestant thought at the end of the nineteenth century showed the strong influence of science and idealism. Let us see what the results were.

As concerns the impact of science upon liberal Christianity, the general tendency was to deny or at least to minimize the significance of those aspects of Christian belief which science found it difficult or impossible to establish. Accordingly, the activity of God in natural happenings was generally denied. God might still be thought of as influencing the general course of events, but not specifically. Such orthodox beliefs as the virgin birth of Jesus, the nature miracles, and the physical resurrection, which in earlier centuries were used to demonstrate the validity of Christianity and its supremacy over its rivals, were not accepted by liberals just because scientific thought found no place for exceptional happenings. The effect of this approach to religion was to make the discoveries of science the standard of truth. If conflict arose between science and theology, it was the theological belief that was the more readily sacrificed. The lesson learned in the controversy between theologians and scientists after the time of Copernicus was taken to heart by Protestant thinkers. Liberals generally refused to hold a materialistic view of reality, insisting that nature requires the supernatural, yet some were even prepared to take the final step of denying God and becoming "non-theistic humanists," stressing the importance of improving the lot of man. For them science had become the final arbiter in matters of truth, and not only in questions directly investigated by science but in a naturalistic world view which scientists as such did not directly support.

Since they denied God, extreme liberals questioned the value of religious exercises, like prayer. The science of physics appeared to rule out any way in which prayer might affect the physical universe. The laws of mechanics seemed to govern the future entirely. As a psychological exercise, possibly as a kind of autosuggestion, prayer and worship might have a legitimate function, but no values other than the psychological could be expected from it.

Idealism was no less significant in its effects upon liberal Christian thought than was science, even though idealism was felt not to be so radical in its challenge. Absolute idealism accepted reason as the principal means of discovering truth, since Hegel and his disciples believed that reality is itself rational. God was conceived of as divine mind, and the laws of nature were believed to be used by God for his purposes. In agreement at this point with a scientific approach, idealism held that exceptional occurrences are not likely or possible. God was believed to act always in rational, consistent ways, not miraculously. He was thought of as immanent in the universe, acting from within rather than transcendentally, after the pattern of man's own self acting in and through his body.

Particular Christian truths were taken as symbols rather than as literal facts in the idealist view. Calling Jesus divine was interpreted as a way of pointing to the divine in all life, and the miraculous birth of Jesus was a reminder of the miracle in every birth. In short, as influenced by idealism, liberal Protestantism insisted upon the rational, teleological, regular, nonmiraculous nature of the world. Everywhere regularity is to be found, a regularity influenced by God who in some manner directs the whole purposively.

This line of thinking, of course, had significant implications. Revelation was denied or questioned, for it is in his use of reason that man approaches God most closely. The exceptional events of Christian belief were dismissed or minimized. That Jesus was in any unique sense the Son of God or the bringer of salvation, that miracles occur, that special revelations come to particular individuals, that Christianity is unique among the world religions—all such claims were questioned. Generally speaking, liberals tended to think of Jesus as a teacher, leader, and ethical and moral example who was to be followed as "lord," as the ideal man, not as "savior" in the orthodox sense. Indeed, idealists rejected the belief in man's original sin, for since man is rational and reason is good, man is basically good. His sin comes in not being as fully rational as he might. Salvation in the idealist meaning is deliverance from sin, selfishness, fear, and guilt.

In the doctrine of evolution, liberals generally saw a promise of God's supporting and directing activity in the world. The progress theory of history seemed quite obviously true to many liberals. They believed that in the not-too-distant future the kingdom of human perfection would appear. Understandably, they were in the forefront of those who accepted the critical approach to the Bible, and they were leaders in the "social gospel" movement which stressed the need for Christian men to cooperate with God in the establishment of the kingdom of a just and loving human society.

It can be readily seen from the brief description above that liberalism covered a wide spectrum of views which differed from each other more in degree than in kind. On its right fringe it touched upon orthodoxy, on its left upon humanism, and it showed every possible shade between. As an organized movement it no longer exists, but its influence has by no means disappeared. It still continues among many Protestants with regard to both specific beliefs and, even more markedly, attitudes. Elements that stand forth as representative of the basic nature of liberalism are its emphasis upon the place of reason in religion and its assertion that religion itself is basically belief; its wide acceptance of scientific discoveries as providing truth that must be taken seriously by religious thought; its optimism about the nature of man and the future of the world; and its willingness to put aside points in Christian orthodoxy which do not fit into these approaches. Orthodox beliefs tended to be rejected, and many liberals felt that instead of conceiving of man as a sinner standing before the awesome judgment of God, he is actually best understood as a partner with God who ought to cooperate with God in the divine purposes being worked out. In short, liberalism was a very vigorous, optimistic, activistic movement within Protestantism that displayed all the outstanding characteristics of the Enlightenment, thus proving itself a true child of that period. Its critics claimed that it had surrendered the very heart of Christianity and had sacrificed depth for breadth.

Recent Protestant Thought

Social and political changes inevitably affect philosophic and theological thought. Even when the codifications of theology remain unchanged in *form*, as they do in the Roman Catholic church, they pass, however slowly, through changes of emphasis and viewpoint. As we saw, liberalism provided a reflection of optimistic views derived from the Enlightenment, modern science, and idealism. But as we know from earlier sections of this chapter, the political and social environment went through great changes in the first three decades of the twentieth century, changes which were accompanied by equally radical shifts in theological perspective. Those who felt "the disillusion with the laboratory" questioned the early optimism about the promise of science. But far more crucial in the thinking of twentieth-century men was, of course, the effect of the two great world wars. These made visible an abyss of evil and destructiveness at the very heart of human nature—and that in the most rational of men, namely, those of Europe and America—which made it appear quite impossible to many thinkers to regard man as fundamentally good or dependable in the use he made of his abilities.

The first powerful Protestant voice to be raised in strong and direct challenge of the liberal interpretations of Christianity was that of the German *Karl Barth* (1886——), formerly himself a liberal, in his *Epistle to the Romans*, which appeared just after the close of the first World War. Behind Barth's thought stands Kierkegaard, previously mentioned as a founder of extentialism, with his despair, paradox, and passion. Barth started a theological revolution which, echoing Luther, emphasized Biblical religion again. He had no great interest in science, placing his predominant emphasis upon the Word of God. He charged that liberals based their theology upon their own reason and experience instead of upon historical revelation, and failed to take the measure of the great crisis in which the modern world stands. Theirs was a man-centered and therefore false religion—it was actually a form of idolatry in which they worshiped themselves. He stated that the optimism which characterized the eighteenth-century rationalists and those who held to a progress theory of history was proved false by the threatened breakdown of society. Modern liberals, he charged, failed to understand their world, since not man but God is ultimate reality, who confronts man in the crises of human life. "Man's crisis in God's opportunity," for as man realizes his true condition, which is one of powerlessness and perversity, he becomes willing to turn to God in humility and true faith.

God has spoken his Word directly in and through Jesus Christ, Barth continues. The Bible, which gives the account of Christ, contains the record of that Word. It is heard by each man individually, not simply as he reads the record but as he knows it to be spoken to himself. His response is self-giving trust and commitment, which is what the word *faith* means for Barth. God's revelation is a personal matter, between God and the individual man in his particular situation in life. And revelation reveals what man most needs in his situation; it is never simply abstract knowledge about the nature of God or man. In these emphases we recognize a strong resemblance between Barth and the Hebrew prophets, for whom also God's revelation was a message for the times.

Barth also discusses the nature of God at length. He rejects the liberal view, derived from absolute idealism, that God is completely immanent in the universe. God transcends the world completely—not that Barth thinks, in the manner of the deists, that God is out of touch with the world, but rather that the nature of God is "entirely other" or "wholly other" than the nature of the world and man. God is the creator, without whom the world could not be, and the world is the created; God is in eternity, the world is in time. There is a fundamental otherness or difference between man and God. For this reason it is impossible to speak of him directly, as we might of other parts of nature. Only paradoxical statements can be made about God.

Barth also reaffirms man's sinfulness. Between man and God lies a great gulf, caused by man's rebellion against God as he attempts to establish his own independence. The gulf of separation is of man's own making, but he cannot unmake it. He finds it impossible through his own efforts to cross from the human side to the divine. As orthodox Christianity has always insisted, salvation can come only from God. And God has come to man, very directly, in the man Jesus Christ and in him alone, in whom God has taken the form of man. Since he was in the form of man, he was able to speak understandably to men. In this way he made his Word available for the saving of men, which takes place when the response of faith is elicited.

This form of Protestant theology is frequently called neo-orthodoxy for the reason that it is not actually orthodoxy as such and yet it agrees with orthodoxy at various points and uses much of its language. Neo-orthodoxy is opposed to aspects of both orthodoxy and liberalism. In contrast to orthodoxy after Calvin, it does not regard the Biblical writings themselves as literally authoritative, for they are not the Word of God but are simply the words used by their authors to tell the story of God's deed of grace in taking on human form for the salvation of men. Christian faith is not intellectual belief about God, although such belief is present. True Christianity arises, Barth insists, only as man meets God, hears his Word, and responds in faith. Also, Barth does not emphasize miracles, apart from the supreme miracle of the incarnation of God in Christ.

In contrast to liberalism, Barth holds what he calls a Biblical theology. He attacks reason because, like everything in man, it is infected with human pride and sin. He emphasizes strongly the sinfulness of man, his inability to escape his sin, his standing under judgment, and his guilt. Barth reaffirms the Christian belief that Jesus Christ was both God and man. He cannot accept the liberal optimistic faith that any social order, now or in the future, can be the ideal society, for all men's societies will be infected by human sin. In brief, he opposes liberalism and agrees with orthodoxy in his central interest in religion rather than in science and in his teaching on the majesty of God, the universality and terrible nature of sin, the availability of God's grace, the drama of salvation, Jesus Christ as the Word of God, and salvation through God's grace.

Barth's thought introduced a God-centeredness and a seriousness into

Protestant theology in this century which it had largely lost. His influence has been felt very strongly in many men of stature, among them Emil Brunner in Switzerland and Reinhold Niebuhr in this country. While that influence is no longer as powerful as it once was, it has become a constituent part of twentieth-century Protestant thought.

Space does not permit us to go further into these very important issues, not even to comment on such significant figures as Richard Niebuhr, Rudolf Bultmann, and Paul Tillich. We note, in summary, that during this century many Protestant theologians have returned to understandings of God, man, Christ, and salvation much closer to those of the Bible than was the case during the period of liberalism, and yet that values remain from the liberal tradition. For these contemporary thinkers, the study of nature does not hold the primary position it held for liberals. This is partly the result of the political and social circumstances which have turned their attention to the position of man himself in his world and before God and have made it impossible for them to subscribe to the earlier optimism and the belief in inevitable progress and the goodness of man. But partly also it reflects the fact that the challenge of science has been lessened; that the scientific dogmatism and materialism of nineteenth-century science has largely disappeared.

While it is true that science is no longer as outspokenly materialistic as it once was, the relation of science to religion remains one of the greatest problems facing thinkers in religion at this time. Protestants may well agree with Catholics in stating that, since truth is one, there *can* be no real conflict between revealed and scientific truth; while this is true in principle, the fact remains that in practice it is far from clear how the two may be brought into unity. The precise relation of nature to God—of nature's regularities to divine purpose and knowledge, for example—is a problem for which no generally accepted solution has yet been found. It suggests the kind of questions waiting to be answered. No doubt the heart of this problem is the being of God himself, but how physical nature is truly and most inclusively to be understood is also a part of the question.

Conclusion

As we conclude this study, we remind our readers again that our Western heritage is an immensely rich and varied one. Within it the two primary strands of religion and philosophy wove a pattern that was further enriched by the scientific thread to construct the world of thought and physical reality in which we live. Our heritage is an open-ended one which looks toward a future that is at many points unimaginable to us. It may be, as some have said, that only now does man stand at the threshold of his genuine humanity because of his knowledge and the power it has brought him. Now, for the first time in human history, he is capable of freeing himself from drudgery and of developing a life of leisure, beauty, and well-being such as has never before been generally possible. Everything in the future depends upon how well he uses his powers and for what purposes. Many of his old purposes will have to be eliminated—his use of war, old forms of narrow nationalism, and all that denies human oneness. Love in its widest meaning appears to be the one necessity for man to survive the dangers to which his powers have given rise. And great faith and hope must accompany love if modern man is to have purposes noble enough to challenge and draw from him all that can give his life value and meaning.

Questions for Study

1. Why is it true to state that our own cultural period is heir to the Enlightenment?
2. Explain the seeming paradox that anxiety and despair have become common at a time when man's powers of reason have been used most fully. What is the basis of this modern mood, and why did it not appear during the Middle Ages?
3. What is it in religious belief that gives life meaning and values? What is meant by values, and why is it probably true to state that values do not support themselves?
4. For what reasons do modern thinking men find it difficult to hold the kind of religious belief which was possible in the Middle Ages?
5. What significance can you see in the restoration of the state of Israel and in the ecumenical movement in Christianity? What possible consequences can you imagine of the confrontation of Christianity with Eastern religions?
6. What aspects of life seem most significant to existentialists? Precisely what *is* existentialism? If you were Plato, how might you criticize and evaluate it?
7. How does Kierkegaard understand the word *faith*, and why does it arise from despair? What does he mean by saying that truth is subjectivity? Explain why you would agree or disagree with him.
8. What positive qualities do you see in Sartre? Why is responsibility so closely related to anguish in his thought? How does this form of existentialism arise from factors in the Enlightenment? Be specific.
9. What interests do linguistic analysts have? How do their interests and procedures differ from those of logical positivists? In what sense can their results be termed scientific?
10. What dominant interests and concepts from the Enlightenment were crucial in Protestant liberalism? What good points do you see in liberalism, and what

errors or weak points do you think it had? Why did it deny miracles, special revelation, and Jesus as savior? What did liberalism absorb from science, and what from idealism?

11. Why did neo-orthodoxy arise? What are its primary emphases, and in what ways is it neither liberalism nor orthodoxy?
12. Exactly what does Barth mean by the Word of God? How does his understanding of God differ from that of liberals, and why did he call liberals idolaters? If you were a liberal, how would you criticize Barth? If you were a Roman Catholic, how might you criticize him?
13. What do you think are going to be the main lines of thought and interest appearing during the next century? What do you think might happen to classical Christianity, and to classical philosophy as represented by Plato, Aristotle, and the great idealists? How do you think science will be evaluated by the end of another century?

Selected Readings

Brinton, Crane, *Ideas and Men,* New York, Prentice-Hall, Inc., 1950.

Copleston, Frederick C., *Contemporary Philosophy,* London, Burns, Oates & Washbourne, Ltd., 1956.

Dillenberger, John, *Protestant Thought and Natural Science,* Garden City, Doubleday & Company, Inc., 1960.

Herberg, Will, *Protestant–Catholic–Jew,* Garden City, Doubleday & Company, Inc., 1955.

Hordern, William, *A Layman's Guide to Protestant Theology,* New York, The Macmillan Company, 1956.

Hubben, William, *Four Prophets of Our Destiny (Kierkegaard, Dostoevsky, Nietzsche, and Kafka),* New York, The Macmillan Company, 1952.

Kaplan, Abraham, *The New World of Philosophy,* New York, Random House, Inc., 1961.

Levi, E. W., *Philosophy and the Modern World,* Bloomington, Indiana University Press, 1959.

Lippmann, Walter, *A Preface to Morals,* New York, The Macmillan Company, 1929.

Olmstead, Clifton E., *History of Religion in the United States,* Englewood Cliffs, N. J., Prentice-Hall, Inc., 1960.

Scott, Nathan A., Jr. (ed.), *The Tragic Vision and the Christian Faith,* New York, Association Press, 1957.

Williams, Daniel Day, *What Present-Day Theologians are Thinking,* New York, Harper & Brothers, 1952.

Students are referred to primary works of the men mentioned in this chapter, many of which are available in paperback.

Index

Format by Faith Nelson
Set in Linotype Janson
Composed, printed and bound by The Haddon Craftsmen, Inc.
HARPER & ROW, PUBLISHERS, INCORPORATED

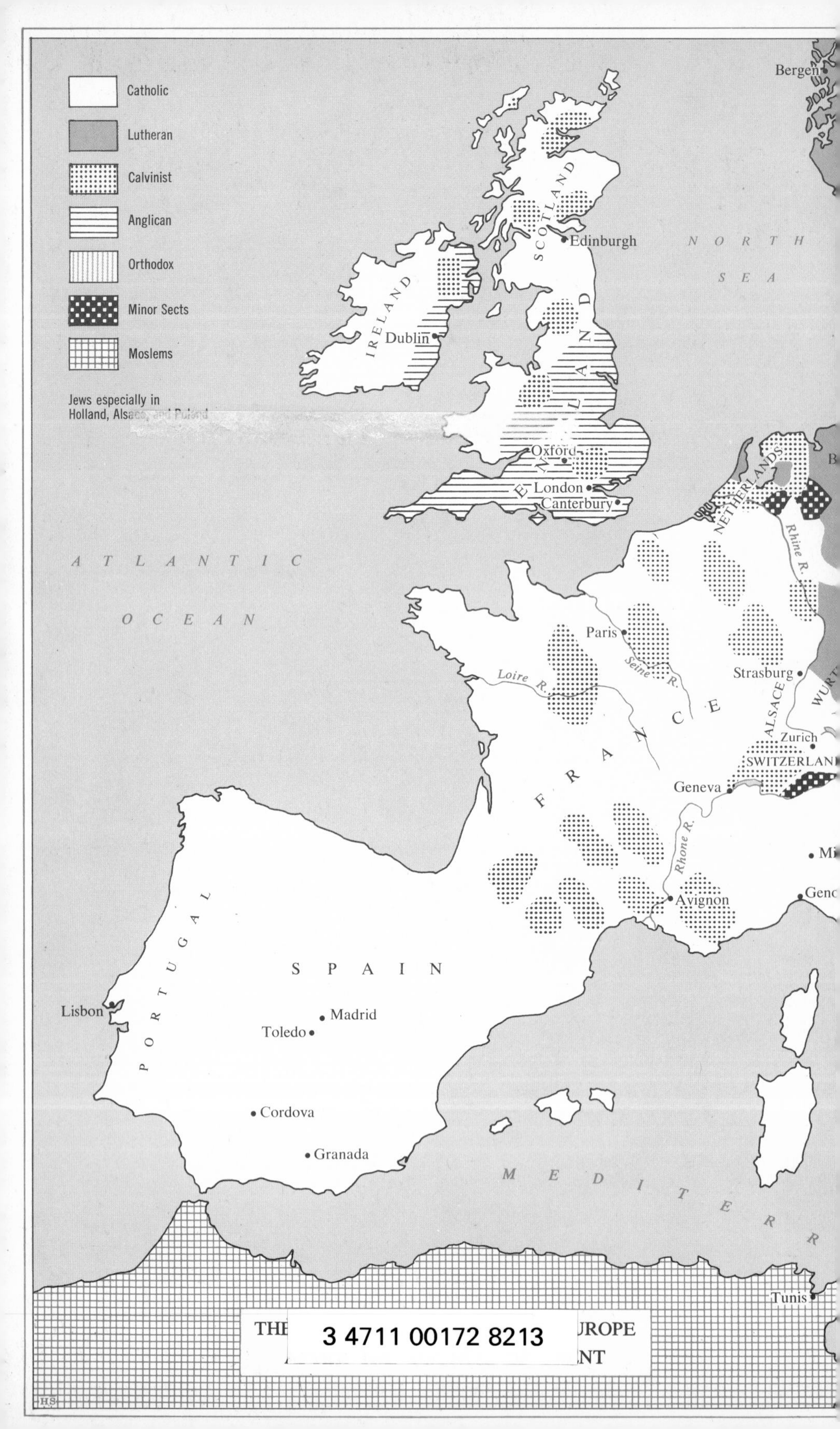

Catholic
Lutheran
Calvinist
Anglican
Orthodox
Minor Sects
Moslems
Jews especially in
Holland, Alsace, and Poland
Bergen
SCOTLAND
Edinburgh
NORTH SEA
IRELAND
Dublin
ENGLAND
Oxford
London
Canterbury
NETHERLANDS
Rhine R.
ATLANTIC OCEAN
Paris
Seine R.
Loire R.
Strasburg
ALSACE
FRANCE
Zurich
Geneva
Rhone R.
Avignon
PORTUGAL
SPAIN
Lisbon
Madrid
Toledo
Cordova
Granada
MEDITERR
Tunis
HS